Date of Birth... 6th June. 1868.   Place of Bir[th]...

Name and Profession } J.E. Scott Esq JP.   Date and Place of } 2 Sept 98
of Father ... } Outlands Plymouth.   Marriage ... } Edith Bruce

11/08)

Examinations.	Special Attainments or Qualifications.

Rated Midn without Examination   July 1893 Qualified as Torpedo Lieut. 1st Cl. Cy
Passed Seamanship 1st Cl. Cert. 980 marks
" College March 1888 1st Cl. Cert. 1445 marks
" Torpedo May 1888 1st Cl. Cert. 178 marks
" Gunnery Oct r 1888 2nd Cl. Cert. 516 marks
" Pilotage Dec 88 1st Cl. Cert. 928 marks
ly 92 obtained 1st Cl. Cert. at RN Coll. in Exam n
n Torpedo Lieut July 93 Passed practical
mine 1st Cl. Cert. 860 marks.

Judgment.	Temper.	Professional Knowledge.	If Temperate.	Physical Qualities.	Performance of Special Duties.	If deserving of advancement.	REMARKS.
							Captain Wells
—	.	Fair	yes	—	—	—	, Church
	.	✗	yes	—	—	—	–"– –"–
	.	VG	Yes	sketches &	zealous & attentive	–"–	–"–
		VG	Yes	paints well	promises very well.	–"–	–"–
	.	VG	Yes	An able & promising	young officer	"	Noel

Lord Byron's Jackal: A Life of Trelawny

*The Kindness of Sisters: Annabella Milbanke
and the Destruction of the Byrons*

SCOTT of the ANTARCTIC

SCOTT of

the ANTARCTIC

A Life of Courage and Tragedy

David Crane

Alfred A. Knopf   New York   2006

THIS IS A BORZOI BOOK
PUBLISHED BY ALFRED A. KNOPF

www.aaknopf.com

Originally published in Great Britain by HarperCollins
Publishers, London, in 2005.

Library of Congress Cataloging-in-Publication Data.

Crane, David.
    Scott of the Antarctic : a life of courage and tragedy / David
Crane.—1st American ed.
        p. cm.
Includes bibliographical references and index.
ISBN 0-375-41527-0
1. Scott, Robert Falcon, 1868–1912. 2. Explorers—Great Britain—
Biography. 3. Antarctica—Discovery and exploration—British.
4. British National Antarctic Expedition (1901–1904) 5. British Antarctic
("Terra Nova") Expedition (1910–1913) I. Title.

G875.S35C73 2006
910.92—dc22
[B]   2006045262

Manufactured in the United States of America
First American Edition

Contents

vi
Contents

Illustrations

Outlands: the "sleepy hollow" of Scott's childhood. (Scott Polar Research Institute, University of Cambridge)

Hannah Scott: "If ever children had cause to worship their mother, we feel we have." (Scott Polar Research Institute, University of Cambridge)

John Scott: "The inherited vice from my side of the family is indolence . . . My father was idle and it brought much trouble." (unknown photographer)

Scott at thirteen. (Scott Polar Research Institute, University of Cambridge)

Scott's discipline sheet from the naval training ship *Britannia*. (Royal Naval College, Dartmouth)

Sir Clements Markham, KCB, FRS: "the father" of the *Discovery* expedition "and its most constant friend." (Royal Geographical Society)

Discovery's officers, 17 July 1901. (Scott Polar Research Institute, University of Cambridge)

The first balloon ascent: "If nobody is killed it will only be because God has pity on the foolish." (Royal Geographical Society)

Football on the ice: a "good deal of promiscuous kicking and foul play." (Scott Polar Research Institute, University of Cambridge)

Discovery in the ice. (Royal Geographical Society)

Return from the Southern Journey: Shackleton, Scott and Wilson. (Royal Geographical Society)

Escape from the ice: *Discovery*, *Morning* and *Terra Nova*. (Royal Geographical Society)

Captain Scott, ambition fulfilled: among "the ranks of the advancers." (Scott Polar Research Institute, University of Cambridge)

Maps

Note on Distances, Temperatures and Weights

Unless stated, all distances are given in geographical (i.e. nautical) miles. One geographical mile equals 1.15 statute miles, or c. 2,025 yards (1,852 metres). Temperatures are given in Fahrenheit and weights in imperial measures.

SCOTT of the ANTARCTIC

One: St. Paul's, 14 February 1913

I am more proud of my most loved son's goodness than for anything he has done and all this glory & honour the country is giving him is naturally a gratification to a Mother's heart but very little consolation—you know how much my dear son was to me, and I have never a bitter memory or an unkind word to recall.

HANNAH SCOTT, *21 February 1913*

Your children shall ask their fathers in time to come, saying "What mean these stones?"

JOSHUA IV. 21. *Scott Memorial, Port Chalmers, New Zealand*

In the early hours of 10 February 1913, an old converted whaler "crept like a phantom" into the little harbour of Oamaru on the east coast of New Zealand's South Island and dropped anchor. For many of the men on board this was their first smell of grass and trees in over twenty-six months, but with secrecy at a premium only two of her officers were landed before the ship weighed anchor and slipped back out to sea to disappear into the pre-dawn gloom from which she had emerged.

While the ship steamed offshore in a self-imposed quarantine, the officers were taken by the nightwatchman to the harbour master's home, and first thing next morning to the Oamaru post office. More than two years earlier an elaborate and coded arrangement had been set in place to release what everyone had then hoped would be very different news, but with contractual obligations still to be honoured, a cable was sent and the operator confined to house arrest until Central News could exploit its exclusive rights to the scoop the two men had brought.

The ship that had so quietly stolen into Oamaru harbour was the *Terra Nova*, the news was of Captain Scott's death on his return from the South Pole, and within hours it was around the world. For almost a year Britain had been learning to live with the fact that Scott had been beaten by the Norwegian Amundsen in the "Race for the Pole," but nothing in any reports from the Antarctic had prepared the country for the worst disaster in her polar history since the loss of Sir John Franklin more than sixty years earlier. "There is a dreadful report in the Portuguese newspapers," a bewildered Sir Clements Markham, the "father" of British Antarctic exploration and Scott's first patron, scrawled from his Lisbon hotel the following day, "that Captain Scott reached the South Pole on January 18th and that he perished in a snow storm—a telegram from New Zealand . . . If this is true we have lost the greatest polar explorer that ever lived . . . We can never hope to see his like again. Telegraph if it is true. I am plunged in grief."

If there had ever been any doubt of its truth in London, it did not last long, and with Scott's widow, at sea on her way to New Zealand to meet her husband, almost alone in her ignorance, the nation prepared to share in Markham's grief. Less than a year earlier the sinking of the *Titanic* had brought thousands to St. Paul's Cathedral to mourn, and within four days of the first news from Oamaru the crowds were out in even greater force, silently waiting in the raw chill of a February dawn for a memorial service that was not scheduled to start until twelve.

There could have been nowhere more fitting than the burial place of Nelson and Wellington for the service, no church that so boldly embodied the mix of public and private sorrow that characterised the waiting crowd. During the second half of the old century Dean Stanley had done all he could to assert the primacy of Westminster Abbey, but as London's Protestant cathedral, built by a Protestant for a Protestant country, St. Paul's spoke for a special sense of Englishness and national election as nowhere else could. "Within the Cathedral all is hushed and dim," recorded *The Times*'s correspondent. "The wintry light of the February morning is insufficient to illuminate the edifice, and circles of electric light glow with a golden radiance in the choir and nave and transepts. Almost every one attending the service is in mourning or dressed in sombre garments. Gradually the building fills, and as it does so one catches glimpses of the scarlet tunics of distinguished soldiers, of scarlet gowns, the garb of City aldermen, and of the golden epaulettes of naval officers shining out conspicuously against the dark background of their uniforms. The band of the Coldstream Guards is stationed beneath the dome . . . and this, too, affords a vivid note of colour. Behind the band sit a number of bluejackets."

For all the trappings of the occasion, however, the statesmen, foreign dignitaries and diplomats, it was the simplicity of the service that was so striking. On the stroke of twelve the King, dressed in the uniform of an admiral of the fleet, took his place, and as the Archbishop of Canterbury, the Bishop of London and the Dean of St. Paul's processed with the other clergy into the choir, the congregation sang "Rock of Ages." The Lord's Prayer was then read, followed by the antiphon "Lead Me Lord in Thy Righteousness," and Psalms XXIII—"The Lord Is My Shepherd"—and XC—"Lord Thou Hast Been Our Refuge."

It was a short service, without a sermon. "Behold I shew you a mystery," Dean Inge read from 1 Corinthians XV:

> *We shall not all sleep, but we shall all be changed,*
> *For this corruptible must put on incorruption, and this mortal*
> *must put on immortality.*
> *So when this corruptible shall have put on incorruption, and this*
> *mortal shall have put on immortality, then shall be brought to pass*
> *the saying that is written, Death is swallowed up in victory.*
> *O death where is thy sting? O grave where is thy victory?*

As St. Paul's ringing challenge faded away, the sounds of a drum roll swelled, and the Dead March from *Saul* filled the cathedral. For all those present this was a moment of almost unbearable poignancy, but with that ceremonial genius that the imperial age had lately mastered, the most memorable and starkly simple was still to come.

As the Prayer of Committal was read, the names of the dead—Robert Falcon Scott, Lawrence Oates, Edward Wilson, Henry Bowers, Edgar Evans—filled the "stricken silence" of the dimly lit church with their absence. "As we go down to the dust," the choir sang, just as they had done to the same Kieff chant at the memorial service for those lost on the *Titanic*, "and weeping o'er the grave we make our song: Alleluia! Alleluia! Alleluia! Give rest, O Christ, to Thy servants with Thy Saints, where sorrow and pain are no more, neither sighing, but life everlasting."

With a final hymn sung by the whole congregation, and a blessing from the Archbishop, the service was over. The National Anthem was sung to the accompaniment of the Coldstreams' band, and as the sound reached the streets outside the vast crowd of some ten thousand still waiting took it up. The King was escorted to the south door, and to the strains of Beethoven's "Funeral March on the death of a hero," the congregation slowly dispersed.

For all its simplicity and familiarity, it had in some ways been an odd service, combining as it did the raw immediacy of a funeral with the more celebratory distance of a memorial. It might have been only four days since the news from Oamaru reached England, but by that time Scott and his men had been dead for almost a year, their bodies lying frozen in the tent in which they had been found. "There is awe in the thought that it all happened a year ago," the *Daily Sketch* had written on 11 February, shamelessly milking the idea for all the pathos it was worth. "When Amundsen came back in the spring of last year and Polar discussions were in all men's mouths and newspapers—even then, the Englishmen, the goal accomplished, lay quiet in the snows. Through the months since . . . while wives and friends set forth for meetings and counted time, they lay oblivious. All was over for them long ago."

For the families of the dead there could be nothing but bitterness in the thought, but for the nation as a whole it made the transition from grief to celebration that much easier. In its columns the *Sketch* might "quiver in unison" with the "lonely pathetic figure" of Scott's wife "on the far Pacific," but the lapse of time had an important psychological impact, subsuming the recent past into a longer historical narrative in a way that enabled the country to metamorphose the reality of that tent into an icy shrine, and Scott and his men into the quasi-legendary heroes they immediately became.

Above all else, however, it was a sense of *absence* rather than *presence* that contributed most profoundly to the mood of national mourning in a way that looked forward to the psychology of the Cenotaph and the Unknown Soldier rather than back to any precedent. During November of 1920 the hundreds of thousands who filed past the tomb of the Unknown Soldier could all superimpose their own image on the nameless and rankless corpse, and in a similar way the men and women who mourned Scott all had different ideas of precisely what they were mourning.

To some the meaning of the deaths of Scott and his men was religious, to others secular; to some they were the embodiment of Christian sacrifice or English chivalry, to others again of pacific courage or scientific dedication. "No more pathetic and tragic story has ever been unfolded," *The Times*'s leader announced on the twelfth, just twenty-four hours after the country had begun to digest the news, "than that of the gallant band of Antarctic explorers whose unavailing heroism now fills the public mind with mingled grief and admiration . . . Nothing in the painful yet inspiring narrative is more touching than the fidelity with which CAPTAIN

SCOTT and his comrades, fighting for their very lives with the remorseless forces of Nature, clung in ever increasing peril and weakness to the scientific records and geological specimens which it was the primary object of their expedition to secure. It is thus that they snatched victory out of the jaws of death ... The admiralty regards them, and the Navy honours them, as 'killed in action,' and the civilized world will endorse the verdict."

There was something, however, about the response to Scott's death that differentiates it sharply from the mourning over the grave of the Unknown Soldier. There can be no doubting the reality of people's grief when the news reached England, but it was a grief shot through with a sense of gratitude to the men who had restored to them their emotional birthright as Englishmen. "The keynote of this wonderful 'In Memoriam,'" the *Daily Sketch* proudly wrote, "was at once its simplicity and its quiet exultation." "To mourn!" it demanded, the day after the memorial service. "Yes, we had come to mourn—yet not with wailing and lamenting, but rather with a song of thankfulness for that these sons of our common country had died as they had lived, in the spirit which is the noblest heritage of Englishmen ... Could Nelson, sleeping in the crypt below, hear those mighty trumps of a nation's requiem, he would know that though the years roll on, yet, as long as England expects, there are heroes of her blood and race to answer truly to the call."

The real value of their deaths, *The Times* insisted, "is moral and spiritual, and therefore in the truest sense national. It is a proof that in an age of depressing materialism men can still be found to face known hardship, heavy risk, and even death, in pursuit of an idea, and that the unconquerable will can carry them through, loyal to the last to the charge they have undertaken. That is the temper of men who build empires, and while it lives among us we shall be capable of maintaining the Empire that our fathers builded ... So we owe honour and gratitude to Captain Scott and his companions for showing that the solid stuff of national character is still among us, and that men are still willing to be 'killed in action' for an idea."

The news of Scott's death would have struck a chord at any time, but what is easily ignored in all this is that it came at a moment when Britain was in urgent need of the kind of reassurance it seemed to offer. The horrors of the First World War have cast so seductive a glow over the age that immediately preceded it that it is easy to forget what it was really like, seeing it instead as a last Golden Age, a final swansong of patrician ease and self-confidence before the watershed of the Somme and Jutland destroyed its certainties for ever.

There is something about the iconography of the period, too—something about its ripeness of institutional expression, its imperial gravity, its command of ritual—that no amount of historical deconstruction can shake. This has nothing in any crude sense to do with the mere exercise of power, but from the rent rolls of its statesmen to the flickering cinematographic dumb-show of the old Queen's Jubilee parade, the age before the Great War still projects an illusion of ceremonial and functional harmony that seems to paralyse dissent.

It was, after all, little more than a decade since a cabinet that boasted a marquess for Prime Minister, another at the War Office, a duke for Lord President, the son of a duke as Secretary of India, an earl, a viscount, three barons and a brace of baronets, seemed to hold out to Englishmen a promise of social and historic permanence. In the United States—the power of the future—and France—the historic enemy of the past—politics and social status had long parted company, but faced with a government that seemed to reconcile privilege and responsibility, heredity and power as effortlessly as Salisbury's did, it is hard not to succumb to the illusion.

Yet if images of the King presiding at Cowes, of Balfour golfing at North Berwick, or Sir Edward Grey fly-fishing on the Itchen, seem to extend the shelf-life of the "Splendid" in Splendid Isolation long beyond its doctrinal usefulness, it certainly did not seem a Golden Age at the time. The Poet Laureate Alfred Austin's idea of heaven might be to sit in an English garden and receive telegrams alternately announcing British victories by land and sea, but after the humiliations of the Boer War at the hands of a nation no bigger than "Flintshire and Denbighshire combined," it was not just Kipling who could see the writing on the walls of Tyre.

There are certain moments in modern British history that have a psychological impact out of all proportion to their practical consequences, and the war in South Africa is one of these. In the past even such defeats as Majuba Hill could be transmuted into allegories of British heroism, but as Europe howled in moral outrage at British concentration camps, and British troops came invalided home in their thousands, the jubilant vision of Herbert Bismarck, the Anglophobe son of the "Iron Chancellor," of a country "smothered in its own fat" seemed something more than Prussian wishful thinking.

It was as if Britain, as it began the long retreat from empire and abandoned its historic isolation for the entanglements of European alliances, had collectively glimpsed the possibility that the whole fabric of its power was nothing but a show. From the moment that naval architects had created the *Dreadnought* the navy that had reigned supreme at the Queen's Jubilee was so much scrap. But what if the whole edifice of power was a charade? What if the obsessions with espionage and invasion in the popular fiction of the day were justified? What if the paranoid hatred of decadence and homosexuality and "foreign influence" was no more than a last, dying protest of a stricken empire? What if the very texture of national life, the physical and imaginative landscape of its identity, its historical sense of self, were all equally flawed? What if "The great house, the church, the village, and the labourers and their servants in their stations and degrees," as Wells wrote, had "even now passed away"? "The great houses stand in the parks still, the cottages cluster respectfully on their borders, touching their eaves with their creepers, the English country-side . . . persists obstinately in looking what it was. It is like an early day in a fine October. The hand of change rests on it all, unfelt, unseen; resting for a while, as it were half reluctantly, before it grips and ends the thing forever. One frost and the whole face of things will be bare, links snap, patience end, our fine foliage of pretences lie glowing in the mire . . ."

In such a climate of doubt and self-questioning, the outpouring of national pride over Scott was no demonstration of imperialist triumphalism but its reverse, its militancy the militancy of weakness, its stridency the stridency of a country desperate for assurance that the moral qualities that once made it great were still intact. "Children," Arthur Machen—the great mythologiser of "The Angel of Mons"—began the story read to hundreds of thousands of schoolchildren across the country as Scott's memorial service at St. Paul's opened, "you are about to hear the true story of five of the bravest and best men who have ever lived on the earth since the world began. You are English boys and girls, and you must often have heard England spoken of as the greatest country in the world, or perhaps you have been told that the British Empire . . . is the greatest Empire that the world has ever seen . . . when we say that England is great we are not thinking of the size of the country or of the number of people who live in it. We are thinking of much more important things, and if you listen to the story that is to be read to you, you will find out what greatness really does mean."

"Oh! England! oh! England! What men have done for thee," responded one eleven-year-old girl, Mary Steel, and her sob of relieved gratitude found an echo across the country. "Amundsen says he won the Cup," began one extraordinary poem sent to Scott's bereaved family by an E. Clacy—a poem that in its grotesque fusion of sporting and religious symbolism brings into single focus every outdated fantasy of Arthurian chivalry and games-playing, dog-loving, xenophobic English pre-eminence that ever floated an empire.

> *Amundsen says he won the Cup*
> *Then why do our men guard it?*
> *Two lie prone, but one sits up*
> *Over his hands there hovers a Cup*
> *Amundsen says he won that Cup*
> *Then why does our man hold it?*
> *"Devil's Ballroom" and "Devil's Ravine"*
> *Naming the vastnesses! What does he mean?*
> *"Shambles," the dogs explain that name*
> *Where they lie butchered—exhausted and lame*
> *With bringing him up! . . .*

> *Over the tent and into the tent*
> *Floats the wonderful Cup*
> *Hovers and touches those that lie prone*
> *And then to the Master—who sits alone*
> *Fire—Blood—or Wine?*
> *He sees right into the Thing Divine*
> *For he sits up*
> *Into his hands—the Holy Grail*
> *Into his body—cease of pain*
> *Into his heart—a voice says "Hail"*
> *And he knows he has won that Cup.*
> *Amundsen says he won the Cup*
> *Then why does our man hold it?*

If ever a man needed saving from the enthusiasm of his admirers, in fact, it was Scott. During the course of his life the impassioned support of Sir Clements Markham would invariably be as much a liability as a help, and in death the jingoistic and imperialist uses to which his name and story were pressed guaranteed that when the reaction came it would be bitter and violent. "I found an essentially *little* man," Trevor Griffiths, the dramatist and influential populariser of the hostile modern "Scott myth," wrote in 1985, "of deeply ordinary talent: light, conventional, fearful, uncertain, manipulative, ill-tempered, irrational, secretive, driven, at times touching in his misery, trapped inside a particular class-specific Englishness, unequipped, uncharismatic."

Were the sentiments expressed in E. Clacy's poem the only ones heard at Scott's death, the backlash that has seen his reputation plummet over the last years might be understandable; but his tragedy touched the popular imagination in ways that had nothing to do with imperial destiny, "class-specifics" or "Englishness." The race for the Poles in the Heroic Age of Exploration had certainly excited intense national rivalries, but as the telegrams, donations and letters of condolence poured in from Toronto and Lyttelton, and from Tempico and Christiania, all that was forgotten in a sympathy that predicates a shared—and almost proprietorial—pride in his end.

This picture of universal sorrow is not the whole story, of course—even in these first days the doubts and questions were there—but when Dean Inge declared Scott's triumph over the grave, it was not just an expression of Christian hope but an absolute conviction that Death had no sting to wound a man who had lived and died as Scott. When he was interviewed in New York, Shackleton might publicly wonder how Scott's party could have succumbed to a mere blizzard, but not in even his most sanguine moments could he have seen what would happen, or anticipate his own posthumous metamorphosis from Edwardian freebooter into middle-management guru while the *beau idéal* of English chivalry became a byword for bungling incompetence.

There are few things that more poignantly signal the remoteness of Dean Inge's age from our own, because while nothing is more inevitable or healthier than historical revisionism, what has happened to Scott's reputation requires some other label. It might seem odd from this distance that neo-Georgian England should find in a Darwin-carrying agnostic of Scott's cast the type of Christian sacrifice, but the historical process that has shrunk the rich, complex and deeply human set of associations that once clustered round his story into an allegory of arrogance, selfishness and moral stupidity is every bit as extraordinary. How has a life that was once seen as a long struggle of duty been transformed into the embodiment of self-interested calculation? How has the name of the meticulous and "cautious explorer" his men followed become synonymous with reckless waste? How has the son and husband his mother and wife described become the type of English emotional inadequacy? By what process does a tenderness for animal life become a pathological disorder that belongs to the psychology of military incompetence? What is it that stops a whole age

hearing in the cadences, the measure and the sentiment of Scott's last harrowing appeal to the public, the words of the dying Hamlet?

The most tempting answer is suggested by the cultural and political
overtones implicit in Trevor Griffiths' use of the word "Englishness,"
because if Scott was once celebrated as the incarnation of everything an
Englishman should be, he is now damned as the sad embodiment of everything he actually was. It is very hard to imagine that Scott's reputation
would have taken the battering it has if he had been Irish or Australian, but
in his real and perceived "Englishness" the hero of St. Paul's has answered
the revisionist needs of a post-colonial age as perfectly as General Gordon
once did those of Bloomsbury.

But if the historiography of the Heroic Age has always been as political
as the expeditions themselves—polar archives bear witness to that—it
would be too easy to take this as the full answer. From the early 1960s historians and biographers were constantly exploiting one or another partisan
line, yet buried beneath their different cultural or partisan agenda lies a
more fundamental lack of sympathy for Scott's age that has nothing to do
with nationality or bias.

In many ways, of course, the simple truth is that we know more about
Scott's weaknesses and the failures of his leadership than did the congregation at St. Paul's, but it is not that we see him differently from the way they
did, but that we see him the *same,* and instinctively do not like it. As an age
we no longer hear what A.C. Bradley called the "Othello Music" of high
eloquence, no longer, mercifully, believe it. At the time of Scott's death
men and women clutched at the proof he offered that the qualities that
had once made Britain great were not extinct, but with the knowledge of
what lay only two years ahead—the hidebound failure of Jutland, the
hopeless heroism and obscene waste of the Western Front—the ideals of
duty, self-sacrifice, discipline, patriotism and hierarchy associated with his
tragedy take on a different and more sinister colouring. This is too seminal
and too valid an insight to give up, but somewhere between the Scott of St.
Paul's and the Scott of modern myth lies a profoundly more complex and
interesting figure. Of all the explorers of the Heroic Age he is the most
interesting, and if Scott had never gone to the Pole, and we had never
heard of him, his life, with its alternating rhythms of obscurity and fame, of
duty and ambition, of success and failure and the corrosive temptations of
them both, would still be the stuff of the English novel from George Eliot
to George Gissing.

It was Scott's fate, however, to be plucked from the pages of a domestic novel and placed, quite literally, between the covers of an A.E.W. Mason tale of heroic adventure. It is the moral of Gray's "Elegy" in reverse: a life destined for Stoke Poges rerouted to St. Paul's. This is its fascination. It would be moving enough in any context, but set it against its Antarctic background, against a world where every hairline crack becomes a fissure, every inadequacy is ruthlessly exposed, every motive publicly interrogated and every resource of moral and physical courage challenged, and one has the unique appeal of Scott's story.

"To me, and perhaps to you," wrote Apsley Cherry-Garrard, one of the party who found the frozen bodies of Scott and his companions, "the interest in this story is the men, and it is the spirit of the men." Of no one is this more true than of Scott himself. It is this that makes a rounded sense of his whole life and personality so crucial to any understanding of the successes and failures of his two great expeditions. History can take one so far; science can answer so many questions. But those ultimate questions that still swirl about Scott's last tent can be resolved by neither. They belong to a sense of Scott the man and to the imagination in a way that lifts his story out of the esoterica of polar history and places it in the mainstream of human experience.

Two: Childhood and Dartmouth

There was a time, and not so long ago either, when gentle people were so gentle that the males could not with the countenance of their families enter upon any profession other than the Army, the Navy, or the Church.

GILBERT CANNAN, *The Road to Come* (1913)

T wo years before the outbreak of the First World War, at just about the same time that Scott was refining the concept of gentility for a whole age, a Royal Naval officer confidently told an Admiralty committee, set up to explore the question of commissions from the lower deck, that it took three generations to make a *gentleman*.

If anyone was searching for a clue to the simultaneous social durability and decline of Britain as a great industrial power, they could do a lot worse than settle on that. For many a European the only surprise about the formula would have been that the process could be so rapid; but it has always been Britain's genius and curse to dangle the hopes of gentility before an aspirant population, absorbing and anaesthetising the nation's energies and talents into the comforting and inclusive orbit of respectability encompassed by that word "gentleman."

There is a case, anyway, for arguing that only pedantry, snobbery or family romance could ask for a longer genealogical perspective, and certainly none is needed for Scott's family. His early biographers liked to detect a likeness to the "great Sir Walter" in his features, but for all the family traditions of Border raiders, Buccleuch connections and Jacobites hanged at York, the only family history that had any relevance to Scott himself begins with his grandfather Robert.*

The son of a schoolteacher who had come to the West Country from France, where the family had gone after the '45, Robert Scott was born in 1784, and after four years "in a subordinate capacity" was promoted in 1806 to purser in the Royal Navy. At the end of the Napoleonic Wars he was serving—prophetically enough in the light of his grandson's future career—in HMS *Erebus,* and within five years had amassed enough from prize money or graft to buy with his brother Edward a brewery in Plymouth for £4,782. Robert Scott had married in 1816, and in the same year that the two brothers acquired the Hoegate Brewery took the lease from Sir John Aubyn on a house at Stoke Damerel on the outskirts of Devonport. The house was more a Regency cottage than anything grander when Robert bought it, but by the time he had finished adding to it, "Outlands" had become the outward symbol of the Scotts' ambitions, a country gentleman's residence in miniature, complete with servants, outbuildings, shrubberies, paddocks, orchard, governesses, nurses, pets, peacock and stream.

In a small way Robert Scott was the nightmare of Jane Austen's Sir Walter Elliot made flesh, the Napoleonic War carpetbagger come good. It is not clear how close an interest he ever took in his brewery, but while it was certainly enough to lead to quarrels with his brother, he had other ambitions for his children, sending four of his five sons into the army or navy,

---

*In the light of Scott's own posthumous reputation, however, it is fascinating to see the way in which his earlier biographers were determined to give him a family history more in keeping with the romance of his reputation. "The Scotts were, before the union of the two kingdoms, 'the greatest robbers and fiercest fighters among the border clans,' " wrote Stephen Gwynn, the first of Scott's biographers, in the 1920s, to write with the active cooperation of the family: "By the eighteenth century, even the Border was tolerably settled, but the Scotts 'kept a wild trick of their ancestry,' and when the Jacobite risings came, they were in the fighting also. Sir Walter tells us, in a fragment of autobiography, that he was made a Jacobite in his childhood by the stories told in his hearing of the cruelties exercised in the executions at Carlisle and in the Highlands after the battle of Culloden. 'One or two of our own distant relations,' he says, 'had fallen on that occasion.' It is possible that one of these may have been the great-great-grand uncle of Robert Falcon Scott. It is certain at all events that Captain Scott's great-great-grand uncle was hanged upon this occasion . . . at York."

There is a kernel of truth in this tradition—church registers record a wide network of Scotts living, marrying and inter-marrying in the parishes around the Jacobite battlefield of Prestonpans in the first half of the eighteenth century—but the only historical certainty is that no Scott was hanged at York. There were certainly three Scotts captured at Carlisle by the Duke of Cumberland's forces as the Jacobite army retreated north, and it is possible that one of the two tried and condemned at York in 1746, Alexander or William—both members of Colonel Stuart's regiment and recruited in Perthshire the previous year—was a relative, although neither was in the end executed but instead, like so many other Jacobites, reprieved and enlisted into the Hanoverian army.

and leaving only the youngest, John Edward—Robert Falcon Scott's father—to maintain an increasingly distasteful connection with trade.

If the brewery had ever made very much money, it had ceased to do so by the time of Robert's death, and Scott's father was left with the tastes of a gentleman and very little on which to support them. The death of Robert also led to a protracted family challenge over the ownership of Outlands, and in 1862 John played the only card available to a man spoiled for business and useless for much else, and married a Hannah Cuming, the twenty-one-year-old daughter of a prominent figure in the Plymouth insurance and maritime world.

John and Hannah Scott had six children who survived infancy—Ettie, Rose, Robert Falcon (always known as "Con"), Grace, Archie and Katherine—and it is in their memories that this marriage and Outlands' life most vividly survive. "Mr. Scott girded against the enforced restriction of a business life which was uncongenial to his tastes," wrote George Seaver, the last biographical link, through Con's sister Grace, with that generation of the Scott family, "and although he interested himself in local affairs in Devonport where he was magistrate and Chairman of the Conservative Association, these pursuits provided no adequate outlet for a man of his capability . . . Lack of means, lack of health, and lack of opportunity bred in him a baleful sense of inferiority, the result of inhibitions, which gave rise to the most explosive temper—by no means improved by the periodical visits of his brothers, who stirred his envy by their accounts of thrilling adventures in foreign fields."

It is hard to know how just this is, or how much it reflects the resentment of a daughter who always had to take second place to her two brothers. The few surviving letters from Con's early days certainly suggest an affectionate and easy-going relationship between father and son, but a letter written in a tent in Antarctica just before his death conjures up the John Scott of Grace's memory. "The inherited vice from my side of the family is indolence," Scott warned his wife about their own son; "above all he must guard, and you must guard him against that. I had to force myself into being strenuous as you know—had always an inclination to be idle. My father was idle and it brought much trouble."

Side by side in photographs, Scott's parents certainly look an oddly suited pair, John Scott bearded, irresolute, almost characterless, his wife Hannah refined, intelligent, discriminating and kindly formidable. It seems unlikely that the Cuming family ever let John Scott forget that it was their money that had kept Outlands in the family, and it was Hannah who ruled, and her brand of genteel, slightly compromised, mid-Victorian Evangelicalism that set the moral tone of the household. "Whatever we have cause to bless ourselves for, comes from you," her devoted elder son would later write to her at a moment of family tragedy. "If ever children had cause to worship their mother, we feel we have, dear . . . you can never be a burden, but only the bond that keeps us closer together,—the fine example that will guide us all . . . What is left for you to do is to be the same sweet kind mother that you have always been, our guide and our friend."

Not that there was anything gloomily oppressive about her influence— their Plymouth Brethren cousins thought the Outlands Scotts "damned" —and the children grew up to a normal, uncomplicated life. "As children we were always very happy and ordinary and simple," Grace recalled in a bucolic memoir of their Outlands childhood, "and though we had a comfortable house and a nice biggish garden there was no money for travel or even simple excitements. As a matter of fact, we did not want them or think about them, for we were brought up a much quieter generation . . . Our great yearly treat to look forward to was a visit to the Pantomime at the Plymouth Theatre! Though the house was small for such a crowd—seventeen persons when the boys were at home—thanks to the garden, fields, and outhouses, during the day-time we could disperse. We had entire liberty within these bounds which excluded a blacksmith's forge just outside the shrubbery gate, and a small general shop—good for boiled sweets. I may say that to get the sweets we had to climb a high gate, which was kept locked to keep us from temptation, and failed."

Robert Falcon Scott was born into this modest Victorian idyll on 6 June 1868, and first "enters history," as J.M. Barrie, his most influential and unscrupulous mythologiser, put it, "aged six, blue eyed, long haired, inexpressibly slight and in velveteen, being held out at arm's length by a servant and dripping horribly, like a half drowned kitten. This is the earliest recollection of him of a sister, who was too young to join a children's party on that fatal day. But Con, as he was always called, had intimated to her that from her window she would be able to see him taking a noble lead in the festivities in the garden, and she looked; and that is what she saw. He had been showing his guests how superbly he could jump the leat, and had fallen into it."

This probably says more about the author of *Peter Pan* than it does about Scott, but if it is hard to see how a nation could swallow it, it does highlight the problem of everything to do with Scott's youth. There is no reason to imagine that anyone would invent Barrie's anecdotes for him, but they belong to the world of medieval apocrypha rather than biography, exemplary tales chosen to illustrate either latent greatness or the triumph of will over the sickly, dreamy, introspective, "pigeon-chested," slovenly "Old Mooney" of Barrie-inspired legend.

There is no evidence that Scott was any weaker-chested than many another child, or any "dreamier," but the anecdotes flow with the same dire mix of saccharine charm and cautionary humour—the stream, the "ocean" that only adults could call a pond, the holly tree, the dangers of the glass conservatory, the much-loved pony, Beppo, who would throw any other rider. "His first knife is a great event in the life of a boy," wrote Barrie, "and he is nearly always given it on condition that he keeps it shut. So it was with Con, and a few minutes after he had sworn not to open it he was begging for permission to use it on a tempting sapling. 'Very well,' his father said grimly, 'but remember, if you hurt yourself, don't expect any sympathy from me.' The knife was opened, and to cut himself rather badly proved as easy as falling into the leat. The father, however, had not noticed, and the boy put his bleeding hand into his pocket and walked on unconcernedly. This is a good story of a child of seven who all his life suffered extreme nausea from the sight of blood; even in the *Discovery* days, to get accustomed to 'seeing red' he had to force himself to watch Dr. Wilson skinning his specimens."

For all of Barrie's efforts to press it into significance, it is the utter normality of Scott's childhood that is most striking. In later life he, Archie and his oldest sister, Ettie, would always form a kind of distinctive triumvirate within family councils, but as children they all mucked in together, left pretty much to their own devices by a father busy pottering about his gardens and a mother nursing her ailing parents. "Our tastes for sailing were very much encouraged by my uncle Harry, my mother's brother," Grace remembered. "On holidays we, that is four girls and two brothers, had glorious days sailing about Plymouth Harbour in an eighteen foot boat with a big lug sail. We were taught to work the boat and had thrilling days out by the Mewstone (the parental limit seawards), or up one of the rivers, where we had been known to be stranded in the mud for hours on a falling tide. Considering our lives were so very sheltered then, so small and bounded, it seemed wonderful to have our sailing freedom."

Close as the children would always be, it was not within the circle of his siblings that Scott's childhood was shaped, but by the dynamics of family ambitions that stretched back to his grandfather Robert. In any sensible society—or European nation of his own day—a child of Scott's type would have ended up as an engineer or scientist, but for a boy of his class in Victorian England the future was circumscribed by the deadening monopoly of the old professions, and at the age of eight, home and his sisters' governess were exchanged for a day school at Damerel, from where, at eleven or twelve, he was packed off by his father to board at Stubbington House in Fareham, a naval crammer that prepared boys for the entrance exams to the training ship *Britannia*.

If Scott had any say in the choice it has gone unrecorded, but it would be hard to imagine a better berth for a training ship or for a child of any imagination than the River Dart. Sheltered by steep hills on either bank and protected from the sea by a sudden bend in the river, the *Britannia* lay moored just above the ancient port of Dartmouth, ideally positioned for the rough training ground of the open channel and the quiet waters of the river.

There can be few more beautiful ports anywhere, and if a boy from Plymouth needed no lesson in England's maritime past, Dartmouth's history was just as rich. The natural harbour had become too small to retain its old importance by Scott's day, but even after its historic role in the old triangular trade of cod, salt and wine had been usurped by Liverpool, the town still preserved links with the New World and English naval life that stretched back through the Dutch and Civil Wars to Sir Humphrey Gilbert and Elizabeth's reign.

The *Britannia* was a product of the mid-Victorian navy's determination to control and standardise its officer intake. In the first half of the nineteenth century a boy's education was dependent on the goodwill and interest of the individual ship's captain, but in 1857 an Admiralty circular announced a new regime of training and examinations for all future officers that would include a period of time on a stationary ship before they were allowed to go to sea. The initial training ship had been established at Portsmouth, but *Britannia* had first been towed to her mooring on the Dart in September 1863, and in the following year, as numbers grew, was joined by a second vessel, the *Hindostan*. In 1869 the *Britannia* herself was replaced by a bigger ship, and it was this *Britannia*—the eighth of her name—that Scott knew, an old sailing vessel of over six thousand tons, with a draught of thirty-one feet and a length of 251 feet, a gangway linking her to the *Hindostan*, and a fully rigged foremast to test the seamanship, agility and courage of her cadets.

And it was in this *Britannia*, too, for the next thirty years, until she was replaced by a shore-based college, that the navy trained its future leaders. At the time of the First World War there was scarcely a senior officer who had not passed through Dartmouth, not a man above the rank of lieutenant-commander who had not been moulded by the same ethos and training that produced the men who fought at Jutland or went south with Scott. "That training," the biographer of Earl Beatty—the navy's most flamboyantly glamorous admiral since Nelson—wrote of *Britannia* in the mid-1880s, the years immediately after Scott was there, "was based on forcing cadets into a pre-conceived and rigid mould by the application of harsh, even inhuman discipline. Obedience to orders was the hallowed principle of the system, and woe betide any boy who was deemed to have transgressed that tenet. Any signs of originality or independence were seriously frowned on—if not actively suppressed; while intellectual accomplishments always came a bad second to athletics."

In many ways, this makes it little different from any Victorian public school in its aspirations. From the days of Thomas Arnold the ambition of every public school was to produce a "brave, helpful, truth-telling" English Christian gentleman, but whereas the Arnoldian ideal was to mould the men who would run the Empire or clear out slums, the aim of *Britannia* was to take the sons of these gentlemen and refine—or brutalise—them into the more specialist incarnation of the British naval officer.

This might have mattered less if the navy still recruited from a more inclusive social base, or if the curriculum in Scott's day had been any wider, or had more strenuously faced up to the realities of the age of steam. When *Britannia* was first established twenty years before, the range of subjects was more or less typical of the wider educational world, but by 1883 this had shrunk back to a far more vocational training—Arithmetic and Algebra (to read across Scott's Final Examination Results); Geometry; Trigonometry, Plain and Spherical; Practical Navigation; Theoretical Navigation; Charts; Instruments and Observations; French; Essay; Physics and Drawing.

In practice little attention was ever given to "Extra Subjects," or, in fact, to study at all—in Scott's term, or intake, only three cadets got so much as "Fair" for "Attention paid to Study"—and with no engineering workshop, no gunnery officer, no instruction in command and a heavy emphasis on seamanship, a *Britannia* training put a cadet firmly in the camp of the dinosaur. "I call the whole system of our naval education utterly faulty," the young Jellicoe—future First Sea Lord and Commander-in-Chief of the Grand Fleet at Jutland—writing under the *nom de plume* of "A Naval

Nobody," protested in *Macmillan's Magazine*: "I say that we, the Navy's youth, are in some professional matters most deplorably ignorant, and the day will come when we, England, will wake up to the fact with a start. It sounds impossible, inconceivable, that it is only a privileged few who are allowed to make a study of gunnery . . . only a privileged few who are initiated into the mysteries of torpedos; only a privileged few who are taught . . . surveying and navigation; not even a privileged few who are taught the science of steam; and yet all this is so!"

It was an education for an age of sail, designed for a profession that envisaged no scope for individual responsibility, and enforced with all the rigour of nineteenth-century naval discipline. From the moment that Scott woke, his day was regulated to the sound of bugle calls or drum rolls, to the barking of orders and the running of feet, as the cadets were marched from bath house to inspection deck, from inspection to Euclid, from Euclid to breakfast, and from their breakfast across the gangway to *Hindostan* and back to *Britannia's* poop for another inspection, prayers—and all that before the day proper had even started. Even their swimming was controlled by bugle call, even the casual brutality of the discipline institutionalised by a system of numbers. For severe offences there was the cane and the captain, but for everything else, the Commander's Punishments ranged from 1 to 7, with "No. 4"—Scott's most common penalty—including "an hour early in the morning, an hour out on the deck after evening prayers, extra drill and stopped pocket money." "19 Oct, '81," Scott's charge sheet typically reads:

> Entering an orchard whilst on Half holiday . . . March 11th 1882, Skylarking at Morning Study, [punishment] 1 days 3; Sept 18th Late for Muster, 1 days 4; Oct 3rd Not being into his place in the ranks when 2nd bugle sounded, 1 days 3; Oct 6th Talking in his Hammock after hours, 1 days 3; Oct 11th Being into Hindostan Contrary to regulations, 1 days 4; Oct 13th Going on the Middle deck in his night shirt, 1 days 4; Oct 15th; Creating a disturbance on sleeping deck, 1 days 4; Oct 16th Making a noise in his Hamk after hours, 1 days 3; Nov 5th Talking in his Hamk after hours, 1 days 3; Nov 9th Improperly dressed at Muster, 1 days 2; Nov 22nd Delaying to come out of the bath, 1 days 3 . . .

There were other infringements—most memorably, "Did as Cadet Captain allow some of the Cadets to humbug Mr. Poynter Chief Capt. in the

Sanctuary, and did also take part in annoying him"—but there is not much here to alarm anyone who has ever been to a boarding school, and still less to suggest the delicate child of Barrie legend. From time to time the *Britannia* regime or some bullying scandal would make the national newspapers, but if it always tottered on the edge of bullying, it was probably no different from any other school in Victorian life or fiction.

There was a lighter side to *Britannia* life, too, and if there was little privacy, there was the band and dancing in the evenings, the playing fields, the tennis and racquets courts, the ship's beagles, and Totnes and the freedom of the river on summer half-holidays. On these occasions the cadets would be given hampers of food and lemonade and ginger beer, and after rowing upstream past the Anchor Stone in the middle of the Dart where Raleigh had smoked his pipe, would swim and watch the salmon-netting before drifting back downstream in the evening, tying up among a small flotilla of boats behind the Totnes pleasure steamer while trippers threw them cakes.

There are no surviving letters of Scott's from *Britannia*—nothing to suggest that he was there except the memorial in the chapel erected by his term—but for a fourteen-year-old grandson of a despised ship's purser, anonymity itself was a victory.* It is no coincidence that the future Earl Beatty was a failure there, but if Scott's aim was assimilation he could not have done it better, coming out of *Britannia* the average product of an average term in a system designed to produce the average—tenth of his term in his first exams, sixth at the end of his second and eighth in the third, with a numbing catalogue of "Satisfactories" and "Very Satisfacto-

---

* A glance at Scott's term underlines how marginal a figure the son of a man in trade was in the late-Victorian navy. Among his intake was the son of a viscount, the son of a baronet, the sons of admirals, colonels and clergymen, and the scions of some of Britain's great naval families. In more general terms, this did no more than reflect the professionally disastrous narrowing of the social range from which the service recruited its officers that had occurred since the end of the Napoleonic Wars. In 1815 almost 7 per cent of officers came from a working-class background, but within a generation this had dropped to none. Over the same span the children of peers entering the service increased from 7 to almost 11 per cent. The sons of baronets almost doubled, the gentry and traditional professions similarly increased their numbers, while only business fell, with the 4 per cent of the eighteen thousand officers who had once been prepared to acknowledge a background in trade dwindling to just three individuals. In one sense, however, Scott was lucky. In 1881, the same year that he joined *Britannia*, John Scott sold the failing brewery and retired to his gardens. In the census returns of 1881 he is already described as "Magistrate for Devonport, retired merchant," and if that conjures up a more prosperous situation than was the actual case, it at least allowed his son the luxury of filling in at the top of his Service Record, under "Name and Profession of Father," "J.E. Scott Esq, JP, Outlands, Plymouth."

ries" relieved only by a brace of "Fairs" and one "Unsatisfactory" in French.

His final examinations in July 1883 followed the same pattern. He scored a total of 1,457, coming sixth in Mathematics, ninth in Extra Subjects, thirteenth in seamanship, and seventh overall in a term of twenty-six. He passed out with First Class Certificates in Mathematics and Seamanship, and a Second in Extra Subjects. Of a possible year's sea-time—to count against the time needed, in the slow grind of promotion, to qualify for his lieutenant's exams—he was allowed eleven months. His "Attention Paid to Study" was rated "Very Moderate," his abilities "Very Good," and his conduct "as noted on Cadet's Certificate in Captain's own writing," also "Very Good."

He would have looked at those above him in the list and those below and seen nothing either to fear or to hope. Four years before him there had been Jellicoe, the year behind him Beatty, but there were no stars in his term. There were any number of future admirals there, and fourteen out of the twenty-six would make the crucial step of post-captain, but there was no one except Scott himself whose name would ever reach the wider public. None of this, though, helped. Without money, without "interest," without a naval pedigree, without a war to fight, he was ready for that gentlemanly anonymity the Outlands Scotts had been aiming at.

Three: Scott's Navy

The Naval Salute is made by bringing up the right hand to the cap or hat, naturally and smartly, but not hurriedly, with the thumb and fingers straight and close together, elbow in line with the shoulder, hand and forearm in line, the thumb being in line with the outer edge of the right elbow, with the palm of the hand being turned to the left, the opposite being the case when using the left hand . . .

Should a Petty Officer or man be standing about, and an officer pass him, he is to face the officer and salute; if sitting when an officer approaches, he is to rise, stand at attention, and salute. If two or more Petty Officers or men are sitting or standing about, the Senior Petty Officer or man will call the whole to attention and he alone will salute.

Manual of Seamanship (1908)

I have *never* realized to such an extent the truth that "familiarity breeds contempt" as this last year during which I have seen a little of the inside of the "Royal Navy," God help it.

EDWARD WILSON, *diary, 18 August 1902*

It is impossible to understand Scott's character or the expeditions he led unless it is remembered that from the age of thirteen until his death at forty-three, his whole life was led within this world. In everything but name *Discovery* and *Terra Nova* were naval expeditions, and nothing in their triumphs or failures, in the process of decision-making or the centralisation of control, in the cult of man-hauling or the chivalric traditions of sledging, in the relationships of its members with each other, of "insider" and "outsider," of navy and civilian, navy and scientist, navy and soldier, navy and merchant service and even navy and navy—wardroom and mess deck, executive and engineering—makes any sense unless seen against the background of the world that had closed round Scott when he entered *Britannia.*

For any boy joining *Britannia* at this time, as a novel based on Scott's life put it, there was a weight of history and expectation that was both a burden and an inspiration. The origins of the Royal Navy in anything like its modern form date back to the seventeenth century, but it was in the 120 years after the Glorious Revolution of 1688, and the long series of wars with France that established Britain as a world power, that its traditions, reputation and special place in the national life were set in stone.

From the St. Lawrence River to the Indian Ocean, from the West Indies to the Mediterranean, from the Baltic to the Southern Atlantic, the navy saw active service, carried out sieges, supported amphibious operations, fought fleet actions, defended Britain's trade routes, and acted as a potent instrument of diplomacy. During this period there were certainly some spectacular reverses, but in the almost continuous years of warfare that followed on the War of Jenkins' Ear in 1739—the navy was fighting for fifty out of the next seventy-five years—a tradition of professionalism, brotherhood, mutual confidence, experience, aggression, courage, flare and independence was created that reached its apogee in the charismatic genius of Nelson. "An Englishman enters a naval action with the firm conviction that his duty is to hurt his enemies and help his friends without looking out for directions in the middle of the fight," wrote a Spanish observer after the battle of Cape St. Vincent in 1797, in which Nelson had displayed just these qualities,

> and while he thus clears his mind of all subsidiary distractions, he rests in confidence on the certainty that his comrades, actuated by the same principles as himself, will be bound by the sacred and priceless law of mutual support. Accordingly, both he and all his fellows fix their minds on acting with zeal and judgement on the spur of the moment, and with the certainty that they will not be deserted. Experience shows, on the contrary, that a Frenchman or a Spaniard, working under a system which leans to formality and strict order being maintained in battle, has no feeling for mutual support, and goes into action with hesitation, preoccupied with the anxiety of seeing the commander-in-chief's signals, for such and such manoeuvres.

Nelson, Collingwood, Jervis, Duncan, Rodney, Hawke, Howe—Trafalgar, the Nile, Cape St. Vincent, Camperdown, Quiberon Bay, the Glorious First of June—these were names and battles that still held their place in

the popular imagination in the Victorian age, and if the nineteenth-
century navy could not match them, that was not entirely its fault. The
defeat of Napoleon in 1815 had left Britain as the sole global power and her
navy in undisputed possession of the seas, and in the "long calm lee of
Trafalgar" it was inevitable that her role would change from that of the
fighting force that had won Britain's eighteenth-century empire to the service that would have to police it.

If in many ways, however, the navy was no more than a victim of its
own unparalleled success, in the transition from a war footing to peacetime duties it had undoubtedly lost its way. In every generation there
were individuals who could see what needed to be done, but as the old
fighting machine settled into its new role, the old "purser" turned into the
new "paymaster" and the old working-class "tarpaulin" captain disappeared from the bridge, the instinctual, lateral-thinking, individualist, anti-
hierarchical "autocrat" of Nelson's navy gave way to the "authoritarian
personality" and the culture of deference, inflexibility, secretiveness, me-
ticulousness, obsessive cleanliness and social rigidity that dominated the
Victorian service.*

The period in Royal Naval history in which Scott joined the service has
not been called the "Dark Ages" for nothing, and few institutions have ever
offered so many hostages to satire as the late-Victorian navy. At the height
of its prestige in the 1880s it was the equal in size of any other five navies in
the world combined, and yet within a generation its ships and its reputa-

---

*The terms "autocratic" and "authoritarian" are used here in the technical sense that Nor-
man Dixon employed them in his dazzling On the Psychology of Military Incompetence. If
most people are undoubtedly a mixture of the two types, there are enough personalities that
manifest an overwhelming preponderance of one or other sets of characteristics to make it a
fascinating working model for any study of naval or military life. It is, though, a distinction that
is perhaps more easily illustrated than defined. Among Dixon's "autocrats" are Wolfe, Wellington, Nelson, Fisher, Lawrence of Arabia, Allenby, Slim, Rommel, Shaka, Napoleon, Zhukov
and, for all his megalomania, Douglas MacArthur. From his long list of "authoritarians," it is
perhaps only necessary to select Rear Admiral Albert Markham, an important figure in Scott's
life, and the officer who rammed and killed his admiral rather than disobey an order, to convey
what he means by the term. As a young midshipman in the China Seas and as a commander
on Nares's 1875 Arctic expedition Markham had amply proved his courage, but as he climbed
through the naval ranks all the gloomiest aspects of his sternly evangelical soul were given
their head. "A gentleman may be forgiven the occasional cigar," he once told his officers, "cigarettes are only for effeminate weaklings, but the low, filthy, and nauseous black pipe can only
be compared with gin and other disreputable liquors which ruin mind and body." With his
emotionally precarious childhood, his habit of subordination, his chivalrous and distant devotion to women, his intense fastidiousness, his harsh religiosity, tetchiness with juniors, rigidi-
ties, anxieties and Freemasonry, Albert Markham in fact comes as close as anyone to
embodying Dixon's concept of "authoritarianism" in its most purely unalloyed form.

tion were both gone, leaving behind only memories of whitewashed coal piles and exquisitely choreographed collisions, of choleric captains, holy-stoned decks and the endless "bull" of a peacetime service devoted to order, cleanliness, appearance, uniformity and uniforms.

Almost every memoir of the nineteenth century enshrines some particular favourite—the officer who thought he was the ship's boiler, and lay in his bed all day puffing out imaginary steam; the young Lord Charles Beresford, who kept an elephant on board; the captain who would fly-fish from the poop deck for his first officer; the fitness fanatic Sir Robert Arbuthnot, who sentenced a sailor to death for blistered feet—but against stiff competition, perhaps Sir Algernon "Pompo" Heneage gets the nod.

A man of wonderful and unabashed vanity, Heneage would break two eggs over his blond hair every morning, and take off his uniform for prayers because no Royal Navy captain should be seen kneeling to a higher deity. It was the same Algernon Heneage who instituted the practice of white kid gloves for the captain's inspection, progressing through a terrified ship, his cox'n behind him carrying another dozen clean pairs on a silver tray, as Heneage groped behind pipes and down lavatory bowls for the traces of dirt that could damn an executive officer's career for ever.

Perhaps the most alarming thing, however, about the dandified Heneage—he had 240 dress shirts in the Pacific, and sent them home to be laundered in London and returned in air-tight crates—was that he was by no means unique. There was a kind of magnificence about his self-esteem that gave him a semi-legendary status even during his lifetime, but as the letters and recollections of junior officers from future First Sea Lords down to the young Scott make plain, the petty tyranny and small-mindedness he embodied was the norm rather than the exception in a navy bent on turning its officers from fighting men into what the great naval reformer Jacky Fisher called "a sort of upper housemaid."

It is not the whole story, of course, and even during the *Pax Britannica* of the late Victorian age, a number of Scott's term in *Britannia* would see active service before they were out of their twenties. It is certainly true that the navy had fought no fleet action since the last bizarre fling of the Nelson navy at Navarino in 1827, but for most of the years since it had been on duty somewhere or other, its midshipmen and junior officers learning their trade and winning some forty-odd VCs in the long, unglamorous war against slavery or in campaigns that ranged from the Baltic to the Crimea and from the Sudan and the relief of Lucknow to China, Burma and the South Seas.

The oddity of it was, however, that in a service where captains would rather jettison shells than risk dirtying their ships by firing them, the most insidious temptation for a young midshipman of Scott's generation lay in everything that had been best in the navy rather than what was worst. From the day in 1757 that Admiral Byng was shot on his own quarterdeck "*pour encourager les autres*,"* every naval cadet was brought up to know that valour was the better part of discretion, and for a man like Scott, Shackleton's famous quip that a "live donkey" was better than a "dead lion" could have been no more an option than it would be for those other *Britannia*-reared officers who unswervingly followed Admiral Craddock to the bottom of the sea in the hopelessly unequal Battle of Coronel less than three years after Scott's own death.†

In Scott's case it would always be the virtues of naval life—the call to duty, the demands on courage—that exercised their tyranny over him, and casting its seductive, deadly light over these values was the Victorians' obsession with medieval chivalry and a mythical Camelot. The cult of medievalism this stemmed from went back to the Romantics and the novels of Sir Walter Scott, but over the succeeding generations it had somehow entwined itself round other concepts of English gentility, lending a pseudo-historical legitimacy and glamour to those ideals of amateurism and clean-living, games-playing Christianity that became such an integral part of an ethic that elevated the Grail-like *quest*, with all its attendant hardships and inbuilt glorification of failure, above any vulgar insistence on mere *victory*.

The history and traditions of naval polar expeditions during the nineteenth century, which will be examined later in their proper context, would eventually confront Scott with this culture in its most absolute form, but there was another and no less chimerical development that had an equally injurious effect on the training of the young nineteenth-century naval officer. One of the great mysteries of the Victorian service is the way

*In 1756 Rear Admiral John Byng, in command of a woefully inadequate squadron, failed to relieve a British garrison under siege on Minorca, and was subsequently court martialled and executed. Byng was acquitted of "cowardice or disaffection," but found guilty of failing "to do his utmost to take, seize and destroy the ships of the French King, which it was his duty to engage."

†On 1 November 1914, an outnumbered and badly outgunned British squadron under Sir Christopher Craddock engaged Count Maximilian von Spee's five cruisers off the coast of Chile and was destroyed. Craddock's ambition, according to the fitness fanatic Rear Admiral Sir Robert Arbuthnot, had always been to die in battle or break his neck hunting. Among the sixteen hundred men who died with him when the obsolete *Good Hope* and *Monmouth* went down were some of the last pre-war intake at Dartmouth—young boys still—who had been rushed, mid-match, from the cricket field to join their ships when the single-word cable "Mobilize" arrived on 1 August.

in which it succeeded in misinterpreting the Nelson legacy as badly as it did; but nothing in its catastrophic misunderstanding of its own past was more perverse than its belief that the secret of Nelson's genius lay in his total mastery of the battleground, rather than an ability to promote individuals of the same independent stamp as himself.

The result of this reading of history—abetted by crucial developments in flag signalling that gave any commander a potential 330,000 signals*— was a culture that made independent thought a crime and raised abstract theory and complex orders above the traditional empiricism that had been the great strength of the British navy. To all intents and purposes Nelson had left his captains to get on with their jobs, but by Scott's day the only prerequisite of a good subordinate was not "Duty" in the overmastering sense that Nelson had used the word, but blind, unquestioning obedience. "A good deal has been said of late as to the freedom being given to inferiors to question and disobey the orders of a superior officer," the Duke of Cambridge told cadets in the aftermath of the *Camperdown* tragedy of 1893, when in the depths of peace and the clear light of a Mediterranean summer's day Albert Markham had rammed and sunk the *Victoria* with the loss of Sir George Tryon, Britain's greatest admiral since Nelson, and 433 other lives rather than disobey a patently ludicrous order. "Discipline must be law, and must prevail. It is better to go wrong according to orders than to go wrong in opposition to orders."

Conformity, obedience, centralisation, abstract reasoning, unthinking bravery, chivalric idealism, unswerving duty in the narrowest sense of the word—these, then, were the battle cries of the navy Scott joined, and even if he could have foreseen the tragedy they would bring him to almost thirty years later it is unlikely that he would have had the strength to resist them. There were obviously Young Turks in every generation who had the self-confidence or the independence of means to buck the system, but for a fifteen-year-old of Scott's background and circumstances, without the connections or social assurance of a Tryon or a Beatty, conformity was not just a temptation but a *sine qua non* of survival.

---

*This seemingly abstruse development of a signalling culture has a profound relevance for Scott. The signalling inadequacies of the old navy at least meant that her officers had to *talk* to each other face to face, but under the new system that tradition was broken, with an admiral effectively cocooned from his subordinates in his own private world. The system also fatally ignored the realities of battle, in which smoke, dismasting, human error and the sheer, ungovernable chaos of war could make nonsense of any abstract planning. The implications of this culture for naval officers operating in Antarctica, often at great distances from each other, and in conditions that mimicked the confusions and unpredictability of war, will be evident.

The mature Scott would be only too bitterly aware of the cost of conformity, but it is hard to know whether the young cadet already felt it. There is a vast wealth of correspondence, journals, notes, memoranda and jottings surviving from the second half of his life, but from the summer of 1883 when he first went to sea until he took over *Discovery* and became a "public man" there are no more than a few dozen letters and a couple of diary fragments to give any sense of an interior life.

The career of a peacetime naval officer leaves so faint a biographical trace that almost everything beyond a skeleton of dates and ships is conjecture. From the time Scott left *Britannia* to the day he was appointed to command *Discovery* there is scarcely a day that cannot be accounted for, but apart from the dry details of a ship's movements or the laconic entries on a service record there is nothing but the occasional "RFS" initialled in a log book to lift him out of the anonymity of a service that spanned and policed the world.

It is curious to know at once so much and so little about a man, and yet, as in *Britannia*, it is the opacity of surviving records that offers the bleakest clue to Scott's new life. After a last boyhood summer at home he had sailed out to South Africa in the *Euphrates* with a fellow cadet from the same term at Dartmouth to join HMS *Boadicea*, and the ship's log for 4 October 1883 records with characteristic indifference their arrival: "9 a.m. Read articles of war and returns of courts martial, out launch and P boat. Joined Lieut Roope and Messrs Dampier & Scott, mids from HMS Euphrates."

As a midshipman Scott was still a pupil under instruction, and in many respects life in *Boadicea*'s gunroom would only have been a more bruising extension of his *Britannia* existence. His mornings would at least in theory be spent in navigation lessons, but with watches to keep and sights to take, men to manage and the ship's boats to run, instruction invariably lost out to the endless demands of ship life.

It was only twelve months before, too, that the fleet at Alexandria had fired its guns for the first time since the Crimea, and as long as Rear Admiral Nowell Salmon, with a face that wouldn't look out of place on Mount Rushmore, was flying his flag in *Boadicea*, Scott would need no reminder of what was ultimately expected of a naval officer. In the Crimean War Salmon had served against the Russians in the Baltic, and then as a young lieutenant in the *Shannon*'s Naval Brigade during the Indian Mutiny made his name winning one of the four naval Victoria Crosses awarded at the relief of Lucknow.

And even in the depths of peace, the occasional entry in the ship's log betrays the kind of personalities and frictions that lay behind the orderly façade of naval life. "Mr. Kirkby gunner was cautioned by Capt and his leave stopped for 1 month for not being fit for duty in the morning supposed from having taken too much liquor the night before," records the log for the day after Scott's arrival. "Sublt the Honble Francis Addington," runs a second entry, for 2 January 1884, "was cautioned by Capt for unofficerlike conduct in using abusive and disgraceful language to one of his shipmates in the gun room on Xmas day." "British barque Guyana in want of medical assistance arrived," the *Boadicea*'s log for 29 January notes with a wonderfully mild detachment, "Capt having stabbed the 2nd mate and assaulted one of the crew with an iron belaying pin." For the most part, though, the life of the ship, with its interminable provisioning, coaling and sailmaking, its mending, scrubbing and drilling, its cutlass exercise, sail and signalling drills, its exchanges of courtesies and diplomatic visits, went on with the unruffled calm of an organisation supremely sure of its role in the world.

There are no surviving letters of Scott's from his time in *Boadicea*, but in the ship's log one can follow him over the next two years, as the wooden-cased iron corvette did its imperial rounds from Simon's Bay and the Congo to Accra and Lagos and back to repeat the same leisurely sweep all over again. "All yesterday was spent at Sierra Leone," a future shipmate of Scott's wrote home of another such cruise with the Duke of Connaught aboard, giving a vivid glimpse of the assumptions, prejudices and cultural *remoteness* of the world that lay behind all these anonymous entries in the *Boadicea*'s log book, "and a most amusing time we had of it. We arrived there at 7 a.m. and landed at 9 and never, never, in my life, have I seen such enthusiasm as was displayed by all the niggers and seldom have I seen more ludicrous contrasts. Addresses were presented at the Town Hall which were read out by The Town Clerk, a large typical nigger with rolling eyes, who was in a barrister's wig and gown . . . In the garden at Government House the Duke received deputations from native chiefs in all sorts of ridiculous garments—some of them with tinsel crowns, and one in a naval cocked hat with military plumes . . . A deputation from the Coloured Freemasons and from the African Ladies of the Colony. We were all quite intrigued to know who the African Ladies were, when there appeared about a dozen negresses, dressed in the very latest Parisian fashions picture hats, hobble skirts and all the rest of it . . . one had to rub one's eyes to be sure one wasn't dreaming—it was more like a scene from a very extravagant musical comedy than anything else."

St. Helena—where in the 1880s naval visitors would have a woman in her sixties pointed out to them as Napoleon's daughter—Ascension, River Gambia, Sierra Leone, Monrovia, Accra, Lagos—it was August 1885 before Scott would again be in England, but his time in *Boadicea* had gone well. There is a sameness about captain's reports that gives very little away, but if a "VG" for conduct and abilities, and "Temperate" for habits, are no more than the standard comments, Captain Church was sufficiently impressed to take the seventeen-year-old Scott with him when he moved from *Boadicea* to *Monarch*.

Before *Monarch*, though, there was the rest of the summer, and Grace would always remember these last family holidays, when Con came home from sea and Archie, bound for the Artillery, was on leave from Woolwich or his station at Weymouth. There was still their eighteen-foot boat with the big lug sail, and "As to horsemanship, Con was a fairly good rider—good enough to win trophies when he was stationed at Lima—but not so good as Archie who was an exceptionally good huntsman, though he never possessed a horse of his own. The two brothers seized all opportunities of being together for a few days' leave; Archie coming home in his cheery way described days of golfing when he had to find both balls—Con being lost in day-dreams besides a bunker or on a green, maybe enchanted by a view or lost in a problem, anyway quite oblivious of his surroundings."

By the middle of September, however, Scott was with his new ship, and a part of the Channel Squadron in the armour-plated *Monarch*. It was the same life and the same routines as in *Boadicea*, and if his time under Nowell Salmon had brought him face to face with the navy's past, HMS *Monarch*, with both Rosslyn Wemyss, a future First Sea Lord, and John Jellicoe lieutenants in the ship, afforded an equally uncompromising vision of its future. It is a moot point whether or not this glimpse would have been reassuring, but it must at least have brought home to a young midshipman with almost nothing in the way of "interest" to call on that promotion would be a long, slow haul. From his earliest days in *Britannia* Jellicoe had clearly been destined for the top, but if "Old Biddy"—as Rosslyn Wemyss was familiarly known in court circles—was going in the same direction it owed as much to all those social, political and royal connections that Scott lacked as to any transcendent abilities.

The descendant on his father's side of the last Scottish Lord High Admiral, and on his mother's side of the last English one, the great-grandson of William IV and his mistress Mrs. Jordan, the heir to one of the great names in Scottish history and to a lineage that fancifully traced itself

behind this passage, its tone inevitably draws attention to the one period of Scott's naval life over which there is any uncertainty. A lot has been made of a brief gap in his service record while he was on the Pacific Station, and while there is not a shred of evidence to suggest he had put up any sort of "black" that was later covered up, it does seem likely that Scott was ill on the Station's depot ship, *Liffey*, at Coquimbo for a few weeks in the autumn of 1889.*

The only professional risk Scott ever ran, however, was not that he would be a bad naval officer, but that he would turn himself into only too good a one, and whatever lay behind the diary entry never surfaced in his work. He had been lent by Hulton to *Caroline* and then *Daphne* shortly after they had arrived at Esquimault in British Columbia, and an independent account of Scott's journey back from Acapulco in the *City of New York* to rejoin his ship hardly suggests anything like a physical or mental crisis. "In the late winter a quarter of a century ago," Sir Courtauld Thom-

---

*If one looked no farther than the Naval Lists or at Scott's service record, he would seem to have served in *Amphion* from December 1888 until the summer of 1891, but as *Amphion's* log records, on 15 April 1889 he was in fact lent to another cruiser serving on the Pacific Station, HMS *Caroline*.

The discrepancies between Admiralty documents and ships' records add up to nothing—Admiralty instructions would often be countermanded at a local level—but over the last twenty years a whole conspiracy theory has grown up around the next months of Scott's career. In the original scenario Scott left *Amphion* and went inexplicably "missing" for eight months, and although a more careful examination of ships' logs soon reduces this to a mere eleven weeks, the substance of the original suggestion of some indiscretion, possible breakdown, flight and establishment cover-up has been allowed to stand. "But what happened at this time is obscure," wrote Roland Huntford, the original advocate of the conspiracy theory and Scott's most persuasive and influential critic. "Circumstances point to being discreetly kept on *Liffey* for observation, medical or otherwise. There is the hint of an irregular trip home, the protection of a superior officer, and a cover up."

It is not only the clear discrepancies between local and central documents that are adduced in support of this theory, but the incompleteness of Admiralty records for this phase of Scott's career. It is certainly true that letters and papers which might be useful are missing, but Admiralty files represent nothing more nor less than the day-to-day work of a vast organisation, concerned only with its own immediate business, and utterly indifferent to the demands of history or biography. For certain periods or events they can be wonderfully complete, but that is purely a matter of chance, and for every document that is preserved or every letter that is logged and minuted and still in its right place there are likely to be half a dozen that have been innocently lost, misfiled or routinely destroyed.

In such a tight-knit world as the nineteenth-century navy—vast but clannishly inward-looking—it is hard, too, to see how a young officer with as little social, political or family clout as Scott had could have buried all trace of an indiscretion. It is easy enough to imagine an officer on the spot doing whatever he could to tidy up some folly or another, but when half the admirals subsequently involved in Scott's appointment to command *Discovery* were scrutinising his record for some excuse to block it, it is inconceivable that anything serious could have remained hidden.

son later wrote in a letter that Barrie wove into his legend of the Young Scott,

> I had to find my way from San Francisco to Alaska. The railway was snowed up and the only available transport at the moment was an ill-found tramp steamer. My fellow passengers were mostly Californians hurrying off to a new mining camp and, with the crew, looked a very unpleasant lot of ruffians. Three singularly unprepossessing Frisco toughs joined me in my cabin, which was none too large for a single person. I was then told that yet another had somehow to be wedged in. While I was wondering if he could be a more ill-favoured or dirtier specimen of humanity than the others the last comer suddenly appeared—the jolliest and breeziest English naval Second

---

So much has been made of this alleged "gap" in his career, so vague but so damaging a shadow been allowed to darken Scott's reputation as a naval officer, that it is again important to let the few facts that are known speak for themselves. After joining *Caroline* on 15 April 1889 Scott remained in her until 1 August of the same year, cruising between Callao, Coquimbo, Valparaiso and Juan Fernández, the uninhabited Pacific island on which Alexander Selkirk—the inspiration for Defoe's Robinson Crusoe—lived for five years at the beginning of the eighteenth century.

Something of the *ad hoc* nature of such employment—and something, too, of the conditions of service in the southern division on the Pacific Station—can be gauged from the one mention of Scott during his time in *Caroline* that has survived among Admiralty records. On 1 May her captain, Sir William Wiseman Bt, informed their Lordships that the Supernumerary boatswain had been "invalided home from heat, having tried to kill himself by jumping overboard. Under such altered circumstances on the arrival of 'Champion' I telegraphed you, Sir, for permission to retain Acting Lieutenant Scott, until the arrival of some officer from England."*Caroline* was at Callao, the port for Lima, at the time, and was again there on 1 August, when the ship's log for that day notes that Sub Lieut. Scott was "Discharged . . . to SS Serena," a steam vessel plying the Americas' west coast. The *Serena* headed south and on 12 August arrived at Coquimbo in Chile, where the log for HMS *Liffey*, the depot ship for the southern division, records her arrival: "SS Serena arrived at 8:15 a.m., sailed 12:20."

There is no mention of Scott in the *Liffey*'s log, but there is virtually no mention of anyone else either, so that means nothing, and it seems almost certain that he remained in the depot ship until 26 October, when her log records the discharge of fifteen supernumeraries to HMS *Daphne*. On the following day the *Daphne*'s log notes the arrival of Sub Lieut R.F. Scott, and from that moment onwards Scott's career can again be traced in Admiralty records, leaving not the originally alleged eight months to make an illicit trip to England and back again, but just the seventy-seven days between 12 August and 27 October.

And if the *Liffey*'s log only very rarely names individuals, it is meticulous in recording the arrival and departure of every ship in and out of Coquimbo, making it simple enough to see what opportunities Scott might have had for getting home. During the eleven weeks in question there were daily movements of vessels involved in the South American coastal trade, but in all that time only one ship, HMS *Cormorant*, sailed for England, and she was still nowhere near home waters when Scott reported for duty on the *Daphne* on 25 October.

Lieutenant. It was Con Scott. I had never seen him before, but we at once became friends and remained so till the end. He was going up to join his ship which, I think, was the Amphion, at Esquimault, B.C.

As soon as we got outside the Golden Gates we ran into a full gale which lasted all the way to Victoria, B.C. The ship was so overcrowded that a large number of women and children were allowed to sleep on the floor of the only saloon there was on condition that they got up early, so that the rest of the passengers could come in for breakfast and the other meals.

I need scarcely say that owing to the heavy weather hardly a woman was able to get up, and the saloon was soon in an indescribable condition. Practically no attempt was made to serve meals, and the few so-called stewards were themselves mostly out of action from drink or sea-sickness.

Nearly all the male passengers who were able to be about spent their time drinking and quarrelling. The deck cargo and some of our top hamper were washed away and the cabins got their share of the waves that were washing the deck.

Then it was I first knew that Con Scott was no ordinary human being. Though at that time still only a boy he practically took command of the passengers and was at once accepted by them as their Boss during the rest of the trip. With a small body of volunteers he led an attack on the saloon—dressed the mothers, washed the children, fed the babies, swabbed down the floors and nursed the sick, and performed every imaginable service for all hands. On deck he settled the quarrels and established order either by his personality, or, if necessary, by his fists. Practically by day and night he worked for the common good, never sparing himself, and with his infectious smile gradually made us all feel the whole thing was jolly good fun.

I daresay there are still some of the passengers like myself who, after a quarter of a century, have imprinted on their minds the vision of this fair-haired English sailor boy with the laughing blue eyes, who at that early age knew how to sacrifice himself for the welfare and happiness of others.

Scott himself always looked back with particular fondness to his time on the Pacific Station, and he made friends there that he would keep all his life. In professional terms Esquimault was possibly the least interesting of all the navy's global stations, but if the dress code spelled out in Standing Orders is anything to go by—Helmets to be worn with White Undress; Frock coats to be buttoned close up; Undress Coats with Epaulettes, Gold Laced Trousers and White Waistcoats for Balls; Mess Jackets for Dinner; Dress, White or Blue for Dinner; Undress, Dark Coats and Hats for Sundays ashore—there were all the social compensations of naval life at the apogee of British seapower.

Such a life came at a cost, of course, and a lieutenant's pay of £182.10s a year can only have been just enough to keep up those appearances about which Scott was always morbidly sensitive. In his future years he would have to watch every wardroom drink he bought and pass over every entertainment that had to be paid for, but at Esquimault at least he seems to have been able to hold his own in a society eager to embrace an engaging and attractive young naval officer. He rode, canoed, dined out, and in the handsome Victoria home of Peter O'Reilly, a prominent figure in local life, and his wife, found a welcome that helped ease his homesickness. For many years after Scott kept up a fitful but affectionate correspondence with Mrs. O'Reilly and her daughter Kathleen, and in 1899, on the eve of his new life in polar exploration, was still writing of "ever fresh memories of good times" at Esquimault.

There was never a suggestion at the time, however, or in any of the subsequent correspondence, of a warmer friendship with Kathleen, and Scott was just one of any number of officers who washed through the O'Reillys' hospitable home. "Warrender & Scott called," Peter O'Reilly noted in his journal for 4 May, six weeks after Scott's return to *Amphion*. "Warrender & Scott called," he wrote again three weeks later; "Warrender & Scott arrived in their canoe"; "Scott called"; "Scott came to supper"; "Scott dined with us"; "Scott supper"; "Scott accompanied the Admiral to church & returned to supper"; "Kit: Warrender & Scott on horseback." "How lovely it must be at Victoria now," Scott wrote to Mrs. O'Reilly on his return to England and the summer rain of Devon the following year. "I can imagine the delightful weather even in the midst of all the rain we are forced to endure here. What jolly times those were for me at Victoria! If anything were needed to recall them to memory—which nothing is—the strawberries and cream on which I chiefly keep my spirits up at present would be a constant reminder . . . I often feel I shall never have such times again as those days at Victoria which were so very pleasant thanks to your invariable kindness."

On 19 October 1890 *Amphion's* tour of duty came to an end, and she weighed for Honolulu on the first stage of the long journey back to England. The weather on leaving Victoria was foul, Scott wrote to Mrs. O'Reilly—"as regards physical discomfort some of the worst I have ever endured. We had a gale of wind with a very heavy sea, in our teeth, the motion was awful and the pangs of sea-sickness attacked us all from the captain down to the 'warrant officers' cook's mate' (usually supposed to be the most humble individual on board). The climax was reached on the night of the Government House Ball when it blew really hard: I had the middle watch, the rain and spray dashing in one's face made it quite impossible to see ahead, so I turned my back on it and with a sort of grim pleasure tried to imagine what was going on at the ball."

It is interesting to catch Scott's own voice again—if for nothing else than to be reminded of just how young he still was—and all the more so as he wrote to Mrs. O'Reilly with the same unguarded familiarity with which he treated his own family. "The 'plant' thrives," he went on, clearly referring to a parting gift to him, "& to my messmates this is a matter of supreme wonder . . . it is not for nothing that I have learned the elements of botany . . . that plant has had a treatment which I venture to suggest, no plant has ever had before; once it grew very yellow, I dosed it with iron and other tonics, gave it nitrate, sulphurite, in carefully measured proportions, to my horror it seemed to grow worse, but I persisted in my treatment and eventually it recovered and has since flourished. In fine weather I take it on deck when I go on watch but I don't spoil it, it is not allowed too much to drink nor too much fresh air."

On the way home Scott and his messmates raced each other in growing beards, with Scott "bound to confess," he wrote, that "I was a bad last—a brilliant idea struck me that checking my hair proper, would help to 'force' the beard, so I had my back cut with one of those patent horse-clipping arrangements: it didn't seem to do the least much good, but it gave me a very weird appearance."

With a long voyage ahead of them, he continued, the "Admiral" (Warrender, a future admiral, so a prophetic nickname for Scott's friend, as it turned out) and Scott "hit on a capital method of employing this spare time" in writing a book—"not a novel, but a grave and important technical work," designed to "epitomise" the various seamanship manuals into one pocket-sized volume. "With this great end in view, we set and lay out our places, divide into heads and sub-heads, chapters and paragraphs and generally succeed in building up scaffolding, which would contain books about three times the size of any seamanship manual in existence. At first this was amusing, but after a bit it gets quite irritating. This is of course a state secret, and naval officers must not be told what is in store for them, nor, in case of non-publication, must they know what they have missed."

It was ten days' sailing from Victoria to Honolulu, where a week was spent in those social and diplomatic functions dear to Captain Hulton's heart. "At Honolulu we employed our time firing salutes and anathematising mosquitoes," Scott wrote. "Besides such necessary visitors as the King etc, the Captain in the fullness of his heart must needs invite calls from all the consuls and other dignitaries in the place, their name is legion and they all have to be saluted, so we are everlastingly popping off guns."

There were other things for Scott to worry about, apart from Hulton or the mosquitoes. He had applied for a place on the Torpedo course at HMS *Vernon*, and as the *Amphion* made its slow way back to England via Hong Kong, Aden and Suez, he became increasingly anxious over his prospects. "I was very despondent," he later confessed to Mrs. O'Reilly, in a letter that probably shows as well as anything what anxieties lay behind the tone of his short-lived diary, "on account of my small chance of being selected for this Torpedo business; after that my spirits got lower & lower; each mail brought me what I considered to be worse & worse news—I knew there were only five vacancies and every letter from home informed me of an increased number of applicants for them—the number swelled from 20 to 30 and at last to 49—I was in despair and gave up all hope; but a day or two brought the welcome telegram informing me that I was chosen and on the 20th of June I was on my road to England—I really think if I had not been taken this year I should have gradually lost all interest in the Service—it seems such a dismal look out to go on year after year with that dreary old watch keeping, going abroad for three years and coming home for six weeks and so off again. As it is there is a great deal of interest in the speciality I have adopted and at any rate there are a certain two or perhaps three years in England."

If Scott had been anxious, he was right to be. Ambition, for a naval or army officer of intelligence, is not an option but a necessity. Cultural traditions might dissemble the fact, but the alternative to promotion is too dire to leave any alternative. Fail to get on the right Torpedo course, fail to get a Staff College nomination, fail to get on the "pink list," fail to be seen doing the right job, fall six months behind your contemporaries—and the endless vista of naval or military life in all its undifferentiated and unimaginative dullness, stagnation and impotent subordination opens up.

For a young officer without interest, ambition was even more vital. It was, alongside his talent, all he had. It was not, in any narrowing sense, a mere matter of self-interest. It was not about power, or self-promotion, or any authoritarian instinct, but about professional fulfilment—about finding the space to think and develop—the mental and physical *lebensraum* that the naval and military life institutionally denies to failure or mediocrity. And for Scott, as he set foot on English soil again for the first time in two and a half years, and went down to Outlands to see his "great stay-at-home" of a father, it would soon be about more. It would be about survival.

Four: **Crisis**

> *Lives there the man with soul so dead,*
> *Who never to himself hath said*
> *This is mine own, my native land*
> *Whose heart hath ne'er within him burned*
> *As home his footsteps he hath turned*
> *From wandering on a foreign strand.*
>
> SIR WALTER SCOTT, *(mis)quoted in Scott's address book*

The twenty-three-year-old Scott his family welcomed home in the summer of 1891 was not the homesick boy who had gone to sea in *Amphion*. In their memories of these last, unclouded months together as a family, his sisters would recall a more physically and mentally alert Con, stronger, more robust, more incisive, more curious, more *navy*. "He felt that things requiring to be done," Grace recollected, "must be well arranged, and must not attend on slower wits . . . matters once well considered and decided upon must not be allowed to be hampered by afterthoughts and questions. Details should be minutely arranged, then off and get it done with."

His few surviving letters from this time convey the same impression, though the final phase of his journey home from Esquimault hardly bears it out. He had gone down with fever at Malta and been forced to miss Cannes, where the *Amphion* was on guard duty for the Queen, and on his recovery made his own way back by land from Brindisi. He had "looked forward to a few days in Paris," he wrote to the O'Reillys, but "hating timetables and all those sorts of things," had "attached" himself to a civil engineer he had met, and woke up in Milan "where I didn't ought to have been" with no luggage and nothing to do but "console" himself with a day in the cathedral.

He was not united with his luggage again until Calais, and so had to miss Paris, but with the exception of his father all the Scotts that could be rounded up were waiting for him in London. For a family whose idea of excitement was the Plymouth Theatre pantomime, the capital must have seemed about as remote as Esquimault, and for the next three days the Scotts gorged themselves on it, cramming in the Handel Festival and *Ivanhoe* at the English Opera—music a "trifle insipid"—between exhaustive sweeps of the naval exhibition and—that symbol of everything the service still thought it was—Nelson's *Victory* moored on the Thames.

Scott had been appointed to *Sharpshooter* for summer manoeuvres before he joined *Vernon*, but as she was conveniently anchored at Plymouth there was time first for Outlands. "When Con, at the age of nineteen, was wildly in the throes of his first love," Grace again recalled, in an elusive glimpse of a side of Scott's life that has vanished without trace, "and longing to rush off to his charmer, who had a very short-tempered husband, Archie alone could speak to him and try to dissuade him from his project; Con at the time was very impressionable, and remained so. The sailor's life and his romantic nature caused him to idealise women. He had his youthful loves and flirtations. His affections were easily caught though not easily held. He had a capacity for appearing wholly absorbed in the person he was talking to, while all the time he was really quite detached. This was misleading. As far as I know, he had two real loves only; one, a girlhood friend of ours who later married, but was always in the background of his affections, no matter who from time to time interested him for a while, and she remained so, I think, until he met his wife."

This is a sister talking—and a younger sister, at that, who saw him only rarely—but if there was any other woman of whom Grace never knew, no name survives. Many years later Cherry-Garrard would write of Scott's astonishing power to charm when he wanted to, and at least one married American woman, a Minnie Chase, a friend's sister Scott met briefly in San Francisco on his way north to rejoin the *Amphion*, would happily have signed up to the proposition. "The night has a thousand eyes," she copied into the front of an address book she probably gave him,

> And the day but one,
> Yet the light of the bright world dies,
> With the dying sun.

The mind has a thousand eyes,
And the heart but one;
Yet the light of a whole life dies,
When love is done.

Conventional enough stuff—the verses are by Francis Bourdillon and were well known at the time—and Scott was in San Francisco only a few days, but those days fixed themselves in Minnie Chase's memory. "Do you remember Mrs. Chase 24 years ago," Scott's widow would write to her husband from California in 1913, ignorant that he had already been dead ten months. "She fell on my neck because of what a darling you were 24 years ago. She couldn't believe that you'd remained unmarried so long—the more I think of it the more I wonder with her."

At twenty-three Scott was slightly below average height, trim and broad-chested, with fair hair, blue, almost violet eyes, an odd, attractively ugly face not unlike Jacky Fisher's, and a smile that went a long way to explaining the impact of his charm. "Well-built, and alert," one man who saw him lecturing a few years later described him. "Neither tall nor short, he yet conveyed the impression of vigorous quickness. Nine people out of ten, seeing him, would have said, 'Naval Officer.' " It was certainly a role he was well on his way to making his own. "Lieutenant Scott is a young officer of good promise," his last captain had written in forwarding on his application to *Vernon*, "and has patience and tact in the handling of men. He is quick and intelligent and from all I've seen of him I think likely to develop into a useful torpedo officer. I recommend him for the class which commences in October next."

After his holiday at Outlands and nearly six weeks of manoeuvres in *Sharpshooter*, Scott took up his place in HMS *Vernon*, the navy's Torpedo School Ship at Portsmouth. He would only have had to see a Lieutenant Philip Colomb—another great name in the Victorian navy—on the same list as himself to know what he was still up against, but if there was anywhere that might have symbolised a different navy, it was *Vernon*, an elegant and streamlined relic of the age of sail that had been laid up, dismasted and brutalised into shape to serve the service's newest technical arm.

The *Vernon* had begun its new life as a tender to HMS *Excellent*, the naval gunnery school, but as the importance of the new weapon became obvious, *Vernon* broke away from *Excellent* to become an independent command in her own right. She was lucky enough to have Jacky Fisher for her first captain, and when he was followed in turn by another formidable naval legend and future First Sea Lord, "old 'ard 'art" Wilson, who had hacked and brawled his way to a VC at the Battle of El Teb in 1884, the future of the school was assured.

By Wilson and Scott's time, *Vernon* had grown in size and importance, with a motley collection of hulks, workshops and a flat iron gunboat with a horizontal funnel jutting out of her stern added to the original establishment. In some ways the unsanitary, rat-infested warren of vessels must have conjured up memories of *Britannia* and *Hindostan* for Scott, but the filth and bustle of nineteenth-century Portsmouth was about as far a cry from the quiet beauty of the Dart as *Vernon* was from anything in the navy Scott had known before.

It was an exciting time to be there, with the torpedo undergoing constant improvements since the first above-water-launched model had been slid into the sea off a mess table. The year before Scott arrived had seen the introduction and testing of a new eighteen-inch weapon with a greater range, speed and accuracy than anything tried before, and for the first time in his life he had the chance to develop—or discover in himself—the technical and scientific aptitude that would so strongly mark his future work.

Even in *Vernon*, however, the most modern and innovative of establishments, Scott found himself in a culture that paradoxically reinforced those centralising, controlling, anti-initiative tendencies that were the hallmarks of the nineteenth-century service. In his brilliant study of Britain's pre–First World War navy, Andrew Gordon identified four key institutions—*Vernon*, the Royal Geographical Society, Royalty and Freemasonry—as comprising a kind of "checklist" of naval "authoritarianism," and what he says of *Vernon* holds a special resonance for anyone interested in Scott's later record as an explorer in the unpredictable world of Antarctica. "The work of the Torpedo School took place on the frontiers of practical physics," he wrote. "The staff formed (at least in their own opinion) a naval science vanguard, and their leadership of their profession away from art and into science may have inclined them towards a highly regulated 'Newton's clock' view of the universe, in which the unpredictabilities concomitant with devolved authority had no place."

If there was one other aspect of *Vernon* life that was regressive in its tendencies, it was a Raglanesque assumption that any future enemy must be French. During the summer of 1890 exercises around Portland and Plymouth had showed how dangerous boats issuing from creeks on the French coast could be, and over his two summers in *Vernon*, Scott was involved in similar manoeuvres to counter the threat.

It was the first time that he had commanded anything bigger than a ship's boat, and he could not have made a more disastrous start. On 12 August 1893 he headed for Falmouth as part of the torpedo flotilla, but the next day somehow succeeded in running Torpedo Boat 87 aground, suffering the humiliation of having himself towed back into dry dock at Keyham with "severe injury to propeller."

It was an acute embarrassment for a young officer—"due care and attention does not appear to have been exercised," Scott's service record reads—but it was no more than that. In the official report on the incident he was "cautioned to be more attentive in future," but *Vernon*'s commander, George Egerton, would always remain one of Scott's greatest admirers, and a First Class in his theory examination, and a First Class Certificate in his practical, certainly suggest that the incident led to no lasting damage to his prospects.*

It is just possible, though, that it cast a shadow over his first appointment as a qualified Torpedo Officer to the unglamorous Depot ship *Vulcan*. The appointment was not "considered good in the *Vernon*," but in the dogged way that would become typical of Scott, he was determined to make the best of his opportunities. His reasons for remaining with the ship, he wrote to his anxious father from *Vulcan*,

> are firstly that I look upon her as a latent success, as a splendid but undeveloped and misused experiment dependent on her present handling to establish her utility, a utility which in war time would be apparent and patent to all. For this reason I take a very great interest in her welfare and do as much as lays in my

---

*Admiralty logs show an alarming number of collisions in the nineteenth-century navy. This would not be the only incident involving Scott, and nor was it even the first time that Torpedo Boat 87 had suffered from the incompetence of its officers. In exercises the previous year Lieutenant Greatorex had collided with another vessel while in command, holing her below the waterline. The *Vernon* authorities, however, were perhaps not in the strongest position to take action. In 1885 Albert Markham, while in command of the school, had rammed and sunk a passenger steamer in fog off Land's End, killing thirteen civilians. Neither that, however, nor his subsequent performance in sinking Sir George Tryon's *Victoria*, stopped him ending up as Masonic District Grand Master of Malta or making rear admiral and KCB. A collision and a severe reprimand never did any harm, either, to Scott's future best man, Henry Campbell, another future knight and admiral.

power to forward it. Secondly, and in consequence of my first reason, I have hopes of establishing a reputation for myself.

Thirdly, I am losing nothing; in fact gaining a very great deal in general service experience — In general service work, of which we do as much as most other ships, I have a stake and take a position far above that which I should have in other ships — In addition I keep watch at sea with the fleet, and as they generally put us in the fighting line, am precisely in the same position to gain experience as if on board a battleship . . .

To fall back on the torpedo work again at which I have worked exceedingly hard, I look upon this ship as the best practical experience that could possibly befall an officer; in fact I look upon myself now as an authority on the only modern way of working a minefield and such like exercises — but what is better, the Captain and Currey do likewise.

Even if I fail, the practical knowledge and experience will be invaluable. I am conscious that by self-advertisement I might make myself heard now, but the position is a delicate one, and I should be sorry to advocate anything in which I did not believe. Meanwhile things constantly annoy and irritate one — but as you see, I work for a larger than ordinary stake, and with this I will conclude adding, that the welfare of body if not of career remains good.

It would be another decade before Scott would be able to tick off the other three boxes on Gordon's "authoritarian checklist" — the RGS, Freemasonry, and Royal connections — but the inevitable process of institutionalisation had begun. "We are getting very well known in the fleet," he told his father in the same letter, sounding alarmingly like some embryo "Pompo" Heneage; "no function takes place but that we come pretty well out of it, the athletic sports, the rifle meetings, the regattas, events which though very far from you are very near to us out here; fate has kept us before the public in all. But best of all we had a most triumphant inspection, the Admiral said publicly that he should report us as the most creditable to all concerned, and privately that we were the cleanest ship he'd inspected, an opinion fully endorsed by Levison and others who accompany him on these occasions, they adding that no ship could 'touch us.' "

This was no momentary aberration either. "The ship is still very dirty," he complained to his mother of his new ship, the *Empress of India*, "but I think improving—a great improvement has been commented upon in my small share of the cleaning part and I feel if only we could get the commander to smarten up a bit we should get the ship all straight—but he is unfortunately lamentably slack." Just over a week later, virtue was rewarded when a "somewhat disastrous" admiral's inspection confirmed "that the only clean parts of the ship were the torpedo department—and also that at drills etc the torpedo department shone by a mere absence of doing wrong . . . Altogether I was pleased with my own show. I have some sixty men numbered whom I fell in at the beginning and told them things must be altered altogether."

This thickening of the professional arteries, the slow but inexorable process of assimilation, might well have been inevitable, but by the time that Scott wrote this last letter, "choice" had largely been removed. There had always been an assumption within the family that John Scott had been living off interest since his retirement, but in the autumn of 1894, while his son was still in *Vulcan*, it emerged that for the last twelve years he had been running down his capital and that they were virtually bankrupt. "On the 23rd October," Hannah Scott recorded with an almost preternatural calm, "a crushing blow came of heavy losses. At once we decided to let our house and hope that some occupation will come that will please my dear husband and bring him comfort in the loss of his old house. On November 12th our dear Rose commenced work at Nottingham Hospital, under three weeks after the loss. The others all anxious to be up and doing are only restrained by the occupation at home in getting things in order for letting the furnished house. From Con comes a fine manly reliable letter offering help . . . Truly sorrow has many compensations and with God's help we shall yet if He wills it return to our old home."

They only returned, in fact, to let Outlands permanently, and all it meant in terms of respectability, security and position was gone. It would be impossible to guess from the tone here what this must have meant to Hannah Scott, but for a woman of her age and gentle snobberies, it was as if she had gone to sleep in the cosy, familiar world of some West Country Cranford, and woke within the harsh landscape of a Gissing novel, staring at the prospects of rented rooms, poverty, ostracism, trade and working daughters.

But if there seemed nothing for Hannah Scott except humiliation, for the girls—poised on the brink of a new century with new expectations, aspirations, possibilities—there was at least the chance of a different and more expansive world. Within weeks Rose had begun a career in nursing that would take her to the Gold Coast, and the others soon followed her from home, the ebullient Ettie to a theatre school at Margate and briefly onto the stage with Irene Vanbrugh's touring company, and Grace and, eventually, Kate into the dingier dressmaking business.

Of all the children it was probably Archie who suffered most, being forced to abandon the Royal Artillery for a post in Nigeria as secretary to the governor, but from the start it was Con who carried the emotional burden of the disaster. For a few months in 1895 the family rented a Devonshire farmhouse, and it was there, in Barrie's account, that the metamorphosis from "Old Mooney" to "head of the family" was completed. "He never seems to have shown a gayer front than when the troubles fell," Barrie wrote in his inimitable mix of family lore and hagiography. "Not only must there be no 'Old Mooney' in him, but it must be driven out of everyone. His concerts, in which he took a leading part, became celebrated in the district; deputations called at the farm to beg for another, and once in these words, 'Wull 'ee gie we a concert over our way when the comic young gentleman be here along?' "

If there is again as much Barrie as Scott in this, the family collapse does provide the first real insight into the qualities that distinguished the mature man. In his later years he could talk about "duty" and "patriotism" with the best of them, but whether it was to ship, colleagues, service or country, Scott's sense of loyalty and duty was always rooted in real obligations, affections, ties and responsibilities. And at the heart of this nexus of relations was his family, and above all his mother. There is a species of family feeling that is little more than an enlarged and clannish selfishness, but as with his ambition there was nothing narrow or "laager-like" in Scott's devotion, only a generous and unpossessive openness to their sorrows, happiness and opportunities.

In her memoir of her brother Con, Grace described his facility for *appearing* to be absorbed in the person he was talking to, but his letters to his family reveal a much profounder and more genuine empathy than that remark suggests. It is one of those aspects of personality that is always going to elude definition, but there seems to have always been something almost Keatsian in Scott's capacity for submerging his own identity and "absorbing" himself—Grace's word—in the fragile, anxious interior lives of a mother, brother or sister.

As his subsequent career in the Antarctic—and in particular his response to human or animal suffering—would underline, the barriers between "self" and "other" would never be very firmly established for Scott, and never was this more true than when his family needed him. There was nothing he actually "did" for them during their troubles that Archie or Ettie did not match, but in terms of understanding and explaining, and interpreting one to another, he was central to their recovery.

With his mother, in particular, he needed all his tact and sympathy to nudge and cajole her into accepting the different world the Scotts found themselves in with financial failure. Some time towards the end of 1895 or 1896 John Scott secured a job as manager of a Somerset brewery, and while it brought a house and some financial stability, the descent back into trade left Hannah Scott more rawly exposed than ever to the indignities of her position. There can have been no escaping it, either, because even the transition from the rich Devon landscape to the mean, straggling village of Holcombe offered a Hardyesque mirror to their fortunes. Under the fields around the old perpendicular church of St. Andrew's lay buried the ancient pre-plague village, but it was the great mass of the Holcombe Brewery that dominated the new village, with its miserably ugly church, its Wesleyan chapel, its vestiges of the old coal industry and its brewery employees, defining the physical and social perimeters of the Scott family's decline.

There had been nothing in the bourgeois, provincial, God-fearing, servant-padded world in which Hannah Scott had lived the first sixty years of her life to prepare her for this, and nothing her son would not do to protect her from it. In his memoir of Scott, Barrie spoke feelingly of *his* hardships at this time, but whatever the humiliations of tarnished braid or a threadbare uniform for a naval officer of Scott's stamp, he felt the family's poverty more keenly for his mother than himself. "I hate to think that you did not go and see her before she left," he wrote to her at Holcombe after Ettie had left for the stage. "I hate to think I had not the forethought of writing to urge you to go—that you should have studied economy in such a matter makes me feel very bitter—Promise you won't do it again—but you really shan't, for when she comes back I am determined you shall go and see her act and shall yourself see the life and some of your many unknown admirers (who have seen your picture only). I can't forgive my own want of forethought in not writing about it . . . I have another great fear about you dear, which is that you don't get any society.—I do hope people will come & call—you don't speak of any as yet. I rather feel that people round you are not inclined that way and that you are having rather a slow time—But I suppose time only can correct this and the gradual appreciation of how nice you really are."

For all Scott's chivalry, there was nothing emasculating in his devotion to his mother, and while she always remained at the centre of his loyalties, that never stopped him fighting his sisters' corners when they needed him. "Dear Mother," he wrote in the same letter to Holcombe, "I am afraid that you must be grieving over Ettie's absence very much, but think dear what it means to her. What prospects of independence and the pleasure of really living, working & doing."

"My Own Dearest Mother," he wrote in the same vein, this time of Kate and Grace's new lives as working women, "You cannot think how delightful it was to find you all in such good health and spirits. The prospect for the future seems brighter than it has been for years and above all things I rejoice to see that you are beginning to appreciate that by this honest hard work the girls are anything but sufferers. The difference in them since they have been about, meeting all manner of people and relying on themselves, is so very plain to me. Just the same sort of difference that Ettie felt and valued so much. They have gained in a hundred points, not to mention appearance and smartness. I honestly think we shall some day be grateful to fortune for lifting us out of the 'sleepy hollow' of the old Plymouth life. Personally, I cannot express the difference I see in the girls since their London experiences."

For a few brief months in the mid-1890s it must have seemed that he was right, and home on leave at Christmas 1896, the two brothers took up where they had left off in their rented farm. A "mixed entertainment and fine farce called Chiselling" was put on for the brewery's workers and customers, the local paper reported. "Lt A Scott RA. Lt R Scott RN and the Misses K and M. Scott of Holcombe House [were] extremely funny . . . continuous roars of laughter."

It was no more than a last, poignant codicil to the family's collapse, though, and within twelve months both John Scott and his younger son, "Arch," were dead. It seems somehow appropriate that the last public glimpse of John Scott is of him being pushed in a wheelchair to his daughter Ettie's wedding, but while his death from heart disease cannot have been a complete shock, or even blow, to his family, nothing had prepared them for Arch's.

"I am longing to see old Arch," Scott had written in the summer of 1897, "and tell him how hopeful I think it all," and the following year he got his wish. Arch, home on leave from Lagos, joined him, with the use of the admiral's spare cabin, for a cruise off the Irish coast in Scott's ship to thrash out the details of the family's finances. "My dearest girl," he wrote to his sister Ettie, "Arch has been staying with me for the last few days, he is in great form & looking very well — we have of course talked matters out & I think arrived at a clear understanding as regards the situation." "Isn't Arch just splendid," he wrote to his mother on 15 October. "He is so absolutely full of life and enjoyment and at the same time so keen on his job. I expect he has told you about his hope of becoming a commissioner. He seems to have done most excellent work and shown tact and energy in an extraordinary degree. Dear old chap, he deserves to be a success — Commissioner, Consul, and Governor is the future for him I feel sure."

Within a month, Arch was dead. He had gone to Hythe to play golf, and went down with typhoid. Just what the news meant to Scott can be felt in his letter to Ettie. "My dearest Girl, It is good to hear there was no pain and it is easy to understand that he died like a man. All his life, wherever he went, people felt the better for his coming. I don't think he ever did an unkind thing and no form of meanness was in him. It is a strange chance that has taken him who perhaps of us all found the keenest pleasure in life, who was always content and never grumbled. Of course, now we know he never ought to have gone to West Africa. After watching him carefully, I saw that despite his health he was not strong and I meant to have a long talk with you on the subject. Too late — doesn't it always seem the ending of our wretched little mortal plans? Good God, it is past all understanding. He and you and I were very close together, weren't we? I know what your loss is, knowing my own."

To his mother, however, none of the bewilderment or anger was ever allowed to surface. "My Own Dearest Mother," he wrote to her from Gibraltar,

> I got your letter this morning. Don't blame yourself for what has happened, dear. Whatever we have cause to bless ourselves for, comes from you. He died like the true-hearted gentleman he was, but to you we owe the first lessons and example that made us gentlemen. This thing is most terrible to us all but it is no penalty for any act of yours . . .
>
> In another matter I think I can afford a key other than your construction. Arch and I discussed his commissionership in all lights . . . and it was in regard to that, that his remark about leav-

ing the artillery fell from him. Of this I am sure: he never regret-ted leaving Weymouth. Often and often when we were about there he said, "Well, old chap, this is all very narrow. I am awfully glad to have got away and seen the world a bit."

Of course he loved his corps, but he never thought of it as a thing left behind and never was anything but glad to have left the dull routine of garrison duty.

I'm glad you got that nice letter from the Governor. Oh, my dear, it is something to know that everyone thought him a fine chap. His popularity was marvellous—he was such a fine gentle-man. God bless you . . . Don't be bitter, dear.

> *Your loving son*
> *Con.*

Hannah Scott had joined her daughters in Paris for six months, where they had gone to learn the dressmaking business, but with his father and Archie both dead, the financial burden for the family now fell on Scott, gener-ously helped by Ettie's new husband, the old Etonian, Unionist MP for Antrim and Parliamentary Secretary to the Admiralty, Willy Ellison-Macartney. "It seems to me to boil down to this," Scott had written to Ettie only weeks before Arch's death:

> that you & Willy are proposing to act in a most generous man-ner in the matter of the insurance; mother and the girls (espe-cially the former) have been given new life by the proposal, (which if the business succeeds only moderately well will prove satisfactory all round . . .)
>
> The saving of Mother's money has an enormous effect on her peace of mind, as of course was to be expected. Therefore the future arrangements seem to be
>
> You are insured for £1500 & pay something like £45 per annum
>
> Arch pays to the ménage £120 & I some £70
>
> The above £190 plus £30 from Outlands & £30 interest on Mother's capital—£250 forms the home income
>
> But of above is paid £40 as interest on loan £1000 leaving a net income of over £200
>
> All expenses in connection with the business to come out of the £1000

Expenses of the Paris scheme [the dressmaking] to be deb-
ited on the £1000 advance.

It was a bathetic world for an ambitious young naval officer to find himself
in, but Scott did not flinch. He had been prepared to sacrifice his career
prospects in the immediate aftermath of the financial crash so that he
could be at Devonport near his family, but with Archie dead and another
£120 to be found, the only thing that concerned him now was promotion.

He might still sometimes wonder "whether the game is worth a candle," but that was just idle talk. In letter after letter he comes back to the
subject, and the endless speculation, manoeuvring and jobbing that the
whole business of joining "the ranks of the advancers" entailed: "if this can
be worked I shall have little to grumble at"; "in with all the Flagship now";
"the Flag Captain is rather a friend of mine thanks to Ettie"; "Fraser would
of course be only too delighted for me to succeed him"; "I can only hope
to become known to their successors"; "I trust he will not forget me."

Even before his father's death he had been aiming high, applying for a
berth in the senior Royal Yacht, *Victoria & Albert*, that would have put him
at the heart of that unrivalled nexus of connections and patronage that
effectively ran the service. "I want you to tell father the following about the
Yacht of my year," he wrote home with that clear thinking and lack of
resentment that always characterised his attitude to what he called the
navy's "much gilded" youth: "I fear it will disappoint him—next to my name
in the Navy List he will find Stanley—Michael Colme-Seymour & Goodenough—Stanley is a godson of the Queen, son of the Earl of Derby, a nice
chap, popular and has war service (though only Egyptian)—Michael Seymour is of course the son of the Admiral which is saying a great deal as by
the time of selection, his father will be at Portsmouth in command . . .
Goodenough is very well connected, has been in the Yacht and in the
Mediterranean Yacht, has many personal friends in high places, war service
and altogether an excellent chance. Mike Seymour tells me all three people
will try for the billet—so you see I fear there's a very poor chance for me."

Scott was right—Colme-Seymour got the post—but if he failed with
the Yacht, he was more successful in his next ambition, joining the flagship of the Channel Fleet under the command of Prince Louis of Battenberg in July 1897. Among all the ships Scott served in, the *Majestic* and
"Majestics" would always hold a special place, and over the next three
years he forged many of those key loyalties and friendships—Skelton,
Barne, Evans, Egerton, Campbell—that would last his life. It was in

Majestic, too, that Scott established himself beyond any question in his profession. He was not sure whether Prince Louis "liked" him or not, "but at any rate," he told his mother, "he thinks me able for my work which is the main thing." "I think I said I would tell you about our doings at Palma Bay," he reported home in the same letter.

> Well, they were most successful. We had a great time at our various exercises and everything went swimmingly; they left everything in my hands and I was a great man bossing the whole show. On the second day the Admiral came ashore and I showed him around the different arrangements—of course he knew very little about it, but by judiciously working his fads in, I think we made the whole thing popular . . . I am quite pleased with myself because it is the first time anything of the sort has been done in the Channel. On the last day we had a night attack of which I drew out the whole scheme; altogether I feel the torpedo department has asserted itself to some purpose. Now that Hickley leaves they are about to give me his work as well as my own—having no one else they can entrust it to. It suits me on the whole as having now established myself as a competent torpedo man, my policy is to show myself able to do the general duties . . . and I think there is no doubt I shall be able to manage the "Vernon" next year, if I want it; it is satisfactory to think that promotion is more or less certain within something like a limited time and one joins the ranks of the advancers. Meanwhile I know you will like to hear that everything flourishes with my work here.

For all the cheery triumphalism of this letter—Scott was always wonderfully good in that way with his mother, endlessly ready to indulge maternal pride at the expense of his own innate hatred of "show"—it touches on the one aspect of his career prospects that worried him. "Everything went well," he wrote home from Port Mahon again the following week, "and the Admiral was exceedingly nice about it so that I think my character as a torpedo man is established . . . But I have my eye also on another thing which is I fear a bit out of my reach. When Campbell [his future best man] is promoted I should like to be thought of as first lieutenant. They may not think me sufficiently good as a general service officer however, which worries me a bit, and since it would have to be done against the gunnery people I fear they won't see it in the same light. However I shall wait my opportunity—and as Hickley's work has come down on me as well, it may come that way."

The danger of finding himself typecast as a technical specialist was no idle fear, but in the June of 1899 a change of captain and ship's personnel in *Majestic* gave him the opportunity he wanted. "Egerton joined today," Scott wrote to his mother from Portsmouth on the twenty-eighth; "things have occurred as I expected and I am commander until de Chair arrives in England. He will be telegraphed for when Bradford is promoted but as he is at Zanzibar the journey will occupy some time, so here I am till the end of August or thereabouts—of course it is a wonderful opportunity but means work unending as my own torpedo work has to go on somehow."

If Scott had found in Prince Louis a captain who thought of him first and foremost as a "first rate" torpedo man, in George Egerton, his old commander in *Vernon*, he had secured himself a powerful patron and friend. In the Dixonian dichotomy of "autocrat" and "authoritarian," Egerton's credentials would almost certainly put him on the "wrong" side of the fence, but that did not stop him being in many ways the *beau idéal* of a Victorian naval officer, spirited, brave, charming, well-connected and— best of all in a culture that raised chivalric effort over mere efficiency—an old "Arctic" from the disastrous but heroic Nares expedition of 1875.

Scott was not the sort of young officer who would naturally impose himself, but as the man in *Majestic* who knew the ship better than anyone, he was well placed to make a mark with his new captain. By the middle of September de Chair had taken up his post as commander, but while he was still "green" in the job he, too, inevitably depended "pretty much" on Scott's advice and knowledge. It was, as Scott said, hard work but a comfortable situation. "The new Captain is very pleased with the ship," he reported home the following month, "as I am the only link with the past, so to speak, and knowing the game from experience . . . my position is a very strong one."

Strong as his position was, it is another remark of Scott's, a chance comment from a diary fragment—"The naval officer should be provided by nature with an infinite capacity for patiently accepting disappointments"—that probably more accurately reflects his mood at this time. "In 1899," Grace recalled, "coming home in H.M.S. *Majestic* he said he must look out for something to take him out of the general rut of the Navy, a service he was devoted to, but he wanted freedom to develop more widely. All this time he had been realizing that he had really something to say, in some form or other as yet unknown. How could he express himself fully?"

It was the old angst of the *Amphion* diary fragment, only maturity had sharpened a vague adolescent dissatisfaction into a more intelligent need for growth. The 14,900-ton, first-class, twin-screw, armoured *Majestic* was hardly a "sleepy hollow," but in its own way it was every bit as restricting and stultifying. Including Dartmouth, *Vernon* and that "farce" of an institution, as Jellicoe labelled the Royal Naval College at Greenwich, where Scott had gone in preparation for his lieutenant's examination, he had been doing more or less the same thing for nineteen years, and again the *Majestic*'s ship's log is the best guide to just what that meant: Weighed for Vigo. Anchored Vigo. Weighed for Gibraltar. Anchored Gibraltar. Weighed for Aranci. Anchored Aranci. Governor visited ship. French Admiral visited ship. Italian Royal Yacht Savoia with King and Queen of Italy passed through the lines. Royal salute. King and Queen arrived on board. Royal Salute. Weighed for Cagliari. Anchored Cagliari . . . Ship dressed in honour of King and Queen of Portugal. Royal Salute. Annual pulling regatta. Sailing regatta. Vice Admiral's Cup.

At the end of March 1900 *Majestic* was at anchor at Berehaven, in attendance on the old Queen on her historic visit to Ireland. "We leave here on Saturday, arriving at Kingstown on Monday," Scott wrote home with a barely restrained irony, as if the whole purpose of the navy was to amuse some Imperial reincarnation of Miss Havisham. "The Queen comes on Tuesday, when we man ship and cheer and fire guns and generally display our loyalty."

Grace was right. Scott needed something different. Her memoir, like those of all Scott's early biographers, shows the same desire to give shape and meaning to his early years, to see them in quasi-biblical terms as a kind of preparation for the ministry of sacrifice that was his polar career. Nevertheless, Grace's portrait of frustration rings true. Again, brother and sister, speaking from their very different worlds, the one from the dressmakers' shop, the other from one of the most formidable battleships of the pre-Dreadnought age, could see things in the same light. "What he wanted," she went on, were "great interests and expansion of life with new experiences . . . in contact with men of the big world [with] all sorts of experiences and interests."

In the same year Scott, at least, found what he was looking for. In his letter home from Berehaven, he had announced with mock pomposity that June should "bring me to greater dignity." That "dignity"—commander's rank—duly arrived on 30 June 1900. And with it came the command that was to transform his life.

Five: Enter Markham

It is almost a reproach to civilization that we have arrived at the close of the nineteenth century without knowing the whole of the superficial appearance of this
little planet.

THE DUKE OF ARGYLL, 1897

To the right of the main entrance of the Royal Geographical Society in
London's South Kensington is a portrait bust that once seen is hard to forget. It is not a particularly impressive piece of sculpture or portraiture, but
there is something in the expression of the face, in the fastidious curl of the
lip and the shape of the brows, that wonderfully evokes the personality of a
man who for more than forty years lorded it over the Society with all the
democratic instincts of a Renaissance prince-bishop.

The man was Sir Clements Markham, official Geographer to Sir
Robert Napier at the sack of Magadala in Ethiopia, introducer of the qui-
nine tree into India, President of the Royal Geographical Society, President of the Hakluyt Society, great Panjandrum of Victorian clubland
and—with the exceptions of Scott's mother and wife—the most important
figure in his life.

In recent years the reputation of anyone who was ever close to Scott has
tended to suffer by a simple process of contagion, but it is fair to say that
had their paths never crossed, Markham's unrivalled capacity for self-
serving, misrepresentation, scurrilities, slanders, snobberies, affectations,

infatuations and vindictiveness was well up to earning him his own posthumous opprobrium without help from anyone else.

For all that, it would be a mistake—a mistake his enemies never made more than once—to underestimate this formidable man or what he achieved. For the best part of two decades he was the driving force behind British polar exploration, and for every flaw in his character there was its opposite quality in equal measure—a chivalry to soften the snobbery; a hatred of cruelty to temper his waspishness; a largeness of imagination to match his pettiness; and, above all, a capacity for loyalty and friendship as complete, unshakable and intemperate as any of his hatreds.

Clements Markham was born in 1830, the son and grandson of clergymen, the great-grandson of an admiral, and the great-great-grandson of the formidable William Markham, Archbishop of York. Like so many families of a similar social and financial position the Markham generations had regularly alternated between Church and navy, and after school at Cheam and Westminster the fourteen-year-old Clements duly reported with his fellow applicants aboard the *St. Vincent* at Portsmouth to be examined for a naval cadet. After writing out half the Lord's Prayer, he was told he had passed, and then "a fat old doctor made his appearance, and, punching them violently in the wind, asks 'if it hurts?' On their replying in the negative, he reported them medically fit for the service."

An exquisite drawing of him done about this time by George Richmond shows a "ringer" for the young Thomas de Quincey, but it is a moot point whether it was the faculty of imagination or just temper that most severely disabled Markham for naval life. By the time he had finished his first cruise to South America he had more than had his fill of it, and not even a brief foray "in the vanguard of English chivalry" during the long search for Sir John Franklin in the Arctic was enough to reconcile his "volatile, emotional, strong willed and impulsive" nature to the discipline or brutality that marked the old navy in the last years of sail.

For all his loathing of the harsh punishments of naval life, and his deep resentment of any authority other than his own, Markham never lost his deeply romantic and nostalgic attachment to the service itself. During his first cruise in *Collingwood* he had fallen under the spell of the son of the Prime Minister Sir Robert Peel, and in many ways the charismatic and brilliant William Peel—VC, KCB and Byronically dead by the age of thirty-three—is the clue to Markham's whole character, the "Rosebud" he would eternally mourn, the unattainably glorious, handsome, well-connected model of manliness and gentility that as an old man Markham would scour the gunrooms of the Royal Navy's ships in a rheumy-eyed search to replace.

There seems little doubt that there was a homosexual strain in this passionate attachment to youth—there would be "talk" of it in *Discovery*—but what exactly that means is harder to say. There was clearly nothing that Markham liked more than an evening "larking" with some good-looking "middie" in a ship's gunroom, and to the fastidious taste of the epicure the old man brought an almost Linnaean rigour and method, cataloguing, listing, and ranking his newest favourites in journal entries of ten and twelve pages long that ranged, in his small spidery hand, from pedigree and family coat-of-arms to colouring, shape of lip and tilt of nose. There is not a shred of evidence, however, nothing in fact but the odd snatch of naval gossip, to suggest that his predilection for youth was anything more than that. Throughout his life he had a fierce and dogmatic hatred of exploitation in any form, and if his interest in young midshipmen had an erotic tinge, it was of the sentimentalising, romantic and snobbish kind, homage to the pedigree and birth of a chivalric caste for which physical good looks merely stood surety.

The whole question of Markham's sexuality would be an utter irrelevance if it were not for its slight bearing on Scott's reputation, and for the broader concern that it has diverted attention from the achievements of a remarkable man. After leaving the navy, in 1851, Markham had entered the civil service, and with the influence he achieved there, and subsequently in the India Office, exploited a position at the heart of the Victorian establishment to push the geographical and historical interests that alongside the navy and its young officers were the ruling passions of his life.

If there was nothing in which Markham was not interested, however, and nothing that a life of travel, exploration, research, archaeology, collecting, writing and power-brokering did not entitle him to an opinion on, it was polar exploration that brought the disparate sides of his personality into sharpest focus. In many ways no one would ever challenge the hold of Sir William Peel on his imagination, but alongside Peel loomed those other titans of his youth, obscure heroes of even more obscure voyages, naval officers like McClintock, Osborn, Mechan, and Hamilton, who had so heroically retarded the cause of human knowledge and British exploration in the nineteenth-century navy's long quest for those twin chimeras of a North-West Passage and the North Pole.

The modern history of polar exploration dates back to the years immediately following the end of the Napoleonic War. For centuries before then seamen and speculators had dreamed of a navigable northern route linking the Atlantic and the Pacific oceans, but it was only when reports from whalers of changing ice conditions off Greenland coincided with a glut of unemployable naval officers that the Admiralty decided that the Arctic offered a perfect solution to the baleful spectre of peace. "To what purpose could a portion of our naval force be . . . more honourably or more usefully employed," demanded John Barrow, the influential Second Secretary to the Admiralty, in 1816, "than in completing those details of geographical and hydrographical science of which the grand outlines have been boldly and broadly sketched by Cook, Vancouver and Flinders, and other of our countrymen?"

The Arctic was by no means Barrow's only goal—he was as happy to commit lives and money to Timbuctoo as to Baffin Bay—but it was in the polar regions that his obsessions bore the bitterest fruit. Within two years of his call a dual expedition under the command of John Ross and David Buchan had been dispatched, the first of a long series of futile and harrowing journeys in search of the Passage or the Pole that reached its tragic climax in 1845 when Sir John Franklin, that "knight sans peur et sans reproche"—or "the man who ate his boots," as he was more familiarly known—disappeared into the ice with the *Erebus* and *Terror* and was never seen again, perishing with all his men in a prolonged agony of disease, starvation, cold and cannibalism that gripped and horrified the nation for more than a decade.

The long, rancorous and ruinously expensive search for Franklin ought to have put paid to public and Admiralty enthusiasm for good, but when it came to polar exploration memories were notoriously short, and by 1875 Britain was ready to try again. "No one on board our two ships can ever forget the farewell given to the discovery vessels," wrote the expedition commander, George "Daddy" Nares, of the scenes at Portsmouth in May of that year when *Alert* and *Discovery* sailed for the Arctic. "Closely packed multitudes occupied each pier and jetty . . . troops in garrison paraded on the common, the men-of-war in port manned their rigging, and as we passed greeted us with deafening cheers, whilst the air rang with the shouts of spectators on shore and on board the steamers, yachts and small craft which crowded the water."

The object of the Nares expedition was the Pole, the motive the old one of national prestige, but for all the excitement and confidence, the result was very much what any dispassionate observer of British Arctic exploration might have predicted.* By the autumn of 1875 *Alert* had hit an impenetrable wall of ice in 82°27'N, and the next spring, after a brief flirtation with dogs, Nares's men reverted to doing what naval expeditions traditionally did best in these circumstances, and settled down to the grim business of man-hauling their massive sledges towards the distant Pole.

In the culture that had grown up over the previous half-century, in fact, no other mode of exploration was really acceptable. As early as 1822 Parry had experimented with Eskimo dog-sledging, but long before Nares's voyage the heroics of men like Leopold McClintock, criss-crossing the ice in the search for Franklin with their heraldic pennants flying above their sledges, had made man-hauling with all its attendant miseries the *British* way.

Nares had warned his officers that "the hardest day's work" they "had ever *imagined*, let alone *had*, would not hold a patch" on the miseries of man-hauling, and he had not been exaggerating. He had put Sir Clements's gloomily evangelical cousin Albert Markham in command of the northern sledging party, and by the time Markham had hacked, stumbled, dragged and prayed his way through a nightmare ice-scape of hummocks and fissures to a dispiriting and utterly meaningless farthest north of 83°20'N—celebrated with the Dean of Dundee's whisky and a rendition of "The Union Jack of Old England"—two-thirds of his ill-equipped, ill-fed, ill-clothed and scurvy-ravaged team were all but done. "Hardly one of them was recognisable," Dr. Moss, the *Alert*'s surgeon, wrote on their eventual return to the ship—a miracle in itself of endurance and courage that is almost impossible to comprehend. "The thin, feeble voices, the swollen and frost-bitten faces and crippled limbs, made an awful contrast to the picked body of determined men we had seen march north only two months before."

There are many more tragic episodes in British Arctic exploration—only one of Markham's team died—but as a vignette of the culture that sent ship after ship out in search of the polar Grail, the Nares expedition would be hard to beat. It had been absolutely plain to John Ross forty years

---

*A portrait of Edward Trelawny, Byron's companion in the Greek War of Independence, by Sir John Millais, illustrates one aspect of this. It depicts Trelawny as an old sea-dog, a sailing-boat visible through an open window, a portrait of Nelson on the wall, and a map of the Arctic spread on a table. The title—jingoistic, Imperial, high Victorian, all those things Trelawny had spent a lifetime hating—reads: "It might be done and England should do it." Britain was not the only country motivated by national pride. "Americans can do it—and *will*," the *Cincinnati News* announced on the eve of Isaac Hayes's attempt on the Pole. An emerging Germany's attitudes to Arctic exploration were no different. "It rests for German inquiry to open up new domains," Karl Koldewey, the captain of the *Germania*, wrote, "in order to show that German sailors are as qualified, as bold and as persevering as those of other nations."

earlier that there was nothing of any commercial or national value to be gained out of the Arctic. But to see it in utilitarian terms of miles surveyed, rivers charted or the Magnetic Pole located, or money wasted, is to miss the spirit that underpinned the whole venture, from Barrow's first expedition to the moment when, with only nine of his fifty-three crew fit for service, Nares abandoned hopes of the Pole and blasted a path out south for his ice-bound *Alert*. "In laying down their lives at the call of duty our countrymen bequeathed us a rich gift," Leopold McClintock—the only man in Markham's eyes to compare with Scott—said on the fiftieth anniversary of the Franklin expedition of the navy's legacy to future British explorers, "another of those noble examples not yet rare in our history, and of which we are all so justly proud, one more beacon light to guide our sons to deeds of heroism in the future. These examples of unflinching courage, devotion to duty, and endurance of hardships are as life-blood to naval enterprise."

The British were not the only ones drawn to the Arctic by Franklin's ghost: there were Germans, Austrians and Americans—notably Elisha Kane, that most successful of self-publicists, Isaac Hayes, and the tragic figure of Charles Hall—but nothing in their history of disputed claims, alleged poisoning, desertion, mutiny and incompetence could seriously threaten British complacency. By the end of the nineteenth century explorers like the American Robert Peary and the great Norwegian Fridtjof Nansen had introduced new techniques and new approaches to polar exploration, but for Markham the only model was the unwieldy, over-manned and ill-equipped British expedition perfected during his youth, the supreme virtues those British virtues of endurance, courage, discipline and duty that had taken his cousin Albert to the empty triumph of his farthest north. "In recent times much reliance has been placed upon dogs for Arctic travelling," he told a Berlin audience in 1899, in defiance of all that skis and dogs had done to revolutionise polar travel, "yet nothing has been done with them to be compared with what men have achieved without dogs. Indeed, only one journey of considerable length has ever been performed in the Arctic regions, with dogs—that by Mr. Peary across the inland ice of Greenland . . . and all his dogs, but one, died, owing to overwork, or were killed to feed the others. It is a very cruel system."

In the greatest of all polar books, *The Worst Journey in the World*, Apsley Cherry-Garrard called polar exploration "at once the cleanest and most isolated way of having a bad time which has been devised," but for old Sir Clements, comfortably ensconced in Ecclestone Square with his blank maps in front of him, that was the whole *point* of the Poles. There is no doubt that his interests in exploration and geography were as genuine as Barrow's had been, and yet it was the purity and the misery of the adventure that seduced him, the opportunity it offered the chivalry of England to test itself in a quest that united pointlessness, patriotism and personal heroism in ways that nothing before the Somme would ever equal.

Above all—and again here is an echo of Barrow—it was the opportunities exploration offered the young naval officer to distinguish himself in peacetime that drew Markham's eyes to the ice. Even he could see that in the age of the great pre-Dreadnoughts seamanship of the old school was of only limited value, but at a time when professionals, politicians and journalists were all exercised by the problems of a peacetime navy, Markham saw in the challenge of polar exploration an answer that united his own faith in youth with the demands of the nation. "Although it is not the same work as is required in general service," he wrote in 1900 to George Goschen, First Lord of the Admiralty, ex–Chancellor of the Exchequer and just the sort of "inimical," half-foreign, and half foreign-educated financier most in need of a lecture on the traditions of the Royal Navy and the virtues of man-hauling, "the work involved in the stress of contest with the mighty powers of nature in the Antarctic regions, calls for the very same qualities as are needed in the stress of battle."

A muted, but real, sense of national disappointment at the failure of the Nares expedition to return with any real achievement to its credit had effectively forfeited Britain's interest in the north to other nations, but that still left the south. In the mid-1880s a committee including Markham had been set up by the British Association for the Advancement of Science in order to promote a government-funded expedition, but it was not until 1893, when he became President of the RGS, that Markham at last had the position, contacts and institutional clout to push his interests successfully.

It was a long and stubborn fight, involving lobbying, fund-raising, begging and bullying, but the man and the hour were well matched. In 1887 the Treasury had turned down the BAAS request with barely a second thought, but by the middle of the 1890s, national, maritime, commercial, patriotic and scientific interests were all beginning to converge on the Antarctic region as an essential theatre of future exploration. There were outstanding questions of meteorology, geology, marine biology, geodesy, currents, tides and atmospheric electricity that only an expedition could answer, but above all it was in the unresolved navigational problems of the southern oceans that Markham saw the sprat to land his mackerel. The key to these navigational problems lay in a fuller understanding of terrestrial

magnetism, and for the fifty years since Sir James Ross's voyages the position of the South Magnetic Pole had effectively been "lost," making it impossible for scientists to verify for the southern hemisphere Carl Gauss's calculations for predicting the forces of the earth's magnetic field.

Interesting as these questions were to Markham, however, and willing as he was to play the scientific card when it suited, they took second place to the limitless opportunities for geographical exploration that the Antarctic regions offered. It is almost impossible now to grasp just how little was then known of the region, and for an Englishman imbued, as Markham was, with a deep scepticism of anything in the way of exploration not carried out under the aegis of the Royal Navy, the short history of Antarctic discovery was shorter and more problematic still.

The history of cartographic fantasy had a long and colourful pedigree, but in British eyes it was only with James Cook's voyages of the 1760s and 1770s that the age of speculation ended and polar exploration in any modern sense began. Before Cook's discoveries it was still possible to believe in the existence of habitable regions of unknown size in the south, but once he had become the first navigator to cross the Antarctic Circle and circumnavigate the globe in a high southern latitude, the limits and nature of any such continent were fixed. "The greatest part of this Southern Continent (supposing there is one)," Cook had written, with the authority of a sixty-thousand-nautical-mile journey behind him, "must lie within the Polar Circle where the sea is so pestered with ice that the land is thereby inaccessible. The risk one runs in exploring a coast in these unknown and icy seas, is so very great, that I can be bold to say that no man will ever venture [by sea] farther than I have done, and that the lands which may lie to the south will never be explored. Thick fogs, snowstorms, intense cold and every other thing that can render navigation dangerous one has to encounter, and these difficulties are greatly heightened by the inexpressibly horrid aspect of the country, a country doomed by nature never once to feel the warmth of the sun's rays, but to lie forever buried under everlasting snow and ice."

For almost fifty years there was nothing to suggest that Cook would be proved wrong, but in the first half of the nineteenth century the drive of the whaling and sealing men and the journeys of Bellingshausen, D'Urville and the American Wilkes in 1840 began a piecemeal discovery of southern land. By the time that Wilkes returned to civilisation something like a seventy-degree arc of the Antarctic Circle south of Australia had been claimed, while farther west detached sightings of Kemp Land, Enderby Land and—still farther west again—Graham Land, Alexander I

Land and Peter I Island had sketched out the possible configurations of a southern continent.

In the eyes of the British establishment, though, a faint but disparaging air of scepticism hung over these foreign voyages, relegating them to the margins and even the mythology of Antarctic exploration. In 1823 James Weddell had extended Cook's farthest south by more than a degree into the sea named after him, but for all the inroads made by commercial skippers like Balleny, Biscoe and Weddell himself, it was left to another Royal Navy officer, Sir James Ross, to take the next decisive step in the process begun by Cook. Sailing in two old bomb vessels, *Erebus* and *Terror*, slow but strong, and strengthened in the bows against southern conditions, Ross crossed the Antarctic Circle in longitude 171°E on New Year's Day 1841, and smashed his way into the heavy pack. Up until this point any captain faced with pack could do nothing but skirt it, but after five days buffeting a path through the ice, Ross "burst forth to the south in an open sea," and on 8 January 1841 discovered the glorious mountainous country of Victoria Land.

In two journeys to this great open sea, Ross laid down with some accuracy the coastline and high mountain ranges of Victoria Land from Cape North in latitude 71° to Wood Bay in latitude 74°, and less definitely to McMurdo Bay in 77 1/2°. In that same latitude and slightly to the east he discovered the two volcanoes subsequently named after his ships, and to the east of them, the ice wall of the Great Barrier now named in his honour. "After all the experiences and adventure in the Southern Seas," Scott himself later wrote of Ross's achievements, "few things could have looked more hopeless than an attack upon that great ice-bound region which lay within the Antarctic Circle; yet out of this desolate prospect Ross wrested an open sea, a vast mountain region, a smoking volcano, and a hundred problems of great interest to the geographer; in this unique region he carried out scientific research in every possible department, and yet by unremitted labour succeeded in collecting material which until quite lately has constituted almost the exclusive source of our knowledge of magnetic conditions in the higher southern latitudes. It might be said that it was James Cook who defined the Antarctic Region, and James Ross who discovered it."

More than a generation later, however, the problem for the geographers was still how to interpret the accumulated knowledge of a century of piecemeal discovery since the pioneering journeys of Cook in the 1770s. In 1874, *Challenger*, under the command of George Nares had shown by dredgings and soundings that there must be continental land within the

Antarctic Circle, but with still only a little over one-tenth of the Circle broached neither *Challenger* nor the subsequent *Southern Cross* and *Belgica* expeditions did much to clarify the problem of its extent.

The *Belgica*, under the command of Adrien de Gerlache, sailed from Antwerp in 1897 for the south with the intention of landing a small party at Cape Adare on Antarctica's South Victoria Land. Before the ship got anywhere remotely near her target winter had set in, and *Belgica*'s resentful crew were condemned to the first Antarctic winter spent within the Circle, frozen helpless in the pack of the Bellingshausen Sea, at the mercy of the currents and the ice, ravaged by scurvy and tottering on the brink of madness as they brooded on the thought of a dead shipmate, his feet weighted to take him to the bottom, swaying backwards and forwards on the ocean bed hundreds of fathoms beneath their captive hull.

If Carsten Borchgrevink had been a British naval officer, it is possible that the *Southern Cross* expedition might have done more to dispel the ignorance and fear that was *Belgica*'s chief legacy to Antarctic knowledge than it actually did, but a Norwegian seaman/schoolmaster was never going to be taken seriously. In 1894 Borchgrevink had become the first man to set foot on Victoria Land when he rowed ashore from a small Norwegian whaler. Five years later, with the backing of the publisher Sir George Newnes, and in the teeth of the hostility and contempt of Clements Markham and a geographical establishment outraged to see British money financing a foreign adventurer, he took down the first expedition to overwinter on Antarctica.

Borchgrevink was "in many respects . . . not a good leader," as the physicist on *Southern Cross* and on Scott's first expedition, Louis Bernacchi, charitably put it, but whatever his faults he has never received the credit that he is due. The site of the expedition's hut on the shore edge at Cape Adare effectively ruled out any of the serious geographical exploration so beloved of Markham, but for a "small pioneering expedition without influence or backing," the work carried out by *Southern Cross* across a range of scientific disciplines from magnetism to marine biology, penguins to atmospheric circulation and Antarctica's cyclonic winds, "stands unchallenged."

The *Southern Cross* and *Belgica* expeditions were the first expeditions of a "Heroic Age" of Antarctic exploration that is often dated back to the day in 1893 when, at a lecture at the RGS, Professor John Murray of *Challenger* fame called for an expedition to resolve the outstanding geographical questions still posed in the south. "All honour," he declared, "to those

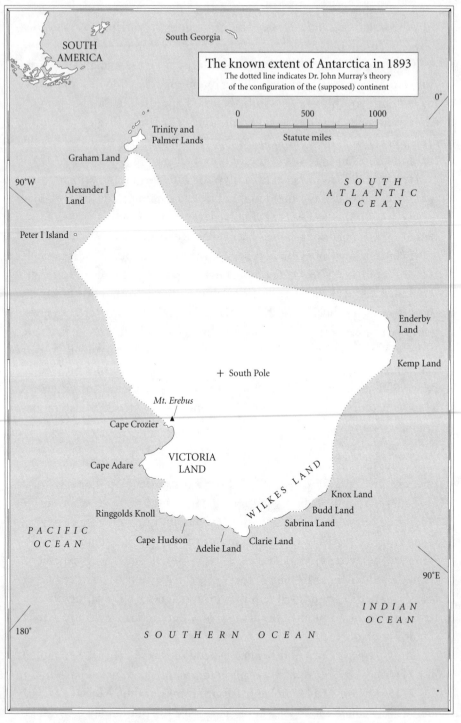

SOUTH GEORGIA

SOUTH
AMERICA

The known extent of Antarctica in 1893
The dotted line indicates Dr. John Murray's theory
of the configuration of the (supposed) continent

0°

0   500   1000

Statute miles

Trinity and
Palmer Lands

Graham Land

90°W

S O U T H
A T L A N T I C
O C E A N

Alexander I
Land

Peter I Island

Enderby
Land

Kemp Land

+ South Pole

Mt. Erebus

Cape Crozier

VICTORIA
LAND

Cape Adare

W I L K E S   L A N D

Knox Land

Budd Land

Sabrina Land

Ringgolds Knoll

P A C I F I C
O C E A N

Cape Hudson

Clarie Land

Adelie Land

90°E

180°

I N D I A N
O C E A N

S O U T H E R N   O C E A N

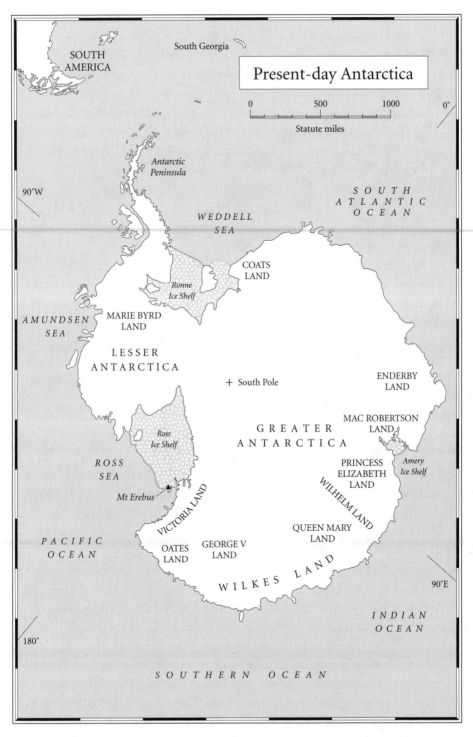

SOUTH
AMERICA

South Georgia

Present-day Antarctica

0   500   1000

Statute miles

0°

Antarctic
Peninsula

90°W

*SOUTH
ATLANTIC
OCEAN*

*WEDDELL
SEA*

COATS
LAND

*Ronne
Ice Shelf*

AMUNDSEN
SEA

MARIE BYRD
LAND

LESSER
ANTARCTICA

+ South Pole

ENDERBY
LAND

MAC ROBERTSON
LAND

GREATER
ANTARCTICA

*Ross
Ice Shelf*

*Amery
Ice Shelf*

*ROSS
SEA*

PRINCESS
ELIZABETH
LAND

Mt Erebus

VICTORIA LAND

WILHELM LAND

PACIFIC
OCEAN

QUEEN MARY
LAND

OATES
LAND

GEORGE V
LAND

90°E

WILKES LAND

180°

*INDIAN
OCEAN*

SOUTHERN   OCEAN

who venture into the far north, or far south, with slender resource and bring back with them a burden of new observations. A dash to the South Pole is not what I now advocate, nor is it what British science desires. It demands rather a steady, continuous, laborious, and systematic exploration of the whole southern region."

If Markham was in need of an ally, he could not have found a more influential one; but between Murray's plea and his ambition lay a fundamental difference that was to bedevil the whole future of British Antarctic exploration. In his lecture Murray had argued for two largely civilian parties to be landed at widely separate points, but to Markham any scheme that relegated the role of the navy to little more than a glorified ferry service and robbed her officers of an opportunity to test their courage defeated the whole point of polar exploration.

And here in miniature is the history of the next twenty years, the clash of visions between the scientific establishment, determined to fund an expedition in its own image, and a Clements Markham equally bent on reliving the naval glories of the Franklin era. In terms of argument there ought never to have been a contest, but in Markham, Murray and all the other scientists of the Royal Society who followed him to the slaughter were up against a natural street-fighter prepared to bully, beg, lie and do anything else required to get his way. In letters, speeches, articles, memoranda, conferences and lectures—lectures to the Royal United Services Institute, to the Imperial Institute, on the role of the colonies, the role of the navy—the same vision was pushed with an energy astonishing in a man of seventy. Over the next six years meetings both within and without the RGS would generate violent outbursts of temper, and yet whenever it came to the point, it was inevitably Markham who would stand his ground, Markham whose vision, energy and sheer persistence could grind his opponents into acquiescence, submission or—better still—resignation.

It was the same, too, when it came to prising funds out of a government reluctant to commit money or naval personnel at a time when British isolationism was looking particularly exposed. When he first approached the government the response was no more encouraging than it had been a decade earlier, but Markham was not a man to be deflected from a sense of Britain's destiny by international embarrassments like the Jameson Raid or tensions with the United States over Venezuela, and the following year another approach extracted a more sympathetic response. "Referring to the communications which have passed between the First Lord of the Admiralty and yourself," he was told in that *de haut en bas* tone so typical of Admiralty communications, ". . . I am commanded by my Lords Commissioners of the Admiralty to state that they have taken the matter into careful consideration, and while they regret to be unable to take any direct part in the organising of such an expedition, at the same time they regard the enterprise as one which is important in the interests of science. Although the present exigencies of the Naval Service prevent them from lending officers, as they would necessarily be out of reach for a protracted period in case of being required for the active duties of the Fleet, Their Lordships will watch the results with great interest and will be prepared to aid in the outfit of an Expedition by the loan of instruments, further they would be happy to place at the disposal of those chosen to conduct an Expedition any experience which may have been gained in the past and which might possibly be useful."

It was not much, but it was enough for Markham, and forging a reluctant partnership with the Royal Society, he launched a public appeal to fund an expedition under the joint auspices of the two Societies. At the beginning there seemed little more public enthusiasm for the cause than there was in government circles, but when in 1899 a gift of £25,000 was followed in quick succession by a promise of royal patronage and an invitation from Germany to collaborate on a scientific programme, Markham knew he could go back to the Treasury with an irresistibly strong hand. "On grounds of polity alone," read a letter almost identical in tone to that sent by the Royal Society to the government of the day before Cook's first great voyage over a century earlier, "we submit that it is not the time for our country, so long the mother of discovery and of maritime enterprise, to abdicate her leading position."

At a time when the situation in South Africa made Britain's isolation seem chillier than ever, it was more than even Lord Salisbury's government could resist, and a meeting with the First Lord of the Treasury Arthur Balfour on 2 June 1899 produced a promise of £45,000 on the condition that the Societies could match the sum from private funds. The grant still left the Societies three thousand short of the £90,000 they required, but with Markham's again the crucial voice, the RGS voted to raise the money through the sale of investments, and Markham had won.

The danger for Markham was that at the moment of victory he was going to have to pay the price for having brought the scientific establishment, in the form of the Royal Society, into partnership to get his way. He was realist enough to know that he could never have won over the government without its support, but now that the British National Expedition—

as it was somewhat euphemistically called—was a reality, differences over where it should go, why it should go and who should lead it could no longer be fudged.

At the heart of all Markham's problems was the lumbering Joint Committee, set up in June 1899 and comprising members of both Societies, appointed to oversee every aspect of the planning of the expedition. With its greater prestige and authority there had always been a danger that the RS would dominate this, and with little but his own willpower and the record of the RGS in raising funds to help him, Markham faced an endless struggle to control "the rag, tag and bobtail professors" and the endless sub-committees they spawned. "We initiate the whole thing," he bitterly complained in August 1900, only two months after Balfour had given the go-ahead to the expedition, "raise all the funds, for geographical exploration, and then these mudlarkers [the biological sub-committee] coolly ask us to turn our expedition into a cruise for their purposes."

"Murray talking rubbish," he scrawled in one typical complaint. "Murray very troublesome and wasting our time." "I think Murray is trying to wreck the expedition." "He is an ill conditioned bully." "Murray's conduct looks as if he was trying to do all the harm he can . . . This committee will strangle the Expedition with red tape if not checked . . . Futile chatter." "Greely pompous and egotistical . . . all progress all work impossible." "Professors know nothing and only care about their own hobby." "The important questions must be left to one man"—from June 1899 till the sailing of the expedition, Markham's diaries and letters are peppered with expressions of his frustration at sharing power and at the sheer dilatoriness of committee life.

At the core of these battles were real principles—the nature of the expedition, the integrity of British science, the quality of international cooperation—and the one battle that mattered more than any was over the appointment of the expedition's leader. There was room in even Markham's universe for give and take over the location or duration of the expedition, but if there was one thing over which he would rather have seen the whole project collapse than give in, it was his vision of a National Antarctic Expedition sailing with a naval officer and not a scientist at its head. There was probably no subject to which Markham had devoted more time, either, and none on which he felt himself so uniquely qualified to judge. From the middle of the 1880s the search for the right man had been his personal quest, and over the fifteen years since there could hardly have been a suitable midshipman Markham did not get to know, and whose name, appearance and background did not find their way into his journals.

He knew what he wanted, which historical models to copy and which to avoid, and with his customary obsessiveness had made charts, drawn up lists, cross-referenced expeditions and compared performances in page after page of meticulous notes. Parry, he noted, was twenty-nine when he did his best work, Franklin thirty-three, McClintock twenty-nine, Osborn twenty-eight to thirty-two, Mecham twenty-two to twenty-six, Vesey twenty-one to twenty-five, Ross less successful at forty-three than he had been when younger. At fifty, Crozier was a quarter of a century too old. In the search for Franklin all the real work was done by the young. Nares was fine in *Challenger*, but no good for "really severe work" in the north. The young men on that expedition had been excellent then, but were now past it. "He should be a naval officer," Markham summed up the evidence; "he should be in the regular line and not in the surveying branch, and he should be young, not more than 35; but preferably some years younger than that. All previous good work in the Polar region has been done by young officers in the regular line: those in the surveying branch who have been employed on Polar service have been failures. Old officers, all past 40, have failed and have been unable to take the lead in expeditions they nominally command." There were various reasons for this, he went on, because while surveying called for "close attention, diligence and endurance, it does not bring out those other qualities which are needed in the leader of an expedition into unknown regions. Nor is the discipline and order of a surveying vessel, the sort of system . . . essential for the well being of an exploring expedition."

The other objection to the surveying branch, in Markham's eyes, was that it had never been a path to promotion or distinction, and did not attract the kind of officer "conscious of ability, or who are ambitious, the class of man we want." "Such are the young men to be found in the regular line," he triumphantly concluded, prejudice and snobbery gloriously vindicated by precedent, "generally as gunnery or torpedo lieutenants, because they see that to excel in those lines is the quickest way to promotion. Among them are many young officers ambitious for distinction, enthusiastic, anxious for opportunities to win a name; at the same time able, resourceful, lovers of order and discipline, and accustomed to the management of men. It is among these that the best leader of an expedition is to be found."

If Markham had got his expedition ten years earlier, his choice of leader would have been Scott's new captain in *Majestic*, but at forty-six Egerton—"the beau ideal [a favourite phrase] of a Polar commander"— was too old. Over the years other possibles on the list had also fallen away for one reason or another, but on 11 June 1899, less than a fortnight before the crucial meeting with Balfour, the officer whom he had already identi- fied as "the best man next to Egerton for the job" appeared at Markham's Ecclestone Square home. "(Sun) to church with Minna," Markham's diary for 11 June bathetically recorded the historic occasion. "Mrs. & Miss Nut- tall came to bid us farewell, then young Robert F. Scott wanting to com- mand the Antarctic Expedition."

The two men had in fact met in the street a few days earlier, when Scott first learned of the expedition, but it would have been more than Markham could have borne to leave the decisive moment of his life to a chance meeting or an afterthought to Mrs. and Miss Nuttall. "On June 5th, 1899"—not the eleventh of the diary—"here was a remarkable coinci- dence," he later wrote with a more suitable eye for the workings of destiny, "a remarkable coincidence. I was just sitting down to write to my old friend Captain Egerton about [Scott], when he was announced. He came to vol- unteer to command the Expedition. I believed him to be the best man for so great a trust."

And Markham had had his eye on Scott for so long too, had seen the potential in him so early, that there must have come a time when he forgot that Scott had once been no more than sixth on his list of possible leaders for the Antarctic. The two men had first come across each other twelve years earlier when Scott was a midshipman in the Training Squadron, and Markham's diary recorded the occasion. "In the forenoon there was a ser- vice race for cutters," the entry for 1 March 1887 reads. "The *Rover's* boat won (mid-Scott) but the *Calypso* (Hyde Parker) held the lead for a long time."

That race made enough of an impression on Markham for him to recall it in detail a dozen years later, and yet Scott was just one of a score of midshipmen to catch his eye that spring. Markham was cruising—if that is the right word—with the Training Squadron as a guest of his cousin Albert, and not even the death of another boy in *Rover* who fell overboard and drowned was enough to dispel the rosy haze through which he looked out on a world of young men dressing up as girls or listening to his yarns against a backdrop of Caribbean skies and seas. "The day was lovely," Markham's diary happily runs on, "with a smooth sea, and light breeze. The ships crowded all sail. 'Calypso' shooting ahead. It was the prettiest sight imaginable . . . Went with Woollcombe to the tailor, to try on his female attire . . . Told ghost stories to Woollcombe [later captain of the *Valiant* at Jutland and a future admiral], Tremayne [despatches at Jutland, and another admiral], Smyth, and Ommaney, during the first watch . . . Skylarking with Smyth under the poop . . . I never met nicer, better mannered, more warm hearted young fellows. God bless them!"

It was, in fact, another nineteen-year-old from the same term in *Britannia* as Scott, Tommy Smyth, who for a long time, before he went off the rails, commanded Markham's deepest affections and hopes. Smyth had passed out of *Britannia* in second place, five above Scott, and in terms of family, looks, temperament and aristocratic connections was everything that Markham wanted. "My bright young friend Tommy Smyth brings such sunshine into the house," he wrote on their return from the West Indies. "The boy has a very warm place in my heart: he has rare gifts of intellect and heart, not weak but a little wild—and all the better for that— brimming over with merriment and fun . . . went fast asleep with his head on my shoulder."

If it was a Tommy Smyth that Markham wanted, in fact—and looks, birth, connections and a sunny nature the principal criteria of judgement— then the wonder of it is that he should have ended up with Scott at all. It is certainly true that Markham had identified him as an officer of "great ability," but it is doubtful if he had any more idea of what he had got himself when Scott came to see him than the navy had when they let him go.

It would have been odd if he had done, because anyone who could dismiss the whole surveying and engineering branches with Markham's breathtaking arrogance was unlikely to have recognised the practical and scientific bent that was at the heart of Scott's genius. He would have known that as a torpedo officer Scott possessed a certain technical aptitude, but for all the subsequent claims over the appointment, the truth is that Markham—and those who allowed him to wield such unfettered powers— were luckier than they knew or deserved when they found themselves Scott.

It would be harsh to blame Markham, though, because the navy establishment was not designed to recognise the worth of an officer like Scott. He did not have a great naval name like Hyde-Parker, the boy he beat in the cutters' race. No one said that Scott reminded him of his father or his uncle. Nobody suggested he would sooner go into battle or spend a polar winter with him than any man in the service. No captain thought him one in a thousand. All, when brought to think of him, spoke simply in terms of "entire satisfaction" . . . "a most promising officer" . . . "a zealous and painstaking young officer . . . of most value to the service." "You have nothing to thank me for," Prince Louis of Battenberg had written to him on quitting *Majestic*, as if Scott's existence in his ship had come as something of a surprise to him. "I required a reliable first Lieut. & was glad to get him."

Only George Egerton—Lord Louis's successor in *Majestic*—seemed to have any real conception of Scott's abilities, and even he had to warm himself to the task. "I am at a loss to name any officer who is likely to be more suitable," he had written in his initial response to Markham's appeal. "Lieutenant Scott is an officer of great capabilities and possesses a large amount of tact and common sense. He is of strong physique and robust health—a scientist and an expert in electricity. Very keen, zealous, of a cheerful disposition, full of resource and a first rate comrade." "You certainly could not do better than put Scott in command," he wrote again from on board *Majestic* in Dublin Bay when he had had more time to think about it; "he is just the fellow for it, strong, steady and as keen as possible. Genial, scientific, a good head on his shoulders and a very good officer. I am in hope he will get his promotion in June, he deserves it."

Scott himself was the first to admit that he had no knowledge of Antarctica and no great "predilection" for polar exploration, but it is not hard to see what took him to Ecclestone Square. The idea that exploration on the eve of the "Fisher Revolution" that would haul the navy into the twentieth century offered some magic route to promotion is utter nonsense, and yet what it did offer was both a physical and intellectual release from the straitjacket of service life that Scott had been craving since his days in *Amphion*.

And if he lacked the charisma and pedigree of Smyth, or even the focused ambition for exploration, he had a charm and tact that immediately sealed Markham's support. "I told Captain Egerton about your wish," Markham wrote to him after his visit to Ecclestone Square, the first of a long stream of hints, warnings and instructions. "There could not be a better adviser. You will make a great mistake if you do anything at the Admiralty before you get the signal. I very well remember the way you won the service cutter race at St. Kitz when you were in the 'Rover,' and with the same combination of good judgement, prudence, and determination you will win again."

It was a steep and unfamiliar learning curve for Scott. The appointment was not going to be straightforward, Markham explained three days later. Quite apart from the hostility of the Royal Society members who wanted a scientific leader, the factions within the RGS element also posed a difficulty. Sir George Nares wanted his son on the expedition. The powerful surveying lobby grouped around Sir William Wharton, the navy's Chief Hydrographer, was going to demand a surveyor for the post. Lord Walter Kerr, the First Sea Lord, would be in Scott's favour, Markham added with a final cautionary word, but it would be best "to do nothing until October beyond making interest with the naval officers on the Joint Committee."

"I see no possible danger in seeing the naval members of the Committee personally," Markham was warning again just two days later; "the mistake would be to make any application until the right time. Lord Walter Kerr would be the most important person to get on your side. Unluckily people are out of town until the autumn . . . Hoskins and McClintock are the most important to get on your side, as regards the Committee. Vesey Hamilton is luckily dead against Wharton and his surveyors . . . Sir George Nares is for the surveyor, but he seems to me to be getting into his dotage, and keeps maundering about his son going, whatever the subject of the discussion may be. He will be no good."

"You have your hands full indeed," Markham wrote once more on 1 August, determined to mark his protégé's card as fully as possible. "I have told them to send you . . . Murray's Antarctic paper of 1890, which is worth reading . . . They made (yesterday) Admiral Markham Secretary of the 'Ship' sub-committee, so it is very desirable that you should square him . . . I have mentioned you to him . . . Success attend you." "I am glad you saw Sir Leopold McClintock and Admiral Markham," he wrote from Norway three weeks later. "The great thing will be to talk it over with Captain Egerton and get him to recommend you. His opinion will carry most weight . . . The only thing I am afraid of is that you will be considered too good—that the Admiralty may give leave to one of Wharton's people about whom they care nothing, but may hesitate about a rising officer in the regular line."

"The hydrographers are directly responsible for all former disasters," Markham was complaining just over a month after he had first seen Scott, "for the Franklin catastrophe, for the searches invariably being sent in wrong directions . . . for having jobbed other failures into commands . . . for jobbing an old woman like Nares into the command in 1875 . . . Wharton has continually harassed and annoyed me, and now it is a success he wants to do the same; job the appointments, and get all the credit. If he succeeds there will be blunder after blunder ending in disaster like everything else they touch."

To Markham the answer to any such impasse was always the same — "the important questions *must* be left to one man," he insisted — and in the spring of 1900 he wrote directly to the Admiralty to put forward Scott's name. "I have written to Mr. Goschen," First Lord of the Admiralty, applying for the release of two officers, he told Lord Walter Kerr, one "to take charge of the executive work of the Antarctic Expedition, and one to command."

> On this permission will, I consider, depend the efficiency and success of the expedition. If a young commander and one lieutenant are allowed, no doubt the other watch keeper can be found among smart young fellows in the naval reserve; but these two are essential to give a tone to the expedition and leaven the rest as well as because such leaders cannot be found elsewhere.
>
> Of volunteers, Lieut. Robert F. Scott, now in "Majestic," is much the best man to command the expedition I think; and Lieut Charles Royds ("Crescent") would be the best as the one lieutenant . . .

With the heavy demands made on the service by the Boxer Rebellion in China and war in South Africa, the Admiralty were reluctant to lend anyone, but by 5 April the appointment of Scott and Royds had been confirmed. On the following day Markham wrote to congratulate Scott and reassure him on the score of promotion, and it was probably as well that he did not tell him just how strong the opposition remained. "I read my letter to Mr. Goschen," Markham noted in his diary for 18 April, after he had finally broken the news of his *fait accompli* to the odd alliance of naval hydrographers and Royal Society entomologists his years of bullying had conjured into existence, "and the reply from him, and from the Secretary of the Admiralty appointing Scott and Royds. Captain Tizard immediately became most insolent, questioning my right to write to Mr. Goschen, cross-questioning, and making a violent attack on the professional character of the officers. His real meaning is that no officer in the regular line is fit, only those serving in the surveying branch. His manner was most offensive."

After all Markham's manipulation and deceptions, there was probably no protégé of his the hydrographers could have accepted, but their opposition to Scott was not simply a matter of revenge. He might, they conceded, have the paper certificates to prove his "thorough grounding in seamanship, navigation, surveying, chemical & mechanical science." He might well have got the best marks of his year—980 out of 1000—in seamanship. He might equally have done a special course in surveying at Greenwich, and written up the "whole question of mining survey." None of that answered to their point. "That officer's [Scott's] certificates are without doubt remarkably creditable & show him to be possessed of a rare combination," Captain Mostyn Field—"Scott's chief enemy," Markham called him—wrote on 12 May, in a letter that remains as crucial now to any valuation of Scott's capacities as it was then,

> but qualifications for the command of an expedition to the Antarctic should, in my opinion, include experience as a responsible officer in a masted ship . . . Not less essential in the officer in Command, is a practical acquaintance with the practice of deep sea sounding, dredging, running survey, and magnetical & astronomical observations both afloat & ashore . . . Mere courses of instruction in these subjects cannot adequately take the place of years devoted to their practice under varied conditions, however talented an officer may be. All experience must be purchased, and if an officer inexperienced in these matters be appointed, the price will be paid in time and material, neither of which can be afforded in an Antarctic Expedition . . . It is one thing to take observations in a hut at Kew or the courtyard at Greenwich observatory, but quite another thing to get the same observations under conditions of service & especially such as prevail in the Antarctic . . . I regret that I cannot concur in the appointment of that officer.

The tone here is so disarmingly reasonable, so apparently unarguable, that it is easy to forget that the same objections would have applied to any young naval officer at the end of Victoria's reign. It is certainly true that a candidate from the hydrographers' branch would have been in a better position to carry out the oceanographic and surveying work of the expedition, and yet after a gap of more than twenty years in naval polar exploration, Field's ideal of a commander no more existed among the junior officers of the surveying branch than did Markham's incarnation of Arthurian chivalry in the executive line.

If Field thought arguments were going to win him the case, however, he had misjudged his enemy. At the next meeting of the Joint Committee the old alliance of hydrographers and professors fought one last stand, but with the control of the vital naval sub-committee set up to resolve the issue slipping away from them and into the hands of Markham's old "Arctics" clique, they were finished. "There were six distinguished Naval Officers most of them with Arctic experience, who would insist upon Scott's appointment," Markham wrote of the final, bitter end game. "Wharton's hydrographic clique also numbered six, and they would strive to secure & job for the survey department with obstinate perversity . . . I saw the R.S. Secretaries and told them that if Wharton was allowed to continue the dead lock they would be responsible. But they could do nothing with him. At last I persuaded McClintock to have one more meeting and divide. The Committee met once more on May 24th, when Wharton and Tizard both heard some home truths. Some of the Clique were ashamed and staid [sic] away . . . On a division there was a good majority for Scott's appointment, Wharton and Tizard had been the only dissentients."

Markham had won. Wharton, unwell at this time, and presumably no better for his drubbings in committee, had given in. The following day Markham called a meeting of the Joint Committee to endorse the appointment. Markham proposed Scott, and Lord Lister, the President of the Royal Society—"always courteous, never taking a decided line, and caring nothing"—seconded him. The motion was adopted unanimously. "We take the opportunity of offering you our congratulations, on assuming the conduct of an enterprise involving difficulties and responsibilities of no ordinary character," the two presidents wrote to Scott with an inscrutable show of unity.

Scott, in his turn, was no less silkily diplomatic. "My Lord and Sir," he replied on 11 June 1900, a year to the day since he had followed Mrs. and Miss Nuttall into Ecclestone Square, "I am keenly alive to the great honour done me in the selection and sincerely hope that the trust reposed in me may be justified in my conduct of the enterprise and in my earnest wish to further its great scientific aims. I am grateful for your kindness in the applications you have made on my behalf to my Lords Commissioners of the Admiralty and feel that while in your service, I can confidently leave in your hands, my interests in a profession to which I am devotedly attached."

Scott had learned fast. But if he thought that his troubles were over, he was in for a brutal awakening. Wharton and his clique had been no more than stalking horses for a far more dangerous challenge.

Six: Preparations

Oh Lord! What an expedition, but order will come.
GEORGE MURRAY, *26 February 1901*

It had been an odd twelve months for Scott. In the week before Markham finally brought Wharton to his knees he had been up in London on leave, but for most of the year during which the RS and the RGS had been locking horns over his nomination, Scott was in *Majestic* and more concerned with ship and home life than any remoter prospect of command.

With his appointment at the end of May this changed, and although his duties in *Majestic* did not officially end for another two months, he immediately found himself plunged into Antarctic business. In his book on his great 1893–96 journey in the *Fram*, Nansen described the preparation as the hardest part of any expedition, and for a thirty-year-old naval lieutenant with scarcely more experience of the hostile world of the Royal Society than had his dressmaking sisters, it was harder again.

There is possibly nothing in Scott's whole career that so clearly demonstrates the competence of the man—his intelligence, grasp of detail, ability to get on with people, or, for that matter, his tact and charm—than the astonishing way in which he rose to the challenge. There were times over the next year in which he came very close to buckling under the strain, but one only has to look at the letters and memos that poured from his desk to recognise that in his new independence here at last was a man who had found himself.

It is to Sir Clements Markham's everlasting credit, too, that having for so long sung the song of youth, he was prepared, when the time came, to give it its head. "I am delighted to see your promotion in the Times," he wrote generously on 2 July 1900, the day after Scott was appointed commander. "In taking charge of Antarctic matters, you may rely on my support always . . . I consider that the commander is the man whose opinion should prevail, on all points. The old fossils (including myself) can compose the committees, can make themselves very useful from their experience and knowledge; but decisions should rest with a clearer and younger head."

It helped that they saw things in virtually identical terms, but it would be a mistake to assume that when one reads Scott he is simply writing to another man's dictation. "I must have complete command of the ship and the landing parties," he wrote in the first crucial letter after his appointment, a memo that bears the stamp of Scott's mature style as clearly as it does that of Markham's coaching.

> There cannot be two heads.
> I must be consulted on all matters affecting the equipment of
>   the landing parties.
> The executive officers must not number less than four, excluding
>   of myself.
> I must be consulted on all future appointments both civilian
>   and other, especially the Doctors.
> It must be understood that the Doctors are first medical men, and
>   secondly members of the scientific staff, and not vice versa.
> I am ready to insist upon these conditions to the point of resignation
>   if, in my opinion, their refusal perils the success of the
>   undertaking.

If there was a certain amount of shadowboxing here, behind that first point lay a quarrel that went to the heart of both Scott's and Markham's understanding of the position of commander. From the earliest planning stages of the expedition two distinct naval and scientific elements had been envisaged, but what had never been satisfactorily established in all the arguments of the previous year was either the balance of power between the two or the ultimate authority over any landing party.

In Markham's own mind, fixed as it was with a theological fury on the indivisibility of a naval command, there had never been and never could be any confusion, but in a lapse of concentration he had opened the door to his opponents. In October 1899 he had received a request for a testimonial for Melbourne University from a Professor Gregory of the Natural History Museum, and in an unusual show of unity with his Royal Society opponents, met Gregory the following month with the counter suggestion that he should become the Director of Civilian Staff on the forthcoming expedition. With the benefit of hindsight, Markham managed to convince himself that Gregory's size, voice and habit of "nervously pulling his moustache" had never inspired confidence, but at the time he seemed the ideal candidate for the job. "I was influenced by his proved success in organisation and the management of men in a most difficult expedition (British East Africa)," Professor Edward Poulton, an Oxford zoologist with a speciality in butterflies, and an object of particular contempt to Markham, later wrote of Gregory, "by the wide grasp of science which enabled him to bring back valuable observations and collections in so many departments. His ice experience in Spitzbergen and Alpine regions was also of highest importance, together with the fact that his chief subject was geology, a science which pursued in the Antarctic Continent would almost certainly yield results of especial significance . . . No one was more competent to state the probable structure of the Antarctic Continent and its relation to that of the earth. This opinion of Prof. Gregory's qualifications for the position of scientific leader of an Antarctic expedition is I know widely held among British scientific men. In their wide combination and united as they are to tried capacity as a leader they are unique, and an expedition with Prof. Gregory for its scientific chief, with as free a hand as English law would permit, was bound to yield great results."

If Markham had paused for a moment, he must have known that the last thing he wanted on his *naval* expedition was a scientist of this kind of stature, but by the time he realised the threat the damage was done. In the early January of 1900 Gregory had sailed for Australia with what seemed to him a clear understanding of their agreement, and in a letter posted in Egypt on his way out, he spelled out his idea of the command he was accepting. Gregory envisaged a small and carefully chosen landing party, with two scientists supported by a cook, porter, two sailors, one reserve, a "medical man of endurance, resource and pluck," equipped with a three-roomed house, two observatory huts, stables, two boats, sledges, dogs and fuel for two years. "As the main object of the landing party would be to solve the problem of the nature of the countryside," he had written in a letter that in some bizarre aberration Markham had "approved," "which is a geological and geographical problem, it seems to me that it would be better for the organization of the land party to be placed in the hands of the scientific leader . . . The captain would, I hope, be instructed to give such assistance from the crew as may be required in dredging, tow-netting etc, to place boats where required at the disposal of the Scientific staff . . . In regards of the Captain, it seems to me that the main desiderata are considerable experience of sailing ships and of ice navigation which would be most likely combined in a whaling captain." The advantages of a naval commander, Gregory conceded, were obvious, "but sailing is a neglected art in the navy. Further, it seems doubtful whether a first-rate naval officer would in the present condition of affairs be willing to bury himself in the Antarctic for three years, and whether the admiralty would give the necessary leave of absence to one of its best men."

It seems likely that Markham's "approval" of this plan is one of the first signs of old age and failing powers that would become increasingly worrying over the next three years. For some time he had been suffering from sporadic ill health, but it is impossible to believe that the younger Markham would have allowed gout or pneumonia or anything else to cloud his judgement in a way that was so potentially crippling to Scott's prospects.

With Gregory not expected back from Australia until December, however, there was nothing to do but go on as if nothing had happened, and after a crash course in magnetism at Deptford, Scott joined Markham in Norway to look at equipment and meet the men whose experience he so badly needed. "It is quite clear that our Hydrographer Dept is behindhand & old fashioned as regards all these matters," Markham had written to him after a cruise with Nansen had opened his eyes to the oceanographic advances being made abroad, "while it will not be to our credit if our Antarctic work is not quite up to date. I think it quintessential that you should come out here in September . . . Nansen and Hjort will be delighted to see you."

Scott never needed much encouragement to bring himself up to date with technical innovations, and while his magnetic course kept him busy through September, he was in Oslo by 9 October. From Oslo he went up to a new health hydro to join Markham and his wife Minna, and on the next day, he recorded in the blue hardcover notebook he had bought himself for the journey, boarded the *Michael Sars*, the state-owned oceano-graphic ship.

It is unusual to have a diary of Scott's from this period, because unlike most naval officers, to whom a journal was second nature, he never seems to have kept one before going south. It is possible that they have simply disappeared, but if the odd, aborted fragments from his early career are any guide, there would seem to have existed in Scott an ingrained habit of reserve that extended even to the private page. There is certainly nothing in this journal to suggest anything of a private life; what it conjures up instead is the curiosity, excitement and openness that Scott brought to almost everything he did at this time. In her memoir of him his sister spoke of his need for a wider and more challenging world than the navy, and in Norway he found himself in his element, doing what he did best with the kind of men for whom science and practical invention merged in the precise way he admired.

Scott would, in fact, have made a good Norwegian. "So many things discussed that it becomes absolutely necessary to start this journal," he scrawled on the tenth, and the next two weeks were filled with notes, memos, questions, sketches and snatches of conversation. Nansen, too, was as generous with his time and advice as Markham had promised. "Nansen joined us for dinner . . . Nansen rejects asbestos . . . Many interesting scraps of conversation with Nansen . . . N. spoke of Borchgrevink as a tremendous fraud . . . Nansen's name will go far here . . ." From scurvy to the size of boats, from sledges to ski, sextants, theodolites, ships' plans, insulation, thermometers, propellers, drag nets, matting, moccasins, wool, provisions, grain and even dogs, Scott got all he could out of him. "Discussed dogs," Scott recorded a conversation on the eleventh with the arch-man-hauler of Ecclestone Square. "He [Markham] is evidently yielding—and we must do something soon."

The note of urgency—of impatience, even—in that entry is typical, because the more Scott was impressed with what he saw and heard in Norway, the more alarmed he was at the gaps the journey had exposed in British preparations. In memo after memo to himself he noted issues that would have to be raised back in England, and if he found that for all his "very nice manners . . . there was not much to learn" from the Duke of Abruzzi, he was the first to recognise his own ignorance. "Saw many instruments but could not quite follow what each was for." "Nansen, and two Germans at the Grand Hotel," he noted on the fifteenth—"terrible trouble not knowing any language but my own." "Met Nansen who gave me some papers on titration—must look the matter up but confess to being considerably at sea at present."

That same evening Scott dined with Nansen and his wife and daughter, and after hearing Markham lecture at the university on Peru, left for Gothenburg and Copenhagen. On his first day in Copenhagen he had dinner with Maurice Baring from the embassy, and after an evening at the music hall was "trotted off" to the zoo the next day to see a musk-ox by a "dear simple minded old gentleman with equal simple minded wife." But even with the occasional musk-ox, music hall, concert recital—"horrible looking person with magnificent voice," he noted of the Marquis de Souza—to leaven his journey, the coming expedition was never far from his thoughts. "What was principally brought to my attention notice and serious consideration," he anxiously scrawled in Copenhagen, "is . . . that the crew is ridiculously large in the eyes of all foreigners—this point is again & again driven home—*the crew must be largely reduced.*"

It was not all one-way traffic, however, and if Scott's sense of national pride had taken a denting in Norway, it was wonderfully restored by reading the American Frederick Cook's account of his Antarctic experience on the train journey on to Berlin. Cook had been a member of de Gerlache's *Belgica* expedition that had been trapped for a year in the ice of the Bellingshausen Sea, and his maudlin narrative of emotional breakdown and moral disintegration among a foreign crew was just the tonic Scott's patriotism needed. "Read Cook," he noted on the twentieth; "they must be a poor lot except Lecointe whom alone appears to have had some guts—the food seems to have been very bad."

If this seems a sweeping judgement on a crew that also included the young Roald Amundsen, Scott was soon brought back to a less insular view of international exploration by the forwardness of German preparations. "Two personal points of great interest transpired," he wrote on the twenty-first, his own unresolved relations with Gregory clearly in his mind after a meeting with the *Gauss*'s expedition leader, Erich von Drygalski: "He has emancipated himself from all control. He has refused to be subject to any orders."

The following day Scott was in Potsdam with Drygalski, looking at instruments and discussing magnetism and the chemistry of seawater. After paying a final visit to Baron Richthofen, Markham's opposite number in Berlin, he left for Hamburg on the twenty-third and the next day caught the train for England, "fully impressed with our backwardness" and determined to "put things in order." "The German expedition was to sail from Europe at the same time as our own," he later wrote, "but its preparations were far more advanced. In Berlin I found the work of equipment in full swing; provisions and stores had already been ordered; clothing had been tried, special instruments were being prepared, the staff of the expedition had been appointed and were already at work, and the 'Gauss' was well on towards completion. I was forced to realise that this was all in marked contrast with the state of things in England, and I hastened home in considerable alarm. I found, as I had expected, that all the arrangements which were being so busily pushed forward in Germany were practically at a standstill in England; many of them, in fact, had not yet been considered."

At the root of the problem, and in marked contrast to the freedom Drygalski enjoyed, were the various committees that controlled every aspect of expedition planning. It was hard to imagine that anywhere but England a national venture of such a scale should have to wait on the social movements of men who were as likely to be on the grouse moors as anywhere else, but until Scott could extract himself from the financial shackles of committee control, there could be no real hope of narrowing the gap with the Germans.

Another month—and another bad-tempered rearguard from Wharton—was wasted before Scott was allowed a measure of financial independence, but he still had nothing like the support that Drygalski enjoyed in Germany. At the end of June Markham had appointed the young Cyril Longhurst to the post of expedition secretary, but with the first lieutenant and engineer busy with the ship's preparations in Scotland, the third naval officer on the China Station, his biologist working out his notice at Plymouth Museum, his senior doctor just back from Brazil, his navigator still unconfirmed in the job, and half the scientific staff as yet unappointed, the vast bulk of the administrative work inevitably fell on Scott himself.

His energy, though, seemed inexhaustible. He was now living with his mother and sisters again, above a shop in the upper half of a house at 80 Royal Hospital Road in Chelsea. "The horror of slackness," Barrie wrote, "was turned into a very passion for keeping himself 'fit' . . . Even when he was getting the *Discovery* ready and doing daily the work of several men, he might have been seen running through the streets of London from Savile Row [the old RGS building] or the Admiralty to his home, not because there was no time . . . but because he must be fit, fit, fit."

The difficulties only increased when at the beginning of December Gregory arrived back from Melbourne to oversee the scientific preparations for the expedition. At their first meeting he had given Scott a copy of the original plan that Markham had so inexplicably endorsed, and a dinner on the tenth to thrash out their differences only showed how far apart they were. "I may as well say," Gregory wrote to Poulton, irritated at what he saw as Scott's trespassing on his territory,

> I do not think Scott at all a good man for the post.
> His forte is that he is very prepossessing.
> It is his first command & for a man who talks so much about discipline I think it is a pity for his first command to be so unusual.
> I think he is a poor organizer, his departments are in arrears & he is so casual in all his plans. He appears to trust to luck things which ought to be a matter of precise calculation.
> He has no experience of expedition equipment.
> Instead of looking after his own work, he has apparently devoted most of his time to making himself acquainted with mine . . . On questions of furs food sledges ski ie things which are in his department his ignorance is appalling.
> He is a mechanical engineer not a sailor or surveyor. And he does not seem at all conscious of these facts or inclined to get experience necessary.
> Personally I like Scott but I am sorry he does not stick to his own work, instead of devoting so much of his energies to jumping mine.

This was rich coming from a man who had just swanned in from Australia, but he had no more intention of giving in to Scott, than Scott had of playing ferry master to Gregory. "Before perusing your article," Scott wrote to the RGS librarian, John Scott Keltie, some time in January, in a letter marked and triple-underlined "Strictly Private," "I am writing to tell in strict privacy that the situation between Gregory & myself is in the nature of a deadlock. It is a great matter of regret to me but I still hope he may take a view more consistent with mine."

If Scott really still had hopes that he could "manage" him, they did not last long, and on 22 January—the same day that the old Queen died—Gregory sent a memorandum to Markham reiterating his demands. "A preposterous draft of instruction for himself arrived from Gregory," Markham noted in his diary that evening—"quite inadmissible," as he later wrote. "He wanted a position equal to Scott's, to have a deciding voice as to the route, to be consulted in everything, to have charge of observations and sole command on land, but he conceded that Scott might be in charge during times of stress and danger at sea . . . I sent the draft back, telling him it was out of the question."

Behind Scott stood Markham, behind Gregory the Royal Society, but for both sides the issue—scientific or naval command?—was the same, and for both sides the one tactic was to produce a definition of the commander's role that would force the other into resignation. "Dear Gregory," Markham wrote on 30 January, conveniently forgetting his own earlier endorsement, "I am exceedingly sorry if you have been inconvenienced and led to suppose that the organization of the expedition was other than it is, and must be. I thought my views were perfectly well known . . . I must regret the loss of your services if this is to be, but trust that you will not have been much inconvenienced, as I believe you were coming home on leave at this time, under any circumstances."

As far as Markham was concerned, Gregory had only himself to blame for his "misconception," and two days later he circulated a memorandum among RGS members of the Joint Committee reminding them exactly where their loyalties lay. Dr. Gregory had turned down a position analogous to that of Sir Wyville Thomson in *Challenger*, Markham explained with all his old economy of truth, demanding instead "that he should be Director of Science generally, that he should have executive control with regard to routes, the sole executive command of landing parties and of everything on land. This is impossible because Captain Scott has already been appointed by the two Presidents . . . to be Commander of the Expedition, involving executive control of everything connected with it, and undivided responsibility. It would be a breach of faith to take away from that position, and it would ruin the Expedition, for it would lead to the loss of Captain Scott's services . . . A divided command is but another name for failure and disaster. Your President could not agree to the change, and, if it is made, would have to give up all responsibility and withdraw from all active concern in the Expedition."

With rather more enemies about him than friends, one would have thought the threat of resignation a dangerous card for Markham to play, but the old ragtag alliance of professors, hydrographers, time servers, jobbers, incompetents and half-senile apostates was playing a still riskier one. As early as 27 January, Poulton had sounded out the expedition's newly appointed second-in-command, Albert Armitage, suggesting to him that if they could force Scott into resignation, the position could be his. "How far," he concluded, with an Iago-like instinct for the weak spot of a merchant service man, "anything but the ambition of a few young naval officers is likely to be satisfied by this Expedition you may judge by this article in the PG [a piece on the coming expedition in the *Pall Mall Gazette*] . . ."

"It was a rotten letter from someone who might have known better," and Poulton probably knew it himself the moment he sent it. He had only written it in the first place because he believed Scott responsible for the piece of naval self-glorification in the *Pall Mall*, but by the time he realised his mistake it was too late to prevent his letter escaping into the public domain—"If a murderer were to write to you," Scott had asked Armitage with a nicely sophistical twist, "saying that he intended killing someone, and marked it 'Confidential,' would you hold it so?"

If Poulton's attempt to withdraw his bribe represents a certain restoration of decencies, however, it did not represent any weakening, and at a meeting of the Joint Committee a week later, the Gregory faction countered with a set of Instructions that would have given their man the final say in all the key questions touching the expedition. "My Dear Armitage," Scott wrote on the ninth, "Things are now in a condition from which I can see no way out but resignation."

"I called and found him very much depressed over the whole business," Armitage recalled. "He said that he would resign and that I had better take over, etc etc. I persuaded him to wait and talk the matter over the following day. Sir Clements, Scott and I had a pow-wow over it, and the two of us got Scott to stick to his guns."

Other than Armitage's account—and he always had a tendency to be the hero of his own narratives—there is no evidence that Scott thought of giving in, though Markham too noted the "visible effect" the whole business was having on him. Even Markham himself was beginning to feel the strain, but after another bad-tempered committee meeting that saw him jeered out of the room, he bounced back with a series of manoeuvres and counter-coups that restored the critical control of the ship's future movements and overall control to Scott. "Scott came in the morning," Markham triumphantly noted in his diary for 7 May, "and told me that yesterday Goldie's [Markham's henchman] committee telegraphed . . . asking Gregory if he agreed. Gregory answered *no*, which the committee considered to be a resignation."

The "Gregory question" had been "a tale of dullness, intrigue . . . spite . . . malignity" and "incompetence" from the first, as Markham put it, but that did not stop it having its repercussions for Scott. It is impossible to say whether the science carried out by the expedition would have been any better or different if Gregory had been in charge, but the price of Markham's victory was not just the continued hostility or scepticism of the RS towards all the expedition's scientific results, but the grotesque association of Scott's name with naval amateurism.

If there is any one certainty in all this, it is that the only man who emerged from the whole tawdry business with any credit is Scott. It was not his fault that the RS and the whole scientific establishment lacked the guts to stand up to Markham. He was not to blame, either, for that mix of arrogance and *folie de grandeur* that Gregory brought to all their negotiations. "It will be understood what an enormous weight of anxiety and worry was added . . . by this intolerable nuisance," Markham for once wrote without exaggeration. "It would have driven most men out of their senses. It had a visible effect on Scott: but he bore it with most wonderful prudence, tact, and patience."

It was not just Markham who was impressed, and even Gregory and his circle could scarcely find a hard word for him personally. "I admire immensely Scott's powers of organization," Gregory's friend and scientific successor for the duration of the journey to South Africa, George Murray, wrote to Markham at the height of the controversy, "even among affairs that must have been unfamiliar to him. Moreover I am sure we will be all of us happy on board which means so much as regards getting the best work out of men." "I went to see Scott," recalled Armitage, "and dined with his mother and sister and him. I was charmed by him from the first . . . I will say at once that I never met a more delightful man than Scott to work with during our collaboration in our preparations of all matters in connection with the expedition."

The relations between Scott and his second-in-command would deteriorate badly in the Antarctic, but there is an interesting illustration of just how close they were at this time. On 9 April Scott was initiated into Freemasonry at Drury Lane Lodge No. 2127, and in the following month "passed" at an emergency meeting of the same Lodge, the first step on a ladder of Masonic enlightenment that saw him "raised" at the St. Alban's Lodge No. 2597 in Christchurch, New Zealand, in 1904 before finally resigning from Navy Lodge No. 2612 in 1906.

It is hard to imagine Scott attracted to the flummery of Freemasonry—difficult to hear him asking to have his Throat cut and his Tongue ripped from the Roof of his Mouth, and his Heart plucked from under his Left Breast before being staked out a Cable's length from the Shore if he broke his vow of secrecy—but there can have been nothing in its more benevolent tenets that would have been at odds with his own principles. It is impossible to be sure what if any were Scott's beliefs at this stage of his life, but for a naval officer Freemasonry would have been more of a career move than anything else, a gesture of belonging that knitted him more closely to a powerful, if largely invisible, service establishment. Albert Markham, George Egerton, Lord Charles Beresford, Francis Bridgeman, Pelham Aldridge, John Jellicoe—the list of senior naval officers Scott knew who had Masonic links is a lengthy one, but perhaps the most interesting name in this connection is that of his proposer, Albert Armitage. Only another Mason would be able to say with any certainty what if any obligations that relationship postulated, but if there is probably no cause for anti-Masonic hysteria here, it is at least worth bearing in mind in the light of the two men's mutual conduct on the expedition.*

With only months to go, however, both Scott and Armitage had other things to think of, and after the best part of a year had been wasted, preparations were multiplying by the day. There were food and medical supplies to be worked out, applications to be sifted and interviews held, medicals and dental examinations to be arranged, and the myriad other tasks that poured into the two rooms that Scott and Cyril Longhurst shared in the Burlington Gardens University Building. "To Savile Row," the tireless Markham noted in his diary, "where Crease had prepared a feast of Pemmican and other samples of preserved meats, for Scott"; "with Scott to Savile Row, where we had a long consultation with Dr. Koettlitz, respecting the provision and the scale of dietary . . . ship committee where Scott distinguished himself . . . Scott on estimates . . . Scott came with an excellent memorandum on the magnetic observations . . . Scott came to settle about letters to Berlin with reference to co-operation . . . Scott about a notice to invite volunteers . . . Scott . . . asking the War Office for a captive balloon . . ."

As well as the expedition work, there were also the social obligations that went with the command. "Scott at the RGS evening . . . Scott to dinner . . . Scott at paper on Lake Rudolph—Nile journey . . . Anniversary dinner—Scott there . . ." Exhausting though all this may have been, he was becoming very good at it. There was nothing Armitage admired in

---

*In addition to Armitage, two more of Scott's officers would become Freemasons before the expedition was over: Charles Royds, his First Lieutenant, who was initiated in Christchurch, and Ernest Shackleton. If the relations of these four men are anything to go by, the world has nothing to fear from a Masonic conspiracy.

Scott more than his deft touch with the difficult men who were his employers, but behind the charm there was real metal. "I am of course aware that the latter amount has been definitely ordered," he wrote smoothly to the American Compressed Food Company, having first explained that he was halving his original order, "but I do not think it would be satisfactory to you that the fact should be known that we were obliged to leave behind a quantity of your pemmican owing to its not being up to our requirements."

If the burden of things still fell on Scott, at least his staff was beginning to take shape. Albert Armitage had joined from the merchant service in December, and most of the naval and scientific personnel were in place by the spring. A medical doubt still hung over the choice of a second doctor, but by the end of February the list of executive officers was complete with the appointment of Michael Barne—"a charming young fellow . . . and a relative of mine which is also in his favour," Markham noted—and a twenty-three-year-old merchant officer with the ear of the expedition's greatest benefactor, Llewellyn Longstaff, and valuable experience in square-rigged ships, Ernest Shackleton.

If there was one thing too that hydrographers, "Arctics," scientists and Clements Markham were united in, it was the recognition that the key to success lay in the right ship and the right men to handle it. In the earliest days of planning Markham had looked for a suitable whaler to do the job, but with the delicacy of the instruments required for their magnetic programme ruling that option out, it was decided to commission a purpose-built ship. The obvious place for this was Norway, and the obvious man to build it Colin Archer, the designer of Nansen's *Fram*, but national sensibilities made this a delicate issue. "Colin Archer is no doubt a man of great skill and experience," Sir William White, the greatest of all British warship designers, warned Markham, "but it would be a matter of great regret that a ship to carry a British Antarctic expedition should be built outside these islands. We have only a few wooden-ship builders left, but they are quite capable of doing all you want."

If public money had been involved at this stage, White might have had a valid point, but it was Longstaff's donation that had made a new ship possible, and the advice effectively cut the expedition off from both Archer's expertise and the stocks of seasoned timber at his disposal. The consequences of this would later be felt by those who had to sail her, but no Ship Committee chaired by Sir Leopold McClintock was going to ignore an appeal to patriotism, and in the place of a new design emerged a modified version of the old *Discovery* that twenty-five years earlier had gone with Nares to the Arctic.

The design of the vessel was put in the hands of the Admiralty's chief constructor, William Smith, and with the contract awarded to the Dundee Shipbuilders' Company, the keel was laid on 16 March 1900. The ship that rose on the stocks over the next twelve months was 172 feet long and thirty-four feet at the beam, barque rigged, with a displacement of 1,620 tons, a comfortable speed under steam of something like seven knots, an iron exclusion zone of thirty feet around the magnetic observatory, an over-hanging stern to protect the "Achilles' heel" of the ship, a massively rein-forced and raked stem, and an "internal arrangement" — Scott recalled with a blind affection he never showed for any other home — of a strength that no one who had only travelled in a modern steel ship could conceive. "The frames, which were placed very close together," he wrote, "were eleven inches thick and of solid English oak; inside the frames came the inner lining, a solid planking four inches thick; whilst the outside was cov-ered with two layers of planking, respectively six and five inches thick, so that, in most places, to bore a hole in the side one would have had to get through twenty-six inches of solid wood.

"The inner lining," Scott went on, "was of Riga fir, the frames of En-glish oak, the inner skin, according to its position, of pitch pine, Honduras mahogany, or oak, whilst the outer skin in the same way was of English elm or greenheart. The massive side structure was stiffened and strength-ened by three tiers of beams running from side to side, and at intervals with stout transverse wooden bulkheads; the beams in the lower tiers were espe-cially solid, being eleven inches by eleven inches in section, and they were placed at intervals of something less than three feet."

A measure of this strength can be gauged from photographs of her on the stocks, and that must have been how Scott first saw her when he came off the night train for Dundee at the beginning of December 1900. The day-to-day supervision of her progress was left in the capable hands of his engineer, the tirelessly hard-working, inventive and cheerfully irascible old "Majestic" Reginald Skelton, but there were always details that needed Scott's attention. In "1¼ days," George Murray wrote to the RGS librarian Hugh Robert Mill two months later, "I have settled the deck plan for winches, reels, sounding gear, trawling and dredging gear, special tow net-ting and thermometer and water bottle gear, and the fittings for the Biolog-ical and physico-chemical workshop. Many matters which could have

version of the old *Discovery* that twenty-five years earlier had gone with
Nares to the Arctic.

The design of the vessel was put in the hands of the Admiralty's chief
constructor, William Smith, and with the contract awarded to the Dundee
Shipbuilders' Company, the keel was laid on 16 March 1900. The ship that
rose on the stocks over the next twelve months was 172 feet long and thirty-
four feet at the beam, barque rigged, with a displacement of 1,620 tons, a
comfortable speed under steam of something like seven knots, an iron
exclusion zone of thirty feet around the magnetic observatory, an over-
hanging stern to protect the "Achilles' heel" of the ship, a massively rein-
forced and raked stem, and an "internal arrangement"—Scott recalled
with a blind affection he never showed for any other home—of a strength
that no one who had only travelled in a modern steel ship could conceive.
"The frames, which were placed very close together," he wrote, "were
eleven inches thick and of solid English oak; inside the frames came the
inner lining, a solid planking four inches thick; whilst the outside was covered with two layers of planking, respectively six and five inches thick, so
that, in most places, to bore a hole in the side one would have had to get
through twenty-six inches of solid wood.

"The inner lining," Scott went on, "was of Riga fir, the frames of English oak, the inner skin, according to its position, of pitch pine, Honduras
mahogany, or oak, whilst the outer skin in the same way was of English
elm or greenheart. The massive side structure was stiffened and strength-
ened by three tiers of beams running from side to side, and at intervals with
stout transverse wooden bulkheads; the beams in the lower tiers were especially solid, being eleven inches by eleven inches in section, and they were
placed at intervals of something less than three feet."

A measure of this strength can be gauged from photographs of her on
the stocks, and that must have been how Scott first saw her when he came
off the night train for Dundee at the beginning of December 1900. The
day-to-day supervision of her progress was left in the capable hands of his
engineer, the tirelessly hard-working, inventive and cheerfully irascible
old "Majestic" Reginald Skelton, but there were always details that needed
Scott's attention. In "1¼ days," George Murray wrote to the RGS librarian
Hugh Robert Mill two months later, "I have settled the deck plan for
winches, reels, sounding gear, trawling and dredging gear, special tow net-
ting and thermometer and water bottle gear, and the fittings for the Biological and physico-chemical workshop. Many matters which could have

Scott more than his deft touch with the difficult men who were his employers, but behind the charm there was real metal. "I am of course aware that the latter amount has been definitely ordered," he wrote smoothly to the American Compressed Food Company, having first explained that he was halving his original order, "but I do not think it would be satisfactory to you that the fact should be known that we were obliged to leave behind a quantity of your pemmican owing to its not being up to our requirements."

If the burden of things still fell on Scott, at least his staff was beginning to take shape. Albert Armitage had joined from the merchant service in December, and most of the naval and scientific personnel were in place by the spring. A medical doubt still hung over the choice of a second doctor, but by the end of February the list of executive officers was complete with the appointment of Michael Barne—"a charming young fellow . . . and a relative of mine which is also in his favour," Markham noted—and a twenty-three-year-old merchant officer with the ear of the expedition's greatest benefactor, Llewellyn Longstaff, and valuable experience in square-rigged ships, Ernest Shackleton.

If there was one thing too that hydrographers, "Arctics," scientists and Clements Markham were united in, it was the recognition that the key to success lay in the right ship and the right men to handle it. In the earliest days of planning Markham had looked for a suitable whaler to do the job, but with the delicacy of the instruments required for their magnetic pro-gramme ruling that option out, it was decided to commission a purpose-built ship. The obvious place for this was Norway, and the obvious man to build it Colin Archer, the designer of Nansen's *Fram*, but national sensi-bilities made this a delicate issue. "Colin Archer is no doubt a man of great skill and experience," Sir William White, the greatest of all British warship designers, warned Markham, "but it would be a matter of great regret that a ship to carry a British Antarctic expedition should be built outside these islands. We have only a few wooden-ship builders left, but they are quite capable of doing all you want."

If public money had been involved at this stage, White might have had a valid point, but it was Longstaff's donation that had made a new ship pos-sible, and the advice effectively cut the expedition off from both Archer's expertise and the stocks of seasoned timber at his disposal. The conse-quences of this would later be felt by those who had to sail her, but no Ship Committee chaired by Sir Leopold McClintock was going to ignore an appeal to patriotism, and in the place of a new design emerged a modified taken weeks of committees (joint and disjointed) Scott and I have settled quietly . . . Scott is a good chap and a first class organiser. I think he will go all the way and Armitage too."

Just over three weeks later, Scott, along with Armitage and Sir Clements and Lady Markham, was again heading north, via the Waverley Hotel in Edinburgh. It had been only eleven months since the keel had been laid, but the ship was ready for launch. At midday on 21 March 1901 Scott showed Markham over her, and after lunch with the President of the Dundee Council of the Scottish Geographical Society, invited forward Markham's wife, Minna, to perform the ceremony.

It had been Scott's decision to ask Lady Markham, a graceful tribute to the man who had almost single-handedly battered the expedition into being. "After waiting a short time in the office," Markham proudly recorded in his diary, "Minna was conducted to the platform before the stern . . . I followed, and there were also Mrs. Peterson, the other directors, Scott, Armitage, Royds and Koettlitz . . . Keltie, Mill etc. Minna was presented with a pair of gold scissors, and at a signal she cut a ribbon. The bottle of wine was smashed against the bows, there was a pause of two minutes, and then the good ship 'Discovery' glided into the sea—a beautiful sight—amidst tremendous cheers."

The name "Discovery" had only been finally chosen the previous June, but with Markham's sense of history, it is hard to imagine her being called anything else. With certain modifications and nods in the direction of Colin Archer, she was to all intents and purposes Nares's old ship, the sixth of a long line of "Discoveries" that linked Scott's vessel in an unbroken tradition of exploration with the great voyages of Vancouver, Cook and William Baffin.

If Scott was as alive as anyone to the romance of the name, however, he was more concerned with performance, and he would have been pleased with the successful trials in the middle of May. It had been estimated beforehand that she would make seven knots under steam, but in trials both with and against the tide, an average mean of nine knots and the performance of the engine gave them all the encouragement they needed. They might have been less sanguine if they had been able to test her capabilities under sail, but without either the money or the crew to do this, Scott would have to wait until the journey out to South Africa to discover how seriously she under-performed. Her sluggishness under sail would have serious consequences for the costs and timetable of the southward journey, and yet as with everything connected with the expedition, the sheer pressure of time and business meant that no one had the luxury of their German colleagues to think or plan properly ahead.

Back in London, Scott was busier than ever, ordering furs and sledges, negotiating the purchase of dogs, and cadging and wheedling his way to a full crew. From the day that he had taken on the command he had seen the expedition as an essentially naval affair, and he was determined to squeeze as many men out of a reluctant Admiralty as possible. "1 senior carpenter's mate—F.E. Dailey (Ganges)," an Admiralty file records his shopping-list and its own irritable—and belated—approval:

> 1 senior boatswain's mate
> 1 ER artificer
> 4 leading stokers
> 6 petty officers
> 10 seamen

At the end of May, Scott and Markham were again in Dundee to take possession of the completed ship and steam her down to London. As they were being shown over it, an incident nearly cost Scott his life. "Went over Discovery with Scott etc," Markham's diary records. "We then, including Royds, all went to see the screw lifted by tackle from the spanker boom, used as a derrick. We were all standing round watching, when the iron hook came in two, the block crashed down, and the screw went down—2½ tons. Scott was standing exactly under the block, and would have been killed if Mr. Smith had not got him to move a little, just a few seconds before. Mr. Smith saved Scott's life."

Scott was none the worse for the episode, but the screw had jammed in its lifting shaft, and for two days the Discovery was back in dry dock. With time to spare for the first time in months, Scott took out the ship's dinghy, and the next day drove with his hosts to see Glamis Castle ten miles north of Dundee. On 3 June, though, Discovery was again ready, and in "fine weather with a smooth sea" and Markham "very comfortable in the captain's cabin," began the first leg of her long journey south.

By the next day Discovery was off Flamborough Head, and passing Yarmouth on the fifth, came into her East India Dock billet on the Thames at 2 p.m. on the sixth, Scott's thirty-third birthday. Even at this late stage they were still eight men short of a full crew, and with the Admiralty authorising only twenty-three volunteers, Scott was forced to recruit the remainder where he could, taking on four unknown men from the great pool of London's maritime labour force, and another three from Dundee with experience on northern whalers.

The last thing that Scott had wanted was to mix naval and merchant men in this way, and with the defection of Gregory and the loss of his one outstanding scientist, George Simpson, to the Admiralty's medical board, there were also still gaps in his civilian staff. It seems astonishing that a National Antarctic Expedition could have brought itself to such a pass, but with little more than a month to go Scott was still without a physicist and a geologist, the two men most crucial to the expedition's geographical programme and cooperation with the German *Gauss*.

It was not as though the scientists he already had — Reginald Koettlitz, a former member of the Jackson-Harmsworth expedition, or the "exceedingly bald" Thomas Hodgson, his marine biologist — were national *names*, but not even Poulton can have envisaged the situation now facing Scott. He was luckier than he might have been in getting another old polar hand in Louis Bernacchi to accept the vacant role of physicist, but with nobody of proven ability to fill Gregory's shoes, he had no choice but to fall back on a twenty-one-year-old Cambridge oarsman with a Second in the Natural Science Tripos from Cambridge that summer, Hartley Ferrar.

It was little wonder that a scientist like Poulton thought it would have been better that the expedition should be abandoned than sail on these terms, but it was Scott who had to live with the consequences, and no one could have denied him the one piece of real fortune he had with his scientific staff. The previous November he had interviewed a talented ornithologist and water-colourist called Edward Wilson for the post of second doctor, and had been impressed enough to ignore a history of tuberculosis and an infected arm and put him straight onto the books.

A subsequent medical board — at which the scrupulous Wilson had gone back into the room to confess to his tuberculosis — had advised against the appointment, but Scott had no intention of losing a second good man. At such a late stage it would have been almost impossible, anyway, to find a replacement, and so long as Wilson was willing to risk his health and life, Scott was happy to abet him. "I think," Wilson wrote with that absolute trust in the controlling purpose of a beneficent God that stayed with him to the end, "I am intended to go. If I had tried to get it I should have many doubts, but it seems given to me to do. If the climate suits me I shall come back more fit for work than ever, whereas if it doesn't I think there's no fear of my coming back at all. I quite realize that it is kill or cure, and have made up my mind that it shall be cure."

There was one more scare, when their engineer, Skelton, found a leak in *Discovery* and she went again into dry dock, but with coaling and stowing still to be done, no one could be persuaded to take this with the seriousness it deserved. It must have seemed to Scott, in fact, that a greater threat to the ship came from the visitors, with a chaotic scrum of families, friends, admirals, donors, old "Arctics," ticket-holders and sightseers all pressing to see *Discovery* before she sailed. The visitors were so numerous, Thomas Williamson, a young naval seaman recruited from HMS *Pactolus*, complained, "you had scarcely breathing." "The relatives were frequently on board," Markham recalled with all his old, almost forensic, fascination with the peculiarities of human behaviour, "and it was most interesting and rather pathetic to see them finding great consolation in furnishing and arranging the cabins. Scott had his dear old Mother, and his sisters Mrs. Macartney, Mrs. Campbell, Mrs. Brownlow, and Miss Scott. Charlie Royds had his mother and his sisters. Barne had his mother Lady Constance and sister. Shackleton had his fiancée and her two sisters. Dr. Koettlitz and Dr. Wilson had their wives. Mrs. Armitage was near her confinement . . ."

With the leak apparently mended, the filthy scramble to coal the ship could at last begin, and 240 tons were loaded into the main bunker, and another sixty into the small bunkers either side of the engine room. On 15 July, another ceremony took place on board that brought home to crew and families the imminence of departure. "The bishop came up from below in his robes," Markham recalled, "preceded by his chaplain with the Crozier." Drawn up, waiting for him between the hatching and the main mast, stood the officers and men, and behind them, crowding the ship, their families. "The Bishop's address" — "Behold how good and pleasant it is for brothers to dwell together in unity" — "was excellent and very impressive," Markham noted, "and the men, led by Royds, sang their hymns well." "Oh! Almighty God," the Bishop finally prayed, "Who has appointed all things in heaven and earth in a wonderful order, be pleased to receive into Thy most gracious protection all who sail in this ship. Grant that our labours may show forth Thy praise and increase natural knowledge, preserve us in all dangers of body and soul, nourish us in one spirit of gentle unity, and bring us home O Father in love and safety through Jesus Christ our Lord. Amen."

It is an image to savour. The Bishop's blessing, the final prayer of dedication that Scott cherished all his life, the First Lieutenant in his naval
uniform leading the lower deck in the hymns, the choice of hymns themselves—"Fight the good fight," "Lord Thou hast been our refuge" and the
great sailors' hymn, "Eternal Father"—no service could have better captured the peculiarly English cultural baggage that the men of the *Discovery* took with them when they went south. In his account of the first
nightmare winter ever spent in Antarctica, Frederick Cook recalled that
there was not so much as a bible on board *Belgica*. In *Discovery* that would
have been inconceivable. For an English and *naval* expedition, uneasily
straddling the nineteenth and twentieth centuries, the institutional trappings of late-Victorian religion, along with the sense of order, hierarchy
and deference they underpinned, were as real and ever-present as the science, the modernity, agnosticism and spirit of enquiry that drove them.

With only days left before they sailed, there was little time for anything
more spiritual than the last, rushed preparations. There were still a hundred things to do, and as many again that would never be done in time.
The novelist A.E.W. Mason wanted to see over the ship. Sir Erasmus
Ommaney, one of the last frail links with Ross's expedition, wrote begging
Scott to escort him around her. Sir George Nares and Sir Joseph Hooker,
old adversaries, had to be accommodated. There were lectures to give,
speeches to make, the *Worcester* training ship to be visited, pay scales to be
finalised, wills to be completed, teeth to be stopped, and a last ritual dinner
at the Athenaeum with the very men who had spent the last year trying to
stop Scott going to be endured. "The venerable white President down
from his stellar regions . . . the great physiologist . . . the equally great
physicist . . . the man responsible for the safe navigation of the world's
waters . . . the one who had revolutionised surgical practice" were all
there, Armitage recalled twenty-five years later, in a richly Orwellian
image of Pig and Man sitting down in amity together, "to show us, the officers and scientific staff of the expedition, that although there might have
been differences of opinion between the two great societies, there was
nothing but a feeling of utmost friendliness for us . . . We were quite con-
vivial at the close of dinner . . . Before we left the room with the famous
round table we sang 'For they are jolly good fellows,' to which they
responded in like fashion."

A week later on 31 July, Scott and *Discovery* were at last ready to make
their escape. At twelve o'clock Markham and his wife, Minna, along with
Scott's mother and his sister Grace, went on board at the dock gate. There,

also, were Sir George Goldie, Markham's staunchest ally in the last battle against the RS, Cyril Longhurst, the expedition secretary, relatives and a watching crowd of hundreds. "At 1 sharp," Scott noted in the first entry of his Expedition Journal, "left E.I. Docks . . . Ship's company not so disorganised as I had expected. Naval people splendid—three merchant seamen intoxicated."

As *Discovery* moved slowly down river on the tide, "all the steamers on the Thames," the expedition's new geologist, Hartley Ferrar, wrote in his diary, "blew their horns," and the boys of the *Worcester*, manning the rigging of the training ship, "sang Auld Lang Syne." At Greenhithe most of the visitors were put ashore, and by next evening *Discovery* had crossed Spithead and was anchored off the pier at Stokes Bay. On 3 August George Murray arrived with Dr. Hugh Mill, the RGS librarian, who was accompanying the ship as far as Madeira, and two days later the last of the men returned from leave, including among them Wilson, back from a brief honeymoon, having been married less than three weeks before.

At nine that morning *Discovery*, with Sir Clements Markham and his cousin Albert, McClintock and Scott's mother aboard, steamed across to Cowes and made fast to a buoy near the Royal Yacht *Osborne*. Scott had come a long way since he had been turned down for a berth on the Yacht, and at twelve the new King and Queen came alongside, with Princess Victoria. "As His Majesty came over the side," Markham noted with a wonderful bit of courtier's mummery, "he called me, and I knelt and kissed hands, being the first time I had seen him since the accession, also the Queen." Markham then introduced Scott to the King and Queen, and Scott presented his officers. The men, drawn up on the port side, were inspected, and then Scott's mother presented. "The King and Queen then went round the upper-deck, and the living deck," Markham continued, "taking the greatest interest in everything. On returning to the upper deck the King came and talked to me, speaking in high terms of Scott and his crew. The men were drawn up on the starboard side. After mentioning his grief and anxiety over his sister who was dying [Victoria, the Dowager Empress of Germany and the Kaiser's mother, died that same day, one more small incident in the deteriorating relations between Britain and Germany], he spoke to Albert and McClintock. Then he made an excellent speech to the men, and turning to Scott, His Majesty decorated him with the Victorian Order (MVO)."

If the biologist Thomas Hodgson is to be believed, the only thing that really excited the Queen was Scott's terrier, Scamp, but as Hodgson had not even recognised the Queen—"Very young . . . lame and deaf"—he is possibly not the best witness. "We have had millions of visitors while we have been here," Hodgson wrote to his mother, as if numbers might some-how explain his failure of identification, "mostly aristocratic yet very mixed. We went in a mob to sign the King's book on board the Osborne and as we came back a boat fouled us at the gangway and a fool went and jumped overboard and we had to haul him in like a drowned rat." The "fool" had actually dived in to rescue one of the Queen's Pekingeses, but even an anxious Skelton, "in spite of being much troubled with numerous ladies," thought it "on the whole rather a good show."

For Scott himself, it was a mixed occasion. He always hated fuss of any kind, especially anything that singled him out. In his journal entry for the day he forgot even to mention his MVO, only pencilling it later in the mar-gin as an afterthought. For his mother, though, he was pleased. "My Dear little Phoebe & Esther," he wrote in big writing to his sister Ettie's chil-dren, "This letter is to tell you that the King has made dear Uncle Con a Member of the Victorian Order, that is to say he has been given a very pretty medal which dear Granny Scott pinned to his coat." He was grate-ful, too, to his old captain for his thoughtfulness in arranging things. "It was entirely due to Egerton," he explained to the girls' father, "that mother remained on board, and nothing as you say could have been more gratify-ing to her at such a time."

It was a kindness that was not wasted on her. On holiday with Grace in France, where Scott had sent them to take her mind off his leaving, she wrote to him with a disarming pride of meeting the King and Queen. "Peo-ple here like hearing about them. I never *begin* the subject, but of course if I'm asked I am only too pleased to tell them and recall my time of triumph in my son, for, after all, it is only the very few who actually shake hands with Royalty. Apart from that I like to think of the sweet sympathetic face that looked at me and smiled such interest in all she was looking at. And now, dear, one word of thanks for the holiday you are giving us both, and then good bye. God bless, keep and preserve you, my best of sons." Royalty was not enough, however, to take her mind long off her sadness at losing him. "I am not going to say one word about our feelings," she wrote three days later, "as your beautiful ship grew less & less till we lost her altogether: I shall rather tell you of the great kindness everyone showed us."

Even the landscape of the coast brought back memories: "It was so lovely sitting on the shore," she wrote to him again a week later, "but this sort of life is too much like the old life at Devonport & brings it much to the front . . . Monsie [Grace] went to the stores about your V.O. ribbon and was directed to Spink & Sons and I hear from them that they have sent it." By the time she wrote that, *Discovery* was already off Madeira. After one last hectic day, she had sailed on the sixth. Scott and Murray had gone ashore for a final breakfast with Markham, and then returned to the ship, "sad to see the last of this Grand old man and his companion Longhurst."

Just before twelve o'clock *Discovery* finally slipped from her buoy, the house flag of the RGS and Blue Ensign and burgee of the Harwich Yacht Club—the Admiralty had forbidden them use of the Royal Navy's White Ensign—fluttering at the mast. Slowly she made her way through the bobbing mass of boats and yachts crowding the Solent for Cowes Week and westward towards the Needles Channel. Off the small town of Yarmouth on the Isle of Wight the last of the families were put ashore—"a sad time indeed," Scott scrawled in his journal, "but the womenfolk are always brave." "How willingly one would dispense with these farewells," he later wrote in a passage that might have come straight out of Jane Austen's *Persuasion*, "and how truly one feels that the greater burden of sadness is on those who are left behind! Before us lay new scenes, new interests, expanding horizons; but who at such times must not think sorely of the wives and mothers condemned to think of the past, and hope in silent patience for the future, through years of suspense and anxiety?"

Early the next morning the Start was still in sight, "but gradually it shaded from green to blue, till towards noon it vanished in the distance, and with it our last view of the Old Country."

Seven: South

This is an awful ship for keeping our whites clean.

CHARLES ROYDS, *diary, 22 August 1901*

The same routine, all day at work & keeping watch & watch at night, a little bit rough I think.

THOMAS WILLIAMSON, *journal, 9 August 1901*

For all his anxieties over his mother, Scott would have been an odd creature if he had not been relieved to see England finally dip out of sight. With the forgettable exception of Torpedo Boat 87 almost a decade earlier, this was his first command, and if he had been in control of *Discovery* for over a year, it had been only the most notional authority, beset by the hydrographers and professors on the one side and the benign but autocratic presence of Sir Clements Markham on the other.

But now it was his ship, and if the Instructions he carried with him ran to twenty-seven paragraphs and thousands of words, they at least enshrined the principle of autonomy for which Markham had fought so hard. "INSTRUCTIONS TO THE COMMANDER OF THE NATIONAL ANTARCTIC EXPEDITION AND THE DIRECTOR OF THE SCIENTIFIC STAFF," the document was headed:

1: INSTRUCTIONS TO THE COMMANDER
The Royal Society and the Royal Geographical Society, with the assistance of His Majesty's Government, have fitted out an

expedition for scientific discovery and exploration in the Antarctic Regions, and have entrusted you with the command.

The objects of the Expedition are (a) to determine, as far as possible, the nature, condition and extent of that portion of the South Polar lands which is included in the scope of your Expedition; and (b) to make a magnetic survey in the southern regions to the south of the 40th parallel and to carry on meteorological, oceanographic, geological, biological and physical investigations and researches. Neither of these objects is to be sacrificed to the other.

There was a genuine value in a set of instructions of this kind, in as much as it established the notional *priorities* of the expedition, but it was the clauses that freed Scott and didn't tie him to London that were so crucial. "Owing to our imperfect knowledge of the conditions which prevail in Antarctic seas," Markham had written in Paragraph 17, emancipating Scott at a stroke from any prearranged assumptions about the ship's movements in the south, "we cannot pronounce definitely whether it will be necessary for the ship to make her way out of the ice before the winter sets in, or whether she should winter in the Antarctic regions. It is for you to decide on this important question after a careful examination of the local conditions."

Scott soon had early reminders, too, of how important it was that he should be free to make his own decisions. At the Dundee trials in May *Discovery* had only been tested under steam, and they had not crossed the Bay of Biscay before it became obvious that it was only in a force 7 or 8 on the Beaufort scale that they were going to manage anything like the eight knots needed under sail. The problem, as Scott saw it, was the "terribly small" area of sail that *Discovery* carried, a design deficiency he dressed up rather differently for the benefit of his worried mother. "The ship is a magnificent sea boat," he wrote to her from Madeira, where *Discovery* had moored on 15 August, "smooth and easy in every movement, a positive cradle on the deep. We only sigh for more sails. Ours are made for temperate seas, so they look rather like pocket handkerchiefs in a light Trade; they are so small that even in a hurricane they couldn't capsize the ship."

"It is quite impossible for me to describe the delight of getting your letter," she wrote back from Arromanches in Normandy, where she was still on holiday with Grace. "It is so good of you to tell me all the details of the ship and her sailing powers & so sweet of you to tell me of small sails & the safety of these in high winds. I prize *every* detail and read and reread what you say . . ."

Discovery was in fact no more sluggish than might have been expected, and certainly outperformed the German *Gauss* on the voyage south, but if anything was to be done during the first season in the ice, there was no margin for delay. In his first official "Letter of Proceedings" Scott estimated that the best that could be hoped for was an average speed of 6¾ knots, and even if they missed out Melbourne and headed straight for Lyttelton, that still put their original estimates for arriving well out of reach.

There was soon a more serious problem, with the leak that had been discovered back in the East India Docks on the Thames. Skelton and Royds had been trying to warn Scott about it since London, but it was only when two feet of foul-smelling water was found washing around the forward holds a week out of Madeira that, as an irritable Royds wrote in his diary, "the skipper at last woke up to the fact that the ship leaked." The cause of the problem was almost certainly unseasoned timber, which only added to a growing disillusionment with the work of the Dundee Shipbuilders' Company. Scott had already sent off a long list of their "enormities" to the ship's designer, and it is not just his journal from these first weeks that is littered with outbursts against *Discovery*'s contractors. The "ship building firm was in my opinion most dilatory in performing the work," Skelton had complained the day they sailed; "not only were they dilatory but I consider them to have performed their contract in a most scandalous manner." "Those responsible for the leakage out [sic] to be strung up," was the twenty-four-year-old seaman Thomas Williamson's more succinct verdict, and by the time they had finished rescuing, cleaning, disinfecting, restoring or jettisoning slime-covered cases there would have been few dissenters on board.

A week later an exhausted Skelton was complaining that things were still as bad as ever, but one unscheduled benefit of the leak was that the stores had all to be systematically repacked. There had been so little time to complete preparations in London that no one on board really knew where anything was, and with half the stores going separately to Melbourne, and the one man who knew anything about the system going with them, equipment was endlessly being lost or turning up buried "in the cutter or some other marvellous stow hold."

The work had at least given Scott a chance to gauge the men under him, and if he was impressed with Shackleton, he was doubly grateful that he had persuaded Skelton to join him from *Majestic*. "I cannot sufficiently express my admiration for their efforts," he reported in his second Letter of Proceedings, after a dead calm and temperatures in the 140s had turned the stokehold into a living hell, "and more especially for the unfailing perseverance and skill of Mr. Skelton the Chief Engineer and Mr. Dellbridge the artifice engineer."

In spite of these teething problems, however, and the inexperience of the crew in handling a sailing ship or taking soundings, the atmosphere on board was good. "It's a blessed thing we get so much heavy work," Edward Wilson wrote contentedly after three weeks at sea, "because none of us need ever feel the want of exercise at all. The Captain turns to with all of us and shirks nothing, not even the dirtiest work. Royds works well and had most of the work on the ship itself to do. Shackle and Barne and I are a trio, and one is never dirtier than the other two, and all three as a rule are filthy. We three generally sleep down aft the poop in moonlight as bright as day, except when driven below by rain. Hodgson is always on the go. I think that Shackleton has so far done more hard work than anyone on board."

Wilson was in no doubt either of the pivotal role Scott played in the well-being of the ship. "He is a most capable man in every way," he wrote again later in the voyage, when he had had time to take fuller stock of his skipper, "and has a really well-balanced head on his shoulders. I admire him immensely, all but his temper. He is quick tempered and very impatient, but he is a really nice fellow, very generous and ready to help us all in every way, and to do everything he can to ensure us the full merit of all we do. He is thoughtful for each individual and does little kindnesses which show it. He is ready to listen to everyone too, and joins heartily in all the humbug that goes on. I have a great admiration for him, and he is in no Service rut but is always anxious to see both sides of every question, and I have never known him to be unfair."

There were obviously tensions and irritations—the state of the bald, untidy, hopelessly civilian Hodgson's laboratory, Koettlitz's idleness, the ever-present threat of having Shackleton spout Swinburne or Browning at you on watch—but Hugh Mill had never been in "pleasanter company." "Captain Scott has shown a power that I must own surprised me in mastering the details of the scientific work," he reported home, as clear as Wilson as to where the credit lay; "he is greatly liked and respected by everyone on board, and has I believe mastered the art—more difficult than any of the scientific work—of preserving the necessary discipline & the equally necessary confidence and friendly feeling between all on board."

If there was any early difficulty on board, in fact, it was curiously not between navy and civilian, or navy and merchant, or wardroom and mess deck, but between Scott and his First Lieutenant, Charles Royds. By the end of the expedition there was nothing that the two men would not have done for each other, but in these first weeks differences of temperament and habits—and differences at heart, one suspects, between Scott's style of command and Royds's *amour propre* as the First Lieutenant responsible for the running of the ship—spilled out in the stream of grumbles that bubble up time and again in Royds's journals.

It was invariably Scott's impatience that upset him—"I expected to be blamed for it and was not disappointed . . . Captain much upset and of course I got the blame, someone has to, so it might as well be the 1st Lieut."—but he was as new to his job as Scott was to his. Many years later one of the seamen on the expedition recalled "Charles Rawson Royds" as "absolutely Navy from top to toe," and of all the ship's executive officers he seems to have found it hardest to adjust to the grime, the stench from the flooded holds and the slacker codes of *Discovery* life.

There was a decency about Royds, a deep sense of loyalty, and a refined civility that would all come out strongly in the south, but as a young man there also was a certain prissiness—"girlishness" his mess-mates called it— that had somehow grafted itself onto the conventional stiffness of the well-connected naval officer. To the rest of the wardroom the state of the ship was a matter for nothing more than the occasional good-humoured comment, but for Royds every speck of coal dust that got on his whites was a personal affront to a soul ideally created for the Mediterranean Squadron and the Grand Harbour at Valetta.

If he was right about one thing, it was Scott's "impatience," a recurring theme of journal after journal of the men who served under him. When the terrible Jacky Fisher was at the Admiralty he would "emblazon" his papers—and people, he claimed—with the word "RUSH," and as *Discovery* made its slow way south there were times when Scott's men must have imagined the same demonic stigmata blistering itself on his brow— " 'Knock off everything,' " a weary Royds parodied Scott's style of command, " 'up anchor,' 'No steam up,' 'clean lower deck.' "

Like Fisher, wandering around with a plaque around his neck saying "Give me something to do," Scott wanted things done and he wanted them done immediately. He could never understand how anyone could waste the opportunities that *Discovery* had dropped into their laps, and like some reprieved victim, liberated at last from the deadening torpor of naval life, he was determined to press his own, exhausting freshness of vision on everyone around him.

Discovery's sluggishness under sail also fretted at his patience. "A better pace," he confided to his journal, "produces better spirits," and if he added "in me at least," he could not imaginatively grasp any different view of things. How could the scientists not seize every opportunity to perfect their skills, he would wonder in letters home. Why were they not as endlessly eager as he was? "These delays are very damping to the spirits," he complained in his journal after one altercation over tow-netting. "Patience is difficult but the daily tasks proceed. Had to expostulate with Murray on the disgusting state of Hodgson's laboratory with fruitful results—but I fear there are still pangs to be endured from the latter's untidiness & want of hygienic perception—Oh for more wind."

It was not just Royds Scott could annoy; he could just as easily bring the lower deck to a full and historic sense of its grievances. The *Discovery* had not been three days into her voyage before Williamson was complaining of his workload, but there is an underlying feeling that a lot of this is no more than routine lower-deck grumbling. Seamen like Williamson—one of the great moaners of *Discovery*, and one of the first to serve with Scott again on his second expedition—*knew* that it was an officer's world. They knew, as any self-respecting able-bodied seaman or army private has always known, that the promotions and the credit would not be coming their way. They knew, with all the force of the biblical injunction to the serpent, that between them and the officer there could be no accommodation. They were not *meant* to like their captain. Complaint was not just a pleasure and privilege, it was a duty. They might see things partially, but they saw them plain. Read Royds's journal, and one can almost see the hairs rise on the back of his neck as Scott reads out the Bishop's prayer; read Williamson, and it is just the "usual amount of church Service."

It is this persistent note of scepticism that gives *Discovery*'s lower-deck journals their interest, adding an almost Shakespearean texture to the picture of expedition life. In Markham's or Scott's accounts it is inevitably the *nobility* of the work that is played up, but in the journals of Williamson or James Duncan what we hear is the *antidote*—the voice of a Dolabella puncturing the glory of a Mark Antony—of the Clown eating away at the narcissistic tragedy of a Cleopatra—of Robert Bolt's "Common man" casting his jaundiced eye over the vanities and self-delusions of heroism and martyrdom.

With one single exception, however, the other quality that marks all these journals is an utter lack of resentment of "things as they are." What-ever the different politics of the men in *Discovery*, there seems to have been a vein of almost Salisburyesque conservatism running through the ship, a good old-fashioned John Bull belief that the barbarian was at the gate, and that only the familiar structures of discipline and self-discipline stood between them and the chaos of egotism, megalomania, betrayal, greed, brutality, stupidity, mendacity, murder and cannibalism that the long history of nineteenth-century Arctic exploration suggested as the alternative.

It would be a mistake, in any case, to read any more into these journals than into the occasional spasm of irritation that similarly marks Royds's or Scott's diaries. In some ways they bring us as close as we can ever get to *Discovery*, and yet of their very nature they are dangerous historical tools, safety valves for all the petty and momentary resentments of day-to-day life among thirty-odd men living together in the cramped discomfort of a ship for three years.

And given how claustrophobic this world was, the astonishing thing is not that there were so many rows or discontents in *Discovery*, but so few. The eleven officers lived and worked in a wardroom no more than thirty feet by twenty, with a long table down the centre, a large stove at the after end, a pianola, and a warren of small cabins leading off on both sides that provided them with their solitary, fragile measure of privacy. It was a world in which there was no escape for Scott, and no escape from him, and the conditions for the men were worse again. In terms of warmth and physical comfort they would certainly be better off than the officers in the ice, but as *Discovery* steamed slowly through the tropics, with the temperatures in the stokeholds stuck fast in the 140s, it was almost inevitable that the cramped, stifling conditions of a mess deck where a combustible mix of naval and merchant men ate, drank, worked and slung their hammocks in a space scarcely bigger than the wardroom, should spark off the first ugly incident of the voyage.

It occurred at the end of August, just three weeks into their journey, as *Discovery* crossed the equator, and Neptune and his consort hailed the ship and came aboard. A large seawater bath had been constructed amid-ships out of a sail, and a scaffold built above it, with a ducking stool secured by a rope for the victims. In the bath below, well primed with "a go of grog," waited four tritons, and high on the platform, Neptune and his court, "with the doctor and his greasy soap pill, the barber and his foaming tallow lather and huge razor. After the victim had been interviewed, he was handed over to the tender mercies of the Tritons; and it was generally a gasping, almost breathless creature that emerged from the other end of the bath. Wilson was the first on Neptune's list, and was the most lucky one, for the chair slipped and before he was even lathered, he was shot into the bath, so he escaped with merely a ducking. Ferrar, the geologist, did not take very kindly to the attentions of the operators, so on the platform he received a double dose, and he struggled a lot in the bath not knowing that under the disguise of wigs and oilskins were hidden the strongest men on the ship. The whole affair went off well, 'though the men got a bit rough towards the end.' "

If that had been the finish of it, no one but Ferrar would have had anything to complain about, but by the end of the evening a combination of drink and heat had taken its toll. At the bottom of the trouble was a Brixham seaman taken on in London called John Mardon, and by the time things had been brought under order, one of the Dundee whaler men, Walker, had had his thumb bitten through to the bone and two more of the men had got themselves lined up for reprimands. "The party was rather too lavishly regaled with whisky," Scott primly wrote on 31 August, "and the merchant seamen appear to have saved their rum for the occasion. The result was an orgy in the evening with Mardon and his confreres behaving insubordinately. It gives an excellent opportunity of putting one's foot down."

The problem was not of Scott's making—and there is no need to waste a second's sympathy on Mardon—but what he lacked was the imagination or will to find anything other than naval solutions to the difficulties of a mixed lower deck. It is always very hard for anyone within the services to realise how their world might look from outside, but Scott in particular seemed incapable of seeing the surly independence of merchantmen as anything other than an affront to naval—and his—authority.

It was the first time he had to exercise any discipline, but it would not be the last; because the navy had treated its own seamen like children for so long that it was little wonder that they behaved like them whenever they had the chance. The root of the problem this time might have been the merchant recruits, but in these early days Scott's own seamen were scarcely any better, only ever needing to sniff land or drink for ship standards to dissolve into the drunken indiscipline, irresponsibility and desertions that were endemic to any port the Royal Navy visited. "Some of the naval people thought they were in for a sort of picnic from which as they had signed articles they could not be excluded," an irritated Scott wrote back to George Egerton, his old *Majestic* skipper. "Nothing much happened but there was a bad feeling creeping in which I couldn't lay hold of until it came to the surface on a little drink following the function of crossing the line . . . so having my opportunity I just walked into them properly—I pointed out that I could stop half their pay, all their grog and reduce them to starvation diet without even taking trouble to report the fact further, that I could discharge either naval or merchant seaman and make it pretty hot for them afterwards."*

It was not just on the lower deck that the voyage was beginning to take its toll. As a south-easterly trade wind pushed *Discovery* helplessly westward towards the South American coast, a sense of drift seems to have filled the ship. The southern night sky, with its Southern Cross—that great symbol of loneliness and despair in A.E.W. Mason's *The Four Feathers*—brought home to everyone just how far they were from home. In the privacy of his cabin Wilson could take "spiritual communion" and imagine himself in St. Philips with his wife Ory, but there were days when the mere talk of England could make "old Shackles very homesick . . . and myself nearly as bad." "Moderate wind and sea!" Shackleton himself wrote in his journal. "Just think of it! Moderate wind and sea—instead of golden grain and harvest fields, and gentle winds that waft the warm scent from the hay ricks. We are nearly 6,000 miles from home."

They were six days behind schedule, and Scott had already abandoned the idea of stopping in Melbourne, but these faltering spirits were enough to prompt him to break their journey at the "weird, blighted island" of South Trinidad. The island was sighted on the morning of 13 September, and dropping anchor on its western side, Scott took two small boats and a landing party in on the heavy, shark-infested breakers that smashed up against its rocky shore. It was a dangerous operation, and if it is typical of Scott that he should have first checked that everyone could swim, it was even more so that he should have pushed on even when he found out that they couldn't.

It says something too for the monotony of ship life that a place like South Trinidad could seem an attractive diversion, but after five weeks at sea "the shore looked too enticing . . . to be abandoned without an effort." "There is not a single beast on four legs on it," Wilson, always the most visually acute of Scott's men, wrote of it, with "thousands of white

---

* Even in this case, however, Scott's bark was a lot worse than his bite. He ordered Mardon to be discharged and handed over to the authorities in South Africa, but in the event simply discharged him without involving the police.

bleached tree trunks everywhere, and not one living tree of the kind to be seen." The island was alive, he went on, "with birds that knew no fear, and with myriads of quick scrabbling shore-crabs that were the prey of fish; and land-crabs, large fat bloated anaemic-looking beasts with strange black eyes, sat in every hole and corner of the whole island and just slowly look at one. We fed them on potted meat and cheese and chocolate, and they ate it slowly and deliberately without ever taking their eyes off us. There was something horribly uncanny about these slow things; one didn't know a bit how old they were; they might have been there since the island came up."

A new specimen of petrel—*Aestralat wilsoni*—seemed reward enough for a six-hour delay, and that same night *Discovery* was again under steam and searching for the westerlies that would help preserve their depleted stocks of coal. With the winds as fitful as ever Scott soon had to accept that they could never make South Africa on time, but as so often with him acceptance brought with it no easing of spirit. Ross, he impatiently noted in his journal, "had crossed the line on December 3 1839 . . . with the aid of steam we beat him by a day. So much for 1/2 a century & more or what has happened to the trade wind."

"These twists of fortune are truly exasperating," he complained again on 24 September, eleven days on from South Trinidad, "& when the luck is adverse one feels inclined to profanity." Only Scamp seemed completely indifferent to conditions. "Best of the sport on board was our mischievous little dog Scamp," Williamson wrote the next day; "every time we ran along the deck Scamp would sure enough run in between our legs and capsize you, therefore causing much merriment & laughter . . . all's well."

He was equally disrespectful of Divine Service, which his agnostic master would no more have missed than he would a wind or temperature reading. "Morning service as usual with interruptions," Wilson noted one Sunday. "Scamp, the dog tried to enter church when Koettlitz, who was sitting nearest the door seized him by the tail and swung him out again. Scamp gave tongue in a high-pitched voice and in three minutes pelted in again, having got past Koettlitz, and was silently applauded by the blue jackets who beamed upon him. Scamp is an Aberdeen terrier with all the cunning of a Scotchman and a blue jacket rolled in one, and an appetite which bears no mathematical relationship to his full stomach."

Six days after South Trinidad, *Discovery* at last picked up the westerlies, and though they were again weaker than expected, progress was "slow but sure." With the Cape less than a week away, Scott took a last opportunity to catch up on his letters home. "It is always woe betide me when I take a rest—as regards letter writing," he told his sister Ettie. "I did so for a whole month after leaving England regarding my desk full of letters with a most complacent and devil-may-care attitude result is when I once come to tackle the matter I find myself once more in a rush to get things off before our arrival at the Cape. There are so many and such different tasks to be floored in this time and I never could drive my pen at a respectable speed so this is only going to be a very short letter to be followed by a more flowery epistle for the general perusal of the family & which of course must first go to headquarters. It's nice of you to write all those pretty things about 'Cowes.' Whatever natural expansion my chest assumes under the small piece of ribbon, it is speedily deflated when I think of the very small deserving of it."

On the afternoon of 3 October, after nearly two months at sea and with reserves running low, *Discovery* rounded Green Point and entered Table Bay. The next day Skelton began the hated business of coaling the ship, feeding 230 tons of coal down canvas chutes that passed through hatches in the wardroom ceiling and floor to the coal hold below. "Coaling is filthy," Royds characteristically complained (a complaint, it should be said, that Scott would have echoed—he never missed a chance as captain to get in a round of golf when there was coaling to be done), "and the ship is simply crowded with visitors, black, white and indifferent. Soldiers in uniform, some in plain clothes, Generals, Colonels, Captains, etc, all come to see the ship and gaze on the heroes to be!!! I say Rats to them all."

It was not just the ship that was in a filthy state and "inundated with sightseers"; the crew were no better. "I had great trouble with some of my men," Skelton was writing within hours of *Discovery* docking, "in fact throughout the ship, the men were unsatisfactory—chiefly owing to the fact that their friends from the shore [were] bringing them drink." "From tonight my behaviour to the men will be a trifle different," an equally irascible Royds threatened. "If they won't behave themselves for kindness, we will see what the other thing does, as things are now too much of a good thing, and can't go on."

Scott had not been at the Cape since his days in *Boadicea*, but with a troublesome crew and the town under martial law, he cannot have been sad to see the back of it the moment coaling was finished. In his brilliant study of the role of "ice" in the English imagination, Francis Spufford makes the point that a naval officer could sail from London to the Antarctic and back without ever really *leaving* England, happily travelling down a "corridor of Britishness" without touching a land where he could not find familiar faces or a familiar tongue, where he could not stay in a Government or Admiralty House, or where "the coins were not the same size and shape and denominated in sterling, where the officers were not fed mutton and sherry at dinners given by local notables and the men could not go to the pub." It is a compelling vision—and one only has to think of Scott tongue-tied in Berlin for the want of a foreign language to recognise its truth—but Cape Town in October 1901 might possibly have provided the one exception. There might not have been much difference in physical terms from the place Scott had known as a midshipman, but in the course of three years of the Boer War something radical had changed, undermining in the process the assumption of English superiority that *Discovery* was supposed to embody.

It was not primarily that Britain's military complacency had been severely dented, because for all the gloom and fear of guerrillas at the Cape, the army was at last beginning to bring the situation under control. The early reversals of the war had brutally exposed the amateurishness and incompetence of Britain's forces, and yet in a sense what was even harder for a nation that prided itself on its moral superiority was the disgust of the international community and its own liberals for the barbarism of a conflict that had left twenty-eight thousand Boer women and children and more than fifty thousand Africans dead in her camps. "Now that I know what the duties of a soldier are in war," wrote Wilson, whose own brother was in the fighting, "I would sooner shoot myself than anyone else by a long, long way . . . It [the bombardment of Kronje] made me cry like a baby and I threw away the paper in perfect disgust. A nation should be judged on exactly the same ground as an individual. As a nation we have the vilest of sins which everyone extols as the glories of Imperialism."

This was not the sort of heroism that had been dreamed of when *Discovery* sailed, and Scott seemed more than usually grateful to get away to the reassuring world of the naval base at Simonstown. "Took up my quarters at Admiralty House," he wrote in his journal on the fifth, after they had made the rough journey round from Table Bay: "found Armitage & Barne already installed there."

The main object of their stay at the Cape was to prepare for the magnetic programme ahead, and for the ten days *Discovery* was at Simonstown, Armitage and Barne were installed in an Admiralty tent on the plateau behind the base, comparing their variable sea instruments with absolute values only attainable on land. While this was being done the resources of the naval dockyards were put at Scott's disposal. *Discovery's* rigging was reset, the ship was recaulked to the waterline, and naval divers were sent down to scrape the barnacles off her hull. In spite of the tensions of the war, Admiral Moore also provided Scott with three more men. In addition to these, another two were recruited, Robert Sinclair, an employee of the Union Castle Line, and an Australian soldier called Horace Buckridge, who would bring to *Discovery* his own characteristic brand of colonial dissent.

Cocooned once more in a familiar world, however, there were the inevitable dinners to be endured, entertainment to be returned, speeches to be made — "As usual didn't know what to say but stumbled through a few sentences with more than customary credit" — and the regulation hordes of visitors eager to see the ship. "Heard an amusing yarn of lady being asked why she was coming on board this ship," Royds noted, "replied that in case of any disaster think how interesting it would be to know that she had actually spoken to and seen the officers!! Nice way of looking at things and not very bright for us."

By 14 October the refitting was complete, Armitage's and Barne's magnetic work done, and *Discovery* ready to leave on the next leg of the journey to New Zealand. As she made her way out between the warships of the fleet, Scott was moved to one of those hymns to the corporate, interdependent life of the navy that sit so touchingly alongside his own private frustrations. "As we got under weigh," he recorded in his journal, "all ships cleared lower decks & cheered—a grand send off—our small company did their best to respond. Thus ends an experience that makes one totally proud of a glorious profession—added to the practical benefits of our visit, one is deeply touched by the real kindness and sympathy shown by all; men and officers have had a glimpse of the real efficiency and meaning of our navy."

The dismissal of Mardon had done the trick, and with the men "working very well," and "little to complain of on the score of wind," as Scott put it with a nice understatement, the ship was at last coming into her own. In the heavy following seas she was a mite "livelier" than Williamson found comfortable, but while rolls of up to forty-seven degrees each way were commonplace, "it was rarely, if ever necessary to shorten" those "handkerchief" sails that Scott had reassured his mother about. The "worse all this gets," an exhilarated Wilson wrote in the middle of the Roaring Forties, "the more we all enjoy it! Our dinner was all over the ward-room this evening," he cheerfully recorded, "the crockery is fast disappearing in small pieces. It is the funniest sight . . . everything all round seems to be tumbling about one's head. The noise is indescribable."

Wilson's good humour is wonderfully engaging, and there is something deeply English in a sensibility that could "domesticate" even the southern oceans. "The waves we are amongst now," he was writing five days later, as if *Discovery* were in some neo-Georgian landscape that a Brooke or a Housman might have found comfortingly familiar, "are, without any exaggeration, comparable in length and height to the rise from our pigeon gates, at the foot of the Crippets [the family home on a low spur of Leckhampton Hill in the Cotswolds], up to the rabbit warren above, and about the same depth."

The next day the whole of Leckhampton Hill almost came down on them when a "monstrous sea," "towering" to the topsails, hit *Discovery* side on. Wilson was on the bridge with Barne and Scott when "an enormous wave broke right over the ship. We all three hung on to the stanchions and rails and were swept clean off our feet. We were simply deluged, and I burst out laughing at the Skipper who was gasping for breath. He had been nearly a minute under water. The whole of the upper deck was afloat. The water had flooded the magnetic house; laboratories, fo'c'sle and wardroom; galley filled with steam, winter clothes just brought up from the hold for distribution all swamped, and they call this a dry ship!" "Didn't we just laugh," he added, and not even the sight of a corpse from some unknown ship floating past or Williamson's conviction that his "checks were in" were enough to dispel the sense that this was "indeed . . . living."

After the torpor of their voyage through the tropics, there was a palpable excitement that they were at last approaching the edge of an unknown world. There are few things still that can feel so excitingly *alien* as the first sight of ice at sea, and on 16 November, as Scott temporarily altered course and took *Discovery* southwards to record the changes in the magnetic force and dip* as they approached the Magnetic Pole, they saw it for the first time. "Fast ice seen about 10 a.m.," Scott noted in his report for the two Societies, "and amid much excitement we watched small pieces of decayed drift ice gradually growing in size and number and assuming more fantastic shapes . . . The intense blue of the small sea-swept holes and caverns . . . was noticed with delight." "A most marvellous sight," an excited Skelton noted in his journal, "quite the most wonderful I have ever seen." "The sky was grey with snow falling," Wilson wrote, "the breakers were white on a dark grey sea, and the ice only had its whiteness broken

---

*Dip: the vertical angle through which a freely suspended magnetic needle dips from horizontal.

with the most exquisitely shaded blues and greens, pure blue, cobalt, and pale emerald, and every mixture in between them. I never saw more perfect colour or toning in nature."

"At 4 a.m.," Scott continued, with that meticulous eye for "technical" detail that would characterise everything he looked at in the south, "a strong ice blink"—the reflection of ice in the sky—"was observed to the left and right and a line of white ahead, and in half an hour we had run into a loose pack of drift ice, amongst which were occasional small fragments of glacier ice showing blue and heavy in contrast." "The wind had died away," he later more atmospherically wrote, "what light remained was reflected in a ghostly glimmer from the white surface of the pack; now and again a white snow petrel flitted through the gloom, the grinding of the floes against the ship's side was mingled with the more subdued hush of their rise and fall on the long swell, and for the first time we felt something of the solemnity of these great Southern solitudes."

Six days later they had their next glimpse of what lay ahead, when the long, grim ridge of Macquarie Island, isolated in the southern ocean hundreds of miles from the nearest land, was sighted. Having lost time on the way to South Africa, Scott was anxious to press on, but with Wilson bribing Armitage with a bottle of liqueur to act as mediator, he was persuaded to make a brief landing. It was the first time that anyone on board had seen a penguin rookery, and it was a toss-up who was most excited, Wilson by the chance of collecting specimens, or Scamp, who spent his time in "a series of short rushes, made with suppressed growls and every hair bristling, but ending at a very safe distance."

If Scamp was reluctant to mix it with Macquarie's inhabitants, Shackleton and the rest of the crew were not so easily discouraged. "We saw great flocks of Penwings"—and a sea elephant that they shot—the difficult but touchingly curious Dundee whaling man James Duncan wrote, with his inimitable spelling, "some hands started to skin him & this being their first attempt there was some sport in the finish they were blood from head to foot . . . we continued on our way Doctor spoting every little plant or moss & bagin it."

It was not just the men's first introduction to a penguin colony, but to penguin meat, and Scott was surprised to find "no prejudice more difficult to conquer than my own." He knew well enough from Cook's account of the *Belgica* the consequences of any squeamishness over diet, and was glad of the chance to introduce the crew to a regime "which it will so often be essential to enforce." "Had penguin for dinner & penguin eggs for breakfast," he wrote in his journal on the twenty-fourth, "must own to a weak stomach in these matters but am rejoiced to see the excellent spirit shown by the crew—they all ate and most pronounced favourably where I rather expected a kicking against the pricks in a matter where they are usually so pig headed & obstinate."

With Macquarie Island behind them, they were now less than six hundred miles south-west of New Zealand, and Scott could sit down to his 3rd Letter of Proceedings with a real sense that men and ship had come well through their "baptism of fire." The experience of the voyage, he reported, "has been of excellent service to officers and men in learning to handle the ship and the sails, it has given confidence in the ship & in themselves which cannot be overvalued and I am pleased to say that the charge of inexperience which might reasonably have attached to the whole crew, in view of the small amounts of time they had spent in sailing ships, can now no longer be applied."

Scott also felt that he had got to know his officers. To his mother he confessed—"entre nous"—that of all the wardroom, he had most warmed to Barne, Skelton and Wilson. Wilson, in particular, impressed him. "He is indeed a treasure [one of Scott's favourite terms] in our small company," he wrote in his journal just before they reached Lyttelton, "whose quick eye for every detail of colour & form, every action and every attitude of his studies can I think have rarely been equalled."

"There is one thing your husband will not have told you," he took the trouble to write to Wilson's wife Ory, "and that is what a fine fellow we all think him. His intellect and ability will one day win him a great name; of this I feel sure. We admire such qualities . . . but his kindness, loyalty, good-temper and fine feelings are possessions which go beyond the word admiration and can simply be said to have endeared him to us all. How truly grateful I am to have such a man with me . . ."

His officers had also had the chance to get to know Scott. "I like Captain Scott better than ever," Armitage, his second-in-command, wrote home. More to the point, as Discovery dropped anchor that night at Lyttelton, and the last stage of their journey came into focus, was Wilson's judgement. "One of the best points about him too is that he is very definite about everything," he wrote home; "nothing is left vague or indeterminate. In every argument he goes straight for the main point, and always knows exactly what he is driving at. There will be no fear of our wandering about aimlessly in the Southern regions."

Eight: Into the Ice

New Year's morning . . . Memories of Old turning my thoughts to My Dear
Loved ones at Home. We being about 14,000 miles from them & in latitude
whare thare has not been any ship for a century & I may say cut off from the
Civilised World our return as yet being doutfull. Hooping for the Best.

JAMES DUNCAN, *journal, 1 January 1902*

If Scott thought that his troubles were at an end when he got rid of Mardon, Lyttelton proved a rude awakening. From the first day in port his crew
seemed determined to relapse into "shore" mode, and with the whole of
New Zealand desperate to show its hospitality, there was no shortage of
opportunities to make up for lost time.

They were young men in their early twenties who had been at sea for
almost four months, and Scott was neither prudish nor unrealistic in his
expectations of them. "Mayor Rhodes who appears the Croesus of the
neighbourhood called with his wife, a pretty woman," he wrote the day
after their arrival. "Fear I rather seemed to throw cold water on entertainment of men but what can one say to a tea social for such thirsty gentry."

The tolerance did not last long. "It is awful," Royds complained two
days later, "and the men are asking to leave the ship and in fact are all very
unsettled. How I wish they could keep away from the drink, as they are
excellent while at sea, but when in harbour, they absolutely forget themselves, and go wrong." "We have dismissed . . . servant and cook," Skelton
wrote the same day, grateful at least for one mercy—though he would have
been less pleased about it if he had known the cook they were getting in his

place; "they were very poor men & I believe scoundrels . . . men behaving very badly . . . good deal of fighting & drunkenness."

This was a problem that was so endemic to naval life that it is hard to see what Scott could have done to prevent it, but now that trouble had broken out, it was a test of discipline that he had to pass. To a certain extent he was tied by the fact that *Discovery* had sailed under the Merchant Shipping Act, but if he ever hoped to cope in the ice without the draconian measures of the Navy Act to prop up his authority, he was going to have to assert himself now. The "men very fat-headed," he wrote angrily that night; "heard of great disturbance on night before . . . spoke to men in evening, little to be said, they disgust me—but I'm going to have it out of them somehow—there are really only few black sheep but they lend their colour to the flock."

If there were going to be problems, it was as well they should happen in Lyttelton and not in the south, while Scott still had the chance to weed out the troublemakers. The Australian warship *Ringarooma* had already been helping with their refit, and now the navy came to his rescue again, taking his worst offenders into custody, and releasing in their place two volunteers, a "big AB named Jesse Handsley" whom Scott "liked the look of," and another "very fine strapping AB" destined to play a major role in Antarctic history, the twenty-four-year-old Kerryman Tom Crean.

It was not just the crew that was a worry. After *Discovery*'s brief exposure to ice, the old problem was compounded by a fresh leak in the bow compartments. Back in England her immense strength had seemed a triumph of design, but now that the leaks had to be found, the very thickness and complexity of her linings became a serious drawback, making it virtually impossible, even after two sessions in dry dock, for men unfamiliar with her construction to trace the trouble to its source.

For all the difficulties, however, it would be perverse for these weeks in New Zealand to be remembered for them, because in many ways there was no happier period in *Discovery*'s history. From the day she arrived there had been far more enthusiasm for the expedition than had ever been shown in England, and with all the hospitality ashore and endless crushes of visitors on board, Scott's only "puzzle" was "How we get along with our work."

With the curious exception of Wilson, in fact, who did not like the naval officers they met, did not think much of Maori women, and thought the Haka a bogus piece of Sunday-school flummery, a strong note of gratitude runs through all the journals and letters from the time. "We had a visit from the Maorie ladies," a more appreciative Duncan recorded. "They are all original Natives of New Zealand, some of them were rigged up in their own style of dress & they looked splendid." "I for one will never forget this," wrote Williamson of all the kindness they had been shown, and Scott was every bit as thankful. After the initial drunkenness the men had begun to behave "in a manner worthy of the ship," and with that worry off his shoulders, he was able to enjoy a temporary respite from ship life at the home of a cousin — "an excellent chap" — called Robert Scott, and his wife — "was a Miss Bowan — Mrs. Bowan is Sir Clements' sister," he threw in for his mother's benefit, "a charming woman . . . delightful simple & nice . . . overflowing with kindness & good nature," who seemed to touch Scott's heart in a way that few people ever did. "For my own part," he wrote in his journal, "I must ever remember with gratitude the extraordinary kindness shown me . . . it has been truly delightful to find in this far spot . . . English flowers, birds & trees, English faces and English welcomes."

In spite of Scott's fears, the work *was* getting done, and by 21 December *Discovery* was ready to leave. A service of blessing was held on board by the Bishop of Christchurch, and to the cheers of the huge crowds and the sound of bands, *Discovery* cast off her warps and steamed slowly out of the great, drowned amphitheatre of Lyttelton harbour, her Plimsoll line sunk beneath the weight of coal, stores, huts, dogs and sheep that now crammed every inch of her upper deck. "Cheers followed cheers," Scott wrote, "until, as we entered the open sea, with a last burst of cheering and a final flutter of handkerchiefs, our kind friends turned away, and slowly we steamed out between the war-ships that seemed to stand as sentinels to the bay."

With his troublemakers safely out of the way, and the distractions of the shore receding behind them, Scott must have been counting his blessings when disaster struck from nowhere. One of the young naval seamen called Charles Bonner had climbed up earlier to the crow's nest on the main mast to return the cheers, and was scrambling up higher to stand on the wind vane when the spindle snapped, a cry was heard below, followed by the hideous "thud of a fall" as "the poor fellow hit the corner of the winch house with his head, completely smashing his skull & scattering his brains." "He appears to have been sober when he went up," a shaken Scott wrote that night on a scrap of paper inserted in his journal, "but it afterwards transpired that a bottle of whisky was handed to him by another seaman named Robert Sinclair, whilst he was at the main mast head . . . his remains were placed on the poop . . . a dreadful example of the effects of our revelry."

The death cast a pall across the whole ship. "Very dull day, on board, not a word spoken scarcely," Williamson wrote in his journal the next day, "every man going about his work as silently & quietly as possible, afraid that the least sound would disturb the dead. In the evening myself and another of his messmates washed poor Charlie put a union jack over him and laid him quietly to rest on the poop all ready for the internment [sic] tomorrow on our arrival at Port Chalmers."

The captain of *Ringarooma* had steamed on to Port Chalmers to arrange the funeral, and at the inquest Scott made sure there was no word of the whisky. That same evening, at six o'clock on 23 December, the twenty-three-year-old Able Seaman Bonner was buried with naval honours in the graveyard high above the harbour, looking out to open sea and the flanks of hills that might have been Scott's Devon. "We gave full naval honours of course," Scott would later write of another funeral to his mother, "you know how solemn & impressive such a ceremony is—but after such a funeral as you know the band plays a quickstep & the signs of mourning are discarded—This I think, is in the spirit as well as in the act and it is right and proper."

Bonner had been hugely popular on the mess deck, but even in the small, tight-knit community of *Discovery*, life left "little time for sad thought." "The cheers of the accompanying ships did not seem to stir so much," Williamson wrote on the next day, "for we still had sad memories of the last few days, when we passed HMS Ringarooma they gave us three hearty British cheers & a few more besides, & of course as Englishmen & brothers in arms as most of us are, we could not hold it any longer, so we bucked up spirits & gave them something of a return, the best we could under our circumstances."

For Scott there was the aftermath of Bonner's death to deal with, his few possessions to be sent home, and the man who had passed him whisky to be considered. On the day of the funeral, Sinclair had stolen a pair of trousers belonging to the cook's mate and deserted, "much depressed" at his role in Bonner's fall, and doubting if he could ever live it down in the ship: "On the whole," Scott added in his journal, "I am inclined to doubt it also and think he took the wisest course and the best for all concerned."

In the circumstances Scott decided to postpone their Christmas celebrations, but they headed south with his mind relieved of at least one worry. He still could not know at this stage whether *Discovery* would winter in the ice or return to Lyttelton, but the news from London that had reached them in New Zealand, that Markham had raised the funds for a relief ship at least meant that if things turned bad their "line of retreat" was "practically assured."

On board, minds hovered between what lay ahead and what they had left behind. At dinner on Christmas Day, the toasts were "The King" and "Absent Friends." Even Scamp now was gone, left behind at Christchurch, where he had "continued to distinguish himself on all sides." "My dear girl," Scott had scribbled to his sister Ettie in a sudden spasm of affection, "Give the chicks my love & a kiss for yourself . . . You know what you have been to & what you will always be to your loving brother Con."

"At home they are just going to bed," wrote Shackleton, in an improbable maudlin blend of sentimentality and *faux* high-mindedness, "and all the little ones were hanging their stockings up for the wonderful Father Christmas, who never fails to think of the children who believe in him so. We, but children in the greater world, pray that our request may be granted to do high good work, not just for ourselves, but for the name of England [Celts note], and for all those who have trusted us with the great adventure that we are setting out upon."

"Rather erotic lines," he wrote more convincingly the next day about a volume of Swinburne's poetry given him by one of the officers in *Ringarooma*, and the lightening of spirits was general. Even the unpoetical Skelton was more than usually prepared to indulge Shackleton's cultural evangelicalism. Reading Stephen Phillips's "Paolo and Francesca" to Skelton, Shackleton recorded optimistically, "though as a rule he thinks poetry of any description rubbish, thinking it, perhaps, not in keeping with the idea of an up-to-date engineer; he rather likes these."

The West Siberian dogs that had joined them at Lyttelton were also playing their less cultured part, carrying on where Scamp had left off. Scott had deputed the arrangements for them to Armitage back in London, and a Whitstable seaman, Isaac Weller, had been signed on to ship them over to New Zealand and look after them in the ice. Each dog now, though, was assigned to the special care of a seaman, and the move was soon paying some unexpected and ambiguous dividends. "Had to make an example of Page & Hubert," Scott noted a week into their voyage, after there had been complaints over the food, "later very annoyed to find that half a joint of meat being given to the dogs—when will these people wake up to the fact that they are not on a picnic." "I myself call mine Clarence," Williamson engagingly recorded, "after a young boyfriend of mine in Lyttelton NZ."

They were also making good progress southward, and with the wind fair and all "handkerchiefs" spread, they were in a latitude of 61°s by the last day of the year. That evening Bernacchi felt sure enough to bet a bottle of champagne and port that they would see ice before dinner, but if there were bergs out there, Armitage's hot punch was enough to guarantee that no one in the wardroom saw them that night. On the stroke of midnight, Ferrar, as the youngest member of the wardroom, struck the bell sixteen times, "which is the custom on this occasion," and grog was served to the men. "Midnight," Skelton's journal recorded, ". . . several glasses—joined hands & sang 'Auld Lang Syne.' Everybody very merry—walking the bridge & joking until nearly 2:00 a.m." "What indeed may or may not the next two months see?" Scott asked himself. "All one can say is we are prepared—the rest is in the hands of an all seeing Providence, we can only hope for good fortune."

In the months to come he would look back on an entry like that, and wonder how they could ever have been so innocent. Over the last eighteen months he had done all that any single man could do to "prepare" himself for his command, but though he could not yet know it, his whole professional life had been a kind of *anti-preparation* for the job, an indoctrination into habits of thought and ways of doing things that would be a positive danger in the conditions they were now entering. As Scott stood on the bridge, or peered into the fog from the crow's nest, searching for a lead through the pack, there was *nothing* out there that he could control, *nothing* he could predict, *nothing* that behaved as he wanted or expected it to, or prayed that it would. In a world where the bergs flowed one way and the current another, where the old stable landmarks shifted and changed, where nothing under you or around you was what it seemed, what use were the rational certainties of the *Vernon* technocrat? In a world in which each man would have to think and act for himself, what price was going to have to be paid for the habit of childlike dependency the navy had foisted on its lower decks? In a world where visibility might be no more than a few feet, what hope was there for a culture of communications or chains of command that had made initiative in its officers a crime?

Nobody could have been less "prepared" than Scott as they entered into this world, but for the time being "Providence" was doing its best to keep them alive. By the morning of 3 January 1902 they had crossed the Antarctic Circle, and were through the scattered "outriders of the pack" and battering a path through the real thing, their eyes trained in a constant vigil on the sky for those telltale darker patches that meant open water.

"The position of the officer of the watch" in these conditions, Scott recalled, "was no sinecure: he had to be constantly on the watch in the pack to avoid contact with the heavier floes and to pick out the easiest path for the ship. When the pack was open his best position was in the 'crow's nest,' where he could first see the open patches of water and the heavier streams of ice, but in thicker pack he could often handle the ship better by 'conning' from the bridge, and at such times he had to be constantly giving fresh directions for the movement of the helm."

With this new world they had entered, wrapped in a heavy pall of leaden skies, came new rhythms, new wildlife, and a new diet. At the edge of the ice the albatross, their constant companion in the southern seas, had fallen away, leaving them to their own gruesome business. The slaughter of the sheep had started, and to their frozen carcasses, hung from the rigging as in some grisly Ottoman man-of-war, were now added the first seals. "My seal started off at a tremendous rate around the floe," a jubilant Skelton wrote on the fifth, celebrating their delayed Christmas Day with his own joyous slaughter of the innocents; "with Michael heading it off and sticking it with his knife—it was a most amusing sight; they chased it into the middle, & then the Skipper gave it a shot through the head with his pea rifle, which stopped it—we then hauled them both on board, mine still alive so it was killed with a knife—must have been very game; they were both small young bulls, very good skins, no scars—We had seal liver for breakfast, neither of them very nice. Church in forenoon with Christmas hymns." Scott might not have shared his engineer's bloodlust—"he hates the sight of our butcher's shop," Wilson wrote—but he was again determined to make sure that *Belgica*'s errors were not repeated. Whenever a sheep had to be killed Scott would move himself to the other side of the bridge until it was over, but that did not stop him drilling into his Dundee whaling men the need to conquer their historic aversion to the taste and stench of blubber. We "are now eating seal flesh regularly," he wrote with satisfaction, throwing in for good measure their newest and most *recherché* term of culinary comparison, "and most of us like it. I must own to some squeamishness myself but even I [thought] the steaks & joints good though the kidneys & liver come amiss . . . the meat is certainly greatly superior to penguins."

Two days later, with their luck still holding, and *Discovery*'s massive overhung bow doing its job, they emerged from the pack into a world of clear seas and blue skies. "Our pleasure in once more reaching open water may be imagined," Scott wrote, and the pleasure was increased when at

10:30 that night their champagne celebrations were suddenly broken "by the shout of 'Land in sight.' It made us almost feel like explorers," Scott wrote in his journal that night, and "All who were not on deck quickly gathered there, to take their first look at the Antarctic Continent; the sun, now near the southern horizon, still shone in a cloudless sky, giving us full daylight. Far away to the south-west could be seen the blue outline of the high mountain peaks of Victoria Land, and we were astonished to find that even at this great distance of more than 100 geographical miles we could easily distinguish the peaks of the Admiralty Range."

With the worst of the pack behind them, a course was set for Robertson Bay, an inlet formed by the long peninsula of Cape Adare where Bernacchi had spent the winter of 1896 with Borchgrevink's *Southern Cross* expedition. After a tortuous path through another stream of pack forty miles from the coast, they forced their way through a last heavy band of ice guarding the entrance to the bay and, the next afternoon at 4 p.m., dropped anchor in the shelter of a low, triangular spit of land. With Royds left in charge of the ship, a boat was lowered and Scott and the rest of the wardroom made their way through the fringe of grounded floe and onto the desolate plateau of pebbled basalt that stretched back three-quarters of a mile to the foot of cliffs.

In the centre of this beach, an incongruous relic among the great colonies of Adélie penguins to whom the world seemed to belong, stood Borchgrevink's hut. Around it were scattered provisions and, inside, a letter addressed "to the Captain of the next Expedition." Scott read it out aloud to his men. It was "rather ridiculous," wrote Skelton, another John Bull convert to the anti-Borchgrevink movement, "& one only wonders how such a man could have ever impressed anybody with his fitness to command an expedition—full of bad spelling & punctuation, there wasn't a word of use to anybody."

Meteorology, geology, biology, climatology—in every discipline, in fact, except the geographical exploration that was all Markham really cared about—Borchgrevink had bequeathed a legacy *Discovery*'s men might have envied, but if the sight of the first grave on Antarctica was not enough to dent English complacency, the ice soon exacted its revenge.* After leaving a canister with details of their progress for the relief ship Markham had obtained, they stood out to sea and almost immediately

---

*The grave is that of Nicolai Hanson, the *Southern Cross*'s zoologist. He is buried high on the cliffs above the bay.

found themselves caught in a stream of pack that carried them helplessly towards a chain of grounded bergs.

It was the first time they had seen what the pack could do, and become aware of what Scott at his most Markhamesque called "its mighty powers." With Armitage aloft in the crow's nest, they twisted and turned *Discovery* in an effort to avoid the heaviest floes, struggling desperately against the tide that was forcing them consistently towards the shore. It was one of those hours, Scott recalled, "which impress themselves on the memory for ever." Above them, the sun shone out of a cloudless sky, its rays reflected in myriad gleams among the pack. Behind them were the snow-covered mountains and the glassy water of the bay. The air, Scott remembered, was "almost breathlessly still; crisp, clear and sun-lit, it seemed an atmosphere in which all Nature should rejoice; the silence was broken only by the deep panting of our engines and the low measured hush of the grinding floes; yet, beneath all ran this mighty, relentless tide, bearing us on to possible destruction."

It was the bewildering contrast of appearance and reality that baffled Scott's imagination, the co-existence of beauty and danger in so extreme a form. At such an early hour of the day, too, only the few men who were on the bridge were aware of their predicament, and the knowledge that down below the rest of the crew lay asleep in their hammocks, unconscious of any danger, seemed to heighten further the incongruity of the scene. Slowly, though—so slowly that no one recognised the moment of release—the tide began to slacken, the tight-packed floes loosened, and by 8:20, five hours after they had weighed anchor, *Discovery* "won through" to open sea and safety. "For me," Scott wrote, "the lesson had been a sharp and, I have no doubt, a salutary one; we were here to fight the elements with their icy weapons, and once and for all this taught me not to under-value the enemy."

If this sounds ominously like the language of naval chivalry, Scott's men soon had to accustom themselves to another "naval" aspect of his leadership. "The Captain is strangely reticent about letting a soul on the ship know what even his immediate plans are," Wilson complained after a sudden decision of Scott's to land on Coulman Island, another in the chain of possible "post-boxes" chosen in London for *Discovery*, "so we are all taken more or less by surprise whenever a landing is made. I think perhaps he is right as a rule, because it means that we must have things ready at all times, but in the case of letters one would like more notice."

"The only objection to the work is that the Skipper is so capricious,"

Hodgson wrote home in a similar vein a week later, "and no-one knows what is to be done till 5 minutes before it is done." It is intriguing to think what the young Scott might have thought of his own behaviour, but between the midshipman who railed in *Amphion* at his captain, and the commander who could do a fair imitation of him when he chose, lay that familiar, time-honoured gap that separates a hospital consultant from his houseman self.

These were only momentary irritations, and as Scott took *Discovery* slowly southwards, holding close to the coastline, they were soon too busy again, laying down food for the winter, to worry about much else. "As so often in the Antarctic," he wrote, they "resolved to turn night into day," and began the wretched job of stocking their rigging with all the seal they could kill. "It seemed a terrible desecration," Scott wrote, "to come to this quiet spot only to murder its innocent inhabitants and stain the white snow with their blood . . . Some of us were glad enough to get away on our ski and to climb the steep slopes at the end of the creek." Their slaughter, though, had given them a chance for their first successful dredge, and Hodgson and Koettlitz were in their element. "Hodgson was awfully pleased & tremendously excited about it," Skelton recorded, one hunter delighted for another. "Sponge, starfish, sea-eggs, worm—70 different species in all."

"Hodgson is glorified," wrote an equally happy Scott, but that was nothing compared to Koettlitz's joy five days later. Throughout the voyage old "Cuttlefish" had been something of a figure of fun in the wardroom, a combination of touchiness and a certain residual "foreign-ness" making him the natural butt in particular for Shackleton's high spirits. " 'Moss! Moss!!' " Koettlitz's tormentor recorded in his diary on the twentieth. " 'I have found moss!!!' I said, 'go on, I found it!' He took it quite seriously, and said, 'Never mind, it's moss, I am so glad!' The poor fellow was so over-joyed that there were almost tears in his eyes."

With the season pressing on, there were other concerns, and for the last few days Scott had been searching with increasing urgency for a suitable wintering place. The natural harbour where Shackleton had found Koett-litz his moss seemed to offer one plausible fallback if nothing else could be found, but on the night of 21 January, as they pushed their way into the loose pack of McMurdo Sound, Scott saw for the first time the landscape that was to provide the backdrop to all his polar hopes. "To the right," he wrote, vividly conveying a sense of anticipation and uncertainty that had nothing to do with hindsight, "is a lofty range of mountains with one very high peak far inland, and to the south a peculiar conical mountain, seemingly ending the coastline in this direction; to the left is Mount Erebus, its foothills, and a glimpse of Mount Terror. The Parry Mountains cannot be seen ahead of us. In the distance there is a small patch like a distant island. Ross could not have seen these patches, and a remnant of hope remains that we are heading for a strait and not a bay."

In technical terms Scott was right—McMurdo is a sound—but by eight the next morning the contours of the landscape ahead had resolved themselves into what for all practical purposes is a massive bay. As they pressed on southward into it, the apparent smudges of islands broadened out to suggest its southern limits, but if there was clearly no route through for *Discovery*, there seemed to be the next best thing. Without doubt, Scott added to his first description, McMurdo was a bay. "But," he went on—a possible gateway to the south, and the "great prospect of very good sledging work" in his sights—"it is highly satisfactory to note that there were no mountains in the background and that as far as the eye can see there must be a straight or smooth level plain stretching far away directly south."

He was again right—it was the northern edge of the Ross Ice Shelf—and with a second likely winter harbour sighted through binoculars on the west side of McMurdo Sound, Scott turned *Discovery* eastwards. Rounding Cape Bird at the north-west extremity of Ross Island, they steamed eastwards beneath the twin peaks of Erebus and Terror until at eight the next evening they found a gently shelving beach to the west of Cape Crozier with enough protection from grounded bergs to provide a landing.

Lowering an overladen whale boat, complete with sixteen men, magnetic instruments and a tin message cylinder, they pulled through the surf for the shore and launched themselves on the crest of a wave onto the beach. Scott found himself a spot in the middle of the biggest penguin colony they had seen to erect a post, and anchoring it with boulders, left their final message for the outside world. It did not, at the time, seem the most secure of connections. Even at a few hundred yards, for all their efforts to mark the spot, "it was almost impossible to distinguish it, and one could not help thinking, should disaster come to the expedition, what a poor reed was this on which alone we could trust to afford our friends a clue to our whereabouts."

Once the post was up, and Bernacchi and Barne busy at their chilly magnetic observations, Scott, Royds and Wilson began the climb up to the highest of the nearby volcanic cones. With penguins occupying every available inch of land they were reduced to whatever scree was available, but after hard scramble and a still steeper climb up the rock faces above, they were at last above the stench-line, with a view to the south and east across the Great Barrier—Scott's first sight of his final resting place—that extended indefinitely away in an immense blue-grey plain of ice.

One of the chief objectives of their first season was to discover whether there was land to the east of this ice shelf, and back on the ship Scott ordered Armitage to take *Discovery* close under the cliff that formed its northernmost edge. With only Ross's description to go on, the endless variety and mutability of the ice wall came as a surprise to them, and "every few hours some new variation showed itself," Scott wrote, with "now a sharp inlet or other irregularity of outline, now a change in appearance showing a difference in the length of time that the ice-face had been exposed."

As they steamed steadily eastwards, taking meticulous observations as they went, *Discovery* passed the farthest south of any ship, and on the twenty-ninth reached the point where Ross had reported a strong suggestion of land to the south-east. Scott had already been in the Antarctic long enough to know how deceptive appearances could be, but soundings of only one hundred fathoms and rapid changes in the conformation of the Barrier suggested land must be close, "But what a land!" Scott wrote. "On the swelling mounds of snow above us there was not one break, not a feature to give definition to the hazy outline. Instinctively one felt that such a scene as this was most perfectly devised to produce optical illusions in the explorer, and to cause those errors into which we had found even experienced persons to be led. What could be the height of the misty summit? And what the distance of that shadowy undulation? Instruments provide no answer—we could but guess."

The discolourations of sand and dirt in the grounded bergs meant that it was more than a "moral certainty" that they had discovered land, but as a thick fog descended over everything the clear visual proof they wanted was still missing. Throughout the next day *Discovery* groped her way slowly along the line of ice, but it was only as the bell sounded for their evening meal, and all but the officer of the watch were going below, that above the summit of an ice island ahead appeared two or three little black patches—"Two little points of bare black rock," a jubilant Shackleton wrote, "but Oh! how glad we were to see them, for it was land, real land, and the end of the great barrier was really found by us, and the theories and ideas can now be settled." "New Land. All's well," a contented Williamson recorded, and Duncan was prepared to go one better, noting in his usual style that "Its local name is being Edwards land." "It is intensely satisfactory to have seen the land," Scott wrote in his journal that night, "for although we were morally certain of its existence—In such a stupendous glaciation doubts of all kinds are always on the top of one's mind."

This was hardly the extensive exploration of an unknown eastern land that Markham had envisaged, but that same evening, as they continued in a north-easterly direction, a near disaster made up Scott's mind that it was enough. *Discovery* had steamed through thick fog into a narrow channel between pack and land before anyone realised they were in trouble, and was soon deep into a cul-de-sac of ice, lost among a shifting chaos of bergs and heavy pack with no way out but the southern end through which they had entered.

With Royds on watch, however, they continued along the same north-easterly course, until at 7:30 the next morning a massive wall of ice blocked their way. By this time Michael Barne had taken over from Royds, and with no other possibility open to him, began a series of manoeuvres that took them round every point of the compass in a lop-sided figure of eight that left them heading north into deeper trouble. Twelve hours after the nightmare had begun, Royds recorded the critical juncture: "There was a panic, and I was sent for hurriedly as it appears that Barne, finding no clear water, had turned and was in reality going back into the bay again. There was much swearing as to which was the way out, which was the berg we had watered close to etc., but I saw at once purely by luck that we were going wrong, and at last managed to convince the Capt., so we again turned back and at last got out of what at one time looked a very nasty position as young ice was forming thickly and very quickly."

"A strange thing happened during the night," an amused Wilson recorded. "The three watch-keepers spent the whole night in wandering round the big bay." Scott, though, was shaken. A kind of unspoken Masonry among the executive officers kept the extent of the danger to themselves, but they knew exactly how close they had come to sharing the *Belgica*'s fate. "The courses were logged and could have been eventually worked out," Scott wrote—the first entry in the new volume of his Antarctic Journals, and within a whisker of being the entry that marked the end of the expedition—"but the fact of one officer relieving the other and the similarity of the bergs and ice edge was most bewildering . . . the situation was very typical of the ease with which a ship could lose herself in the ice."

And if tempers had frayed, it is not surprising, as Scott cannot have been the only officer who had had virtually no sleep. For several days the

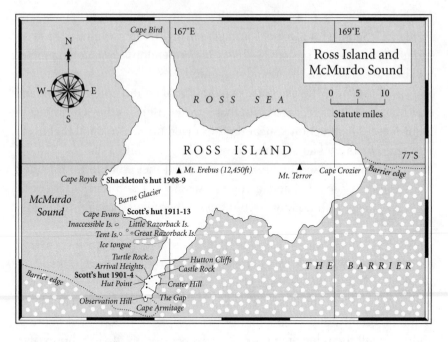

search for land had kept most of them up on deck around the clock, and Scott for one had been on the bridge for the whole of the night of the thirtieth/thirty-first, before taking his first brief rest after twenty-three hours of constant vigil. These were rhythms of life an executive officer was used to, but they were not conditions that any of them were familiar with, and after one more, half-hearted, attempt to find a passage north, Scott decided to turn back before new ice could threaten their McMurdo harbour.

There was time, however, for one detour, and on 3 February Scott took *Discovery* into a deep bight in the Barrier wall, and pushing on down a narrow creek, secured her with their anchors to the ice walls. While Armitage took a small party out onto the Barrier for their first incompetent experience of sledge work, the balloon equipment was set up, and the next day Scott made the first precarious ascent above Antarctica.

Quite why Scott should have gone up first is hard to say, but if the charitable explanation would have him leading boldly from the front, a rare case of "rank pulling" seems more likely. "The Captain said he would like to go up first," Shackleton wrote in his diary, equally pleased at his skipper's indignity and his own satisfaction at outdoing him, "so I got out, though I thought it a rather risky thing for he knew nothing about it, and we had to give him a number of directions just before he started." Once up, Scott jettisoned first a couple of handfuls of ballast and then a whole bag. "We shouted out that he must not throw the ballast out like that," Shackleton continued, "and then a thin piping voice came back 'but I was coming down so fast!' After a short time he had had enough of it, and we hauled him down to earth, and I then went up and realised a height of 650." "If nobody is killed," Wilson added tetchily, "it will only be because God has pity on the foolish."

With a torn fabric and a faulty valve developing, the ballon ride was not just a "first," but a "last," and the first game of football played on the Barrier seems in retrospect the more significant precedent. But if the balloon they had had such hopes for had failed, and the first sledging party had been a chapter of amateurish errors, there was clearly nothing wrong with spirits on board that a mild embarrassment for the captain could not put right. "The good spirits and willingness shown by all hands is beyond praise," Scott wrote gratefully that night. "If an individual can be selected, it is the boatswain—the work, hard manual labour he gets through in the course of the day is little short of wonderful."

The next day—as if to underline what kind of thanks a man might expect for such heroics in the navy—the boatswain's cat was killed by one of the dogs. In spite of that, as Williamson philosophically concluded his one-line obituary, all was "well" in *Discovery*. Two days later they had rounded Cape Bird, and by ten o'clock in the evening of 8 February they were deep into McMurdo Sound again, with *Discovery*'s bows grinding gently on a bank only yards from the shore. Backing away, they found deep water along the northern side of a projecting ice foot, and secured the ship. "We have now to consider the possibility of making this part of the bay our winter quarters," Scott wrote, and from the point of view of future sledging operations, it seemed that nowhere could be better. To the south-south-east a smooth, even surface stretched away into infinity, with every probability that the Great Barrier continued in that direction. Across the strait, the main coastline and all the geological opportunities it offered, was in easy range, while the proximity of Cape Crozier and their "post office" hopefully kept open their connections with the outside world.

The following day they set out to explore the immediate surroundings, and found on the southern side of their ice foot "an excellent little bay." Alongside it was a sheltered space that would do for their huts, and water shallow enough to preserve them from the threat of floating bergs. There was still sea ice on it, but it was cracked, and it seemed only a matter of days before it broke away. Crucially, too, there was no evidence of pressure from any direction.

Scott had now all but made up his mind to winter here, and *Discovery* was brought around the ice tongue into the bay. With the ice anchors well bedded and the small kedge buried in the snow for good measure, he took off across the sea-ice on a long exploratory walk with Skelton. After a momentary anxiety with some dangerously thin ice, they worked themselves into a position from which they could take fuller stock of where they were. It was only now that they could see for certain that they were on an island. From their vantage point a smooth, clean snow plain stretched to the furthest ridge of Terror, close to Cape Crozier, where the great ice-wall of the Barrier edge met land. To their right, through an angle of 120 degrees, was nothing but the vast, white expanse of the Barrier, and the way to the south. Safety and opportunity stood hand in hand. Mill's suggestion of McMurdo, made on the way down to Madeira, had borne fruit. They had found their winter harbour. And if Markham's vision of eastern exploration had been quietly shelved, what else could he have expected of a naval officer on his first independent command?

Nine: Harsh Lessons

All experience must be purchased, and if an officer inexperienced in these matters be appointed, the price will be paid in time and material, neither of which
can be afforded in an Antarctic expedition.

CAPTAIN MOSTYN FIELD

It would be hard to exaggerate how little Scott and his men knew of the
world they had chosen for themselves. Armitage and Koettlitz had the dubi-
ous pleasure of an Arctic winter together during the Jackson-Harmsworth
expedition to call on, but when it came to interpreting their immediate
environment that was of no more real use than Bernacchi's experience with
Borchgrevink some three hundred miles to the north of McMurdo Sound.

"The whole place had a weird and uncanny look and reminded me of
the desert in 'Childe Harold to the Dark Tower Came,'" Shackleton
decided, but in practical terms that was of only limited help. They were
deep in a "bay" formed on the east side by Ross Island, on the west by
mainland Antarctica, and on the south by the Great Barrier. Were the conditions that they had met with typical of McMurdo for this time of the
year? When did the ice in the harbour they had chosen go out? When
would they be able to find a secure anchorage for *Discovery*? How big were
the tides?

With the end of the summer season only a matter of weeks away, the
clear priority was to ready themselves for winter. A convenient spot had been
found on a bare, flattish plateau close to *Discovery*, and work immediately

got under way erecting the three huts brought with them from New Zealand. "We have landed all the dogs," Scott was soon noting with characteristic impatience, "and their kennels are ranged over the hillside below the huts. They complain bitterly, but they are a good riddance from the deck, which is again assuming some appearance of cleanliness . . . It is surprising what a number of things have to be done, and what an unconscionable time it takes to do them . . . Much work is before us when the huts are up: we must land a store of provisions and a boat for emergencies; then there are the instruments to be seen to, more seals to be killed for the winter, arrangements made for fresh-water ice, sledges and tents to be prepared, and a hundred-and-one details to be attended to."

At the heart of this growing shantytown was the ironically dubbed "Villa Gregory," a thirty-six-foot-square "settler's bungalow" with overhanging eves and veranda that had been constructed in Australia and shipped down with their other stores. It had been designed originally with an independent shore party in mind, but one look at it on the quay at Lyttelton had been enough to leave Scott's men knowing there was nothing they would sooner avoid. "There was . . . the uncertainty of the long Antarctic night," Bernacchi wrote with the nightmare memory of Borchgrevink's *Southern Cross* expedition to sharpen his relief, "which I had experienced at Cape Adare, in a tiny hut, fifteen feet square, lashed down by cables to the rocky shore. The night there had been shorter than we would now experience, as we had been farther north, but officers and men, living together in so restricted a space, ten of us in all, had found tempers wearing thin long before it passed. To those who had not yet experienced the polar darkness, anticipating was probably worse than realisation, and some feared the results of nervous irritation before the winter passed. That was an experience, however, from which *Discovery* saved us. A winter in 'Gregory's Lodge' might have been little better than a repetition of the boredom and irritation engendered at Cape Adare. With *Discovery* our home, each officer had his own sanctum, and the men in their quarters could enjoy their leisure in their own way. The friction of conflicting tastes was eliminated from the beginning."

With every available day of light precious, there was little chance of boredom for officer or man in these first weeks ashore. In addition to the Villa Gregory there were two asbestos-covered huts for magnetic observations, the larger of the two for differential instruments and the smaller for absolute instruments against which daily observations could periodically be checked. "They and all that pertained to them were Mr. Bernacchi's special business," Scott wrote of the arcane mysteries of these huts, "and many times a day this officer could be seen journeying to and fro in attendance on his precious charge. Within the larger of the huts, mounted on a solidly bedded oak plant, could be seen three small instruments, set at different angles, but each containing a delicately suspended magnetic needle . . . [recording] on rolls of sensitised photographic paper . . . the declination, horizontal force, and vertical force . . . of the earth's magnetic pull."

It was a tyrannous routine at the best of times—still more so in winter, on the "international term days," when comparative readings in *Discovery* and the German ship *Gauss* had to be taken every two hours—but for sheer despotic misery it probably took second place to Royds's. As Scott's First Lieutenant he was responsible anyway for the day-to-day running of the ship, and on top of his normal duties he was also the expedition's meteorologist, condemned summer and winter, fair or blizzard, to an icy two-hourly circle of the expedition's barometer, thermometers and anemometer.

With each of the officers doing a night shift in turn, and their own separate disciplines to look after, there was no one in the wardroom who was idle. There was such a disparate range of tasks to cover that they tended only to meet at meal times, dispersing in between to their specimens and microscopes, their rocks and ice-holes and dredging equipment or, in the case of Michael Barne—utterly indifferent to cold or hardship—to his lonely treks across the ice in a thankless search for variations in sea temperatures.

For the men, too, there were seals to kill, penguins to hunt, snow ramps to build, ship sides to bank, water to collect and *Discovery*'s winter awning to be prepared. "Routine while the light lasts," Williamson recorded in his journal:

a.m.
5:45—call hands, coffee
6:15—hands fall in for work, ice ship generally
7:00—one hand from each mess to clean out mess deck
8:00—breakfast
9:00—hands turn to work as necessary

p.m.
12:00—dinner
1:30—hands turn to, work as necessary
5:00—supper, finish for day, if all goes well.

From the first, however, Scott had made it clear that he was not interested in making work for its own sake, and for a man who obsessively filled his own time he was surprisingly tolerant of what the men did with theirs. On the nineteenth-century naval expeditions in the Arctic officers had traditionally taught their men to read and write, but in a different world and a different navy Scott recognised that there were no courses that would not either patronise or bewilder a crew who filled in their spare hours with anything from Darwin's *Origin of Species* to interminable games of shove ha'penny.

But for all that he allowed a fairly relaxed regime, he could be tough when he needed to be, and their first days in McMurdo provided him with an unwanted opportunity to put down his marker. "The cook Mr. Brett getting troublesome," the Dundee shipwright James Duncan noted with a nice understatement in his journal for 10 February, "had to be taked two [sic] by the Captain." "Had trouble with the cook this morning," Scott recorded more explicitly. "He had been insolent to Shackleton on Saturday & when brought up was insolent to me—I put him in irons, being much reviled during the process. 8 hours brought him to his senses and a condition of whining humility—He is a wretched specimen of humanity."

This might not sound very attractive, but if journals are anything to go by, there was not a soul on the ship who would have raised a finger to save Charles Brett from a lot worse. Brett had been taken on at the last minute in New Zealand to replace the original cook who had been dismissed, and even before they had reached McMurdo his blend of idleness, dirtiness and empty brag had made anything that Scott could do to him seem no less than his due.

Considering the mix of men on board, in fact, and the restrictions and strains they had to live under, there was astonishingly little need for Scott to use a heavy hand at any time in the south. "There was one [William Hubert] who found himself in serious trouble for his epicurean tastes," Bernacchi recalled of one of the rare exceptions to this general harmony,

> a merchant seaman who must have signed on in a moment of mental aberration. He was not made for Polar exploration. He did not like the Antarctic or anything to do with it, and had been heard, during one of the very cold autumn sledging journeys, to sit up in his sleeping-bag and with chattering teeth apostrophise the night—"Fancy me from bloody Poplar, on the bloody Ice Barrier, in a bloody sleeping-bag, gorblimey!"

No doubt on the mess deck he applied the same adjective to the cake which caused the trouble, though when the ship's company was paraded in strict naval style, so that he might make his complaint with due ceremony, he only demanded mildly of the captain, as he fished an offensive lump of something from his pocket—"Do you call this caike?" Scott had no sense of humour when discipline was infringed upon, and discipline demanded surely that a man who approached his commanding officer in such a way be ordered to instant execution.*

With the routines of wardroom and mess-deck life firmly established, the scientific work under way and the shore settlement taking shape, Scott's next priority was to come to grips with *Discovery*'s immediate environment. "Names have been given to the various landmarks in our vicinity," he wrote in the middle of February of their first, touching steps at appropriating the alien landscape of Ross Island. "The end of our peninsula is to be called 'Cape Armitage' after our excellent navigator. The sharp hill above it is to be 'Observation Hill'; it is 750' high, and should make an excellent look-out station for observing the going and coming of sledge-parties. Next comes the 'Gap,' through which we can cross the peninsula at a comparatively low level. North of the 'Gap' are 'Crater Heights,' and the higher volcanic peak beyond is to be 'Crater Hill'; it is 1,050 feet in height. Our protecting promontory is to be 'Hut Point,' with 'Arrival Bay' on the north and 'Winter Quarter Bay' on the south; above 'Arrival Bay' are the 'Arrival Heights,' which continue . . . to a long snow-slope, beyond which rises the most conspicuous landmark on our peninsula, a high precipitous-sided rock with a flat top, which has been dubbed 'Castle Rock.' " "Eyes," too, "were turning to the south, the land of Promise—" Scott noted on 13 February: "many are the arguments as to what lies in the misty distance, and what nature of obstacles the spring journey will bring to light—the optimistic look for a smooth clear ice-foot but I fear there will be many surprises when we get beyond our present vision."

Four days later the work on shore was sufficiently in hand for Scott to think of their first sledging reconnaissance towards the nearby islands on

---

*Scott had gone off to the wardroom when Hubert complained, returning with an identical piece of cake to show that the officers got no better fare. Whatever Hubert's punishment was, it was not severe enough to be mentioned in any diary. The only other noted case of indiscipline involved a man smoking through the Sunday service, and he seems to have received nothing but a severe dressing-down.

the Barrier, and on 17 February Shackleton won a toss of a coin with Barne
for the pleasure of leading it. The ice around the end of their peninsula
was showing signs of breaking up, and the next day Scott told three seamen
to haul a sledge over the "Gap" in readiness for Shackleton, Wilson and
the young geologist Ferrar to start the next morning.

It was a historic occasion, because it was not only the first test of the
men, but the first test, too, of the equipment over which Scott had struggled
so long before *Discovery* sailed. The tents they had brought were bell-
shaped and made of either a green Willesden canvas or thin gaberdine,
stretched out over five bamboo poles that met at the top to give a height of
five foot six and a diameter of about six feet. There was an entrance hole two
and a half feet in diameter with a funnel-shaped door, another hole at the
top for ventilation, and a valence or "skirting edge" that could be weighed
down with blocks of snow and ice to keep out drift. With a waterproof canvas floorcloth that could double up as a sail, the whole weighed about thirty
pounds—the minimum, Scott reckoned, to withstand Arctic conditions.

The *Discovery* expedition had the advantage of recent polar experience
to call on when it came to their tents—among Markham's papers survives a
note on tent design from *Belgica*'s Frederick Cook—but their sleeping bags
show how much a matter of trial and error their equipment necessarily was.
On this first journey they were experimenting with a kind of "night suit"
made out of reindeer or wolf furs that had been bought in Norway, but
experience would soon prove these virtually impossible to get in and out of,
and Scott had them converted into bags—either single or, more typically,
"three-man bags" weighing forty pounds (twice that by the end of a long
journey with the accumulation of ice)—made with the fur inside, an over-
lap at the head and the sides, and a large flap that could be drawn over when
everyone was inside and toggled down. "The warmest position," Scott
wrote—almost anticipating, it would seem, one of the posthumous criticisms that he always took the centre berth—"was the middle, but it was not
always preferred. As an offset for his increased comfort it was the duty of the
centre occupant to toggle up the bag—a task which, with bare cold fingers
was by no means pleasant, and generally occupied a considerable time."

The sleeping bag was an even more vital piece of equipment than the
tent, Scott reckoned, and not far behind it was their cooker. He was prepared to concede that the nutritional value of the food would in theory be
the same hot or cold, but "as regards the heating of food," he later
remarked with measured understatement, "I can only say that I should prefer to be absent from a party who had decided to forgo it."

The cooker they used was of Nansen's design—his greatest contribution to sledging requirements, a grateful Scott believed—an adaptation of a modern form of heating lamp that consumed paraffin in a vaporised state. The most vital requirement of any cooker in Antarctic conditions was heat efficiency, and Nansen's design of concentric lightweight aluminium containers, with the heated gases circulating around the central pot, usefully expended 90 per cent of the heat coming from the lamp beneath.

It was not just for the cooker that they had to thank Nansen, because their sledges, made in Christiania, similarly showed the benefit of his experience. The typical soul-breaking, iron-shod ten-footer of the McClintock era had taken seven men to pull, but Scott's ash sledges were lighter, narrower and more flexible, with most of the joints made of lashings to allow for an almost snake-like movement, slightly wider runners, rounded beneath, an overall width of one foot five inches, and a length that varied from seven feet (too stiff) to the ideal, forty-odd-pound eleven-footer, and a twelve-footer that was "just beyond the limits of handiness."

As important as their sledges was their sledging costume, and give or take individual touches of whimsy, this was the same for officers and men. A warm thick suit of underclothing formed the innermost layer, followed by a flannel shirt or two, a sweater, pilot-cloth breeches and loosely cut jacket, lots of pockets for knives, matches, goggles and whistles, and an outer suit of thin gaberdine from Messrs. Burberry to keep out the biting wind.

For the hands there were fur or felt mitts—Scott swore by his wolf skin—over long, woollen half mitts—but when it came to headgear, there was more individualism. In the glare of summer a broad-rimmed felt hat would usually be worn over a balaclava, and in the colder weather a camel-wool helmet with gaberdine cover, or simply two woollen balaclavas under the gaberdine cover—Scott used just one, augmented by an extra thickness of material to protect the ears—and a pair of goggles made out of smoked glass, slitted leather or, in Scott's case, a sliver of wood, blackened on the inside and pierced with a cross-shaped aperture.

Most vital of all on the march was the protection of their feet, and for this there was nothing to touch the reindeer-fur boot or finneskoe made in Norway. The pressure of time had meant that their supply was of a variable quality, but a properly made pair, bulked out with a couple of pairs of socks, or in Lapp fashion, an insulating nest of *sennegrass*, would stand weeks of hard travelling on the ice.

There was one further, more controversial piece of equipment that stemmed from Scott's journey to Norway, and that was their skis. Since

Nansen completed the first crossing of Greenland on ski their possibilities for polar travel had been obvious, but between a man who had had his first pair of skis at two and a party of British seamen using them for the first time lay a gulf that no cursory practice on an ice floe in the pack or on the slopes above the *Discovery* hut was going to close. There was a profound disagreement on the subject from the start—Armitage loudest in the anti-skiing faction, Skelton noisiest in their defence—but Scott himself would always remain oddly ambiguous about their use. Alongside the ultra-competitive Skelton he was probably the best skier in the party, but after an early conversion to the pro-ski faction he relapsed into a scepticism that nothing in his expedition experience could shift. "It was found that in spite of all appearances to the contrary," he would later write—and not from any doctrinaire opposition, but with the experience of months on the ice behind him, "a party on foot invariably beat a party on ski, even if the former were sinking ankle-deep at each step; while to add to this, when the surface was hard, ski could not be used, and had to be carried as an extra weight and a great encumbrance on the sledges . . . It will be seen, therefore, that our experience has led me to believe that for sledge work in the Antarctic Regions there is nothing to equal the honest and customary use of one's own legs."

That Scott was wrong would be only too bitterly demonstrated, but whether he was wrong at the time, with the men and equipment that he had at his disposal, is another matter. If he was guilty of anything it is probably that he was enough of a believer to *make* his men more competent, but against that it has to be recognised in his and their defence that, hauling on foot, Scott's men would comfortably match in terms of miles anything that Nansen achieved with skis on the Greenland icecap.

All these matters, however—and the all-important issue of sledging rations that the long journeys of their first full season would expose—still lay in the future as Shackleton and his party finally set off.* The weather was fine, but with a bitter southerly wind soon getting up, and White Island seeming to recede with every step they took towards it, it was not long before any illusions of knight errantry were brought to a brutal end. "At 11:30 the wind was worse than ever and we were all simply done," Wil-

---

*A photograph shows their eleven-foot sledge as they prepared to march off—the first party to leave from McMurdo for the south—with the personal pennants designed by Sir Clements Markham fluttering proudly above it. It is interesting that of all the officers in *Discovery* Scott alone was resistant to this piece of chivalric flummery, but Shackleton certainly had no such embarrassment, insisting in the teeth of all Markham's cod-heraldry and irritation on a square pennant to distinguish his from the swallow-tailed design that every other officer had dutifully followed.

son wrote after a day's hauling that had seen them manage no more than an exhausting mile an hour,

> so we decided to camp at once and wait until the wind had dropped. Up to this time Shackle's face had suffered most from the cold. His cheek was constantly going dead white in one place, and Ferrar's nose went too. My face wasn't troubled, but the moment we halted and started to unpack . . . the cold and the snow drift and the wind were so bad that we all began frost-bites . . .
>
> However we dug out our trench and shoved the poles into the flapping business and . . . got our footgear off. The ski boots were frozen to the socks, so that both came off in one and it took us all we knew next morning to tear the socks out. The sweat of one's feet had lined the boots with ice. We got into our long fur boots and our feet began to get comfortable. Then we got our supper cooked, hot cocoa and pemmican and biscuit and jam and butter, and then we began to get our furs on, an awful job in a small tent, but it was too bad to go outside, as our furs would have been filled with drift in no time. The other two were bricks to me now. They dressed me first, as I was constantly getting cramp in the thighs whenever I moved, and having dressed me, they put me on the floor and sat on me while they dressed each other. At last we were all in our wolfskins . . . and settled off to sleep huddled together to keep warm . . .

By 3:30 a.m. they had had as much as they could take, but exhausted again after four hours' marching, they pitched camp still two miles short of White Island and slept until four that afternoon. After a meal they trudged on to the island, and with their tea frozen in the water bottles beneath their tunics, roped themselves together to begin the freezing climb to the 2,300-foot summit of the highest crater. "As far as the eye could see was a level ice plain," Wilson wrote of the view from the top, all the misery of the journey momentarily forgotten in the significance of what they were looking at: "the true Great Barrier surface, and no Antarctic Continent at all. On the west coast-line ran a series of promontories formed by splendid mountain ranges, and beyond them all was the setting sun just dipping below the horizon. Shackle took bearings and angles and I made a sketch, though we were nearly frozen doing it."

The sun was actually setting due south of them—Wilson's misorienta-tion of the mountain range would have serious consequences—but their ascent had at least shown that beyond the long finger of land jutting out from the foot of Mount Discovery the Barrier stretched away in an unbro-ken expanse towards the Pole. "Altogether we felt that our outlook on affairs was considerably enlarged by this small journey," Scott wrote after Shackleton had arrived back late the next day, "very tired, but full of talk as was expected," "and we stopped up late as we discussed its bearings and lis-tened to the woes of the inexperienced sledger."

"It is strange now to look back on those first essays at sledging," he later wrote of this first venture, "and to see how terribly hampered we were by want of experience. Perhaps the most curious note I have of the report of these three is that in their opinion our pemmican wouldn't do at all. It was far too rich, they said, and when made into soup it was so greasy that none of them could touch it. Our pemmican contained 60 per cent of lard, but after knowing how it tasted to a true sledging appetite and seeing the man-ner in which it was scraped out of the cooking pot in later times, it needs such a reminder as this to recall that it might not always be grateful to a more civilised taste."

The reconnaissance journey had actually produced as much misinfor-mation as hard knowledge, but it had at least given them some idea of just how hopelessly unprepared they were for the work ahead. On the day that they returned Scott had complained in his journal that a lecture on frost-bite Koettlitz had given had not been the graphic frightener he had hoped for, but even to him the scene around them could seem so deceptively beautiful that it was hard to equate it with danger. An occasional Adélie penguin might play rough at a football game; out in the bay the killer whales patrolled the open leads; but with the sun just beginning to dip at midnight, and "the effects of sunset & sunrise" merging into an hour-long pageant, the scene was "wonderfully beautiful." "The most characteristic feature is a wonderful violet light that tinges the snow slopes and ice foot and fades into the purple outline of the distant mountains—Here & there a high peak is radiantly gilded by a shaft of sunlight and the cumulus clouds that usually hang about some of the slopes & valleys are thrown [into] a striking contrast of brilliant light & deep shadow."

But if a broken leg for their steward, Reginald Ford, and an unscripted swim for Royds were not enough to warn them just how fragile a truce they were living under, their second expedition provided all the reminder they needed. At the end of January a skiing injury had put an end to Scott's own sledging plans for the season, but by 4 February a party of four officers, eight men and two teams of dogs under Royds and Barne was ready for a journey to their Cape Crozier "post-office" with details of *Discovery*'s winter quarters. "I am bound to confess," Scott later wrote of their leavetaking, "that the sledges when packed presented an appearance of which we should afterwards have been wholly ashamed, and much the same might be said of the clothing worn by the sledgers. But at this time our ignorance was deplorable; we did not know how much or what proportions would be required as regards the food, how to use our cookers, how to put up our tents, or even how to put on our clothes. Not a single item of the outfit had been tested, and amid the general ignorance that prevailed the lack of system was painfully apparent in everything."

Hopping around "like a bear with a sore head," as Hodgson put it, Scott could only watch as the chaotic caravan of men and dogs disappeared over the hills and on to the eastern side of their peninsula. Royds and his party had taken enough supplies with them to be away for three weeks, and with the weather at Hut Point fine, even a report of a distant speck on the hillside five days later set off no alarms in *Discovery*.

There was no way that Scott could yet know such a thing, but Hut Point was no guide to conditions only a few miles away, and after a brutally hard slog through deep, soft snow, Royds had decided to send Barne and the rest of the party back while he went on with Koettlitz and Skelton. In his written instructions to Barne, Royds had left the return route to his discretion, and finding a gentler slope up from the ice abreast of Castle Rock, Barne had opted to take it in preference to the steeper route by which they had originally come down.

With visibility good, there was nothing wrong with his decision, but as they reached the top of the ridge some half a mile short of Castle Rock, the weather suddenly broke and a south-east wind swallowed the ridge in drift. Before the landscape had disappeared completely from sight, Barne spied an outcrop of stone that he thought might provide some shelter, and half an hour's blind and disorientating trudge through the driven snow brought them to the spot which he thought he had marked to pitch their tents.

The only sensible course was to stick where they were, but with the winds threatening their temporary encampment, Barne decided to abandon tents and equipment and try to make their way down with the dogs. He might have been all right still if they had been where he thought they were, but without realising it they had strayed in the blizzard onto the seaward rather than the landward side of the ridge, with only a steep ice slope and a sheer cliff between them and the invisible water below. "Before leaving," Barne later reported, "I impressed on the men, as strongly as I could, the importance of keeping together, as it was impossible to distinguish any object at a greater distance than ten yards . . . Our progress was very slow, as we were greatly delayed by the men in fur boots, who had difficulty in walking on the slippery, uneven surface. As we proceeded the surface inclined to our right front until it was evident we were crossing a steep slope, on which it was more and more difficult to keep a foothold . . . About ten minutes after we had left our sledges, Hare, who was at the rear of the party, was reported missing, and at this moment an unusually violent squall prevented us from seeing even one another."

Still not realising his original error, and what lay beneath, Barne had just ordered his men to fan out in a search formation, when Seaman Evans stepped on a patch of bare, smooth ice "and shot out of sight immediately. Thinking the slope to be one of the short ones so common in the folds of the hills, Barne cautioned his men to remain where they were, and sitting down, deliberately started to slide in Evans's tracks. In a moment or two the slope grew steeper, and soon he was going at a pace which left him no power to control his movements; he whipped out his clasp knife and dug it into the ice, but the blade snapped off short, and failed to check his wild career. In the mad rush he had time to realise the mistake that had been made and to wonder what would come next. In a flash, ice changed to snow, which grew softer until, in a smother of flying particles, his rapid flight was arrested, and he stood up to find Evans within a few feet of him."

Barne and Evans had no sooner exchanged a few words of greeting than the figure of Quartley came tumbling out of the drift, and crashed in a pile at their feet. The three men knew that there was no way back up the icy slope, but with the downward route the only option they had not gone four paces when "they found that the slope ended suddenly in a steep precipice beyond which they could see nothing but the clouds of whirling snow. Even as they recoiled from this new danger and dimly realised the merciful patch of soft snow which had saved them from it, a yelping dog flew past them, clawing madly at the ice slope, and disappeared for ever into the gloom beyond."

As Barne, Evans and Quartley began a desperate crawl along the cliff edge, the sea gaping beneath them, the rest of the party were still waiting above in complete ignorance of their fate. With visibility now virtually zero and temperatures in the region of −18°F they knew that they could not just stay where they were, and eventually set off in what they hoped was the direction of the ship, slipping and blindly stumbling in single file behind Frank Wild until, as Frank Plumley recalled, in just one of the confused and confusing versions of events, "All five of us slipped and went sliding down the edge of the precipice bringing up on some soft snow. Poor Vince having fur boots on was not able to stop himself and went over into the sea directly under us."

"It was difficult to discover from the men's account exactly what had happened after this catastrophe," Scott later wrote, but "in some sort of hazy way they realised that they must make upwards and away from the danger. All spoke of that ascent with horror, and wondered how it was ever accomplished . . . Literally their lives depended on each foothold, and they possessed no implement to make these more secure . . . As they crept laboriously upwards, the slope became steeper and more icy, but now, here and there, they found a stone which had rolled from the heights above and become firmly frozen in the icy surface . . . The storm still whirled the snow about them with unabated fury, but they pushed upwards in its teeth from stone to stone, until to their joy the stones grew thicker, and close above them they saw the black outline of the rocky summit. A final scramble, and they were once more on safe ground, with the nightmare of the climb behind them."

The single surprise in this tragedy was that only two men had disappeared, but when Wild and his frostbitten, stupefied companions eventually stumbled out of the dusk and into the camp it seemed at first as though it was even worse. In the roar and chaos of the storm none of them could make much sense of what had happened, but more in desperation than hope a search party was sent out under Armitage, and a whaling boat under Shackleton to scour the cliff edge beneath the ridge. Scott knew that the young seaman George Vince was gone. He probably knew that Clarence Hare had been the first to lose his footing and disappear into the swirling drift. He almost certainly thought—as did Frank Wild, the one man who had held his four colleagues together—that Barne, Quartley and Evans had also slipped to their deaths. "The hours which followed the departure of Armitage and his search party on this fatal night were such as one could scarcely forget," a helpless Scott wrote; "exhausted as our returned wanderers were, we questioned them again and again to get greater light on the accident, but nothing could alter the fact that five of our small company were lost or wandering helplessly about in this dreadful storm. Hatefully conscious of my inability to help on account of my own injured leg, my own mind seemed barren of all suggestion of further help which we might render."

There was nothing to do though but wait, and with Scott expecting the worst, it seemed almost more of a miracle than a disaster when, three hours later, Ferrar brought in a shattered Barne, Evans and Quartley. At one stage Scott had thought that it was Royds and the whole party who were gone, and if he could never have consciously compounded for a tragedy that would cost them two lives, it was the horror of what might have been that filled the ship. "As we prepared to snatch some few hours of rest," Scott wrote, "we had sadly to realise the calamity that had befallen us in what appeared to be the certain loss of two of our comrades; but as the details of the story were unfolded, we could well appreciate that we have been almost miraculously preserved from a far greater tragedy. It seemed almost wonderful that the whole party had not disappeared, to leave us only the terrible discovery of the abandoned sledges or perhaps a frozen silent figure in the snow."

It seemed for some days that Barne's hands would be lost to frostbite, but that sense of the miraculous was soon increased when two days later Williamson saw a figure bending down at the edge of the camp to pat the head of a dog, and recognised the missing Hare. "He must have been under the snow for thirty-six hours," Scott wrote in his diary, the natural scepticism of the agnostic in headlong retreat, "has been forty hours without food, and sixty without warm food . . . A wholly miraculous preservation."

If the dead had walked in, Wilson wrote, Scott could not have been more amazed, but no amount of relief or euphoria or talk of "Providence" could disguise the fact that the expedition was in serious trouble. The brief journey that Wilson, Shackleton and Ferrar had made to White Island had been inept enough, but the fiasco of Michael Barne's first foray into leadership had exposed levels of incompetence and amateurishness that left *Discovery*'s whole future in question. Incapable of even the most basic task of loading a sledge properly, incapable of handling their dogs properly, incapable of dressing properly, incapable of navigating a safe route within only a few miles of the ship—the list of failures would have been grim enough if the death of Vince had not brought Scott face to face with a more fundamental challenge to his most cherished beliefs.

From his first day in *Discovery* he had seen it as an essentially naval expedition, and if he had been asked where its—or for that matter his own — strengths lay, he would have had no more hesitation than Markham in identifying the ethos and training of the naval officer. Throughout his career Scott had constantly kicked against the pricks of service life, but the two things he never seems to have questioned were the fundamental competence of the *Britannia* man to command, and the superiority of the naval rating over any mere merchant man. The performance of Michael Barne and — with the notable exception of Frank Wild — the naval men in the party had left that belief in tatters. In a real sense, poor Barne was no more than a victim of the collective inexperience of the whole crew, but while Scott was quick to defend him in public, there was no escaping the truth. "There can be no doubt," he wrote in his journal on the eleventh, "that there was complete & utter demoralisation from which Providence alone rescued the greater number of the party. I can scarcely bring myself to think of what happened in all its aspects."

It only made it worse, too, that of all his officers Barne came closest to a certain naval ideal. "He was tall and rather thin," Reginald Ford fondly remembered him sixty years later, and "used to wear his uniform cap at a rakish angle — His face was frequently set in a bright and winning smile. In fact this is how he always comes to my mind. He was never self-assertive, always generous to others, ready to accept blame & shield others and equally ready to share praise if it were being given. He was my ideal of an Englishman."

There was nothing here that Scott would not have agreed with, but it was an "ideal" that Vince's death had left looking brutally exposed. "Now that one can reflect more calmly on the situation," he continued the next day, after he had given himself time to digest the different versions of events, "one can appreciate the fatal wants of judgement that produced it. The full responsibility must rest with the officer in charge and one cannot but see that he committed a series of errors. He does not seem to know exactly how his men were dressed and altogether seems to have neglected that proper care for their well being which is so essential to the man in command."

Barne's omissions ranged from his men's footwear, to his failure to put up a tent. "But the crowning and disastrous error," Scott went on, "lay in the fatal decision to abandon the baggage & push on when overtaken by a heavy blizzard . . . The madness of the act is the more glaring in that he had no knowledge of the country over which he was travelling — Everyone who has since visited the cave in which the sledges were left is astonished by the whole proceeding."

It was not just Barne that Scott was concerned about either, because while the safe return of Royds's party from Cape Crozier on the nineteenth relieved him of one anxiety, it left him with another. The party had been no more successful than anyone else in *Discovery* that first season at achieving its primary objective, but it was not so much the failure to reach their post-office that was the real worry as the first faint, unexpected question mark over the courage of his First Lieutenant. Sensitive, thoughtful, kind and meticulous, Royds was also brave, one suspects, more as a matter of *noblesse oblige* and basic human decency than raw animal instinct. There are men like Barne, and perhaps even Scott himself, who seem utterly impervious to the horrors of crevasses, but to an imaginative soul like Royds—or to Cherry-Garrard on Scott's last expedition—there was something in the thought of the bottomless, hidden chasms of ice travel that made every step a nightmare.

There can become, after a while, something sinister even in the beauty of ice, in the endless and deepening gradations of blue, disappearing into a pure, utterly inhuman realm of cold and darkness, and it was this that "got to" Royds. "Honeycombed with crevasses, awful places, deep and dark and no bottom visible for hundreds of feet," he wrote in his diary, wrestling with his fears of a world that surrounded the secure haven of their tent. "Lay awake most of the night, deciding what was best to be done . . . no good . . . and yet I didn't like the idea of having to give up the trip and the object, which especially lent itself to my liking as it was Uncle Wye who joined up the 'Alert' with the 'Discovery' [on the Nares expedition], and it was in my hands now to join up the 'Discovery' with the relief ship."

It is a measure of the man that Royds—and Cherry too—got on with it in spite of his fears, but the age that gave us the White Feather and shot men with shell shock had little time for such sensitivities. There is no way of knowing from the surviving evidence whether Royds had really "funked" it on this first expedition, but it is plain from their subsequent comments that Skelton and Koettlitz both clearly thought so. "Yesterday the skipper called me into his cabin," Skelton wrote in his diary on their return from a second attempt to reach the post-office,

> and asked me plainly "What our Terror party had done, and why we were back so early?" I said I was afraid we hadn't done much, but I had not anything to do with the matter—so seeing I suppose that there was not much to be got out of me, he said

"Well look here,—between you and me why are you back so early" . . . Of course as he put it in a confidential way, I gave him a few details . . . Royds' poor spirit under the circumstances—the discomforts he causes others in a tent by his awkwardness and "girlishness" . . . I also said I didn't consider Royds was cut out for sledging, that he was the wrong man for it. From what he said I should say that evidently he had got much the same yarn from Koettlitz—I certainly didn't give Royds away half so much as I might, particularly leaving out the incident of his "sprained" ankle—the most discreditable incident to my mind.

Later in the day, Royds seems to have got a talking to—he was much cut up about it—the skipper told him the opinion of the mess was that he funked sledging . . . I did my best to buck him up—but of course if he made any row I wouldn't hesitate to tell him my opinion of what the skipper got from me privately—There is no doubt that though he doesn't actually funk sledging,—he is next door to it, & in fact is never feeling happy—too girlish, and he certainly has very little brains, & no observing powers at all for scientific or interesting matter.

It was a moment of real crisis for Scott, because if it did not really matter to him whether the "mail cairn" was reached at the end of the first season or early in the spring, the last thing he could afford was doubts over the fitness of his two senior officers. Many years later Reginald Ford wrote to assure Barne that no one had held Vince's death against him, but in a ship that was as self-consciously divided between navy and merchant men as *Discovery* was during this first year, it would have been odd if some of Scott's own doubts had not percolated down to the mess deck.

It was not, either, as if the mistakes and questions could be discreetly contained within the walls of the wardroom. It was easy enough for Scott to speak to Barne or Royds in the privacy of his cabin, but if the dogs were running loose or the sledges had to be repacked, or a party had to return because they had forgotten equipment, then Scott and his officers had the whole ship there for an audience. "All Fools Day & no doubt we looked it," a laconic Duncan wrote from the middle of one such fiasco at the end of this first season, and no one was in any doubt as to where the blame lay. "I have *never* realized"—it is worth quoting Wilson's comment again in this context—"to such an extent the truth that 'familiarity breeds contempt' as this last year during which I have seen a little of the inside of the 'Royal Navy,' God help it."

It was not as though the men had no alternative in front of them, because with Armitage and Shackleton in the wardroom, the possibility of a different and more informal kind of leadership was always in the air. There was no one on board, in fact, who was more loyal or determined to impress the skipper than Shackleton, but the mere presence of such a natural maverick inevitably offered its own wry commentary on the more absurd aspects of naval hierarchy. Shackleton "was rather an enigma to us in a way," J.W. Dell remembered, recalling a final conversation with him on the night before he died and left Dell with the last duty of sewing his old boss into his shroud; "he was both fore and aft, if you understand, due to the fact that he didn't fall in with all the views of all the Naval officers. And he never did. And you know, the night before—the same night as he died—we were on the bridge together, him and I, and he was in a very reminiscent mood, and he was speaking and saying . . . 'Do you remember when we used to go to Divisions every morning, and come out there and Scott used to come out and read prayers, every morning of his life.' He said 'The thing that always tickled was the way Charles Rawson Royds always used to put the snow on the upper deck, getting the dirty stuff up before Divisions.' "

Much of this is hindsight—Shackleton was not anti-navy enough at the time to stop him trying for a commission on his return to England—but Scott was too self-critical to need comparisons to point up their failures. In the organisation of the expedition back in London and on the voyage south he had flexed his muscles as a commander, but he knew as well as anyone that the ice and the unknown had already presented challenges which he had been helpless to meet. The problem for Scott was that his style of command—the naval style—was all he knew, and all in a sense he wanted to know. The mysteries of "charisma" and leadership were something that would exercise him all his life, but while Scott was always perfectly aware that he could never cut the kind of figure that Shackleton would so brilliantly do, the fact is that his whole background and training made any cult of personality not just redundant but deeply suspect and vulgar.

If Scott was "absolutely navy"—as Dell would put it—in anything, it is in that he had got to the age of thirty-three without ever desiring to fix his authority on anything other than the simple and non-negotiable fact of *rank*. This is not a model of naval or military life that any modern theorist or practitioner would willingly recognise, but the effectiveness of any armed service is in the end dependent—like that of that other great authoritarian structure, the Roman Catholic Church—on the fact that it creates orders (or Holy Orders) that enjoy a validity and authority utterly independent of merit or intellectual consent.

There is something to be said for this, in so far as it recognises that there are not enough Nelsons to officer a navy any more than there are St. Francises to stock the world's parishes, and it has an austere charm about it that is very characteristic of Scott. To a man like Shackleton, any expedition he led was first and last an extension of his own personality, but for Scott in these early years there was none of the same egotism involved—no alignment of authority and personality—but only a submersion of individuality and ambition in a corporate venture and code of conduct that made no allowances for either captain or cook. The paradox of this, however—and the weakness—was that the hostile world of the Antarctic called for a higher degree of individual responsibility than was compatible with the men he had under his command. It was no coincidence that Scott would always be at his best with scientists who only wished to be left to get on with their work, and to expect the same motivation and commitment of a crew who had known no other discipline or education than that of a battleship was in these first months a recipe for near disaster.*

It is a moot point, in the end, whether this intolerance of Scott's was a failure of imagination, of sympathy, or a fear of something he had successfully suppressed in himself, but whichever it was, it inevitably defined the type and limits of the kind of leadership he was able to offer. It would have surprised many of his crew, in fact, if they could have witnessed the thoughtfulness and generosity that surfaced in his private diaries, but in public at least Scott was by training and conviction a leader who pushed himself to the limits, and was not ready to brook anyone who lacked the resolve or stamina to do the same.

---

*There is another side to this that the endless complaints about the "childishness" of the lower deck obscure. Naval officers in South Africa during the Boer War were struck by the superiority of the sailor over the average British soldier, and in some ways the sea ought to have been an ideal training for the ice. There are disproportions of scale—the alarming conjunction of the enclosed and the immense—common to both worlds, but on a more mundane level anyone in a sledging tent who has not mastered those essential shipboard disciplines—dexterity, quickness, the ability to tie a knot that stays tied, to move in confined spaces, to lash and unlash things and lash them all over again—in short, to buckle down to the sheer, unremitting tedium of ship or expedition life with something other than mutinous hostility, is not just useless but an actual menace.

After the "phoney war" of the voyage south he was facing his first real test, and he needed no more warnings of the certain consequences of failure. It would have been expecting too much of Scott for him to have seen that the navy was in part the "problem" and not the "cure," and yet, hamstrung as he was by background and polar tradition, he still had to find the guts and independence of mind to see that the amateurism, institutional complacency and second-hand assumptions that were Markham's lordly bequest to them had no place in the ice.

There are endless moments in Scott's naval career, as in his private life, that seem to illuminate his character with a peculiar sharpness, but it is the death of Vince and its aftermath that first shows his real powers and originality as a leader. A bigger man would have broken with the conventions that shackled *Discovery* in so many ways. But if Scott was not able to see that far, he had the clarity of thought and force of personality—that slow, dogged persistence he would later confess to in a letter to his wife—to make the very best of a deeply flawed system and his own imperfect character. And if this inevitably meant "casualties" among those who fell below the standard he demanded, or the occasional explosion of anger, or the odd ruffled feather in the wardroom, it would also mean the difference between a failing expedition and one of the most successful of all polar ventures. In his obituary notice on Charles Royds, Skelton wrote of his tremendous influence in making *Discovery* the "happy ship" she was. He was right. And yet, as almost everyone on board knew, if the harmony of the wardroom was largely down to Royds and Wilson, it was Scott whose urgent impatience wrenched the expedition back from the edge of disaster to stamp his character and values on everything they would achieve.

And if this was not done with Shackleton's feeling for the outsider, with his ability to touch the imagination of those under him, or his humour, there was little room for those things at the end of their first season in the ice. In some notes on *Discovery* written in his eighties, Clarence Hare contrasted the Scott he remembered smiling at Shackleton's witticisms in the wardroom with the stern disciplinarian the crew knew during this opening year. It is not surprising. With one man dead from drink and another from incompetence, Scott can have found precious little to smile about. It was not just a matter of success or professional pride, but survival, and Scott knew there was no room for indulgence, tolerance or relaxation. "Our autumn sledging was at end," he wrote, "and left me with much food for thought. In one way or another each journey had been a failure; we had lit-

tle or nothing to show for our labours. The errors were patent; food, clothing, everything was wrong, the whole system was bad."

What he needed was time. And as the days began rapidly to shorten,
and the temperatures in late March dropped to −40°, the skuas departed
and *Discovery* was at last frozen hard into her winter quarters, time was
what he was given. The long Antarctic night, the horror of the *Southern
Cross* and *Belgica* expeditions, came to his rescue. As the winter awning
was prepared for *Discovery*'s deck, and the ship readied for darkness, Scott
began to plan for the season ahead. So far, the expedition had been
Markham's: when the sun rose again he was determined it would be
his own.

Ten: Antarctic Night

I have often thought what a remarkable group of men it was that we could live together for 3 years in harmony and without any serious quarrel which I can ever remember. This was partly due, of course, to Captain Scott's leadership.

REGINALD FORD, *16 March 1960*

I turned in about 1 am. What a ridiculous thing it must seem to other people to read a diary where such a statement as "I turned in at 1 am" appears as if they were interested in the time another fellow mortal at the other end of the world went to bed . . . Those sort of items are the penalties that one's friends must pay when struggling to gain a little real information in these reams of paper.

E.H. SHACKLETON, *diary, 14 July 1902*

No one had ever wintered so far south before, and to the last days of autumn the conditions kept Scott and his men guessing. One of the nagging anxieties of their first season had been the state of the ice, and with the ship's boilers let out and the engine dismantled, every rise of temperature or shift of wind during these last brief days was watched with a nervous eye for *Discovery*'s anchorage.

As late as 13 April open water appeared ahead of the ship around Hut Point, but with the ice in their small bay holding firm, preparations for winter accelerated. The bay had taken so much longer to freeze than anyone expected that there was still a lot to do, but with the ice sheet now fast, the meteorological screen was erected to the stern of the ship, a snowbank built at the ice foot to make a road to the huts, and *Discovery*'s boats hauled over towards the ice foot, where, Scott optimistically wrote in his diary, "it is to be hoped, they will remain safely during the winter."

As things transpired it was an idle hope—Bernacchi had warned Scott that the weight of snow would sink them, and got an earful for his pains—but by the last short days of autumn their preparations were in place. On

22 April the sun bathed the top of Observation Hill in a "soft pink light" for the last time, and two days later it was gone, leaving *Discovery* to the darkness of the long Antarctic night.

On the mess deck the event was celebrated with an extra ration of Dutch courage, and it would have been odd if Scott had not needed some himself. For good or ill, as he put it, *Discovery* was "now a fixture" nearly five hundred miles south of any point where anyone had previously wintered, and what awaited them was very largely guesswork. They had done, though, everything that could be done to make the ordeal as safe and comfortable as possible. The ship, under her awning of wagoncloth, lay snug in "Winter Quarters Bay." The link with the shore, the Villa Gregory and the magnetic huts, marked out with a ropeway, was secure. The supply of seal, augmented by two culls in April, was enough to guarantee that there would be fresh meat four times a week, and their clothes—whatever problems there had been out sledging—were at least ideal for hibernation.

For a few brief weeks there was even the promise of electric light to lift morale. "The windmill is in full swing," a jubilant Scott crowed on 1 March, technocrat rampant at this victory of science over the horrors of the Antarctic night and Skelton's Jeremiads, "which is a great triumph after all the disparaging remarks that were passed on it. The electric light is certainly a great boon and if our mill continues to behave well there will be no reason to regret the trouble & expense connected with it."

The first fierce "southerly" of the winter did for Scott's dream and temper, but as they settled into winter quarters it was not so much the cold or light deprivation that was their main discomfort, as condensation. "It would be idle to say that we live in complete comfort below," Scott conceded six weeks into the darkness—quickly adding, with that note of puritanism that was never far from British polar exploration, that "perhaps it is as well that there should be difficulties to overcome . . . We have several weak places as regards damp and cold; the mess-deck is the best part of the ship; except for a little damp there is not much to complain of; but the wardroom in general, and the after cabins in particular are not so happily situated."

At the root of the problem was the fact that while the upper deck was lined with asbestos, the ship's sides had been left unlined. Once the heavy May gales had banked up snow around her conditions improved, but for these first weeks life in the cabins for the officers was a misery, with ice accumulating around the bolts and freezing their mattresses to the ship's side in a hard, spiky mass. At the end of Scott's cabin, where the asbestos lining had slipped behind the iron bulkhead, was a solid block of ice, but the worst problems came from the floors. The conditions for the men were not so bad, but before the ship had reached the south the caulking had fallen from the wardroom deck, leaving only a strip of linoleum to insulate them from the bunker below, and reducing Scott to sitting at his desk with his feet in a box of hay.

If it was not the ice, it was the thaw; if it was not the constant drip of water, it was the back-draught from their stoves; but for all the physical discomforts, the first months of winter passed with an ease that surprised them all. There was the occasional *froideur* over bridge or chess, that invariably involved Scott and the touchily humourless Koettlitz, but the very formality of naval life exerted its own civilising restraint.

This was certainly true of the mess deck, where the vestigial traces of man-o'-war life imposed a discipline and structure on the unchanging weeks, but in its different way it was just as important in the wardroom. "The traditions of the naval service," wrote Bernacchi—the one man in the party in any real position to judge—"which in some things might have proved a disadvantage, in the trivialities of day to day living, were of infinite benefit. It was the wardroom regulation that each member took his turn as President of the mess. Installed at the head of the table, and invested with a little wooden mallet, he was charged with the duty of keeping order between the grace—'Thank God' with which our dinner started, and the drinking of the King's health. No betting was allowed, nor any suggestion of a mild oath, and if anyone offended the gavel fell, and the President pronounced his sentence, usually a fine . . . in the form of a round . . . I remember on one occasion fining Shackleton five times during one meal, for offering to bet that someone was wrong. Payment for many rounds of port made opinion open to modification."

There were also debates to vary the routine—Tennyson v. Browning (Tennyson won), spiritualism (Royds superstitious, Shackleton downright *wet*), women's rights (Hodgson against), sport (Hodgson again against—he presciently thought England football matches "simply an exhibition of drunkenness")—and in the second half of the winter a series of lectures for both messes.* The more earnest performers at these would invariably find

---

*There was no shortage of more informal arguments, either. On 4 June Royds recorded a wardroom debate over whether it would be better to lose an arm or a nose. Armitage, Barne and Skelton were strongly in favour of sacrificing the nose. Royds, characteristically, would rather have lost an arm.

themselves at the mercy of Shackleton's "unruly gang," but if "debate" tended to create more disruption than light, there was always some excuse to reconcile the warring factions—the "Glorious First" to be celebrated, the Duke of York's birthday, "Skipper's birthday," the anniversary of *Discovery's* sailing, or the May Day concert in the Villa Gregory. "This is Victoria Day," Shackleton noted on 24 May, loyalty or wine getting the better of his logic for the moment, "and the late Queen's health was drunk— or rather the memory of the late Queen was drunk by the whole ship's company."

Shackleton was also editor of the *South Polar Times*, *Discovery's* version of the "School Mag"—and just about as interesting—so beloved of British polar expeditions, but all the officers still had their work to keep them busy. The brunt of the scientific observations fell as before on Royds and Bernacchi, but with Scott refusing to pull rank and duck out of his share, not even Koettlitz or Armitage—the two old "Arctics" in the party and notoriously the idlest—could escape the brutal night rounds of anemometer, thermometers and barometer that the whole wardroom did in rotation.* "I have been reading 'Through the first Antarctic Night' by Dr. F.A. Cook," Royds noted in the middle of June, pride and prejudice neatly balanced as he compared *Discovery's* regime with that in *Belgica*, "and have been thoroughly disgusted with it . . . To begin with, what sort of men can they be, who sit and cry over the thought of 'sweethearts' far away, who brood over their solitude, who imagine every sickness possible to these regions, who grow their hair long because they are too tired to cut it, and one hundred and one things they did, which an ordinary man in the same circumstances wouldn't have thought of doing . . . could anything be more hopeless; and simply because—to my mind—a little strength of mind was wanting; just a little will to fight against despondence, and a lack of moral courage to appear happy and contented when they were not—I remember in Uncle Wye's journal he used to talk about the mood of the WR in barometric terms, and at one time I thought of doing it here, but I

---

*Even with a ropeway connecting *Discovery* to the huts, this could be dangerous in winter conditions. On one occasion Bernacchi and Skelton were lost for two hours in a blizzard, stumbling blindly around between ship and shore, unable to see *Discovery* even when in virtual touching distance of her. In a second incident, late at night and before the ship was firmly iced in, Royds fell into the sea while scrambling up a grating lashed to the ship's side. With the water temperature only 29°F, the air zero, no one to hear him and weighed down by boots and coat, he swam the length of the ship until he reached the stern, hauled himself up a ladder, swung himself over the side and eventually appeared in the wardroom, "clothes dripping and his teeth chattering." Very "girlish."

have as yet never had to bring the barometer to any low level, and it would have been somewhat monotonous to be always saying 'A high barometer' sometimes varied with 'A very high barometer.'"

A particularly fetching performance by the young Gilbert Scott as "a really awfully pretty servant girl" at the mid-winter concert might have had something to do with Royds's spirits, but not even the other Scott was immune. "Taking one thing with another," he had written the night before, when, with the whole ship *en fête*, mid-winter day had ended with a wardroom dinner of turtle, soup, mutton, puddings, jellies and mince pies washed down with champagne, port, liqueurs, speeches and—Scott noted with a mix of embarrassment and pleasure—"much unmerited praise, though one rather hates being sung at as 'jolly good fellow' and it's rather trying when all hands insist on doing it a second time, yet it is very gratifying to feel we are all pulling together and to know that people really mean what they say—come what may the present moment finds us as happy & contented a ship's company as ever wintered within the polar circles and the prospects are entirely hopeful."

In the early hours, officers and men all went out to "cool brows." Save for the crack of ice on the invisible rise and fall of the tide, McMurdo was as "still as the grave." It was a scene that Scott never tired of, calm and clear, with "a full moon, high in the heavens," flooding "the snow with its white, pure light. Overhead," he wrote, "a myriad stars irradiated the heavens," and "the pale shafts of the *aurora australis* grew and waned in the southern sky. It was sacrilege to disturb a scene of such placid beauty, but for man it was a night of frolic, and as the dogs quickly caught the infection, the silence was soon broken by a chorus of shouts and barking which continued long after the bare ears and fingers should have warned their possessors that the temperature was nearly into the minus thirties."

The sense of well-being was not all drink—the doctors' monthly examinations bore that out—but not even the beauty of McMurdo, or moonlit football or golf with red balls until the club shafts snapped in the cold, could disguise the fact that *Discovery* was a prison. "The idea that we could get . . . sick of one another is foolish," Shackleton could still write at the end of June, but as the winter dragged on, and the habitual cry of "Girls, girls," no longer seemed enough to put an end to wardroom frictions, the Antarctic night began to look less of the "fraud" that Shackleton had so confidently denounced.

"Say what you like," Royds wrote, "the absence of the sun has, and must have, a depressing effect on the best of men." The caricatures in the *South*

Polar Times seemed less funny to the victims. The weekly debates—raucous, opinionated, but invariably good-humoured—sometimes now took on a new and surrogate edge. "If one couldn't work and hadn't more than one can get through, this life would be quite unbearable," Wilson wrote in mid-August. "Men don't improve when they live together alone, cut off from all the better half of humanity that encourages decency and kindliness. Some of our mess have quite dropped the mask and are not so attractive in their true colouring."

"Scott came into breakfast and told hands that he had heard every word of conversation," Royds wrote after one terminally acrimonious evening's bridge, "and so the barometer is decidedly low and has been all day, and although we played our usual game in the evening, he wouldn't join. I'm afraid this is just the time when one wants to curb the hasty word more than ever, as a thoughtless word or act would cause a lot of trouble and one can't be too careful. After the sledging everyone will be as right as rain, but up to that time tempers will be most uncertain and not to be played with."

It was not surprising that Scott was as often as not at the bottom of these barometric readings, because it would be hard to imagine anyone less suited to the boredom of confinement. Lying in bed one night, Barne thought he had been struck down by an attack of *Polar melancholis*, but it was only poor Royds's clock, maniacally striking eighty-four times on the hour after he had taken it to Scott to mend because it was running slow. Scott could not bear *anything* running slow, and with nothing running slower than an Antarctic night, inaction was a misery. "The Captain spoke up at once very strongly," an exasperated Royds wrote after another dose of Scott's impatience; "it was rather abrupt, and once more only shows to others what a 1st Lt's work is, that is if there is one of that class in this ship. I wonder if the rest of the mess think that it is the usual thing in a man of war . . . The Captain I know did it quite unthinkingly, as he had me in and explained afterwards . . . which point I quite see, but can't help thinking it might have been put differently. It was thoughtless of me to have said it at breakfast, as one is never quite certain how the land lies with the Captain until that meal is well over."

But if, "like all human beings," as Ford put it, Scott "had some failings . . . these were nothing when placed alongside all his good points," and Royds would have been the first to agree. For all the occasional bruised *amour propre* in the wardroom, there was a genuine affection and admiration that Scott never lost, and even on the mess deck the occasional outburst was little more than water off a duck's back to seamen and Dundee whalers used to a good deal worse. "My first job every day," Clarence Hare, their young New Zealand steward, recalled in a portrait of Scott during this first winter that nicely captures the easy-going way in which the ship took the rough and the smooth of their skipper's character,

> was waking the Captain in the morning with "Captain Scott Sir; your bath is ready" . . . the water I heated from melting ice, & this often caused trouble with the cook when I wanted space on the galley stove. The Skipper was a very clean living man, & shaved every morning before breakfast. I got on very well with him and he appreciated any extra attention I could do for him. He would not let me wash his clothes, he said every man should do his own & keep them clean . . . When he was writing in his day cabin, his pipe was always going. He told me I should not smoke as it would stop my growth at my age . . . at the dinner table, he ate whatever was put in front of him, always with many thanks. He was rather absent minded & one time I remember he poured milk on a plate of curry & was just going to sugar it when I quickly changed with another plate. I would not say Capt Scott was a bad tempered man in the ordinary sense of the word. He was over sensitive and got worked up if things did not go as planned. Being used to having his orders obeyed at the double in navy ships, the easy going responses of the merchant shipping men was the cause for what was called temper. Normally his expression was pleasant & he had a very happy smile when pleased.

Royds had been right, too: all that Scott or any of them needed was activity — and *light*. Throughout the winter Scott had been "the moving spirit" in every experiment and wardroom debate, but it was the coming sledging season and their own colossal ignorance of the task in front of them or the precedents behind them that absorbed his every free moment. "I find time also to read up Arctic literature," he confessed in the middle of July, "of which I am woefully ignorant; most unfortunately, our library is deficient in this respect, as owing to the hurry of our departure many important books were omitted. We have Greely, Payer, Nares, Markham, McClintock, McDougall, Scoresby, Nansen's 'Greenland,' and a few others . . . but, sad to relate, Nordeskjold, Nansen ('Farthest North'), and Peary are absent, and two of these at least would have been amongst our most valuable books of reference."

It might seem rather late in the day for the leader of a national expedition to be doing his polar reading, but that was hardly Scott's fault, and with instructions to draft, diets to calculate and logistics to be worked out, he threw himself into it with the same energy that he had shown in London. "I had a long yarn with the Skipper about sledging"—it was invariably "Skipper" when Skelton was pleased with Scott, "Captain" when not—his engineer wrote towards the end of August; "he has very fairly sound practical ideas on the matter—I had hardly any ideas to give him."

The key problem that faced Scott in his sledging calculations was the balance of food and weight, and with nutritional science in its infancy, the impact of extremes of cold on the body imperfectly understood, the variable effects of altitude unknown, and even the causes of scurvy—the great horror of the Nares expedition—still a mystery, it was no easy task. In Arctic conditions McClintock had allowed for forty-two ounces of food per day per man, Nares forty, Greeley thirty-six, Parry—for far shorter periods—only twenty-two. By these standards Scott's eventual figures were on the parsimonious side of average—biscuit 12.0 ounces, oatmeal 1.5, pemmican 7.6, Red Ration 1.1, Plasmon 2.0, pea flour 1.5, cheese 2.0, chocolate 1.1, cocoa 0.7, sugar 3.8*—a total in all, excluding the twelve ounces of tea, eight ounces of onion powder, four ounces of pepper and four ounces of salt allowed to each tent each week, of 33.3 ounces per day per man.

The figures Scott was planning for the first season were actually lower than this—and that 33.3 ounces masks only twenty-nine ounces of concentrated food—but the balance was as crucial as the quantities. It was already "pretty generally known," as Scott put it, that "ordinary food" could "be placed under three headings," but by the light of contemporary knowledge the balance of proteins, fats and carbohydrates that made up his diet was inefficient—like Nansen's on his Greenland crossing, too much protein (over 30 per cent, or three times the modern ideal) and not enough fats (15 per cent, or just half of what is required.)

That could only be found out the hard way, however, and with a new season approaching, and Scott at his desk, feet in his box of hay as he mulled over figures and calculated sledging weights, something of his sense of urgency and expectancy began to percolate down through the whole ship. "The Capt called me in for a talk," Wilson wrote in his jour-

---

*Red Ration was a "nondescript compound of bacon and pea flour" of uncertain food value, but taken because it was starchy enough to thicken their nightly soup and "make it a mixture which, as the sailors said, 'stuck to your ribs.' " Plasmon was an extract of soluble milk proteins.

nal, after Scott had mapped out the coming season's sledging plans to his officers,

> . . . then the Skipper told me he had taken the long journey towards the South Pole for himself, and had decided that to get a long way south the party must be a small one . . . Would I go with him? My surprise can be guessed. It was rather too good a thing to be true it seemed to me. Of course I reminded him that I hadn't got a clear bill of health and that if either of two broke down on a three months sledge journey it would mean that neither would get back. He said some nice things and also that he didn't feel more certain of himself than he did of me and that he had quite decided to take me if I would go.
>
> I then argued for three men rather than two. "Who then was to be the third?" he said. So I told him it wasn't for me to suggest anyone. He then said, he need hardly have asked me because he knew who I would say, and added that as a matter of fact he was the man he would have chosen himself. So then I knew it was Shackleton; and I told him it was Shackleton's one ambition to go on the southern journey. So it was settled and we three are to go . . . we are quite determined to do a big distance towards the South Pole.

"I was called into the Captain's Cabin this morning," Shackleton wrote the following day, "and overjoyed to hear that he has selected me with Wilson to go on the long South Journey with him in the Springtime . . . The Captain tells me that I am not to talk about the Southern Journey yet as it is private, and we have to be examined very carefully for our health."

It was enough to make up for any winter privation, and it was not only Shackleton who was pleased at the thought of action. "This is to be a big job," the normally disgruntled Duncan proudly wrote on 22 August, after Scott had briefed the lower deck on the coming season; "it will be mountainious work."

By the time Duncan was writing, the worst was behind them. They had come through their first winter intact. The party's health was good, and the one man who had shown any signs of mental stress, a hypochondriacal seaman called Smythe, much better for some thoughtful handling by Scott. The weekly inspections and Sunday battleship routines were no more now than a faintly comic memory, the occasional grouse more a matter of self-respect than anything else. On 22 August Shackleton and Scott climbed up to the top of Crater Hill, a thousand feet above their hut, and saw, for the first time in almost exactly four months, the sun. "For long," Scott wrote, the occasion getting the better of his prose, "our blinking eyes remained fixed on that golden ball and on the fiery rack of its reflection; we seemed to bathe in that brilliant flood of light, and from its flashing rays to drink in new life, new strength, and new hope."

"Old Jamaica," Williamson more pithily noted, was back. "I must say," he wrote, "it looked lovely, it was a tremendous size & almost bloodred."

Eleven: Man Proposeth . . . God Disposeth

Nothing could be more promising for good travelling to the south but it is easy to imagine the coming monotony of such a journey.

SCOTT, *diary, 30 September 1902*

At the heart of Scott's plans for their first full season were two main goals: the southern exploration of the Great Barrier, and the discovery of a western route through the mountains and to the Magnetic Pole. When Scott had first outlined these aims six months earlier he had seen them in two distinct phases, with the Southern Party setting off in the first half of the season, and the second expedition, under the command of Armitage, being landed two hundred miles to the north at Wood Bay by the relief ship some time in late December or early January.

With their greater experience of ice and weather conditions, a winter to think it over, and doubts about the feasibility of Wood Bay as a starting base, Scott realised that this original plan needed modifying. By the end of August they were calculating that Markham's relief ship would probably arrive sometime in January, and as their own experience of March sledging had shown just how short a season they had in front of them, it was clear that Armitage needed to start earlier and find another route into the mountains.

Before either of the major objectives could be attacked, however, there were reconnaissances to be made, trials to be carried out, and all the new modifications in clothing and equipment to be tested. For all his winter planning, Scott was under no illusion that they had mastered the problems of sledging, and impatient as ever — "& determined to start off at all costs," as that great connoisseur of his shortcomings, Hodgson, wearily recorded — Scott set off into a near blizzard on 2 September to conduct the dog trials essential to his plans for their Southern Journey.

He began the short journey towards Turtle Rock with four separate dog teams and sledges, but while the teams went well enough so long as they were kept apart, all hell broke loose the moment they could get at each other. "In a moment there was a writhing mass of fur and teeth," Scott wrote, "and almost inextricable confusion of dog traces. Even in the short interval that elapsed before the drivers were amongst them, beating right and left, it was possible to see that the code was observed; each dog confined his attentions to the 'enemy,' and did not attempt to attack his comrades. It was rather surprising to find even this amount of honour among such unscrupulous creatures."

If nothing else, the experience resolved the question of large versus small teams that they had debated over the winter, and with the dogs rearranged into two teams, and the sledges pulled in line astern, the rest of the journey passed off without incident. "Even in this short trip of four days," Scott decided, making the best of a thoroughly incompetent job, "we had gained some experience. There were evidently good reasons for not dividing the dogs into small teams. We had also learnt to distinguish between the strong and the weak, and, what was of more importance, the willing and the lazy; and we saw that we should require a good deal of alteration in our harness and in some of the fittings of our sledges."

While Scott was busy with these trials, Armitage had taken out another party onto the Barrier, and five days later Royds set out on a south-westerly reconnaissance of the approaches to the interior of Victoria Land. "Royds and Koettlitz started away today with Evans, Quartley, Lashly and Wild," Scott noted with some relief on the tenth. "The party looked very workmanlike, and one could see at a glance the vast improvement that had been made since last year. The sledges were uniformly packed. Everything was in its right place and ready to hand . . . One shudders now to think of the slovenly manner in which we conducted things last autumn; at any rate, here is a first result of the care and attention of the winter."

Both the navigator and the puritan in Scott were appeased, too, when the sledge-meters that Skelton had cobbled together over the winter proved their efficiency. "Against our sledging records," he wrote in his journal on the same day, "will stand the sledgemeters with their deadly accuracy. Dead reckoning may be honestly undertaken but it is human nature to err on the one side . . . our parties will be able to claim no more than their small instruments."

In spite of some real improvements, however, the old "childishness" in the men that Wilson and Shackleton had both complained of was no better, and the return of Royds's party within two days—minus Lashly's lost sleeping bag—was a severe jolt to confidence. The "party much done up by heavy travelling," Scott wrote in his journal. "His men have had a great lesson but there is no doubt men cannot face these hard conditions like the officers. Even his party, the best of our people, gave him anxiety at critical times; they don't seem to know how to look after themselves in small ways."

Long before *Discovery* left the Antarctic, Scott would gratefully revise this opinion, and he did not have to wait long to learn that the lower deck had no monopoly on carelessness. The weather had kept him shipbound for a week after the dog trials, but on the morning of 17 September he was finally ready to set out on his own southern reconnaissance, taking with him Shackleton, Barne and thirteen dogs to haul the five hundred pounds of provisions they intended to depot.

After the enforced idleness of winter neither he nor Shackleton was as fit as he might have been, and by the time they had camped that first night they were both done in. In their exhaustion they forgot to pile up enough snow on the skirting of the tent to keep it secure through the night, and the next morning a bewildered Scott awoke to find himself in the middle of a white drift of snow, with not a sign of tent or companions to be seen. There was a violent gale raging, with the air thick with blinding snow, but eventually he made out the outline of the tent flapping wildly over the foot of his sleeping bag. Wriggling in his bag towards it, he succeeded in pulling himself under the billowing canvas, only to find that things inside were as bad as they were out, the tent filled with whirling snow and Shackleton and Barne covered in white where they lay struggling in their bags.

The tent itself was now threatening to take off, and all the three could do was cling on to the skirting, and with frozen fingers try to pull it down until they could half-sit on it and half-clutch it against the wind. In these conditions there was no question of letting go for even a moment, but time and again for all their efforts the skirt would work its way out from underneath them, flapping madly until they could again grab it with slush-filled mitts or bare hands and haul themselves back on top of it.

"Without exception this was the most miserable day I have ever spent," Scott wrote, and for hour after hour they clung on, shouting their warnings of frostbite above the noise of the gale. "An inspection . . . showed that we had all been pretty badly frost-bitten," Scott wrote, when after six o'clock that night they had at last managed to secure the tent well enough to take stock of their woes, "but the worst was poor Barne, whose fingers have never recovered from the accident of last year, when he so nearly lost them. To have hung on to the tent through all those hours must have been positive agony, yet he never uttered a word of complaint."

Wriggling deeper into their icily sodden bags, with the snow piled up inside the tent around them, they lay stoically waiting in the growing darkness for the blizzard to blow itself out. The one consolation through all this had been the thought that their dogs would at least be comfortable enough under the drift, but they were just about to feed themselves some cold pemmican and chocolate when there was a "sad whimpering" at the tent door, and a shivering "Brownie," "whining piteously with cramp," had to be let in to share their shelter and food.

With the temperature at −50°, their sleeping bags and clothes solid with ice, and just one meal in thirty hours, they decided the next morning to return to the ship and dry out before setting off again. After "a grand hot meal of cocoa and pemmican" they collected their scattered belongings, roused the rest of the dogs from the "soft nests" in which they had slept out the storm, and, with a rising sun bathing the western mountains a soft pink, began the stiff, miserable march back towards Hut Point.

Given his subsequent reputation, and his hatred of being beaten, it is curious to find Scott giving up so tamely, and it did not pass unnoticed on their return to the ship. "Shackleton and Barne had got several frost-bites," Skelton noted censoriously in his journal that same night, "& it seems to have been the former who was so keen on returning;—one can't tell of course, but it doesn't seem a very creditable thing returning—looks rather like a lack of determination."

It is the voice of the court that sent Admiral Byng to his death, and the fact that it comes out of the mouth of the engineering branch only gives an added finality to those "gallant, uncompromising, uncerebral imperatives" that underpinned the code *Discovery*'s naval officers lived by. There can be no doubt that Scott would have hated giving up every bit as much as

Skelton himself would have done, but if there was any friction out on the Barrier, or suspicions—as Skelton's and Hodgson's diaries both suggest—over Shackleton's resolve, other codes made sure that the Barrier was where they remained. "So here we are," a philosophical Scott wrote that evening, "having accomplished nothing except the acquisition of wisdom." "It will," he added, without any attempt to shift the blame, "certainly be a very long time before I go to sleep again in a tent which is not properly secured."

It was not as if the Barrier was not dangerous enough without the complicity of the sledging parties, as they were reminded again ten days later. The state of his hands had kept Barne to the ship on their return, and when Scott set out again on the twenty-fourth to complete the reconnaissance and depot supplies, he had with him in Barne's place the boatswain Feather. "The latter has been working so splendidly all through," Scott wrote the day before they set out, generous as always in his assessment of his warrant officers, "and has taken such a keen interest in every detail of the sledging, that I am glad to give him the chance of accompanying us."

Scott's route was to take them between White and Black Islands, and to establish before the main Southern Journey whether the most direct path to the Bluff and the Barrier beyond was in fact practical. By the twenty-sixth they had climbed the stiff slope between the two islands and were down again on the other side, and the next morning were in among a chaos of "torn and twisted" ice, surrounded on all sides by bewildering ranges of blue-ice hummocks set in a sea of ice ridges or "sastrugi."

The dogs hated the going, but next morning they were away again by 7 a.m., marching into wind and drift across the heavily crevassed ice. It seemed that in the hollows at least the snow might be deep enough to bear their weight, and with Scott taking the lead, and the two teams tracing his every twist and turn, they made their tortuous way forward, trusting to their eyes and luck to avoid the hidden crevasses and fragile snow bridges. "In this manner," he wrote, "we proceeded for some time, but suddenly I heard a shout behind, and looking round, to my horror saw that the boatswain had disappeared; there stood the dog team and sledges, but no leader. I hurried back and saw that the traces disappeared down a formidable crevasse, and to my relief the boatswain was at the end of the trace. I soon pulled him up and inquired if he was hurt, to which, being a man of few words, his only reply was 'D—n the dog!' from which I gathered that 'Nigger' had cut a corner . . . This evening the boatswain has shown me his harness; one strand was cut clear through where it fell across the ice-edge. Altogether he had a pretty close call."

It seems astonishing after this warning that they still did not rope themselves together, and it took a second brush with the inside of a crevasse to inject the first note of caution into the march. Looking back on the day, Scott himself was ready to concede the "extreme rashness" of the whole business, and yet as ever in his leadership the flaws and strengths are mixed, the risk-taking part and parcel of a daring that set the tone of every journey he took. There is no doubt that Scott's men responded to this—it was Feather who had himself lowered down the second crevasse to unpack the sledge—and Shackleton and the boatswain would no more have thought of turning back than Scott himself.

In a worsening light that distorted and amplified the landscape, they pushed on in a zig-zag course, marching first east until they had cleared the crevasses and then south, before pitching tent at lunch some ten miles east of the end of the Bluff. Behind them to the north lay those islands and foothills that they had spent the winter gazing on, wondering what lay beyond. Now, for the first time, they could see. To the west of where they were camped, "the Bluff ended abruptly, being but a long peninsula thrust out into the great ice-sheet. Beyond the Bluff our eyes rested searchingly on the new country that rose above our snow horizon. It seemed to stretch in isolated masses ever increasing in detail; but beyond the fact that the coast curves sharply away to the west we could make little of it. But the most impressive fact of all was that from this new western land through the south, through the east, and away to the slopes of Terror, there stretched an unbroken horizon line, and as the eye ranged through this immense arc and met nothing but the level snow-carpet below and the cloudless sky above, one seemed to realise an almost limitless possibility to the extent of the great snow-plain on which we travel."

There were errors implicit in this that would have important consequences for both Armitage's party and for future Barrier exploration, but for the time being the only thing that mattered was the safe depoting of supplies. They had hoped originally that they might find land to mark the spot, but with nothing but the featureless snow-plain of the Barrier around them, they settled instead for a point at which a sharp crater at the end of the bluff stood in perfect alignment with the cone of Mount Discovery. A hundred yards to either side and the alignment was disturbed, and so the next morning, eight miles south-east of the end of the Bluff, they deposited six weeks' worth of provisions and 150 pounds of dog food and marked them with a large black flag. With a last curious gaze on their future route to the south, Scott and his party turned again to the north, and aided by the enthusiasm of the dogs for a homeward trip, set off "for all their worth."

It took them less than three days to complete the sixty-seven miles back, and on 3 October they were again in *Discovery*, the job done, with a degree of satisfaction that Scott rarely allowed himself. "I did not realise that the ship could be such a delightful place as I have found it tonight," he wrote that evening, experiencing for the first time that almost euphoric relief that was always the constant counterpoint of his sledging life; "the sense of having done what one wanted to do, and the knowledge that we have a far clearer problem before us to the south, have much to do with one's feelings of satisfaction, but it is the actual physical comfort of everything that affects one most; a bath and a change into warm, dry clothing have worked wonders . . . but the greatest delight of all is to possess the sledging appetite in the midst of plenty."

As he sat down to his meal in the wardroom that night, Scott was right to be satisfied. For the first time since their arrival a sledging party had accomplished what it had set out to do, and if it was as much by luck as good judgement that no one was injured, they had laid their depot and opened up what looked like a clear route to the Pole. The journey had also produced other, less tangible, rewards. Not only had Scott found his own *métier*, but any lingering doubts there might have been over Shackleton had been answered. In Feather, too, he had received his first instructive glimpse into where the real strengths of the *Discovery* expedition would lie.

His satisfaction, however, did not last long. Scott was too well "pleased with [him]self and the world in general" to take much in, and it was only towards the end of a noisy meal that he realised that something was being held back from him. After dinner he asked his second-in-command into his cabin, and was told the news that Armitage had not planned to break until morning. Scott's calculations, his timetable, everything, were on hold: the expedition had an outbreak of scurvy on its hands. As Wilson had written in his diary when Scott had first unfolded his sledging plans to him during the winter, "*L'homme propose, mais le bon Dieu dispose.*"

Twelve: The Southern Journey

A dread disease its rankling horrors shed,
And death's dire ravage through mine army spread.
Never mine eyes such dreary sights beheld,
Ghastly the mouth and gums enormous swell'd.
And instant, putrified like a dead man's wound,
Poisoned with foetid streams the air around.

LUIS DE CAMOËNS, *The Lusiad*

There was probably no word that carried so much cultural and historic baggage for the seaman of the age of sail as *scurvy*. During the first decade of the new century a lot of work was being done on the disease, but twenty years before the isolation of vitamin C it was still hard for a nineteenth-century naval man brought up on the tribal memories of the service not to feel almost *morally* tainted by its presence in his ship. "We were in the unsatisfactory state of being unable to trace the cause of the evil," a defensive Scott later wrote of this outbreak, his language betraying something of the associations of the disease, "and in that state we still remain, for amongst the various circumstances of our daily life we can find none that definitely contributed to it. The surprise which this unpleasant discovery brought to us has not been lessened by time. We are still unconscious of any element in our surroundings which might have fostered the disease, or of the neglect of any precaution which modern medical science suggests for its prevention."

Behind this prickliness lay centuries of ignorant prejudice and an association in the popular and scientific mind with venereal diseases that time had done little to lessen. The irony of it was that for all practical purposes, science had left Scott in a worse position for combating scurvy than it had his predecessors a hundred years earlier. As early as the 1740s the young Scottish surgeon James Lind had demonstrated the curative powers of lemon juice, but after the virtual elimination of scurvy from Royal Navy ships, a shift from the use of lemon to the less effective West Indian lime had combined with the confusing evidence of polar expeditions to leave Lind and his remedy discredited.

The cause of scurvy is, in fact, a vitamin C deficiency, resulting in an inability of the body to produce collagen, a connective tissue that binds muscle and other structures together. Three years after *Discovery*'s return Axel Holst and Theodor Frolich were close enough to an understanding to demonstrate that scurvy was a dietary problem with a dietary solution, and yet even then prejudice, professional jealousies and institutional resistance—those classic symptoms of scurvy's medical history—meant that there was still nothing like a consensus on its causes. "I understand that scurvy is now believed to be ptomaine poisoning," Scott could still write in 1905, innocently taking his cue from both Nansen and Koettlitz, "caused by the virus of the bacterium of decay in meat, and, in plain language, as long as a man continues to assimilate this poison he is bound to get worse."

The first signs of the disease on Scott's expedition had appeared in Armitage's own party, as they probed the western shore of McMurdo for a way up into the mountains. They had set off from *Discovery* the day after Royds had marched off in the direction of Mount Discovery on a similar mission, but had scarcely done more than scratch at the foot of a possible glacial route before Armitage had been forced to send back Willliam Heald, one of *Discovery*'s redundant balloonists, with an exhausted Hartley Ferrar.

It was only thanks to the young Heald that Ferrar got back to camp at all, and yet even when Heald also began to exhibit signs of exhaustion, Armitage does not seem to have glimpsed what was wrong. "Several men had complained of sprains and bruises which seemed to give pain without much cause," he later told Scott, but if "it seemed curious that such an active officer as Ferrar should have collapsed," he was prepared to put it down to a mere lack of sleep.

By the time they got back to the ship, though, with his men almost incapable of pulling their feather-weight sledges, the symptoms were too obvious to be missed. "The result of Wilson's medical examination of this party has been handed to me," Scott wrote on 4 October, after he had had a night to digest the implications for their season's sledging programme;

"the gist of it is that Heald, Mr. Ferrar and Cross have very badly swollen legs, whilst Heald's are discoloured as well. Heald and Cross have also swollen and spongy gums. The remainder of the party seem fairly well, but not above suspicion. Walker's ankles are slightly swollen. Of course there is no good blinking our eyes to the fact that this is neither more nor less than scurvy, but whence it came, or why it has come with all the precautions that have been taken, is beyond our ability to explain."

It is hard to know whether Armitage should have spotted the symptoms earlier—and he might well have done if there had not been a faint air of scepticism surrounding "the great Cambridge athlete," Ferrar—but he could not have handled the ensuing crisis any better. On the same day that he returned from his western journey he had called a meeting with Royds and Wilson, and between them they had hammered out a new regime to contain the threat. "Our conclusion was," he wrote in his report for Scott five days later, "1st Fresh meat daily. 2nd A liberal diet in every way. 3rd Every possible means to be taken to ensure warm dry quarters . . ."*

---

*If the reasons were not understood, it was known from both Arctic and Antarctic experience that the best remedy for scurvy was fresh meat, which contains some Vitamin C. Among Sir Clements Markham's papers in the RGS is an undated memorandum that interestingly fleshes out the results of Armitage's initiative. "Prior to September 26th 1902 seal meat was cooked every other day only and then always as steaks," it reads. "From that date until October 11th seal was served once a day at least. After October 11th no tinned meats were issued at all except on feast days and tinned soup every Sunday.

"The attached routine of meals was then, with occasional variation, adhered to.

The Cooking

Owing mainly to its not being made palatable, any form of stewed seal was not eaten. Nearly everybody in the Expedition made their breakfast off porridge, except the mornings when liver formed part of the menu. Liver was always enjoyed.

During the summer 1903–4 the following dishes of seal meat were tried and successfully made. Doubtless in the hands of a skilful cook these would be vastly improved and seal might be made into many other savoury and palatable dishes.

Hashed Rissoles
Hashed aux Petits Pois Stewed
Cutlets & tomato sauce Curried
Seal olives Devilled
Minced on toast Haricot
Hotch Potch

The skuas and penguins were tried roasted, fried, hashed and curried. In each way they were excellent. They were skinned and not plucked.

It was found advisable to lightly roast the seal before stewing, hashing or mincing it. The mode of cooking it was identical with that of beef. The dishes mentioned above, except the curry, were made up from recipes in Mrs. Beeton's Cookery Book. Recipes for the cooking of beef were used for the seal and those for duck and goose for skua and penguin.

Quantity Used

Seal The average number of seal used for food was four or five when all hands were on board

It is hard not to think, in fact, that the outbreak was as much an opportunity as a disaster for Armitage, a chance at last for this gloomy and unhappy man to impose his character on an expedition in which he was feeling increasingly marginalised. The son of a Yorkshire doctor, Albert Borlase Armitage had attended the training ship *Worcester* as a boy, and at the age of thirty-six, and with the explorer's equivalent of a "good war" under his belt in Franz Joseph Land, was on his way to a successful career with the P&O Line when Markham offered him the position of navigator and second-in-command to Scott. "I felt that we would be friends," he recalled of their initial meeting. "I consented to go, even though it was against my better reasoning. Scott had no experience of the work he was undertaking; I had three years knowledge of it. I was to be his adviser, a sort of dry-nurse, and knew enough of human nature to fear the result. I threw my reasoning aside. I will say at once that I never met a more delightful man than Scott to work with during our collaboration in the preparation of all matters in connexion with the expedition."

It is unlikely that Scott would have been willing to be dry-nursed by anyone, and the Mason who initiated him into the Drury Lane Lodge was not the man to fill the role unobtrusively. "We were the greatest friends during that six months and for many months afterwards," Armitage continued, "in spite of the fact that I had not seen eye to eye with him as regards to many things in the conduct of affairs. Athletic, brainy, with a keen quick intelligence, great courage and charming manners, he had not to my mind that magnetic quality which would have made me follow him in all things. This I recognised from the beginning, and put forward certain conditions for Sir Clements Markham and Scott to consider before I signed the agreement. These they consented to. Had they been kept, it would have been well."

The terms of Armitage's appointment, as he remembered them, were to make him "independent" of Scott, "although of course I was under his command. I was to be landed, if possible, with a hut and equipment sufficient for two years, eight men, including one of the surgeons, and a team of dogs. There was to be no restriction put on my sledging . . . On arrival at our Antarctic base Scott implored me to forgo the other conditions,

---

Liver The livers of two full grown seals were sufficient for a meal for all hands.
Skua One skua, roasted, made a meal for two persons. When hashed rather less was required.
Penguin One Adelie penguin made a meal for four or five persons. One Emperor, stewed, was sufficient for a meal for all hands."

although they were quite feasible. He put forward the plea, not only would it cripple his own efforts to a great extent, but that he could not do without me. Naturally I consented to stay with the main party . . . I was necessary at first; later I was an interloper."

There is not a scrap of evidence among surviving records to back up any of this, and for all his doggedness and competence—for all those qualities that should have made him an ideal second-in-command—there was a streak of vanity in Armitage that had baulked from the start at a subordinate role. "Ice navigation is very fascinating work," he later wrote in a revealing, proto-fascist hymn to the Olympian loneliness of power. "Perched aloft, almost at the very summit of the main mast, snugly ensconced in the crow's nest . . . It always seemed to me that I had more absolute control of the ship when I was in that situation than in any other. Beneath me is the ship itself, the whole upper contour sharply and gracefully delineated, and one feels, as it were, quite separated from her, and yet directing her every motion."

It was not as anybody's second-in-command that Armitage saw himself, but as a leader, and a leader in the mould of his two great heroes. "What a wonderful pair of men were Nansen and Peary!" he eulogised. "Together they might have conquered the world. But two such men would never hold together for long; their wills would clash. People often speak about the conceit, the swank, the self-assurance of men whom they secretly envy, but what man ever held others, ever led them, who has not complete faith and belief in himself?"

It was never likely that any man with such a brace of heroes—the one, for all his genius, a transcendent egotist, the other a full-blown megalomaniac—would be impressed with Scott, and he had not been able to hide his sense of superiority. "Armitage made rather a fool of himself," Skelton had noted after one wardroom debate, "& took unfair advantage in his speech to make a covert sneer . . . referring to the Skipper & one or two others as 'Great Experts'—singularly bad taste—but he will of course get 'in the soup' if he does much of that." "The Pilot has been talking 'through his hat' pretty considerably lately . . . Armitage is supposed to be our authority on skiing . . . Armitage is inclined to talk in a very superior way of his knowledge of sledging . . . Armitage is . . . rather inclined to be one who will not take information or points, useful for sledging from anyone else . . ."

Armitage had done all he could to make his sense of isolation a reality, but in the outbreak of scurvy he had his chance of revenge, his opportunity to wrest the expedition from an ignorant and younger naval clique who could not appreciate his worth. He was good at it, too—even Skelton had to concede that—and in the disaffected and unloved he had a natural constituency on which he soon went to work. "I had the cook"—that "wretched specimen of humanity," Brett—"before me," he reported to Scott, "and told him that now that Sledging Parties were going out I desired him to make use of his really important position . . . and I took the liberty of informing him that on his efforts in this direction would depend the return of his bonus."

"Render the daily lives of the Ship's Company as cheerful as possible," Armitage had added as the fourth plank of his reforms, and if Scott was too generous to see the implications of that, no one else on board was. It would not be long before the men would feel the other side of Armitage's character, but for the moment he was in clover. "Service conducted by Armitage," Hodgson noted with satisfaction the Sunday before Scott's return, "who makes a better skipper than the Captain." "During Armitage's regime he has walked into the question of food and it is now a pleasure to eat," he wrote again on 4 October, broadening his attack to embrace another of the recent absentees: "I don't think Shackleton likes the reflection on him as Mess Caterer, but that is his fault."

Old grudges were also coming out. "Shackleton has fairly got blight & is very quiet," Hodgson went on the next day, tossing in for good measure the slight cloud that hung over his performance on the Barrier with Barne and Scott: "Koettlitz has been rubbing it in & it now appears that someone else has had another smack on a different subject. It was on his a/c that the Captain's sledge party was so quick to return. A thorough clear out of the ship begins tomorrow."

If Scott himself noticed this undercurrent there is no sign of it, but after the lingering content on that first evening back from sledging, he was too busy with the problems thrown up by the scurvy to worry about much else. The doctors' examination of the remaining crew had turned up nothing serious, but Scott was taking no chances, and although it could have no practical effect, picked up where Armitage had left off. "We have had a thorough clear out of the holds," he recorded on 15 October, "disinfected the bilges, whitewashed the sides, and generally made them sweet and clean." The clothes and hammocks were the next to be tackled, the bedding aired, the deck-lights cleared to allow in more light, the decks scrubbed, and all the holes and corners cleared out until everything was "as clean as a new pin." "We have got a new ministry officiating with the working of the ship now," Williamson grumbled at the return to the well-known obsessions of Royal Navy life, "the executive officer being away sledging & who before going could afford to let us knock off work at 4 p.m. but now it seems all work & no play & for what reason I'm at a loss to know."

But for all the concerns with health, there was still an expedition to run, and preparations "were pushed on . . . as though no such cloud" hung over *Discovery*. Scott had wisely put back the start of his own Southern Journey to the end of October, but with the body of the crew still in perfect health, there seemed no reason to delay Royds from completing the Cape Crozier "mail drop" he had attempted the previous autumn.

The successful return of Royds's party on 24 October, with the additional news of an Emperor penguin colony at Cape Crozier, freed Scott of his last worry over the relief ship, but it gave Wilson an unexpected problem. He had been as delighted as Shackleton when he was first asked by Scott to go on the Southern Journey, but now that it came to it, the thought of the visual monotony of a featureless and unchanging Barrier, "where we shall see neither beast nor bird, nor life of any kind, nor land, and nothing whatever to sketch," disturbed both the artist and the zoologist in him. But "anyhow," he wrote in his diary the day after Royds's return—a sense of history getting the better of his professional scruples for the moment—"it is *the* long journey and I cannot help being glad I was chosen for it."

And in those last days of October, even with their hopes of the Pole dented by their enforced late start, there was a palpable sense of expectation in *Discovery* that they were on the brink of history. The expedition instructions had sketched out a range of scientific ambitions for the expedition, but there was no one in the ship unaware that the Southern Journey offered the most spectacular opportunities for the kind of geographical advances Markham treasured.

As Scott completed his final preparations and orders, life on board was visibly and noisily geared to the same end, with everything and everyone else relegated to a subsidiary role. When Scott and his depot teams had completed their tasks there would be time to think of Armitage's Western Journey, but until that time *Discovery* life revolved almost exclusively around the demands of the Southern Journey. "His party have only one subject of conversation," an irascible Skelton was already complaining more than a month before the unwieldy southern caravan finally set off: "the sledging of their own party—never a word about any other party—& it is generally carried on in a jocular manner at meals—gets a bit tiring—but perhaps I might be a bit 'livery' — anyhow I have got beastly sick of the subject." Even Skelton in the end was not immune, however, bellicosely hoping for "a good record" for them, or if not that at least for "something impassable so it will be no good for those blooming American record breakers & such like."

Scott had planned to get away with his dogs on 31 October, and on the thirtieth his support party was at last ready, with Barne's swallow-tailed pennant floating above the first of their five sledges, and the lower deck's own ironic commentaries on naval chivalry streaming out on their own home-made flags behind—"No dogs need apply," "Hope on, hope ever," and—a wonderfully prescient inversion of Oates's parting heroics—"Now we shan't be long." "It was an inspiriting sight," Scott wrote, "to see nearly the whole of our small company step out on the march with ringing cheers, and to think that all work of this kind promised to be done as heartily."

That night there was champagne in the wardroom for Scott's party, and after a frustrating day's hold-up from the weather, they finally got away on the morning of 2 November, to the cheers of the ship's company. "Dogs in splendid form, could hardly be held at first," Scott scrawled in pencil in his small, nine-by-five-inch black sledging journal of the Southern Journey— the most compelling and impressive of all the thousands of documents generated by *Discovery*, "but later of course had to be driven & not yet accustomed to voice, the whip was in some request. However we did very well—great enthusiasm at ship all officers & some men accompanying us a considerable distance."

That same evening, fourteen miles off the northern end of White Island, they caught up with the support party, who without the help of dogs had managed no more than a mile an hour. "The difficulty is the slipperiness of the wind-swept snow," Scott noted, "the surface being particularly hard amongst the *sastrugi* opposite the gullies of the island. They can get no hold with their fur boots, and find the leather ski boots dreadfully cold for the feet."

A new, and not altogether convincing, note of patience had crept into Scott's journal since the outbreak of scurvy, and he saw that there was little to be done but put up with the delay. It was clearly going to be impossible to keep the two parties together at their different speeds, and so, relieving Barne of 150 pounds of provisions, they pushed on independently, leapfrogging each other as Scott and his party adjusted ambitions and pace to the performance of their support team. "Very comfortable," Scott noted in his sledge journal, content for the time being with a regime that even gave him room for evening readings from Darwin's *Origin of Species*. "Last night we could scarcely have been more comfortable than we were . . . sledging under such circumstances is scarcely a hardship."

Already, though, there were the first indications from "a persistent and annoying cough" that all might not be well with Shackleton. As early as July, Wilson had harboured his doubts over Shackleton's fitness for the journey, but loyalty had kept him silent. "I feel more equal to it than I feel for Shackleton," he had confessed then; "for some reason I don't think he is fitted for the job. The Captain is strong and hard as a bull-dog, but Shackleton hasn't the legs that the job wants; he is so keen to go, however, that he will carry it through."

He might not have been so confident had he heard Shackleton's night-long fit of coughing three weeks earlier, but the dogs were pulling well when conditions allowed, and a ten-mile run on 10 November brought them safely to their Bluff depot. "The dogs, I find today, will drag 2,100 pounds," Scott wrote in a message for Armitage, sufficiently pleased with their performance to release Barne early to carry out his own independent exploration of the south-west approaches to Victoria Land. "This modifies my plan; I shall send Barne back in two days, going on from that date with twelve weeks provisions, plus 70 pound of seal for our party, and about forty days food for the dogs. We see nothing but a vast white plain to the south, though the weather is quite clear. Barne has done splendidly, and I want to give him all possible aid in his south-west trip which I think should prove most important, as it seems about certain the land must trend north round from the farthest point we see."

Given the state of their knowledge, nothing made more sense, but underlying it was a crucial misreading of the evidence that would have profound consequences for the whole expedition. From the site of Scott's depot it looked as though the farthest visible land was the southernmost extreme of an *island*, but what he could not know—and in sending Barne back early would not find out—was that these delusive land sightings were in fact part of that unbroken continental range that Shackleton would finally see seven years later.

It seems a bitter irony that at that moment, when the three great ambitions they had set themselves—the Southern Journey, the route to the Magnetic Pole, and the exploration of the south-west—all seemed within their grasp, Scott had taken the one decision which effectively scuppered them. "Barne leaves us tomorrow," he wrote again to Armitage, his confidence that Victoria Land was an island stronger than ever. "The land certainly trains west-south-west from the Bluff, ending in a cape from which there is little doubt that it trains north again; but there is no high land behind this coastline, and the western hills form a very distinct ridge with an obvious descent on the opposite side. Whether you will come to barrier level again one cannot say at this distance; but I certainly think it looks as though Victoria Land was very narrow at this end."

It was Wilson's and Scott's old errors compounded, and the irony is only increased by their mounting optimism over the dogs. "If former moments of parting have seemed unpropitious, the same cannot be said of today," Scott wrote the day they said goodbye to the support party in a "Farthest South" of 78°45'. "The sun shone brightly on our last farewells, and whilst behind us we left all in good health and spirits, it is scarcely to be wondered at that our hopes ran high for the future. We are already beyond the utmost limit to which man has attained: each footstep will be a fresh conquest of the great unknown. Confident in ourselves, confident in our dog team, we can but feel elated with the prospect that is before us."

Out on the vast desert of the Barrier, however, "so utterly unlike anything experienced before," it did not take long for the mood of confidence to evaporate. "The day's work has cast a shadow on our highest aspirations," Scott wrote the same day that Barne and the support party that could have propelled him farther south turned back, "and already it is evident that if we are to achieve much it will be only by extreme toil, for the dogs have not pulled well today; possibly it may be something to do with the surface, which seems to get softer, possibly the absence of the men in front to cheer them on, and possibly something to do with the temperature, which rose at one time to +20 and made the heavy pulling very warm work."

With the dogs worse the next morning, there was nothing to do but relay, and yet even the half-loads now seemed beyond them. "A full day," Scott noted, "but we plodded on in the same monotonous style. Starting at 11 a.m., we pushed on two and half miles by our sledge-meter, with half the load, then returned for the second half; the whole operation took about four hours and a half, after which we had lunch and then repeated the same performance. It was 11 p.m. before we were in our sleeping-bags, and at the end of the march the dogs were practically 'done.'"

The next day was even worse, with a gain of only four and three-quarter miles, and even that achieved only at the price of the constant, brutal driving of their "poor animals." "When one goes out in the morning," Scott

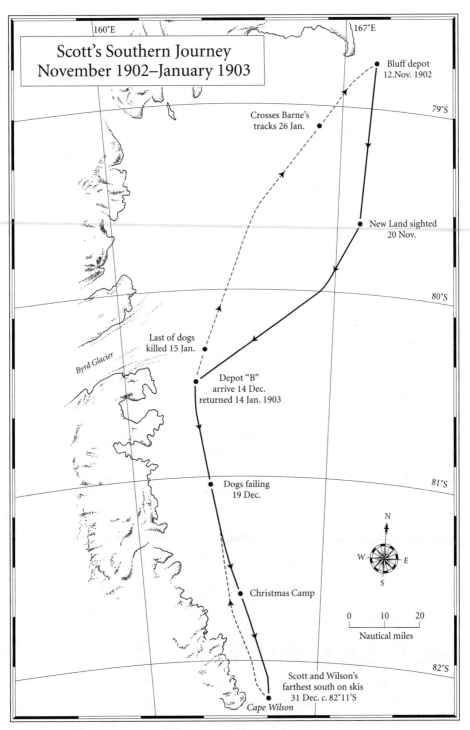

160°E   167°E

Scott's Southern Journey
November 1902–January 1903

Bluff depot
12. Nov. 1902

79°S

Crosses Barne's
tracks 26 Jan.

New Land sighted
20 Nov.

80°S

Last of dogs
killed 15 Jan.

Byrd Glacier

Depot "B"
arrive 14 Dec.
returned 14 Jan. 1903

Dogs failing
19 Dec.

81°S

N

W   E

S

Christmas Camp

0   10   20

Nautical miles

82°S

Scott and Wilson's
farthest south on skis
31 Dec. *c.* 82°11'S

Cape Wilson

wrote, with a plain, almost lapidary quality to the writing that has a strange, dulled eloquence, "there is now no joyous clamour of welcome; one or two of the animals have to be roused out of their nests, then we start in a spiritless fashion. We take our duties in turns; one of us attaches his harness to the head of the trace, and whilst he pulls he endeavours to cheer on the flagging team. A second takes the best position, which is to pull alongside the sledges in silence; the third does not pull, but carries the whip and has to use it all too frequently. Thus our weary caravan winds its slow way along until the sledge-meter has reeled off the required distance. When we halt, the dogs drop at once . . . The afternoon march is of the same nature as that of the forenoon, but is made worse by the increased fatigue of our wretched animals. It is all very heart-breaking work."

It was also becoming difficult to ignore the possibility that at the root of the problem lay the stock fish that in "an evil moment" Scott had allowed Nansen to persuade him into bringing. In his original plan he had intended to use ordinary dog biscuits for the journey, and in the change to the fish no one had thought of first checking the effects on it of a passage through the tropics. "It is easy to be wise after the event," Scott wrote defensively, touchy even three years later at the memory of the horrors this carelessness had inflicted, "but unfortunately for our dogs, this probability escaped our notice, and as there was no outward sign of deterioration it was carried on our sledge journey. As a result the dogs sickened . . . from what one can only suppose was a species of scurvy."

The distant land, too, to which they had turned to make their next depot, taunted them with its apparent closeness. By the twenty-seventh it was still probably fifty miles away, and nine hours' hauling had produced just four miles' progress. "It was my turn to drive today," Scott wrote in a passage filled with a weary mix of fatalism and self-disgust.

> Shackleton led and Wilson pulled at the side. The whole proceedings would have been laughable enough but for the grim sickness that held so tight a grip on our team: Shackleton in front, with harness slung over his shoulder, was bent forward with his whole weight on the trace; in spite of his breathless work, now and again he would raise and half-turn his head in an effort to cheer on the team . . . Behind him, and obviously deaf to these allurements, shambled the long string of depressed animals . . . all by their low-carried heads and trailing tails showing an utter weariness of life. Behind these, again,

came myself with the whip, giving forth one long string of threats and occasionally bringing the lash down with a crack on the snow or across the back of some laggard . . . On the opposite side of the leading sledge was Wilson, pulling away in grim silence . . . This then is the manner in which we have proceeded for nine hours today—entreaties in front and threats behind—and so we went on yesterday, and so we shall go on tomorrow. It is sickening work, but it is the only way; we cannot stop, we cannot go back, we must go on, and there is no alternative but to harden our hearts and drive.

By the middle of December, on a diet that gave them little more than half the calories they were burning, the men were scarcely in better shape. As early as the thirteenth Shackleton was wondering in his diary how much longer they could go on relaying, and the next day they found a site to depot their supplies for the return journey and begin a last "dash for the South." "We have arrived at a place where I think we can depot our dog-food," Scott wrote that night, as close to a "secure" place for their cache as a mountainous jumble of ice and chasms would allow them to get, "and none too soon, I doubt if we could go on another day as we have been going . . . The bearings of our present position are good but distant." The site was anything but ideal, the defining rock patches were twenty or thirty miles away and would be invisible in bad conditions, but with a sixty-foot chasm barring their way and time running out, it had to do. Naming this site Depot "B," they made the camp secure, marked it with "a conspicuous flag," got "excellent cross bearings" to make doubly sure of its position, and prepared to drive on south.

They had pared their supplies and weights down to the absolute minimum for the "dash," rearranged them onto four sledges, and taken just enough food to allow for a few days' leeway at the end to find their depot again. "As I write I scarcely know how to describe the blessed relief it is to be free from our relay work," Scott wrote at the end of a month in which three hundred miles of hauling had produced just 1½ degrees—ninety miles—of latitude. "For one and thirty awful days have we been at it, and whilst I doubt if our human endurance could have stood it much more, I am quite sure the dogs could not. It seems now like a nightmare, which grew more and more terrible towards its end."

Every mile marched now was a mile south, but this was the only consolation they had. Rheumatic pains, brutal headaches, the constant gnawing of hunger, the perpetual strain on the legs and back and lungs—"It would be difficult to convey what marching is like under present conditions," Scott wrote the same day. "The heel of the advanced foot is never planted beyond the toe of the other, and of this small gain with each pace, two or three inches are lost by back-slipping as the weight is brought forward. When we come to any particularly soft patch we do little more than mark time."

For Wilson, in particular, were added the agonies of snow blindness, with its effulgent, almost billowy light, and a pain that can pass from mild irritation to the endless jagging of broken glass. "Wilson spent 3 hours sketching this morning," Scott noted on the eighteenth, "& as a result broke down in the eyes on the march both Shackleton & he are now bad in this respect & my left eye is giving some trouble though I wore goggles." "Wilson's eye giving trouble," Scott noted again, "giving him such pain that I thought it best we camp . . . The eye gave intense pain; he is not at all a demonstrative person but it was too painful even to see such suffering—we had a try at rolling back his lid but it was too swollen—he is using a good deal of cocaine [taken topically] but it only affords relief for a short time . . . poor chap he is having a beastly time."

Beastly or not, it did not stop Wilson painting with the use of only his right eye when his left went, or hauling blind and bandaged in his harness when they had both gone, but by this time hunger had virtually inured the men to any other pain. "We are really hard pressed with hunger," Scott wrote, throwing in almost as a footnote the "burnt and blistered" nostrils and lips, and "chapped and broken fingers" they were all suffering from— "But hunger drowns all other troublous feelings and a hot pemmican or hoosh [their thick sledging "soup"] drives away all other ailments for the time being."

"We are gradually passing from the hungry to the ravenous," he admitted, comforting himself that at least he had his pipe to assuage the hunger; "we cannot drag our thoughts from food . . . The worst times are the later hours of the march and the nights . . . At night one wakes with the most distressing feeling of emptiness, and then to reflect that there are probably four or five hours more before breakfast is positively dreadful." "The talk constantly turns on what we should like & what we shall hope to get," he went on, and Wilson's nights were racked with the same dreams. "Dreams as a rule of splendid food," he noted, "ball suppers, sirloins of beef, cauldrons full of steaming vegetables. But one spends all one's time shouting at waiters who won't bring one a plate of anything, or else one finds the beef is only ashes when one gets it, and a pot full of honey has been poured out on a sawdusty floor."

And just occasionally—"very rarely"—"one gets a feed in one's sleep." "One night I ate the whole of a large cake at Westall," Wilson recalled two months later, "and was horribly ashamed when I realized it had been put there to go in for drawing-room tea, and everyone was asking where it had gone . . . One night Sir David Gill, at the Cape, was examining me in divinity, and I told him I had only just come back from the farthest South and was frightfully hungry, so he got a huge roast sirloin and insisted on filling me up before he examined me."

It was as well that there were dreams to eat in, because on the most frugal diet of any British explorer since Parry—about a pound and a half a day—there was precious little anywhere else. There was tea, pemmican and biscuit for breakfast, and then "Each of us carries a small bag," Scott wrote a few days before Christmas, containing their "small piece of seal-meat, half a biscuit, and eight to ten lumps of sugar which . . . is stowed away in the warmth of a breast-pocket, where it thaws out during the first march . . . Supper is of course the best meal; we then have a *hoosh* which runs from between three-quarters to a whole pannikin apiece, but even at this we cannot afford to make it thick. Whilst it is being heated in the central cooker, cocoa is made in the outer. The lamp is turned out directly the *hoosh* boils, usually from twenty-eight to thirty minutes after it has been lighted; by this time the chill is barely off the contents of the outer cooker, and of course the cocoa is not properly dissolved, but such as it is it is the only drink we can afford."

Even with a diet as meagre as this, it was only Shackleton's invention of "shut eye"—a kind of blind lottery—that prevented the day's cook from cheating himself. That, though, was only typical. As astonishing as any of the miseries of this journey is the spirit with which they were borne. "Wilson is the most indefatigable person," an admiring Scott wrote. "When it is fine and clear at the end of our fatiguing days he will spend two or three hours seated in the door of the tent, sketching every detail of the splendid mountainous coast. His sketches are most astonishingly accurate. I have tested his proportions by actual angular measurements and found them correct."

Wilson was not alone in his powers of observation, and the startling gunshot crack of the ice-crust, the prismatic effects of snow crystals, atmospheric phenomena, a "thistle-down light" carpet of jewels—it does not matter how grim the day, Scott could always find from somewhere the energy to record them as accurately as his "sledging pencil" would allow. "Shortly after four o'clock today we observed the most striking atmospheric phenomenon we have yet seen," he noted. "We were enveloped in a light, thin stratus cloud of small ice-crystals; it could not have extended to any height, as the sun was only lightly veiled. From these drifting crystals above, the sun's rays were reflected in such an extraordinary manner that the whole arch of the heavens was traced with circles and lines of brilliant prismatic or white light. The coloured circles of a bright double halo were touched or intersected by one which ran about us parallel to the horizon; above this, again, a gorgeous prismatic ring encircled the zenith; away from the sun was a white fog-bow, with two bright mock suns where it intersected the horizon circle."

Alongside this intellectual buoyancy went a determination that not even the first suspected symptoms of scurvy in Shackleton could deflect. It had been clear from the dogs' first failure that they would never get the high southern latitude they had hoped for, but with little more than the sad, Pyrrhic victory of the 80th parallel or a sight of the western mountains to keep up morale, they drove themselves on. "Misfortunes never come singly," Scott noted, on the night that Wilson confided in him his fears about Shackleton's condition. "Certainly this is a black night, but things must look blacker yet before we decide to turn."

They were already fifty miles south of the final depot they had put down seven days before, and with nothing more than a few days' safety margin built into their rations, they knew they were near their limit. "We calculate we were pulling about 170 lbs per man," Scott wrote the same day, after they had tried hauling without the dogs. "Either the surface is extraordinarily bad or we are growing weak. It is no use blinding ourselves to facts: we cannot put any further reliance on the dogs. Any day they might give out and leave us entirely dependent on ourselves. In such a case, if things were to remain just as they are, we should have about as much as we could do to get home; on the other hand, will things remain just as they are? It seems reasonable to hope for improvement, we have seen so many changes in the surface."

The hopes of a "dash" were as much ashes as Wilson's sirloin. The previous day's sightings had put them in 81°33's, but each march was now producing grimmer milestones to record their progress. On 19 December "Wolfe" had been killed; on the twentieth "Poor Grannie" died; the next day "Stripes" and "Brownie" were vomiting. Scott's target was the end of the year, the spur, Christmas. "We are looking to our special Xmas dinner tomorrow," he wrote on the twenty-fourth, "& wondering tonight what is going on at home . . . it would be difficult to set down all that it [tomorrow's food] means to us in our present ravenous state."

"A red letter day in all respects," Scott wrote on the twenty-fifth. "The sun bright & warm the sky perfectly clear and the land in full view . . . We have not had such a feast for a long [time] now as lunch for a treat we have reverted for this day only & plasmon hot with biscuit & another spoonful of jam—supper must be described after that meal but we anticipate its delights."

Even the day's marching was easy, and then, after a "Christmas wash & brush up," "supper & such a supper," Scott wrote, as the sun circled their small tent in a cloudless sky and he looked forward to the promise of a dream-free sleep, "that we have not known for many a day. Redolent of soap, we sat around the cooking-pot, whilst into its boiling contents was poured a double 'whack' of everything. In the *hoosh* that followed one could stand one's spoon with ease, and still the primus hissed on, as once again our cocoa was brought to the boiling-point. Meanwhile I had observed Shackleton ferreting about in his bundle, out of which he presently produced a spare sock, and stowed away in the toe of a sock was a small round object about the size of a cricket ball, which when brought to light, proved to be a noble 'plum-pudding.' Another dive into his lucky bag and out came a crumpled piece of artificial holly. Heated in the cocoa, our plum-pudding was soon steaming hot, and stood on the cooker-lid crowned with its decoration . . ."

It was the last peace any of them were to enjoy in forty days. The next day Wilson's eyes were worse than they had ever been. "I have never had such pain before," he wrote. "The Captain and Shackle did everything for me—nothing could have been nicer than the way I was treated." "From start to finish I went blindfold," he recorded on the twenty-seventh; "luckily the surface was smooth, and I only fell twice. I had the strangest thoughts or daydreams as I went along. Sometimes I was in beech-woods, sometimes in fir-woods; sometimes in Birdlip woods . . . and the swish-swish of the ski was as though brushing through dead leaves, or cranberry undergrowth, or heather or juicy bluebells—could almost see and smell them . . . It was delightful."

Nowhere on the planet could have been less like Birdlip Woods. The last living thing they had encountered was a solitary skua, conjured out of nowhere when they had butchered Snatcher over two weeks before. The grim slaughter of their dogs continued to mark their slow progress south across the white plain. "Shackleton is butcher tonight," Scott had written on the twenty-sixth, "and Brownie the victim poor little dog." No one could hate what they were doing more. Nigger, Jim, Spud, Snatcher, Fitz-Clarence, Stripes, Birdie, Nell, Blanco, Grannie, Lewis, Gus, Joe—born at Cape Adare, on Borchgrevink's trip, and contentedly domesticated in London drawing rooms before coming south again with Bernacchi—Wolfe, Vic, Bismarck, Kid, Boss and Brownie, "charming as a pet, but . . . a little too refined and ladylike for the hardest work"—Scott lists them all, a kind of canine Agincourt Roll of those who died or were butchered, as Hodgson tartly put it, in the cause of science.

But if "science" had had little to applaud so far, new sightings of land were adding a growing hope that their journey might not end in a whimper. With faces "burnt black & very sore in the chilly winds," and their Christmas food a receding memory, they edged over the 82nd parallel. Wilson, eyes bandaged, could not see the vistas that were opening up, but Scott acted as his guide. On the twenty-sixth he had noticed that they were approaching a "deeper bay than usual," and the following day, as they altered its bearings, this rolled back "like some vast sliding gate, and gradually there stood revealed one of the most glorious mountain scenes we have yet witnessed. Walking opposite to Wilson I was trying to keep him posted with regard to the changes."

With "some excitement" Scott reported new mountain ridges as high as anything they had seen to the north, and "to my surprise, as we advanced the ridges grew still higher, as no doubt did my tones. Then, instead of a downward turn in the distant outline came a steep upward line; Pelion was heaped on Ossa, and it can be imagined that we pressed the pace to see what would happen next, till the end came in a gloriously sharp double peak crowned with a few flecks of cirrus cloud."

The opening in the coastline now seemed more like an inlet than a bay, but all attention that evening was concentrated on the new twin-peaked mountain. It was "a giant among pigmies." Nothing they had seen so far could compare with the "monster." They had at last found, Scott wrote, something grand enough to be named after Sir Clements, "and 'Mount Markham' it shall be called in memory of the father of the expedition."

There could have been no more fitting end to a journey that had embodied everything Markham most prized. As if to symbolise the spirit that had brought them through so much, Wilson was again led bandaged to the sledge to preserve his eye for sketching in case Shackleton's camera

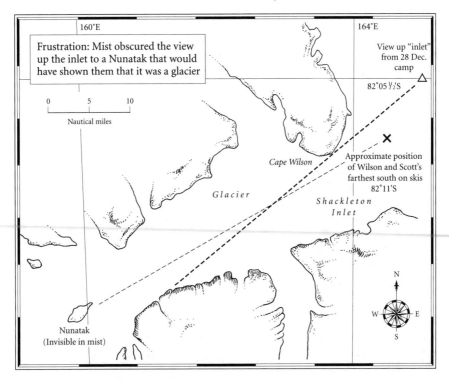

Frustration: Mist obscured the view up the inlet to a Nunatak that would have shown them that it was a glacier

160°E

164°E

View up "inlet" from 28 Dec. camp

82°05 ½'S

0   5   10
Nautical miles

Cape Wilson

✕ Approximate position of Wilson and Scott's farthest south on skis 82°11'S

Glacier

Shackleton Inlet

N
W   E
S

Nunatak
(Invisible in mist)

failed them. "Marched again the whole day with both eyes blindfold," he wrote on the twenty-eighth, "as I want to be able to sketch this new range, the biggest we have met with and the farthest south we shall see . . . My left eye still quite useless, but I got a sketch of the whole grand sight with one eye."

Given the conditions under which he had to work, Wilson's drawing accords wonderfully with Shackleton's photograph. What both miss, though, is the one detail that would have redeemed every misery. It was the old story again. High up in the mist, invisible to them both in the middle of their vast "bay," jutting out above the ice, stood what is now known as the Nunatak. Their "inlet" was a glacier, and the new land they could see to the south not another island but part of the same coastline they had been trudging down for the last two months.

The Antarctic continent had eluded them again. At the end of the march they pitched their "farthest camp," some ten miles from land. Scott reckoned it at 82°11's, but modern maps, correlated with Shackleton's photograph and Wilson's drawing, put them at 82°05½'s, 165°E. After taking angles, sketching and attending to camp duties, they settled into their sleeping bags, hopeful that one last, short dash on ski the next day might resolve the outstanding question of the "inlet."

The next morning, however, a strong southerly blizzard put paid to these plans, keeping them holed up in their tent. "To be idle & hungry is no joke," Scott wrote impatiently, true to himself to the last. Towards night the wind dropped, but the drearily familiar bank of fog that succeeded it only added to their frustration. "Only occasionally to-day have we caught glimpses of the land," he complained, "and it is not inspiriting to lie hour after hour in a sleeping-bag, chill and hungry, and with the knowledge that one is so far from the region of plenty."

At six o'clock the next day they again rose to "thick fog, and nothing in sight." Leaving camp in such conditions was clearly out of the question, so packing their traps, they started out on a south-south-west course, marching for over an hour before the fissured ice towards the land blocked any further progress. After a short lunch, Wilson and Scott continued on skis while Shackleton looked after the dogs, in one last futile hope that the weather would clear. Within a mile or so they had given up. "This camp we have now decided must be our last," Scott wrote, "for we have less than a fortnight's provision to take us back to Depot 'B,' and with the dogs in their present state it would be impossible to make forced marches; we have, therefore, reached our southerly limit. Observations give it as between 82°.16s and 82°.17s; if this compares poorly with our hopes and expectations on leaving the ship, it is a more favourable result than we anticipated when those hopes were first blighted by the failure of the dog-team."

It was cold comfort. "There's something wrong with our bloody system," a baffled Beattie would famously complain at Jutland. Scott beat him to it. He had planned and calculated and measured to the last ounce every mouthful of food, and got it wrong. There were excuses. The fish; the failure of the dogs; the release of Barne; the Barrier surface. But "looking back now," he wrote on their return to England, "the original mistake is evident, and . . . it is clear that we were slowly and surely sapping our energies and reducing ourselves to the condition of our more willing dogs . . . and expending our energies at a greater rate than we were able to renew them with our inadequate supply of food."

All that was left was the grim misery of the journey back and their own courage to get them through it. Invisible in the fog, the Pelion of Mount Markham might have nodded across to the Ossa of Ecclestone Square. As Williamson would have put it for them: "Alls well."

Thirteen: **Survival**

A fool always wants to shorten space and time; a wise man wants to lengthen both.

JOHN RUSKIN —*who had never tried to walk to the South Pole—
quoted with some irony in Wilson's sledging journal, 11 December 1902*

T here is no journey in polar history except Scott's last that has generated as much argument as this first Southern Journey. If one looks at a map of Antarctica and traces on it the faint line of their march, an almost imperceptible scratch across the surface of a floating ice shelf the size of France that never once touches land and left its secrets almost as obscure as it found them, it is hard to see why.

They had unveiled new coastline, named new mountains, and "pushed mankind's knowledge to the 83rd parallel," but one might as well try to survey Switzerland from a fogbound rowing boat in the middle of the English Channel as decode continental Antarctica from the Barrier.* For

---

*It was only with the benefit of another season's experience that Scott was able to make retrospective sense of the geology of the coastline they had seen. "At this time we were all under the impression that these rocks were of the same recent volcanic nature as those about the ship," he later wrote, "but later on, after my visit to the western hills, I came to doubt this belief. It is possible that if at this time we had known more of the structure of the mainland to the north we should have been able to note points of similarity or difference . . . but it is doubtful whether in any case we could have discovered much that was definite at the distance from which we saw it." His hopes of collecting rock samples that would answer their questions on their return journey would be thwarted.

two months Scott and his two companions had marched along the flank of a vast and unbroken chain of mountains that forms the formidable rampart of Antarctica's polar plateau, and at the end of it all they could scarcely be more certain of what they had seen or the geology of the terrain than they would have been if they had sat out the sledging season in *Discovery*.

In technical terms too—as an exercise in polar travelling—the journey demonstrated all the competence one might expect from a Cheltenham doctor, a merchant officer and a torpedo specialist making their first serious venture on ice. There was no prejudice or unwillingness on any of their parts to experiment or learn, but whether they travelled during the day or night, whether they drove the dogs or gave them a lead, used their skis or travelled on foot, they simply lacked the skills and knowledge to overcome their inexperience. "Taken altogether," Scott could write after nine weeks on the Barrier—and this of a method that would enable Amundsen to cover twenty-three miles a day across the same surface without extending himself, "so far, our ski have been of doubtful value, I much doubt if they have got us any further than we could have managed on our own feet."

It is not as though their journey has a monopoly on courage, suffering or selflessness either—the forgotten men of the Ross Sea party on Shackleton's trans-Antarctic venture would outdo them in all three—but in its own grim way there is nothing that matches it. This is in part due to Scott's pen—or sledging pencil—of course, but that is in a sense only another way of recognising just how right Apsley Cherry-Garrard was when he insisted, after a lifetime's brooding on the subject of polar exploration, that the importance of Scott's story lay in "the spirit of the men" rather than in anything "they did or failed to do."

There is another dimension to this Southern Journey, in as much as it led ultimately to the discovery of the Beardmore Glacier and the route to the Pole, but Cherry is still right. At the heart of its successes or failures might lie questions of diet or sledge-runners or dog harnesses, but only a pedant could imagine that these are the real issues at stake, and not mere by-products of the personalities and backgrounds of the men themselves.

This is no soft biographical evasion, because the "Heroic Age" was not called that for nothing, and personality and character went on playing a decisive role in polar exploration long after it had been relegated to the margins of other history. It is inconceivable, for instance, that Shackleton would have gone back to the Antarctic but for this Southern Journey, and that in turn has nothing to do with what they did or did not do or find, and everything to do with what he discovered about *himself*.

And for all three of them, once the misery and the hunger were gone, the lasting legacy of the journey was what they learned of each other. For more than a year they had lived and worked together within the confines of a thirty-by-twenty-foot wardroom, but if any of them imagined that they knew each other, the Barrier and the tent were a revelation. "Sledging draws men into closer companionship than can any other mode of life," Scott himself wrote in an unconsciously autobiographical description. "In its light the fraud must be quickly exposed, but in its light the true man stands out in all his natural strength." In its baldest form that smacks too much of the Markhams for comfort, and yet if it leaves little room for a Ferrar or a Royds—or a slipped disc—it is supremely true of Scott himself. There was probably not a man in the wardroom who had less control over his moods or tongue than Scott, but underneath all the surface unpredictability was that bedrock of integrity and consistency that only fully came out *in extremis*.

It is interesting to pick up on Scott's use of language here, because whatever else he was, whatever his drawbacks as a leader or man, however irascible or impatient he could sometimes be, there was not a trace of anything *fraudulent* in his nature. "What pulled Scott through was character," Cherry would later write of him, "which ran over and under and through his weaker self and clamped it together . . . For him justice was God." Only those who had sledged with Scott could ever really know him, Cherry would say, and if that was not an attractive proposition to everyone, it clearly touched Wilson's imagination in ways which caught him by surprise. From the first days in *Discovery* on their voyage south he had liked and admired his skipper, but it was only during the Southern Journey that he recognised in him the integrity and seriousness of character he demanded of himself.

The admiration was mutual. "Behold, how good & joyful a thing it is: brethren to dwell together in unity!" Scott inscribed in the front of his fourth journal, and if there are times when that seems about as appropriate as Mrs. Thatcher quoting St. Francis from the door of 10 Downing Street, it was undoubtedly his sledging ideal. Sledging is "a sure test of a man's character," Scott went on—though it could just as easily be Wilson speaking—"and daily calls for the highest qualities of which he is possessed. Throughout my sledging experience it has been my lot to observe innumerable instances of self-sacrifice, or devotion to duty, and of cheerfulness under adversity; such qualities appeared naturally in my comrades because they were demanded by the life."

For Scott nobody came closer to this ideal than Wilson. In his first letter home to his mother from *Discovery* he had singled him out, but in much the same way as Wilson recognised a different Scott out on the Barrier, it was only through sledging together that Scott came to rely implicitly on Wilson for advice, affection and, when needed, restraint. And for all their differences—the irascibility, remoteness and agnosticism of one, the patience, the "lovableness" and the absolute Christian faith of the other—Scott and Wilson recognised in each other an integrity that bridged any gap. On the surface no two men could have been more different in temper, but the very patience and kindness that made Wilson so crucial to wardroom life were as much a triumph of will over temperament as were any of Scott's victories over himself.

If the wardroom could have seen their respective journals laid side by side, they would have been as astonished at the bitterness that seeped into Wilson's as they would have been at the endless tolerance of Scott's. In the privacy of Wilson's journal the dislike and contempt for human frailties could sometimes assume a kind of medieval intensity, and if Wilson loved his fellow man, he loved him for Christ rather than for himself. "I am more thankful than I can say for having been brought to this life," he could write home in his best hair-shirt mode, "because it is such an education. But God knows it is just about as much as I can stand at times, and there is absolutely no escape. I have never had my temper tried as it is every day now, but I don't intend to give way."

They were alike in other ways, too. For all his simple, St. Francis–like exultation in the natural world, there was something in temperament—as well as in looks—of the great Jesuit poet Gerard Manley Hopkins about Wilson. In his happier moments and prayers Wilson shared all of Hopkins's sense of wonder at the natural world, and yet alongside this delight in God's creation ran that gloomier, self-denying streak of Hopkinsian asceticism that was a natural bedfellow of Scott's secularised puritanism.

No man's faith ever served him better, though. There was nothing intrusive or ostentatious about it, and it was only twenty years later, when his old companions had a chance to see his letters, that they realised precisely the source of that strength so many of them had relied on. "How far was his courage based upon his faith?" Cherry-Garrard, who knew Wilson as a sledger better than any man except Scott himself, wondered. "After all, courage alone will not take you far in the Antarctic as we knew it in the old man-hauling days. The lady gave the bus-conductor a penny and said 'how far will it take me?' 'To the door of the Ritz,' was the answer, 'but it will not take you far inside.' Courage, or ambition, or love of notoriety, may take you to the Antarctic, or any other uncomfortable place in the world, but it won't take you far inside without being found out; it's courage: and unselfishness: and helping one another: and sound condition; and willing- ness to put in every ounce you have: and clean living: and good temper: and tact: and good judgement: and faith. And the greatest of these is faith, especially a faith that what you are doing is of use. It's the idea which car- ries men on. There, if I am not mistaken, you have Bill Wilson."

And there too, one suspects, one has the key to the friendship between Wilson and Scott, because if Wilson brought his prayer book to the Barrier with him, and Scott his Darwin, they shared the same absolute commit- ment to "the idea." For Wilson the cause of science and human knowledge was always inextricably linked to the discovery of God's purpose, but in Scott's agnostic, scientific nature he recognised the same deep seriousness, the same hatred of anything shoddy, the same selflessness, wonder and belief in something larger than individual ambition.

Cherry's pen-picture of Wilson perhaps also points to the underlying cause of the gradual and probably unconscious marginalisation of Shack- leton over the course of this Southern Journey. Scott would never have taken him in the first place if he had not admired him, and yet if Cherry's checklist of sledging virtues—and above all that sense of purpose, of self- effacement, of "faith in the idea"—is to be the test, then he and Wilson must have equally sensed in Shackleton a lack of substance that was not so much at odds with his charm and popularity as an essential part of it.

Shackleton needs defending against no one—his later record speaks for itself—but it would not have occurred to anybody in *Discovery* that he would go on to achieve what he did. Like Scott he had come south without any particular "predilection" for the Antarctic or polar exploration, but whereas Scott came to see it as his life's work, Shackleton's attitude never changed—it was an opportunity to him, an opportunity for making his name, for adventure, for proving himself, for success, glamour, for all those things, ironically, that Scott was in the process of achieving without really wanting. It clearly would have made no difference to Shackleton if they had gone to the Amazon rather than the Antarctic, and of all the jour- nals that survive from the *Discovery* wardroom, his is perhaps the least interesting or intellectually engaged. There is not a page of Scott's diaries where you don't feel the weight of personality and intelligence behind them, but turn from them to Shackleton's and the same questions prompt nothing more than a quotation or a vague piece of whimsy: " 'Our little systems have their day. They have their day and cease to be,' " he quotes Tennyson after a wardroom debate on the existence or not of an Antarctic continent. "But do they cease to? What in the Dickens does he know about their 'ceasing to be.' Ah well!"

For a man who based his future success and dominance so firmly on "character," there is also a curious lack of "focus" to these journals, an absence of any centred personality, that again contrasts strongly with Scott's. There is no shortage of a vague kind of "Anglo-Irishness" running through them, and yet even that feels if not exactly bogus, at least "experimental," as if, somehow, it was just one of a number of characters he was trying on for fit. "I do not seem to have had the same regard for him as for Scott, Wilson or the others," Reginald Ford—the most naturally charitable man in the ship—later wrote, reluctantly circling round a similar point. "This I think was due to a certain lack of consistency in his character—you did not know where you were with him as certainly as with the others . . . His early charm appears to have become in part a pose and showmanship."

If there was none of Scott's unity of character about Shackleton, however, there was no lack of his courage, and it is too easy to exaggerate the differences between men who were in many respects so similar. In so many accounts of this journey the differences of temperament and personality are analysed as if the Barrier were Bloomsbury, and yet when it came to most of the things that ultimately *counted* out on the ice—courage, willpower, drive, resourcefulness, guts, hardiness—they were, in a good Bloomsbury phrase, so close to each other when compared to the rest of mankind as to be "practically identical."

It was these qualities that were needed as the three men slowly packed up their "farthest camp" and finally turned to the north. If there was one consolation in the thought of what lay ahead it was that they would soon be on their own—not even the turn for home could raise a flicker among their surviving dogs. "HOMEWARD," Scott printed in large letters in his diary for the last day of the year, "we had to do nearly all the pulling ourselves today," he added, "& as far as I can see we shall do so from henceforth." A month before, that would have spelled disaster; now it brought only relief, because for all their hard-headedness none of them had acquired the ruthlessness of an Amundsen when it came to their animals. In the sanctuary of the ship Scott and Wilson might calculate how long the meat from one dog could last sixteen or seventeen dogs, but it was one thing to draw up a tidy pyramid of slaughter on paper, and another to live with the reality.

Throughout his life Scott had a revulsion for the sight of blood, and though this never stopped him killing animals when science or the crew's health demanded, that never eased his own moral or physical repugnance. To those who prefer Bismarck the dog to Bismarck the Chancellor no defence for this will be required, but to his own deep shame Scott could never face his share of the butchery on the Barrier, leaving the filthy task to Wilson and Shackleton.

The next day after turning back it was Spud's turn to give up the ghost. Falling in his tracks, he was put onto a sledge, but within an hour of reaching camp was dead. Most of the others were not far from it. Gus and Bismarck were tottering, Lewis and Birdie about to go, and only Jim and Nigger capable of pulling at all. "It is ludicrous to think of the ease with which we expected to make our return journey in comparison with the struggle which it has become," Scott wrote on 2 January 1903. "I hope all will be well but there are times in the day when the driving our wretched tired beasts & feeling tired & done oneself the result almost seems doubtful & the inclination to shorter marches is hard to resist."

Thick weather was a reminder, too, that Depot "B" still had to be found. By 3 January Mount Markham had disappeared, but their food margins were too tight to allow any sense of relief. A sail was improvised out of the floorcloth and a bamboo pole, but even with a southerly breeze to fill it, there could be no stopping now even in the event of blizzards.

The same day, Nell died, rapidly followed by Gus and, "to our greater grief," Kid. It seemed pointless now to eke out the remaining dogfood, and at the end of the march the seven remaining animals were fed all they wanted. With the three men, though, it was a different story. "*Le Bon temps viendra*," Wilson noted on the fourth, but there was precious little sign of it. "To add to our difficulties," Scott wearily wrote, "Shackleton has a sharp attack of snow-blindness & is suffering badly . . . [He] has been blindfolded all day poor chap but it has had a good effect & I hope he will be well right tomorrow—the disability of one in our small party is not only felt by the individual but greatly adds to the work of the others though we have now reduced everything to such system that we get through our camp very speedily."

The next day they were cheered by the sight of their first skua in over a month, but within hours a southerly blizzard was making a straight course

virtually impossible even with a reefed sail. At first they tried to steer by the
direction of the wind, but with the air thick with swirling snow and visibility no more than twenty or thirty yards, even that was soon impossible. "At
length I made up my mind that we could only hope to hold an approximate course," Scott wrote, "and getting Shackleton well ahead of me, I
observed the manner in which the snow was drifting against his back, and
for the remainder of the day I directed him according to this rough guide."

It was the most exhausting march they had yet done. The blizzard drove
them on at a speed they could barely cope with, forcing them sometimes to
run to keep up with their sledges, sometimes to pull back on them, sometimes sideways, "and always with our senses keenly on the alert and our muscles strung up for instant action." It would have been enough to knock them
up at any stage of the journey, but with Scott and Wilson now "very much
'done'" and Shackleton "a good deal worse," they were in real trouble.
Their sledge-meter had also broken, making distances guesswork. "We cannot be far from our depot," Scott wrote on the tenth, "but then we do not
exactly know where we are; there is not many days' food left, and if this thick
weather continues we shall possibly not be able to find it."

The next day was even worse. Their condition was now such that they
could not tell whether it was their own weakness or the state of the snow
that made their "ridiculously light" loads such a burden. At noon the sun
peeped through for just long enough to enable Scott to take a sighting, but
with no glimpse of land in twenty-four hours, it was "impossible to avoid a
sense of being lost . . . and looking at the diminished food-bag we are
obliged to realize that we are running things very close."

The closer they got to the depot, the smaller it shrank in their imagina-
tions. They still had just enough food in reserve for a search, but with
progress down to something under three-quarters of a mile an hour, distance seemed to increase in inverse proportion to their ebbing strength
and dwindling food bag. "And so here we lie," Scott scrawled as they hud-
dled in their tent on the thirteenth, faces burned black, hair long, and
everything they had—clothes, sleeping bag, kit—sodden wet. "Little has
been said, but I have no doubt we have all been thinking a good deal. The
food-bag is a mere trifle to lift; we could finish all that remains in it at one
sitting and still rise hungry; the depot cannot be far away, but where is it in
this terrible expanse of grey? And with this surface, even if we pick it up,
how are we to carry its extra weight when we cannot even make headway
with our light sledges. I have been staring up at the green canvas and asking myself these questions with no very cheering result."

Even at this stage, however, all they needed was the smallest bit of luck—a clearing of the sky, a glimpse of land—because they knew that they must now be very close to the depot. A sighting Scott had got two days earlier had placed them ten or twelve miles to the south of it, and they had just agreed on another two hours' northward march, when a glimpse of sun had Scott out of his sleeping bag and sweeping the horizon with his telescope: "suddenly a speck seemed to flash by, and a wild hope sprang up. Slowly I brought the telescope back; yes, there it was again; yes, and on either side of it two smaller specks—the depot, without a shadow of doubt. I sprang up and shouted, 'Boys, there's the depot.' We are not a demonstrative party, but I think we excuse ourselves for the wild cheer that greeted this announcement."

They had cut it fine—they knew they would, had always known it—but it was a triumph of depoting, sheer courage and good navigation. Within minutes they had their sledges packed, and if the work was as heavy as before, Scott wrote, "we were in a very different mood to undertake it. Throughout the morning we had marched in dogged silence; now every tongue was chattering and all minor troubles were forgotten in knowledge that we were going to have a *fat hoosh* at last."

With three weeks' worth of food to last them the 130 miles to their next depot, the only anxiety now was sickness. Neither Scott nor Wilson was as strong as he should have been, but it was Shackleton who was again showing the clearest symptoms of scurvy. The next day the hauling finally took its toll. "Truly there appears no freedom from anxiety on this journey," Scott wrote in his journal on the fourteenth, all the euphoria of finding the depot brutally pricked; "we are all tainted with scorbutic symptoms—Shackleton is worst—his gums are not good at all and add to that he has a congested throat which causes him to spit blood—I have very slight signs in the gums & a very slight oedema in the legs with many spots—Wilson has one well marked sign in the gums. Shackleton is of course our weak point and must at all hazards be nursed back from his present condition—we have relieved him of all work about the camp & I have cautioned him not to pull for the present."

"During a halt my cough which had been troubling me for some days became more severe and a haemorrhage started," Shackleton noted the same day, "so I was not allowed to do any more camp work or pull, only doing little jobs such as cooking; it is most annoying. The other poor fellows now have 270lbs [each] to pull while I am only allowed to walk along. They are awfully good to me."

That evening Wilson confided in Scott just how alarmed he was, and a minor accident two days later more than bore out his fears. "Both I and Shackleton slipped our feet in deep cracks," a worried Scott recorded on the sixteenth; "this shook Shackleton up considerably & at lunch he was very groggy—I am still very anxious about him . . . but he has a terribly excitable temperament & it is impossible to keep him as quiet as we should wish."

The only thought now was of the next depot, and to save dragging the extra weight of food the last dogs were killed. Throughout even the worst days Scott had clung to the hope of getting some of them back, and even as nine dwindled to seven, and seven to five, he had hoped, at least, that the last remaining pair might be saved. With Shackleton's life now at stake, this was no longer possible. "This morning 'Nigger' and 'Jim' were taken a short distance from the camp and killed," Scott wrote. "This was the saddest scene of all; I think we could all have wept. And so this is the last of our dog team, the finale to a tale of tragedy; I scarcely like to write of it."

An increase in their seal ration soon had an effect on Scott and Wilson, and even Shackleton showed some improvement. It was "easy to see he is much relieved," Scott wrote on the seventeenth; "we cannot of course talk the matter out as the patient is always within earshot. I cannot but imagine that the scurvy picks out the weak spots in a man; Shackleton was by far the most tainted and in his case his chest is decidedly weak."

Shackleton had stopped spitting blood, but there was still no question of his doing any real hauling, and that left Scott and Wilson with over two hundred pounds to drag each. "It is difficult to describe the trying nature of this work," Scott wrote, physical and mental weariness exacerbated by the difficulties of navigating in a featureless landscape where neither sun, land nor compass could offer any help. "For hours one plods on, ever searching for some . . . definite sign. Sometimes the eye picks up a shade on the surface or a cloud slightly lighter or darker than its surroundings; these may occur at any angle, and have often to be kept in the corner of the eye. Frequently there comes a minute or two of absolute confusion, when one may be going in any direction and for the time the mind seems blank. It can scarcely be imagined how tiring this is or how trying to the eyes; one's whole attention must be given to it, without relaxing for a moment the strain on the harness."

They tried everything—the bearing of a cloud, a shred of wool attached as a wind vane to a bamboo pole—but the constant wearing away at the eyes took its toll. Again, it was Wilson who suffered most. On the eighteenth, after a spell leading, he told Scott his eyes were on the point of failing. After a day's seeming respite, too, Shackleton was once more as weak as ever. "Shackleton gave in with a bad pain in his chest," Scott wrote on the eighteenth; "it was a disappointment not to be able to go on and still more so as it puts the old serious aspects of Shackleton's case again before us—it is no use being down about it, we must evidently be prepared to carry him as a lame duck sooner or later he does not pull at all and if he cannot even walk we shall have a rough time."

The next day brought a slight improvement, and with the first, familiar sight of Mount Discovery to buoy spirits, Shackleton felt strong enough by the twenty-first to manage an hour in harness. It was a triumph of will, courage and pride over constitution. "Shackleton is improving," Scott noted, "and very obedient to his enforced rest much as he longs to join in the work. Poor chap! He has felt his breakdown very severely." With the breeze behind them doing most of the work, Shackleton rode on the sledge to steady it, or skied on at his own pace while Scott and Wilson hauled and talked. "The Captain and I had long talks on every subject," Wilson noted in his diary on the twenty-third, "and indeed he is a most interesting talker when he starts."

They were still talking and still "plodding" the next day when—"to our great joy"—they caught their first glimpse of the Bluff. For Shackleton each day was still "a cruel time," but with every march and every sighting the sense of "home and safety" that their first view of Mount Discovery had brought grew stronger. "Old and familiar landmarks have been showing up one by one," Scott wrote on the twenty-sixth, just after they had crossed the reassuring tracks of Barne and his party. "Erebus raised its head above the Bluff range; Terror opened out to the east; the western range developed in better-known shape. It has been grand to watch it all."

On the twenty-eighth they reached Bluff Depot, with a week's supply of food still unused, held back by Scott in case the weather had seriously delayed them. News and messages left there of the other parties all seemed good—a knighthood was being confidently predicted for the Royal Marine private Arthur Blisset's discovery of an Emperor penguin's egg at Cape Crozier—but even that took second place to their first real "binge" in months. "Meanwhile our *hoosh* is preparing," Scott wrote in anticipation. "We are putting a double 'whack' of everything into the cooking pot, and when in doubt as to what is double, we put in treble. The smell of this savoury mess is already arising, so I cease."

A half-hour of "pure joy" followed the meal, and then "there slowly crept in on us a feeling that something was going wrong. Our clothes seemed to be getting extraordinarily tight, and the only conclusion we could come to was that the concentrated food was continuing to swell." Shackleton had been in no state to eat, but for Scott the discomfort soon turned to agony. It seemed a gratuitous insult that after weeks of hunger the worst night of the whole journey was the result of eating, and for hours Scott could only pace around the outside of the tent, little comforted by Wilson's amusement or the knowledge that the cause of his distress was his own greed. "However, when at length my pangs subsided sufficiently to allow me to return to the tent I had some revenge, for as I was about to enter, Wilson realized his acutest suffering had only been deferred, and as I approached he burst into the open with a pea-green face, and I had some consolation in knowing that we had changed places."

The next day, though, their own misery was put in perspective by Shackleton's condition. The regime and the march had nearly finished him. "I am feeling worse today," he had confessed in his diary the day before, after more than a week's silence on his health, "have not done any pulling and am not allowed even to cook now. Kneeling down to get in or out of the tent I find the hardest thing to do." The next morning he was even worse, his breathing loud and laboured, his face pinched and worn, his whole body racked with coughing. For the first time even his spirit seemed broken. A blizzard had blown up, keeping them where they were camped, but after another miserable night punctuated by paroxysms of coughing, it seemed more vital than ever to get him back to the ship.

Wilson knew that Shackleton could never survive another blizzard, and that his only hope now was a clear sky and a hard surface. He had been "livid and speechless, and his spirits . . . very low" the morning after this last bout, but with a combination of skiing and riding he somehow dragged himself on. By 2 February they rounded White Island and could see the well-known shapes of Castle Rock and Observation Hill no more than a dozen miles ahead. "That it is none too soon is evident," Scott wrote. "We are as near spent as three persons can well be. If Shackleton has shown a temporary improvement, we know by experience how little confidence we can put in it, and how near he has been and still is to a total collapse. As for Wilson and myself, we have scarcely liked to own how 'done' we are, and how greatly the last week or two has tried us. We have known that our scurvy has been advancing again with rapid strides . . . Wilson has suffered from lameness for many a day; the cause was plain, and we knew it must increase. Each morning he has vainly tried to disguise a limp, and his set face has shown me that there is much to be gone through before the first stiffness wears off."

Scott was also suffering, his ankles badly swollen, but as there was nothing to be done about it, he kept his symptoms to himself. "One and all we want rest and peace," he wearily concluded his sledging diary, "and, all being well, to-morrow, thank Heaven, we shall get them."

On a brilliant, cloudless morning they packed up their last camp and set off towards Observation Hill. After some hours two specks were seen in the distance, and soon Bernacchi and Skelton were with them. There were "no dogs with them," Skelton noted in his diary that night—the first independent view of the three men in almost two months. "Wilson & the Skipper pulling two sledges on foot, Shackleton walking alongside on ski. They looked as if they had had a pretty rough time—the Skipper & Wilson looked fit, but Shackleton looked very weak & seedy & his hair very much bleached. The Skipper's first question was about the ship & if everybody was all right; he seemed rather anxious and was tremendously pleased to hear everything was all right."

Watchers on the hill had also seen them, and the ship had been hastily dressed "in honour of capt's return." At 4:30 Scott, Wilson and Shackleton at last arrived on board. "Amidst cheer upon cheer," Williamson recorded, "we manned the rigging & gave them a hearty welcome back home, which they or any other sledge party undoubtedly deserves but more especially them."

"A lovely day," Royds wrote, delighted especially to have Wilson back, and more pleased than he would once have ever guessed to have his skipper on board again, "and just the right sort of day for Captain Scott's return . . . they all looked in excellent health, the Captain especially." As they got alongside the gangway, "the men cheered like mad. The Captain said a lot of very nice things about the ship to me, in fact he seemed very pleased with everybody and everything . . . After dinner the men mustered outside the wardroom and sang 'Captain Scott and all his lot.' "

It was a proud ship. In the wardroom there was "champagne unlimited & Bernacchi's liquors," and on the mess deck they spliced the mainbrace "no less than 3 times in honour of the furthest South Latitude of 82°17's." That night Scott was heard from his cabin: "I say, Shackles," he called out, "how would you fancy some sardines on toast?" The three men had survived in more than just the literal sense.

Fourteen: A Second Winter

Shackleton & nine others [gone], some invalids & some undesirables & the ship is much better for the change.

THOMAS HODGSON, *journal, 31 March 1903*

Scott had a lot to catch up on. While he was away, *Morning*, the relief ship, had arrived. She had sailed from England in July under an experienced and skilful merchant officer who had been on Borchgrevink's expedition, Captain Colbeck, and had reached Cape Adare and found Scott's first message on 8 January.

There had been no guarantee when *Discovery* left England that finances would even stretch to a relief ship, but Scott knew even before the news reached them in New Zealand that if anyone could find one, it would be Markham. It is perhaps a measure of Scott's confidence that he had taken their prearranged chain of post boxes as seriously as he had, but what must have seemed a fragile enough system back in London must have felt even more so in the immensity of the south. The risks inherent in the chain became obvious when Colbeck was blocked by ice from Coulman Island and Wood Bay, and drawing a blank at Franklin Island, was forced to pin his last hopes of finding *Discovery* on Cape Crozier. On 18 January he led a landing party ashore in search of the elusive message, and after some hours' searching was about to give up when a small post was seen against the horizon, and the tin cylinder left by Royds was found.

It was an improbable, imaginative success that had "Markham" written all over it; but then *Morning* had been his child from the first, born of tribal memories of Arctic disasters and his own sense of responsibility for the men he had sent south. In his original brief Colbeck's job was to provide any assistance that Scott might require if he was in trouble, and to place himself if all was well at his disposal while Scott continued his explorations by sea along the lines laid down in his Instructions. "Early in 1903 your ship should be free from the ice of winter quarters," those read, "and you will devote to further exploration by sea so much of the navigable season as will certainly leave time for the ship to return to the north of the pack ice. Having recruited at your base station, you will then proceed with your magnetic survey across the Pacific and return to this country."

If there were any doubt as to the clarity of that instruction, the point was enforced in the letter carried out by Colbeck. "You will then be in command of the two ships," Scott was told, "and you are to take what you require from *Morning*, and extricate yourself from your winter quarters with as little loss of time as possible. You are then to do as much exploring and scientific work as the time will admit with the two ships, during the navigable season of 1903. The direction you will take, and the methods you may adopt in performing this service, are left entirely to your discretion. You will return to Lyttelton in March or April 1903."

Few things involving Markham were that simple, however, and even when they were, he had a track record of duplicity so long that his opponents were always looking for a hidden agenda. As early as May 1902 he had been angling for a second season in the ice for Scott, and within both Societies there was an unjustified but immovable suspicion that along with their jointly and publicly drafted instructions, Colbeck was carrying a secret letter from Markham authorising another year.

This would later have damaging consequences for the expedition, but as Scott at last lay in the comfort of his own bunk that night, after ninety-three days out on the ice, not even the letters from home brought by *Morning* could keep him from the "dreamless sleep of exhaustion." During the day he had struggled about as best he could, but he had felt the journey more than he cared to admit, and to badly swollen legs and gums was added a "lassitude" that he could not shake off: "And this lassitude was not physical only; to write, or even to think, had become wholly distasteful, and sometimes quite impossible. At this time I seemed to be incapable of all but eating or sleeping or lounging in the depths of an armchair, whilst I lazily scanned the files of the newspapers which had grown so unfamiliar. Many days passed before I could rouse myself from this slothful humour, and it was many weeks before I had returned to a normally vigorous condition." Even in such a state of physical and mental exhaustion, however, the idea of leaving McMurdo with the job only half-finished, and with so little in hard, measurable terms to show for all his winter planning, must have been anathema to a man like Scott.

He would not have been human if he had not felt his own disappointment most keenly, but the Southern Journey had been only one part of a three-pronged assault on Antarctica that had "failed" on all accounts. Between them Scott's and Barne's journeys had succeeded in unveiling 375 miles of coast adjoining the Barrier, but the same weather that had thwarted Scott's party at their last camp had similarly prevented Barne from "joining up the gap" farther north that would have resolved a fragmented "archipelago" into the great continental chain of mountains it is.

The one important piece of exploration rather than endurance to show for the season came when Armitage's Western Party were the first men to breach this formidable wall of mountains. No brief summary can begin to conjure up the scale of this achievement, but with a group of seamen who had never before had any experience of glacial work—and quite possibly had never in their lives been higher than the rigging of a ship—Armitage not only found a route up to the summit of Antarctica, but in the teeth of blizzards, crevasses, altitude sickness, and in one case a heart attack, brought his whole party down safe again. "On all sides," he reported to Scott on the first, historic sighting at almost nine thousand feet of the plateau, "the surface was quite smooth, and there was very little sign of wind; it looked as though the plateau on which we stood was the summit of the ice-cap."

For all the real achievements of this journey, however, there was ultimately the same lack of resolution, and a vague but disappointing sense that Armitage had not pushed as hard as he might. By any normal standards his ascent of the unknown Ferrar Glacier still appears a model of bravery and good sense, but by the lights Scott had set himself and his expedition it came to seem almost the opposite—a lost opportunity, a victory of caution over ambition, of dully plodding "age" over youthful vigour and imagination. "On the way up the Ferrar Glacier, Armitage was not energetic and purposeful," Skelton wrote over forty years later, as irritated as ever by the pig-headedness and caution that had cost the expedition its chance to "crack" the secrets of the plateau, and often obstinate against proposals made by some of the men and myself;—we were keen, but marches were slow, and the day's work far too short—Scott would have been horrified . . . At the top of the Ferrar Glacier, some of the men were not well—notably McFarlane [sic], and in his case I think it was "cold feet" [heart attack in fact];—but some were very fit and it was suggested to Armitage to split the party, send half back, and half to push on to the limit;—he was again obstinate or nervous of responsibility.—what a chance missed?

During the winter Scott wormed the story out of me—he must have heard rumours from the men;—I had no desire to be disloyal to Armitage, who, after all, was in charge. Had Armitage divided the party and done some real pushing, it would have made Scott's journey the 2nd year unnecessary and other important explorations could have been made.

The Western Journey marks a watershed in Armitage's career, as after the charm offensive that had followed Scott's departure on the Southern Journey—"What would Capt. Scott say if he could see a commoner in the Ward Room sitting at the table drinking whisky & smoking cigars," a delighted Buckridge had wondered*—his popularity on the mess deck had also begun to wane. For a while Armitage's determination to give the crew "endless privileges & [feed] them" had been enough to sustain his credit, but it never seemed to occur to him that the demarcations of naval discipline that he was out to break were as integral and cherished a part of mess-deck *freedom* as they were of wardroom *privilege*. "Sing song in Ward Room above all places," an uneasy Williamson wrote after his return with the depot party, "which to us has been Holy Ground up to now, for ever since our absence (Lt Armitage being in charge) the[y] have been holding sing song & concerts etc."

There was, more importantly, a core of selfishness to Armitage, and a sort of slow, deep-seated indolence that was bound eventually to catch him out; and the arrival of *Morning* exposed his apparent interest in crew

---

*This comment is in Williamson's journal, but not in his hand. While he was away from the ship sledging, another member of the mess deck kept it up for him. This was almost certainly Horace Buckridge, the clever, wayward Australian taken on in South Africa who would come to a sticky end in suspicious circumstances shortly after leaving *Discovery*. Buckridge despised Scott and his naval ways with a good colonial contempt. For his part, Scott was increasingly—and rightly—distrustful of Buckridge's influence on the lower deck, and would be glad to get rid of him.

welfare for the disloyalty to Scott it actually was. After more than a year in a naval wardroom the sight of the relief ship must have seemed like a glimpse of home to him, and taking a party across the sound the next day to where she was anchored at the limit of the fast ice, he ensconced himself in her and refused to budge, stubbornly indifferent to the rump of the crew still waiting back in *Discovery* for their first mail in fourteen months. "I was quite ready to start at any time with a sledge," Skelton noted in his journal, having tried two or three times to budge him, "but Armitage seemed rather callous about it, & took a delight in 'hanging on.' "

While *Morning*'s guests fed "like fighting cocks" and regaled their hosts with stories of naval discipline, Royds was left to deal with the consequences back in *Discovery*. Hubert, he reported on the twenty-fifth, was "beside himself" at the wait. The "men have been in almost mutinous condition at the delay with the mails," Hodgson wrote the next day, "& the feeling against Armitage is intensely bitter. My own opinion is that it is excessive but there are grounds for it." There was "very great discontent," Skelton recorded the same day, "because they had not been brought it before—Royds says they have been in a frightful state—'falling in' to complain officially, & one or two of the bad characters making use of insubordinate language about it. Of course that sort of thing must be squashed—but in their place I almost sympathise with them."

In the whole of the first year under Scott there had been fewer than a handful of disciplinary incidents of any kind, and this near-mutiny over the mail brought home what a fine line separated *Discovery* from the moral and psychological collapse of other polar expeditions. It cannot have escaped anyone's notice that such a breakdown could never have occurred under Scott's leadership, and the genuine sense of pleasure at the return of the Southern Party was as much as anything else a tardy recognition of just what his presence and standards meant to the ship.*

And as the ice in the bay stubbornly refused to move, holding *Discovery* a helpless prisoner, it became increasingly clear that Scott was going to be given a third season to mould the expedition in his own image. Mentally exhausted after the Southern Journey, however, it took him some time to realise it. Day by day, through February, he passively waited for the ice to break up, seemingly incapable of grasping that conditions were different from those of the previous year. "I was vaguely surprised to learn that the

---

*Jacob Cross, for one, wrote in his diary that they would have had their mail inside twenty-four hours if Scott had been there.

'Morning' had experienced so much obstruction in the Ross Sea," he later confessed, still puzzled at his own mental torpor, "and I was astonished to hear that the pack was still hanging in the entrance to the Sound, and as yet showed no sign of clearing away to the north; but it was long before I connected these facts with circumstances likely to have an adverse bearing on our position, and the prospect of the ice about us remaining fast throughout the season never once entered my head."

On 8 February, the anniversary of *Discovery*'s arrival in McMurdo Sound, the first inkling of the truth appears in his diary. In a week *Morning* had advanced no more than a quarter of a mile, and though two days later another mile had been made, it was clear that she could not afford to wait for *Discovery* if she was to be sure of getting out herself. "There is no doubt things are looking serious," Scott wrote a week later, after a futile attempt with explosives had produced nothing more than a twenty-foot hole in the ice and the odd crack. "The ice is as stagnant as ever; there has been scarcely any change in the last week. I have had to rouse myself to face the situation. The 'Morning' must go in less than a week, and it seems now impossible that we shall be free by that time, though I still hope that the break-up may come after she has departed."

There was nothing disingenuous here—and no truth in Royal Society suspicions that he had always intended to keep *Discovery* in the ice—but there is equally little doubt that Scott was happy to have another season forced on him. He had decided some time previously that in the event of another year in the ice he wanted a slimmer crew, and on 24 February he mustered the men to offer anyone who wanted it a passage out in *Morning*. Perhaps the only man he would have wished to keep of the eight who took him up was Clarence Hare, the young New Zealand steward who had "risen from the dead" the previous March. Hare had only joined *Discovery* in the first place out of a sense of adventure, and as he recalled sixty years later, the sight of *Morning*'s sails and the thought of freedom was too much to resist. "A good boy," Scott noted, "but above his station. I was sorry to lose him but had some sympathy with his obvious distaste for the work."

With that single exception, however, the list was exactly what he would have drawn up himself. "A thorough hypochondriac," he noted of Macfarlane on 7 March. "An idler and at bottom a bad sort of man [Page] . . . An ignorant Poplar cockney and a bad hat altogether [Hubert] . . . never got on with the rest [Duncan] . . . A rolling stone & a queer character strongly suspected as a bad influence in the ship but too intelligent to misbehave himself [Buckridge]," and finally—and Scott and the rest of the ship's *bête noire*—"that dirty little rascal [Brett]."

It is hard not to feel some sympathy for Macfarlane, a victim of medical misdiagnosis if ever there was one, but there was no doubt that *Discovery* was well shot of the rest. A lot has been made of this clear-out, as if it represented some premeditated naval purge on Scott's part, and yet while it is certainly true that it shifted the balance on the mess deck overwhelmingly in favour of the bluejackets, there was not a man—civilian, merchant or naval—left in either mess who would have wanted to keep any of them.

It was a rather different and delicate matter when it came to the wardroom, and one that unfairly exposed Scott to serious misunderstanding. On his return from the Southern Journey Koettlitz had come to him in his cabin with a convoluted story of a letter from his wife saying that Scott's mother had told her that Mrs. Armitage—"a hell of a woman," as Skelton put it—had got herself involved in a boarding house "incident" that had led to the police courts in Richmond. Scott had already heard hints to the same effect, and while he could hardly ignore them, his main concern was to protect Armitage from gossip. "My dear, please be careful yourself in the matter," he begged his mother at the end of February, acutely conscious of the damage that could be done at a distance of half the world and a time lag of a year and more in letters, "for I am sure neither you or I want to be mixed up—the reason for my warning is as follows: I guessed something was wrong from your letter and the only thing to do was to give him a loophole for getting away if he had any doubts himself—he didn't rise, I gathered he had none but Koettlitz who you know is a very indiscreet person, came to my cabin asking if he should tell Armitage what he had heard, he then read me his wife's letter which hinted at things being very wrong and constantly quoted you as partly the authority for what she had heard—Mrs. Koettlitz of course means it very well but under the present circumstances it would be madness to tell Armitage anything about it—I have quieted Koettlitz and all is well at this end."

It might well have occurred to Scott—as it would to his own wife seven years later—that it was as important to choose the *wives* as the *men* for an expedition, because the incident had put him in an impossible position. There had already been enough awkwardness between him and Armitage to make any frank conversation difficult, and yet to leave it dangling in the air as he was forced to do, suspended between a vague invitation and a hint to quit the ship, pandered to every paranoid suspicion Armitage harboured. "After church went for a walk with Armitage," Royds wrote in his journal four months later, the "snub" clearly as fresh in the pilot's mind as if it had been delivered with the collect that morning, "and he told me about his row with the Captain. It appears that Armitage had very strong feelings about the Captain giving him the option of going home in the relief ship, and he took it as a personal thing, instead of which the Captain was in reality meaning a kindness, as he had heard of something which he didn't wish to tell the Pilot, but give him the chance of going home if he wanted to. This and various other things he told me, and they all helped to convince me that he had ill feelings for naval officers generally, and that he is not being treated fair and above board, which I told him I thought was an absurd notion."

To be fair to Armitage, there was enough historical "edge" between the two services to add a certain substance to his paranoia, and it cannot have been eased by Scott's decision to send home the one other merchant officer in the wardroom. On their return from the Barrier Shackleton had recovered more quickly than anyone could have expected, but it was clear in Scott's mind still that his health remained a weakness that they could not afford with the prospect of another full season in the ice.

Four days before he wrote the report to be carried home by *Morning*, Scott wrote a memo to Koettlitz, asking him if there were any on board whose health would be threatened by another season's hauling in the Antarctic. Scott was not so worried about a man like Hodgson, whose duties more or less excluded him from sledging, but with Shackleton particularly in mind he emphasised those duties as sledge leader that would fall to any executive officer remaining with the ship. Shackleton had "recovered" from his scurvy, Koettlitz wrote back, but, "Referring to your memorandum as to the duties of [this] executive officer, I cannot say that he would be fit to undergo hardships and exposure in this climate." It was a decision that Wilson sadly agreed with, writing in his diary that "It is certainly wiser for him to go home," and there is no reason to think that the decision was based on anything more than medical reasons. There was certainly talk in the *Discovery* at the time of *Morning's* departure that "personal feeling" lay behind Shackleton's departure, and yet all the evidence makes it clear that any animus on his part came as a *result* and not as a cause of Scott's decision.

There clearly had been tensions on the Barrier—it would have been astonishing if there had not been—but the only specific "incident" comes with such a doubtful provenance that it is probably best ignored. "During the winter, Wilson told me the following story, which Shackleton confirmed later," an embittered Armitage wrote in 1922, after anyone who might contradict him was safely dead. "On the Southern Journey, Wilson and Shackleton were packing their sledges after breakfast one morning. Suddenly they heard Scott shout to them: 'Come here you BFs.' They went to him, and Wilson quietly said: 'Were you speaking to me?' 'No Bill,' said Scott. 'Then it must have been me,' said Shackleton. He received no answer. He then said: 'Right, you are the worst BF of the lot, and every time you dare to speak to me like that you will get it back.' Before Shackleton left he told me he meant to return to prove to Scott that he—Shackleton— was a better man than Scott."

And with Macfarlane—popularly suspected of malingering—and the wretched Brett—who had now added the symptoms of syphilis to his other attractions—completing Koettlitz's list, it is not surprising that Shackleton was humiliated by the decision. There was not a man in *Discovery* who had cared more passionately about his part in the expedition, and to a natural disappointment was added a psychological preoccupation with strength and health as a kind of index of moral worth that made him intensely vulnerable to so public a suggestion of failure.

There is no doubt, either, that the decision to send him home fuelled all Shackleton's future ambitions, but that had everything to do with him, and nothing to do with Scott. It is impossible, of course, to know the "truth"—if there is such a thing—of what happened between the two men out on the Barrier, but after his total and public collapse Shackleton would not have needed to see his own doubts reflected back in Scott's eyes to feel he had something to prove.

There is a second story, originating again with Armitage, and carefully reserved until Scott and Shackleton were both dead, that Shackleton came to him after he had learned of his dismissal and asked him to intercede. "He was in great distress," Armitage wrote to H.R. Mill, the future biographer of Shackleton who had sailed in *Discovery* as far as Madeira, "and could not understand it. I consulted Koettlitz and he informed me that Scott was in a worse condition than Shackleton. I then went to Scott, and asked him why he was sending him back. I told him there was no necessity from a health point of view, so after beating about the bush he said: 'If he does not go back sick he will go back in disgrace.' "

It would be odd if there were any more truth in this than in Armitage's first contribution to the Scott/Shackleton mythology, and there is certainly nothing in Scott's official or private papers to suggest any hidden agenda. "This gentleman has performed his work in a highly satisfactory manner," he wrote of Shackleton in his report for the RGS, "but unfortunately his constitution has proved unequal to the rigours of a polar climate. It is with great reluctance that I order his return and trust that it will be made evident that I do so solely on account of his health and that his future prospect may not suffer." "All the 'crocks' I am sending away & am much relieved to be rid of," he told his mother in a letter that is frank enough about the rest of the wardroom to leave no doubt that he meant what he was saying here, "except Shackleton who is a very good fellow & only fails from the constitutional point of view. He has promised to go and see you and if you can understand him (you know how Irish he is) will no doubt tell you many a tale of our doings."

Even for those reluctant to see any good in Scott, there is a problem of *motive* that makes any other explanation than the "official" one almost impossible to understand. In the light of subsequent events it is tempting to see it in terms of an incipient rivalry between the two men, and yet to imagine Shackleton as a figure who in some way posed a threat to Scott's authority is as much an insult to his instinctive loyalty as it is to the good sense of the wardroom. When Reginald Ford was asked—in one of those biographer's questionnaires specifically designed to elicit the answer "Yes"—whether Shackleton stood out as a future leader, his reply was "no more than the others on the ship." Ford is perhaps not the most representative figure from the lower deck, in so far as he did not much like Shackleton, but even to a lifelong follower like Jimmy Dell, Shackleton was a marginal presence in the serious business of *Discovery*, a maverick and an outsider—a mere merchant "cargo shifter" in the eyes of Royal Naval colleagues who would have been no more capable of seeing the leadership potential in him than they would have of forgoing Divisions.

He was certainly popular throughout the ship—"a grand ship-mate, and good company," as Barne called him—but "leadership" was simply not among the terms in which they thought of him. He was, instead, the man who lifted cutlery from New Zealand receptions and planted it in Koettlitz's bags. He was the man who would disrupt Ferrar's tedious lecture on geology. He was the inevitable target of Bernacchi's fines at wardroom dinners. He was the man who could make Scott smile. He was the natural leader of the "rowdy element"—he was, in short, "Shackles," the life of the wardroom, full of talk, full of Browning, and—if Skelton is to be believed—full of air.

Scott was not just "the last person on earth," as Dell recalled, who would have listened to Shackleton's "wild-cat schemes," he was the last person who would have seen him as a possible rival. It is clear from all his letters and journals that he *liked* him well enough, but he was no Barne or Wilson, nor was he—in defence of Scott's judgement—the Shackleton who later commanded the *Nimrod* and *Endurance* expeditions.

It is only hindsight that injects any significance into Shackleton's return, and at the time Scott was as much concerned with his other officers. "Royds has improved wonderfully," he told his mother with a certain smugness that his first lieutenant might well have had something to say about; "his bumptiousness has entirely vanished and the really solid good nature of the man come to the top, for which I take to myself much credit. Michael Barne is always in the front rank in health & spirits. Nothing daunts him, nothing dispirits him and the more work he gets the better he seems pleased.—when we spent 36 hours together holding onto the corner of a tent in a temperature of minus 40° whilst his fingers were being badly frostbitten, he was quite in his most cheerful frame of mind."

With the sole exception of Armitage, perhaps, who "*entre nous*" was "a little old for this work—It wants men with the fire & dash of Barne, Skelton & the others," there was nobody who Scott was not happy to have staying on with him in the ship. In the privacy of his letters to his mother he might voice the odd qualification, but from Koettlitz to Hodgson—"the most solid sound old person imaginable," and from Bernacchi to that "conceited young ass" Ferrar—"a changed youth . . . was objectionable . . . now a nonentity & knows it, and therefore in time . . . will be an acquisition"—Scott's comments on his wardroom reflect the sense of optimism and confidence with which he looked forward to another Antarctic winter.

There was a widespread feeling in both messes, too, that with the "crocks" gone, *Discovery* was going to have a happier mess deck. On 1 March Shackleton left the ship for the last time to the cheers of the remaining crew, but though there was a real sadness at seeing him go, it was nothing to the sense of buoyancy and expectation among the naval officers that they were at last to have the ship and the standards they wanted—"just first class I call it," Royds noted in his journal the following day with the same satisfaction that stamped Skelton's delighted valediction on his own departing "bad characters."

And as *Morning* prepared to leave, and the last of the discharged men settled into her, everyone was too busy with their own thoughts and letters to spare much time for Shackleton or anyone else. In his letter to his mother Scott apologised for making her the victim of his other commitments, but with the relief ship offering the only communication with the outside world for a whole year there was not just family, official and naval correspondence to be got through, but letters to all the new friends *Discovery* had made in New Zealand.

And even at his busiest, Scott always made time for children. "We are all very well on board the 'Discovery,' " he wrote to Marie and Taku Rhodes, the daughter and son of the Croesus of Christchurch who had sent cakes to them in *Morning* inscribed in icing with the children's names, "but we have not yet seen the South pole. There are lots of great big ice bergs down here; some of them are twice as high as the ship's masts and nearly as big round as the whole of Christchurch—There are no polar bears you know but lots of big seals; on fine days they come out of the water and stretch themselves out on the ice to sleep; you never saw anything so fat and lazy; they puff & snort when you go near them."

On the afternoon of 1 March, almost the whole ship's company trudged across the ice for the last time to where *Morning* lay at anchor. After a long night that only ended in the early hours around the piano, officers and men rolled themselves into blankets to snatch a few hours' sleep before mustering again on the floe the next day to wave them off. "Cheer after cheer was raised as she gradually gathered way," Scott wrote, "and long after she had passed out of earshot our forlorn little band stood gazing at her receding hull, following in our minds her homeward course and wondering when we too should be permitted to take that northern track."

"A wave of depression has just come over *Discovery*," Hodgson noted in his journal the same day. But with another winter in prospect there was no time for moping. After the scurvy shocks of the previous sledging season Scott was taking no chances with their winter diet, and whenever the weather permitted, he had the ship's "killing parties" out "on their murderous errand," augmenting the great hecatomb of seal carcasses they had in store with another five hundred skuas that the epicurean Skelton had just introduced to their diet.

As the last hopes of following *Morning* out were finally abandoned, and the skua were hung unplucked from the rigging, the crew began to prepare the ship for another winter, running down the boilers, dismantling the engines, disconnecting the steam pipes, coiling the ropes, preparing the awning, piling up the snow, and generally undoing all the hard work Skelton, Royds and their men had slaved to complete while Scott was on his Southern Journey.

Even as the rest of the ship readied itself for winter, Scott's thoughts were already on the coming season. On 20 March he went up on skis to

Castle Rock to see the state of the ice in the sound, and although it had gone out a good way since *Morning*'s departure it was still three and a half miles to open water. "On my walks I can rarely think of much else but our position and its possibilities," he confessed. "What does our imprisonment mean? Was it this summer or the last which was the exception? Does the ice usually break away around the cape, or does it usually stop short to the north? For us these must be the gravest possible questions, for on their answers depend our prospects of getting away next year or at all. It is little wonder that I think of these things continually and scan every nook and corner in the hopes of discovering evidences to support my views; for I hold steadily to a belief that the answers are in our favour, and that our detention is due to exceptional conditions."

At least the ship and her crew offered encouragement, with a "beautifully clean" mess deck a sure sign that the navy was back in the ascendant. The disappearance of Brett had also made a world of difference, with a sort of rolling mess deck "committee of taste" overseeing his old assistant Clarke. "Shackleton & nine others" had gone, Hodgson noted at the end of March, his stomach getting the better of sentiment over the loss of their old catering officer. "Some invalids & some undesirables & the ship is much the better for the change. The feeding arrangements have been wonderfully improved."

He would have been less pleased to see the arrival of that other harbinger of the British polar night, sports out on the ice. The favoured game for this second winter was an anarchic version of field hockey. In temperatures of −40° they played games of half an hour each way, with the Officers taking on the Men, the Marrieds the Singles, and "Fossils" the "Colts"— fossils, the over-twenty-eights and the colts under. There were almost no rules, or none that anyone took any notice of, and no umpire because nobody would take on the job. The only man who seemed to mind was Royds, the best player by far, and the only one who could not bring himself to cheat and use both sides of the stick. It went against everything he stood for to see so much "promiscuous kicking and foul play" go unpunished, but if he had to suffer the indignity of losing to men whose only qualification for the game was total ignorance, he at least had the slight consolation in one game of giving Scott a "glorious black eye."

With the coming of darkness, too, all the old scientific routines had to be resumed, and with them all their attendant anxieties and miseries. "The Captain's night" on meteorological duties, Royds was soon wearily noting, as if nothing in the life of a first lieutenant could ever change, "and, of course the light goes wrong, the candle not standing the wind, and the electric battery was run down . . . he is now busily engaged in filling up the battery and putting new cells in, and I expect cussing me roundly." But for all Royds's comic forebodings there was a new note in his journal, a fresh spring and self-confidence to it, as he gradually came to see the occasional outburst of Scott's for what it was. In his letter to his mother Scott was happy to take the credit for this transformation in his first officer, but the more likely truth is that with time and the experience of command Scott himself was getting better at what he was doing. The old racing saw that confidence "travels down the reins" was proving its truth. During their first months in the ice Royds probably had to pay the price of his skipper's own insecurities, but as Scott became more sure of himself and—crucially— sure of those under him, much of that confidence and content inevitably filtered down through the ship.

By nature Scott can never have been a natural delegator, but whether he liked it or not, his long absence from *Discovery* on the Southern Journey had forced the virtue on him, and his men responded in kind. When he had left the ship in November there had still been a real question mark hanging over his first lieutenant, but in his absence Royds had blossomed in his role, teaching Scott an important lesson in delegation and trust that would serve him well with men like Pennell and Bowers in the future.

There was still the occasional wardroom *froideur*, almost inevitably caused by bridge and involving Koettlitz, but every journal told the same story of an essentially happy ship. A "polar winter could scarcely be imagined more internally comfortable than this second one of ours has been so far," Scott wrote expansively after a mid-winter dinner in the wardroom for the warrant officers; "there has scarcely been a friction—every element of trouble & discontent has disappeared with the crew so happily sent back in the 'Morning' . . . if there are quarrels they never come to my ears."

Perhaps it was only Armitage's punch talking—"Captain . . . quite as much excited as was necessary to his dignity," Hodgson noted—but whatever it was, it was certainly not due to the Heidsieck '95 that had been put on board for Edward VII at Cowes. "The carpenter asked me what it was about three parts through dinner," Wilson recorded in his diary. "He said it wasn't like any champagne he had ever drunk, because it 'didn't seem to do you any good.' He had done his best and been unable to get any forrarder on it."

But that dinner, and the next day's hangover, were rarities. For the most part the second winter slid past almost unnoticed. "Altogether the work is

precisely what it was last year, and carried out even more keenly and properly," Wilson noted in his diary towards the end of May. He was also reading hard, busily reconciling God and Darwin and ploughing somewhat
reluctantly through Wells—"full of stuff to make one think, but written by
a hard-minded, unpleasant scientific socialist . . . surely *not* a gentleman."
Skelton was reading A.E.W. Mason and Kipling's *Kim*—"very good."
Bernacchi had taken over Shackleton's position as editor of the *SPT*. Koettlitz could as often as not be found getting the "ump" over bridge or
because Barne had dressed up as a bear and ambushed him on the floe.
"Time passes fairly quietly & pleasantly," an unusually benign Skelton
wrote at the beginning of August. "We have several more or less heated
arguments in the Ward Room, which almost always end up all right & very
good things they are in their way. One or two people don't quite 'cotton' on
to it; old Koettlitz doesn't quite understand a little harmless leg-pulling
though he is a first-rate old chap in the main; Bernacchi gets his 'rag out'
over the most absurd things occasionally due apparently to a lack of a
decent public school training; & Mulock [Shackleton's replacement from
Morning], newly joined, is distinctly peculiar for such a youngster, a mixture of sulkiness, attempts at sarcasm, great readiness to take offence where
none is meant, a little conceit, a very unnecessary seriousness in general;
the Pilot is a little crude in his repartee & has most peculiar arguments,
but the rest are first rate, & 'give & take' in the proper manner. The Skipper joins in everything with the greatest tact."

Only Armitage felt out of it. There are lengthy gaps in his journal, and
pages torn out at crucial moments, but splicing his account with other
wardroom diaries it is clear that there was a major break between pilot and
skipper. Scott himself might not have particularly noticed it—he was
either remarkably above all pettiness or curiously blind to atmosphere on
occasions—but everyone else did. "I had another dose of the Pilot's opinions of things in general," Hodgson noted on 29 April, and Royds's diary for
the thirtieth fills in the background: "Apparently he has asked permission
to try his luck on a Southern Journey, and in my opinion his sole wish is to
beat the Captain's record. This the Capt wouldn't allow, not for that reason though by any means, and I am certain if he could see his way clear
that the Pilot really could get further south, and do good work, he would
let him go, but in his own mind he doesn't think he could, and so deems it
a waste of time to try, and so now I don't expect the Pilot will go at all, and
he has told both Barne and self that he doesn't wish to stand in our way at
all etc etc which is all bunkum, but it is so like the chap; what he is driving

at I don't know, but there is more to it than meets the eye, and he has some reason for talking to us like this."

The end of all this was a "coldness" that Armitage's diary speaks of, but even if Scott had wanted to give him his day of glory, resources and the absence of dogs would have ruled it out. He had decided to lead a western expedition himself to complete the work that Armitage had left undone, and on 28 July drew up the whole crew to sketch out plans. No one "should have any grievance about the journeys," Skelton recorded, "supposing one man was not getting as much sledging as another;—it was impossible for everyone to go everywhere; & that as far as they were concerned he would like to take all of them, in fact that they were all suitable men for the work."

It was a moot point whether anyone needed consoling at the idea of missing out on the Barrier or the plateau. Sledging was, though, as Williamson had philosophically noted in his journal, "the thing that has to be done." Winter, too, was taking its toll in a certain weariness that even Scott found hard to shake off. The health of the crew was good—Wilson put down soreness of the gums on the mess deck to the foulness of the language rather than scurvy—but the whole ship was more than ready for another season.

The most startling news from the doctors, in fact, was Wilson's discovery of a hard, calcareous growth on seals' hearts that suggested they suffered from gout. And as winter finally came to an end, and Williamson's "Old Sol" reappeared, the wardroom, at least, did its best to follow the seals' example. "Turtle soup, fish, seal-liver, roast beef, plum pudding & jellies," Scott noted, "all washed down with what is known as the King's Champagne—Heidsick [sic] '95." "Things rather more modest on the mess deck," Williamson wrote, "but they in the Ward Room made up for our quietness by playing up old Harry until late this morning."

Scott could not wait. The previous season might have brought its disappointments, but the one thing he now knew was that he could "feel absolute confidence" in the "pluck and endurance" of his men. They, and he, had come a long way since their first stumbling attempts. "All disappointment at our enforced detention has passed away," he wrote as the sun reappeared, and "All thoughts are turned towards the work that lies before us." And for himself he had, as he put it with nice understatement, the prospect that "this year's trip should be more interesting than the last."

Fifteen: Last Season

We are all very proud of our march out. I don't know where we are, but I know
we must be a long way to the west . . . besides which we cannot have marched so
many hours without covering a long distance. We have been discussing this matter at supper, and wondering whether future explorers will travel further over
this inhospitable country. Evans remarked that if they did they "would have to
leg it," and indeed I think they would.

SCOTT, *The Voyage of the Discovery*

O f all Scott's journeys, there is none that is so characteristic of his mixture of boldness and brinkmanship as the great summer explorations of
1903. In its own desperate way his Southern Journey with Wilson and
Shackleton remains a yardstick of a kind, and yet that was essentially a triumph of courage and sheer slog without any of the variety, imagination or
daring that marks his assault on the western mountains first pioneered the
season before.

With his resources stretched to their limits, manpower short, dogs non-
existent and sledges in short supply, Scott had been forced to work out his
priorities with a rigour that left no room to indulge Armitage's ambitions.
From early in the winter he had seen that they could mount no more than
two major supported journeys, and the tantalising omissions of the previous season naturally determined that one should complete Barne's surveying work at the southern extremes of Victoria Land and the other "find out
the nature of the interior of the ice-cap" that Armitage had left unexplored.

There were just sufficient resources for one further, unsupported journey, under Royds and Bernacchi, to the eastern Barrier, but from the first
the emphasis was on those geographical questions that could only be

answered to the west. With the pressures of time and the need to give *Discovery* every chance of getting out of the ice, Scott had only the first half of the season to work in, but by the end of the first week in September, just nineteen days after he had watched the returning sun from the top of Arrival Heights, he was ready to set off on a preliminary reconnaissance.

The previous year Armitage had shied away from the risks of a direct assault on the foot of the Ferrar Glacier, but Scott knew that if they could find a route up it they could save priceless time. Leaving the ship on the ninth, he and his party of six were across the strait by the thirteenth, and after a hard day's struggle camped at the start of the great ice and morainic turbulence that had confounded Armitage. That night "was an anxious one," Scott remembered. "On each side of us rose the great granite foothills. The light had been poor in the afternoon march, and now that the sun had sunk behind the mountains in a crimson glow, we were left with only the barest twilight. We had been forced to camp when we had suddenly found ourselves on a broken surface, and all about us loomed up gigantic ice-blocks and lofty morainic heaps. To-morrow was to decide whether these obstructions could be tackled; meanwhile the temperature had fallen to −49°, and in the frigid gloom our prospects did not look hopeful."

Back in *Discovery*, Scott had argued to himself, *a priori*, that there *must* be a way up from here, and with the sun shining cheerfully the next morning, the party pushed up the frozen bed of a stream that ran along the glacier's southern flank. It looked to begin with as though the distorted pinnacles and faces of the glacier wall were going to be unscalable, but the end of the stream bed left them with no option, and after a difficult, intricate climb and some heavy "porterage" they were onto the glacier and camped well into it in a small dip.

As they gazed upwards to the great sweep of the glacier the next morning, it looked "like a smooth polished road—a ribbon of blue down the centre of which ran a dark stream caused by a double line of boulders." There still lay four or five miles of uncharted ice between them and their prospective depot site, but with their luck again in, this proved no problem and by afternoon they were two thousand feet above sea level and abreast the cliffs of Cathedral Rocks towering four thousand feet above them.

It had been a brilliant performance, and even with time lost to a blizzard in the sound, it had taken them just a week to Armitage's three to reach this spot. With temperatures in the −50s, though, there was little temptation to hang around, and after depoting their provisions they

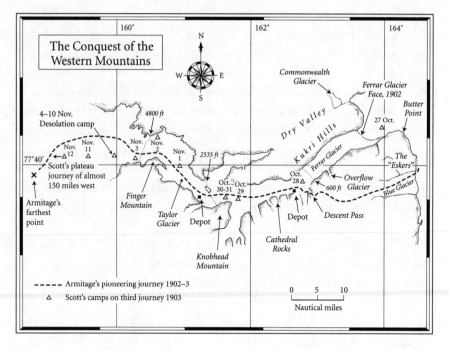

The Conquest of the Western Mountains

- - - - Armitage's pioneering journey 1902–3
△   Scott's camps on third journey 1903

0   5   10
Nautical miles

headed back down the glacier by a more northerly route that cut out the
need for any portering.

Understandably smug with themselves after a fifty-mile march in just
two and a half days, they were mildly put out to find their temperatures
were nothing compared to those the other parties had experienced on the
Barrier. "Nothing is more delightful," Scott wrote in his journal two nights
later,

> than to arrive back with a real sledging appetite after our hard
> experience & compare notes . . . Whitfield lost 10lbs on his Ter-
> ror trip, he is described as standing outside the tent door smok-
> ing his pipe with his hands in his pockets at a temperature of
> −61 & the air of cheerful satisfaction of one who contemplates
> his garden in the evening of some summer day at home . . .
>
> Evans suffers from frostbites on nose & fingers but he treats
> them with such comical indifference that it is impossible to do
> other than laugh.
>
> Barne takes everything as it comes in his usual smiley fash-
> ion, disregarding frostbites on his own person & ready to do
> anything to pull others through . . . The seriousness of things is

never exaggerated with him and one feels somehow that his pluck & stamina are unfathomable qualities.

Scott was entitled to his satisfaction—as Ferrar had written, the mood in *Discovery* was very much his doing—and they had come through hardships and difficulties that would have sunk them two years before. By this time, however, he knew the Antarctic too well to permit any complacency, and the ship was soon as busy again as ever, with the wardroom resembling "a pawnbrokers shop" as sleeping bags and garments were hung from every available space to dry before the next journeys got under way.

The restriction on time meant that the Magnetic Pole itself was probably out of reach, but with Bernacchi's party out on the Barrier and Scott on the plateau, results could be obtained that made its strict geographical conquest unnecessary. For Scott himself the real prize, anyway, lay with the discovery of Victoria Land's imagined "western coast," and by 12 October he and his party of twelve—advance, geological, and support—were ready to go.

Scott was determined that it should be done by "hard marching" "first and last," and, in spite of loads of two hundred pounds a man, they had their four eleven-foot sledges at the Cathedral Rocks depot by the sixteenth. Williamson and Dailey had felt the effects of the severe pace on the way up, but the next morning the whole party was on the march again, and by the afternoon of the sixth day was at a height of 4,500 feet and crossing the glacial basin terminating in the "Knob Head Moraine" that had taken Armitage twenty-seven days to reach.

Even after almost two years in McMurdo Sound, Scott was stunned by the grandeur of the scene. Their route up from Cathedral Rocks had been hemmed in on both sides by lowering cliffs of greyish-black gneiss and rich brown basalt, but now they were in the open, with every "wrinkle and crease" of Mount Lister visible, and the two great, converging arms of the glacier—the south-west arm of the Ferrar and the north-west arm of the Taylor—rising up ahead of them.

Scott, however, was not given much time to enjoy it, as that same night, while they "were still absorbed in the beauty and the novelty of the scene," the carpenter came to tell him that the German silver had split under the runners of two of their four sledges. In soft snow where the wooden runners needed no protection that would not have mattered, but on the hard ice of the glacier it was a disaster, and when a third sledge split its runners the next morning there was no choice but to turn back.

"Things which have gone fast in the past," Scott wrote ominously on the eighteenth, "will positively have to fly in the future," and he was as good as his word. With eighty-seven miles to cover and six thousand feet of glacier to be negotiated, he had the party away next day at the crack of dawn, scrambling their way down as best they could, pausing only to snatch a quick lunch, before they "were off again over the rugged, slippery ice." "If he can do it, I don't see why I can't; my legs are as long as his," was Thomas Kennar's constant mantra as another series of forced marches took them back to *Discovery* in record time. "In spite of [their] marching," though, Scott admitted, "it was a blow to be back in the ship so soon after we had made our first hopeful start, and as can be imagined, I did not allow time to be wasted in preparing to be off again."

Such a phrase in Scott is normally code for what Skelton would have called a "panic," and it is clear from Armitage's diary that the frustration was taken out on the man whose dilatoriness had put him under such pressure. On the night of the twenty-fourth the pilot went to see Scott in his cabin, asking him why he had been so unfriendly since his return, ignoring him entirely or only speaking briefly when he did. For a moment Scott said nothing, and then replied—at which point the pages are torn out of the journal, leaving the explanation lost.

It is impossible to know what is missing, or whether it was Armitage himself or someone else who excised the pages, but the timing suggests that the Western Journey must have been at the root of it. Scott was seldom above lashing out in the heat of the moment when things went wrong, and now that he had pioneered and mastered for himself the route Armitage had ducked the previous season, his second-in-command's "failures" of reconnaissance, initiative and determination must have struck him as little short of a spineless dereliction of duty.

More prosaically, Scott had little time to waste on Armitage if he was to salvage anything from the shortened season. Out of the scanty materials left in the ship the carpenters managed to cobble together one eleven-foot and one seven-foot sledge, and within five hectic days a reduced party of nine—Ferrar and Skelton the only other officers—were again on their way and crossing the sea ice on the march to the mainland.

There was more trouble with their sledge runners on the lower slopes, and on the morning of the thirtieth another sharp reminder of the dangers when a sudden wind swept down on their camp and took off the sleeping bags, socks and finneskoes that lay scattered around them on the ice. In other circumstances they might have enjoyed the comedy of the chase that followed, but with their bags well on their way to the precipitous north fall of the glacier, no one was in any doubt as to the potential consequences.

It was not just around their camp that the winds had been blowing, and after two days stuck in their tents, they reached their old depot to find a more devastating loss than the odd piece of clothing. "In travelling to the west," Scott later explained, they were going to be out of sight of any landmark for weeks on end, and thus effectively in the same position "as a ship at sea," dependent on the sun and stars for their navigation and on "an excellent little publication issued by the Royal Geographical Society and called 'Hints to Travellers' " for the necessary declination and logarithm tables with which to make their calculations.

It has such a wonderfully inappropriate ring to it, that "Hints to Travellers," so redolent of Baedekers and English clergymen in Florence, that it is hard to grasp the significance of the discovery that it was gone. "The gravity of this loss can scarcely be exaggerated," an appalled Scott wrote on realising that it had been swept away with Skelton's goggles when the winds had wrenched open their instrument case; "if we did not return to the ship to make good our loss, we should be obliged to take the risk of marching away into the unknown without exactly knowing where we were or how to get back."

Now "we shall never know where we are," a more laconic Skelton wrote in his journal, but if he believed that they should turn back, he kept the thought to himself. For his own part Scott was determined that they were not retreating a second time, and when he spelled out the options to the rest of the party, force of personality, argument—or simply the fear of showing fear?—carried the whole team with him without one demurring voice.

And for all the risks it involved, it was not completely foolhardy, because Scott realised that if they could work out the sun's noon altitude they could at least use the sun compass to hold to their latitude. This meant in effect that any thoughts of heading northwards towards the Magnetic Pole were finally ruled out, but it still in theory left the option of following a due west course across the plateau in search of that illusory coastline and an eastwards retreat along the same line to the head of the "right" glacier.

There were still the upper reaches of the glacier to be overcome first, but by 4 November they were at seven thousand feet, and there was a real sense that the summit was in reach. The peaks of the mountains on each side still towered high above them, but the glacier itself had changed and opened out, with the boundary cliffs that had pressed in on them lower down now cut through by the wide channels of tributary ice flows. After heavy pulling into a bitter and strengthening wind, the party drew breath in the shelter of Armitage's "Depot Nunatak" before pushing on towards the foot of the last immense ice-fall at the top of the glacier. Scott knew that once they were past this final obstacle the destructively hard blue ice would be behind them, but before they had got more than halfway to it they were caught up in the blinding, driving snow of a full-blown gale.

Everyone was soon badly frostbitten in the face, but with nowhere to camp, they forced their way on at a virtual run, desperate to find shelter while they could. In the wretched visibility there was no question of leaving equipment for even a minute, and with their runners again split, the next hour became an increasing nightmare as they dragged the crippled sledges backwards and forwards in a desperate search for a patch of snow soft enough to pitch their tents on. "I shall not forget the next hour in a hurry," Scott wrote. ". . . At last we saw a white patch, and made a rush for it; it proved to be snow indeed, but so ancient and wind-swept that it was almost as hard as the solid ice itself. Nevertheless, we knew it was this or nothing, and in a minute our tents and shovels were hauled off the sledges and we were digging for dear life. I seized the shovel myself, for my own tent party, but found I could not make the least impression on the hard surface. Luckily, at this moment the boatswain came to my relief, and managing the implement with much greater skill, succeeded in chipping out a few small blocks. Then we tried to get up the tent, but again and again it and the poles were blown flat; at last the men came to our assistance, and with our united efforts the three tents were eventually erected."

As they finally crawled exhausted into their sleeping bags, hands, feet and faces all badly frostbitten, Scott knew how close they had come to disaster. "The temperature tonight is –24°," he wrote in his sledging diary, "and it is blowing nearly a full gale; it is not too pleasant lying under the shelter of our thin, flapping tent under such conditions, but one cannot help remembering that we have come mighty well out of a very tight place. Nothing but experience saved us from disaster to-day, but I feel pretty confident that we could not have stood another hour in the open."

With every hold-up he watched helpless as rations and ambitions for their plateau journey contracted together. "The skipper gets very impatient under these delays," Skelton noted that evening, "and says rather hasty and unkind things but," he added with that experience of Scott that they now all had, "I don't think he means anything at all, and certainly the weather we are having is enough to try the patience of Job."

Job he was not, but Scott would have been even more grateful to their luck and experience if he had known that a week later they would still be in the same place. Even after his experience of the Barrier with Wilson and Shackleton, he had no hesitation in calling this the worst week of his life, and for seven days they lay in their bags twenty-two out of the twenty-four hours a day, entombed by the drifting snow in the precarious, isolated world of their tents. "It is impossible to describe how awful the past week has been," Scott later wrote; "it is a 'nightmare' to remember . . . To sleep much was out of the question, and I scarcely know how the other long hours went. In our tent we had one book, Darwin's delightful 'Cruise of the Beagle,' and sometimes one or another would read this aloud until our freezing fingers refused to turn the pages. Often we would drop into conversation, but, as can be imagined, the circumstances were not such as to encourage much talking, and most of the commoner topics were threadbare by the end of the week. Sometimes we would gaze up at the fluttering green canvas overhead, but this was not inspiriting."

With the ice inside their sleeping bags becoming a threat to circulation, there was an attempt on the sixth morning to break out, but within ten minutes both of Scott's hands were "gone," and Skelton and the boatswain in an even worse state. "I think the wind and drift have never been quite so bad as to-day," Scott wrote, "and the temperature is −20°. Things are looking serious; I fear the long spell of bad weather is telling on us. The cheerfulness of the party is slowly waning; I heard the usual song from Lashly this morning, but it was short-lived and dolorous." "Luck is not with us this trip," he continued characteristically, "and yet we have worked hard to make things go right. Something must be done to-morrow, but what it will be, to-morrow can only show."

By the time Scott had finished this Western Journey, in fact, he would have used up a lifetime's worth of luck, and the change of fortune began the next day. The air was still "thick as a hedge" with snow when they turned out of their tents, but a lull in the wind was all Scott needed, and dashing off breakfast, and bundling everything "anyhow" onto the sledges, he had his men into their harnesses and stumbling away from "Desolation Camp" towards the last ice-fall before the wind could imprison them again.

And "since that we have got to the top," an incredulous Scott wrote later the same day, "but how, I don't quite know, nor can I imagine how we have escaped accident. On starting we could not see half-a-dozen yards ahead of us; within a hundred yards of the camp we as nearly as possible walked into an enormous chasm; and when we started to ascend the slope we crossed any number of crevasses without waiting to see if the bridges would bear. I really believe we were in a state when we none of us really cared much what happened; our sole thought was to get away from that terrible spot."

At Desolation Camp Ferrar and his geological team had peeled off to explore the glacier, but that day, 11 November, the ascent party climbed seven hundred feet, and the next day the same again. By the thirteenth the incline had at last flattened out, and their aneroids at evening camp showed an altitude of 8,900 feet above sea level—the farthest point reached by Armitage's party. The following day, too, the weather cleared enough to give them their first real sense of the upland world they had entered. "We found ourselves on a great snow-plain," Scott wrote, "with a level horizon all about, but above this to the east rose the tops of mountains, many of which we could recognise. Directly to the east and to the north-east only the extreme summits of the higher hills could be seen, but to the south-east Mount Lister and the higher peaks of the Royal Society Range still showed well above our level."

The prospect was vital to Scott, because it gave him the chance to work out their latitude, and to fix identifying landmarks for the return journey to the top of the glacier. He had also been wrestling with the problem of the lost "Hints" on the ascent, and had come up with a rough but imaginative solution, realising that if he could find some way of calculating the sun's declination he could at least keep an approximate idea of their latitude. "With this idea"—"and for the benefit of explorers who might be in like case in future"—Scott engagingly explained, "I carefully ruled out a sheet of my notebook into squares with the intention of making a curve of the sun's declination. I found on reflection that I had some data for this curve, for I could calculate the declination for certain fixed days, such as the day when the sun had returned to us . . . To make a long story short, I plotted all these points on my squared paper, and joined them with a freehand curve of which I have some reason to be proud, for on my return to the ship I found it was nowhere more than 4° in error."

Nothing could better illustrate Scott's blend of imagination and daring, but faced by the undifferentiated monotony of the great ice-cap, even he was reluctant to place the trust in his calculations that they deserved. "I do not think," he wrote, "that it would be possible to conceive a more cheerless prospect than that which faced us at this time, when on this lofty, desolate plateau we turned our backs upon the last mountain peak that could remind us of habitable lands. Yet before us lay the unknown. What fascination lies in that word! Could anyone wonder that we determined to push on, be the outlook ever so comfortless."

It was perhaps as well that last question was a rhetorical one, because nobody in his party can have been under any illusions as to the risks they were running. The wind up on the plateau was never more than 3 or 4 on the Beaufort scale, but with the thin air and biting temperatures, every step they took into this "unknown" was almost visibly sapping their dwindling energies.

For three days of alternating hard, worn ice and clinging soft snow, they managed a pace of something around a mile an hour. By this time the sledges had been separated in an attempt to speed up progress, but though that marginally improved things it was plain that Skelton, Handsley and Lashly could only keep their more cumbersome twelve-foot sledge in sight of Scott's at a serious cost. On the afternoon of the seventeenth, Skelton warned him that they might have to form two separate parties, "which he readily accepted. I told him I thought the strain rather too much and might damage some of us, but he said the Boatswain and Evans both wished to go on as at present, so I said I was willing to abide by his decisions and if we couldn't keep up, work longer hours and so arrive in the same camp every night. So it was arranged that Evans and myself should change tents."

It was important for Scott to have with him a man like Skelton, the one officer in the party other than Wilson with the courage and independence to fight his men's corner, but in the naval culture in which they were all immersed his engineer might have saved his breath. "Handsley came to me to-night to beg that he might not be made an example of again," Scott wrote on the twentieth, after they had been reduced to relaying by the collapse with altitude sickness of the imposing seaman who had joined *Discovery* in New Zealand. "I tried to explain that I had no intention of reflecting on his conduct, but apparently nothing will persuade him but that his breakdown is in the nature of a disgrace. What children these men are! And yet what splendid children! They won't give in till they break down, and then they consider their collapse disgraceful. The boatswain has been suffering agonies from his back; he has been pulling just behind me, and in some sympathy that comes through the traces I have got to know all about him, yet he has never uttered a word of complaint, and when he knows my eye is on him he straightens up and pretends he is just as fit as ever. What is one to do with such people?"

In an expedition narrative of almost a thousand pages, with scarcely a false note, this sounds very much like one of them. This is something that has to be treated with the caution that every different age demands, of course, and yet if it is clear that it was precisely this culture that brought the best out of Scott's men, the line between a shared set of values uniting wardroom and mess deck and a species of moral intimidation was a much finer one than Scott's encomium here would suggest.

Scott could not afford to watch his western ambitions gutter away in the same fashion as they had on the Southern Journey, and after two more disappointing days he called Skelton into his tent to tell him that he was sending him back with Handsley and Feather. "Those told off to return took it extremely well," Scott recorded, but "they could not disguise their disappointment." "I said I hoped we hadn't delayed him at all," Skelton wrote, "and that it was hard lines to come up here a second time and not get farthest west, to which he answered that it was hard lines, that he was very sorry to part company, but that he was anxious about Handsley having already had experience of chest breakdown last year, so that something must be done."

There were few men that Scott would have less liked to lose than Skelton, but in Leading Stoker Lashly and Seaman Evans he had the perfect colleagues for the hard, gruelling slog ahead. "Evans was a man of Herculean strength," Scott wrote with that "Edwardian" admiration for "physique" so typical of him, "very long in the arm and with splendidly developed muscles. He had been a gymnastic instructor in the Navy, and had always been an easy winner in all our sports which involved tests of strength. He weighed 12st. 10lbs. in hard condition."

"I suppose you would follow Scott to hell if he had decided to go there?" an officer once asked Evans, and his answer, "Yes I would," could equally have come from William Lashly. From the earliest days in *Discovery* Skelton had identified his stoker as far and away the finest man in the ship, and that was, improbably, a judgement with which the lower deck would have agreed. Dependable, hard-working, good-natured and "a fine clean living man," as Clarence Hare fondly remembered him, the thirty-five-year-old Lashly was physically and mentally a different type altogether from "Taff" Evans. Over their years in the Antarctic together Scott and Evans would develop a particularly close bond, but in terms of all those sledging virtues that were now needed—resourcefulness, indifference to hardship, cheerfulness and sheer brute strength—Scott knew that there was nothing to split the two men. "Lashly, in appearance, was the most deceptive man I have ever seen," he wrote in another little burst of muscle-inspired lyricism. "He was not above the ordinary height, nor did he look more than ordinarily broad, and yet he weighed 13st, 8 lbs., and had one of the largest chest measurements in the ship. He had been a teetotaller and non-smoker all his life, and was never in anything but the hardest condition."*

And as they trudged westwards across the great, featureless plain, with the wind constantly in their faces, that officer's suggestion that Evans would have followed Scott to hell could not have seemed such a hypothetical one. "The wind is the plague of our lives," Scott wrote on the twenty-sixth. "It has cut us to pieces. We all have deep cracks in our nostrils and cheeks, and our lips are broken and raw; our fingers are also getting in a shocking state; one of Evans's thumbs has a deep cut on either side of the nail which might have been made by a heavy slash with a knife . . . There is a good deal of pain also in the tent at night, and we try to keep our faces as still as possible; laughing is a really painful process, and from this point of view jokes are not to be encouraged."

They had set the end of the month as their outward limit, but with clouds threatening the use of their one navigational tool, even Scott was thinking of turning back early. With every mile covered westward, the illusory hope of another coast—or at least coastal mountains—that might have been some reward, receded with it. "The *sastrugi* now get on my nerves," he wrote on 30 November, with an almost prevenient hatred for a landscape that seemed to belong to some "evil dream": "they are shaped like the barbs of a hook with their sharp points turned to the east; from which direction many look high and threatening; and each one now seems to suggest that, however easy we may have found it to come here, we shall have a very different task in returning."

But they had, at least, reached their farthest point, and if they had found no mythical coast they had opened up men's minds for the first time to the immensity of Antarctica. "We have finished our last outward march, thank heaven!" Scott wrote the same day, a strain of Hardyesque romanticism bedding down oddly with the masochistic traditions of McClintock and Albert Markham:

---

*Not, of course, an entire irrelevance if you are man-hauling together. Scott was not the only one in *Discovery* to be concerned with chest measurements. The regular winter inspections stirred enough interest for Duncan to record his statistics in his journal: "Chest empty 35 Chest full 38½ Waist 28½ Bisops 13 Forearm 11¾ Caff 15 Weight 188 lbs Blow 277 Grip right 138 left 136."

Nothing has kept us going during the past week but the determination to carry out our original intention of going on to the end of the month, and so we have pitched our last tent . . .

Here, then, tonight we have reached the end of our tether, and all we have done is to show the immensity of this vast plain. The scene about us is the same as we have seen for many a day, and shall see for many a day to come—a scene so wildly and awfully desolate that it cannot fail to impress one with gloomy thoughts . . .

But, after all, it is not what we see that inspires awe, but the knowledge of what lies beyond our view. We see only a few miles of ruffled snow bounded by a vague wavy horizon, but we know that beyond that horizon are hundreds and even thousands of miles which can offer no change to the weary eye, while on the vast expanse that one's mind conceives one knows that there is neither tree nor shrub, nor any living thing, nor even inanimate rock—nothing but this terrible limitless expanse of snow. It has been so for countless years, and it will be so for countless more. And we, little human insects, have started to crawl over this awful desert, and are now bent on crawling back again. Could anything be more terrible than this silent, wind-swept immensity when one thinks such thoughts.

They were already "terribly hungry," too, and soon after turning back were again held up by bad weather. As Scott lay in his sleeping bag in the middle of the day, he reckoned that they were seventeen marches out from the glacier, with fourteen days of full rations and—"perhaps"—twelve of oil. As ever, he had based his calculations on the assumption that things would go as he *needed* them to go, and he knew that any delay now would put them in "Queer Street." "At the high altitude to which we had climbed," he later wrote with some puzzlement, "and with the low temperatures . . . to find banks of cloud still above us was unexpected and added a most alarming circumstance . . . we had placed ourselves in a position from which we could only hope to retreat by relying on our hard condition and utilising all our marching powers; a simple arithmetic sum showed that we could not afford an hour's delay."

Luck this time was with them, though, and after two hours' incarceration in their bags, Evans put his head out of the tent and announced "in his usual, matter-of-fact tones that the sun was shining." They had their sledges packed and the sail hoisted in record time, and had soon recovered the lost hours and distance, marching in the better light at a great pace over a surface that in the earlier gloom had seemed so hazardous.

Scott was lucky in another way, too, because whatever his own private anxieties, Lashly and Evans seemed "undefeatable," as hard as ever on the march, and as good-humoured in the tent. Scott never quite mastered the single verse of the single song that constituted Lashly's full repertoire, but as they lay in their sleeping bags at the end of the day's march, arguing through long evenings over naval matters and deciding that the three of them could run the service a good deal better than any Board of Admiralty, "rank" clearly came to matter as little as could have ever have been possible in the Edwardian navy.

By 3 December they had lost the last, fading signs of their outward tracks, and though they picked them up momentarily again the next day, that was the end of the navigational assistance. Two days later Scott was concerned enough about their oil supplies to add another half-hour to their daily march, but by the ninth a "sandy layer of loose ice crystals" had made underfoot conditions bad enough to render any such marginal tinkering futile.

They were also getting hungrier. The same ritual that Shackleton had devised for dividing rations on the Southern Journey was employed again, and with about as much satisfaction. The imaginary menu Scott dreamed of was different, but that was about all. On the Barrier it had been beefsteak pies and Shackleton's "three-decker puddings." Now, on the plateau, all Scott could think of was a bowl of Devonshire cream. "I think Evans's idea of joy is pork," he wrote, "while Lashly dreams of vegetables, and especially apples. He tells us stories of his youth when these things, and not much else, were plentiful."

Even with another hour added to their marching time, it was looking inevitable that they would have to cut back on food, when after five gruelling hours of hauling the next day, they got their first distant sighting of mountains. The relief was immense, but while it meant that they now knew that they were approaching the edge of the plateau, that was all they did know. Somewhere at the back of his mind, Scott had imagined that their problems would be over once they saw mountains, but with visibility poor and low clouds hanging over the peaks, it was impossible to recognise a single landmark. The cloud cover over the Barrier had made it difficult already with his makeshift chart, and though he thought they were probably to the south of the right glacier, there was no way of being sure.

And, hungry, hollow-cheeked and frostbitten—"gaunt shadows of their former selves"—they could not afford to get it wrong. Evans's nose in particular suffered almost constantly from frostbites, rendering him a "most curious-looking object. He speaks of it with a comic forbearance," Scott wrote with a kind of Dickensian relish, "as though, whilst it scarcely belonged to him, it was something for which he was responsible, and had to make excuses. When I told him of its fault to-day, he said in a resigned tone, 'My poor old nose again; well, there, it's chronic!' "

So long as they continued east they knew that they must eventually reach the plateau edge, and on the thirteenth they were at last beginning to descend. But in the swirling drift of a storm, without "any notion" of where they were, they "might have been walking over the edge of a precipice" for all that Scott knew to the contrary. In any other circumstances he would not have dreamed of pressing on, but conditions now were an irrelevance, and they went to sleep knowing that nothing outside could be worse than the certain starvation that faced them if another blizzard entombed them in their tent.

The next morning the all-important mountain peaks were still obscured, and Scott called the "council of war" they had all known was coming. It was "bitterly cold, and the only result of our deliberations was to show more clearly that we did not know where we were. In this predicament I vaguely realised that it would be rash to go forward, as the air was becoming thick with snowdrift, but then to stop might mean a long spell in a blizzard camp . . . I asked the men if they were prepared to take the risk of going on; they answered promptly in the affirmative. I think after all our trying experiences we were all feeling pretty reckless."

Heading straight for the ice disturbance that blocked their path, they began to thread their way through a maze of hummocks and crevasses, until after a while the surface became at once smoother and steeper. The danger now was that the sledge was beginning to overrun them, but with Scott at the front picking out a path and the two men behind acting as brakes, they successfully edged their way down the steepening slope, until suddenly Lashly slipped. In a moment he was on his back and hurtling past Scott, followed an instant later by Evans. The three men were tied together, and the moment Scott braced himself to arrest their fall he too was whipped off his feet, and sent "flying downward with an ever-increasing velocity." As he fell he had time to shout out a fatuous warning, before in a state of curiously "vague wonder" as to what would happen next, he found that the smooth surface had given way to a rougher incline that pitched them down in a series of immense bounds onto a slope of rough, wind-swept snow.

It seemed a miracle that there were no broken bones, but they were all badly shaken and bruised, with Lashly the worst sufferer. As the lightest of the three, Scott had probably come out of it best, and as he pulled himself together and took stock of the three-hundred-foot drop they had just survived, he realised that they had quite literally fallen into the right glacier: "ahead and on either side of us appeared well-remembered landmarks, whilst behind, in the rough broken ice-wall over which we had fallen, I now recognised at once the most elevated ice cascade of our valley . . . I cannot but think that this sudden revelation of our position was very wonderful. Half an hour before we had been lost; I could not have told whether we were making for our own glacier or for any other, or whether we were ten or fifty miles from our depot . . . Now in this extraordinary manner the curtain had been raised; we found that our rule-of-thumb had accomplished the most accurate 'land fall,' and down the valley we could see the high cliffs of the Depot Nunatak where peace and plenty awaited us."

It had been an astonishing navigational achievement of Scott's—fourteen days across an unknown, featureless plain with virtually no aid—but they were not home yet, and between them and Depot Nunatak lay the second cascade. Under the conditions there could be no thought of hunting round for an easy descent, and harnessing themselves together in an arrowhead formation, with Scott in the middle, Evans to his left and Lashly to his right, they had just begun to pick a slow path down when Scott and Evans "stepped on nothing" and disappeared from view.

Dangling at the end of his trace, with showers of ice-crystals tumbling around him, the blue walls of ice on either side and "a very horrid looking gulf below," Scott took off his goggles to see Evans suspended just above him. Swinging himself from side to side in an attempt to secure a foothold, his leg hit a projection, and pulling himself up, he managed to get just enough of a purchase to take stock. "I found myself standing on a thin shaft of ice which was wedged between the walls of the chasm—how it came there I cannot imagine, but its position was wholly providential; to the right or left, above or below, there was not a vestige of another such support—nothing, in fact, but the smooth walls of ice. My next step was to get Evans into the same position as myself, and when he had slipped his harness well up under his arms I found that I could pilot his feet to the bridge."

They had fallen about twelve feet, and above them they could see the silhouette of their broken sledge bridging the crevasse, the one frail support that was keeping them from the chasm beneath. It was clear to all of them that it could not hold for long, and while Scott and Evans balanced on their ice bridge, Lashly—who had miraculously escaped the drop—edged himself down to the sledge and, clinging on with one hand, somehow managed to extract their skis with the other and slide them beneath.

With Lashly's whole body braced against the strain, and the skis making the bridge that much more secure, Scott began to climb. The cold of the crevasse was already taking its toll of faces and hands, and with heavy clothes and frostbitten fingers even twelve feet seemed impossible. "But it was no use thinking about it, so I slung my mitts over my shoulders, grasped the rope, and swung off the bridge. I don't know how long I took to climb or how I did it, but I remember I got a rest when I could plant my foot in the belt of my harness, and again when my feet held on the rings of my belt. Then came a mighty effort till I reached the stirrup formed by the rope span of the sledge, and then, mustering all the strength that remained, I reached the sledge itself and flung myself panting on the snow beyond. Lashly said, 'Thank God!' and it was perhaps then that I realised that his position had been worst of all."

Scott's hands were white to the wrist, but after five minutes hugging them to his chest, circulation was restored enough for him to help Evans. Lowering his own harness down the crevasse, he and Lashly hauled from above while a frostbitten Evans climbed up from beneath, emerging at last with the first words of astonishment Scott had ever heard from him—"Well, I'm blowed."

With a bitter wind again blowing, there was no time to stand around admiring their escape, and harnessing themselves in single file as a precaution, they dragged their stricken sledge down to the shelter of Depot Nunatak. "As long as I live I can never forget last night," Scott wrote the next day of that evening, as they had sat in temperatures above zero, drying their clothes on the ground outside and luxuriating in their first warmth and release from danger in weeks. Battered and weary, Lashly sang over his cooking pot, as the smoke rose in a thin vertical trail, and Evans mulled over the events of the last hours. "With his sock half-on he would pause to think out our adventures in some new light," Scott wrote, "and would say suddenly, 'Well, sir, but what about that snow bridge?' or if so-and-so hadn't happened 'where would we be now?' and then the soliloquy would end with 'My word, but it was a close call!' "

The fourteenth marked the end of their difficulties, and over the next two days they rapidly covered the route down to their old camp at Knob Head Moraine. The contours of the glacier meant that they still could not see into the sound below, but anxious as he was to discover the condition of the sea ice, Scott decided on one last detour down a northern outlet running out of the great glacial "basin" that he had noticed on the way up. It was a historic decision. As they set off down it, Scott was expecting nothing more than a six-thousand-foot drop down to the sea, but at the end of a rough descent and a narrow *schist* between towering cliffs, he was rewarded instead by the bizarre sight of the first dry valley found in Antarctica.

It was a discovery that had almost been Ferrar's. It seems only right, though, that it should crown this journey, because it is hard to imagine anyone but Scott having the energy, curiosity or physical strength to make such a detour at the end of it. A good place for growing spuds was Lashly's one response to the Martian landscape, and if that underplays the significance of their find, it captures perfectly the element of understatement that accompanied one of the great journeys of polar history. It had spanned fifty-nine days and over seven hundred miles. It had revealed the nature of Antarctica's plateau and the existence of dry valleys. It was the journey on which the lower deck had come of age. It was the journey, too, when Scott matured into a leader of real stature. Luck had constantly been on his side, but he had earned it. Courage, daring, speed, endurance, leadership and imagination—the Western Journey had the lot. All they needed now to complete their satisfaction was the sight of open water in the sound below that would spell *Discovery*'s release. As they approached their second depot beneath Cathedral Rocks, McMurdo at last came into view. Below them, dashing all Scott's hopes, lay an unbroken sheet of ice.

Sixteen: A Long Wait

I am afraid that [Sir Clements] has brought it on himself as he would not be advised . . . were you his son he could not consider your interests more . . . The truth is I fear he is getting a little too old.

HANNAH SCOTT, 8 *July 1903*

There were only four men in *Discovery* when Scott returned on Christmas Eve, with the rest out on the sea-ice to the north, where the sawing operations that Scott had pre-arranged with Armitage were now well under way.

Scott already knew from messages left at their glacier depots that Skelton had got his men back safely, and over the next days he caught up with the other expeditions. It was a long time now since Ferrar had been a liability to the expedition, and after parting from Scott at Desolation Camp he had repaid his confidence with a systematic exploration of the glacier valley under immensely difficult conditions that produced the first fossilised plant remains from Antarctica then known. It is a moot point whether Ferrar grasped the full significance of his finds—he was certainly modest enough about them—and it was over twenty years before he got the credit he deserved. Their charred condition meant that they produced no great excitement when they were first examined in London, but in 1928 the same palaeobotanist who had earlier dismissed them broke open a sample while he was rearranging the Natural History Museum collection, and found inside "undoubted fragments of the leaf *Glossopteris indica*" that gave "the first physically recovered evidence of the continent's place in the great southern super-continent of Gondwana."

There was other news, too, that finally resolved a debate that had been running within the wardroom since they had first arrived in McMurdo. From the first Scott had argued that the rhythms of disturbance on the Barrier suggested that the Great Barrier was a floating ice shelf, and Royds set out to test the theory with a series of temperature readings down crevasses. Close to land he found that the temperature fell with the depth to a mean level of −9°, but at a distance of ten miles from the coast the temperature first fell and then steadily rose, until at a depth of 154 feet it showed zero.

This was an increase that could only be explained by the presence of water beneath, and more by chance than judgement, Michael Barne was able to arrive at a figure at which the great ice Barrier moved over it. In 1902 Scott had set up a depot for his Southern Journey just off the bluff, aligning its position with a small peak on the bluff itself and with Mount Discovery. On visiting the same depot just over a year later Barne was surprised to find that the alignment no longer held, and subsequent measurements showed that in the intervening thirteen and a half months it had moved 608 yards in a direction a little to the east of north.

There were important magnetic readings from out on the Barrier by Bernacchi, too, some valuable surveying work from Shackleton's replacement, Sub-Lieutenant Mulock, and a glimpse of new land up what is now the Byrd Glacier; but no one knew better than Scott that all these results would count for little back at home if *Discovery* was stuck in the ice. Since he had got back to the ship he had been getting conflicting accounts of progress with the sawing work out at the ice camp, and on the last day of the year he went out with Lashly, Evans and the fully recovered Handsley to see for himself.

After the privations of the plateau they had more than made up for it in *Discovery*, and with Evans "swelling visibly" and Scott looking "awfully well," they had little to show for their hardships when they tramped into camp to the cheers of the ship's crew. There was a magic about these returns from a long sledging trip that never palled on Scott, and as he sat that evening on a packing case out on the ice, swapping stories with his men, or lay in his sleeping bag listening again to the "farmyard" sounds of McMurdo life, to the whistles and moans and grunts of the Weddell seals and the cawing of the skuas, to the squawks of the penguins and "the familiar snores of humanity," he knew for the first time that he had succeeded with *Discovery* in ways that simultaneously had everything and nothing to do with his own personal achievements.

It had taken him more than two years, and there had been casualties and mistakes along the way, but the crew were at last what "Birdie" Bowers would famously call "Scott's men." After their years in the ice they were looking fitter and healthier than they had ever been, but that was merely the external sign of things, the physical manifestation of a strength and self-reliance that ran the whole way through the crew from Scott himself to their makeshift cook. "It is a real treat to be amongst our people once more," he wrote as he looked on the results of his handiwork, "and to find them in such splendid condition and spirits. I do not think there is a whole garment in the party; judging by the torn and patched clothing, they might be the veriest lot of tramps, but one would have to go far to find such sturdy tramps. Everyone is burnt to a deep bronze colour by the sun . . . I do not think I ever saw such exuberant, overflowing health and spirits as now exists in this camp."

The only blot on this was Armitage and the hopeless failure that all their attempts at cutting a path through the seven feet of sea-ice had proved. The men had been at work on their eighteen-foot saws since the middle of December, but it had been obvious within days that it was point-less, and that only Armitage's stubborn refusal to rethink his orders was keeping the parties at an "absolutely futile" task. To be fair to Armitage, he was doing no more than carrying out his instructions, but those instruc-tions had been drawn up under different circumstances and with a differ-ent projection of the conditions they were likely to meet. When Scott had departed on his Western Journey he had nothing but the previous season's timetable to work on, and everything from the position of the camp to the date of starting sawing had been predicated upon a single shaky precedent that events had rendered obsolete.

It was hard for the other officers to know whether Armitage was press-ing on with orders in an attempt to make Scott seem ridiculous, or whether he was simply too timid to change them, but either way his last, failing credit was spent. The sawing, Skelton wrote on his return from the plateau, "was the most fearful waste of time one could possibly think of. One would think Armitage was entirely devoid of common sense, & that his only idea was to say that he had carried out orders . . . he also seemed to me to have been making himself particularly unpleasant to all hands especially Royds—absolutely tasteless."

Armitage was up to his old tricks, too, "stirrer" and bully to the fore. "To me it seems as if he was trying to spread dissention amongst us," Royds himself wrote ten days before Scott's return, "but if I can help it, he won't succeed . . . Spoke to Bunny about Armitage . . . just what I thought: he has twisted my words about and in general is trying to make a row . . . Poor Boatswain! I'm afraid he gets a rotten time from ABA."

"Glorious day," wrote Hodgson, a late but enthusiastic convert to naval ways. "Everybody is now denouncing the utter futility of continuing this farce. The Skipper arrived from the ship about 4:30 p.m. just as we were coming off watch & the sawing was suspended pro tem. There is no doubt that Armitage is in hot water."

Scott was, in fact, notably conciliatory in the way he handled Armitage, but his officers had been right, and the moment that he saw the farce for himself he immediately called it off. The men had been working with giant saws that were raised and lowered by ropes and handles from tripods, and in a fortnight's backbreaking work, Williamson noted a few days earlier, had "cut 174 yards of ice since we started, not so bad but only a flea bite to what we have to do."

By the time Scott arrived that figure had increased to two parallel cuts of 150 yards each, and with twenty miles still to go, and each exhausting stroke of the saw cutting no more than a fraction of an inch, there was no need "to work this sum out to appreciate the futility of further operations." "I have been much struck by the way in which everyone has cheerfully carried on this hopeless work until the order came to halt," Scott went on. "There could have been no officer or man amongst them who did not see from the first how utterly useless it was, and yet there has been no faltering or complaint, simply because all have felt that, as the sailor expresses it, 'Them's the orders.' "

For all the gratitude and sense of belonging, however, it was almost inevitable that Scott would suffer a reaction to his journey, and if he succeeded in disguising it from his other officers, he did not even try with Wilson. "The Captain asked me to come with him and camp on the shore at the mouth of the strand," Wilson's journal recorded on 1 January 1904, the day after Scott's arrival at the camp; "really he is feeling the effects of his journey pretty badly—he has very bad indigestion—and wants to get away from the ship and everyone and rest a bit."

Leaving only Evans, Lashly and two others to stock their larder in case *Discovery* remained trapped in the ice, Scott sent the rest of the officers and men back to the ship and set off with Wilson to the north. There was some vague talk between them of an attempt on the lower slopes of Erebus, but as after their Southern Journey the previous year, neither of them relished the prospect of hard work, and Scott settled for a nervy vigil at the ice-edge while Wilson contentedly set about exploring the region's wildlife.

The site they found for their tent was the sheltered plateau next to a small Adélie colony among the rocks of Cape Royds where Shackleton would later erect his *Nimrod* hut. "Words fail me to describe what a delightful and interesting spot this is," Scott wrote. "From our open tent door we look out onto open sea, deep blue but dotted with snowy white pack-ice. Erebus towers high above us on our right, and to the left we look away over the long stretch of fast-ice to the cloud-capped western mountains. We hear the constant chatter of the penguins, and find a wonderful interest in watching their queer habits; the brown fluffy chicks are still quite small, and the adult birds are streaming to and from the sea. Close about us skuas are nesting; they naturally regard us as intruders, and are terribly angry. The owners of one nest near by are perched on a rock; whenever we move they arch their necks and scream with rage, and when we go out of the tent they sweep down on us, only turning their course as their wings brush our heads."

A century later the Adélie colony is still there, the skuas still providing the same angry fighter cover for their nesting chicks, and as Scott sat staring out across to open sea, he must have wondered if *Discovery* was to become as permanent a fixture of the McMurdo landscape. There were few things that he hated more than an impotent passivity, but the two weeks wasted on the saws had shown that there was nothing to be done but to wait on that old and indifferent standby of his, "Providence."

However pessimistic he might have been about their chances, nothing could have prepared him for the blow awaiting him the next morning. He was sitting in the tent staring idly out onto the patch of open sea beyond the fast ice, when to his "blank astonishment" the startling sight of a ship framed in the doorway was "trumped" by an exclamation from Wilson, " 'Why there's another' . . . and sure enough a second ship heaves into sight." "We had of course taken for granted that the first ship was the 'Morning,' " Scott wrote, "but what in the name of fortune could be the meaning of this second one? We propounded all sorts of wild theories of which it need only be said that not one was within measurable distance of the truth." Scribbling an instruction for Armitage to send out a sledge party for the mails, Scott and Wilson set off across the fast-ice in search of Evans and Lashly, packing them off with the news to *Discovery*, while they traipsed across the fast-ice to where the two ships lay.

As Scott and Wilson approached, a party came out onto the ice to meet them, a mix of familiar faces from *Morning*'s last visit, and some that "were quite strange. Of course I learned at once that the second ship was the 'Terra Nova,' " Scott wrote that night, "but it was not until I had a long talk with my good friend Colbeck that I began to understand why a second ship had been sent and what a strangely new aspect everything must wear . . . I can only record that in spite of the good home news, and in spite of the pleasure of seeing old friends again, I was happier last night than I am tonight."

Nothing could have been more of an understatement, and nothing more humiliating than the dawning realisation that the second ship had been sent down in order to "rescue" him. It was some time before Scott could grasp the full significance of what lay behind this development, but there was nothing elusive or ambiguous about the first letter handed him by Colbeck, a blunt instruction from the Admiralty ordering him to abandon *Discovery* if she was not free from the ice by the time that *Morning* and *Terra Nova* had to sail.

The command was so patently a reprimand, too, that Scott can have been in no doubt what it meant for him personally; and yet even so it was the injustice and the sheer *folly* and waste that rankled most. He had never been in much doubt that Markham would find the means of sending *Morning* down again, but even with hindsight he found it difficult to see how the report he had sent home with the relief ship the previous autumn could have led to this. He had written to the Presidents at the end of March 1903 with details of the work carried out so far, but in reporting the outbreak of scurvy and alerting them to the probability of a second winter in the ice he had said nothing that could remotely have been interpreted as a plea for help.

With *Morning* to bring down fresh provisions, and a limitless supply of seal and penguin, Scott knew that *Discovery* could survive indefinitely in the ice, but in the emotional and ageing Markham's mind the spectre of Franklin had been raised. That might not have mattered so much if the funds had been available to send *Morning* down under the aegis of the Societies, but as estimates of cost swelled beyond their capabilities and Markham was forced to beg for aid, he unwittingly embarked on a course that would have serious consequences for Scott.

In Markham's over-excited imagination, the money needed for the relief had soared from an initial £6,000 to £15,000 before contracting again to £8,000, and in April 1903 he persuaded the RGS Council to approve a joint appeal with the RS to the Treasury for a sum that finally settled at £12,000. By the time this appeal had been passed by both Societies an extra ship had been added to requirements, and when, in his old inimitable style, Markham attempted to force the Treasury's hand with newspaper and parliamentary pressure, all the disparate political, scientific, academic, hydrographic and naval enemies he had made before *Discovery* even sailed were waiting to pay him back for a decade of hectoring autocracy.

To be fair to the old man, he never had anything but Scott's welfare in mind; but the problem was that while his judgement was showing signs of faltering powers, age had robbed him of none of his old, destructive talent for invective. "That wretched obstacle Wharton" . . . "That malignant cur Montefiori" . . . the Royal Society "sneaks" . . . "the wretched story of Treasury insolence and malignity" . . . "the jackal Tizard . . . that sneaking cur Balfour"—all the old targets were there, and a few new ones, as Markham launched himself into a campaign that seemed almost designed to antagonise the few people in establishment life who might still have felt sympathetic or at least neutral towards *Discovery*. From the Prime Minister designate to the Chief Hydrographer, Markham succeeded in alienating them all, and although the government only finally gave its answer in June, the conflict had spelled the end of Markham's reign. The Treasury agreed to shoulder the costs of the two "rescue" ships, but only on the punitive and humiliating condition for Markham that the operation should be placed in naval hands and *Morning* ceded "absolutely and at once to the Board of Admiralty."

"I have scarcely as yet grasped the true meaning of the news brought by 'Morning,' " Scott wrote in his journal two days after her arrival, as he tried to digest the implications of this coup for the expedition and himself, "but cannot but feel very depressed at present condition of affairs. Colbeck is to try his men on saws, we shall do all we can at our end to free 'Discovery' & Providence must do the rest, from the futility of our labours up to the present it is obvious the greater part of the work must be done by 'Providence.' The ice shows no inclination to go out, the pack is growing thicker . . . I feel very despondent with such a dismal alternative to the ship getting out."

It is arguable that Scott would never be so effective as a leader or an explorer again, and the bitterness of it for him was that he was being told to abandon *Discovery* at that precise moment when he was most conscious of success. On his last expedition he would assemble an infinitely more experienced and intellectually gifted staff, but with a young and varied crew and an almost ludicrously underpowered scientific team, he had succeeded with *Discovery* by sheer willpower and leadership in defining the geographical and physical parameters of Antarctic exploration for the whole Heroic Age.

The irony of it all was that if *Discovery* had escaped at the end of the second season, with all the achievements of the last year left undone, Scott would have gone back to public and professional acclaim, and in all probability a knighthood. In the letters from home brought down by *Morning*, Hannah Scott could scarcely contain her pride as she reported to her son what this or that admiral had said about him—Admiral McClintock was full of praise, Admiral Carr had given the toast of "The King & Con," Scott Keltie was all admiration—and Scott Keltie was a "sound man & a word from him means a great deal," she added, as if her mother's delight in hearing her son's praises sung had the smallest iota of discrimination about it.

"Are you not a proud woman," had been Scott Keltie's greeting at the RGS Antarctic Night, and mother and her "four good-looking daughters" had clearly wallowed in the reflected glory. "Ettie dined with us and she is so handsome & looking so well," Mrs. Scott went on, sounding more than ever like Jane Austen's Mrs. Bennet. "She did not of course wear the splendour of diamonds but she had an emerald on worth a large amount and became it well . . . Willy thought [Sir Clements] might have made a point of this by saying more about [the hardships undergone] but I feel sure it is the work done & not your powers of endurance that *you* would wish to have set before the public."

"I really think I am so proud of you that I am almost beside myself," she wrote again, after receiving the Patron's Medal on his behalf. As she had "no wish to rival Mrs. Baden Powell," she wonderfully told him, she had "asked Willy to go up on the platform" and bring it to her, "which I think is more dignified for me than going myself." "What an extraordinary conquest you have made of Mr. Royds!" she went on in the same letter; "the high praise he gives you in his letter to me and Mr. Ferrar is also full of good expressions of your power & fitness for the work, saying 'no-one could have been so good a leader.'"

At any other time Scott would have been happy to indulge his mother's pride, but coming after the Admiralty news, her letters must have made bitter reading. He "seems very down in the mouth," Hodgson wrote sympathetically, and something of his mood permeated the whole ship. "Oh what joy, we all started jumping around like the wild one," Williamson had exclaimed on the fifth, but his tone soon changed. "In the evening the Capt & officers came out on mess deck," he wrote five days later, "to hear the different reports & orders issued from the Royal Society & Royal Geographical Society . . . The Captain seems to be quite upset about it & said that he cannot realise the fact of deserting the ship, as abandoned she'll have to be this year if we cannot get her out, in clewing up his yarn he heartily thanked us one & all for having stuck to him through thick & thin, & after reading out his different orders he seemed to be quite greaved [sic] so we gave him 3 cheers to buck him up a bit & there's no doubt he deserves it if ever a man does."

This was a side of Scott his men had not seen. Nearly sixty years later, their gentle, civilised and accident-prone steward Reginald Ford recalled the speech. "Now for the incident," he wrote. "Captain Scott took an action which was almost unthinkable in those days for a Naval Commander. He assembled the ship's company on the main deck, first giving instruction that the water-tight doors leading into and out of the main deck should be closed. This was so that some members of the relief ships crews, which were on board, should not come in. He then read us all the Admiralty instructions. He had tears in his eyes and told us what a blow it was to him and said something to the effect that he must have had some enemy in the Admiralty as the orders were couched in such stringent terms as they gave him no option to even take a slight risk."

"Not one of us would voluntarily have abandoned the ship," Ford insisted, but the Admiralty orders left Scott no room for manoeuvre, and the next day his officers began drawing up lists of instruments and collections that had to be transferred to the relief ships. It was one thing to draw up plans, though, and another to implement them, and Scott could not bring himself to give an order that so clearly spelled defeat. A flagstaff had been erected on Tent Islet ten miles to the north of the ship, and first thing every morning *Discovery*'s telescope would be trained on it in the hope of seeing the signal that the ice was breaking up.

Through the first fortnight of January it seemed that the ice would never change, and on the fifteenth Scott at last ordered the transfer to begin. He had managed to convince himself that their scientific collections might as well go back in the relief ships as in *Discovery* whatever the outcome, but behind that reasoning was the starker truth that it was better to be doing something—*anything*—than just sitting and waiting for conditions to take their course.

In much the same spirit, he had the sawing parties resume working at Hut Point, and sent Royds northwards to experiment with their explosives. He knew the ice was too far out for any good to be done at either end, but the frustration and anxiety of the wait were beginning to take their toll. "Whitfield has been acting oddly since the mail," he wrote anxiously on the twenty-fourth, "when he seems to have received bad news, but I had no idea he would go off in this way by himself . . . It is to be hoped that there is nothing seriously the matter but I have great fears."

"Whitfield returned last night," Scott added the following day. "He says that he forgot to tell the boatswain he was going down to ships & afterwards knew he was in the wrong—all very weak but he says it with a most plausible air and one can detect absolutely no symptom of light headedness in his talk—still it is all very fishy—I have arranged for him to be kept in the ship & looked after."

On top of the anxieties over Whitfield, there was a scare, too, with Hodgson's health. "Yesterday morning Hodgson had a slight apoplectic seizure which alarmed us very much. He seemed perfectly fit & was going about his work when this occurred. Suddenly the nerves on the right hand side of his face & neck became affected he felt extremely sick and could not talk without mouthing his words . . . There is clearly something wrong with [Whitfield]—He loosened the puppies & either they alone or he with them succeeded in killing our poor little black cat."

Even the conditions had turned against them, impeding the relay teams with drifts of deep, soft snow "such as one would come across in England." "Things look very bad here," he wrote to his friends the Rhodeses in New Zealand, confessing himself "a great deal too bad tempered to write long letters. It keeps one's spirits at a very low ebb and the dismal foreboding that the ship will have to be abandoned is most distressing to us all."

Even so—and however often he cautioned himself against it—Scott found it impossible not to hope. In his diary he might complain of the "irresistible tendency" of the relay parties to exaggerate progress, but that did not stop him or the rest of the ship "constantly dashing up the hill to the look-out station" or wandering fretfully over the hills searching for some hint of change in the bay beneath.

And there was just enough movement of the ice now to keep their hopes alive. On the twenty-fourth the sledge parties had brought back news that the relief ships had edged closer during the night, and four days later Scott woke in his bunk for the first time to "the pleasant music" of *Discovery* creaking and stirring on a long, rhythmic swell.

It was the most promising sign so far, and with the whole ice sheet swaying to the movement of the sea, the ship had soon worked herself sufficiently loose to move "an inch or two in her icy bed." "One scarcely dares to hope for the best," Scott nervously wrote in his diary, and yet he knew that if they could just be given a good northerly breeze to assist the swell, they were at last in with a real chance.

"*Everything depends on the swell*" . . . "oh for a northerly wind" . . . "spirits are steadily going down" . . . "The whole outlook is most depressing" — day after day, his journal recorded his oscillations of mood as hope and confidence flared and died with the changing conditions. By the end of January the relief ships were close enough for him to see their crews through his telescope, but no sooner had Scott allowed himself to begin to believe, than the wind and swell would drop to leave *Morning* and *Terra Nova* helpless against the ice.

The ships were at least close enough now to make it worthwhile trying the effects of explosives, and Scott ordered a series of holes in a line parallel with the ice edge. He had been watching the way in which the floe broke away along such transverse lines, and hoped that if they could use their explosives to mimic the action of the swell, they might be able to anticipate the natural results of sea movement on the ice sheet. If they were going to employ explosives, he decided, they were going to do it in style, with the coordinated use of charges containing thirty-five pounds of gun-cotton each. As soon as three holes had been cut along a line that Scott had marked out, the charges were lowered to a depth of five fathoms and simultaneously set off, lifting the whole floe, he wrote, "as though there were an earthquake," and sending "three mighty columns of water and ice" shooting into the sky high above the ships' masts.

It was a tense operation handling the charges, with a nervous wait to follow, as the debris of ice fell back in a hail of shattered fragments to reveal nothing but three gaping and blackened holes. To the casual glance it looked as if the floe itself was undamaged, but within minutes a network of minute cracks had appeared, radiating out from each hole until an extended fissure perhaps a quarter of an inch wide linked them into one decisive faultline.

That was, Scott wrote, the "beginning of the end," and an hour or two later an isolated fragment of sheet—"small enough in area but containing many hundreds of tons of ice"—had quietly detached itself and floated "calmly away to the north." It was impossible to be sure how much of the credit for this was down to the gun-cotton and how much to "Nature," but with an advance of a third of a mile gained on that first day, no one in the relief ships or *Discovery* cared, "as long as the advance is made."

Even with the help of explosives, conditions in the bay lagged behind those of the previous year, and by 10 February Scott had at last accepted that he would have to make arrangements to abandon ship. At the very latest he reckoned that *Morning* would have to be away by the twenty-fifth if she was not also to be trapped in the ice, and even if the stronger *Terra Nova* could hold on for a week more, time had run out. He had tried patience, he had tried explosives, he had tried superstition—he had accelerated the transfer of stores on the grounds that "Nature with its usual cussedness" would free *Discovery* the moment they prepared to abandon her—and despair was clearly the last shot in the locker. "Last night I thought things out well," he wrote the next day, "& came to the conclusion that little short of a miracle could now free the ship . . . I have abandoned all hope and am trying to take in the situation. It is cruel work." There had been few days since the death of Vince when things had looked so bleak, "and yet, as always," he wrote when it was safely over, "when things look blackest the sun breaks through." A light southerly wind and a sky filled with snow on the morning of the eleventh had done nothing to suggest they were going to get their miracle, and he had just despatched a final instruction to Colbeck for the abandonment of the ship when news came back that the ice was going out, and going out fast.

With a second message that night confirming the news, and asking for more men out on the floe for the explosives, *Discovery* was a ship reborn. "I was standing by Captain Scott late in the night," Ford recalled the scene, as Scott turned to him among the piles of newly made-up packing cases that crowded the decks, and said with an almost vengeful sense of release, " 'You can shake those cases now, Ford.' This being a naval expression for knocking them to pieces."

Within half an hour Royds and a party of ten were on their way to the ice edge, leaving Scott too drained for anything more than his journal. "I can't think that much excitement of this sort would be good for us," he wrote, but he could as easily have shifted the ice in the bay as hope to contain it. "What a day it has been! and how we shall be able to answer the croakers!" he scrawled with a savage triumphalism. "It is just splendid . . . It would be difficult to describe the excitement & enthusiasm of the moment."

It was still an anxious wait, but two nights later

> a voice sang out down the hatchway "The ships are coming, sir!"
>
> There was no more dinner, and in one minute we were racing for Hut Point, where a glorious sight met our view. The ice was breaking up across the strait, and with a rapidity which we had not thought possible . . .
>
> I have never witnessed a more impressive sight; the sun was low behind us, the surface of the ice-sheet in front was intensely white, and in contrast the distant sea and its forking leads looked almost black.
>
> For weeks we had been struggling with this mighty obstacle . . . But now without a word, without an effort on our part it was all melting away, and we knew that in an hour or two not a vestige of it would be left, and that the open sea would be lapping on the black rocks of Hut Point.

Within hours the relief ships had weaved and battered their way through the last of the ice, while Scott and his crew in their "nondescript, tattered garments" watched entranced from the shore. "It seems unnecessary to describe all that has followed," he gratefully wrote, "how everyone has been dashing about madly from ship to ship, how everyone shook everyone else by the hand, how our small bay has become a scene of wild revelry, and how some have now reached that state which places them in doubt as to which ship they really belong."

With the three ships lying almost side by side, and a rope from *Terra Nova* secured to *Discovery*, "Much," as Scott said, could "be excused on such a night." It must have been the first moment in the six weeks since his return from the plateau that he could breathe easily, and yet the reversal of fortune was so sudden and so unexpected that it was almost as if he could not quite take it in. "Who could have thought it possible?" he asked, and gave the answer, "Certainly not we who have lived through the trying scenes of the last month."

There was still a last sheet of ice girding *Discovery*, but Scott had no intention of waiting for nature to take its course. The next day officers and men were digging holes in it for gun-cotton, and at one in the morning, utterly indifferent to anyone still asleep, Scott exploded a sixty-seven-pound charge just fifteen yards off *Discovery*'s bow. The ice around the ship was up to seventeen feet thick, but one more explosion was all that was needed. Early the following morning the charges were forced down a crack alongside the ship's stern, and when everyone had taken cover, Scott pressed the firing key. For a moment after the deafening roar it seemed that nothing had happened, and then suddenly, Williamson wrote, *Discovery* "gave a lurch & leap right out of her cradle of ice, where she had been imprisoned for two years, the 'Morning' and 'Terra Nova' sending up cheer after cheer as the ice gave way under her." Slowly the last great sheet of ice on her port side drifted out to sea, and *Discovery* swung quietly round on her anchors, blue water surrounding her. "Three cheers were once more given for the old ship," Williamson fondly added, "which has come through an ordeal not much the worse I don't think from a terrible position."

It was a note of proprietorial affection and gratitude that Scott shared. "Thus it was that after she had afforded us shelter and comfort for full two years . . . our good ship was spared to take us homeward. On February 16, 1904, the 'Discovery' came to her own again—the right to ride the high seas."

Seventeen: Escape from the Ice

Let no one think the worst is over until he is dead.

SOPHOCLES

If ever a man had cause to listen to Sophocles it was Scott. One would have thought that after two years in the ice he might have learned, but for all the occasional "black dog" there was a buoyancy about him—or perhaps just a plain, self-induced capacity for amnesia—that left him endlessly crying out for one more lesson.

This is a quality that serial explorers must all share to some degree, because no one who remembered things as they really were would ever voluntarily return to the Barrier or the plateau. It would be difficult to keep track of the times that Scott's journal records the miseries of Antarctica, but put him back in the ship for a couple of days—or in England for a couple of years—and the sledging life took on that retrospective glow of comradeship, character-moulding and hardy purity that suffused the memories of all his great journeys.

It was typical of the continent that at that precise moment when Scott was confidently re-dedicating himself to "Providence," "Nature" and all those other abstractions in his curious rationalist's pantheon, it should deal him one last blow. "The afternoon was beautifully calm and bright," he recalled with an air of surprise that is the only surprise about the sudden reversal of fortune, "and the weather seemed to smile peacefully on the termination of our long and successful struggle with the ice. We little guessed what lay before us, and assuredly if ever the treacherous nature of the Antarctic climate and the need for the explorer to be constantly on guard were shown, it was by our experience of the succeeding twenty-four hours."

While the *Terra Nova*'s crew began the filthy task of coaling *Discovery*, Scott's men had rowed ashore to hold a memorial service for George Vince at the foot of the plain wooden cross they had erected on the summit of Hut Point the previous day. The water was an oily calm and the sky heavy as they rowed back, but they had grown so used to ignoring conditions in the ice-bound security of their snug bay that they thought nothing of it.

That night the *Terra Nova*'s skipper, Henry McKay, and his men came aboard for dinner, and were midway through their penguin and seal when Scott was called up with the news that the wind was freshening. It was clear from the sky that they were in for a "stiff blow," and McKay took "one glance" at it and "was over the rail like a shot," desperate to get his ship out from alongside *Discovery* and into the safety of the sound as quickly as he could.

Scott was reluctant to get up steam at the risk of later engine damage, and so had little option but to trust to their ground tackle. An anchor of two tons and a decent drift of cable out meant that he was fairly confident they would not drag, but with a full gale now blowing and the captain of *Morning* and eight of the *Terra Nova* crew and officers still trapped in *Discovery*, their small fleet had managed to get itself into an extraordinary jam in a very brief space of time.

At about eight the next day *Morning* reappeared out of the gloom, and in a freshening wind Colbeck managed to get across to his ship just before the gale hit them with a "redoubled fury." There was still nothing Scott could do until Skelton could get up steam, and the word had just come up from the engine room that they would need another half-hour when *Discovery* finally began to drag towards the "wind-beaten cliff" of the ice-foot.

It was a question of which came first—cliff or steam?—and as Scott paced the deck, with the breaking waves now crashing over the poop, and the distance between *Discovery* and the ice foot decreasing by the minute, a sudden, shuddering blow provided the answer. The ship's stern had struck the ice. *Discovery* "rebounded and struck again, and our head was just beginning to fall off and the ship to get broadside on (heaven knows

what would have happened then) when steam was announced. Skelton
said he could only go slow at first, but hoped to work up. I told him to give
her every ounce he could, when he could, and he fled below to do his
best."

Even with the engines going ahead, and anchor raised, *Discovery* could
do no more than hold her own against the gale. Scott knew that if they
could get into the open water they would be all right, and as he began to
edge *Discovery* out to the point a quarter of a mile away, their luck looked
like holding until a strong cross current caught them up and spun them
"like a top" onto the shoal, where they "stopped dead . . . masts shivering."

"Dead to windward of the bank, with wind, sea, and current" all driving
them more firmly ashore, they were "in the worst possible position" they
could have found. "We took the shore thus at about 11 a.m," Scott recorded
in his journal, "and the hours that followed were truly the most dreadful I
have ever spent. Each moment the ship came down with a sickening thud
which shook her from stem to stern, and each thud seemed to show more
plainly that, strong as was her build, she could not long survive such awful
blows."

An attempt to drive her over the bar only made things worse, and with
the seas breaking heavily over her stern and Skelton reporting the engine
inlets blocked, they were helpless. By three o'clock "we had come to the
end of our resources," Scott confessed, "and the situation seemed to have
no ray of comfort. On the deck the wind was howling through our rigging,
the ship was swaying helplessly and rising slightly each moment, to crash
once more down on the stony bottom . . . Towering above us within a
stone's throw was the rocky promontory of Hut Point; on its summit, and
clearly outlined against the sky, stood the cross which we had erected to
our shipmate. I remember thinking how hard it seemed that we had rescued our ship only to be beaten to pieces beneath its shadow."

It was as bad below as it was on deck, with the ship seemingly alive, her
doors flying open, decks buckling, timbers groaning and her very form distorting out of shape under the heaviest blows. "When it was known that
there was nothing more that could be done," wrote Scott, "it was curious to
see how different temperaments took it. Some sat in stony silence below,
some wandered about aimlessly, and some went steadily on with an ordinary task as though nothing had happened. I almost smiled when I saw our
excellent marine Gilbert Scott [the man who had raised blood pressures
with his appearances as a girl, and who would later die at Gallipoli] dust-
ing and sweeping out the wardroom and polishing up the silver as if the

principal thing to be feared was an interference with the cleanly state in which he usually keeps all these things. For myself, I could not remain still. How many times I wandered from the dismal scene on deck to the equally dismal one below I do not know, but what I do know is that I tasted something very near akin to despair."

It made Scott look ten years older, Royds later told Hannah Scott, but it was still the old Scott sure enough, "continually on the panic," as Royds noted wearily, "just the same as ever, expecting everything to be done at once and rows if nothing is done." Hour after hour the ship ground on the bottom while they waited, impotent, for the gale to drop. At about seven it at last showed the first sign of abating, and with the wind slackening above, the officers assembled in the wardroom for dinner—"not that any of us wanted to eat, but because it never does to disturb a custom." As they sat down to their food, with the rocky promontory of the point still lowering over the masts, Scott wrote, "never was there a more despondent party . . . I myself have never felt so dispirited at any time; it seemed such poor luck to have got the ship out only to lose her a few yards away on the following day."

They were halfway through a silent meal when Mulock, the officer of the watch, suddenly appeared to say that the ship was working astern. Scott was up on the bridge in a flash, and in an instant could see that the ship was moving a few inches with every successive wave. The wind, too, had dropped, and the current that had driven them onto the bar had reversed itself. Within minutes every officer and man was up on deck, running together from side to side, rolling the boat in time, until "with a sponta-neous cheer from all hands" and a last, steady grating noise from below, *Discovery* "slid gently into deep water."

Scott was never able to understand how he got her onto the bank in the first place, and still less how they had ever got her off, but the latter at least he was prepared to label a "miracle" and gratefully accept. Their escape seemed even more miraculous when a first inspection revealed nothing worse than damage to her false keel, and with full steam astern ordered, *Discovery* was soon clear of the shoal and steaming out into the sound to join *Terra Nova*.

There was an anxious wait the next day for Colbeck, who had been blown forty miles to the north, to join them, but late in the afternoon *Morning* was again united with Scott's small squadron to complete *Discov-ery's* coaling. "Officers & men worked together like demons," Scott reported in his diary. "At about midnight we had finished with TN and I took the ship round & alongside the 'Morning' from which vessel we immediately commenced to coal & received 25 tons—a very undue proportion as compared with TN—but Colbeck is a most generous chap and McKay a type built on other lines & liberally endowed with Scottish caution."

This was a theme Scott returned to in a long letter to his old captain— now an admiral—George Egerton. Commenting again on Colbeck's self-lessness, he went on: "but Terra Nova ought & in fact could have given us a good deal more than they did—old McKay the captain is a very good sort but there is no doubt that he was thoroughly upset by the Antarctic and had only one desire, to get out of it as soon as possible."

McKay's parsimony or nerves spelled an end to any ambitious explo-rations planned for the rest of the navigable season, but it would not be long before Scott would be happy enough to be robbed of his chance. Their last task before leaving McMurdo was to take on water at the glacier tongue, but with a problem developing with their steam pipes, and another southerly blowing up, there was no option "but to run to the north and hope to get our water elsewhere."

After two years of calling McMurdo Sound "home," there was inevitably a certain sadness as they watched the familiar landmarks fall away to the stern for the last time. "Away to the south-west behind the ragged storm clouds could be seen the deep-red of the setting sun," Scott recalled, "against which there stood in sharp outline the dark forms of the western mountains and the familiar cone of Mount Discovery. On our right in a gloomy threatening sky rose the lofty snow-clad slopes of Erebus and the high domed summit of Cape Bird . . . and yet whatever sorrow we may have felt . . . it is not surprising that after our recent experiences the last entry in my diary for this night should have been, 'Oh but it is grand to be on the high seas once more in our good ship.' "

By the morning of the twenty-second, however, after they had taken on more water to the northern side of the immense snout of the Drygalski Ice Tongue, Scott was singing a different tune. In the early hours Skelton came to tell him that the pumps were not working, and with the water gaining on the ship all the time, Scott was left with no choice but to allow his engineer to stop the engines and condemn *Discovery* to sit broadside on to the strong south-easterly swell.

A roll of thirty degrees each way would have been uncomfortable enough in any circumstances, but with the water above the stokehold plates and washing heavily from side to side, they were in real trouble.

From the way the water was gaining it was only a matter of time before the fires in the main boilers were drowned, and to avert another accident Scott ordered them to be drawn. "Altogether," he wrote in his diary, "things looked very uncomfortable and at first almost worse. I'm bound to confess I passed some very bad hours—all the engine room staff were at work all night—Dellbridge was magnificent—when I asked if the pump would work he said 'It must work.' "

With the steam pump out of action, and the main boilers it depended on drawn, Scott tried the hand pumps, only to find them choked up with ice. It was impossible to see—or subsequently discover—why the ship should suddenly leak so badly, but leaking she was, and as the water continued to rise, Dellbridge set to work mending the steam pump while another party rushed to get the small boiler under the forecastle lighted.

It was five torrid hours before the trouble was solved, and no sooner were the pumps unblocked than the discovery of a damaged rudder forced them into Robertson Bay to change it for the smaller spare. Scott's original intention had been to follow the coast as it turns at right angles to the west here, but with a mass of heavy pack and bergs blocking their way, he was forced instead out to sea, eating into their dwindling coal supplies and taking them farther away from the coastline they were trying to explore with every mile north they steamed.

They had already parted with *Morning*, and by the twenty-ninth they had lost sight of *Terra Nova*, but with a pre-arranged rendezvous of all three ships at Auckland Island, Scott was not unduly worried. In the prevailing conditions it would have been virtually impossible to re-establish contact anyway, and when the end of the pack finally gave Scott the chance to turn westward, *Discovery* was again on her own in their last bid to see what could be salvaged of their season's programme.

Five days later, as they at last turned for New Zealand, their coal stocks depleted to the limit, the answer was less than nothing, with Ross's "Russell Islands" erased from the map and Wilkes's mythical Eld's Peak and Ringold's Knoll following suit. "We have done exploring and our last piece of work has been one of destruction," Scott wrote ruefully in his journal on 5 March, only too conscious after twenty-six months in the ice of the tricks that light and distance could play in the Antarctic; "it will undoubtedly raise some trouble and almost one wishes it had not been done. Without the least intention or desire to discredit former Explorers we have during the past few days brought to light a grave error of Ross's and found Wilkes & his companions to have been complete frauds."

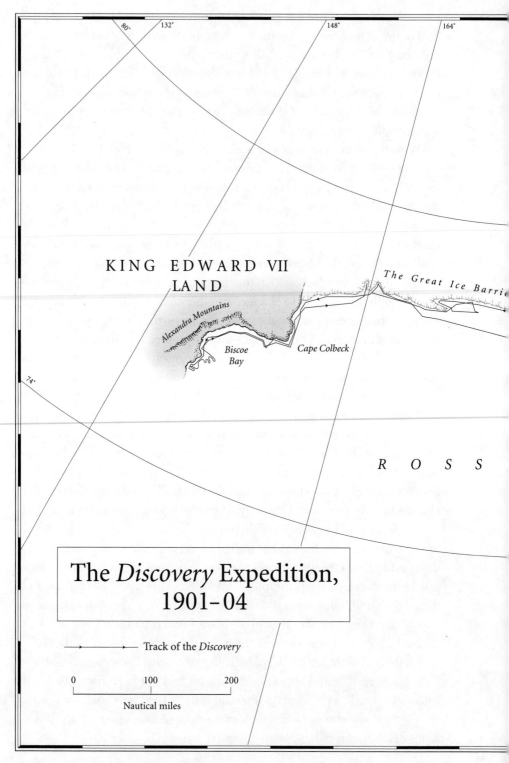

KING EDWARD VII LAND

Alexandra Mountains

The Great Ice Barrie

Biscoe Bay

Cape Colbeck

R O S S

The *Discovery* Expedition,
1901–04

→————→ Track of the *Discovery*

0	100	200

Nautical miles

Cape Goldie

Cape Lyttelton

Cape Wilson

Beaumont
Bay

Scott's Southern
Journey 1902-03

Barne 1902-03

Royds 1903

Scott's Western Journey 1903

Depot A

Armitage 1902-03

Ross
Island

Cape Crozier

McMurdo
Sound

SOUTH VICTORIA
LAND

Prince Albert Mountains

74°

S E A

Terra
Nova
Bay

Cape Washington

Lady
Newnes
Bay

Admiralty Rang

Cape Adare

Cape North

180°   164°   148°   132°   80°

It was an anticlimactic end to the season and the expedition, and as *Discovery* crossed the Antarctic Circle that same day, Royds's hopes "that I will never cross it again" might well have found a more general echo. It is difficult to imagine that there was a soul on board who was not relieved, because if their run of "bad luck" was precisely that, there was also possibly a certain "ring rustiness" among officers and crew after two years in the ice that made an Antarctic autumn a threat to their lives. There is also a feeling that at some level Scott half-sensed this. If there was nothing he could do about the bergs and pack, he seems to have accepted defeat with a goodish grace that was utterly alien to him. In his later account of the journey he described their failure to penetrate westwards as "grievously disappointing," though there is almost nothing in his journal entries of the frustration and impatience that invariably characterised him at such moments.

It was the condition of the surviving dogs, all born in the Antarctic, that seems to have upset him most. "The worst sufferers are the wretched dogs," he wrote in the middle of a gale, "which are wet, shivery, frightened & wholly lost under such conditions." "Born in the South, they have absolutely no experience of damp conditions, and . . . show the same horror of a wet deck or a wet coat as a cat might. But the most curious result of their ignorance is that they had to be taught to lap; they had never quenched their thirst except by eating snow, and when water was out before them they didn't know what to do with it."

There was one last scare with a berg before they were finally clear of the ice, but apart from sea-sickness and continued anxieties over their coal supplies, there was little to mark a rough passage to the rendezvous at Port Ross. After two years of the visual austerity of the Antarctic, Wilson found himself in a "Paradise" of colour and life, with the rata forests and the "green and russet scrub" forming the luxuriant setting for some of his oldest favourites — "my joy was nearly complete," he wrote, "when I heard the well-known cry of a hawk, and looking up saw a beautiful little falcon fly across . . . What a paradise!"

Scott had taken *Discovery* into the deepest arm of Port Ross, a winding inlet at the northern end of Auckland Island, and dropped anchor out of sight of the open sea and only yards from the scrub-covered shore. To his surprise neither *Terra Nova* nor *Morning* was yet there, and so while Wilson shot and painted to his heart's content, all hands went to work to make *Discovery* look "as though she had spent her three adventurous years in some peaceful harbour." Four days after her arrival, *Terra Nova* hove into sight, followed the next day by *Morning*, and as soon as *Discovery* was coaled—they were down to their last ten tons—the small fleet set off on their final leg to Lyttelton. The following day they sighted Stewart Island, and at daybreak on Good Friday were off the familiar Heads of Lyttelton.

Scott had addressed the men in Port Ross, "calling on their self-respect to behave themselves," but the welcome they received as they berthed alongside Lyttelton's jetty must have made any such warning seem redundant. "It is little wonder," Scott wrote, that after all the kindness they had received there, "each one of us felt that we were returning to what was very nearly our home—to a place where we should find rest and peace after our wanderings, and to people who would greet us with sympathetic friendship. And all this we found in fullest measure; New Zealand welcomed us as its own."

During the greater part of their time in New Zealand he stayed in Christchurch with his Scott cousin, but as a guest of Lord Ranfurly he also found himself part of the gubernatorial entourage on a farewell tour of the country. For a man who had spent the best part of two months on the Ferrar Glacier, the attractions of the Mount Cook region must have worn fairly thin, but after Canterbury—"nearly all people of good family and refinement," he reassured his mother—and Wellington "in much royal state," the hot springs of Rotorua were just the antidote to McMurdo he needed. Scott was fascinated, and rewarded with "one very good shot" of a geyser shooting "hundreds of feet up into the air with terrific force . . . on the whole as you may imagine it was a very delightful little trip," he wrote home. "The Governor was really extremely kind and went much out of his way so that we should miss nothing and indeed I shall know more about N Zealand when we leave than most of its inhabitants."

He had to sing for his supper—"I never seem to be able to go anywhere without making a speech"—and there were other, more pastoral responsibilities that went with the job. "Most of our people are away on the north island," he continued in the same letter to his mother, comfortably slipping back into the kind of gentle snobbery she appreciated. "Barne is playing the duffer, he has taken up with some people of doubtful antecedents—I hope nothing comes of it but I feel pretty confident they have designs & am therefore a good deal exercised—you must not mention this business however. I shall do my best to keep him clear."

The girl in question, the younger sister of the *Morning*'s Teddy Evans's fiancée, would have earned herself quite a reputation with explorers by the time Scott came back in 1910, and he was worried enough to think it "high

time we were off as all our young men are getting engaged. Skelton is actually caught," he told his mother, unfortunately to "one of six," but "very
nice."

Scott had his own pressing reasons to be on his way, too, as from the day
Discovery crossed the Antarctic Circle his mind had been on his own
future and the reputation of the expedition. "I fear there is no doubt that
our old friend Sir Clem started this," he wrote to his mother on the voyage
north, still brooding on the likely consequences of the Admiralty decision
to send down *Terra Nova* to "rescue" them; "it was he who first adopted the
note of 'brave fellows in distress'; of course the reason is obvious and does
him honour, but from our point of view it was extremely annoying . . .
when one is feeling perfectly comfortable & contented quite prepared to
take things as they come it is not surprising that one feels some chagrin at
being suddenly and overwhelmingly 'saved.' "

It was not just the humiliation of "rescue" that exercised him, but the
implications it held for his future career, and a rather frosty cable from the
Admiralty congratulating him on his safe return can have done nothing to
allay his fears. The problem was compounded by an interview he gave in
New Zealand that found its way into the London papers. "Commander
Scott emphatically protests against the despatch by the Admiralty of the
Terra Nova," the report read, "which he declares to have been a waste-
ful expense of money. He says that had the proper position of the *Discovery* been made known, it would have been obvious that she was perfectly
safe, and no assistance beyond that which the *Morning* could render was
requisite."

At the best this could only sound like ingratitude, at the worst gross
impertinence, and either way Scott knew he was in trouble. It did not help
that those were precisely his opinions on the subject, but in a barrage of
letters and cables to *The Times*, to Reuters, to the RGS, to the Admiralty —
to anyone in fact he could think of — he protested that he had been misrep-
resented and had never said anything of the sort. "I have always been most
careful to point out that we thoroughly understood the reason for the
Admiralty's action," he explained to his brother-in-law William Ellison
Macartney, the one man in the family who might have the clout to help
him out of a hole. ". . . There is here a dear old gentleman who is a
brother-in-law of Sir Clements Markham. With the best intentions in the
world he has promulgated the doctrine that the *Terra Nova* was a waste of
money. I found everyone ready to tell me so on arrival, but I always replied
that the Government could do nothing less than make a certainty of the

relief by sending a second ship . . . However I suppose it will all be put right some day—meanwhile I foresee their Lordships will not be anxious to do much for me and they must do something or I shall be out of the running altogether. By Regulation I have two more years to put in [as Commander] and if that is adhered to I shall be a very antiquated post-Captain as things are going now."

The key point here is a technical one, because before Scott could make captain—*the* crucial step on the promotional ladder—he had to complete his sea-time or hope for an Admiralty dispensation. "I feel hopelessly out of the running in naval matters," he had confessed in a letter to George Egerton written on the way north to New Zealand before the complication of the Reuters cable had added even further to his worries, "and if they [the Admiralty] keep up to the letter of the law shall I suppose remain so—for as you probably know this doesn't count sea time for the officers; we have nothing to complain of as we accepted the condition, nevertheless I hope the Admiralty will do something especially for the men for I can only regard it as adding to their merit, that they have behaved so loyally without the Naval Discipline Act."

It was impossible for Scott not to worry—he had his mother and sisters to think of as well as himself—but it is likely that distance and delay made things seem worse than they actually were. Even before he received Scott's letter his brother-in-law Willy had been to see Lord Walter Kerr, and had come away with the assurance that Scott was "a marked man" and that there was "no cause for anxiety."

And besides, as a bullish Markham demanded, what could they possibly do about it? "Scott said what was perfectly true," he wrote, "and what everyone knows to be true, though it was not prudent to say it to Reuter. Having been said I do not see what can be done. They would not dare to spite him for saying it. He stands too high now. The *Terra Nova* was a most scandalous waste of public money; and the whole wretched story of Treasury insolence and malignity will have to be made public before long."

If there was anything Markham could do to ensure that Scott did stand "high," he was going to do it. The news from the south was "simply magnificent," he wrote triumphantly, when he had had his first chance to digest Scott's results. "The sledging season of 1903 is quite equal to that of 1902–03. Scott's inland journey is a grand achievement, apparently longer than Armitage's, of course on another route. 60 days, and 270 miles from the ship, 620 statute miles there and back as the crow flies. People should count in statute miles when walking. No dogs . . . Scott has shown much zeal too, in doing as much exploring work as possible on his way back . . . clearing away the imaginary Wilkes Land as far as 56. It is very fine and the two seasons together make the expedition quite unsurpassed."

Even the Royal Society had "woken up considerably since they heard news of your fossil discoveries," Cyril Longhurst wrote, and with the King sending a message of congratulation, Scott's rehabilitation seemed complete. "It is a great relief to hear the Admiralty business was put straight," he wrote to his mother at the beginning of June; "what a trump Willy has been! he seems to think my promotion a good chance. I hope it may prove so. As things are going I feel I can't afford to wait long."

With expedition finances parlous enough to make Scott watch even the cost of a cable, neither could *Discovery*. *Terra Nova* had already left more than a week earlier, and after a last ball given for their New Zealand friends, *Discovery* finally sailed on 8 June, a gift of sheep hanging from the rigging giving her an incongruously "sad" air as she steamed out to the heads through a flotilla of dressed and cheering vessels.

Scott's pessimistic mood seems to have been only momentary. Clarence Hare, the young New Zealand steward during their first year in the ice, had rejoined the ship for the passage home, and remembered how much happier he seemed in the almost exclusively naval world that *Discovery* had become. She was, of course, still sailing under the Merchant Shipping Act, but the overhaul and painting in Port Ross had marked a kind of rite of passage, a transition from the hermetic enclave of McMurdo, with its own standards and informalities, to the familiar, regulated regime of naval life. "Anyone that had seen us down in the ice," Williamson—the same Williamson who two years earlier had complained of scrubbing the decks—proudly wrote of his newly painted ship, "then look at us now they would not know us, she looks splendid, what with nice white & dry decks, woodwork & brasswork polished & all brand new paint makes her look quite a treat."

The return to the old routines, however, brought with it its own anxieties. Williamson's might be the voice of the navy they knew, but that navy was changing, and Scott was not the only man to have apprehensions over his place in it. "A few yarns lately with the Skipper as to what will happen when we get home," Skelton wrote five days out of Lyttelton, "as he says, of course, it will depend on the way the Admiralty look on the expedition & that again depends upon who is at the Admiralty at the time. If there are 2 or 3 people who are interested in exploration it will probably mean that something will be done for the Skipper, & if anything much is done for him we ought also to get something in proportion. Personally it must mean little or nothing to me—I have always considered that little or nothing can be done for an engineer in the navy . . . one must be content, & very often a hard-working one at that . . . Personally I would sooner have gone out to the colonies with £10 in my pocket & started as a labourer."

Skelton, in fact, had less to worry about than anyone on board—he had been born at the right time for an engineer of talent and energy—but for every officer in *Discovery* the first sight of a Navy List in a year had been a reminder of forgotten realities. "I realise that everything possible is being done for my promotion," Scott wrote again, unable to shake off his worries in spite of Willy's assurances, "but of course can't help being anxious. If they wait till we get home it means that 2 or 3 persons will inevitably leap over my head. The question is will they consider it fair to pass me over in June. It is such a close thing that it must make a great deal of difference."

He did not just have himself to think of, and as always in his career he was anxious to do everything he could for the warrant officers and men under him. In many ways the Antarctic had been one long lesson for Scott, an eye-opener as to what the ordinary seaman and warrant officer could do when given the chance, and as a professional, as their captain and—with Evans and Lashly—as a *friend*, he was determined that they should not be wasted. "One of the most gratifying things for me that has happened in connection with the Expedition," he would later write, proud equally of his men and of his own part in their development, "is the manner in which all my people have gone back to their regular work—on all sides I hear the best accounts of them, individually & collectively, and I cannot but feel some pride that this should have happened to men who might easily have become confirmed 'pirates.' "

It is interesting that the final, democratic word in his last expedition diary belonged not to his officers, but to the men who had made *Discovery* the ship she was. "And the deed of high endeavour," he quoted,

> *Was no more to the favoured few*
> *But brain & heart were measure*
> *Of what any man might do.*

Save for a continuing problem with Whitfield's mental health, it was an uneventful journey home. At Port Stanley in the Falkland Islands they completed the last of their magnetic observations and got their first news of the reception Markham was planning for them. The "Father of the Expedition" had not been idle. His plan was to have "a luncheon in the shed at the docks, hung with flags," he wrote to Keltie, followed the next night by a dinner and reception and then an escort up the Thames and a show of flags before a final grand celebration in November. He wanted Lord Selborne there to greet Scott at Spithead, he wanted Fisher, May and Kerr, he wanted the whole of the RGS Council, the Royal Society officers, the Lords of the Admiralty, the Lord Mayor, he wanted more flags, and red cloth, and sledging pennants, and songs—"I want 'all the thousand masts of the Thames to send back an echoing cheer.' " "People do not understand the greatness of the achievement," he lectured from the Schloss Hotel in Heidelberg, where he was off badgering foreigners, "nor the greatness of the results. The sledge journeys *without dogs* are quite unequalled. Easier for Peary or Nansen to make the dogs do the work while they stroll along or guide the sledge from behind. Our people have done a great work, and it will be shameful if it is not officially, as well as generally recognised . . . Scott ought to have the freedom of the city."

"From all accounts people seem bent on making much of us on our return," a nervous Scott complained in a letter to his mother. "I can't look forward with any pleasure to that sort of thing & shall be glad enough when it is all over."

It seemed, however, as if poor Markham could not get it right, because if Scott winced at the thought of their reception, he was clearly still prickly about getting the acknowledgement he felt the expedition deserved. "Scott's complaint is utterly incomprehensible," an ailing Markham protested to Keltie:

> We telegraphed to him when he arrived, and about the medal; but he never answered either of them. I got the King to telegraph to him; I have written three letters to him at Lyttelton full of congratulations, and two to the Falkland Islands, and there was a joint letter of congratulations sent to Lyttelton, signed by the two Presidents. What on earth can he mean about the way his Report was treated. How could we possibly do more than publish it in the RGS Journal.
>
> The press arrangements are his own affair. Surely that long official letter of congratulation signed by me as President RGS

and entering into every detail of his work should have satisfied him. What can he mean!!

He has not written to me.

Their mutual irritation, however, was short-lived. "I am much annoyed that Scott should complain . . . of my want of attention to him," Markham protested again, but the very next day a "very charming letter from Scott to her Ladyship" arrived to make everything "all right." His only fear now, in fact, was that he could not do enough for Scott. "I despair," he told Keltie, "of being able to give the explorers a reception to compare with what they had in New Zealand; but we must do our best."

And if that was the last thing Scott wanted, he too had soon relented. Before *Discovery* reached England, he spoke to his officers and scientific staff about a present from the ship for Markham. Interestingly, though, as the expedition came to an end and they all contemplated their separate futures, the unity of interest that had bound them in the south showed its first signs of cracking. "About the present to Sir Clements," Skelton wrote in his journal, "I don't care either way—still I have always felt myself that his interest in the expedition in a personal way, referred purely to the Skipper, Royds & perhaps one or two others, & outside that his interest in individuals was merely because his own protégés were interested in the other individuals. Some people say he isn't 'straight'—I don't know anything about that,—but I do believe all his actions have been controlled by sentiment,—favouritism etc than by practical commonsense duty towards the expedition as a national undertaking—perhaps for that reason he deserves a present from us—anyway I shall subscribe to it."

At the same meeting the expedition library was divided up, an issue that gave Scott one last chance to show his competitiveness, and Skelton one last opportunity to moan. "There was one slight hitch at the commencement owing to the Skipper thinking he was not getting a fair chance," he wrote, "& altogether it seemed to me very silly and small-minded, but it 'blew off'—that is one thing our skipper cannot do 'play a losing game'—it is most noticeable, even in the trivial little games on deck of cricket—in 'bridge' which we used to play in winter quarters, in fact in almost any form of sport."

This was rich coming from Skelton, but at the end of three tedious months at sea, broken only by Port Stanley and a brief stop to coal in the Azores, it would have been odd if they had not all grown stale of each other. And besides, as *Discovery* made her way up the Channel, and the flash of Bishop's Rock lighthouse was sighted almost three years to the day since England had disappeared into the haze off *Discovery*'s stern, it was Wilson who more accurately spoke for the wardroom. "Without a doubt he has been the making of the expedition," he wrote of Scott, "and not one of us will but feel more and more grateful to him for the way he has acted throughout. Notwithstanding that it is a difficult thing, at least I imagine it is, for the Captain to make intimate friends with anyone, I feel as though we were real friends, and I need hardly say I am proud of it."

Eighteen: The Reluctant Lion

Let's see how it works out. Falkner behaves most gallantly in Africa. Falkner res-
cues Mrs. Ebernoe. Falkner splendidly avenges Colonel Ebernoe's death, and
strikes terror into every slave-dealer's heart. Falkner returns to England covered
with glory. A grateful nation goes into a panic of admiration, and makes itself
slightly ridiculous over Falkner. Falkner is the lion of the season.

HENRY ARTHUR JONES, *The Liars* (1897)

If the reception was not quite everything Markham had hoped for, it was
certainly all that Scott had feared. *Discovery* was first sighted at 8 a.m. on
Saturday, 10 September, and Markham was the first aboard, going over on
the launch carrying across the officer who would take over Armitage's
instruments.

The delay while the final rituals of the voyage were completed was
clearly as much as Markham's patience could bear, but after Armitage had
taken "5 mortal hours" to swing the ship, and Scott's family and other crew
relatives were picked up from a pinnace off Spithead, *Discovery* finally
came in through the ranks of cheering warships to tie up in harbour at 5:30
that afternoon.

There can be no doubt that Scott hated it for himself—he always
loathed anything in the way of public "show"—but he would at least have
had the grace to be pleased for the old man to whom the day really
belonged. Over the last weeks Markham had been unrelenting in his
determination to ensure *Discovery* received the homecoming she
deserved, and the crowds that massed at every vantage point to welcome

Scott's men showed that, if nothing else, he had caught the mood of the public.

It would be years before all the scientific findings could be formulated and judged, and results had to be correlated with the German *Gauss* expedition, which had suffered a torrid time in the ice,* but *The Times* was in no doubt. "The expedition commanded by Commander Scott," it declared in a pre-emptive strike on the scientific establishment, "has been one of the most successful that ever ventured into polar regions, north or south. True to the spirit of his instructions, he has done what he set out to do, and even more. He has added definitely to the map a long and continuous coastline . . . His sledge expeditions, south and west and east have given us a substantial idea of the character of the interior. The geological collections brought home will enable us to read a part at least of the history of this land of desolation. The life of the sea and such scanty life as is to be found . . . has been thoroughly investigated . . . These are some of the spoils which this great British expedition has brought back. Apart from their immense value to science, it is not improbable that the meteorological and magnetic work will prove to be of considerable practical importance in human affairs."

The original battle over the appointment of Professor Gregory, and a subsequent rancorous dispute over meteorological results, would always cloud the expedition's scientific reputation, but *The Times* had not got it far wrong. It is perhaps only a natural bias that enabled Louis Bernacchi to label Ferrar and Hodgson the "fathers" of Antarctic geology and marine biology respectively, but on top of the *Discovery*'s geographical, surveying and geological results, Wilson's work on the fauna of the area and Bernacchi's own observations—magnetic records for something like six hundred days collected under the most appalling conditions—were enough alone to ensure the scientific value of the expedition. His results "entitle him to

---

*The twenty-four volumes of scientific data attest to Drygalski's thoroughness, but in geographical terms the *Gauss* expedition was a disappointment. Their original objective had been "Termination Land," the westernmost of Wilkes's sightings in 64s 97½E, with a view to establishing whether land stretched from there to Kemp Land in 66s 60E or was interrupted by a sea that joined up with the Weddell Sea on the opposite side of Antarctica. Forced back by heavy pack, they headed westwards until the ship became trapped in the ice forty-five miles off the coast they named after Wilhelm II. Without a land base, and threatened with permanent imprisonment, their exploration was limited to the immediate coastline and the discovery of the West Ice Shelf. Short of coal, the *Gauss* returned to South Africa in May 1903, the geographical questions she had set out to answer still unresolved. Drygalski had never believed in the theory of a sea between Wilkes and Kemp Land, but a shortage of funds prevented him returning to prove that he was right.

the sincerest congratulations," J. Milne wrote of Bernacchi in 1908, when the volume on the expedition's physical observations was published, "[and] throw light upon hitherto unsuspected phenomena which take place within and on the surface of our world."

The massive volumes of results and observations that came out under the auspices of the British Museum and the Royal Society over the next nine years are the unarguable legacy of *Discovery*'s scientific work, but what they do not bring out is Scott's role in the achievement. "With regard to Captain Scott," Wilson wrote in his introduction to the second volume of the expedition's records in 1907, "there is a point to be mentioned which finds no place in his book [Scott's expedition history], namely the untiring interest that he took in the Scientific work of those who were placed under his command . . . It is to the interest and goodwill that he showed in all our work that such results that we have been able to collect are very largely due."

Scott would later find himself at the centre of the arguments over *Discovery*'s scientific work, but for the moment at least he wanted only one thing, and he got that when he was taken to the Commander-in-Chief's house to learn that he had been promoted post-captain. In his final letter from Port Stanley he had improbably reassured his mother that he "contained his soul in patience," but it had been a miserable wait. He had, he told her, "a very clear conscience over everything written or said [concerning the *Terra Nova*] but of course that does not prevent misrepresentation and one must be prepared for that. The Admiralty at least by this time ought to acquit one of disloyalty."

The Admiralty clearly had acquitted him, and done so with a better grace than anyone could have anticipated. "Will you tell Captain Scott and his officers and men," a message from the First Lord of the Admiralty read, "the satisfaction of the Board of Admiralty at the manner in which they have so thoroughly upheld the traditions of the Navy, and with what pleasure they greet them on their return to England." Even the Hydrographers had come round. "Commander Scott and his staff have most magnificently maintained the high standard of efficiency of former polar explorers," his old enemy Admiral Wharton minuted Scott's despatch. "I presume steps will be taken about medals."

In a comically symmetrical piece of buck-passing, in fact, Wharton believed the whole "rescue" saga reflected badly on Markham, while Markham believed precisely the reverse, and between the two old mastodons Scott seems to have slid out relatively unscathed. "Dear Lord

Walter Kerr," he wrote to the First Sea Lord, determined to do nothing to upset this happy state of things, "My employers wish me to undertake a narrative of our voyage, to be published in the spring; they have also arranged for a lecture to be given in November with the Prince of Wales in the chair. In addition, the geographical societies and other persons of large towns are anxious for a repetition of the lecture . . . I should be very sorry to do anything that the Admiralty or the service at large thought unbecoming a naval officer. Except in the matter mentioned, I am trying to keep as quiet as possible." For their own part, the Admiralty cannot have been unconscious of the credit Scott had brought them in the wake of a war that had done little for the prestige of British arms, and were happy to grant him the six months' leave he asked for.

Wharton's medals, too, were readily forthcoming. In a widely criticised piece of small-mindedness the government alone did nothing, but with the approval of the King, a new Polar Medal was instituted and awarded to the whole ship's company. The King had also raised Scott to the rank of Commander of the Victorian Order, and with Markham and the RGS Council commissioning a gold medal, the groundswell of international recognition was soon in full flood. Following hard on the RGS's special award came the Patron's Gold Medal, and then among others—they impinged so little on Scott's consciousness that they can all safely be lumped together—the Kane Gold Medal from Philadelphia, the Cullum Gold Medal from New York, the Livingstone Gold Medal of the Royal Scottish Geographical Society, the French Légion d'Honneur, the Vega Gold Medal from Sweden, and the Berlin Geographical Society's Gustav Nachtigal Gold Medal.

Medals were one thing—and, mercifully, could usually be received by proxy or post—but the speeches and lectures were another. The one consolation of having to make so many of them in New Zealand was the practice it gave him, Scott had told his mother, and England and Markham were soon giving him occasion to call on the experience. The Tuesday after *Discovery* arrived, he spoke at the banquet held for her crew in Portsmouth's town hall, and two days later took her up the Channel under full sail to the East India Docks in the Thames. There was a feeling in contemporary newspapers that London had not welcomed them as it might have done, but for men on board who were seeing friends and relatives for the first time in three years, the absence of the Lord Mayor was a loss that they could comfortably sustain.

If the official response was muted, the public were out in force, and no one more eager to meet them than Shackleton. In the year he had been home he had seen—and charmed—Scott's mother a number of times, and his letter of welcome shows no trace of any bad feeling.

> *My Dear Captain Scott,*
>
> *Just a line to welcome you safely back after your long anxious time. I had hoped to have a line from you but I expect you have been very busy all the time. I am so glad the whole show has been such a complete success, and you will now for a time be able to enjoy a rest from your work.*
>
> *As you know, no doubt, I am married and settled down as Secretary to the RSGS, the pay is only £200 a year, but it is better than going to sea . . . I had thought of trying to go on another expedition sometime but have given up the idea now as there seems to be no money about, and besides I am settled now and have to make money. It would only break up my life if I could stand it which Wilson says I could not. I do hope to see you do the NW Passage sometime . . .*
>
> *I will be writing to you officially in a few days that the council of the RSGS have voted you the Livingstone Gold Medal, and I hope you will be able to open our session up here in November and receive the medal . . . You will have a most enthusiastic welcome for all Scotland takes an interest in the Expedition.*

After a "very jolly evening" with Scott and Markham, Shackleton was also there the next day with the whole ship's company to march to the lunch held at the East India Docks in their honour. Naturally the occasion meant another speech for Scott, and as always he took the opportunity to stress the role of his crew in everything that *Discovery* had achieved. Over his time practising in New Zealand he had plainly developed a nice line in self-deprecation, but his modesty was as genuine as it was culturally required. He could sound pleased with himself at times, even slightly smug, but it was invariably over the conduct and achievements of his men rather than on his own account. He knew what he owed them, and he was more than ever determined to see that they got their due. "I feel that it is most difficult to place before my Lords in its true light," he wrote in a long report to the Admiralty at the end of October,

the exemplary behaviour of the officers and men lent to the Expedition.

It is to be remembered that they were not under the Naval Discipline Act, and were perfectly aware of the feeble application of the merchant shipping laws to their unusual position. If it was by my suggestion, it was by their choice, that the true spirit of naval discipline was observed throughout the voyage and I cannot remember a single instance of a man presuming on the laxity of the law, or acting otherwise than he would, had he been on the decks of a man-of-war.

I sincerely believe that the excellent conduct was due to a high sense of duty and that they worked purely for the honour of their ship, their service and their country . . .

Feather, Dailey, Dellbridge, Crean, Wild, Lashly, Evans, they were all singled out, and Scott was just as generous and protective of his officers and scientists. He had asked the Admiralty for leave for Royds and Barne to work up their results, but the old suspicions of Royal Society intentions he had inherited from Markham still clearly festered. "The Royal Society gives me the blight," he bluntly told Bernacchi at the beginning of November. "Things generally are so unsatisfactory for the members of our expedition that I think it best to meet & discuss . . . My sole idea, so far, has been to keep in with everyone for our own sakes but if people want to rob us of our credit I'm prepared to fight & we've got a d—d good case."

For all his attempts to diffuse attention and credit, however, it was inevitably Scott himself who was the focus of interest, and the final imprimatur came with an invitation to Balmoral to speak to the King and his guests. "I must tell you of Balmoral," he wrote to his mother on the Sunday after the ordeal was over.

I arrived here on Tuesday, before dinner I was sent for by the King who gave me the CVO. Dinner 3 round tables. I sat at the King's, Princess of Wales, Duke & Duchess of Connaught, P. Arthur prime minister & two ladies in waiting. Concert that night.

Wednesday busy all day preparing for lecture—walked round castle with equerry for exercise.

Dinner sat at King's table again.

Evening gave lecture (k P of Wales Connaughts PM & many more) Intended an hour but the King asked so many questions & ran into 1¾ hours—all sorts of nice things said afterwards—none nicer than by Prime Minister who said he regarded himself as *Father of the Expedition!!!!* Don't give this away.

The rest of the week took on a more traditional country shape, with the Thursday given over to a grouse drive, and the Friday to stalking and the Gillies' Ball. Scott always enjoyed shooting for the chance it gave him to be in the open air, and a stag and nine grouse—"less than most and more than some"—must have seemed to him just about the right figure for maintaining his social credibility without inflicting too grim a slaughter.

It was clearly relief enough, anyway, that he had not only *not* killed the Prince of Wales—who after instructing him on the grouse drive, had the "temerity to remain in next butt"—but survived the week himself. "Gillies ball," he concluded his account: "long talk with Princess of Wales at supper—said goodbye to King & to bed a little overpowered with Royalty kind & considerate as they are. The King offered me my stag's head . . . I don't think I made a mistake except perhaps in not asking for more but I hate the idea of it. I haven't quite got the hang of matters but I feel I have left an impression that I was not the sort which takes advantage of kindness shown me—which is something though possibly a narrow view."

For his part Markham was in no doubt of Scott's success, even doubling his grouse to eighteen, but Balfour's claim was almost enough to bring on apoplexy. "Balfour's brazen impudence in calling himself father of the expedition beats anything I ever heard in that line," its alternative "Father" wrote to Keltie. "He deliberately announced his intention of abandoning them to perish on two occasions: a nice sort of father!!!"

A civic reception for the captain and crew of *Morning* at Hull, a "Discovery Exhibition" in Mayfair, a presentation and public lecture in front of seven thousand at the Albert Hall punctuated by spontaneous bursts of applause; Scott was becoming a public figure. "Well built and alert," one newspaper recalled the impact he made on his audience, with a figure "neither tall nor short" that "yet conveyed the impression of strength and vigour and quickness. Nine people out of ten, seeing him, would have said 'Naval Officer'; he had that stamp on him; and it was borne out by his clear-cut features, his healthy face, with something about it which told you that the man was used to speaking the crisp language of command."

The crisp language of command might have done for the English, but as he had found with Captain McKay and his Dundee seamen, the Scots were another matter. "The Lecture came off," he reported home after an audience of 2,300 had packed Synod Hall in Edinburgh to see him receive the Livingstone Medal, "my first before a Scotch audience and I didn't take long to realise the difference—I never really felt that they were in sympathy but I continued to exert efforts to please and at the end I received a really big ovation." After the speech came the medal—"a very handsome thing"—and then a reception at the North British Hotel—"I shook hands with 400 people . . . rather trying work but everyone means very well"—and bed at one in the morning.

Scott was staying in the gloomily impressive home of a daughter of David Livingstone, but managed to escape just long enough the next day for lunch with Shackleton, before he was back again for a banquet and another speech. Relations with Shackleton were clearly as warm as they had ever been, and Scott was delighted to report how "pleased" everyone was with him, and what "great energy and business capacity" he was showing. "Shackleton as you will now have heard," he told his mother, "has been chosen as candidate for the Liberal Unionists of Dundee, he doesn't expect to get in but on the whole his plans are sound . . ." On the Sunday after the banquet he was with Shackleton again at Tullicheven Castle, staying with William Beardmore—"a millionaire . . . in the way of becoming the greatest ship builder in England," Scott wrote, mercifully unconscious of what that name would come to mean to him—and after that back to Glasgow for another lecture.

After two months on more or less constant display, however, Scott was beginning to feel the strain. As he crossed and re-crossed the country in his third-class railway carriages to save Expedition money, it was becoming a moot point which was worse, private kindness or civic receptions, Lady Abercrombie's or station hotels, constant company or the loneliness of living out of a suitcase without enough collars to make a decent show "because some stupid man must have forgotten to pack" them.

Glasgow—"a miserable depressing town"—Tullicheven again—"Mrs. Beardmore . . . young & nice looking & I think has social ambitions"—and finally the place that Scott had most been dreading, Dundee. His lecture there was in part a gesture of thanks to the city and the men who had built *Discovery*, but after the jokes over the infamous "Dundee leak," and his slightly equivocal relations with the Dundee whaler skipper of the *Terra Nova*, he knew better than to expect a "home audience." With another full house, however, it turned out better than he had feared. Although all the whaling captains were in "good form and doubtless . . . ready to take exception to anything I might say," he could tell his mother audience of 2,300 had packed Synod Hall in Edinburgh to see him receive the Livingstone Medal, "my first before a Scotch audience and I didn't take long to realise the difference—I never really felt that they were in sympathy but I continued to exert efforts to please and at the end I received a really big ovation." After the speech came the medal—"a very handsome thing"—and then a reception at the North British Hotel—"I shook hands with 400 people . . . rather trying work but everyone means very well"—and bed at one in the morning.

Scott was staying in the gloomily impressive home of a daughter of David Livingstone, but managed to escape just long enough the next day for lunch with Shackleton, before he was back again for a banquet and another speech. Relations with Shackleton were clearly as warm as they had ever been, and Scott was delighted to report how "pleased" everyone was with him, and what "great energy and business capacity" he was showing. "Shackleton as you will now have heard," he told his mother, "has been chosen as candidate for the Liberal Unionists of Dundee, he doesn't expect to get in but on the whole his plans are sound . . ." On the Sunday after the banquet he was with Shackleton again at Tullicheven Castle, staying with William Beardmore—"a millionaire . . . in the way of becoming the greatest ship builder in England," Scott wrote, mercifully unconscious of what that name would come to mean to him—and after that back to Glasgow for another lecture.

After two months on more or less constant display, however, Scott was beginning to feel the strain. As he crossed and re-crossed the country in his third-class railway carriages to save Expedition money, it was becoming a moot point which was worse, private kindness or civic receptions, Lady Abercrombie's or station hotels, constant company or the loneliness of living out of a suitcase without enough collars to make a decent show "because some stupid man must have forgotten to pack" them.

Glasgow—"a miserable depressing town"—Tullicheven again—"Mrs. Beardmore . . . young & nice looking & I think has social ambitions"—and finally the place that Scott had most been dreading, Dundee. His lecture there was in part a gesture of thanks to the city and the men who had built *Discovery*, but after the jokes over the infamous "Dundee leak," and his slightly equivocal relations with the Dundee whaler skipper of the *Terra Nova*, he knew better than to expect a "home audience." With another full house, however, it turned out better than he had feared. Although all the whaling captains were in "good form and doubtless . . . ready to take exception to anything I might say," he could tell his mother afterwards—none nicer than by Prime Minister who said he regarded himself as *Father of the Expedition!!!!* Don't give this away.

The rest of the week took on a more traditional country shape, with the Thursday given over to a grouse drive, and the Friday to stalking and the Gillies' Ball. Scott always enjoyed shooting for the chance it gave him to be in the open air, and a stag and nine grouse—"less than most and more than some"—must have seemed to him just about the right figure for maintaining his social credibility without inflicting too grim a slaughter.

It was clearly relief enough, anyway, that he had not only *not* killed the Prince of Wales—who after instructing him on the grouse drive, had the "temerity to remain in next butt"—but survived the week himself. "Gillies ball," he concluded his account: "long talk with Princess of Wales at supper—said goodbye to King & to bed a little overpowered with Royalty kind & considerate as they are. The King offered me my stag's head . . . I don't think I made a mistake except perhaps in not asking for more but I hate the idea of it. I haven't quite got the hang of matters but I feel I have left an impression that I was not the sort which takes advantage of kindness shown me—which is something though possibly a narrow view."

For his part Markham was in no doubt of Scott's success, even doubling his grouse to eighteen, but Balfour's claim was almost enough to bring on apoplexy. "Balfour's brazen impudence in calling himself father of the expedition beats anything I ever heard in that line," its alternative "Father" wrote to Keltie. "He deliberately announced his intention of abandoning them to perish on two occasions: a nice sort of father!!!"

A civic reception for the captain and crew of *Morning* at Hull, a "Discovery Exhibition" in Mayfair, a presentation and public lecture in front of seven thousand at the Albert Hall punctuated by spontaneous bursts of applause; Scott was becoming a public figure. "Well built and alert," one newspaper recalled the impact he made on his audience, with a figure "neither tall nor short" that "yet conveyed the impression of strength and vigour and quickness. Nine people out of ten, seeing him, would have said 'Naval Officer'; he had that stamp on him; and it was borne out by his clear-cut features, his healthy face, with something about it which told you that the man was used to speaking the crisp language of command."

The crisp language of command might have done for the English, but as he had found with Captain McKay and his Dundee seamen, the Scots were another matter. "The Lecture came off," he reported home after an that he "managed to say just what was right," and thought "everyone went away pleased."

But if he thought that with Scotland pacified the worst was behind him, the north of England soon had him changing his mind. He had given a lecture in Newcastle with the Duke of Northumberland in the chair that had gone quite well, but as he carried on by train to Middlesbrough, Bradford and Hull, his spirits sank with every depressing view of an England that he had plainly not known was there and never wished to see again.

Perhaps the most interesting aspect of this whole lecture tour, in fact, is the way in which it underlines just how little Scott knew of his own country. On the eve of *Discovery*'s voyage it was a commonplace that the world knew more of Mars than it did of Antarctica, but after two years in the ice and a lifetime in the navy, the equally bizarre truth was that Scott probably knew less about England than he did about the Barrier or the plateau. It seemed almost inexplicable to him that "nice people" could live in the sorts of places he found himself lecturing in, because while "a fair sprinkling" of them would turn up for his talks, "where they came from was difficult to guess." He had been lucky enough to see Middlesbrough only in the dark, he told his mother, but even so a "fine audience" and a big hall were not enough to make up for "an apology of a dinner"—and this from a man happy to eat skua when he could get it—or the grimness of narrow streets, wretched shops, artisan dwellings, and a town that could not boast one single decent hotel.

It is not an attractive side of Scott—those same dwellings would produce the children who would listen spellbound to Arthur Machen's tale of his death and would go to their own with much the same courage—but that is no more than to say that he was a man of his time. "I cannot conclude my remarks," he wrote in similar vein to the Admiralty of *Discovery*'s lower deck, Edwardian naval officer and West Country provincial at one again after the education of the plateau journey with Evans and Lashly, "without . . . calling attention to their excellent behaviour since our return to civilization. Both in New Zealand and at home they have been feted, and made much of, and fully exposed to all the temptations which so frequently demoralize men of their class."*

If Scott had to pay the price of being one of the first of the modern,

---

*J.M. Barrie's *The Admirable Crichton* throws an interesting sidelight on these cultural attitudes. It would be nice to know if Evans, Lashly or Crean—the latter two, in particular, in the light of their heroics on Scott's last expedition—ever saw the play or recognised anything of their own position in that of Barrie's eponymous butler.

newspaper celebrities, however, with all its attendant publicity and exposure, he was fortunate also to be one of the last in that long and variegated
tradition of "lions" that stretched back to Byron and William Bankes and
forward to Shackleton and that great "anti-lion," T.E. Lawrence. It had its
disadvantages, of course—Lady Abercrombie among them—but it opened
up a world for him that would have been otherwise unimaginable. There
was a sense of cultural continuity behind the "process" that must have
appealed to the Hannah Scott in him, because while the "lion" might
change from season to season, the "machinery" and the rest of the cast
remained reassuringly the same, with that identical, self-regulating social
elite inviting him to their lunches and blocking Mayfair with their carriages during the *Discovery* Exhibition, whose great-grandmothers had
brought Albemarle Street to a stop in the rush for Byron's "Childe Harold."

But if Antarctica was the new Africa, and Scott the season's "Falkner,"
there was still work to do. "My Dear Keltie," he wrote in January 1905,

> A hundred thousand apologies for not turning up tonight—it is
> now 12 p.m. and until 5 minutes ago I thought your kind invita-
> tion was for the 25th as it is stupidly noted in my engagements. I
> happened to look at your card—to see the time of the dinner
> and the horrid truth suddenly burst on me.
>
> I don't know what you will think but your kindest view must
> be that my brain is "softening" under the weight of the "mag-
> num opus."
>
> I feel nothing less than an "ass" in the largest letters.

The "magnum opus" was the expedition account Markham had been
harassing him over since the previous August. "I wrote to Scott about the
book," Markham had told Keltie, while *Discovery* was still at sea. "His
answer is 'I am not elated at the idea of writing a book; but I will do my best
to get the material together, so that there may be as little delay as possible
in its publication. We have at least the material to illustrate such a narrative thoroughly well.' " Scott was blunter still to Mill. "Of all things I dread
having to write a narrative," he confessed, "and am wholly doubtful of my
capacity; in any event if I have to do it, it will take me a long time. I have
not, like you, the pen of a ready writer."

Before he could think of beginning the book in earnest, however, he
needed not just somewhere to write, but somewhere to live more appropriate to his new circumstances and a captain's half-pay of £410 a year. "The

question is: — How are we going to live when I get back to London," he had written from *Discovery* to his mother, while his promotion was still in the balance. "I shall certainly need a study as well as a bedroom. If the shop room I had before is vacant, it would suffice but if not, it will be necessary for me to have a sitting room somewhere in the neighbourhood — Now in either case we are adding considerably to the rental of the house and the question is whether we could find a domicile which gives us sufficient space and some additional comfort by spending a sum which will not greatly exceed the combined rental."

They were now paying £80 a year, and could go to £120 or £130, he went on, staring soberly into a Gissing-like world of rented accommodation, shop premises and family dependants. "I don't know what one can get for such a sum but one ought to get a fairly decent place. A proper bathroom and electric lights are I think comforts that we deserve. I ought to have a good sum to my credit by this time and have no intention of saving it, so it will tide over such time as I am out of employment; if I am promoted that will not be long and employment as a post captain ensures at least enough for us to live comfortably on. Will you think all this out. I don't know how you look upon London . . . as far as I am concerned one place is as good as another and of course there is Monsie to be considered."

A house in Chelsea's Oakley Street was found, and if Scott felt the incongruity of writing from Balmoral about rental costs, his letter did not betray it. "Will you go ahead with the house," he asked his mother. "I think I should like electric light in the principal study and bedrooms — You seem to think that the whole thing will be a little expensive, if so it can't be helped — I am prepared to go over £100 if we get the worth of our money in comfort. The best policy is I'm sure to have it nice whilst there is the money. I can't be more explicit without knowing details — but you may be sure I should be quite pleased whatever you may decide provided you do not attempt to be economical."

Scott's sole concern in all this was that his mother should have the peace and security she had been robbed of ten years before, but for himself he did not really care. He never found Oakley Street an easy place to work in, and at the beginning wrote at Markham's house in Ecclestone Square before London and the pressure of finishing drove him to one or other country hotel. "I don't like going into horrid financial matters," he wrote in the spring of 1905 from Ashdown Forest to his mother, who was recuperating from a bout of illness at a Bournemouth hotel, "but of course you understand that I shall expect you to charge me with your expenses at

Bournemouth and as you know I shall be only too delighted to send you a cheque when you require it; the only real kindness to me is to spare me the trouble of going into details and to relieve me from the thought that you may be at any time cramping yourself. The book is getting on, not very fast but steadily—I've done half—I find proof correcting is not much trouble, arranging illustrations is rather more but I begin to see a glimmer of possibility of finishing."

"I have been trying harder this week to see how I get on and it won't do," he wrote again from Oakley Street the same month, "so tomorrow I'm off again—I go to Sheringham in Norfolk address The Burlington—I hear I can be very quiet there & in good air* with golf handy—one good month of peace will now see me within measurable distance of the end I hope and I need not add how welcome that position will be . . . I can't tell why I find it impossible to work in London but so it is, my ideas refuse to flow and I get a cramped inexpansive feeling which hinders me badly."

The recently-built Burlington, a large, ugly, red-brick building overlooking the sea, suited him "A1," he told her at the beginning of May, when he was three-quarters of the way through finishing. "I am glad you like the book—Personally I'm very tired of it but I plod along . . . Dearest mother I hope you will be comfortable in Oakley Street and will not think of expenses and those sort of troubles . . . PS It's really very cheap here although my sitting room comes heavy £2 a week it has four windows 4 tables, 4 armchairs & a sofa. My board is only £2 a week which is extraordinarily little for the extreme comfort I enjoy."

He was at least lucky in his publisher, the old Etonian barrister, classicist and senior partner in the firm of Smith, Elder and Co., Reginald Smith, who was to become a lifelong friend to both Scott and Wilson. "It is eight years since Captain Scott walked into the office at six o'clock one Autumn evening," Smith later wrote of his first meeting with the two men, "and said, 'I am back from the Antarctic, and I want you to publish my book.' His perfect comradeship with Dr. Wilson, the closest companion of his first expedition as of the last, was delightful to behold as they sat together in this room and discussed various points in the forthcoming book . . . One scene among these stands out unforgettably among many less defined memories. The question of the frontispiece to the first volume

---

*Something of a euphemism. If there was anywhere in England that could bring back memories of the Barrier, it was the north Norfolk coast in April. Scott remained a member of the golf club until his death. Arthur Conan Doyle was also a member at this time.

came up. It was proposed to give a photograph of the Southern sledge party led by Scott himself. Scott regarded it thoughtfully; then suddenly looking up said, at first tentatively, then with growing emphasis: 'What do you think, Bill? I don't think we ought to be there. The Southern Party wasn't more than any other sledging party. No, we won't have it.' And it was thrown out to take a more modest place in the text. As substitute a sketch of the good ship *Discovery* was suggested. Time was short; one remembers the cheery question, 'How long do you think you would take to do it, Bill?' and the quiet answer, in matter-of-fact tone, 'I can get it done in thirty-six hours if I sit up all night to it.' "

It was not Smith, however, but his chief reader Leonard Huxley, who most brilliantly captured the quality that "made" Scott a writer when he described him as "like wax to receive an impression and like marble to retain it." From all Scott's own letters and journals it is clear that he did not find the business easy, but there is a kind of metaphysical accuracy in Huxley's tribute that distils perfectly the talent that enabled Scott to absorb impressions of light, colour and atmosphere with a sensual passivity and *fix* them with a near scientific precision. There is nothing lifeless in the transformation either, and to pass from the writing of Armitage or Bernacchi, or even an artist like Wilson, to that of Scott is something like moving from the crudest engraving to the most sophisticated mezzotint. In passage after passage in *The Voyage of the Discovery* Scott might lament his inability to describe a scene in front of him, and yet no one writing of Antarctica has better deployed the shades and half-tones of descriptive prose to render the infinite gradations of colour and distance that lie within the white world of ice. This is not simply a matter of "atmosphere"—any travel writer with a pen can manage that—but of close and disciplined observation. *The Voyage of the Discovery* might often enough lapse into overwriting, but even at its "purplest" it is always based on a commitment to the literal as well as the poetic "truth" of a landscape that is so finely and unusually balanced in Scott.

There are two other, if related, aspects of his writing that quotation can less easily convey, and the first of these is the *topographical* accuracy of his accounts. There is too much historical and emotional baggage now attached to the landscape of McMurdo Sound for us ever to be able to see it through Scott's eyes, yet climb Observation Hill and look across to Castle Rock or out to White and Black Islands, and one still feels that shock of recognition and *familiarity* that is the most vivid, involuntary tribute that can be paid to any travel writer. Even the hideous sprawl of the U.S. base below cannot disguise this, and there is the same clarity to his narrative as well, an organisation so limpid and undemonstrative that it almost goes unnoticed. There is at once a sameness and a confusion about polar travel that militates against the sort of simplicity mastered by Scott, and one only has to read other sledging accounts—or paraphrases, summaries and plagiarisms of Scott himself—to become aware of the unusual powers of comprehension and planning that he brought to the business of both exploration and writing.

No one can marshal detail on the page like Scott. Nobody can make the logistical complexities of a journey read so straightforwardly. Nobody can make so lucid and explicable an experience of being lost. Nobody fix a physical feature and make it so palpably real. Cherry-Garrard *knew* McMurdo as he knew his home of Lamer before he ever set foot in the south. When he read Scott's accounts of his sledging, Reginald Smith wrote to tell him that he could almost hear him "speak" in them, and in the same way one is "there" with him, as sure of the position of an ice-ledge halfway down a crevasse as if one's next foothold depended on it. "I had no idea you had been through such trials," Admiral Sir Lewis Bayly wrote to him. "I held my breath as you shot down the ice following your two companions. I trembled when you were down the crevasse."

There are problems with the book—excisions, launderings and "quotations" from the original diaries that are not the literal transcriptions that they might seem—but these are no more or less than might be expected. Behind these silences and evasions lay the long and discreet tradition of Victorian biography, and if Lytton Strachey was already waiting in the wings, it would no more have occurred to Scott to air old grievances and dislikes than it would his modern successor to leave them out. One could read the near-thousand pages of *The Voyage of the Discovery* and never know that there had been any tensions in the wardroom, that Scott had made Ferrar cry, that Barne had nearly lost them half a dozen men, or Armitage had spent the last year sulking in his tent. It plainly suited Scott's purposes to project an image of contented unity to the Admiralty and to the public, and yet the real point is that there would not have been a single man in the ship—not even Armitage at this stage—who would have wanted it told differently or not closed ranks around the "myth" perpetrated in his expedition history.

Only when it comes to the treatment of their dogs on the Southern Journey, perhaps, does Scott lapse from the standards of integrity that survive all the omissions of the book. It is clear from the original diaries that the animals were carried on the sledges to keep them alive as fodder, but although this is plain enough in the published version, there are moments when Scott fights shy of spelling it out, too ashamed, too guilty—and too conscious of his readership, one suspects—to face up to the full cost of his Southern Journey in terms of the cruelty and suffering it caused.*

It clearly worked, and when *The Voyage of the Discovery* came out in the autumn of 1905, reviewers, "Arctics," shipmates, colleagues, friends and—in the case of *Nature*—an old enemy in the shape of Professor Gregory, queued up to heap on the praise. "I worked very hard on my book," Scott wrote to George Egerton in December, "and I don't deny that I am pleased that it has proved popular with the public, but this is nothing to the justification I feel when an old friend and an Arctic explorer like yourself writes in praise of it." "My Dear Sir Joseph Hooker," he wrote in the same vein to the last survivor of Ross's expedition over sixty years before, "no criticism of my book, public or private, has pleased me so much as your letter. My reviewers have been kind, and in some cases discriminating, but nothing they have said can reward my literary labours so fully as the thought that I have really brought vividly before you those scenes of ice and snow which you knew so well."

The book sold, too, with a first edition of three thousand going immediately, followed the next month by a second run of 1,500. By the end of the year Scott had made over £1,500 from the sales, and if that was not a fortune it was almost four times his half-pay as a captain—almost eight times his personal income once his annual allowance to his mother is taken into account.

There was a minor contractual irritation when Armitage brought out his own account of the expedition to compete with Scott's, but money apart, perhaps the most important result of the book was the new friendships it brought him. Among the guests who had crowded onto *Discovery* before she had sailed had been the novelist, politician, yachtsman, mountaineer, actor and spy A.E.W. Mason, and through Mason Scott now met

---

*There was also an unhappy fallout from the book when the *Daily Mail* interpreted a passage describing the Southern Journey when Shackleton had ridden on the sledge as an aspersion on his courage. Shackleton himself had no complaint with it at all when he read it—"It is beautifully got up and splendidly written," he told Scott—and Scott was quick to undo any damage he had unwittingly caused. "The facts were," he wrote to the editor of the *Daily Mail*, "that though Mr. Shackleton was extremely ill, and caused us great anxiety, he displayed the [most] extraordinary pluck and endurance, and managed to struggle on beside the sledge without adding his weight to our burden . . . I assume you will see the reason why in remembering the courage and spirit shown by Mr. Shackleton, I am anxious to correct the statement made in the report."

J.M. Barrie, the author of *Peter Pan* and, alongside Shaw, the most dominant figure in English theatre. "On the night when my friendship with
Scott began," Barrie recalled, "he was but lately home from his first adventure into the Antarctic, and I well remember how, having found the
entrancing man, I was unable to leave him. In vain he escorted me
through the streets of London to my home, for when he had said good-
night I then escorted him to his, and so it went on long through the small
hours. Our talk was largely a comparison of the life of action (which he
pooh-poohed) with the loathly life of those who sit at home (which I
scorned)."

It is an old argument—Byron used to complain that soldiers wanted to
free Greece with the "pen," while poets preferred the sword—but it perhaps pinpoints the secret of what otherwise looks a very improbable friendship. It is hard at this distance to understand the prestige and stature that
Barrie once enjoyed as a writer, and yet for all his whimsy and egotism he
clearly had an innate understanding and sympathy for "men of action"
that in turn won him their trust and affection. "If Barrie liked to be in the
company of explorers, *they* felt a natural sympathy with him," Cynthia
Asquith, his secretary for many years, wrote of him; "it struck me that soldiers as well as explorers were instinctively drawn to Barrie. He seemed to
have an intuitive understanding of what he had never experienced, the different aspects of battle—the hell of it and the compensatory gleams
glimpsed from that hell. I remember my husband paying him a remarkable tribute. 'I would sooner talk about the war to Barrie,' he said, 'than to
any other non-combatant.' "

It was a friendship that would open out Scott's life in new directions,
but as an index of success, a freeze frame as it were of his life, it was not so
much an entrée as an ending. Scott had arrived. And if Barrie's idealised
image of him as a man of "iron self-control" with "a blessed sense of fun"
does not say much for his own powers of judgement, it speaks volumes for
the success Scott had made of his new role as a public man. In the eighteen months since his return he had embraced and been embraced by that
"wider" world he and his sister Grace had dreamed of six years before. It is
a nice point whether a stag shoot with the King or lunch with Henry James
was the greater strain, but the young naval officer had managed both. Only
a very different friendship would reveal the uncertainty that still threatened this success, and that would not be with another man. That, though,
would have to wait. For the time being other imperatives were shaping
Scott's life.

Nineteen: The Pull of the South

As I say, I was very glad to go. The journey was a great experience. Yes, three years of my life were very well spent upon it; but they were very well spent, not because the journey was a great experience, but because it is now the great help to me in getting on, which I always thought it was going to be . . .

I can hardly remember the time when I was not diligently looking for a chance to get on. I was poor, you see.

A.E.W. MASON, *The Turnstile* (1912)

I watched him from time to time as Peary was talking—it was the face of a man transfigured . . . it was the face of a boy, eager, enthusiastic, absorbed in the story of dangers he knew so well.

EDGAR WALLACE, *Daily Sketch*, 11 February 1913

It is unlikely that Scott himself knew when he first decided to return to the south. Of all the officers and men in *Discovery* he was probably the only one who might have contemplated another winter with any equanimity, but "Gold medals," as he had written to Ettie on the voyage back from Antarctica, "are all very fine but they don't pay the rent nor provide for the future."

Eighteen months later—and even with a successful book to his credit—the "rent" remained as much of a motive force as it had ever been. The programme of lectures and his expedition history had inevitably kept him away from service business since *Discovery*'s return, but there seems no reason to doubt that he went back onto full pay envisaging anything for himself but the orthodox naval career his "future" and family had always demanded.

After a short War Course at the end of November 1905, and a temporary attachment at the Admiralty, Scott took up his new post as Assistant to the Director of Naval Intelligence in the middle of January 1906. In some ways a London appointment fitted in well enough with his new life, and while it

was sea-time rather than a desk that he wanted and needed, the job itself—
and in particular work on the possibilities of air power for the navy—was
not without its interest.*

For all the lunches at the Savoy with Barrie and Mason, or weekends
away at Barrie's country cottage, London and life at Oakley Street was soon
beginning to pall. If Scott was going to make up for time lost in *Discovery*
the Admiralty was not the place to be either, and in the summer of 1906, at
the age of thirty-eight, he got what he wanted. "I return to London on
13th," he wrote in early July from Sheringham to his old friend from midshipman days, Kathleen O'Reilly, in England after the death of her father,
"and shall be there on and off for some time. In August I go to sea as Flag
Captain [to George Egerton] in the Victorious—I shall not be sorry as I
am tired of London and its rush."

With the benefit of hindsight this seems not just one of the key
moments of Scott's life, but one of those crises of identity and purpose that
place his biography so firmly at the centre of a wide gamut of human experience. From the day he entered the navy he had aimed at the rank of captain and the command of his own ship, and here at last with his
appointment to *Victorious* was the day of reckoning, the vertiginous
moment when he had to look down from the eminence he had clawed his
way up to, and ask himself if it was worth it.

It had been such a long struggle. Since he was scarcely out of his teens
he had been looking at navy lists and calculating who was above him. He
had taken stock of fellow officers and weighed up their connections, noted
who had war service, who was Queen Victoria's godchild, whose father
was an admiral, who was likely to get the Yacht. He had sweated on the way
back from Vancouver for the news of his appointment to *Vernon*. He had
"contained his soul in patience" on the way home from the south for news
of his promotion. This was what, on behalf of the whole family, his
brother-in-law Willy had schemed at the Admiralty to bring about. This

---

*Among his papers from this time survive some undated notes on the subject, and though
it did not take an H.G. Wells or that visionary prophet of modern terrorism, George Griffith, to
see the shape of things, they show all the intelligence and clarity that characterised his work in
Discovery. It was the "phenomenal progress" made in the two years since the Wright brothers'
first flight that convinced Scott that the future was in the air, and after a visit to Rheims in connection with aviation developments he was already envisaging a role and a strategic influence
for aircraft carriers that in 1906 still lay thirty-five years in the future. By an interesting coincidence, Cecil Meares, Scott's dog-driver on his last expedition, was awarded the Order of the
Sacred Treasure (Third Class) by the Japanese Emperor in 1921 for services to the Imperial
Japanese Navy's nascent air capability. Meares would be dead before his work came to full
fruition.

was what all their financial plans and expectations, the care of his mother and his sisters, had depended on. And he had gambled as well, gambled on who at the Admiralty was in and who was out, who might help and who might consign him to the polar dustbin. He had followed his technical bent, and wondered if he had cut himself off from the main stream of executive life. He had seized the opportunity that *Discovery* offered and spent his time wondering whether a changing navy had left him and his kind behind.

In his long yarns with Skelton on the voyage home, this in particular had been his great fear, but now as he joined *Victorious* in Devonport, it was not the changes that must have struck him, but the similarities to the navy he had escaped five years before. In the intervening years a profound cultural and technical revolution might have occurred within the service, but as he exchanged memories of the 14,900-ton, twin-screw *Majestic* for the reality of the 14,900-ton, twin-screw *Victorious*, the Channel Squadron for the Atlantic Fleet, and weighed for Kingstown and Queenstown in the old familiar routine, it must have felt as though he had never left the service.

While the navy was in many ways still the same, however, Scott was not, and it did not take him long to find out that what he had struggled to achieve all those years was not what he wanted. If there was any man in the service under whom he would have been happy to serve it was probably George Egerton, but after three years of physical and intellectual independence in the ice, there was no one who could have reconciled Scott to that blend of autocratic licence and actual powerlessness that was the reality of a peacetime captain's authority. He had nothing to grumble about, he confessed to his mother just two months after joining *Victorious*, as "all goes smoothly on board," but "I'm afraid that my experience makes it difficult for me to take kindly to being dependent on another person's movements & ideas."

There is nothing unusual in this—outside the monastery or the convent there has never been a great tradition of men or women happily sliding back into anonymity—and for all Scott's humility he had never made a natural subordinate. In all his arguments for polar exploration Markham had stressed its value as a training ground for the navy, and while the record of Scott's men in the First World War might suggest that he was right, the irony of it in Scott's own case was that it had only spoiled him for the drudgery of an orthodox career. "I am dreadfully sick of this routine," he complained again to Ettie three months later, six weeks after leaving

Victorious for *Albemarle*. He wanted to do a job, he told her, and *could* do one, but his admiral, "the dearest nicest man, is always worrying over trifles and frittering away my time and his own over details which might be left to subordinates—can you understand—he has no notion of his mission as an Admiral which is essentially to take a wide grasp of fleet affairs and the larger organization . . . his mind, forever remaining on the minute pros & cons of a question, is incapable of decision until it recalls some obsolete precedent on which it dwells with mulish obstinacy utterly devoid of reason . . . Can you wonder that I consider myself an ass for being where I am."

As he looked at himself, too, he was not at all sure that he much liked what he saw. "Then to some old Misses Morrison," he would write, as he soberly contemplated the price of success,

> the elder, Miss Madeline, told my fortune by palm—she said "inter alia" . . . Extremely indolent—you have stuck to things with pertinacity and yet at times slackened off from mere ennui—you are naturally very logical and yet not a philosopher—you exaggerate troubles, look at the darker side of things, make mountains out of molehills—you are irritable, not exactly bad tempered but quick to take offence and not too quick to forgive, you are untidy but fond of comfort liking to have everything in place and hating little inconveniences . . . you like details and the necessity of dealing with them—and so on and so on.
>
> I liked much candour and deemed the description far from ill.

It is impossible to be sure how much of Scott's malaise was personal and how much professional, but it is doubtful if there have been many unhappier periods in naval history than in the years of the "Fisher Revolution." The judgement of history has run so strongly in John Fisher's favour that it is easy to forget that there were once two sides to the question, but it perhaps says something of the atmosphere of suspicion and resentment that his methods bred that an instinctive "modernist" and technocrat like Scott should find himself outside the charmed world of the "Fish pond."

After a naval career that had begun at the age of thirteen—his nomination was secured by his godmother, Lady Wilmot-Horton, the subject of Byron's "She walks in beauty like the night"—and taken him from active service in China during the Opium Wars to the *Warrior*, Britain's first "ironclad," *Inflexible* at the bombardment of Alexandria, and the command of the Mediterranean Fleet, Fisher had become First Sea Lord in 1904. He had already shown his willingness for a scrap as Second Lord with reforms to the recruitment and training of officers, and in an era of rapid technological development and strategic reorientation to combat the emerging threat of German sea power he brought to the navy's top job all the ruthlessness, pugnacity, intelligence, energy, charm and genius for self-promotion that had marked his whole career.

If Fisher's name will always popularly be associated with the awesome Dreadnought battleships, and the heavily armed and fast battlecruisers whose construction he oversaw, his reputation at the time had as much to do with personalities as it did with matériel. There was probably not a man in the service who could have wrenched the navy from its old habits and practices in the way that he did, but the very drive and zealotry that made him the great reformer he was meant that his revolution was achieved at the cost of politicising and dividing the navy against itself in a way that had not been known in generations.

The object of warfare, in Fisher's brutally simple vision, was to find the enemy and kill him, and that left little room for the chivalric culture that had sustained the service through almost a century of peace. To men of the stamp of Markham or McClintock polar exploration had seemed an ideal preparation for war, but to a technocrat like Fisher who saw the future in terms of speed, gunnery, overwhelming force and—that most "un-British" of all forms of warfare—submarines, Antarctica was about as relevant a training as were "shifting" topsails or "holystoning" decks. "Before his arrival" to command the Mediterranean Fleet, one former marine, the future Lord Hankey, recalled, "the topics and arguments of the officers' messes . . . were mainly confined to such matters as the cleaning of paint and brasswork, the getting out of torpedo nets and anchors and similar trivialities. After a year of Fisher's regime, these were forgotten and replaced by incessant controversies on tactics, strategy, gunnery, torpedo warfare, blockade, etc."

This all ought to have been manna to the *Vernon*-trained Scott, but with his RGS and old "Arctic" connections, his own polar record, and above all his organic sense of service loyalty and interdependence, there was a real ambiguity in his attitude. It was typical of him that even when he was one of Lord Charles Beresford's captains he remained fatally able to see both sides of the question; and yet if his head and his whole training put him on the side of the reformers, everything that he most admired in navy life bound him to an opposition rump that was struggling for its professional survival.

It would be wrong to think that it was simply dissatisfaction that drove him back to the south, however, as a conversation with Rosy Wemyss—an arch anti-Fisherite—while Scott was still at the Admiralty underlines. In 1903 Wemyss had become the first captain of the newly founded Osborne College, and when he was looking for a successor two years later and approached Scott—for whom he "had long felt boundless admiration"— he was told "that his whole soul was bound up in exploration and the Arctic [sic] and that no naval appointment had for him any longer either much interest or charm."

This might well owe something to hindsight and the posthumous glamour of Scott's reputation, but if Wemyss remembered correctly, it antedates Scott's disillusion with his return to sea. There is nothing in Scott's own correspondence prior to *Victorious* to bear out Wemyss's recollection, but even if he was conflating different times and conversations, and relocating a lunch with Scott at Gibraltar in February 1907 to London and 1905, it still offers a useful corrective to the usual explanations of Scott's motives.

It is all too easy to picture these in purely negative terms, to identify the professional and financial treadmill he had condemned himself to, to see what Scott was escaping, or to project it in terms of domestic unhappiness, the burden of "destiny" or some equally vague patriotic "duty." It is plain that in the aftermath of *Discovery* and his book success Scott underwent some kind of emotional and professional crisis, and yet it is the other side of the picture that Wemyss insists on—not the "escape," not the tedium of naval life, not the call of "duty," but the *pull* of the south and the unknown.

Scott was always so prosaic about himself that there is little temptation to speak of "soul" in his connection, but it is clear from everything he wrote that the ice exercised a charm over him that nothing else could match. In passage after passage in *The Voyage of the Discovery* he captures the grandeur of a scene or a sense of isolation with an immediacy that Wilson's brush could never match, and in purely physical terms he was never more alive or more intensely *himself*, as Cherry-Garrard would recognise, than when sledging. It is hard to know if he ever fully realised this himself, or when he first knew that the satisfactions of naval or family life were never going to suffice, but they cannot have been easy truths to face up to. Ever since the day he learned from home of his father's bankruptcy he had schooled himself to discipline and caution, and now, inexorably, there were other factors at work, other imperatives that cut across all those ties of duty and affection by which he had steered his life.

There is a fascinating trace of this struggle in a novel by his friend A.E.W. Mason, published in the year of Scott's death. It needs to be remembered, of course, that *The Turnstile* is fiction and not biography, but no one was in any doubt when it came out that the psychological and historical model for Mason's "Henry Rames" was Scott himself. "I had none of those opportunities which money commands," Rames tells an idealistic young admirer in a speech in which the echoes of Scott's own language are too insistent for coincidence.

"I had somehow to create or find them. There's a motto in gold letters above the clock in the great hall at Osborne, the first of all mottoes in its superb confidence;

" 'There is nothing the Navy cannot do.' "

Cynthia turned to him with eagerness.

"Yes," she said, with a smile. "For a boy to have that plain and simple statement before his eyes each day, that's splendid. I suppose a boy would never speak of it, but it would be to him a perpetual inspiration."

"Yes," said Rames, "if all he thought of was the Navy; if his ambitions were bound up with the Navy. But mine weren't, you see, and I used to worry over that sentence even then. 'There is nothing the Navy cannot do.' Very well. But that didn't mean that this little particular, insignificant cog-wheel in the Navy machine was going to do anything special, or indeed anything at all. And I wanted to do things—I myself, not the Navy . . ."

"You speak as if you had thought all these things out," she said.

"I have had to," he replied.

"I wonder that you went into the Navy at all."

"My father put me there," he answered.

Cynthia looked at him over again, noting the strong, square face, the direct, the practical, common-sense, uninspired look of him. He would get on without a doubt . . . He would get on probably by trampling upon others, but he would do it good-humouredly, and with no desire to cause unnecessary pain. There are men, after all, who put nails in their boots to do the trampling.

In many ways what we have here in its *ur*-form is the Scott of modern myth, a man of ambition without direction, of aspirations without vision, of will without conscience, of charm without kindness, of character without *centre*. It is worth conceding, too, that Mason knew Scott well enough to make the similarities to this *grotesque* more than mildly discomforting, and yet if he portrayed a pragmatism and complacent ordinariness in Rames which he did not much like, he also recognised a burning, redeeming idealism that his hero is reluctant to admit even to himself. "She saw something in his face which she had never seen there before," he wrote of the moment when Cynthia, by now Rames's disillusioned wife, discovers that her rival is not another woman but the old Antarctic charts that her husband has kept like a guilty secret in a locked drawer, "which she had never thought to see there at all. He wore the look of a man quite caught out of himself. He was as one wrapped in visions and refined by the fires of great longings. It seemed to her that she saw a man whose eyes, brimful of light, looked upon the Holy Grail."

There is a fascination in seeing what a novelist like Mason "made" of Scott before death had effectively censored all such insights, and *The Turnstile* is useful in the same way as Wemyss's recollections. In the figure of Harry Rames, Mason set out to draw a man of deliberate and calculated ordinariness who is seized unawares by the extraordinary, and nowhere is the portrait more convincing or suggestive of Scott than in the rendering of this self-discovery. " 'I had no suspicion that any longing could get so strong a hold on me,' " Rames confesses. " 'I once told you carelessly that men were driven out upon these expeditions by the torment of their souls. I said that knowing it only by hearsay and by the plain proof of it which they show in what they have written. Now I know it—here,' and he struck his breast above his heart. 'Yes, I have got to go if I am ever to have peace.' "

If Scott's own subsequent claims are to be believed, he had "always" intended to return, but with a naval career to safeguard, the first tentative feelers were only put out in September 1906 when he wrote to Michael Barne asking if he would go as his first lieutenant. Barne had already tried and failed to fund an expedition of his own to the Weddell Sea since their return in *Discovery*, and immediately agreed to the proposal, arranging to go on half-pay from the spring of the following year.

In the gap between leaving *Victorious* and joining *Albemarle*, Scott also sounded out the RGS with a view to possible funding. On 28 January 1907 he wrote to Keltie, spelling out in brief his hopes of another expedition.

"As regards my future plans I saw Goldie and talked to him," he wrote with a fine blend of cajolery and moral blackmail,

> but I don't think he has any heart in the matter though he has promised to do his best and keep an eye to finding a likely millionaire. He will need little reminders and this is a service in which you can assist me . . . You were sanguine—you believe there will be little difficulty in raising the funds with my name—I can't tell but I don't see how it is to be done at present. I'd sooner have a single subscriber as you know.
>
> Well anyway you must do the very best you can to enlist general sympathy. There cannot be a doubt that the thing ought to be done. There is the finest prospect of a big advance in latitude that has ever been before a polar explorer.
>
> Rub all this into Goldie—it's essentially the thing for a Geographical Society and remember what a future generation will think if you lose the experience combined with the will to go when these are at your command. It will soon be on record of course that I want to go and only need funds. I am pretty certain that I could do the whole thing for £30,000. It won't look well for the Society if an inexperienced foreigner cuts in on the thing while we are wasting time. There really is a splendid chance.

Those last words would be only too prophetic—if not in any way he could possibly have imagined—but before they could come home to roost Scott found himself with more immediate problems. He had been in *Albemarle* less than a month when he wrote to Keltie from home waters, but by the beginning of February cleaning and preparations at Chatham were complete, and after coaling at Plymouth *Albemarle* was taken round on the third to join the fleet "safe and sound" at Portland.

Four days later, on 7 February 1907, *Albemarle* weighed anchor for Gibraltar, and on the night of the eleventh was steaming in close formation without lights when the flagship, the *Edward VII*, inexplicably signalled full speed ahead without increasing speed herself. To avoid an inevitable collision *Britannia* swung through forty or fifty degrees to the right, and was followed in turn by *New Zealand*, *Africa* and finally *Albemarle*.

Astern of Scott's ship, *Commonwealth* failed to follow suit until too late, and at 8.16½ collided on her port bows with *Albemarle*. Like all other captains in the formation, Scott was below, "looking out the position of the enemy as signalled." "I think we are as clear of blame as we can be under the circumstances but of course the court of enquiry may have a different view," he wrote anxiously to his mother when they reached Gibraltar, shaken but not "unnerved" for all the complex fleet manoeuvres that had followed the collision. "Finally we came in after dark last night, altering course and coming to anchor in close block formation 1¾ cables between the ships—It was really a wonderful manoeuvre and shows Wilson's ["Old 'ard 'art"] remarkable nerve, no one has ever attempted to have ships so moored at night."

Scott had already had a chance to speak with the captain of *Africa*, and "everyone condemned the signal that governed it." In a private conversation Admiral May—another old Arctic—had bravely taken the whole blame on himself for the signal, he went on, and though there would of course be an inquiry, "intended to be at home when the report came and do his best to hush the whole thing up. He discussed the whole thing very plainly and it is evident he had discussed it and finds Sir A. Wilson in agreement—He acknowledges the fault of the formation & of his signal but he argues that these sort of things must be expected to happen occasionally & that the lessons learned are worth it—It is quite evident he means to do his best but I expect he may have a job to smooth down Sir John Fisher."

By 3 March a relieved Markham had had a telegram from Scott, announcing that he had been cleared of all blame, and "except as an amusing incident," the "affair" was over. "I had quite a long talk with the Queen [of Portugal]," he reported home, reputation and career both happily intact once more, "and a longer with the young Crown Prince—everyone was very nice especially about the accident."

Something, in fact, of his London "lion" status had followed him out to the Rock. "I went to the C-in-C's lunch for Prince Henry of Prussia," he wrote again at the beginning of April, "and was trotted out as usual as a person of note—as our C in C remarked with his usual politeness 'I fear it is the penalty of greatness' however HRH duly produced the usual question 'What was the good of it all'—he is a nice looking man, very keen & alert and a little given to boasting of the efficiency of his German Navy."

Even if it had done his naval prospects no harm, however, there was a synchronicity about the "accident" that must have brutally brought home to Scott the difficulties of pursuing two careers at once. The same day

Albemarle and *Commonwealth* collided in the Bay of Biscay, Shackleton had turned up in Keltie's office at the RGS, announcing that he had the money to launch an expedition to the south. By chance Nansen was there too, and Amundsen, fresh from the first successful navigation of the North-West Passage. Enjoined to secrecy by Scott over his own plans, Keltie could only listen in silence. "He told me had been planning something of the kind ever since he came back," he wrote to Scott a week later, concerned that Scott might already have had wind of Shackleton's plans from a press announcement,

> probably to prove that though he had been sent home, he is quite as good as those who remained. He assured me that he had heard on the best authority that the Belgians had an expedition ready to send out to the Discovery quarters and to make for the Pole, and that is the reason why he wished to rush out with his announcement . . . The position is an awkward one, as you can understand.
>
> I suppose even if you had the necessary funds, you would not think of going down there as a rival to Shackleton? He is very confident of success, but I am doubtful of it myself, and it is just possible that he may have to return within 18 months after he set out without doing much. Then of course it might be our opportunity.

Scott had already heard the news, and the same day was writing the first of a string of letters to Shackleton. "The situation is awkward for me," he wrote.

> As a matter of fact I have always intended to try again but as I am dependent on the Navy I was forced to reinstate myself & get some experience before I again asked for leave, meanwhile I thought it best to keep my plans dark . . . You see therefore that your announcement cuts right across my plans and to an extent that it would not have done two months ago . . . I needn't tell you that I don't wish to hurt you and your plans but in a way I feel I have a sort of right to my own field of work in the same way as Peary claimed Smith's Sound and many African travellers their particular locality—I am sure you will agree with me in this and I am equally sure that only your entire ignorance of my plan could have made you settle on the Discovery route

without a word to me. As I say Michael Barne is now in town I
wish you would meet him and discuss matters as he is in possession of my ideas.

PS I feel sure that with a little discussion we can work in
accord rather than in opposition—I don't believe the Foreigner
will do much, the whole area is ours to attack.

"I ought perhaps to explain to you what has been my attitude with regard
to the South a little more carefully as I wrote in haste," he elaborated
almost immediately:

you know that I support my mother & family, it is therefore
essential for me to have an assured income . . . I therefore
decided to be very quiet about the matter to go back to my profession & accept appointments which would give me a chance
of getting quite up to date in Naval matters . . . perhaps I was
wrong to keep this dark but in the first place I doubt whether
the Admiralty would have liked me to announce that I had such
a plan and in the second I did not want a lot of publicity & press
criticism until everything was on a sound footing.

Of course my intention was to go to McMurdo Sound our
old winter quarters again! I cannot but look upon this as my
area until I signify my intention to desert it—I think this is not a
dog in the manger attitude for after all I know the region better
than anyone, everything concerning it was discovered by our
expedition and it is a natural right of leadership to continue
along the line which I made . . . The foreigners always conceded this when I was abroad or rather they conceded that the
sphere of the Ross Sea was English; indeed they did this in the
case of "Discovery" herself on account of Ross. Surely if a foreigner has the good taste to leave this to the country which has
done the work there, the English must admit the same argument to apply amongst themselves.

. . . I would explain to you that the reason I did not write to
you was because it never entered my head that you had a wish
to go on. I have imagined you as very busy . . . I had naturally
no object in keeping any of our old company in the dark, you
know how attached I am to all and how gladly I would take anyone who cared to come again.

There is no way of judging the rights and wrongs of Scott's claim to priority, other than to say that if it seems absurd now, it would not have done so then. It is hard to feel at this distance that the example of Peary or Africa does much for the morality of his case, but there were gentlemanly codes of behaviour involved here, and with the instinctive anxiety of the outsider, Shackleton was as keen to observe them as anyone—"I would rather lose the chance of making a record," he wrote to Barne, "than do anything that might not be quite right."* And if no one already in the "know" had any doubt as to what the "right" thing was—Keltie thought that Shackleton should have consulted Scott in advance, Markham was indignant, Barne angry—that does not settle the issue either way. It had certainly never occurred to Shackleton that Scott had some quasi-seigneurial rights over the old *Discovery* quarters and men, but even he could see that "as Britishers, the position is clear." "He has evidently been quite upset by your letter," Keltie wrote to Scott on 1 March, "and the letter he has had from Barne, he told me he has not slept for four nights. He has evidently been thinking over alternatives. He talked of the Weddell Sea, and landing there and trying to make his way to the Pole, then he thought of making King Edward VII Land his base of operations, and leaving the old Discovery quarters to you and even hinted that he might turn his expedition towards the North Pole . . . As to Shackleton's capacity as a leader and his staying powers, I think you and I take the same view. He looks strong enough, but it is clear that he is not absolutely sound, and Heaven knows what may happen if he starts on his journey Pole-wards."

It was all the harder for Shackleton, because he had financial backers to placate, but the seeming indifference with which he could talk of the Weddell Sea and the North Pole in one breath perhaps explains the scepticism that surrounded him. With the knowledge of what he would achieve this attitude seems obtuse to the point of idiocy, and yet without that benefit, what did they have to go on? What had Shackleton actually *done* to make Scott's judgement of him seem in any way unfair? "As to his chance of success I do not like to express an opinion," Scott wrote on 2 March; "on the one hand he has lots of energy & he may select his people well—on the other I personally never expect much in this sort of work from a man who isn't straight—it is the first essential for the co-operation necessary for such a venture—of course also Shackleton is the least experienced of our

---

*The great French explorer Jean Charcot certainly thought that the Ross Sea area belonged to the British, and would not have dreamed of trespassing there. And even Amundsen would regard McMurdo as out of bounds.

travellers and he was never very thorough in anything—one has but to consider his subsequent history to see that—he has stuck to nothing & you know better than I the continual schemes which he has fathered."

All this was simultaneously true and untrue, and yet only a serious misunderstanding on Scott's part could possibly have justified his aspersions that Shackleton had not been "straight." The first that Shackleton had in fact known of any rival ambitions was in a letter from Mulock, the surveyor who had replaced him in *Discovery*, turning down an offer to join his expedition. The letter was dated 17 February, Shackleton reassured Scott, six days after he had first been to see Keltie: "I took the letter to the Geographical and saw Kelty [sic]. I said 'What is the meaning of this?' Kelty said 'Oh! Mulock has let the cat out of the bag.' I said 'What do you mean?' I said 'Is Scott going to go?' He said 'Yes.' "

But even with Keltie's assurances that Shackleton knew nothing, Scott was determined to believe the worst: "You do not say that you told him that I contemplated getting up an expedition, but it is impossible to imagine that you omitted to mention it when you saw him. The fact must therefore be that Shackleton deliberately worded his notice so as to forestall *me*—I would not have believed it of any of my own people—and since it is so I cannot express my condemnation of such an act too strongly."

Keltie was in an impossible position, and it was made worse still by Scott's attitude. "Your letter makes me feel very unhappy," he wrote in reply to Scott's. "I feel rather sorry now that when Shackleton spoke to me first about his expedition and told me that he was going to put it in the papers next day that I did not tell him what were your intentions . . . But then I thought that you wanted to keep the whole matter absolutely secret . . . Of course you will understand that my position here is a difficult one . . . I think that you will admit that we could not ignore his expedition altogether."

By this time Scott was too angry to see straight, and if Shackleton was not to blame, then someone else was. "I am sorry to have done you this injustice and I think it right to tell you how it came about," he wrote to Shackleton on 7 March.

> I . . . have the relief of knowing that you did not intentionally wreck my plans and the thought that you had done so was very distressing to me, for it seemed an action of which an old Discovery should have been incapable and one that surprised me beyond measure in you.
>
> I apologise for having thought you guilty of it.

As to Keltie we must now draw our own conclusions—His silence seems to have been deliberately calculated to make trouble—he must have known that I should protest and think evil things of you and that you would be deeply troubled, as I gather you are . . . neither of us I expect is likely to forget it.

Nothing could have been more unfair, because if two things are absolutely clear in this whole business, it is that Shackleton was utterly blameless, and Keltie just about as honourable as it was possible to be in an impossible situation. The worst that he can be accused of is a lack of initiative or boldness in ignoring Scott's injunction to silence, but Scott was incapable of letting it rest. "I confess your silence appears to me inexplicable," he harried Keltie again on the eleventh. "Now that I know the facts I must of course acquit Shackleton of want of loyalty but I cannot think that you acted a friendly part . . . It is beyond me to guess what was in your mind . . . I confess I am at a loss to find your motive and being a plain dealing person I have been exceedingly hurt by your act."

If Scott had been forced to acquit Shackleton of disloyalty, however, he was not prepared to concede him their old *Discovery* base. "The question now is what you intend to do?" he wrote on 26 March. "On the one hand I do not wish to stand in the way of any legitimate scheme of yours—on the other it must be clear to you now that you have placed yourself directly in the way of my life's work—a thing for which I have sacrificed much and worked with steady purpose—Two expeditions cannot go to the same spot either together or within the compass of several years—If you go to McMurdo Sound you go to winter quarters which are clearly mine . . . I do not need to remind you that it was I who took you to the South or of the loyalty with which you all stuck to one another or of incidents on one voyage or of my readiness to do you justice on my return."

By this time the only thing they did agree on was that the one man they could both trust to arbitrate was Wilson. Wilson had already been offered and turned down the position of Shackleton's second-in-command, and now in a double blow he came firmly down on Scott's side. "I do not agree with you, Billy," a disappointed Shackleton wrote back to him, "about holding up my plans until I hear what Scott considers his rights. There is no doubt in my mind that his rights end at the base he asked for, or within reasonable distance of that base. I will not consider that he has any right to King Edward the Seventh's Land [first seen by Shackleton], and only regard it as a direct attempt to keep me out of the Ross quarter if he should ever propose such a thing. I have given way to him in the greatest thing of all, and my limit has been reached . . . just as well might Borchgrevink have objected to Scott wintering anywhere within a radius of 500 miles of Cape Adare."

Scott had, in fact, no objections to any attempt by Shackleton on King Edward VII Land, and all that was left was to put a good public face on the argument and thrash out the details of a private agreement. "If you in consultation with others," Scott wrote to Keltie at the end of March, at a time when it seemed that the Polish Henryk Arctowski might be threatening British hegemony in the Ross Sea area, "think it wise to announce a change of Shackleton's plan and a hint as to my own I am willing that you should do so presuming it is solely to show the world that England intends to operate in the Ross Sea — If you think no such statement is necessary but it will be sufficient to inform foreign rivals more privately it would be a course better suited to my views."

He had also written to Shackleton, he told Keltie, suggesting that they operate "on either side of the 170° W meridian," and on 17 May Shackleton spelled out the exact terms of their understanding. "I am leaving the McMurdo Sound base to you," he conceded,

> and will land either at the place known as Barrier Inlet or at King Edward VII Land, which ever is most suitable. If I land at either of these places I will not work to the westward of the 170 meridian W and shall not make any sledge journey going W. of that meridian unless prevented when going to the South from keeping to the East of that meridian by the physical features of the country . . .
>
> I shall not touch the coast of Victoria Land at all.
>
> If I find it impracticable to land at King Edward VII Land or at barrier Inlet or further to the N.E., I may possibly steam North and then to westward and try to land to the West of Kaiser Wilhelm II Land, going down to the meridian that the "Challenger" made her furthest South . . .
>
> I think this outlines my plan, which I shall rightly adhere to, and I hope that this letter meets you on the points that you desire.

"My Dear Shackleton," a victorious Scott wrote back across the bottom of Shackleton's own letter, "I return you this copy of your letter which is a very clear statement of the arrangement to which we came. If as you say you will rigidly adhere to it, I don't think our plans will clash and I will feel on sure ground in developing my own." If Scott had won, he had won at a cost that, however incalculable, was real enough. On the balance of contemporary opinion he was probably within his rights to stake the claim he did, but whatever else he had been in his dealings with Shackleton, he had not been generous.

There are any number of times when Scott behaved badly, when he was ill-tempered or hasty, but this prolonged territorial battle is the first occasion when these defects of character feel something more than the failures of the moment. It is possible to make any number of excuses for him, but even when these are taken into account and one remembers the pressures of his job, the anxieties over the collision, the constant fears for the security of his mother and family, the boundless room for misunderstanding when letters and counter letters crossed in the post—even when all these are borne in mind something remains that leaves the first real sense of disappointment at anything of human importance Scott did.

In one respect his behaviour only goes to show how deeply Scott wanted to complete the work he had begun in *Discovery*, but there is an air of egotism and self-importance about his ambitions now that was never there before. Scott's secretary in *Albemarle* has left a vivid testimony of Scott's uncertain temper during this row, and while there was nothing unusual in that, what is new is the pomposity—a pomposity that makes one wonder what the young Scott who had poked fun at his captain in *Amphion*, or the man who hung from a harness supported only by Lashly, would have said to this: "On the whole it is premature for me to write more till I hear more," he had told Keltie in the first throes of the battle with Shackleton. "The attitude of the RGS should be noncommittal altogether. It is their duty to encourage exploration but it must be also remembered that an ill-conducted expedition tends to ruin the cause of true exploration . . . Whilst the experience of the 'Discovery' remains available it is a question how far the Society should condone an act of disloyalty. As to the King I shall of course explain the case in the proper quarter."

Scott's struggles and fears are all the evidence one needs of the damage done by a life of care and responsibility, but for the first time here we see the rather different dangers of success. The man who came back in *Discovery* could never have written a letter like that, but whether it was the habit of command or the familiarity of applause, something had happened to him, blinding him to those truths that underlay the language of "loyalty" and "spirit" he deployed against Shackleton. While he could still blithely talk of loyalty, what he now meant was loyalty to *him*, and while he still boasted of *Discovery*'s spirit and achievements, they had somehow with distance become his private preserve. In a shrewd judgement on Shackleton, Reginald Ford once identified the way in which he grew with success into a kind of parody of himself. If the same thing had not happened to Scott, he had come within a whisker of it, subsuming to his own self-interest all the rhetoric of duty, loyalty and patriotism that had made him what he was.

He cannot have been aware of it—human nature does not work like that—and one can almost feel the battle he was fighting within himself, as an overwrought sense of injury and *amour propre* contended with a much saner recognition of reality. "But indeed you mistake me altogether," he lied to Keltie in a letter at the end of May, apologising and retracting again in the same breath, "if you suppose that I have ever attributed any malicious motive to you—in my angriest moment I never did that—no the case was this, I cherished a warm feeling of friendship for you on account of many kind things you had done—amongst them, most conspicuous, the care & attention you gave to my mother & sisters. Then the time came when it seemed to me you might have done something which a friend should have done and you didn't do it.—That's the whole case. I've no claim that you should have treated me differently from a hundred others that came to your office—it is only that I thought & expected that you would and therefore I was deeply disappointed & hurt when it seemed to me that you did not."

It had been a bad year. The twin-pronged assault of poverty and success had had its effect. Scott's personality and sense of his own dignity were firming into something less attractive than they had once been. His ruthlessness had driven a wedge between him and Shackleton, and his habit of secretiveness had effectively put all his own plans on hold. His one spurious consolation in all this lay in his, and almost everyone else's, misjudgement of his rival's capabilities. All he could do was hope that they were right, and wait. It would be a long wait, too, and as Scott sat in his lonely cabin in *Albemarle*, he could never have guessed what was going to fill it.

Twenty: **Of Lions and Lionesses**

Falkner is the lion of the season. Therefore we may be quite sure that Falkner won't make love to any pretty woman who comes in his way. It doesn't seem to work out right.

HENRY ARTHUR JONES, *The Liars (1897)*

At the beginning of 1907, a young nobody of a woman just back from Greece was invited to a "luncheon party of lions" given by Mabel Beardsley. It was one of those occasions in the social zoo of London life when there were no balancing "lionesses" to match the "lions," she recalled, with only the hostess herself, an actress and writer *manquée* and the sister of the dead artist Aubrey Beardsley, even so much as a "lioness" by association.

The lunch was, in fact, largely for his old friends,

but lions they were, and to me very splendid ones indeed, the men whose books I had read, whose pictures I had admired. There was a poet, a politician, and an explorer. I, the humble, sat between Max Beerbohm and J.M. Barrie. I wished they would roar a little louder. I was terribly shy of them both. Englishmen are very difficult, I thought. Far down the other side of the table was a naval officer, Captain Scott. He was not very young, perhaps forty, not very good looking; but he looked very healthy and alert, and I glowed rather foolishly and suddenly when I clearly saw him ask his neighbour who I was. I was nobody, and I knew his neighbour, my hostess, would be saying so. I had heard that he had just returned from a very heroic and rather sensational exploit, and for the last few months had been subject to the torture of intrusive popularity. I was introduced to him after lunch and he wanted to know where I had got my wonderful sunburn. I was of the richest brown which made my eyes a very startling blue. I told him I had been vagabonding in Greece, and he thought how entrancing to vagabond like that. I had to leave immediately to catch a train. He left two minutes after me, hoping to catch me up, but he saw me just ahead carrying a rather large suitcase, and his "English gentlemen don't carry large objects in the street" upbringing was too much for him. He did not catch me up.

It is a curious reflection on Scott's life that, at the age of thirty-eight, this is the first sight of him through the eyes of any woman outside his family that we have. In her memoir of her brother, Grace Scott spoke of a "first love" at the age of nineteen, but for all the trace that or any other romance has left, this might be the first time he had so much as looked at a woman in a life that from *Britannia* to the end of the *Discovery* expedition had been lived in an exclusively masculine world.

There was Minnie Chase in San Francisco, and Kathleen O'Reilly at Victoria, but these are mere names, preserved as biographical trophies in the absence of any serious candidates. "Dear Miss O'Reilly," Scott wrote from Sheringham when he heard the news of her father's death in 1906— twenty-six passionless years after he had first met her, if the tone of his letter is anything to go by,

> . . . *Yesterday I came here for a week's golf with my despatch box and the first thing I saw on opening the latter was your missing letter. I fear this reveals an inexcusable want of method but that is me . . . It seems such a short time since George Warrender first took me to call on you at Victoria and I remember vividly the words he used in preparing me to meet a "type of the finest men the colony possessed." . . . I have been doing the season rather thoroughly for the first time and am here for a small rest. The air is splendid coming pure and sparkling from the North Sea and it's a positive pleasure to chase a golf ball over the links that bor-*

*der the sea regardless of the frequency with which one fails to
strike it.*

   *My address in London is 56 Oakley St—drop a line when I
can call on you.*

      Yrs ever sincerely

A luncheon party for lions with Max Beerbohm and J.M. Barrie was a far
cry from canoeing, riding and going to church with the finest types the
colonies can produce, but there is no evidence that the woman Scott met
in his first London season made any more lasting impression than Kit
O'Reilly. It is plain from family correspondence that Scott was in search of
a wife, or at least prepared to find himself a suitable one, but the two
women who seem to have made any serious impression on him at this time
hardly belonged to worlds from which she was likely to come.

   The first of these was the young American actress and protégée of Barrie's, Pauline Chase, the First Twin in the opening performance of *Peter
Pan*, and Nina Boucicault's and Cissie Loftus's successor in the title role
itself. A portrait photograph of her in costume taken the year before Scott
met her reveals a tiny, almost stunted figure, her head tilted on one side,
the face fixed in a studio smile, a slender child's wrist showing from the
sleeve of her pyjama suit, a spotted hanky knotted into a sack dangling
from a stick slung carelessly over her shoulder—the perfect incarnation of
Barrie's fantasy of arrested physical and emotional growth.

   Scott was not the only man who thought this creature "as pretty as
they're made," but it remains a curious thought that the bulk of his rivals
were to be found among the gender-confused eight- and nine-year-olds of
Middle England. "I DO love you so, Peter dear," they used to write to
her—"No one noes I am writing to you, & I don't ever want them to know,
you will keep it a secret won't you Peter darling"; "Swee'ts Darlingest Peter
Pan"; "You make the most lovely boy imaginerable"; "I loved you so much
that Mother said I was crying in bed for you"; "Fancy you not knowing
what a kiss was! I think you were made for kissing."

   My Darling Peter,
      *. . . I love you so much that I think of you all day long and
   dream at night. I had the happy thought to write to you and I
   would be the happiest little girl in the world if you would write
   me a letter. I am eight years old and live with my Parents.*
         Your loving Mary

The letters that Pauline Chase received as Peter go on and on, from Cadogan Square and Camberwell, from St. John's Wood and Stoke Newington, from Sussex and Hampshire, from an Edwardian world of boarding schools, nannies, birthday parties, sisters, parents, home-made theatres and those miniature English gentlemen who within a decade would get more than the "hour of Herod" Anthony Hope sighed for when he saw the play. "How is the brutal and horrid James Hook," one such child demanded. "Send him round here and I, being an English gentleman will give him what he deserves as I have a sword a razor a South American dagger and a thing that they kill bulls with in Spain. Poor Hook! If he does come he wont forget it."

It would seem probable that Scott also met her at the theatre, at a rehearsal of *Peter Pan* shortly after his first, legendary meeting with Barrie. He had given Barrie a copy of *The Voyage of the Discovery* after they had first met, and "as a sign of his ardent appreciation" an entranced Barrie had reciprocated with an invitation to watch him at work. "So Scott did," wrote Denis Mackail, biographer and friend of Barrie's for more than thirty years, "and was exhilarated and impressed. Was introduced, in turn, to the company, was distinctly fascinated by them too, was modest and irresistible, and found himself—though never forgetting the Navy or the Antarctic— admitted to a circle exceedingly remote from both. Barrie isn't going to let go now. Scott will be meeting Frohman, and staying at Black Lake Cottage, and appearing at another Farnham, in Buckinghamshire, to play golf-croquet—with Miss Pauline Chase coming over from her own cottage—in Haddon Chambers's garden. And Scott will extend his frank admiration to all. He also has an ingenuous and openly-expressed wish to get married."

His flirtation with Pauline Chase, carried out under the slightly prurient gaze of the diminutive Barrie, would drift on late into 1907, but if he wanted to marry anybody on his return from *Discovery* it was probably not her. There is nothing in Scott's own papers that gives even a clue to the existence of any other relationship at this time, but in the fragmentary memories of a generation now gone, the faint trace of a real passion and of a different and unknown Scott are still just discernible.

The woman in question was a Marie-Carola d'Erlanger, the improbably beautiful and accomplished daughter of an Irish baronet and an aristocratic German bluestocking, with an entrée to every salon in Paris and London. Marie-Carola was a widow with two small children when Scott first met and fell in love with her at the home of Rosy Wemyss, but not even the blessing and support of William IV's great-grandson was enough to bridge the gap between a talented and impeccably connected cosmopolitan and an indigent polar explorer.

There is almost nothing now left of this relationship—a linen napkin found shredded beneath Scott's chair at the end of a dinner, the disapproval of a French governess at the sight of his coat hanging in the hall, a man raising his straw hat in a park and smiling as a woman drew her children a map in the dust with the point of an umbrella—but for all their sharpness these are just fragments, *Punch* illustrations without text that survive more as a warning of just how little one actually *knows* of the middle-aged Scott than anything else. There are so many ways in which we *do* know him, and know him in such a mass of detail, that this ignorance is of a kind and extent that is hard to grasp. There is so little of his adult life when we cannot say where he was or what he was earning, what he weighed or what his chest measurement and blood levels were, that it is easy to forget that the interior landscape that lies behind those glimpses of a raised hat or a torn napkin remain as blank as the empty pages of the adolescent midshipman's diary.

To a certain extent this is the case with any life—biography can confidently offer profounder insights only by pretending to a knowledge that it does not possess—but it is all the more relevant to a man like Scott, who by instinct and training was so emotionally reticent. The same might, of course, be said of most men of his time and class who had passed through the *Britannia* mill, yet in the case of Scott it was compounded by a burden of responsibility that bound him from an early age to a kind of self-denying ordinance with those dependent members of his family to whom he might otherwise have unburdened himself.

It is impossible to live with such a discipline of self-restraint and it not to become a habit of mind, a crippling incapacity even, and one only has to look at Scott's *Discovery* journals to see that it had become so with him. In his letters to his mother he would never have dreamed of off-loading his anxieties and fears, but the journals are in many ways the same—not impersonal or emotionally sterile, because they are never that, but guarded and secretive, as if he could not bring himself to commit to paper the unhappiness or the wounds of daily life. There are any number of occasions when some outburst is noted in a wardroom diary and there is nothing in Scott's, but whether that is the silence of self-restraint, indifference, wounded feelings, or of emotional stupidity, it would be impossible to say. There is a kind of fineness about Scott in all his dealings with those closest to him that would seem to preclude that last possibility, but beyond that the answer seems in a sense unknowable, the hidden secrets of a man who had guarded his emotional privacy too well for us ever to penetrate its carapace of silence.

At that stage in life when most personalities have more or less taken on their final shape, Scott would successfully have done so too, if it had not been for that woman at the other end of the table at Mabel Beardsley's lunch party. In his account of the *Discovery* expedition Bernacchi reckoned that Scott had "only a slender knowledge of women," but it is fair to say that all the knowledge in the world would probably not have prepared him for the wonderfully tanned, determinedly virginal, twenty-eight-year-old sculptress with a passion for "male babies" and a critical eye for a prospective father, just back from five months' vagabonding around Greece.

It would be hard to imagine two people more superficially at odds than Scott and Kathleen Bruce, and yet in its own way her life had been the same brave triumph of courage and determination over circumstances as was his. She had been born in the Jacobean rectory of Carlton-in-Lindrick in the Midlands in 1878, "the last of a huge family of about a dozen sturdy children" of an indigent country parson of distantly royal Scottish ancestry and a half-Greek mother of Phanariot descent. Kathleen had been only two when her mother died, and when her father married again, she and most of her brothers and sisters went to live with "an old Presbyterian lawyer who was our grand-uncle in Edinburgh." "Here the blinds were kept down on a Sunday until dinner-time," she recalled with a good Butleresque hatred. "Here no book save a Bible might be read on the holy day. Here at meals no child might speak till she had finished her meat-course. Here surface order and decorum were of the strictest."

And here—she might have added with more honesty—she did pretty much as she liked, and behind the trappings of Presbyterian respectability the Bruce children grew up in an atmosphere of loveless but robust anarchy. In 1892 Kathleen's great-uncle died and she was sent to a "cheap convent school," from where she finally escaped at the age of seventeen to London and art school, with little more than a theatrical, self-dramatising and exuberantly pagan determination to *live* to show for her chaotic, lonely, overcrowded Presbyterian/Catholic "upbringing."

"It is not enough to have this globe at a certain time," she used to quote Whitman, "I will have thousands of globes and all time," and having bought herself a copy of *Leaves of Grass*, Kathleen took him at his word. In the last years before Roger Fry revolutionised English art, the Slade belonged to the grimly autocratic Henry Tonks, but in 1901 London was exchanged for Paris, a room with relatives for her own studio, and the austere draughtsmanship and mild bohemianism of the Slade for the exhilarating and narcissistic world of Rodin and Picasso, of Isadora Duncan and Aleister Crowley, of Gertrude Stein, Anatole France and the dying Wilde, of Conradian anarchists, photographers, suicides, Jews, life classes, suitors and dawn swims in the Seine.

For Kathleen, Paris was followed by the war-torn Balkans, Macedonia by Italy, and Florence by Paris again; but if there might have been enough in all this to alarm and amuse a middle-aged naval officer in about equal measure, it was something else about her that would have attracted him. In an age when a genteel bohemianism was almost *de rigueur*, Kathleen's was in fact probably the least interesting thing about her; but redeeming all the "vagabonding" and posing of a reinvented Parisian art student was an ardour and a passionate commitment to work, life and living that in its startling way was the joyous, affirmative obverse of Scott's own puritanical and duty-filled dedication.

And yet, for a woman who lived life with the hunger and intensity that Kathleen Bruce did, who for forty years lived that life at the heart of Britain's political, artistic and literary establishments, who has left so many hundreds of pages of diaries, letters and autobiography behind her, she remains emotionally and even physically a curiously elusive figure. "She was of medium height," her daughter-in-law, the novelist Elizabeth Jane Howard, remembered her, "with an unremarkable body, rather sturdy and shapeless. She had 'bad' legs and her hands were like a man's, strong and well shaped. Her most beautiful and striking feature was her large head with hair cut very short, shingled at the back, which accentuated its shape. She had a fine complexion, with a large, well-shaped nose, and beautiful eyes of a blue between gentian and cornflower that looked at everything with a penetrating intelligence."

Kathleen would have been in her early sixties at this time, and her daughter-in-law had no very good reason to love her, but—hair apart—it could be a pen-picture of her at almost any time in her life. There is a portrait in profile of her done as a young woman by her friend Charles Shannon that catches a different and softer woman, but in photograph after photograph what one gets is what Elizabeth Jane Howard describes—the same strong, intelligent face, the same powerful sculptor's hands, and the same lumpen figure made all the more sexless by a habitual preference for the "shapeless, sacklike garments" and "aggressive no taste in clothes" that would make her "the worst dressed woman" James Lees-Milne knew.

This is so wildly at odds with the way men saw her that it cannot be the whole truth, any more than the self-portrait that she left in her autobiography and diaries can begin to capture the force and charm of her personality. There are men and women — Scott amongst them — who come off the page better than they do out of life itself, but Kathleen was the opposite, a woman who saved for posterity everything that was most egotistical and self-dramatising in her character, and left the charm, the generosity, courage, spontaneity and vitality to survive only in the letters and memories of friends.

Even that, however, is only half the truth, and when she was alive she could polarise opinion in the way that only the strongest characters do. It is not necessary to believe that every man who Kathleen ever imagined in love with her actually was, but from politicians and explorers to writers and painters, enough of them were to make one wonder how they managed to miss, or at least forgive, what Aleister Crowley saw in her. "She was strangely seductive," "The Beast" recalled. "Her brilliant beauty and wholesome Highland flamboyance were complicated with a sinister perversity. She took delight in getting married men away from their wives . . . Love had no savour for her unless she was causing ruin and unhappiness to others . . . She initiated me into the tortuous pleasure of algolagny on the spiritual plain . . . She made me wonder, in fact if the secret of Puritanism was not to heighten the intensity of love by putting obstacles in its way."

It is impossible to read her diaries, with their endless accounts of frustrated lovers, and not know — algolagny apart — what Crowley meant; but uniting all the contradictions and perversities in Kathleen's own eyes was the vision of maternal destiny that she had nursed since a child. "It's the only thing I do quite surely and always want," she had once told a friend in Paris, appropriating from her convent past a sacerdotal sense of the "boy baby" if nothing else.

> "Well, my dear, you shouldn't find it difficult. You seem to have plenty of eager young men."
>
> If there was a touch of mockery I ignored it, replying, "I know, but none is worthy to be the father of my son." Hermione laughed a little uncomfortably, but said, after a pause quite seriously:

"Do you think you're such a very unusual person?"

"Can't you see? It's not me I'm thinking about, it's my son."

Six years later there were still any number of men willing to oblige, but still not the *one*, and almost a year after her first brief meeting with Scott, the same search brought her back to Mabel Beardsley's. "Then life confirmed the decision it had made ten months earlier," Kathleen recalled twenty-five years later.

> A note came from Mabel Beardsley . . . bidding me to meet him again at tea the following day. The like of him should not go to tea-parties, I thought, as bare footed and still in my nighty I reviewed my two hats, and sitting on the edge of my bed set about, with a pair of nail-scissors and some pins, deftly making of the two hats one . . .
>
> There were a dozen or more people in the room when I arrived at the tea party, mostly men; artists, dramatists, actors and the like, many of them known to me. Sitting on a sofa in the back drawing-room with an elderly lady was Captain Scott. With my instinct to avoid what was attracting me, I moved to the furthermost corner of the party and allowed myself to be diverted by the gay comedy of Ernest Thesiger and the heavy disdain of Henry James. What an unexpected setting for a simple, austere naval officer!
>
> Then all of a sudden, and I did not know how, I was sitting in a stiff, uncomfortable chair with an ill-balanced cup of tea, and being trivially chaffed by this very well-dressed, rather ugly and celebrated explorer. He was standing over me. He was of medium height, with broad shoulders, very small waist, and dull hair beginning to thin, but with a rare smile, and with eyes of quite unusually dark blue, almost purple. I had noticed those eyes ten months before. I noticed them again now, though by electric light. I had never seen their like. He suggested taking me home. I had not been going home; I had been going to dine in Soho with a gentle Academician, Charles Shannon, who was painting me. But without a second's hesitation I threw over my dining companion . . . Not for a moment did I doubt that on leaving the house he would hail a hansom, but no, he started

striding forth westward at a good rate. Anxious but excited I fell
in, and side by side we walked, laughing, talking, jostling each
other, as we lunged along the river-side in hilarious high spirits.
Arrived at my humble little home, I hesitated. "Mayn't I come
and see where you live?" and he did.

Scott was not the only suitor hanging around outside Kathleen's home at
the time, hoping for a brief glimpse of a "sleeping head by the window,"
but over the next ten days, before Scott's work took him out of London
again, they were almost constantly together. And when they were not, he
was sending her notes. "Dearest Professor," he was writing to her by
2 November, the first of hundreds of letters between them that are revealing, intimate, embarrassing, happy, tedious, fresh and repetitive by turns—
much, in other words, like any similar correspondence that no one else
was ever meant to see, "There is no regret but the memory of delight—tell
me the same. You will call on my mother next week as you said will you?"
"I've tried the telephone without result," he wrote again from Oakley
Street, "so now this is to ask if I might take you out to dinner tonight—dinner and the play, dinner and no play, anything you like but do let me carry
you off . . . it would be delightful to find a note from you when I return
and to be rescued from my loneliness tonight."

It did not take much more than ten days for Scott to realise something
of what he had on his hands. "Somebody said Friday morning," he was
soon complaining, "so somebody's young man came to fetch her but dear
Somebody *wasn't* there—what is somebody's young man to conclude?"
"There's such strength of mind being brought to bear to control an inclination to stroll along Cheyne Walk," he scribbled a note in pencil on
7 November, but strength of mind was clearly not enough. "Uncontrollable footsteps carried me along the Embankment to find no light," he
confessed two days later, as he joined the ranks of Kathleen's suitors
reduced to what Pinero's Sir William Gower contemptuously labelled
"troubadoring,"

yet I knew you were there dear heart and it was good to think
of—I saw the open windows and in fancy, a sweetly tangled
head of hair on the pillow within—dear head, dear sweet
face—dearest softest lips—were they smiling?—don't tell me
it's all fancy—

Little lady don't fly away. I've this dread that you can't be quite real and so for this disease there is but one cure—to see you—When is it to be? I'm bewildered & all impatient; therefore I remember no instructions & shall call tomorrow morning—was I relegated to the afternoon?

. . . The thought of you means just a catch of the breath and extra revolutions within—so you shorten life, if it is told by heart beats.

"To 'know only the joy of going forward,'" she answered in her nearillegible scrawl the following day, "only the joy of going forward. It's madness & I cling to my madness & revel in it.—for it is *my* madness every bit, nay more than yours. Fill up the joy—I have such faith joy & life & love."

Whether or not that faith and joy was all for Scott at this time is another matter, but if she was reluctant to give up her freedom or her admirers, she seems to have made her mind up from an early stage that Scott was the father of her child she was searching for. "'Kathleen,'" that artistic exquisite Charles Shannon told her while she was sitting to him shortly after meeting Scott,

"you don't love me at all to-day . . . You've got something on your mind. I know your face too well not to know that."

I smiled and was clam-like. Although this beautiful painter was thirty-eight, I was the first woman he had ever loved. I loved his work so deeply that we had become devoted friends . . . I loved sitting for him in the very exquisite surroundings of his lovely studio . . . There was quiet there and peace. I didn't want to ruffle that quiet content. What a lot of upheavals and severings I saw looming ahead. Yet quite clearly this healthy, fresh, decent, honest rock-like naval officer was just exactly what I had been setting up in my mind as a contrast to my artist friends, as the thing I had been looking for. As I sat there in the quiet, temple-like studio, I made my decision . . .

"Listen," I said, taking the lapels of his coat, "I'm going to marry someone."

The painter leant his back against the door.

"Whom?" he said. "Not X?"

"No, not X. You don't know him; he's not of our world at all. I'm so sorry if you mind."

To Kathleen's infinite satisfaction Shannon minded enough to walk out into Sloane Street, "with his head, I suppose still swimming," and step under a bus (he survived). It was not just the reaction of her "world" that was their problem, however, because if somewhere in the background of Scott's life Peter Pan was still hovering, there was also the less ethereal matter of a dependent mother and family with expectations of a "good" marriage to worry him.

With a captain's salary and royalties from the *Discovery* book, Scott was better off than he had ever been, but even so, with the dressmaking business not going well and Rose now a widow, an impoverished sculptress friend of Isadora Duncan can hardly have seemed the obvious solution to the problem of the family finances. "My Dear Con," Ettie wrote to him on 9 January 1908 from her home at the Royal Mint, where her husband Willy had been Deputy Master since 1903—the first hint of any criticism in all the years of Scott's devotion to his family, "Please come to lunch tomorrow at 1:30 o.c. I shall be here & Willy will be out. As any change that takes place is (I gather from your letter this morning) to be of a permanent nature, I have told Willy. We have looked together at the balance sheet which arrived this morning, & it appears to speak volumes for Rose's housekeeping—The great thing now is to arrive at a suitable arrangement for our mother, & it is a great advantage that matters need not be unduly hurrid [sic], I hope therefore you will allow full discussion."

"My Dear Ettie"—not his more usual "My Dear Old Girl"—Scott replied two days later, sending her back her letter—now torn in pieces—with the word "our" and the final barbed sentence heavily underlined:

> The words underlined are those which I resent as their implication is obvious.
>
> After our conversation on Thursday there was no ground for the suggestion that I wished to avoid discussing the matter yet the charge is made in both notes
>
> Will you return the balance sheet at your leisure.

Behind this exchange lay an argument over expenses at Oakley Street and Scott's plans for a new home for their mother, but it was the implication that he was ducking his family responsibilities that galled Scott. It is clear from other letters that Ettie was more worried about her husband's reactions than anything else, but in the state of high nervousness to which his courtship of Kathleen had reduced him, Scott could see no farther than his own sense of hurt and injustice.

After all his years of self-denial, he had every right to his hauteur, but he was probably made pricklier by a nagging sense that Ettie was partly right. In the time since he had come back from the south he had done everything he could for his mother, and yet slowly but surely he had been drifting away, pulled by new interests, new friends, new commitments and new plans that had no real place in them for the old life. "It's really nice of you to write and I delight in your letters," he had written to Ettie the previous summer, when the first news of his fresh Antarctic plans had provoked a similar alarm, "but you know I'm a poor correspondent—I liked your birthday letter and my dear old chap there isn't any annoyance at your attitude to my plans—of course I didn't expect you to be pleased—I suppose what conscience I have pricked me concerning mother and you helped to prod without meaning it. I suppose we none of us are pleased to have our shortcomings held up before us—however there it is there's no real misunderstanding."

It was one thing, though, when there was nobody but himself to weigh against his family's interests, and another when he and Kathleen were talking of marriage and looking at houses. He had introduced her to his mother the month before Ettie's note of protest had come, and though Scott tried to keep his and Kathleen's spirits up, he can scarcely have missed the fact that the only thing that a pious Victorian Evangelical and a penniless, pagan bohemian could have in common was the man who made them natural antagonists.

If it was bitter for Scott, he knew it was even harder for his mother, and it is difficult to know whether the dignity and bravery she tried to muster would have made it better or worse for him. "My own dear Con," she wrote to him on New Year's Eve 1907, just days before his angry exchange with Ettie,

> This is to wish you the *very* best of good things in the coming year and all happiness & success to you in *all* your undertakings.
>
> I also want to say that *whatever* plans you make for the future will be suitable for me, and you must never let me be a nuisance in any way to your making a home & a life of your own.
>
> With every wish and prayer for your happiness and that God will bless & prosper you my best of Sons

Ever believe in the love of your devoted Mother
H. Scott.

You have carried the burden of the family since 1894 it is
time now for you to think of yourself & your future.

God bless & keep you

However courageous Hannah was, Scott and Kathleen knew their problems were only just beginning. "Dearest Con," she wrote at the beginning
of January 1908, as she swung backwards and forwards between hope and
disbelief that a marriage could ever work,

Don't lets get married, I've been thinking a lot about it & tho'
much of it would be beautiful, there is much also that would be
very difficult.

I have always wanted to marry for the *one* reason & now that
very thing seems as though it would only be an encumbrance
we could scarcely cope with. I know dear that you will be lonely
without me for a little while, but the relief of knowing that you
need not worry or uproot your sweet little mother will soon
compensate . . .

We're horribly different you & me, the fact is I've been
hideously spoiled . . .

It seems a waste of you that you should not be married &
with all my heart I *quite truly* hope that you will find someone
who will fit better.

"I've just had your letter but I don't quite like it—I don't like it at all," he
wrote back the next day.

Dear I want to marry you very badly and . . . I want as much as
you the one thing but it is absurd to pretend I can do so without
facing great difficulty and risking a great deal for others as well
as myself.

If I was very young I should probably take all risks and probably win through. I am still young enough to believe we could
win through, but in facing poverty we should be living and
believing in a better future—The old can only live in the present. My mother is 67—only a strand of life remains—she has
had a hard life in many respects. I set myself up to make these

last years free from anxiety—I can't light heartedly think of events that may disturb that decision. Since my return I have always said that worry was to be put aside and half in joke I added that if I married I should look out that the young lady had lots of money—in the uncertainty of life it is stupid to make promises and though my mother would freely absolve me I cannot quite forgive myself.

But all this is only what you know—that things are difficult. If you care enough however we can put things right—I am convinced of that—but it can only be if you care enough. And dear, heaven knows, when I think of your future I don't want to force you to face a life of poverty . . . if you really believe and think we are "horribly different" in all our ideas and thoughts why of course it would make things impossible. I don't think this a bit. If I did I wouldn't want to marry you.

Little girl if you can, be patient and we'll put things straight—have that faith in me—but you must work with me dearest not against me. But I should be a poor thing indeed if I didn't give you freedom to annul the bargain whenever you feel that it cannot make for your happiness—you wont have to face heroics or troubles of any sort when you decide.

"Estimates for 2 persons living in a small house in London in this year of Grace," he wrote again a few days later, spelling out their prospects in all their reductive dreariness: "Rent, £65 a year, Rates and taxes, £27, Electric light and Gas £12, Coals etc £15, Servants' wages £45, House repairs and cleaning £20, Laundress £25, Papers, stationery & small incidentals £6, Food for four persons at 10/- a head per week, £104, Renewals of Linen, etc, etc, etc, £10," giving a total in all of £329—certainly within their income so long as he was at sea on full pay, but scarcely what either of them wanted for their future. "I'm looking at poverty here as represented by those who live on pay alone," he wrote of his naval colleagues a few weeks later. "I don't find it attractive to them—I don't believe it would be attractive to you or me—lodgings—ceaseless gossip of appointments—what will this or that person do next—constant change—I grow a little despondent—but perhaps that is only tonight as I'm tired too having done much today."

"Your letter made me rather sad," Kathleen wrote back. ". . . I went to see Mabel Beardsley & for about an hour she nobly forbore mentioning you but then she . . . asked me if you wanted to marry me & I said no, I didn't think so besides I didn't suppose you could marry, you were too poor & then she said she supposed anyhow I wouldn't marry a sailor & I said I didn't mind about a sailor but of course one couldn't be poor! One couldn't, could one??!"

For all the financial anxieties, there lurked behind this another and darker fear in Scott's mind, that Kathleen could not love him as he loved her, that he was not worthy of her. "I dare not think how sweet and necessary to me you grow," he had written only weeks after their tea at Mabel Beardsley's, and with this sense of need came a sense of his own inadequacy. "Dear dear sweet heart," he wrote again five days later, "I've been worrying about you—little vague worries—centering round the thought that I may have hurt you in word or deed . . . You know, I'm half frightened of you—and dear I'm very humble before you—I've so little, so very little to offer." "I seem to have a million things to say to you yet [in] a sense of the oppression of forty years wrestling with hard facts I forget myself," he told her. "I fight myself—the devil is in 'the time to think.' One thing dearest—there mustn't be sadness in that sweet face—never—that is the only fixed thought in me just now."

The devil might have been in the time Scott had to brood on things, but he was also lurking in the distance that now separated them, and the misunderstandings, crossed letters and anxieties it led to. After their first few weeks together in London Scott had taken up a new appointment with the Home Fleet at Portsmouth, and for the next eight months their courtship had to contend with snatched days of leave, botched partings and stumbling explanations. "I'm sad tonight," he wrote again, in a letter heavy with sadness and self-knowledge:

> it *is* difficult to know what to do—and all the time I'm conscious of bringing unhappiness to you—It's *I* who make you cry—disappointment in me I think, though your sweet generosity wouldn't admit it—Kathleen dearest don't let your happiness be troubled—sometimes when all the obstacles loom large, I wonder for the future, but always always I know that to take away that dear happy smile of yours would be the most dreadful thing in the world . . . How good it was to be with you! Kathleen, there is no one like you—never a girl looked life so boldly in the face—I love your splendid independence and the unswerving directness & candour of you. I love the unblinking courage which admits no difficulty yet shirks no responsibility—

words are cheap dear heart yet right down in the innermost cells I feel how I love you for all this — God bless you . . .

yet oh my dear there is another side of me, born of hereditary instincts of caution and fostered by circumstances which have made the struggle for existence an especially hard one for me — Can you understand? — I review a past — a real fight from an almost desperate position to the bare right to live as my fellows — Is it strange that I should look at all the consequences of a fresh struggle. My dear I know, as you well think, that this should be no attitude for the man determined to conquer, but sweetheart what I know and you do not is our service, with its machine like accuracy and limitations — it offers place and power, but never a money prize — so that it must be poverty always.

Dear heart — I'm a coward to write like this but it's late now and I've been thinking much — Withal and at last comes the thought that I cannot give your sweetness up — it has grown too dear to me come what will and darling you are the only woman to whom I can tell things — I try to tell you and somehow it is comparatively easy — Will you see in the midst of my despondency that I tell you of my sadder thoughts of the difficulties before us as well as the love I feel for you and the longing I have that you should always be near me . . . Give me your patience.

It is a desolate glimpse into Scott's inner life, into the way he saw his past, and the loneliness that had been his almost constant state. For a man so prone to self-doubt the very vitality and confidence of a Kathleen was an added reproach, too, a warning that on the verge of forty the arteries were too furred by care and habit for his love to do anything but stunt Kathleen's happiness. "I am afraid of what I shall be to you," he confided again; "shall I be trusted — will it come natural to you to tell me things, ultimate things, or will you grow to think me fitted for the outer courtyard of your heart? I'm stupidly anxious tonight," he went on, as he faced up to his own conventionality and her independence of spirit,

but oh dear me how will it all sort out with the disciplined, precedent seeking education of a naval officer. Do you understand a little our naval machine? — from midshipman to Admiral cast in a mould to make parts of a whole — so that having a fine thought or quality is condemned because it does not fit.

And the machine grinds on with wonderful efficiency because it is unyielding and like nature itself atrophies the limbs for which it has no use however great their beauty . . .

Here I see the level, it is the dreamer, the enthusiast, the idealist—I was something of each once—and now it gives me the feeling of being old! . . . and yet in remembering I know that a hard life limited by practical fact was the only thing for me—the dreaming part of me was and is a failure.

This would have been a hard enough letter for a twenty-eight-year-old to answer at the best of times, but it was probably made more difficult by the reappearance of another old suitor in Kathleen's life. The man in question was a "corn-haired," "crooked-smiled" aspiring novelist called Gilbert Cannan, and if she had long known that he was not the gene pool she was after for her son—the closest he came to being that was his delusion in later life that he *was* Captain Scott—she loved him for a "vivid vitality" that after five months of dealing with Scott's implacable sorrow must have been more than ever a welcome reminder of her old life. There was another aspect to his appeal as well, because if Cannan was not to everyone's taste—Ottoline Morrell thought him "a rather vacant Sir Galahad"—it was essentially a Sir Galahad that Kathleen still wanted. There seems no reason to doubt that she was genuinely attracted to his looks and his spurious air of "promise," but as Cannan dismally guessed, it was not so much for himself that she needed him as for the devotion and adulation he could bring to her.

If Kathleen's strange, loveless childhood had left one scar on her, it was the craving for unconditional admiration that not even the love of a man like Scott could satisfy. In his savage pen-portrait of her Aleister Crowley ascribed this to a kind of calculated and sexless harlotry, and yet from all the evidence of her letters and diaries it seems more a vulnerable, almost obsessive, need for an assurance she could only find outside herself.

And nobody—not even Scott—could serve that up like Cannan. "My dear K," he wrote to her at the beginning of April, after he had spent a long night "troubadoring" and wandering the streets of London, entranced equally by Kathleen and her sculpture, "The cause of the wanderings was the wonderful you, the maker of beautiful things, the creator alone and without male assistance of enough lovely babies to stock the whole world . . . That you should have—have—have—I don't know—given me so many hours of yourself. Liked my work. Liked me. Ye Gods. It seems impossible—

Do I sleep, do I dream . . . NO—everything before is the dream . . . and the reality of all the world is concentrated in you."

If it was a dream, it was a dream uncannily like Kathleen's own, a dream of a universe filled with fatherless babies of her own creation, with her at its centre. The difference between Cannan on his long, slow road to the asylum and Kathleen was that when it came to it she knew it *was* a dream, and yet if that knowledge brought with it a grudging recognition of future responsibilities she was prepared to indulge it for as long as Scott would allow her. "Dear you really must not be so afraid," she wrote in answer to his long letter of self-recrimination and doubt,

> afraid of yourself & me & the future & all sorts of things. NON-SENSE Con sweet one. Everything is perfectly harmonious & will be—Why not?—because I let you know that I'm happy when fine natures love me and show their generosity—must I learn to be . . . secretive . . .
>
> I'm in no sort of mood for writing tonight, I just write to tell you that we are both perfect dears & that together we shall be *splendid*.

Scott was not a jealous man—and hated it when any situation made him appear in that role—but only a clod could have remained untouched by the situation. On 21 April, while he was somewhere at sea between Torbay and Spithead, Kathleen was spending the evening with his rival, who wrote the next day to tell her that in nature they were "one," their beings indissolubly united in a con-celebration of "freedom, light, purity and truth." "If 'you and me' is absurd then life is only a silly, silly game played by the gods . . . It is as though I had three pebbles to drop into the well of truth," he told her in an arcane reference to the bizarre triangle that was taking shape. "Each sinks far down and the rings spread over the water so that I cannot see. Then bubbles rise; beautiful bubbles that look silvery truth, but at the surface they are no more and again there are three pebbles in my hand, and until you come to throw one away there will be three—which? . . . Without you it's all nothing . . . 'With you' is incredible and makes to swoon . . . Dear, it was only after you had flung the first stone and we knew that each knew, that the thing grew, flamed up in us and merged the two of us. What can you be but mine, or I but yours?"

It would be enough to make anyone pine for the Antarctic, and the good, clean, simple world of Gilbert Scott dressed up as a serving maid, but Kathleen had not finished with them yet. Towards the end of April Scott was able to get back to London on Easter leave, and on the twenty-fifth all three met in London, three pebbles aflame, or sinking to the bottom, or whatever it is that English pebbles do in such a situation. "Dear You," Cannan wrote to Kathleen, with all the certainty of schizoid promise, "I'm so glad that RS came up this morning. He's a dear clean thing and, 'cept that he don't see things, and never will, 'right.' He could laugh although he was being hurt all the time. You laughed too and I laughed and laughing all together it seems perfectly ridiculous that you can't have both of us since you are so rapacious that the love of the one you love isn't enough for you."

If Cannan's future record is any guide, he was perfectly serious in his suggestion that she should have them both, but she knew that babies—especially the prize boy specimen she had in mind—did not come without the right father, and within days had finally rejected him. "You shall not do this wicked thing," he wrote back. "You belong to me, and no blazing folly that you choose to commit can alter that . . . Dear God-in-me, you are a wicked, wicked blasphemous woman, but I love you. The wild audacity with which you can fling the biggest thing over your shoulder and put out your tongue at life forces an admiration almost shuddering from me."

If she had disposed of one pebble, she was no kinder to the other. "Why no word of you!!" Scott demanded on 7 May. "Why? Why? Why!—I conjure up all sorts of horrible reasons—tell me they aren't true." He was desperate to see her, he told her the next day when still no letter had arrived, "that is if things are the same," he added. "You know if you wish them different I shall have only a silent memory of what has been—I am to be trusted altogether in such a case."

"The weather here has been nice," he wrote from sea to his niece Phoebe on the twelfth—a letter that for all its charm and affection has an air of displaced melancholy to it—"and the sea very smooth so that we enjoy our games also . . . We are quite a long way away from you now and if you want to come and see me you must take the train to Portsmouth and then the second turning to the right over the sea and when you've sailed miles and miles and miles . . . if you look very carefully you will see in front of the hills a long grey shadow and when you see it you will know that it is the Essex with Uncle Con sitting on top of the mast and waving . . . you must write again and send more kisses because the others didn't arrive. I think they must have fallen out of the envelope on the way and taken the wrong turning from Portsmouth."

It was not just his niece's kisses that had gone astray. Kathleen had gone off to Italy on a walking tour with the husband of a distant cousin. In her own later account Scott had been "splendid" about the whole business, telling her in effect to go and write often and not stay too long—" 'Oh this,' thought I, 'is a grand man; no self-pity, no suspicions, no querulousness, no recriminations. Perfect man!' And off I went."

For someone who made such a credo of honesty and transparency, Kathleen could be remarkably disingenuous when it suited, and the separation was not as painless as she pretended. Travelling first to Venice, which she did not like—"I can't breathe here"—she went on to Florence, recapturing as she travelled all the old wanderlust that marriage, respectability and poverty threatened. "You must stop loving a little vagabond," she wrote to Scott from Florence on 23 May. "I've got it in my blood dearest—How I love it. The freedom and irresponsibility of it is very precious to me."

"How dare you tell me to stop loving you now?" he demanded, soaring to a Wordsworthian rhetoric in his own defence. "My precious girl—how dare you. Knock a few shackles off me and you'll find as great a vagabond as you but perhaps that won't do. I shall never fit in my round hole—The part of a machine has got to fit—yet how I hate it sometimes—oh by nature I think I must be a free lance. Among uncertainties this is certain. I love the open air, the trees, the fields and the seas—the open spaces of life and thought. Darling you seem the spirit of all these to me though we have loved each other in crowded places—I want you to be with me when the sun shines free of fog."

There was no hiding the note of desperation, and every expression of vagabonding freedom or picture of Isadora Duncan that Kathleen sent him from Italy only increased his sense of inadequacy. "*Do you* realize that you will have to change me," he pressed her; "change me—infuse something of the joyous pure spirit within you—a year or two hence it would have been too late—I should have been too late to admit the principle of change. It's something that I acknowledge my short comings! But oh dear me what a task you have left before you!! All this because you have met Isadora Duncan and I see the great heart of you going out to her—I see you half worshipful; wholly & beautifully alive—and I love you for it." "Oh I love you and your free joyous outlook on life!" he wrote again the next day, "but it's disturbing sweet—I ask myself why I must dwell in the machine, the mill that grinds small."

There are times as one reads these outpourings of Scott's that Kathleen seems the worst thing that could have happened to him, but that is fair neither to him nor to her. There is nothing more touching about their relationship than its wildly improbable success, and that success is in a sense the best guarantee of each that we could have, the mutual and validating recognition from the two extremes of conformity and individualism of the rival claims of their opposites. From their separate worlds, as mutually and naturally antagonistic as the worlds of the Wilcoxes and the Schlegels in Forster's *Howards End,* Kathleen and Scott looked at each other and embraced their differences. The comfort and support was not all one-way either. Cannan might think Scott a dull penny to his bright, shining sixpence; Kathleen's cousin could cut himself shaving when she broke the news of her engagement to him; Max Beerbohm reassure her that he had never thought Scott "dull and limited"—it did not matter; Kathleen saw what Scott brought to her as clearly as he recognised the vitality and spontaneity she gave him. He was—whether she liked it or not—as she later put it when death had sharpened her sense of what he had always meant, her "god . . . conscience" and "motive power." "I'm really falling desperately in love with you," she told him on her return from Italy. "I'm loving you so much this morning. I can't think why I ever thought of loving anyone else." "Here I am," she robustly answered another outpouring of self-abasement from him, "a little ass of a girl who's never done a thing in her life allowing a real man to talk of her superiority. My sense of humour can't do with it."

And for all his reverence and self-doubt, Scott was more clear-eyed about her and her world than his letters would sometimes suggest. "To be honest," he would later tell her, after an argument over a play and the merits of Barrie, "there's a hark back in the suggestion to a memory—I oughtn't to have bottled it—a long while ago you dined with the Barries, you described the conversation and mentioned names (three, I think) as representing the foremost thought of the country. Two names I remember, Wells and Granville Barker—'The only hopes of England' was the expression—I ought to have told you how often I have pondered over the state of mind which could give utterance to such a diction—In cogitating the activities of this country I will own a confusion in the remembrance of such assertions."

But if he could sometimes wonder if he would shake himself awake one day and find that she was no more than "a dear little girl with a pretty face," they were both confident enough by the middle of June to break the news to family and friends. "And now dear I want to tell you I was most anxious to come and see you," Scott wrote to his mother in Henley, where she had moved from Oakley Street in the spring,

> yet it has been a great annoyance to me not to be able to see you because I have a most especial thing to talk of. Dear mother you know I spoke to you some time ago about Miss Bruce—It is hard for an undemonstrative person like myself to break through reserve—but I think you must have guessed that I had learned to care much for her. It's impossible for me to tell you how awfully hurt and worried I have been over all the misunderstandings and worries that have arisen over this matter. The fault I think has been wholly mine but somehow it has seemed to me that there has been antagonism in the family to my marrying for anything but a sordid motive—and the antagonism has been a little extended to the dear lady who is wholly innocent of design in bringing discomfort—Now dear I must tell you I want to marry Kathleen Bruce—but she and I are agreed that under no circumstances must your comfort suffer—she is content to wait any time but I ask myself how can we wait long—you know I am now 40—she is 28—why should we wait till we lose so much that may mean all in the future . . .
>
> Oh I know that all this is against your hopes, but don't judge until you know all the facts. I do so want to make for a happier state of affairs all round—and Oh dear if you knew it now, as I feel you will know it—that girl has fought so good a fight for herself and yet makes of life the most bright and joyous thing is a great factor—so dear will you please ask Kathleen Bruce to come and see you as my future wife . . . Good night dear mother I do not want to be selfish indeed and I know she does not.

Scott knew his mother's weaknesses well enough to season the news to her taste. "You know of course that she is a lady by birth breeding & association," he assured her, "responsible to no-one," but closest to a "Mrs. Thomson her aunt (wife of the late Archbishop of York)."

For all his attempts to placate his family, his letter is the first sign of just how hurt Scott had been. There is nothing in his correspondence with his mother remotely like it. It seems, however, to have elicited little response. "I'd been hoping for a rather longer letter than your last," he wrote again on 23 June, unable to keep the note of disappointment out of his letter. "Please write dear I hate to think that things are still awry . . . I am anxious to hear from you . . . your last letter was so very short."

He had also written to his favourite sister. "My Dear Old Girl," he wrote to Ettie, his first letter since their falling out in January, "This is just to tell you that I'm engaged to be married to Miss Bruce—you don't know her I think but probably have heard much . . . There are elements of folly about the transaction which will be far from meeting your approval—still I think you will like the lady yourself when you know her. I think I had better bring her to see you or ask her to go—if you wish . . . Dear old chap I feel a great deal could be said if I talked to you—very little by letter—I'd better come as soon as possible—Even your daughter is ashamed of my inability to write."

Ettie at least was everything Scott had hoped. Grace moped and got weepy, and left the room, and felt excluded. Phoebe, his niece, whispered questions in her father's ear, but "Ettie was more than a dear," he wrote to Kathleen three days later; "first we made it up—you know that things had not been right between us and I was feeling it—*you* the peacemaker. Then she said nice things of you—very nice things—there was admiration of your sweet face—the vertical forehead and charm in growth of hair—then better, she saw the truth and honesty of you, the bravery of you—a glimpse of the real you—Oh your little ears should have burned! And they are dear people aren't they? You'll love them when you know them better."

After the first disappointment, his mother had also rallied. The "sweetest letter from your dear little mother," Kathleen wrote revealingly when Hannah Scott did what her son asked and invited her to come and see her, "Calling me Kathleen & wanting to 'welcome me as a daughter.' You don't know my darling how I've felt about it all this time, but now it's presumably over I don't mind you knowing—I can't *bear* to be disliked, distrusted, & I felt (foolishly maybe) that it amounted to that . . . But now I could shriek for joy that the horrid feeling is gone & that she is 'very ready to love me.' She *shall* love me, for I will love her, & *make* her."

It was as hard for Kathleen as it was for Scott. She was unable to accept the invitation immediately, as she was dining and playing consequences with Sir Edward Grey, Harry Cust, Arthur Balfour and Lady Elcho—a congregation of politics, society and "Souls" unlikely to make the prospect of her future mother-in-law and her pair of rather dingy daughters any more enticing. "My Dear Mrs. Scott," Kathleen explained, "I wish I could come down at once but I have things to do tomorrow which I cannot

escape. May I come down before lunch on Wednesday? I have an engagement that evening with Mabel Beardsley. I shall find out from her whether
it would matter if I broke it and will let you know. I do hope you aren't hating me very much. I'm afraid I should if I were you . . . Con tells me such
beautiful things about you, so that I hated never seeing you."

For Scott it was a question of reassuring both women. His mother was
delighted, he reassured Kathleen after the visit. "Of course Kathleen loved
you," he wrote to his mother at the same time, desperate to broker an
understanding, "I felt that she would—she came back full of the visit to
you—she told me again and again how sweet you had been to her and
Rose also—her whole mind has been centred on the hope that you like
her—and she has been longing to hear either directly or through me that
you did."

And "Did you?," he pressed.

> Dear you said something to Kathleen about your love not inter-
> fering with hers—she was touched and puzzled, puzzled
> because the thought that she could come between you and I
> had not entered her head and even your suggestion of it did not
> make it real.
>
> Indeed I fear you don't understand her—long before she
> knew you her thought was of you and her most often expressed
> hope was that she would be able to help you and care for you—
> My dear she may not be all you wish but there isn't an ounce of
> jealousy in her frank nature.
>
> Oh don't you see she came to you feeling very humble and
> hoping you would like her & trust her & since that she has been
> full of anxiety as to the result.

The familiarity of it all does not make it any less painful, and Scott's moods
were up and down with every letter. "So glad—so very glad—I never
doubted they'd love you when they knew you," he would write to Kathleen
one day, and then two days later: "what's making us half unhappy—It's just
simply lack of money—Oh I see it all—my peoples' attitude—delighted
with you personally, ready to love you anyway, yet vaguely disappointed
because their minds have nursed a thought of brilliant worldly things and
in me lay their women's hopes—Ah don't blame them—think how it has
all been and how one is too old to see the end of a fresh struggle. Darling
be very kind & forbearing to all."

Almost everything was a potential source of misunderstanding. They had found themselves a house in a Georgian terrace in London's Buckingham Palace Road for £50 a year. It had eight rooms and a studio for Kathleen. With marriage and houses, though, came lawyers and financial arrangements for their future. "I'm extremely frightened at your lawyer with his 'settlements,' 'life insurance' 'provisions' etc," an anxious Scott wrote to Kathleen in the middle of July, "and you send it on without a word—Girl you do know how all that stands don't you? My will leaves what I've got to my mother—I can't change that can I?—I told you I hadn't a life insurance. And you know also there's a provision of £70 or £90 I've forgotten which for you." "Precious man, how hideously you misunderstand me," she answered. "I only omitted to refer to the lawyer's letter because it didn't interest me. My dearest do be it understood for *always* that if *you* are not there I don't want anything of yours—*of course* [underlined four times] what you have would go to your little mother."

They had also seriously botched the business of breaking the news to their friends. "I'm trying to write to my lady friends but it's difficult!!!" Scott had written to Kathleen at the end of June, "How are you getting on in this respect?" Better than him, was the answer, if the tone of their letters is anything to go by. Beerbohm wrote nicely when he heard, and even Cannan managed to be generous, but the list of people ready to take offence at Scott's reticence seemed to grow by the week. "Con dear I've just heard that sweet little Barne has heard rumours of our—our—our [she hated the word "engagement"]—& is hurt because you haven't told him," Kathleen wrote. "Please write quite by return of post as nice a letter as ever you can think of—he thinks it is *my* fault you've kept it from him . . . Apparently Muriel Paget told the Barries & he is hurt & she annoyed. Hurry up & make it right." "I saw your little Pauline Chase yesterday," she added silkily, "she was supping . . . with three of the stupidest looking youths however she was sweet & charming in her little way."

Sweet and charming as she was, Scott left it to Barrie to break the news to her, while he repaired other bridges. "I've written to Barrie at once," he wrote back to Kathleen. "I feel guilty—also I'm in trouble elsewhere—Mason was not so silent as we supposed, he told the Warrenders. I had a charming note from Miss Eleanor before I wrote to her. There was a frank remark that she was hurt to have to discover it that way first—also Miss Woodehouse heard from Lady Speyer—How did she know?"

As the wedding came closer, too, he found it hard to shake off the conventional, decent, honourable sense that he owed Kathleen a life that he would not be able to give her. "I hate the fact that I can't give you all you ought to have," he told her after she had disclaimed all interest in his will:

> it's so strong sometimes that I'm irritable and wretched about it—and that lawyer with his "settlements" & "insurances" just went straight to my most sensitive spot—God I don't think I was made to understand—to really understand such a splendid creature as you—but be sparing to my meanness when it peeps out. I can cover myself with ridicule at the thought but there are moments when it's horrid to know that Mrs. Scott cannot drive her carriage! And be patient with me Oh girl take me rough and smooth—do you think I have ever grudged my money to my own? Do you think money is the thought with me. Girl don't you see sometimes I'm fearing myself—I want my mother to be happy and comfortable yet I know that *we* must keep up some small state for the sake of my career—that's just the whole rub . . . but girl just for my sake you have to have a nice house and nice clothes so please take that money—and begin to arrange at once how it's all to be spent.

"There is one important thing I wish to say," he wrote again to Kathleen on 28 July, his mood "dreadfully sombre": "I want you to consider your trousseau—stupid man you will say!—yes I know but I want you to consider it from my point of view . . . the serious consideration is that when we are married you mustn't only look nice (which you can't help) but you must look as though there wasn't any poverty—you may say humbug but just let me put it this way too—you've admired my clothes so just think of my feelings when I am so to speak 'expensively' dressed whilst your condition shows a striving spirit—Kathleen dearest am I dreadfully sensitive to appearances."

If he was touchy about appearances, he was equally sensitive about avoiding "show" when it came to the wedding. Kathleen's Aunt Zoe, the archbishop's widow, was living in a grace-and-favour apartment at Hampton Court Palace, and had offered them a flat and the wedding in the Chapel Royal there. "Kathleen's dear heart was much exercised after my visit to Hampton Court," Scott wrote diplomatically to Mrs. Thomson,

"and indeed I think you must have found my reluctance extraordinary—
the truth is I was a little alarmed at so large a company—I appreciate the
more how good of you it was to write comforting things to her."

They both had a large circle of friends, which complicated things, but
a "very quiet wedding" was Scott's ideal. "No, no uniform I think . . . no I
think just quiet plain clothes," he wrote to Kathleen, in answer to her question. "Give me a word of advice as to the ceremony at Hampton Court," he
asked his sister Ettie on 19 August, exactly two weeks before the day:

> organist—2 guineas
> boy choir—2 guineas
> 6 men—2 guineas each
> soloist—2 guineas

1 Which & what of this lot shall we have? (organist says "wedding
   music can be sung by boys alone")
2 Re Naval wedding—I don't want a lot of blue jackets—I don't
   want to wear uniform—Will ordinary morning coat do—Must I
   get a *frock* coat.
3 Can't think of any more for the present but answer these
   conundrums.

Late in August the invitations to the wedding went out, "at the Chapel
Royal Hampton Court Palace on Wednesday, September 2nd at 2:30
o'clock, and afterwards in the Oak Room of the Palace." In response to
Scott's sartorial badgering Kathleen had threatened to dress in a fashion-
able gown the next time they met, just to show him how awful she looked.
In the event, though, she conformed, wearing what the papers described as
"a dress of white satin trimmed with Limerick lace and a body of chiffon
with a wreath of natural myrtle and a tulle veil."

The service was taken by Rosslyn Bruce, Kathleen's brother, who had
been expelled from school at the age of six for looking up the teachers'
skirts and who would preach his sermons with a pet lemur peeping out of
his pocket. She was given away by another brother, Lieutenant Wilfred
Bruce RN. Scott's best man was Captain Henry Campbell, an old "Majestic," and so tall and good-looking that Kathleen whisperingly asked Scott if
she could marry him instead. The King sent a telegram and there were 150
guests, including, on Kathleen's side, Rodin and his wife, and on Scott's

enough admirals to stock the world's fleets.* *Discovery* was well represented, too, with Royds, Barne, Wilson and Bernacchi all there. "I just hated your absence from the wedding," Scott later wrote affectionately to Skelton, thanking him for his share of "the most beautiful and valued wedding present" they had received from his old *Discovery* colleagues; "the only thing that alleviated the distress of that function was to see the faces of Charles Billy & Michael wreathed in many smiles."

"Huge crowds gathered as Captain and Mrs. Scott left by motor car for London and then France," the *Daily Mirror* reported. It was another newspaper, however, that answered the one question that anyone outside their immediate circle was interested in: "The marriage," announced *The Times*, "will make no difference to Capt. Scott's future plans with regard to Antarctic exploration."

---

*It is impossible to be sure who was actually there, as the newspapers all give different guest lists, and some of the names seem highly improbable. The lists were clearly drawn up in advance, and seem to represent a vision of who *should* be there rather than who came. It is hard to imagine, for instance, that Jacky Fisher was invited.

Twenty-one: Marking Time

You *shall* go to the S. Pole. Oh dear, what's the use of having energy & enterprise
if a little thing like that can't be done. It's got to be done, so hurry up.

KATHLEEN BRUCE, 11 *July 1908*

Behind that bland statement in *The Times* lay one of the most difficult
years of his life as Scott had tried to juggle the conflicting demands of
Kathleen, Antarctica and a naval career. He had still been in *Albemarle*
when the news of Shackleton's plans for an expedition first reached him,
and it was not until May 1907, when she was in dock at Chatham for three
weeks, that Scott had his first opportunity to take his future in his own
hands.

There was still little enough he could do, but their time in England at
least enabled him to nudge his own plans into motion. Not a single one of
his old wardroom had accepted Shackleton's invitation, and with a huge
fund of loyalty and reputation to call on, Scott had always known that getting the right men would be no problem. He already had Michael Barne.
Mulock had asked to join. Teddy Evans, who had also come out in *Morning*, had written applying for the post of navigator. The applications from
old *Discovery* hands would pour in. And, above all, he had secured a
promise from Wilson. "Can you really mean that you would like me to go
south again with you," he wrote to Scott at the end of March 1907. "If you
do I may tell you that nothing in the world would please me more, and my

wife is entirely with me . . . As for your good opinion of me I can only say that there is nothing I would not do to deserve it."

At this early stage, however, the man he wanted and needed even more than Wilson was his old engineer, Reginald Skelton. From the very first he had decided that "the key to everything" was motorised transport, and there was "only one person in the world," he told Skelton under a sub-paragraph of a long letter headed *Yourself*, "that combines a knowledge of southern conditions with engineering skill and that is yourself. I have cherished the idea that if I ever went South again you would join—but of course I can understand how your position is awkward by your private affairs as a married man—there is no one I would sooner have than you and I believe that with your help a great journey can be made."

While he was stuck at sea there had been little Scott could do except entrust his plans to Michel Barne, but with the chance of a week in London while *Albemarle* was in dock, he "dived into the motor world," getting to know "a good few leading men"—Charles Rolls among them—in search of a backer "who could & would give not only money but personal interest to the venture." "And at last I found him in Lord Howard de Walden," he wrote to a more than willing Skelton, all the old, mildly cynical charm Armitage had once admired to the fore. "It took time but at length I have worked him up to something like enthusiasm on the subject and he has given his promise to help all he can . . . he is only 27 and has rather a curious manner which may put you off at first but the manner hides great good nature . . . You know his interest in motor boats—this is his especial hobby and you will be wise to draw him out . . . in other words as a matter of policy it will be expedient to let him imagine that his ideas are being worked out instead of yours—But I can trust you to exercise tact."*

With Skelton's services secured, Lord Howard hopefully in the bag, and Michael Barne exploring other alternatives in France, Scott could turn his attention back to the politics of McMurdo Sound. He was still as reluctant as ever to show his hand in public, and had no intention of being "pushed out of that position by a windbag like Cook," he told Shackleton, who was keen on warning off foreign opposition. "My opinion of Cook

---

*A lieutenant in the 10th Hussars during the Boer War, a reserve for the British Olympic fencing team, landowner, stalwart of the Turf and a patron of the arts, a dramatist and librettist in his own right, Howard de Walden was a more richly and bizarrely varied man than Scott's description might suggest.

[the Cook who had sailed in *Belgica* and who would later claim the North Pole] is nil — he is a needy adventurer — seeking notoriety . . . the man who gives Cook money must be an ass."

"As regards the future," he elaborated in a long letter to Keltie — since the ageing Markham's retirement from the presidency in 1905 Scott's key contact at the RGS — "you saw Shackleton's article in the 'Tribune' prompted by Cook's essay — he (Shackleton) wished me to make an announcement but I refused. I saw no reason — as I presume it won't stop Cook if he means real mischief. This leads me to a real point. What is or has been the international position as regards exploring areas and how far do Geographical Societies regulate it?"

"Is the Public Press the only means by which England can signalise her intention of going on in that area?" he wanted to know. "If so what are international geographical congresses for? Will you tell me what are the Society's powers in this matter," he went on in his best protectionist mode.

> Would it be listened to if it assured the American Societies that England was willing and able to go on with the work of exploration in that quarter.
>
> This is a matter of great importance to me. On these lines everything is going well. I have arranged for all the patient & exhaustive trials which I proposed to myself. I never talk idly — so you will not think so when I tell you that I see my way ahead and a road to all the money I want . . .
>
> When I go south it will be with something that promises a great reward but I cannot pretend that I do not wish to keep my field clear. It is not that I fear great things being done by others, but it's the occupation of the field of action by strangers which will render it impossible for me to go to the same field — and possibly waste all my labours.

It is a curious world this letter conjures up — and a world that had moved on a long way in the seven years since Scott had received such generous help in Norway and Germany — but it did not take him long to see just how unreasonable he was being. "I should explain," he wrote to the long-suffering Keltie four days later, anxious to unsay the note of *folie de grandeur* that had crept into his correspondence,

I had no thought of an official letter being sent by the RGS to American Societies. I presumed only that the RGS has sources of information with regard to what is happening in geographical matters which cannot be open to private individuals—it being obviously absurd that two persons of different nationalities should start for the same place at the same time in ignorance of each others intentions.

Of course Cook may be and I think he is a mere adventurer, in that case official authority could do nothing. But it is scarcely right to assume that he cannot be genuine and if he is and continues preparation with the support of American Geographical Societies, both he & the authorities of the Society would be justifiably aggrieved if they were asked to change plans at the last moment . . . I hope I have made the object of my last letter clear. I was not asking for the Society's support in any form—I would not dream of doing so at such a time.

Scott would soon learn how little control the Societies or anyone else had over a determined enough adventurer, but for the time being it was not Cook or any other foreigner who posed the real threat. "Rupert England [another old *Morning* officer] came to see me yesterday to tell me that he is engaged to go with Shackleton as Captain of the ship," Keltie wrote back, clearly nervous of what could and could not be said in the climate of suspicion and secrecy Scott had engendered. "He did not tell me that there was any secret about it, so I suppose there is no harm in my telling it to you. I understand Shackleton has practically bought his ship, I forget its name, I dare say you know it. For they are pushing on all they can to leave about the end of July or the beginning of August."

The ship was the *Nimrod*, "a small . . . old . . . dilapidated" vessel, reeking of seal oil and in urgent need of caulking and remasting, that was still working out of Newfoundland when Shackleton bought her. He had not even seen her when she arrived in the Thames in the middle of June, but by 30 July he had her ready to sail, with stores, hut, equipment and motor car stored aboard, ponies and dogs ordered, a staff that included Frank Wild and Ernest Joyce from *Discovery* days, and a summons from the King to Cowes awaiting him to add the final seal of royal approval. In the face of his own financial worries—let alone the shadow of bankruptcy and worse hanging over his brother Frank—it was a triumph of energy and brinkmanship that reaped the success it deserved.* Scott had not been the only one who had doubted that an Antarctic expedition could be put together in seven months, but just over a week later, and six years and a day after *Discovery* had sailed, *Nimrod* was at sea and on her way to Lyttelton and the south.

The speed of Shackleton's preparations had left Scott's own looking slightly lame, and it was not simply for his mother's peace of mind that he was downbeat in his expectations. "I hope we shall have something ready for trial in September on the result of which will depend all future plans," he wrote of his collaboration with Lord Howard, "but of course the whole thing is very hazy and uncertain at present and my dear it's not worth worrying about so I rely on you not to worry—if the chance comes it is worth taking if it does not come I shall not be heartbroken."

One piece of good news was that Michael Barne had found a potential second backer for their motor sledge in Paris, but having "worked him up to enthusiasm once," Scott had no intention of letting Lord Howard find out that there were other supporters. They had engaged an engineer in Finchley, a Belton Hamilton, to work on the initial design, but until the end of August, when he was due to be replaced in *Albemarle* by William Goodenough—one of the few undisputed successes of Jutland—there was nothing for Scott to do but trust to Barne and Skelton and muster whatever patience he could manage.

After her refit at Chatham *Albemarle* had sailed for Ireland, and with an endless stream of Irish parties and Irish fogs to endure, and an enforced lay-up with an eye cyst, patience did not come easy to Scott. "June is a bad month here," he complained, "so say the wiseacres on shore but possibly they would say the same of any other month . . . When all is said and done I shall not be sorry to get away . . . where we shall find some rest."

In spite of the weather and the collision at the beginning of his command, it had been a successful tour in *Albemarle*, and there was a nicely symmetrical triumph in the fleet regatta to finish it that showed that Scott had lost none of the competitive edge that had first attracted Markham twenty years earlier. He had been beaten into second place in the cutter race on the first day, he boasted with a middle-aged pride in his achieve-

*Shackleton's finances are a shadowy affair. He had told Keltie at their original meeting that he had raised £30,000 for the expedition, but even with a loan of £7,000 from his principal backer, the industrialist William Beardmore, with whom Scott had stayed in 1904, and further guarantees, he had to sail without anything approaching that amount. On his return, a government grant of £20,000 helped pay off debts.

ments, but then had made up for it the next: "to be near getting both cups is rather a unique experience, and gives quite a little flourish to the finish of our time."

The next day *Albemarle* left the fleet for Portsmouth, and on the twenty-fifth, in a double change of command that pointed to a naval future Scott would never know, Jellicoe hoisted his flag, and his protégé Goodenough took over from Scott. "It has been a great pleasure to me to have known and served with you," wrote the outgoing Curzon-Howe, Jellicoe's predecessor, RGS member and Scott's golfing and cycling partner in Ireland: ". . . it is with great regret that [I pen] that unpleasant word 'good bye.' "

With a chance at last to push on with Antarctic plans, however, Scott's mind was already elsewhere. He had written to his mother from Ireland to say how much he was looking forward to "a very special little party" with the Smiths in Scotland, but before that there was a meeting in London with Skelton and their engineer, Hamilton, to review progress on their machine. "I don't want you to keep the servants from their holiday on my account," he wrote again—a sobering insight into his domestic life just two months before his second, fateful meeting with Kathleen Bruce—"you know I can have my meals out and all I want is a latch key. But I think it might be well if the housemaid, whose name I have clean forgotten, could be there one day to help pack away my clothes so that she knows where they are . . . and my dear don't for heaven's sake open the house for me or make any fires, you know I don't appreciate that sort of thing."

On 21 September, Scott travelled up to Scotland to join the Wilsons at the bungalow of his publisher Reginald Smith and his wife at the southern end of Glen Prosen in Angus. Since 1905 Wilson had been hard at work as Field Observer to the Grouse Disease Commission, and the Smiths' house had often been his refuge from the avalanche of dead grouse that landed from every moor across the country on his laboratory table for dissection.

There was nowhere that could have offered a better antidote to fleet or London life for Scott, and no one with whom he would rather be. Beside the narrow road that leads into the heart of the Glen a cairn still commemorates their association with Prosen and the Smiths, and among the curlews and corncrakes the two men picnicked, shot, walked and talked of the Antarctic.

The September date that Scott had spoken of for a motor trial proved to be optimistic, however, and in January 1908, a month after beginning his courtship of Kathleen, he took over command of his new ship, the 9,800-

ton HMS *Essex*, still with nothing in his private or public life resolved. After *Albemarle* it was not the best of commands, but it was sea-time Scott was interested in, and an appointment with the Home Fleet suited his purposes ideally. "Yesterday I walked to Weymouth with another Captain," he told Kathleen, "a nice little man—on returning he said 'I rather wonder you took the Essex'—I explained that it suited my plans—'that's alright' said he 'but you lose £100 a year.' My dear was there ever such a casual idiot as I?—until that moment I never knew that I was receiving £720 a year instead of the £830 or whatever it was I told you."

"Our story is wind wind wind—its been blowing continuously and exasperatingly," he complained in the same letter, but for all his deep-seated unhappiness over certain aspects of service life, it would never quite let him go. "I come next the Admiral in command of our division of the Fleet," he had reported proudly to his mother on his appointment, and the challenge and complexities of gunnery drills and manoeuvres still held an excitement that he freely admitted was incomprehensible to anyone outside the service. "We play at war and fire off big guns all day long," he told his niece, "to try and make as many holes as possible in a little bit of red cloth a mile away from the ship . . . one has to be very careful if one wants to make a lot of holes."

After his experience in *Albemarle*, Scott needed no reminders of the dangers present even in peacetime, but they were nevertheless there to give Kathleen her first hint of what marriage to a naval officer might entail. "I'm writing in the middle of the night as we strain for Portland," he wrote to her at the beginning of April, after the *Tiger* had been involved in one of two fatal collisions that shook the fleet within a matter of weeks. "We were brought up in a heap inky blackness about and lights suddenly flaring out, search rays all on a pitiable object the sinking destroyer—she vanished before boats could reach her—I'm afraid several lives were lost—so far we have only counted 22 saved . . . and the crew must have been nearly fifty."

"Tomorrow we start firing again," he wrote to her again the following day, "but owing to the Tiger disaster we are not to have our night-search for the Dreadnought for which I'm extremely sorry for I'd taken quite a lot of trouble to work out my plan for capturing her." In spite of this disappointment, however, he was beginning "just faintly . . . to see new stepping stones," and at the end of the following month had more definite news. "This very instant night I've been offered a new appointment & have accepted," he wrote to Kathleen on 25 May. "From a service point of view this is a very good appointment—I shall be the most junior captain in separate command of a battleship."

The ship was the fifteen-thousand-ton *Bulwark*, flagship to the Nore Division of the Home Fleet, but scheduled for an imminent return to a "private" or "separate" status. The appointment meant another £100 a year to Scott, but while that came as a major attraction to a man planning marriage, it was the sniff of independence that was the real lure. "It has been a *very great pleasure* to me having you as Flag Captain," Rear Admiral Hon. Stanley Colville—veteran of both Wolseley's abortive attempt to rescue Gordon and of Kitchener's campaign to avenge his death—wrote to Scott on striking his flag: "from a selfish point of view I sincerely wish you were staying on with me but can well understand your wishes to be your own Boss."

As Scott had found in *Discovery*, however, the role of "Boss" brought its own unpredictable range of cares. "The name of Mr. P.F. Hickman, midshipman, is entered in the log by my direction," one entry reads, suggesting that Scott had lost neither his old hastiness nor his willingness to rethink, "for conduct unbecoming an officer [crossed out and initialled by Scott] drinking wine when, suffering from gonorrhoea, he was ordered to abstain from alcohol and in falsity [these two words similarly crossed out] for declaring to me that he had not drunk wine under these circumstances."

But for all the inevitable loneliness of command—"breakfast, lunch and dinner all alone in this palatial palace"—it brought privileges that Scott was not above enjoying. "I ought to explain that taking in coal is very seriously considered," he explained to Kathleen, "because of its importance in war and the average number of tons taken in per hour is one of the pegs on which the reputation of a ship hangs. The Captain made a speech to the men and then went on shore and played 48 holes of golf whilst every other soul in the ship either shovelled coal or wheeled it round in trucks—which shows the captain has the best of it."

There are glimpses in his letters, too, of the wardroom life and ship's characters that made up the texture of day-to-day life for most of his adult years. "Here's a curious thing for you," he wrote again to Kathleen at the beginning of June, just after an Italian-owned and -trained filly with little pedigree and less chance had shocked an Edwardian racing world equally committed to aristocratic owners and thoroughbreds, with victory in the Derby. "The second doctor of the ship went to sleep in an armchair after lunch on Thursday last. When he woke he said 'I've had an extraordinary dream. I dreamt I was at the Derby and I saw quite plainly the colours of a jockey, blue and white, passing the winning post and heard the people shouting "Cinetta." ' " The doctor had no interest in racing, but his messmates had looked up the runners, found a horse called Signorinetta in the Chevalier Ginistrelli's blue-and-white silks, and with the exception of the odd bull-headed rationalist like Scott, invested their one and two pounds. "Today we learn that Signorinetta has won the Derby at 100 to 1 chance," Scott continued with a stuffiness in inverse ratio to his own share of the winnings, "and our Wardroom officers are jointly richer by about £2000 [more than twice Scott's annual income]—To imagine the manifestation of a prophetic spirit is of course too ridiculous; but as a chain of coincidences it is certainly the most curious that has come under my knowledge."*

These reminders of a forgotten naval world are revealing, because by their very nature, Scott's letters to Kathleen or his mother inevitably focused on family interests or his own narrower ambitions. It is worth recalling in this context that the best man at his wedding was a fellow naval officer, and not Wilson or any of the other old "Discoverys," and yet in the main these friendships have left little trace, submerged beneath the volumes of correspondence and dealings with superiors or juniors that represented the reality of a hierarchical service life.

Just occasionally, though, a letter survives—a letter to an "equal" and not an admiral or an AB—and we hear a voice that must have been the one Scott's Dartmouth and ship friends were familiar with. "To what stroke of ill deserved good fortune you owe your present appointment I cannot imagine," one such letter reads, the subject—plus ça change—promotion and prospects, "iniquitous as it is and with every desire to insult you. I am bound to confess that the bestowal of a similar position on Mike S. carries the bun. It is quite evident that one will be lost in the New navy. I note the kangaroo like leaps of certain brilliant officers and sincerely hope you are settling down on your bones ready for the jump which should land you within the fourth ring." (Scott need not have worried. His correspondent—Arthur Craig—would be commanding the Barham by the time of Jutland.) "You felicitate me on command of this noble vessel," he wrote to the same officer on his appointment to Bulwark, "but I've a sneaking envy for narrower quarters and wider horizons—in short if it were possible I

---

*It is a shame the doctor did not nap—in both senses—more often. Two days later Signorinetta romped home in the Oaks for a historic double.

would willingly exchange the Bulwark and the fogs of the English Channel for the Pelorus and a cruise in the South Seas."

Whatever Scott's private preferences, it was a naval world in which his new fiancée, for one, was determined he was going to succeed. "Con dear," she wrote to him, "you must grow necessary in the navy as well as at the South Pole . . . you *must* have the first ship in the Fleet or what's the use of you." It was very much the question Scott had been asking himself for the last year, but on the few snatched days or weekends between manoeuvres, Kathleen did at least have one "use" for him. "Oh girl dear we must meet oftener," he pleaded, "and you will make a baby, not of clay, won't you? because girl I know the pain and trouble, but it'll be ours wont it?"

A "bad pain because I *wasn't* clever," she wrote at the beginning of November, half trying to reassure him and half to reassure herself. "Oh dear Oh dear—I believe you mind more than me now.—It really has lots of things to be said for it—this delay—I shall only begin to be disappointed by January—Anyhow no one can say now 'no wonder they were married in a hurry.' " "Oh I could cry," she burst out a month later, "I was so sure . . . Oh Oh Oh!!!!"

"Oh really dearest is this true?" Scott wrote back at the first glimmer of hope that she was pregnant. "I'm hugging your letter and taking it to bed— My dear My dear—my own wife—I can't write a thing till I get your letter tomorrow. But you mustn't be disappointed girl you really really mustn't— if it is not what we want—oh girl you *are* a dear—."

"Still I'm dreading," he confided at the start of the new year, and two days later, 'My own wife—Can't I throw my cap in the air and cheer? Is it too early? Don't let it be too late—for once its sort of settled, I shall begin to worry about all it means." It was not too early, and if "proper parental dignity" kept his cap on, "not from want of inclination—only I think a growing sedateness of demeanour—I must confess that after the receipt of your letter I rolled Everett on the floor of my cabin from which I must imagine that I'm not altogether normal."

It is utterly typical of Scott that his moment of happiness should be touched by fears for their future. In the months before their marriage he had worried that he was too old and set to respond to Kathleen, and the thought now of a new life and new responsibilities stirred up in him all the same anxieties and feelings of inadequacy. Marriage, in fact, had done little to still them, and letter after letter, reunion after reunion, was darkened by "black dogs" and self-recriminations on his part, and bewilderment on hers. "Oh my Darling I'm so sorry," Kathleen wrote after one such reunion, conscious of a gulf that their brief meetings only widened. "How persistently & brutally we do hurt each other & would it hurt so each time if we were not all important to each other—I wonder." "Oh girl dear I'm so sad to think I was such a brute to you," he told her. "Girl I can't describe what comes over me, it's too indefinite . . . [but] the outward signs are the black moods that come and go with such apparent disregard for the feelings of those dear to me . . . Wife dear my own wife for every lapse believe there's repentance."

It was not that she did not *try* to understand these moods, but for a woman for whom happiness was a principle and a duty, it was an imaginative leap too far. "Dear sweetheart I understand, I do really begin to understand," she bravely lied. "You're powerless about these dread thunderclouds & I'm afraid so am I—we have just to wait confident that it will last no longer than thunderstorms do." "What on earth is all this," she demanded again. "Why have 'things changed' & why am I to write to you 'just how' & oh dear what *do* you mean . . . If you were a woman I would think you wanted to hurt me, but man darling I know you can't do that . . . Oh what's the matter Con—What *is* the matter?"

If Scott could have answered these questions he would not have been the man he was, but the truth was that for all her sympathy Kathleen was as much a part of the problem as she was its solution. During these first months of marriage it must have been clear to them both that he loved and needed her more than she did him, and for a man of his brittle confidence that knowledge could lead to something like panic. "Write, write, write," he begged her from his lonely palace in the *Bulwark*, "you *must* or I shall get the blackest of black blights!—God I've put all my eggs in one basket and the funny little arm that was around me last night grasps a large responsibility."

This was not just paranoia on Scott's part, because it was only with the birth of their son, as Kathleen later wrote, that "a strange thing happened" to her, and "I fell for the first time gloriously, passionately, wildly in love with my husband. I did not know that I had not been so before, but I knew now. He became my god; the father of my son and my god. Until now he had been a probationer, a means to an end. Now my aim, my desire had been abundantly accomplished. I worshipped the two of them as one, father and son, and gave myself up in happy abandonment to that worship. Now my determined, my masterful virginity, sustained through such strong vicissitudes, seemed not, as I had sometimes feared, mere selfish prudery, but the purposeful and inevitable highway to this culminating joy and peace."

But if Scott could share in the joy, he could not share in the "peace," because the kind of peace Kathleen was talking about was utterly alien to his personality. For the nine months of her pregnancy she had spoken and written of the baby as "Griselda" in a superstitious bid to ward off the possibility of a girl. Now, though, she had got the boy she wanted, born on 14 September 1909 and named Peter after Barrie's Peter Pan and Markham after Sir Clements. And with her son she was complete, content to enfold herself in a new and indulgent world of maternal and uxorious happiness.

It is true of all artists to one extent or another, but there was something particularly solipsistic about Kathleen that by contrast left Scott curiously exposed. Throughout the first turbulent year he had consistently wanted more from their marriage than she was easily able to give, and yet paradoxically it was now he and not she who needed something else. Domesticity, in the end, was not enough. "I've been dining with the Admiral," he wrote rather wistfully, conscious of horizons beyond the cocooned world of her deified trinity, "very dull except for a rather pretty American wife of the Captain of the Queen—David Beatty—I remember him a lieutenant on his pay with mediocre prospects & intelligence—he stepped into two wars and will be an Admiral at 38, the record for a century—his wife was a 'Field,' inherited a million and a half and went to America to fight for more and I believe got it." By contrast, "I seem to be marking time," he wrote again, "grudging the flying moments yet impotent to command circumstances—I seem to hold in reserve something that makes for success and yet to see no working field for it and so there's the consciousness of wasting and a truly deep 'unrest.'"

The "working field" was there, of course; he knew precisely what he wanted to do, but until there was news of Shackleton Scott could not commit himself. It was perhaps as well that there had been none. On 25 January 1908, the day Scott took over the *Essex*, Shackleton had reneged on their agreement and, "with a heavy heart," steamed across the 170th parallel for McMurdo and Scott's old base.

Twenty-two: Making Ready

I think all present at the Council wished we'd been able to send you a larger sub-
scription, and I should like to tell you some day why we felt unable to do so.

DR. JOHN SCOTT KELTIE, *Royal Geographical Society*

Nobody could have wanted to break his word less than Shackleton. He
had taken *Nimrod* south along a course designed to strike the Ross Ice
Shelf some two hundred miles from Cape Crozier, and then headed eastward across the all-important 170° W line of demarcation agreed with
Scott in search of winter quarters at what he renamed Barrier Inlet—the
old Balloon Bight, close to King Edward VII Land, where the two men had
made the first Antarctic balloon ascents six years earlier.

It would have been a bold stroke at any time to winter on the Barrier,
but it was bolder still as the ice at this point had calved away in the intervening years to create in its place a long, wide bay subsequently christened
the "Bay of Whales." "This was a great disappointment to us," Shackleton
later wrote, "but we were thankful that the Barrier had broken away before
we had made our camp on it. It was bad enough to try and make for a port
that had been wiped off the face of the earth, when all the intending
inhabitants were safe on board the ship, but it would have been infinitely
worse if we had landed there whilst the place was in existence, and that
when the ship returned to take us off she should find the place gone. The

thought of what might have been made me decide then and there that under no circumstances would I winter on the Barrier, and that wherever we did land we would secure a solid rock foundation for our winter home."

"We had two strings to our bow," Shackleton continued, more jauntily than he can have felt at the time, "and I decided to use the second at once and push towards King Edward VII Land." He knew from his *Discovery* days just how dangerous these waters could be, and within an hour the whole weight of the northerly pack and its huge attendant bergs was drifting in towards the Barrier, threatening to crush *Nimrod* up against its ice wall. "The seriousness of the situation may be well realised by the reader," he recalled, "if he imagines for a moment that he is in a small boat right under the vertical cliffs of Dover, that detached cliffs are moving in from seaward slowly but surely, with stupendous force and resistless power, and that it will only be a question of perhaps an hour or two before the two masses come into contact with his tiny craft between."

Escaping through an ever narrowing channel, with barely fifty yards of open water around them, Shackleton continued a helpless probe of the pack, equally desperate to avoid the dangers of a winter on a calving Barrier or the terrible alternative of McMurdo Sound and a broken promise. "I have been through a sort of Hell," he told his wife, after he had stood on *Nimrod*'s bridge in "snow squalls," wrestling with his conscience and deciding "whether to go on or turn back, my whole heart crying out for me to go on and the feeling against of the lives of the 40 odd men on board . . . I had a great public trust which I could not betray . . . my duty to the country and King . . . and the eyes of the world on us . . ."

There is a fascinating paradox at work here, because to an outsider of Shackleton's stamp, living on the crumbling edges of social and business respectability, the code of honour that bound him to his agreement had an even stronger force than it would have done for Scott himself. In his heart Shackleton might never have accepted Scott's "rights" over McMurdo, but he knew with his outsider's sense how his decision would look back in London, and resented it with all the bitterness of a man who craved acceptance and recognition.

As safety won out over honour, and he steered *Nimrod* towards McMurdo, not even Shackleton could have imagined the contempt which would greet the news in England. "The letter was an agreement and it has been completely disregarded in a manner which is too obvious to need comment," Scott wrote indignantly to Keltie from the *Essex* on

28 March 1908, convinced that Shackleton had always intended to go back on his word. "But unpleasant as this must be I cannot bring myself to associate again with such a professed liar nor to credit any statement he may make which is unsupported by the ample testimony of others."

At a personal level Keltie agreed with Scott, but, worried about the RGS "line" if Shackleton succeeded in his attempt on the Pole, he dangled the hope of mitigating factors. Scott, though, was having none of it. "As for 'cogent reasons' for his act," he retorted, certain, after a conversation with Bernacchi, that Shackleton had never meant to adhere to his promise, "you'll scarcely find Shackleton lacking in verbose explanations if that is all that is required to whitewash him . . . It is worthy of notice that he was in McMurdo Sound before the beginning of February, that is, long before any wintering quarters to the East could be open so that no real attempt to find a base in King Edward Land whatever may be said . . . It is very clear to me now that Shackleton lied to me in London."

To Kathleen and old *Discovery* colleagues he was even more brutal. "I'll send also Shackleton's letter to me," he wrote her, "don't bother to return as I have many copies . . . I had a suspicion he might [make for McMurdo] & find others had the same, also bit by bit I get evidence of similar actions in his history during the past few years he seems to have almost deliberately adopted the part of plausible rogue and to have thrown scruple to the winds. I wonder a little if such tactics can succeed but more I think I feel a shock and the terrible vulgarity which it has introduced to the Southern field of enterprise, hitherto so clean and wholesome."

Scott was by no means the only one thinking and talking in these kinds of terms—"I wish to God you had done any mortal thing in the whole world rather than break the promise you had made," Wilson told Shackleton—but the news hit Scott as it did nobody else. "It is awkward in many ways," he told Bernacchi, enclosing with his letter another copy of Shackleton's agreement. "It puts a stopper on my plans—I can of course have nothing more to do with him when he returns whatever he does and I don't like to be forced into such a false position of apparent jealousy. Further of course for my own part I shall find it impossible not to doubt any result he claims—I am sure he is prepared to lie rather than admit failure and I take it he will lie artistically. The whole thing is sickeningly vulgar and all the Daily Mail rubbish which he pumps into the press alone gives me the creeps."

This letter was written just after his return from France, where, as if to rub in Shackleton's advantage, Scott had gone with Skelton and Barne in connection with the first trials of his motorised sledge. He had hoped initially that they could have been held the previous autumn while he was still on half-pay, but delays and difficulties and blunders had continued to bedevil the project. The petrol supply tank had been broken in transit, and the starting handle fitted the wrong way, but after a day's work at the de Dion factory and an "insufferably hot" night at the Folies Bergères, they were more than ready for the mountains. They had sent three models including the Finchley sledge on ahead of them, and on 10 March left Paris by train, arriving at Le Lautaret on the twelfth—"to bed with open windows thank heavens," Scott scribbled on a card to Kathleen, and then, "on and still up by sledge—but more of that—glory of it!"

Scott's euphoria did not survive the first trials. "Exhaust cam of our engine reversed by Pelissier, de Dion mechanic," Skelton noted in a nice balancing act of technical expertise and John Bull prejudice, "but he failed to get engine to run although trying to do so nearly all day. Failure to do so undoubtedly due to low temperature and petrol not vapourising. A blow lamp would have saved this trouble. M. Courier suggested that engine did not have a fair chance on account of the English additions (high tension trembler, coil and elbow piece in induction pipe), but this opinion was, of course, absolute nonsense."

It was not just the Finchley model that was disappointing. The great French polar explorer Jean-Baptiste Charcot was having little more luck. "Dr. Charcot's sledge made a trial to-day," Skelton noted, "but although it advanced on the sledge road, it did not prove capable of any tractive power and could not do anything in soft snow unless assisted."

The next day they dismounted the engine on their own sledge, and after warming it in a hotel room, managed at last to get it started in the snow. "Snow wheels were depressed about half way and clutch put in," Skelton again noted in his report for Scott: "the sledge advanced a small amount and then stopped, the snow chain clearing a hole in the snow. Snow wheels were then depressed to the full extent, and clutch put in again, when sledge advanced a few yards and engine brought up."

If the problem was not the engine, it was the slats; if it was not Scott's sledge it was Charcot's, and with the distance from McMurdo to the Pole almost eight hundred miles, a downhill record of 120 yards with just one stop was not encouraging. "The conditions were so extremely different from the average conditions of the Antarctic," however, Skelton wrote, in an oddly optimistic conclusion that leaves one wondering what they were doing in Le Lautaret in the first place, it would have been difficult with any machine to gain any reliable information—in fact, the conditions were really unfair to the sledges. Nowhere in the Antarctic was such soft snow met with; neither man, pony, dog or reindeer could have pulled on it . . . The two surfaces are quite different, and require different tractors.

In spite of the failure of the sledge to actually perform hauling work, I do not think the general system was in any way shown to be wrong in principle—the failure was entirely due to details which can be easily put right, and to the especially severe conditions of the track.

There was another setback for Scott when, three months after Le Lautaret, criticisms in the second volume of the scientific reports on *Discovery*'s meteorological work opened up some old wounds. Scott was ready to acknowledge in private that Royds's paperwork at the best of times was "dreadfully slipshod," but an error of their own from the Meteorological Office in misinterpreting Royds's directions as "magnetic" rather than "true" gave him the chance to leap to his officer's defence. Scott was on shaky ground, but even after a thorough trawl of the records by Skelton had exposed other errors, he was determined to press for an official inquiry. The President of the Royal Society firmly counselled against anything that could stir up old dissension, but Scott was determined to have his pound of justice, finally eliciting from Sir Archibald Geikie of the RS a reluctant offer to include in the next meteorological volume a résumé of his objections.

It was an offer, ironically, that was only made good after Scott's death, in a volume that came out the same week as the St. Paul's memorial service, but there can be no doubt that he had not handled the matter well. It was not his officers' fault that they had insufficient training in their equipment before *Discovery* sailed, but Scott's resentment of criticism seems to have taken on a stridency that blurred the bounds between rational defence and pigheadedness. "The hyper-sensitiveness that refuses to accept any criticism is very unfortunate," Mostyn Field, Wharton's successor as Hydrographer, wrote. "I fear Captain Scott will retain his own opinion in spite of what any one may say, but in my judgement by pressing for an enquiry he will do himself . . . much harm."

Field was almost certainly right, but Scott had only to think of the ferocious conditions under which Royds and his other officers had made their observations, to see red when a hydrographer or meteorologist had the nerve to criticise them. From the day of *Discovery's* return he had fought his old officers' battles for them, pushing at one moment for proper recognition for Mulock or lobbying the Admiralty at the next on Royds's behalf, and it woke all his protective instincts as well as his sense of natural justice to see their work undermined by an establishment that had done so little to help them in the first place.

And it was for *them* that he fought, because even Mostyn Field, who had done all he could to block Scott's appointment, acknowledged that *Discovery* could have had no better leader. "I have the highest admiration for the way in which Captain Scott conducted the Expedition," he wrote, "and as a leader of men he showed that no officer could be better qualified for carrying out what he undertook. His misfortune lay in the fact that his officers were imperfectly trained in the scientific duties."

It was not all altruism on Scott's part, because with a new expedition of his own in the planning stage—and an expedition that would have to appeal to the general public for funds—criticism of *Discovery's* scientific record could not have appeared at a worse time. From the day that he had first spelled out his plans to Skelton, he had stressed the scientific as well as the geographical nature of the venture, and the last thing he could afford to read in the papers was the review of *Discovery's* work that appeared in the *Times Literary Supplement*. "How much longer shall we have to wait in England," it demanded, "for those entrusted with national affairs to appreciate a little more seriously the requirements of scientific investigation? Probably until the constant leakage and loss which we suffer in ignorance are made plainer by one or more exceptional disasters."

Coming on top of the news from McMurdo and the sledge failures, it was a blow to both hopes and confidence, but if there was little else Scott could do, he could at least put himself in a position to take advantage of any failure of Shackleton's. His command of the *Bulwark* ran until 24 March 1909, but long before that date he and Kathleen were exploring career avenues that would get him to London at the right time. "Mark Kerr"—the future admiral, and a distant relative of the First Sea Lord, Lord Walter Kerr—"has been here for hours," Kathleen wrote at the beginning of December 1908, determined to do all a successful and forceful wife could do for her husband. "Has got a thing he wants to know if you will take I told him you wouldn't—It's assistant to the 2nd Lord of the Admiralty in April— It will be Bridgeman. Full pay & maintenance pay—I told him you wanted to get in your sea time—He said he was sure you would have by April."

"I think all things considered I'd be inclined to accept the offer made through Mark Kerr," Scott had already written the day before, in a letter that crossed with Kathleen's; "my time will be in by Feb? The pros are—I should be at head quarters ready to pick & choose in the future—I should be in London able to see the sledge business etc—I should be with a small lady I love . . . The cons are certain points in the service experience. From a naval point of view the thing would be good enough and from a private one eminently desirable."

After the stresses of brief weekends and crossing letters, Scott was right, but his timing was better than he could possibly have hoped. The same week that he left *Bulwark*, word reached England of Shackleton's failure to reach the Pole, and in a piece of rich serendipity Scott was on the platform waiting for the London train when his old *Discovery* coxswain, Tom Crean, ran along the platform brandishing a paper with the news. "I think," Scott said, "we'd better have a shot next."

"Failure," though, is hardly the right word—in a brilliant journey from his base in McMurdo Shackleton had got within a hundred miles of the Pole—but the Pole itself was still there unconquered, and that was what Scott was waiting to hear. He was too genuinely interested in the science of Antarctica to view the Pole as the commercial opportunity that Shackleton saw, but if he wanted to interest the public and financial backers in another expedition he was realist enough to know that it was the one goal he could not ignore.*

Before Scott could think about his own expedition, however, there was

---

*There is again a fascinating confirmation of all it meant to Scott from Mason, and an interesting sidelight on a curious episode in which an envelope arrived for Scott from Shackleton with nothing but a blank piece of paper inside. The sheet—now carefully kept in a cellophane envelope—is still in the archives of the Scott Polar Research Institute, with an instruction from Kathleen's second husband that it should be carefully preserved. In Mason's version the stamp on the soiled envelope is from "Rexland"—King Edward VII Land. The writing is that of "Hemming," the Shackleton of the story. Inside, Rames knows, must be the news as to whether the South Pole is still *Terra Incognita* or not. "You open it," he tells his wife.

> "You can tell me what he says . . ."
> "There is nothing but this," said Cynthia . . . "Do you understand it?"
> "Yes. He has failed."
> There was no doubt left to her of her husband's joy. The cry which broke from his lips was not to be denied. It was a real cry of exultation. Cynthia turned pale as she heard it. But she would not acknowledge that she understood it, nor would she look into Harry's face lest she should see the same exultation blazoned there.
> "Poor Hemming," said Rames. "That's bad luck. The disappointment must have hit him hard."

the inevitable fall-out of *Nimrod* to be dealt with. "The private feeling incurred by past incidents cannot affect my judgement of his work," he reassured the President of the RGS, promising that he would do all he could to attend any function honouring Shackleton. "That excites my interest and admiration to an extent that can scarcely be felt by those who have no experience of Polar difficulties." "Shackleton's exploit is very fine," he wrote with more candour to Skelton, "but of course I cannot but share your mixed feelings—However, outwardly, there is only one attitude for me and I shall have to do & say things that go a little against the grain—What a difference it would make if one could be genuinely enthusiastic!—but there's such a lot that tastes bad!"

Within a certain circle there were real doubts over Shackleton's claims, but even Sir Clements, indignant still for his old protégé, could not withhold his admiration. "Thanks for sending me the Shackleton telegram," he wrote after the first details of Shackleton's ascent of the Beardmore Glacier had reached him. "I expected that if the ponies proved a success, he might easily reach 85°. But the way he pushed on after that with weights far too heavy, over a crevassed glacier, in the face of furious gales, and on reduced rations, shows a most extraordinary amount of energy and pluck. Indeed I do not quite see how it is possible, for he speaks of having been confined in the tent for 3 days by gale, that the crevassed state of the ice was such that in one day they only made 600 yards."

Rumours of these doubts over Shackleton's figures found their way into the press, but whatever his private scepticism, Scott was determined, as Markham put it, to be "most generous, giving unstinted praise to Shackleton without the slightest allusion to the breach of faith, or to many other things that might be pointed out."

It is a matter of taste—perfidious Albion or civilised restraint?—but either way, the fact was that there was nothing Scott or anyone could do to mar Shackleton's homecoming. On his journey home in *Discovery* Scott had looked forward to the receptions with something approaching dread, but to Shackleton publicity was the stuff of life, fame and recognition the whole *point* of a polar expedition that again might just as well have been up the Orinoco for all it engaged him intellectually. And with a knighthood from the King, the press well primed, the geographical establishment tamely on board, the public left in no doubt of the time and place of his arrival, and the crowds ready to celebrate a national hero, he had at last all the recognition he could desire.

In spite of all his best intentions, Scott found the occasion difficult to

bear when it came to it, and Mill found him at the RGS "gloomily discussing with Keltie whether he ought to go to meet Shackleton or not. He
did not wish to go, but Scott was always a slave to duty, and we persuaded
him that it was his duty to greet his former subordinate. He went with me
to Charing Cross Station, and took first place at the reception." The two
men were careful not to meet in private, but Scott was there again to pre-
side over a dinner for Shackleton at the Savage Club, and was warm in his
praise of his achievements and "very proud," as the *Observer* reported, to
have "had a hand in rocking his Antarctic cradle."

It cannot have been any easier for Shackleton to listen to his old boss's
praise than it was for Scott to give it, still less so as the occasion gave Scott
the chance to announce his own plans. He told an audience always ready
to hear an appeal to national sentiment that the Pole had to be discovered
by an Englishman, that he been ready to do it for two years, and that it was
time the country organised another expedition before the foreigners cut in
on the territorial advances made by Shackleton.

Scott's patriotism was not of the jingoistic kind, but he was not above
exploiting the sentiment when required, and he knew that over the next
months he was going to need support wherever he could find it. At the
beginning of July he wrote to Shackleton to establish that he had no
counter plans of his own, and with that assurance in his pocket, was at last
ready to launch his own bid. "The campaign is opened," he announced to
Keltie from his home at 174 Buckingham Palace Gardens on 12 September, over two years after his first letter to Skelton outlining his plans, "& I
hope the door closed to interference."

He made it absolutely clear from the start, too, what his principal aim
was. "The main object of this Expedition," he wrote in his public appeal
for the £40,000 needed, "is to reach the South Pole, and to secure for The
British Empire the honour of this achievement." There were other objectives, scientific and geographical—the exploration of King Edward's and
Victoria Land, a fuller understanding of the ice shelf, geological, magnetic
and meteorological work, a full and unprecedented scientific programme—but it was only in defeat that Scott's expedition ceased to be
seen in British eyes as the "race" for the Pole it had always been.

And in that fact lay Scott's problem, because if the public liked it, and if
the French, the Japanese, and above all the Americans, were all beating
the same drum, Scott's natural constituency and power base lay in a geographical establishment that frowned on mere "Pole bagging." There was
no doubt in anyone's mind at the RGS that Scott was the man to do it if it

had to be done, but Admiral Sir Lewis Beaumont and Major Darwin, respectively Vice-President and President of the Society, were in no more doubt than Markham that it was not the business of the Society to promote personal or national "competition." "I have thought carefully over what you told me of the Scott-Shackleton difficulty," Beaumont had written to Darwin the very day that Scott offered himself at the Savage Club, defining the limits of RGS support. ". . . Let him lead another Antarctic expedition if he will. Let it be scientific primarily, with exploration and the Pole as secondary objects—and so add to the fine reputation which he already has. All this long story is to incline you to put Scott off from making what I think will be a great mistake."

Scott was not unaware of the problem. On the same day he published his plans in *The Times*, he wrote to Darwin in an attempt to forestall the objections. "At this juncture in the history of Polar Exploration," he told him, "I think it absolutely necessary to continue those efforts which have given to this country the foremost place in Antarctic Research . . . I believe that the main object, that of reaching the South Pole, will appeal to all our countrymen as the one rightly to be pursued at this moment, but the plan which I present provides also for the scientific exploration of a considerable extent of the Antarctic continent and will therefore I hope commend itself to the Royal Geographical Society."

He was as good as his word, immediately sending off a telegram to Wilson asking him to organise and head the scientific staff. Wilson had once told Markham that he would be happy to fall down any crevasse with Scott, but it was the more cerebral side of Scott's leadership that appealed to him now. "Scott is a man worth working for as a man," Wilson wrote to his father. "No one can say that it will only have been a Pole-hunt, though that of course is a *sine qua non*. We *must* get to the Pole; but we shall get more too, and there will be no loopholes for error in means and methods if care in preparation can avoid them. I can promise you it is a work worth anyone's time and care and I feel it is really a great opportunity. We want the Scientific work to make the bagging of the Pole merely an item in the results."

But if RGS doubts over "Pole-bagging" lingered—even Markham thought him "bitten up by the Pole mania"—Scott was in more than usually robust frame of mind to take it after the birth of his and Kathleen's child. As Naval Assistant to the Second Sea Lord his days were still filled with service matters, but now, in London where he needed to be and home by six each evening, he was at last in a position to get down to the detailed business of planning his expedition.

At this stage Scott's letters were headed "British Antarctic Expedition 1910," with expedition headquarters around the corner from Buckingham Palace Road at 36 and 38 Victoria Street. "The offices of the expedition were in Westminster," recalled the Australian physicist Griffith Taylor, who walked the fifty-odd miles from Cambridge to London to prove himself up to naval standards, ". . . situated in a district peculiarly devoted to the empire's interests . . . In a large room occasionally sat Captain Scott, but he was usually busy with some ingenious foodstuffs or patent appliance in one of the other rooms. Adjacent was the secretary's office, and there he was seen *inter alia*, wading through some of the eight thousand applications from eager souls anxious to get out of the rut by joining the expedition in one capacity or another . . . In a second room at headquarters were samples of patent foods . . . In another corner of the same room an eager inventor is explaining the excellence of his patent stove . . . The other room was almost filled with a huge petty officer who was sorting gear for the sledges . . . An old 1902 sledge was lying in the passage . . ."

More pressing than men or equipment in these early days, however, was the question of money, and nothing could have been more inimical to a man of Scott's temperament. It had never cost Shackleton anything to strut the country's lecture halls, but Scott hated it—hated the embarrassment, the humiliation, the publicity, and hated, one suspects above all, the necessity of selling himself in the kind of terms the public demanded— "Stop Murray's letter," he had told Keltie with a hint of desperation, when George Murray, Scott's old companion in *Discovery*, had fired off a demand to *The Times* that "the men with the money & the honour of their country at heart provide—and Capt Scott will do the heroism!"

From the start it was a tough business. A meeting in October at the Mansion House, presided over by the Lord Mayor of London, generated more goodwill than money, and although Keltie had done all he could to undo the RGS's parsimony, Scott was learning what it was like to live in the private sector. However difficult they had been, powerful institutions and a government had stood behind him in *Discovery*, but now he had only his name and reputation. And reputations, rather like Gold Medals, did not pay the bills. The country might be certain, as Scott assured it, that there would be no doubts over anything they might claim of the kind that had sullied the reputations of Peary and Cook in the north. The press might support the cause; the Earl of Derby announce that every uninhabited part of the globe belonged by right to England. But without the single, decisive donation of the kind Beardmore or Longstaff had made, there was no alternative but to traipse the country drumming up support from a public no keener to pay for its Imperial birthright than it would be now for clean air.

"Ask all the Mayors you can find," he told Kathleen, but it was grim work. "Between £20 and £30 since I went [to] Wolverhampton, *c'est tout* . . . This place won't do—wasting my time to some extent . . . I don't think there's a great deal of money in the neighbourhood . . . Last night dined with rich man at Redcar . . . he will give but not very much, and when he asked others to join his party, hinting broadly the object, there was a mighty poor attendance . . . Things have been so-so here . . . I spoke—not well but the room was beastly and attendance small."

"£40 to-day"—that can be multiplied by something between forty and fifty for contemporary values—he was recording again at the end of November 1909, just after he had left the Admiralty to go on half-pay and only six months before the expedition was due to leave, "nothing from Wales—made an agreement with Bowring to pay only £5,000 on the eighth, don't know how I shall manage even that."

The £5,000 was the first instalment of a £12,500 payment for an expedition ship. When Scott first thought of the south again he had hoped that he would be able to get *Discovery*, which had been sold off on her return to England, but in spite of approaches to the High Commissioner for Canada, Lord Strathcona—another on his Advisory Committee—she could not be prised away from her new owners or her duties as supply ship to the Hudson Bay Company trading stations. That left only a handful of alternatives, including *Morning* and Shackleton's *Nimrod*, and in the end it was another whaler with an Antarctic pedigree, the old *Terra Nova*, that was bought. "Poor little ship," Scott's future second-in-command recalled of his first sight of her in the Port of London, "surrounded by great liners and cargo-carrying ships," stinking of whale from the blubber tanks, and "so dirty and uncared for looking" that he blushed at the state of her whenever an admiral came on board to inspect.

But if she was no beauty, she had proved herself in northern and southern seas, and while £12,500—£1,500 more than Markham had got for *Discovery*—seemed a high price, the expedition received the boost it needed in the new year with an announcement of a government grant of £20,000. Scott had put in an application for funds in the middle of December, stressing the scientific dimension—and above all the geological ambitions—of the expedition with a conviction that he was never able to bring to his drumbeating in the town halls of Britain's northern industrial cities. "It is anticipated," he wrote confidently, "that the accomplishment of very important scientific work will be fulfilled . . . The steps which are being taken will ensure the Expedition being better equipped to deal with scientific problems than any other Polar expedition that has ever left these shores."

After Asquith's government had given £20,000 to help clear Shackleton's debts the previous summer, it could scarcely do less, but it still left Scott short of the £40,000 he needed. There were doubts even at this time in RS circles that he would be able to raise the money for the expedition at all, but on top of the government's generosity Scott had a second, if rather more equivocal, piece of luck, when "Teddy" Evans—the former navigator of *Morning* on her relief expedition—agreed to abandon his own plans for an expedition south and join Scott's as second-in-command. The deal was brokered by Markham, and Evans brought to the fund-raising and expedition affairs all the ebullience and flare for publicity that Scott so conspicuously lacked. After a mildly delinquent childhood that had seen him sacked from the Merchant Taylor's School, Evans had gone to the training ship *Worcester*, from where he had won a naval cadetship that would sweep him, on an irresistible wave of charm, energy, daring, bluster, heroism, opportunism and self-promotion, from reform school to the rank of full admiral, a peerage and national fame.

It would be hard to imagine that the service could have provided two such diametric opposites as Scott and Evans, the one all intelligence, reserve and self-doubt, the other a sort of twenty-eight-year-old puppy in naval uniform, boisterous, extrovert, and given to horseplay and ludicrous feats of fairground physical strength. There is nothing in Scott's correspondence to suggest that Evans had made a particular impact one way or another on him when he had come out in *Morning*, but there is no question of the impact Scott's achievements had made on Evans. "I have heard from Michael Barne that his projected expedition will not be dispatched," he had written with his typical directness three years earlier, in April 1907. "He has also informed me that you will yourself lead another expedition. I am very disappointed that I shall not be Michael's navigator, but will you take me as yours? I am not an 'x chaser,'* but if you will only let me sail with you I promise that you will have no keener officer & no one shall

*The "x-chaser" was navy slang for the equivalent of the prep-school swot. The man "who chased x, y and z," the "three-oner" who got first-class passes in his seamanship board, his *Excellent* course and his Greenwich time was deeply distrusted. "A three-oner," a song went, was an officer who "shouted when the ship was flat aback, 'Let go the starboard alpha cosine theta stunsail tack.' "

work harder than I will." He was "tremendously enthusiastic about Antarctica," he told Scott, "*not* of the class of navigator who does not like watchkeeping," and if he had "no musical accomplishments," and was "not a witty person like Barne & Doorly," loved work and was ready, if "a certificate of good temper and amiability" was wanted, to get his wife to furnish him with one.

Given that Evans's wife was a sister of the girl Scott had spent his time in New Zealand extricating Michael Barne from, it is doubtful that that last reference would have carried much weight, but by the spring of 1910 Scott was in no position to stand on his social dignity. He must have recognised as clearly as Markham did that Evans had the qualities that he and the expedition particularly needed at that juncture, but what was of even more importance was the support and financial backing Evans had already secured for his own venture.

There was in fact a touch of the Shackleton about Evans, and with the new second-in-command deputed to milk Wales and the south-west, and Scott working the northern circuit, things picked up. In his own appeals Scott had half-heartedly dangled the potential commercial advantages of the south, but he could never have matched the bravado of Evans, who was quite happy to hustle the money out of Welsh pockets with visions of the "profits—big profits" that those on the inside knew were to be made down in Antarctica.

There was another and harder side to Evans, however, and Scott had his first unwelcome sight of it when his new second-in-command protested against Skelton's presence on the expedition. As an old and loyal friend who had been involved from the start, Skelton had tacitly assumed that Evans's post would be his, but even Skelton's willingness to sail in any capacity was insufficient to reconcile Lieutenant Evans to the idea of a commander of senior rank serving under him. The dispute came to a head in March, three months before *Terra Nova* was due to sail, while Scott was with Skelton and Kathleen in Norway overseeing fresh trials on a new and improved motorised sledge. "I should be delighted to have you on the Expedition," Scott wrote to Skelton on their return, "but it would be folly for me to indulge in a personal predilection and this may lead to friction— I hope you see my position—Evans would of course assent if I put my foot down but I don't think I ought to do that, for yielding on his part should be voluntary."

With Evans determined not to yield, it was a bleak choice for Scott— loyalty or expedience?—and as in the dispute over McMurdo Sound, he had become keener on his old "Discoverys" seeing his point of view than he was on seeing theirs. "I am forced to realise that it displays antagonism on *both* sides," he wrote after a lengthy and acrimonious triangular exchange of letters—and as an expedition leader who would inevitably be away from base camp for long periods, he added, that was something he could not allow to incubate: "My dear chap," he concluded, "you are bound to feel sore over this matter and I cannot expect you will quite appreciate my motives. I am very grieved that it should be so . . . I have the highest regard for your capabilities, your integrity, & your loyalty to myself."

If the only puzzle in all this is Evans's motives—the cavil over rank will not wash—it can have been small consolation to Skelton that Scott got all he deserved when he backed Evans. It says a lot for Skelton and the strength of their friendship that it survived this bitter falling out, but the incident marks another small step away from the man Scott had once been, and his final word on the subject—"I'm sorry awfully sorry"—seems as consciously an elegy for himself as it does an apology for the pain he had caused a friend.

And among the impersonal details of fund-raising and empty lecture halls that constitute the bulk of Scott's correspondence at this time, one letter to Kathleen does suggest that he himself found it no easier to live with the man he was gradually and deliberately becoming. "I was lying abed thinking last night," he wrote to her from his fund-raising travels on 14 February 1910, "and all you'd done and are doing for me spread itself out—and I saw all the brave attempts to conquer the horrid parts of me, and to-day I must write and tell you . . . When things look bad, when I'm tiresome or petulant, don't think your care is wasted. When I'm away on the snows it will be bad to remember that I've grieved you, but it would be infinitely worse if I thought you didn't know that I understood your sacrifices. My dear, my dear, my heart is very full of you in spite of the hard crust which you find it so difficult to get through."

It hurt not just his wife, but his friends too, to see him behave as in any way less than he was. "I know Scott intimately, as you know," Wilson wrote protectively to one young applicant for a place on the expedition, Apsley Cherry-Garrard. "I have known him now for ten years, and I believe in him so firmly that I am often sorry when he lays himself open to misunderstanding. I am sure that you will come to know him and believe in him as I do, and none the less because he is sometimes difficult."

The "crust" had its uses, though, and if a part of the man inside was shrivelling, Scott had trained himself too well for the most part to let anyone but Kathleen see it. "I was drawn strongly to the famous explorer at my first meeting with him," the photographer Herbert Ponting, another future member of the expedition, recalled of his first introduction to Scott. "His trim, athletic figure; the determined face; the clear blue eyes, with their sincere, searching gaze; the simple direct speech, and earnest manner; the quiet *force* of the man—all drew me to him irresistibly." It was a judgement other members of the expedition endorsed. "Scott is just what I expected," Griffith Taylor noted in his journal after his first visit to the Victoria Street offices. "A sturdily built, clean shaved naval officer, with plenty of humour and decision."

The outward performance—the smart and brisk naval officer, modest yet firm, understated yet confident—had in fact been perfected. In provincial newspaper report after report one glimpses the same man, no Shackleton perhaps, but something in a sense more reassuring, more deeply English, or at least, more satisfyingly what the English would like to be— "nothing of the braggart or blusterer about him," as the *Liverpool Post* put it, little of "the first person singular" and not a trace of the "type of American explorer who announces that he will 'reach the Pole or bust.' "

It was not just "image" either, and never had been, which was perhaps as well. Scott allowed himself a last visit to the old family home, Outlands, where he carved his initials in a tree, but with time running out, there was no room for self-questioning or wondering whether the game was worth the candle. In Wilson and Evans he had two men who gave him immense assistance, but in a rerun of the last hectic weeks before *Discovery* sailed there were still a thousand things to do—funds to be raised, appointments confirmed, commercial contracts negotiated, manufacturers sweet-talked,* ponies and dogs bought, Kinsey, his old New Zealand manager from *Discovery* days, briefed, a courteous exchange conducted with Peary over an Anglo–American "race" for the Pole, and a last, tedious flurry of anxiety over Shackleton's future plans survived.

There was also the *Terra Nova* to be prepared, and at the West India Docks Teddy Evans slaved to complete preparations. Before they could do anything, the reeking blubber-tanks had to be removed, the hold cleansed and whitewashed, the bilges sluiced out, the whole ship disinfected fore

---

*A list of the expedition's commercial suppliers makes familiar reading. Fry & Sons for cocoa and chocolate; Colman for their mustard; Tate & Sons, sugar; Frank Cooper of Oxford for their marmalade; Shippams for potted meats; Abram Lyle & Sons for golden syrup; Gonzalez Byass & Co., port and sherry; Heidsieck, champagne; Jaeger, boots and blankets.

and aft, and "a multitude of necessities—canvas for sail-making, fireworks for signalling, whale-boats and whaling gear, flags, logs, paint, tar, carpenter's stores, blacksmith's outfit—bought, borrowed or 'acquired.' We then 'had her barque-rigged,' " Evans, hustler-supreme in all this, recalled. "A large, well-insulated ice house was erected on the upper deck which held 150 carcasses of frozen mutton, and owing to the position of the cold chamber, free as it was from the vicinity of iron, we mounted here our standard compass and Lloyd Creek pedestal for magnetic work . . . A new stove was put in the galley, a lamp-room and paraffin store built, and store rooms, instrument, and chronometer rooms were added . . . Twenty-four bunks were fitted around the saloon accommodation . . . laboratories . . . constructed on poop, while two large magazines and a clothing store were zinc-lined to keep them damp free."

By 1 June, two months ahead of their 1901 schedule, she was ready. As in *Discovery*, Scott was keen to fly the White Ensign, and at the cost of £100 that the expedition could ill-afford, secured himself the privilege by joining the Royal Yacht Squadron. For any naval man the Ensign carried a talismanic value, but as a registered yacht the *Terra Nova* enjoyed another advantage, being exempt from the regulations and inspections of Board of Trade officials ready to declare that she was "not a well-found merchant ship within the meaning of the Act."

What the same officials would have said of her if they could have seen her as she left New Zealand beggars the imagination, but with the Plimsoll mark painted out, and stores on board, the *Terra Nova* was ready to sail. On the night of 31 May the RGS held a dinner for Scott and his men attended by three hundred of its fellows, and the next day, with Major Darwin's peroration on the "manhood of our nation and . . . the characteristics of our ancestors who won our great Empire" still freshly stale in all ears, the White Ensign and the Burgee of the Royal Yacht Squadron were hoisted by Lady Bridgeman and—*mutatis mutandis*—Lady Markham, the visitors in their mourning clothes for Edward VII were warned off, and the brightly painted *Terra Nova* slipped away from her wharf.

Twenty-three: **South Again**

One does pall of champagne, beer and ginger ale in the course of time. Indeed I can think of nothing more calculated to turn a man a rabid TT than a voyage on the Terra Nova RYS.

CHARLES WRIGHT, *diary, 10 July 1910*

It might not have had much to do with Scott, but a happier ship never sailed than the *Terra Nova* on the first leg of her voyage to the south. In the nature of these things, the ceremonies in London were only the first of a protracted series of farewells, and after leaving the ship in the Thames, Scott rejoined her on the south coast to pass between the looming ranks of the new fleet Fisher had created in his own violent image. "At Weymouth we picked up Capt Scott," one of his new recruits wrote home, "& saw under the land the funnels of a fleet the like of which I have never seen, & I am sure the world has never seen such a squadron. Every 'Dreadnought' & Dreadnought-cruiser was there & the splendid King Edward Class. We were given the honour of steaming through the lines. I must say I was never so impressed in my life with hideous strength. The new monsters are ugliness itself but for sheer diabolical brutality in shipbuilding some of the Dreadnought Cruisers take the cake. The look of them is enough to scare anything & when you pass close enough to look into the muzzles of their guns the effect is something to be remembered. Much as I love ships & particularly H.M. Ships there was something about the look of this squadron that was Satanic."

There was still one last "Mayor (Lord)" along with his councillors—"all absolutely double-barrelled-bevel-edged bounders"—to be endured, but by the fifteenth *Terra Nova* was at last ready to sail. Whatever Scott's crew might privately think of her corporation, the City of Cardiff had done the *Terra Nova* proud, and after taking on a gift of coal and enough drink to ensure that it took six men to get Scott's old friend from *Discovery*, "Taff" Evans, back on board, she finally made her escape, gleefully shedding a stream of religious tracts and pamphlets donated by well-wishers as she went.

Sandwiched between the Mayor and Scott at the Cardiff banquet, Taff Evans had declared that no man but his old boss could have induced him to go south again, but for the time being at least he was going to have do without him. It would probably have been better in the long run if Scott had stayed with his ship, but with so much still to do he had decided to join her at Cape Town, and leave the *Terra Nova* and her motley crew of officers, sailors, scientists and amateur volunteers for the first stage of their voyage to his second-in-command, Teddy Evans.

Back in London, Scott spent his last weeks busy completing arrangements with Central News for syndication of reports of the expedition's progress around the world's newspapers. There were also magazine and cinematograph contracts to be finalised, and the endless bills, small and large, that had been incurred on the ship's refitting and supplying to be settled. The small donations continued to come in, too, including more than a hundred contributions from schools in Britain and the Empire to sponsor dogs (three guineas apiece), sledges, sleeping bags and ponies, and they all required answers. "I enclose P.O for £1.7.6," one letter from the Diocesan High School for Girls, Auckland, read. "Our children were most disappointed to find dogs were so expensive! They hoped to be able to give several, and had chosen names for them, but I am afraid they will not raise enough for more than a leg." "Please convey my personal thanks to the boys and girls," Scott wrote in response to another, more successful sponsorship bid, "and tell them the dog will be called 'Steyne,' as they wish."

Even at this late stage, however, there were insufficient funds to guarantee expedition salaries, and it was as well that some of the party could afford to sail for nothing, or only a nominal wage. With a sliding scale that ran from £10 a week for Wilson as chief of the scientific staff down to 13/6 on the lower deck, it was clear that nobody was there for profit, but with £20 a week salary on top of his naval pay, Scott could at least be sure that his family were not going to suffer financially by his going.

Not that that was enough to release him from a sense of guilt he had been harbouring since his marriage to Kathleen. "I've just had a touching little letter from Mummy full of greetings to us!!!"—the "us" double underlined—he had written to her earlier. "It makes me feel very bad." He knew that he had married in the face of family wishes, and he was now going south again in spite of the same opposition. He could, as he had done when *Discovery* sailed, send Grace money for a holiday—they "must be comfortable," he told her just before he left—but to his ageing mother a Norwegian holiday was cold comfort. "I don't forget to wish for your own prosperity," he wrote to Kitty a year later, conscious of the vast gap he had put between himself and the family that had depended on him for so many years, "in hopes that the critical times are past . . . Dear old girl I know how much you both [Kitty and Grace] deserve to be relieved of the anxieties which have pressed so heavily during the past years—all success to you . . . you will be wishing us well . . . May every good fortune be yours and may the world be all that is cheerful for your brave spirit when I return."

The difference from *Discovery* days, however, was that he now had a wife and son. After long "heart-searchings," Kathleen had decided to accompany Scott to New Zealand. "Looking back over my life I can think of nothing that hurt more hideously," she later wrote, "than unlocking the sturdy fingers that clung round mine as I left the laughing, tawny-haired baby Hercules for four months, four months of enchanting change and growth that I should be shut out from and would never come again."

It was all very well Kathleen writing in this vein, but it was not four months Scott was facing, and he knew what lay in store well enough to recognise that he might be looking at his son for the last time. In these final weeks before leaving England no premonition of disaster ever seems to have troubled his plans or expectations, but when it came to Peter there was something wistfully elegiac in the way he silently, almost unconsciously, painted himself out of any future together. "There is only one person who ought to bring our boy up," he wrote in a letter to his wife to be opened when they finally parted. "I am sure he is going to be a fine fellow, but I want you to have the making of his mind as much as you have of his stout little body. It's good to think you have the boy, you being what you are . . . As I tramp alone, it will be good to feel the [sun's] rays and think that similar ones are falling on a small lady and a still smaller man who is toddling about with her."*

*Another shadow across these last days was a disagreement with Barrie that troubled Scott until the end of his life. Both men were too discreet to leave any trace of its cause, but if dates

Peter was to stay at Henley with Scott's mother and sister while Kathleen was away, and on 16 July, after a quiet farewell at Waterloo station from a small party that included Shackleton and Wilhelm Filchner, a German army officer with ambitions of his own for a trans-Antarctic expedition, Scott and Kathleen boarded the *Saxon* for South Africa.

"See you at the South Pole," a straw-hatted Scott had good-humouredly called out of the carriage window to Filchner as the train pulled out of Waterloo, and long before he reached South Africa he could have been excused for wishing he was already there. Kathleen was never an easy companion on sea voyages at the best of times, and with Oriana Wilson and Teddy Evans's wife Hilda on board to add to a miserable bout of seasickness, she was clearly in no mood to charm.

Kathleen and Hilda Evans could never have had anything in common, except perhaps a mutual suspicion of each other's husband, but between Kathleen and Ory Wilson lay a deeper and more principled antipathy. It was not that either of them had not done her best to like the other, but there was a difference of vision, habits, faiths, and a different kind of *seriousness* about life, that no amount of initial goodwill could bridge. "We were simply delighted by her kindness and abundant hospitality and welcome," Wilson had written to Scott after staying at Buckingham Palace Road with Kathleen. "You have been a good friend to me, no one has had a better or truer, and for such a friend I have no better wish in the world than that he should find a wife as well suited to him as mine is to me."

"We both disregarded the other's . . . sense of humour but otherwise we got on very well," Kathleen wrote more sharply of the same visit, and a more prolonged exposure did nothing to bring them closer. For the whole of her adult life she had been used to mixing with men on terms of absolute equality, and it was never going to be likely that she would quietly accept an expedition ethos that sought to relegate her to its decorative edges with a pair of women she despised. "I gather he thinks women aren't much use," she would later complain of Wilson, irritated to be included in a view of her sex so completely at one with her own, "and expect he is judging from long experience, so I don't bear him malice."

---

can supply a clue, it had possibly something to do with Sylvia Llewelyn Davies, the mother of the five boys who played such a vital role in Barrie's life, who was dying of cancer. Barrie clearly believed that Scott had said something against a close friend of his, and the coincidence of dates suggests that Sylvia, to whom Barrie claimed he was engaged, is the most likely candidate. She died on 27 August 1910, while Scott was still in South Africa on his way to the Antarctic.

She would not be the first newly married woman to take against her husband's friends, but this is a clash of temperaments rather than owner-ship rights, because if anyone can be acquitted of jealousy or possessiveness it is Kathleen. Wilson was "a prig," she told James Lees-Milne more than thirty years later—not "rotten; bad blood and no good at all" like Shackle-ton, perhaps—but "just like a private school boy with no humour whatever. He was a good-looking, honest fellow whom simple sailors could not see through. Mrs. Wilson is still alive, and K. described her as a drab female."

With the *Saxon* beating *Terra Nova* down to the Cape by more than a fortnight, however, there was at least a brief chance to forget the voyage and escape both wives and husbands. Scott had originally decided to stop in South Africa to see what funds could be got there, but while that proved largely unsuccessful, the compensation was a sort of delayed honeymoon in the company of a wife who could still bring to everything they did together that spontaneity, irreverence and *zest* that he had first loved her for. "Met their excellencies Dolly and Herbert Gladstone. To him one made a royalty-bob but she however kissed me . . . Con gave a lecture Lord Gladstone in the chair, & Bishop . . . a most engaging creature—a merry thing to meet of a rainy day . . . went to Con's lecture—arrangements abominable—a screen for the slides the size of a pocket handkerchief & light about one candle power. Very nearly a fiasco . . . Mr. Beresford a pathetic unhappy thoughtful creature, the son of a blind Irish parson & a mother who went mad. He has such bad manners poor boy, & an unbal-anced mind, but we had to become undying friends. I felt the waste of him & an anxiety to be kind . . ."

Scott and Kathleen left Cape Town for Pretoria on 11 August with the Egertons, travelling free "in great luxury . . . & in special sitting room car-riage" across a landscape that had not seen rain in five months. At night they would watch the glow of fires from their carriage, spellbound by the violence of the storms and "lightening [sic] more beautiful than I had ever seen. Con & I sat by the open window far into the darkness watching it."

After a visit down a goldmine, they were back in Cape Town by the twenty-second, where they finally caught up with news of *Terra Nova*. Kathleen had dreamed on the night of the thirteenth that the ship would come in at sundown on the fifteenth, and was delighted to be proved right. "Everybody was charmingly enthusiastic about every one else," a slightly sceptical Kathleen recorded; "only two were not regarded as perfect mar-vels, it will be interesting to see how they turn out—one I didn't think any-thing of when he came to dine in London the other I thought clever."

For the most part these marvels came from two distinct spheres, the one Scott's own world of the Royal Navy, and the other that of Cambridge science. To Scott's great regret, health, and possibly an imminent engagement, had forced Barne to drop out from the expedition, but the Admiralty had been more generous to a captain with a name and reputation than they had been to an unknown commander, and alongside a comforting nucleus of old "Discoverys"—Evans, Lashly, Feather, Crean, Williamson—they had given Scott two lieutenants, the immensely able Harry Pennell as his navigator and magnetic observer, and the rather solider Henry Rennick to look after the hydrographic work. "I wish with all my heart that Pennell was not booked for the ship's cruise," Wilson had written on the voyage down, "for he would make an excellent companion for the hut . . . He gets through a perfectly extraordinary amount of work every day—always cheerful and genial and busy, but never too busy to talk birds and to be interested in other work than his own . . . Rennick will prove a splendid man for the whole show . . . a born humorist, and his humour is of the kindliest."

Another recently retired lieutenant, the Etonian Victor Campbell, the two doctors, G. Murray Levick and Edward Atkinson, the ship's engineer and twenty-six petty officers and seamen made up a strong "home" team, but it was a naval outsider, the Royal Indian Marine Lieutenant, Henry "Birdie" Bowers, who had already stolen the show. "Bowers, whom you will remember by sight," Wilson again wrote, "a short red-headed thick-set little man with a very large nose, is a perfect marvel of efficiency—but in addition to this he has the most unselfish character I have ever seen in a man anywhere."

It had not always seemed so obvious to everyone in *Terra Nova* that in their man from the "Cockroach Navy" they had found themselves what Scott would call a "treasure." The first thing Bowers had done on reporting to the ship was to fall nineteen feet through a hatch, but it did not take long for them to realise that it would require more than that to damage him. "He really was a curious person to look at," Cherry-Garrard later recalled. "When *they* first saw him in London they were all very doubtful about him. They were quite wrong . . . As soon as you knew him you saw that there was no bounce about him at all: it was all genuine and the worse things got the better Birdie became . . . Birdie had very little in the shop window: the best people seldom have; but the goods inside were pure gold."

They were right to be doubtful, because it is hard to imagine that the

British Empire has ever thrown up a more improbable hero than the beak-nosed, red-haired, twelve-stone, five-feet-four-inch part-saint and part-bigot that was "Birdie" Bowers. The son of a sea-going father who died early and a devoutly religious mother, Bowers passed out of the training ship *Worcester* into the merchant service, and from there into the Royal Indian Marine. For the next eight years he served on the Irrawaddy and in the Persian Gulf, immune, it seemed, to fear or tiredness, to ill health or ill luck—immune, in fact, to anything that the East or its native gun-runners could throw at him except spiders and those cultural and racial bigotries that were the natural birthright of the nineteenth-century Indian Marine officer.

Even at the height of the Raj, however, there can have been few better "haters" than Birdie Bowers, and fewer still with such a rich portfolio of prejudices. In a perverse kind of way he retained a soft spot for the "sausage-eaters" for having produced Martin Luther, but that was the limit of his tolerance. Bowers hated the half-caste and he hated the native. He hated the "heathen darkness" of Islam and the fetishistic, crucifix-worshipping antics of Popery. He hated the priest-ridden Irish and the idol-atrous Spanish and Portuguese. He hated the Russians and he hated the "Maccaroni." He hated the "filthy smelly creatures" he found in the Far East and the "Godless heedlessly happy, licentious, desperately wicked 'froggies'" he found in Paris. "If ever I could call a dear little kid like that my own," he wrote home of the offspring of a white father and Asian mother, "it would break my heart to feel that she wasn't 'pure.' Thank God we are white & that our parents were pure, & that we were brought up in a country where purity—at least in name—is not at a discount."*

If many of these sentiments would have found an echo across the Empire, there was another strain to Bowers's bigotry that transformed the John Bull prejudices of an Indian Marine officer into something bizarrely his own. In this same letter home he thanked his family for sending out the latest copy of *The Watch Tower* to him, and in the theology of the nine-

---

*The journey south had already added another prejudice to Bowers's list. "I am afraid there was an atmosphere of immorality that was unmistakable," he had written home from Madeira, "and as for that beast Reid"—the Reid of Reid's Hotel who had fed them, and then taken them into his study, locked the door and shown them "a collection of the filthiest & most disgustingly repulsive curiosities I could ever imagine. I never believed such things could exist & that the hand of man could be employed in constructing such depraved & crude examples of filth. To the surprise of my companions I told him straight—host or no host—that I thought it was the most disgusting exhibition I had ever seen. The mind of that man must be a cesspool."

teenth century's proto–Jehovah's Witnesses Bowers found that peculiar range of beliefs, justifications and eschatological certitudes that helped bounce the bigot into the serenely untouchable, well-nigh invincible fanatic he became. In some ways he remained to the end of his life an evangelical of the old school, with a history of temptation and personal conversion to call on, but it was this American-spawned influence that really stamped his character. In his own imagination he always saw himself as a "staunch Roundhead" riding out to battle with Oliver Cromwell, but even in "The World Turned Upside Down" that was the seventeenth century, Bowers would have been on the outside of mainstream life, at one with all those Ranters, Levellers, Muggletonians and other doomed sectaries who have always so gloriously failed to inherit the earth.

Given his eclectic range of religious and racial bigotries, in fact, he was lucky to be born into possibly the one age in European history when his opinions would not land him at the stake or in gaol. The wonderful thing about Bowers, though, was that neither prospect would have held the slightest fear for him, because alongside his evangelical's faith in Christ ran the liberating conviction that everything must all soon end in the final, imminent Battle that would signal the end of time. "No body will give a thought till their calamity comes," he wrote home from the Far East with a vengeful joy at the fate awaiting the French, "& then the [most] gay, overdressed, pleasure sodden animals ever made in the image of God—will see their hopelessly flimsy castles & hopes dashed from them finally."

It made for a powerful team—Bowers on his own would have been formidable enough, Bowers with God on his side was indomitable—but the redeeming thing about him was that there was something comfortingly theoretical about the wilder reaches of his beliefs. In the privacy of his family letters he might inhabit a world of theological and racial crankiness, but if he hated Russians in theory, no one could be kinder in practice to the two Russian boys hired to look after the expedition's animals, or readier to follow to any hell on earth a leader and companion who he knew in his theological bones must be doomed to quite another sort of Hell.*

Alongside these naval officers—Wilfred Bruce, Kathleen's favourite brother and another old *Worcester* boy completed the list—Wilson had

---

*This was not the limit of Bowers's oddities. An imperialist who looked with glad eyes to the imminent destruction of the British Empire; a patriot who had no time for his King; a little Englander who saw the Church of England as the "Daughter of the Harlot"; a naval officer who could salute a Dreadnought as the instrument of Divine Retribution—contradiction was at the heart of his character.

gathered together as impressive a group of scientists as had ever been on a polar expedition. The only man in the party who already enjoyed an international reputation was their meteorologist, George Simpson, but if subsequent distinction is any guide—there would be four "scientific knights" among them—no blend of promise and experience could have been better designed to lay, once and for all, the ghost of *Discovery* amateurism. "Dr. Simpson is known as Sunny Jim," Kathleen noted in her South African diary, more taken up with their peculiarities, however, than their competence,

> & is very keen & eager—On dit, that one day whilst dressing he was seen standing in the door of his cabin haranguing Mr. Lillie & in a complete state of nudity announcing "When I get married I shall marry a really intellectual woman."
>
> Mr. Lillie [a biologist] had measles on board which coincides with his childlike appearance, he is full of theories (including believing he was a reincarnated Persian and Roman) & has eyes of a mad child. He and I went a long walk along the beach, he taught me much . . .
>
> Nelson [another biologist] I have had no talk with. He spends all his time on shore being "a man about town," which makes him look exceedingly tired.

Three of the scientific team that Wilson had brought together were not joining the ship until New Zealand, but the wardroom was completed by the talented young Cambridge physicist Charles Wright, a young Norwegian ski instructor called Tryggve Gran, and two other supernumeraries who fitted into no obvious category. On his *Nimrod* expedition Shackleton had pioneered the employment of "paying" expedition members, and in a short-sighted, land-owning cousin of Reggie Smith called Apsley Cherry-Garrard, and a thirty-year-old cavalry officer, Lawrence Oates, Scott found himself two men happy to donate £1,000 of their own money for the privilege of suffering with him in the ice.

In many ways the most intriguing of all these men is "Cherry"—the future interpreter, historian and conscience of the expedition—but in terms of Scott's life and reputation the only man who can stand alongside "Birdie" Bowers is "Titus" Oates. With the possible exception of Scott himself there is no one in polar history so wholly obscured by legend as "the Soldier," but if it can sometimes seem difficult to square the Oates of

mythology and Dollman's famous painting with the Oates of his own letters and history, it is some comfort to know it would have been as great a
puzzle in these early days of the expedition to his shipmates.

There was clearly a laconic good-humour about him, as well as great
courage, that made him a popular messmate from the first, but Wilson
cannot have been the only man in *Terra Nova* charitably to assume that
there *must* be more to Oates than met the eye. In recent years he has
become a kind of stick with which to beat the poor repressed Scott, but
all surviving evidence suggests that it was not so much a matter of social
ease or indifference to "appearances" that separated the two men, as a fundamental gulf in intelligence between a naval officer interested in everything and a cavalry captain whose emotional and intellectual life revolved
around his dogs, horses and regiment.

And of all the eight thousand applicants for the expedition, none can
have come with such slender credentials for the ice. A sickly, suburban
childhood, a brief spell at Eton, and a brief but brutal war in South Africa
that earned him a shattered leg, a Mention in Despatches and the soubri-
quet of "No Surrender Oates" had been followed by a decade of garrison
soldiering, manoeuvres, polo and pig-sticking that was only ended by the
"call" to the south. "I have now a great confession to make," he wrote to his
formidably unattractive mother from Delhi, spelling and geography
equally insecure. "I offered my services to the Antarctic Expedition that
starts this summer from home under Scott, they wrote and told me to produced [sic] my referrances [sic] which I did and they appear to have been
so flattering that I have been practically accepted . . . Scott . . . appears to
be a man who can make up his mind and having decided he told me at
once . . . Points in favour of going. It will help me professionally as in the
army if they want a man to wash labels off bottles they would sooner
employ a man who had been to the North Pole than one who has only got
as far as the Mile End Road. The job is most suitable to my tastes Scott is
almost certain to get to the Pole and it is something to say you were with
the first party. The climate is very healthy although inclined to be cold."

There is a tolerance extended to the conjunction of wealth and birth
that is shown to no one else, and if this attitude would have seemed less
engaging in an engineer or paymaster, in a cavalry officer it went down a
treat. "We had pictured a smartly-turned out young cavalry officer," Teddy
Evans recalled of their first sighting of Oates at the Victoria Street expedition office, "with hair nicely brushed up and neat moustache. Our future
companion turned up with a bowler characteristically on the back of his

head and a very worn Aquascutum buttoned up closely round his neck, hiding his collar, and showing a strong, clean-shaven, weather beaten face with kindly brown eyes indicative of his fine personality. 'I'm Oates,' he said."

It was the same at the West India Docks, where no one could "make out who or what he was when he came on board." Tom Crean remembered, "We never for a moment thought he was an officer for they were usually so smart! We made up our minds he was a farmer, he was always so nice and friendly, just like one of ourselves, but oh! He was a gentleman, quite a gentleman, and always a gentleman!"

With the exception of the old "Discoverys" and Simpson, who had only been prevented by the medical board from joining the first expedition, most of these men were little more than names to Scott, and so instead of going on to Melbourne separately he decided to sail out in the *Terra Nova*. It is possible that he already felt he should have been with her from the first, but if he did there was no criticism of Evans implied. "I was very glad," Kathleen wrote, "we felt"—and that "we" is as suggestive as her "simple sailors"—"that he ought to be with his Expedition, & it was very lucky that it was possible. The Evanses were much upset at this decision fearing it would look as tho' he had not been sufficiently capable, but this was more petty of them than was their wont. Con was unaware of this foolish sentiment, & would never have dreamt of crediting them with it."

Scott could not have been more pleased, in fact, with the job Evans had done or with the atmosphere he and Wilson had created in the ship. "I have never seen a more enthusiastic body of people than those in *Terra Nova*," he wrote home to his mother, "and there has been a complete absence of trouble or friction. Everyone is doing so well that it is impossible to single out anyone for special praise."

At the end of a long and happy voyage in which Evans and Wilson had been the dominant figures, it was perhaps inevitable that Scott's second-in-command was not the only one upset at the change. The alteration in the plan meant that Wilson had to take his place with the wives on a liner to Australia, and there was a feeling on board the *Terra Nova* that Kathleen had had more to do with the decision than was proper. Hilda Evans was popular with everyone, but "Mrs. Scott is another sort," Bowers reported back to England. "I don't like to see women out of their provinces (don't tell May [Bowers's sister] this) Mrs. S. is very ambitious & has too much say with the expedition for my liking. She got her brother (Bruce) in against Scott's repeated refusals. She bluffed him in during the rush & worry of

Cardiff—though he is I am sure an excellent chap. In fact she may not do so but certainly she appears to influence her husband & to make this apparent is a crime."

This perhaps says as much about Bowers as it does about Kathleen, but it was clearly time that Scott was on his own ship. "Capt. Scott is another man aboard here & away from her constant suggestions & projects," Bowers went on. "We are as lively and unrestrained as ever in spite of Capt. Scott's presence. Scott is a good sort & an excellent leader though somewhat preoccupied. He makes himself one of us but yet there is a gulf fixed. I think he is a splendid 'Owner' to the show & is most observant & capable. He forgets nothing & is undoubtedly the Captain in every way. One feels that it is impossible to bluff him & that he is a good friend. There is also no doubt that he intends to have no enemies & there is an undoubted 'Out you go if you don't like it' about his manner with anybody who gets up against him. I think he is just the man to push this show off. He is a man anyhow, & one I admire. I can't help thinking that Captain Scott has made this trip suddenly to spy out the land so to speak & to find out anything & everything about everything & everybody before it is too late to make changes."

Bowers was right—over the next weeks and months the observations, judgements, criticisms and reassessments flowed from Scott's pen—but the ship remained as boisterously happy under him as it had been under Evans. "They are a capital lot of chaps on the ship with one or two exceptions," Oates wrote to his mother, catching the mood of wardroom life in *Terra Nova*. "This is the roughest mess I have been in we shout and yell at meals as we like and we have a game call Furl topgallant sails which consists in taking off each others shirts. I wonder what some of the people at home would think if they saw the whole of the afterguard with the exception of the officer of the watch yelling and tearing off each others cloths the ship rolling and the whole place a regular pandemonium." If Scott stood apart from all this, it was not in any disapproving way. " 'The Owner' has a thirst for scientific knowledge that cannot be quenched," Charles Wright, the twenty-three-year-old Cambridge physicist, wrote home to his father. "He takes no part in the sky larking—but always looks on with a grin."

But it was not all skylarking, and if Scott found *Terra Nova's* sluggish progress frustrating—she only had two speeds, Oates complained, slow and dead slow—it at least gave him the chance to work out plans for their first summer. "It was an enormous advantage for us to have our leader with us now," Evans smoothly recalled, his own disappointment at being usurped silently edited out; "his master-mind foresaw every situation so wonderfully as he unravelled plan after plan and organised our future procedure."

It was, in fact, the work of the long *Discovery* winters all over again, with the lower deck busy preparing equipment for the coming sledging season while Scott pored over his figures. "A programme was drawn up for work on arrival at McMurdo Sound or Cape Crozier, weights were calculated for the four men sledging units, sledge tables embellished with equipment weights, weekly allowances of food and fuel, with measures of quantities of each article in pannikins or spoonfuls, provisional dates were set down . . . daily ration lists constructed."

There was also a ship to sail, and as on the voyage down to South Africa, the boundaries of rank and naval status were dissolved in a classless free-for-all that reflected Wilson's influence even after he had gone. "I doubt if a class of Ladies College girls could be more unselfish in looking after each other's interests . . . even if they were all preparing for confirmation," he had written before they reached the Cape. "The way in which every one fights for the worst job is really amusing. The pump is really hard work four times a day, and the competition for it is ridiculous."

For four days in the Forties the *Terra Nova* was held up by contrary winds, but with the wind freshening again, a faint gleam of the aurora australis in the sky, and the first albatrosses caught from their stern lines, they began to make up for lost time. By 7 October they were only a thousand miles from their destination, and five days later, after a savage hammering from hailstones inches in diameter, they came up on the tide in a strong blow and pitch dark into Melbourne harbour, and dropped anchor half a mile from the lightship. "I don't think that things could really be fairly better," Cherry reported back to Reggie Smith. "We have had a splendid trip across from the Cape, it was a great thing Scott coming with us. He seems more than pleased."

And soon adding to his pleasure was Kathleen. Wilson had tried to stop her from going out to the ship, but after a month of Hilda Evans that had reduced her to a "monomania" of women-hating, she was not listening to anyone. "So as I insisted," she wrote bellicosely in her diary,

> the other women must needs come too. Bill was furious with me & protested, the women were cold & hungry. It was very dark & very wet & humours were questionable; but I knew my

man would expect me & in spite of a very difficult opposition I persisted—the little motor launch pitched and heaved horribly but I was far too excited to be sea-sick & it didn't occur to me to be frightened. Bill taunted me through the journey making me feel that the elements & everything else was all my fault, but I wouldn't have him turn back . . . At last we arrived at the ship, & as we came along the weather side our little launch got in a bad swell & the ladies thought it was capsizing, & wanted to return without going to the ship, but I had heard my good man's voice & was sure there was no danger so insisted, getting momentarily more unpopular. Bill said it would be very dangerous to go alongside in this swell but the launch man thought it all right, so after much toing and froing we at last got close to the beautiful Terra Nova with our beautiful husbands on board. The relief of getting back to some folk who understood one was more than can be written about. The others stayed in the launch but I went on board & Mr.'s Campbell and Rennick were so nice & I went down to the wardroom so snug it looked, filled with beaming brown faces & pipes—A cheery scene after the hours of coldness & churlishness. So I went to Con's & Teddy's cabin for they had all but finished changing to come ashore with us & I changed my drenched stockings with a pair of Con's socks, & so ashore—a very happy meeting.

Less happily, there was also a telegram waiting for Scott. "Madeira. Am going south, AMUNDSEN," it read.

Twenty-four: Challenges

Acquiring knowledge involves the reduction of ignorance ... But an unexpected fact is less readily absorbed than one which was expected. If this seems less than crystal clear, consider the following example, cast in a suitable military context. The message in this case consists of an intelligence report which states: "Enemy preparing for counter-attack ..."

Now this message, factually so simple, contains amounts of information which differ greatly from commander to commander. To General A, who anticipated such a counter-attack ... it merely confirms a hypothesis which he already held ... In the case of General B ... It reduced a great deal of ignorance and uncertainty. It gave him plenty to occupy his mind and much to do.

Finally, we have General C, for whom the message was so totally unexpected that he chose to ignore it, with disastrous results. It conflicted with his preconceptions. It clashed with his wishes ... Like British generals after the Battle of Cambrai, or American generals before the counter-offensive in the Ardennes in 1944, he ignored it at his cost. Its information-content was just too high for his channel of limited capacity.

NORMAN DIXON, *On the Psychology of Military Incompetence*

I decided long ago to do exactly as I should have done had Amundsen not been down here. If he gets to the Pole, he is bound to do it rapidly with dogs, but one guesses that success will justify him, and that our venture will be "out of it." If he fails, he ought to hide. Anyway, he is taking a big risk, and perhaps deserves his luck if he gets through.

SCOTT, *28 October 1911*

Of all the names that Scott might have expected to see at the bottom of that telegram, Amundsen's was the last. On the day that Scott was receiving the drunken endorsement of Petty Officer Evans in Cardiff, Amundsen was at sea and a week into ocean trials—as Scott and the rest of the world believed—before he took the *Fram* into the Arctic and towards the North Pole to complete Nansen's work.

Just four years younger than Scott, Roald Amundsen was born in 1872 into a Norwegian seafaring dynasty, the son of a prosperous captain and

ship-owner who had made his first money in the profits to be had by a
canny neutral during the Crimean War. By the time he was fifteen
Amundsen had decided that he was going to be an explorer, and at an age
when Scott was still perfecting his torpedo drills in *Majestic* and worrying
over his sister's dressmaking business, Amundsen already had his master's
licence and the first winter ever spent in Antarctica, as a member of the
Belgica expedition, under his belt.

In 1905 Amundsen became the first man to conquer the North-West
Passage, and as Norway's natural heir to Nansen, the *Fram* and the North
Pole seemed his for the asking. Preparations for a polar drift of the kind
Nansen had so brilliantly pioneered were well under way, too, when in
September 1909—the same month that Scott publicly launched his own
Antarctic bid—news reached Amundsen that his old friend and *Belgica*
shipmate, Dr. Frederick Cook, had reached the Pole. Within a week Peary,
too, was claiming the "Damned Old Pole" after twenty-three years of trying, and with the world immediately dividing over the probity of their rival
claims, the North Pole as a viable target for an ambitious, commercially
driven man like Amundsen was gone. As the rows raged in the press over
Cook and Peary, Amundsen searched for an alternative goal that might
have the same public allure, and within days of Peary's announcement had
turned his eyes to the south.

It was certainly an inconvenience for Amundsen that Scott's hat was
already in the ring, but nothing to the problem he had with the fact that
the *Fram* and all the public and private funding for his expedition was
bespoke for scientific work in the Arctic. With breathtaking audacity, however, he continued to talk piously of science and the north and began to
plan for the south, reaffirming in public his commitment to polar science
and in deep secrecy plotting a raid on the South Pole that could bring him
the financial reward that the North-West Passage had failed to deliver.
Almost no one was in on his secret; not Nansen, not Scott, who had in all
innocence sent Amundsen instruments for comparative recordings in the
north and south, not even his own crew, when at midnight on 6–7 June—
Norwegian Independence Day—the *Fram* slipped quietly away from her
mooring and headed for Madeira and then a non-stop voyage to the
Ross Sea.

If there was no name on that telegram that could have more surprised
Scott, there was certainly none that could have been more disturbing. In
terms of courage or audacity men like Scott and Shackleton were the
equals of anyone, but in all the disciplines, skills and attitudes that made

the polar *traveller*, and that were almost second nature to a Norwegian, Amundsen simply belonged to a different league. It is not just that a Scott could not compete on those terms, but rather that there was no way in which he possibly could have done, because skiing as Amundsen and his men could ski was not the skill of a week or a month or even a year, was not something that could be picked up on the job, or learned on an ice floe on the way down to the south. It is unarguable that British expeditions did not help their cause by recruiting from the Irrawaddy and the Indian *maidan*, but even with the most technically accomplished party that Scott or any other British leader could have put together, there was no chance that any "race" against as skilled and ruthlessly single-minded an opponent as Amundsen could end in anything but defeat.

There might have been people in Britain who did not see this, but Scott was not fool enough to be one of them, and that is what makes the events of the next few days so fascinating. For any leader—as Norman Dixon insists—there will always be a thousand variables influencing and distorting the way in which a message is received, but what if, as he asks, the information that it contains is so at odds with every preconception and wish, so completely contrary to every institutional or personal value system and prejudice, so potentially and profoundly disruptive of every carefully worked-out plan? The history of British—and not just British—military disasters of the "authoritarian" type explored by Dixon, is littered with examples of the kind of non-answer that Dixon's "General C" gives to the question. It would certainly be unfair to Scott to lump him in here with all the "C"s from the Crimea to Cambrai who have bedevilled British arms, and yet there is something so profoundly odd about his reception of the news of Amundsen's challenge that it defies any alternative explanation.

There is a variant here on the dog that did not bark, because—to borrow a famous phrase of Kathleen Scott's—"a strange thing happened" when Scott got the telegram, and that strange thing was that nothing happened at all. For as long as he had been planning his expedition he had worked to his own pace and on his own terms, and now, at the very last moment, when every potential threat had been seen off or died of its own inadequacy, came a challenge from the last suspected direction, which seems to have reduced him to something like denial.

Faced with a man uninterested in anything but the Pole, unfettered by science and unburdened by any of the gentlemanly baggage of a British explorer, there was little that Scott *could* do, but what is so odd is that the news is not even so much as mentioned in his or Kathleen's journals.

There is no way of knowing if they talked over their public response between themselves, but if it is unsurprising that it did not find its way into Scott's diary, it seems astonishing that the news is not there in the partisan, garrulous and impassioned pages of her journal.

If the news seems to have been too crushing, too disorientating, too utterly impossible to be processed properly, though, the usual suspects were predictably less reticent. "I have had a long letter from Norway about Amundsen," Markham wrote to Keltie three days after Scott received his telegram.

> He got the loan of the "Fram" [the specially designed ship in which Nansen had deliberately drifted across the Arctic, locked in the ice, in his bid for the North Pole] from the Government and all the subscriptions, for the North Polar drift. He pretended to be going out to Madeira in the "Fram" to see how she behaved, then coming back to raise more money, and to join the "Fram" at San Francisco. But he had quietly got a wintering hut made and on board 100 dogs from Greenland, and a supply of tents and sledges. His secret design must have been nearly a year old.
>
> They believe that his mention of Punta Arenas and Buenos Ayres is merely a blind, and that he is going to McMurdo Sound to try and cut out Scott . . .
>
> Shackleton's rush and failure was a very dirty trick, more especially as he owed everything to Scott and would never have been heard of if Scott had not befriended him.
>
> Amundsen's is a very dirty trick, but not so bad as he owes nothing to Scott. I have sent full details of Amundsen's underhand conduct to Scott, hoping it may reach him before he sails . . . I always thought Master Shackles was a cad, but I confess I was taken by Amundsen and was under the impression that he was a straight forward and very able sailor. I am afraid Nansen and Johansen were in it but I hope not. If I was Scott I would not let them land, but he is always too good natured.

"What rascals these poles are producing," Markham exclaimed in another letter to Keltie, and if there was some truth in that, at least Nansen can be exonerated. The night he had watched the *Fram* leave Norway had been in some ways the bitterest moment of his life, but it would have been worse still if he had known she was bound on a journey that he had always seen as his destiny to achieve. "And when you pass judgement on me, Herr Professor," Amundsen had written from sea, conscious of how his systematic and drawn-out act of deception must look to the man who had given him his blessing, "do not be too severe. I have taken the only path that seemed open, and now events will just have to take their course."

The one consolation for Amundsen's British critics was that the *Fram* was never built with the southern ocean in mind, and might simply "turn turtle" and sink. "I think the 'Fram' sailed from Madeira on Oct 6," Markham assured Keltie with all his old, misplaced confidence. "She has no more sailing qualities than a haystack, not having been built for that, and I doubt her even reaching the Ross Sea in time."

With nothing but that single bald telegram to go on, however, Scott was even more in the dark than they were in London. He did not even know at this early stage where Amundsen was bound for, and Gran, the wealthy, young, engaging and posturing Norwegian ski instructor Nansen had steered his way, could shed no light on his countryman's plans. Nor, it seemed, could Nansen himself. "Amundsen seems to be acting very mysteriously," Scott wrote to Keltie, "but I can't believe he is going to McMurdo Sound—I wired to ask Nansen, his reply was 'unknown' from which I conclude that he has not thought fit to even inform his supporters in Norway in respect to his intentions—Well we shall know in due course I suppose."

In the meantime, there was nothing to do but get on with the job of dragging money out of the government that had brought him to Australia in the first place. "Lunch with minister," Kathleen noted as one of the constant stream of engagements in her diary. "Mayor's ball . . . Ministers lunched on Terra Nova . . . State Gov. came to see ship." Kathleen was in her element. Even the sight of "Captain Wemyss bearing slight sign of overnight drunkenness" could not spoil the pleasure of being the only woman at a dinner in *Powerful* given by Admiral Poore. "That was a beautiful outing, a lovely moonlight night, an open Admiral's launch, a very nice party of men & myself—All parties should be like that!" Missing the last train back to their hotel, Scott and Kathleen were faced with a long walk, "but it was very pleasant, & we discussed the future from my own little feminine point of view, which was pleasant."

Scott was immensely proud of Kathleen, and pleased to see her so popular, and these weeks in South Africa and Australia seem to have been as contented as any they ever shared. After five days in Melbourne they travelled on to Sydney with George Simpson, watching through the night the bushfires burning close up to the railway line, and the blazing trunks of gum trees, standing in the darkness, Kathleen thought, like "sad and fiery . . . giants." There was a reception party waiting at the station for them, led by Professor Edgeworth David, who at the age of fifty-four had reached the South Magnetic Pole on Shackleton's *Nimrod* expedition. Kathleen found it almost impossible to believe that this "frail & old" look-ing man dressed in "his seediest old top hat & frock coat" could ever have done so remarkable a journey, but Scott and his expedition could have had no better friend in Australia. "He is wonderful," a grateful Scott enthused in his diary, "full of fine enthusiasm unsparing in efforts to help—palpably honest & sincere—simply & openly religious—a great heart carried with great dignity—a really splendid personality." And with the federal govern-ment reluctant to part with its money, Scott needed all the friends he could find. He had hoped initially that it would match the £5,000 dona-tion it had made to Shackleton, but even with a rival Japanese expedition to stir national and Imperial juices, £2,500—£2,000 more than the paltry £500 South Africa had voted—was all that he could get.

On the day that he and Kathleen arrived in Sydney a petition was pro-posed to raise this to £5,000, and the next day his financial luck finally changed. "Dined with Lord Mayor," Scott noted in his diary. "Excellent dinner. David proposed my health in a fine speech full of his fine enthusi-astic personality . . . My reply was poor enough—then to everyone's sur-prise Mr. Sam Hordern got up and after stating that David had convinced him as to the usefulness of the enterprise said that if the Government could not see its way to make up the extra £2500 required he would do so—a splendid round up to the evening." "Isn't it fine of him?" Scott wrote to another supporter the following day. "Of course we have to be very silent about this until we know what the Government intends. We would like to tell the young man we need his £2,500 anyhow, but we don't like to do that."

If the endless begging for funds was not bad enough, there was also the press to deal with, and the inevitable speeches. "His pictures were admirable," Kathleen noted on 20 October, after a lecture in a great, echo-ing barn of a hall, "but the noise of passing trams & general bad acoustics made it impossible to hear him from the back of the hall, he therefore moved & stood on a table in the middle of the Hall, but this tho' an improvement made it difficult for the Governor etc in the front. However Con was noble."

Two days later Scott and Kathleen sailed together from Melbourne for

Wellington in the "wretchedly uncomfortable" *Warimmoo*. From the moment they reached open sea Kathleen suffered from her usual violent sea-sickness, and "the only pleasant recollection" of five days of misery on the open boat deck "was the beautiful way my dear man nursed me."

The voyage to Wellington marks a dividing line in Kathleen's journal, however, because almost alone among the collections of diaries and letters to come out of Scott's expeditions, hers is less than enthusiastic about New Zealand. She was perfectly able to see how kind everyone was to them, but if there wasn't a "pathetic little meteorological parson" in Wellington to irritate her, there were a "rotten mayoral function" and a "stuffy little house" in Christchurch to bring home how dully provincial she found New Zealand and its inhabitants. "They were very kind but I felt stifled," she was complaining of her hosts after only a day there, and a move to the home of some old friends of Scott's only took her "out of the frying pan into the fire." "Mrs. Rhodes is kind and sweet," she conceded, "but the atmosphere of the house is physically & mentally bad—no air & petty scandal & nothing more . . . Con & I were paraded & dissatisfied & things went badly."

Kathleen was as unlikely to take to Christchurch and its provincialism as she was to Hilda Evans, but there were other tensions that had not been there in South Africa or Australia. Just before one dance given for them, Scott had come in with a letter for her from a Mr. Hull, a young "boy" with a romantic devotion to all womanhood, whom she had befriended on the passage over from the Cape. "He didn't like it," she wrote in her diary, "& it certainly did read stupidly, but I was not going to spoil the evening on account of this tiresome mistake. I danced till the end . . . & enjoyed it enormously. Con took my word. If he had not I don't know what might happen as it is I don't think I shall ever lie to Con in all my life."

There were rather different—if familiar—problems, too, with the *Terra Nova*, which had been brought down by Evans to dry dock in Lyttelton. Scott had rejoined his ship to find that his old *Discovery* boatswain, Feather, had been insubordinate to Rennick, and after giving himself two days to weigh up the incident, decided that "he must go." "Mr. Feather is leaving us here, not going any further," Lashly reported back to his old boss Skelton; "there was a bit of friction between him and Mr. Renwick [sic] but really the truth is too much drink this happened the day of our arrival here."

There was another casualty when Scott discharged the ship's engineer, Lieutenant Riley—the one man on the voyage down who had not proved a

"Sahib," as Bowers put it—but compensating for these irritations was the safe arrival of the expedition animals. The motorised sledges, with their revolutionary caterpillar tracks, had offered Scott some encouragement on the final Norwegian trials, but long before *Terra Nova* had reached the ice they had been relegated to a subordinate role in a tripartite transport scheme that depended principally on a combination of ponies and dogs. There had never been anything erroneous in Scott's first, visionary hopes for motorised sledges—he was, as so often, ahead of his time—but the presence of ponies in this plan was another matter. During the first winter in *Discovery* Armitage had vigorously advocated their use, and while one might have thought that that alone would have been enough to damn them in Scott's eyes, their use by Shackleton on the *Nimrod* expedition had planted the idea that they were the answer to the Southern Journey and the Pole.

The principal objection to their use, of course, was that while dogs could live off the land in Antarctica, every mouthful ponies ate would have to be taken down in the *Terra Nova* with them. In deep soft snow or any heavily crevassed area their weight and immobility had inevitably proved a drawback, too, while their vulnerability to the extremes of Barrier conditions would effectively mean that any sledging season Scott planned would have to be delayed till almost a month after it could begin with dogs.

When Scott decided on the use of ponies, he did not know that Amundsen's presence would make that last factor of crucial importance, and yet even so the Shackleton precedent was a curious one to have followed. At the back of his mind he seems to have confused a coincidence of ponies and success for a causal relationship, but while the way that Shackleton had publicly written up his ponies gave Scott every excuse for thinking in that way, there was precious little in Shackleton's actual experience of the creatures to bear his claims out. Pound for pound the pony might be able to drag a heavier load than the dog, but of his eight Manchurian ponies, four were dead before he left base camp, three more within a degree of latitude of Scott's own Farthest South, with only the heroic Socks surviving to plunge into the depths of a crevasse on the Beardmore. If this had somehow meant a measure of cruelty less than that involved in dog-driving there might still have been an argument, but the sanguine note in which Shackleton later addressed the issue seems bizarrely at odds with the misery and exhaustion of the animals out on the Barrier. "The killings of the ponies was not pleasant work," he wrote in a footnote to his expedition history, "but we had the satisfaction of knowing that the animals had been well fed and well treated up to the last, and that they suffered no pain. When we had to kill a pony, we threw up a snow mound to the leeward of the camp, so that no smell of blood could come down wind, and took the animal behind this, out of sight of the others. As a matter of fact, the survivors never displayed any interest at all in the proceedings."

With the unarguable evidence of times and latitudes, however, ponies must have seemed an attractive alternative to the miseries of dog-handling, and the previous January Scott had appointed a Boer War veteran and exotic "Great Gamer" called Cecil Meares with the brief of buying both the ponies and dogs. There is so little in the way of hard facts that is known of Cecil Meares—and so many gaps in his career—that he remains one of the most tantalising figures on Scott's last expedition. Born in Kilkenny, Ireland, in 1877, he was the son of an Indian Army major and a mother who died only days after his birth, and grew up a virtual orphan, a precocious and—one suspects—largely solitary boy, with a gift for languages and a weak chest, who was shuffled from school to school and boarding home to boarding home in a Kiplingesque parody of an Empire childhood.

After two years in Spain and Italy learning the languages, Meares went out to India in 1896 to take up coffee planting, but from that point on the trail is harder to follow.* In an interview he gave a Santa Barbara newspaper he claimed for himself a role with British Intelligence in the Boxer Uprising, the Boer War and the Franco-Russian War—presumably the Russo-Japanese War—but the only thing that can be fixed with much certainty is that by 1908 he was on the western frontier of Szechwan, among the semi-independent tribes of the Chinese/Tibetan border in the company of another adventurer/hunter, J.W. Brooke, "exploring and mapping this little known portion of the earth's surface [for the government in India], and . . . shooting some of the rare animals which are to be found in that part of the world."

This was Meares's favourite part of the world and—in spite of Brooke being brutally butchered by the Lolo tribesmen—his favourite people, but so long as a place was empty he was happy, and he had taken up Scott's offer with enthusiasm. "I have been kept very busy collecting dogs," he wrote in one of his rare letters to his father from his homely "c/o British

---

*Needless to say, Meares's service record is missing. At the outbreak of the First World War, though, he was with the Northumberland Hussars in the ferocious fighting of the First Battle of Ypres. By the end of the war he was in the newly created Royal Air Force, and immediately after it, seconded to the Imperial Japanese Navy as an adviser. British Intelligence records seem to contain no trace of him, though that of itself proves nothing.

Consul, Vladivostok" address, "trying teams & picking out one or two dogs and making up a team & trying it on a run of 100 miles & throwing out the dogs which do not come up to the mark . . . I expect to be back in Vladivostock [sic] by the middle of June where I will collect the ponies . . . It is a very long contract indeed to choose all these animals & carry them down to Australia single handed."

"I have arrived here so far safely with my menagerie, and they are all flourishing for the present," he was reporting again from the Caroline Islands in August. "Captain Scott's brother-in-law came out to help me," Meares went on dismissively; "he is chief officer on a P&O steamer. Quite 'one of the boys' but too 'kid glovey' for this job, he stands on the upper deck & looks on instead of taking off his coat when there is a hard job of work."

The large and easy-going Wilfred Bruce was no more taken with Meares, but it did not stop them getting the job done. "To Quail Island to see dogs and ponies," Scott noted on 31 October, after his first sight of the thirty-four sledge dogs and nineteen white Manchurian and Siberian ponies the two men had succeeded in getting down without mishap; "greatly pleased . . . think dogs finest ever got together—Meares has done his work splendidly."

The problem would not be with the dogs, however, but the ponies, who from the day they reached Lyttelton became Oates's responsibility. With the benefit of hindsight it is easy enough to see that a fluency in Hindoostani or Russian did not necessarily qualify Meares for horse-trading, but among all the prophecies of doom that Oates would send out over the next twelve months it is easy to forget that his first impression of the ponies was that they were all "first class."

But there was no disguising the fact that in giving him the ponies to look after, Scott had burdened him with the likely success or failure of the expedition, and responsibility was not something Oates ever wore lightly. "I don't know how long it is since I have been so anxious about anything as I am about these ponies," he wrote home to his mother a week before *Terra Nova* left Lyttelton. "Scott has left everything to me in connection with them. When I look at the stalls sometimes I think they are too small and the ponies wont go in and sometimes I think they are too big, next minute I think we shall never get them out again if we do get them in until I feel positively sick with anxiety . . . I had a great struggle with Scott about the horse forage [the argument was over quantities—thirty or forty-five tons?] he said, 'not one oz over 30 so its no use arguing' however we argued for one hour and he has given way which shows he is open to reason . . . he told me I was a something nuisance."

"If he [Amundsen] gets to the Pole first we shall come home with our tails between our legs and no mistake," he wrote home again a week later from Quail Island. "I must say we have made far too much noise about ourselves all that photographing cheering, steaming through the fleet etc: etc: is rot and if we fail it will only make us look more foolish . . . if Scott does anything silly such as underfeeding his ponies he will be beaten as sure as death."

If Oates was fretting under the pressure of responsibility, however, Bowers was blossoming. "Scott will have nothing but a straight answer & if the job is yours then you've *got* to know all about it." ". . . Captain Scott has left everything to me in the most extraordinary manner"—in fact the only shadow over Bowers's gratitude and admiration for Scott was again the presence of Kathleen in expedition affairs. "Mrs. Wilson has not been about much owing to the strained relations between Mrs. Scott & Mrs. Evans," he wrote home. "I don't know who to blame but somehow don't like Mrs. S. I don't trust her—though I have always been prepared to give her her due. Nobody likes her in the expedition & the painful silence when she arrives is the only jarring note in the whole thing. There is no secret that she runs us all now & what she says is done—through the Owner. Now nobody likes a schemer & yet she is undoubtedly one. Her brother Lt. Bruce is a nice chap in himself but again one does not like to trust to family. We all feel that the sooner we are away the better. She will go home to her small son & will sow no more discord. I am sorry for her as she has tried hard to be one of us & always does anything she can for any of us. She actually brought our initials & came down & sewed them on our winter clothes for us. Very nice of her, was it not—I wish I could like her but I am suspicious."

The tensions over Kathleen's presence overshadowed the expedition's last days in Christchurch, though it was not until she and Scott rejoined the ship at Port Chalmers that the full extent of the damage became apparent. The *Terra Nova* had finally sailed from Lyttelton on 26 November to the familiar accompaniment of blessings, speeches, "hurraying and saluting," and, followed out to the heads by a flotilla of boats, had made her way down the coast to Port Chalmers to wait for Scott, who was journeying down by train. None of the friction between the wives had been allowed to surface in these public farewells, of course, and mercifully none of it seemed to have touched Scott and Kathleen's last hours together. After leaving the ship at the heads they had made their way back on foot to Kinsey's empty house, and after breakfast the next morning with Scott's cousin, "went a happy climb over the hills . . . A good merry day for our last alone."

The next morning they were up early to catch the train, and although travelling with Wilson, "had a reserved carriage and stayed alone. A nice little journey we were happy & good all the way," Kathleen wrote, "till on the wharf met the Evanses both in a tearful condition. Apparently she had been working him up to insurrection, & a volley of childish complaints was let fly. Such as that Con had cut his wife's dance! & many others too puerile to recount, & that therefore he must retire. If ever Con has another expedition the wives must be chosen more carefully than the men, or better still have none. There is not a vestige of doubt that Mrs. Evans is the root of most such troubles, poor little ignorant one. Once away from her the poor little man was soon brought to order." In Scott's own diary there is nothing but a rather puzzled reference to this. "Found all well," he wrote on the same day, after he had rejoined the ship at Port Chalmers, "excepting [Teddy] Evans—he much excited with very vague & wild grievances . . . the cause of all this not difficult to guess—smoothed him down."

The one reasonable grievance that Scott was willing to concede Teddy Evans involved PO Evans, who had got drunk and disgraced himself at Lyttelton, but Scott's leniency towards him was no more than a side issue. "Mrs. Scott and Mrs. Evans have had a magnificent battle," Oates reported home. "They tell me it was a draw after 15 rounds, Mrs. Wilson flinging herself into the fight after the [first] 10 rounds and there was more blood and hair flying about the hotel than you would see in a Chicago slaughter house in a month the husbands got a bit of the backwash and there is a certain amount of coolness which I hope they won't bring into the hut with them."

Bowers was both more heated and more explicit, and his long letter home is the closest anyone is likely to get to the substance of Evans's "childish complaints." "Only one cloud marred our happy horizon," he wrote when the *Terra Nova* was finally on her way south, and beyond the reach of Kathleen's influence,

> and that was one which looking back dated from my earliest connections with the expedition. I did not understand then as I do now the lengths one woman jealous of another can go to. It came as a rude shock & as I am not keen on scandalizing I must

["not"—a very Freudian omission from the most inveterately gossipy enemy of gossip aboard] say too much. To start with I like Mrs. Scott & admit her many excellent qualities—for myself I can honestly say she has been kindness always . . . invited herself to tea with me over & over again . . . For all this I feel she has done me proud & I should be the last person to crab her on that account. Mrs. Evans is a person apart—in my esteem—She is not my style in most ways but for a womanly woman of remarkable beauty & general charm she stands out of the crowd as almost everything a wife should be. Unfortunately her excellent qualities have laid her open to much jealousy & that's where the trouble has been between Scott & his second-in-command. If you knew as I do how Teddy Evans has upheld his leader through thick & thin you would marvel when the hand of Mrs. S can be seen in Scott's coming out with us from the Cape (owing to Evans's unbounded popularity) & Wilson—the one man to pour oil—removed. In minor ways the influence of the petticoat has raised that uneasy feeling among a party of men whose loyalty was otherwise irrefutable. The hand behind Capt S. could be seen in many minor ways not against anybody but at Mrs. E through Teddy. Finally as if Evans might make a dash for the Pole this season in Scott's absence on the ship—S. has announced his intention of going on the Depot journeys with us. The Pole this year is of course out of the question but it was a slur on Evans's honesty to do that & it was the last straw in the heavy load that broke the camel's back & then the beast fell. Through it all Teddy has never criticised the Owner or run down his wife on the contrary he has been wonderful in his loyalty . . . [but] it was no marvel to us that after the continuing thrusting back of her husband— the man who had made the Expedition—he announced privately to us that he intended to resign unless a clear understanding was established and certain demands acceded to. I never saw a man so determined to throw up all his hopes as Evans was then & rank feeling spread rapidly. May it never be known how very nearly the "Terra Nova" came to not sailing at the last few hours. With hearts like lead we all went like children to that Man among men, the quiet unselfish & retiring Dr. Wilson. "Our Bill" was the turning point & nobly he did his duty. Things were undecided when with hearts far from gay we went to dance on our last night. A Mrs. Edmund had got this up for us . . . I was very half-hearted about filling a programme at all considering my already formed determination — However Mrs. Wilson came over & simply said "All's well" & without a word made for her husband & shook him so violently by the hand that our hostess must have thought us funny. Of course the Expedition could not have sailed without Teddy & Scott like the sensible man he is saw that the feminine affair had gone too far. With the aid of "Bill" point by point things were settled & though no mention of the occasion has been made since we all saw the good it did. Evans is ever-full of keenness and bubbling over with life & energy, Scott all smiles and more one of us than ever before . . . How petty it seems, does it not? — when one thinks of the spirit of us all towards each other — never was a happier selection for mutual good feeling in any ship that ever sailed on a difficult enterprise & yet how nearly all that was destroyed.

It is hard to know what to make of this — equally impossible to see it as fabrication or to accept it as cold truth — but if it is in any way right that the expedition was nearly aborted, it paints an extraordinary picture of these last days in New Zealand. It is such utter nonsense that Evans might have been suspected of "jumping" Scott for the Pole that it is tempting to dismiss the rest with it, but the well-nigh Petrine guilt Bowers felt at his own complicity suggests that the suspicions and animosity were real enough.

"Smoothed him down" was Scott's final, laconic word on Evans's outburst, and if it marked a break of trust that was never fully healed, both men were sensible enough to patch things over. That night Kathleen left the dinner and ball at which there had been such dramas "bored at both," but the next day, after a morning spoiled by the memory of Evans's "tantrums" and a final picnic lunch together, she and Scott walked the last part of the way out to the ship to find Evans "quite recovered" — "told me a string of lies or hot air & I believe as he told lies he believed them," she wrote in her diary, perversely contrary to the very last moments of her brief marriage, "he's a rum little beggar, but there's something very attractive about [him]."

As at Lyttelton, the wives accompanied the *Terra Nova* as far as the heads, where they left her to join a returning brig. "I didn't say goodbye to my man because I didn't want anyone to see him sad & I know enough," Kathleen wrote. For once, too, as the *Terra Nova* made her way out into open sea, the old animosities between the women were momentarily submerged in a sense of mutual loss: "On the bridge of the brig Mrs. Evans looked ghastly white & said she wanted to have hysterics, but instead we both took photos of the departing ship."

It was the last Kathleen and Scott ever saw of each other. Their last fortnight together, after they had exchanged the Rhodeses' home and the flat contours of Christchurch for a small house on Summer Hill and nights sleeping in the garden, had restored her to her pagan best, but it would have been odd if there had not been a small sigh of relief. Scott loved her as deeply as he had ever done. She loved him too, at last, probably just as fully. There feels, however, something immensely fragile about their relationship. Distance, that had once bedevilled their marriage, was now perhaps its making. In the ice Scott could trudge across the Barrier sustained by a vision of Kathleen's bravery and vitality, untroubled by awkward reality. And for her part, safe back in her own world, her "simple sailor" could resume the heroic proportions the last hours in New Zealand had almost done so much to threaten.

Twenty-five: Return to the Ice

What an exasperating game this is!

SCOTT, 1910

It was hardly surprising that Hilda Evans wanted to have hysterics. If the *Terra Nova* had left Cardiff deep in the water under her load, she was now scarcely recognisable as a ship at all. "There is no deck visible," Cherry later wrote of her, sliding almost unconsciously into the present tense as the image of the *Terra Nova* and the voyage south asserted itself. "In addition to 30 tons of coal in sacks on deck there are 2½ tons of petrol, stowed in drums which in turn are cased in wood. On the top of the sacks and cases, and on the roof of the ice-house are thirty-three dogs, chained far enough apart to keep them from following their instinct . . . In the forecastle and in the four stalls on deck are the nineteen ponies, wedged tightly in their wooden stalls, and dwarfing everything are the three motor sledges in their huge crates, 16' × 5' × 4', two of them on either side of the main hatch, the third across the break of the poop."

With every inch below deck similarly crammed, the ship had become a floating hymn to maritime irregularities and Bowers's ingenuity. If it had solely been a matter of comfort this would not have mattered to anyone, but with some of the roughest seas in the world ahead of them, a man did not have to be a sailor to recognise that the chances of even reaching the pack were going to depend as much on luck as judgement or seamanship. He did not have to be a Scott, either, to curl up in shame at the "picture of dejection" their wretched animals made on the upper deck. The dogs had been given what scant cover there was among the coal sacks and packing cases, but with the seas continually breaking over the weather bulwarks and the spray drenching the decks, their only protection was to sit chained with their backs to the weather, a miserable and whining reproach to science and ambition.

The condition of Oates's ponies, crammed into their stalls, "swaying, swaying continually in the lunging, irregular motion," seemed scarcely better. "One takes a look through the hole in the bulkhead," Scott wrote with all the old guilt of his *Discovery* days, "and sees a row of heads with sad, patient eyes come swinging up together from the starboard side, while those on the port swing back; then up come the port heads while the starboard recede. It seems a terrible ordeal for these poor beasts to stand this day after day."

The only solace Scott could offer himself was that their "trial could not be gauged from human standards," but with many of the men sick, and their photographer Herbert Ponting at work with a developing dish in one hand and an ordinary basin in the other, human standards in *Terra Nova* were nothing to envy. The ship had been crowded enough on the first leg of the journey down to South Africa, but with the addition of Meares and Bernard Day, their motor-sledge engineer, and their three last scientists—Raymond Priestley and the Australians "Griff" Taylor and Frank Debenham—there were now not even seats enough to sit Scott's officers in the wardroom.

It was not long, however, before Scott would be glad for every hand they had available, and forty-eight hours out of Port Chalmers the winds had already begun to freshen, the seas rise, and, most ominously of all, the deck cargo shift. The cases had been stowed and lashed with all of Bowers's scrupulous care, but as the *Terra Nova* began to rear and plunge and the water crash over the lee rail, the loose coal bags became inertly alive, swinging with the destructive force of "battering rams" against the packing cases until they had ripped them free of their lashings.

For hour after hour through the night, in mountainous seas, officers and men fought a hopeless battle against "the evil," and it was grimmer still in the stalls. From the moment that the gale had broken Oates had been in with the ponies, struggling to keep them on their feet, fighting to save their lives and with them the expedition. "I can't remember having a

worse time," he told his mother. "The motion up in the bows was very violent . . . I was drenched all night, the water continually forcing the skylight
up and pouring over the fo'castle in a regular torrent. During the night one
pony was down as many as eight times and I was unfortunate to have two
killed."

One of the ponies had broken a leg, and the other was cast so badly it
could not be got up without help, but "Worse was to follow," Scott wrote,
"much worse." They had shortened sail to main topsail and staysail,
stopped engines and hove about, "but to little purpose." Down in the
engine room the pumps had choked, and nothing that Lashly—up to his
neck in rushing water trying to clear the suctions—could do to stem the
rising flood made any difference. For a moment it might look as though
the donkey engine and bilge pump could contain the situation, but "hope
was short lived; five minutes of pumping invariably led to the same
result—a general choking of the pumps. It looked grim . . . the decks were
leaking in streams. The ship was very deeply laden; it did not need the
addition of much water to get her waterlogged, in which condition anything might have happened. The hand pump produced only a dribble,
and its suctions could not be got at; as the water crept higher it got in contact with the boiler and grew warmer—so hot at last that no one could
work at the surface."

Things for the moment "seemed very black." The seas were now higher
than ever, and with most of the lee bulwark gone, washed across the decks
unchecked, submerging the ship from forerigging to the main in a solid
sheet of curling water that swept "like a young Niagara" across the poop
and "over the engine room floor plates." Smashed cases, washing backwards and forwards, took on a dangerous life of their own. Lashings
snapped the moment they were resecured. In the stalls the ponies were
flung helplessly about. On the decks dogs were picked up on a wall of
water, only to be left hanging as it flowed back, drowning, choking and
strangling on their own chains.

"I never wish to see a greater abomination of desolation," Frank Debenham, the young geologist, wrote of that night. The one hope for the ship
was to get the pumps working again, but with the seas still mounting it was
impossible to get at the pump-well through the after-hatch to free them.
After a consultation with Scott, Evans ordered a hole to be cut in the
engine-room bulkhead, while in the meantime a half-naked, retching,
shanty-singing, bucket-bailing chain of men tried to contain the situation.
"It was a sight that one could never forget," Evans remembered, "every-

body saturated, some waist-deep on the floor of the engine room, oil and coal dust mixing with the water and making everyone filthy, some men clinging to the iron ladder-way and passing full buckets long after their muscles had ceased to work naturally, their grit and spirit keeping them going." "If Dante had seen our ship as she was at our worst," Priestley wrote in his diary, "I fancy he would have got a good idea for another Circle of Hell, though he would have been at a loss to account for such a ribald and cheerful lot of Souls."

It was at least light now, and by 10 a.m. the hole in the engine-room bulkhead was cut. Evans wriggled through first, followed by Bowers, Nelson and Davies, the carpenter. Tearing down some planks to get at the shaft, Evans lowered himself down until he was hanging from the bottom rungs of the ladder up to his neck in water, while Bowers shone a torch from above "to find out how matters stood." The problem was coagulated balls of coal dust and oil blocking the suctions of both the hand and the engine pump. For fourteen hours Evans sat on the keel, often completely submerged beneath the "unspeakably dirty water," passing up bucket after bucket of the "filthy stuff." By midnight he had sent up twenty buckets, and four hours later, with the hand-pump in the engine room at last beginning to gain on the water level, the bailing party, that had been working since the previous dawn, could finally be stood down.

"Captain Scott was simply splendid," Bowers wrote to his family at the end of it all; "he might have been at Cowes & to do him & Teddy Evans credit at our worst strait none of our landsmen who were working so hard knew how serious things were. Capt. S. said to me quietly—I am afraid it's a bad business for us—what do you think? I said we were by no means dead yet though at that moment Oates at peril of his life got aft to report another horse dead & more down & then an awful sea swept away our lee bulwarks clear between the fore & main rigging—only our chain lashings saved the lee motor sledge. Then, as I was soon diving after petrol cases, Capt Scott calmly told me that 'they did not matter'—This was our great project for getting to the Pole—the much advertised Motors that 'did not matter.' " "In justice to Capt Scott," Bowers finished, "these incidents must be taken as 'confidences' to be told in his own way & later on. That his account will be moderate you may be sure, still take my word for it he is one of the best & behaved up to our best traditions at a time when *his* own outlook must have been the blackness of darkness."

But Scott knew that they were not safe yet, and that another gale of the same force could mean the end of them. If there had been any lingering question marks over any of the officers and men, however, they had been answered, and he knew just how lucky he was. "We are not out of the wood yet," he scrawled in his diary on 2 December, "but hope dawns & indeed it should for me when I find myself so wonderfully served."

The men in particular sparked his gratitude. In the aftermath of the gale the deck under the ponies' stalls leaked badly onto the hammocks and bedding below, but "not a word" of complaint was ever heard. "Indeed the discomfort throughout the mess deck has been extreme," Scott wrote. "Everything has been thrown about, water has found its way down . . . There is no daylight, and the air can only come through the small fore-hatch . . . The men have been wetted to the skin repeatedly on deck, and have no chance of drying their clothing. All things considered their cheerful fortitude is little short of wonderful."

The cost in animals and stores might have been higher, too—one dog and two ponies lost, ten tons of coal, sixty-five gallons of petrol, and a case of the biologists' spirit—but Scott knew that with their condition deteriorating by the day, the ponies could not take another battering like the one they had just had. "I pray there may be no more gales," he wrote on the fifth. "We should be nearing the limits of the westerlies, but one cannot be sure for at least two days . . . So much depends on fine weather. December ought to be a fine month in the Ross Sea; it always has been, and just now conditions point to fine weather. Well, we must be prepared for anything, but I'm anxious, anxious about these animals of ours."

It was not now the westerlies that were Scott's worry, however, but the pack, and on 7 December the first berg was sighted far off to the west. On the following day Teddy Evans spotted from the masthead two more distant bergs on the port beam, and on the morning of the ninth, in a latitude of 65°8', small worn floes, two or three feet in depth and of the kind that Scott had hoped not to meet until much farther south, gave him the first, stressful indication of what was to come.

"Its impossible to interpret the fact," he noted uneasily in his diary, but for the moment a sense of relief that the ponies could enjoy some respite from the endless pitching of the ship kept darker thoughts at bay. After six years' absence, too, the colours and light at the pack edge exerted all their old fascination. "The sun has just dipped below the southern horizon," he wrote. "The scene was incomparable. The northern sky was gloriously rosy and reflected in the calm sea between the ice, which varied from burnished copper to salmon pink; bergs and packs to the north had a pale greenish hue with deep purple shadows, the sky shaded to saffron and pale green."

For all his lyricism, the pack was as much "enemy" as it was an endless source of wonder and speculation. "To-night we are in close pack," he wrote later the same day; "it is doubtful whether it is worth pushing on . . . We had been very carefully into all the evidence of former voyages to pick the best meridian to go south on, and I thought and still think that the evidence points to the 178 W. as the best. We entered the pack more or less on this meridian, and have been rewarded by encountering worse conditions than any ship has had before—worse, in fact, than I imagined would have been possible on any other meridian."

This is the other side of Scott, indignant that nature does not do what it should do and when he needs it. And nobody who had seen Scott under these conditions had ever thought they were looking at a man at Cowes. Disaster, as ever, brought out the best in him, and stalemate the fretful worst. "The ice grew closer in the night . . . We have lain tight in the pack all day . . . The pack still close around us . . . We seem to be in the midst of a terribly screwed pack." "It is a very, very trying time," he wrote nineteen days after their first sighting of ice, frustrated at their lack of progress and still more so by the sheer inexplicability of it all. "It's all very disheartening . . . The exasperating uncertainty of one's mind in such captivity is due to ignorance of its cause and inability to predict the effect of changes of wind. One can only vaguely comprehend that things are happening far beyond our horizon which directly affect our situation."

For those who had never seen pack before, and had only their own responsibilities to worry about, there was always some diversion or novelty, but for Scott there seemed no respite. Every day in the pack shortened their first season. Every day saw the condition of the ponies deteriorate. Every day under steam saw their coal depleted. "One realises the awful monotony of a long stay in the pack," he wrote in a sudden and rare spasm of sympathy for Norwegians, "such as Nansen and others experienced. One can imagine such days as these lengthening into interminable months and years." "We are captured," he wrote again on Christmas Day. "We do practically nothing under sail . . . and could do little under steam, and at each step forward the possibility of advance seems to lessen."

"Three weeks in the pack worried him a lot," his brother-in-law Wilfred Bruce reported back to Kathleen. "He talked very little to anybody (and sometimes several days passed without my saying more than a few words to him), but I think that Wilson and Evans probably saw a little more of him . . . I can imagine what an awful strain the whole responsibility of a show like this must be, & I thank heaven that I'm here as a volunteer with *none* of it. I always hated responsibility. My position, as we expected, was a trifle difficult but I effaced myself utterly, just kept my watch and did as I was told."

Scott's reserve with his brother-in-law was probably a matter of policy, but in one thing Bruce was right. As Cherry wrote, a captain's was a lonely position. The responsibility, the decisions, were in the end his alone. And however genuinely he might indulge them, the high spirits of the wardroom can only have heightened the inevitable sense of distance from those under his command. "The invitation is peculiar," Frank Debenham noted in his journal of the "call to song" at a dinner for Pennell's birthday. "Everyone repeats quickly and loudly 'Silas [Wright] for a song' 'The skua [Taylor] for a squawk' 'Levick for a Limmerick' . . ." It was, touchingly, enough for the young Debenham simply to be there, to be on nickname terms with his shipmates, or to be "wrestling & scragging with men like Wilson," and this naïveté makes his early journals in some ways the most revealing of all the wardroom diaries. In entry after entry one catches a glimpse of Oates and Meares lovingly debating the relative merits of pom pom and maxim, or "Aitch" ruthlessly teasing their reincarnated Persian. Almost nowhere to be found in them, however, is Scott, a reserved and slightly remote presence in a wardroom still dominated by the "trumpet" voice of Evans and the horseplay antics of a bunch of regressive sixth-formers.

Not that there was anything oppressive in Scott's reserve — except to Bruce — or anaemic in his presence. Nothing, as a leader, gave him more satisfaction than a happy expedition. The anxieties and frustrations of his diary he kept to himself. He was constantly on the lookout for leads, interpreting winds, searching the sky for clues, noting the ice blink. "Capt. Scott who has to face all the anxiety of things is splendid," wrote Bowers on Christmas Day, "he never shows it & is geniality itself always. You could not imagine a more congenial leader or one who inspires more confidence."

Four days later he got his reward, when on 29 December, after almost three weeks in the sunless grip of the pack, they had the first unmistakable signs that it was coming to an end. By six o'clock the following morning the *Terra Nova* was at last well into open sea, and by mid-afternoon, with "the sun bursting through the misty sky and warming the air," Scott was cheerfully thinking in terms of a landfall at Cape Crozier by New Year's Day. The original idea to set up their base camp at Cape Crozier had been Wilson's, and the more Scott had thought about it on

the way down, the more intriguing a location it seemed. The attractions of an Emperor penguin colony so close to hand were reason enough to explain Wilson's preference for the site, but from Scott's point of view it was the logistical argument that was so compelling, with the Cape giving them not just a guaranteed access onto the Barrier, but an uninterrupted southward route free of the crevasses that would have to be negotiated from their old base.

Any thoughts of an early landfall, though, were premature, and a strong wind "dead in [their] teeth" ended all thoughts of reaching Cape Crozier before the year was out. "I begin to wonder if fortune will ever turn her wheel," Scott complained. "On every possible occasion she seems to have decided against us. Of course the ponies are feeling the motion as we pitch in a short, sharp sea—it's damnable for them and disgusting for us."

At 10 p.m. on the thirty-first the clouds lifted to show them their first distant view of Antarctica, and with "some pleasure" Scott wrote the year "1910" in his diary for the last time. For the next forty-eight hours, too, the weather in the Ross Sea gave every encouragement that his hopes for a better New Year were to be answered, but on 3 January it was again "Fortune" as usual—"No good!!" a frustrated Scott wrote in his diary at 6 p.m. "Cape Crozier with all its attractions is denied us."

They had come up to the Barrier five miles to the east of the Cape, where its cliff was no more than sixty feet high, and from the crow's nest could see across its huge pressure ridges to Black and White Island in the distance. As they nosed their way slowly along the Barrier edge it seemed virtually unchanged to the old hands, and even to those who were seeing it for the first time there was something so familiar in it that it felt more like a return than a discovery. "We could see the great pressure waves which had proved such an obstacle to travellers from the *Discovery* to the Emperor penguin rookery," Cherry noted, mercifully unconscious of what that place would come to mean to him. "The Knoll was clear, but the summit of Mount Terror was in the clouds. As for the Barrier we seemed to have known it all our lives, as it was so exactly like what we had imagined it to be, and seen in the pictures and photographs."

A heavy swell prevented an attempted landing from their whaler, and with hopes slowly fading, the *Terra Nova* continued westward, looking for a safe landfall. There were a number of grounded bergs close to the rookery that could have provided a sheltered anchorage, but nowhere was there the access to the beach that they would need to land their equipment. "It would have taken weeks to land the ordinary stores," Scott lamented, "and

heaven knows how we could have got the ponies and the motor sledges ashore."

And the more certain failure became, the more perfect seemed Cape Crozier for their needs. "Every detail of the shore promised well for a wintering party," he wrote in his diary. "Comfortable quarters for the hut, ice for water, snow for the animals, good slopes for ski-ing, vast tracks of rock for walks. Proximity to the Barrier and to the rookeries of two types of penguins—easy ascent of Mount Terror—good ground for biological work—good peaks for observation of all sorts—fairly easy approach to the Southern Road, with no chance of being cut off . . . It is a thousand pities to have to abandon such a spot . . . oh it is a thousand pities."

The sight of the "old *Discovery* post office pole sticking up as erect as when planted" only added to the poignancy of the disappointment, but with no chance of shelter that side of Cape Royds, there was nothing to do but press on. By one o'clock the following morning they had rounded Cape Bird and, steaming slowly through a pack of killer whales "idly diving" off a penguin rookery, at last saw in the distant haze Mount Discovery and the great bastion of the Western Mountains. "It gives one a homely feeling to see such a familiar scene," Scott wrote, and with the bay more open than he had ever known it, there was no shortage of possible sites for their base camp. The crucial consideration was to find a place that would not easily be cut off from the Barrier, and after summoning a council, Scott opted to explore a cape they had known in the past as the Skuary. It was separated from Hut Point to the south by the Glacier Tongue and the two deep bays on either side of it, and with every chance that these bays would freeze early and remain frozen late into the season, seemed to answer to their demands.

The cape lay just behind the *Terra Nova*'s most southerly position, and so, skirting back around Inaccessible Island, Scott had the ship taken in through a fringe of thin ice until she butted heavily up against a sheet of thick bay ice that stretched unbroken to the shore a mile and a half away. After making *Terra Nova* fast to the ice with their anchors, Scott walked across to the cape with Wilson and Evans, and a glance at the land was enough to confirm their hunch.

The site they had found was a gently shelving black beach on one of the numerous spurs of Erebus—"the most restful mountain in the world," as Cherry called it—and was dominated to the east by the smoke-plumed summit first climbed by David, Mawson and Mackay on Shackleton's *Nimrod* expedition. To the north and south of the cape lay deep bays, and

beyond them, Scott continued, "great glaciers came rippling over the lower slopes to thrust high blue-wall snouts into the sea. The sea is blue before us, dotted with shining bergs or ice floes, whilst far over the Sound, yet so bold and magnificent as to appear near, stand the beautiful Western Mountains with their numerous lofty peaks, their deep glacial valleys and clear cut scarps, a vision of mountain scenery that can have few rivals."

It was "a panorama of such austere and desolate grandeur as I had never hitherto seen," Ponting wrote, but until the stores were landed the photographer was no more exempt than anyone else from the job at hand. The first things to be hoisted off the ship were two of the three motorised sledges, and Scott was relieved to find them seemingly none the worse for the tons of seawater that had washed over them on the journey south. He was even happier to see the new lease on life the ponies took on the moment they were on the floe. After their ordeal at sea they had all inevitably lost condition, but it seemed to Scott a virtual miracle to see all seventeen safely picketed on the floe and gently gnawing at each other's flanks to ease their itches. "Poor brutes, how they must have enjoyed their first roll," he wrote, "and how glad they must be to have freedom to scratch themselves. It is evident all have suffered from skin irritation—one can imagine the horror of suffering from such an ill for weeks without being able to get at the part that itched."

The dogs, too, seemed to have survived the journey better than had ever looked possible two days out of Port Chalmers, and were soon at work ferrying light loads across the ice under Meares's control. "The great trouble with them has been due to the fatuous conduct of the penguins," Scott wrote with an almost Dickensian touch. "From the moment of landing on their feet their whole attitude expressed devouring curiosity and a pig-headed disregard for their own safety. They waddle forward, poking their heads to and fro in their usually absurd way, in spite of a string of howling dogs straining to get at them. 'Hullo!' they seem to say, 'here's a game— what do you ridiculous things want?' And they come a few steps nearer. The dogs make a rush as far as their leashes or harness allow. The penguins are not daunted in the least, but their ruffs go up and they squawk with semblance of anger, for all the world as though they were rebuking a rude stranger . . . 'Oh, that's the sort of animal you are; well, you've come to the wrong place—we aren't going to be bluffed and bounced by you,' and then the fatal steps forward are taken and they come within reach. There is a spring, a squawk, a horrid red patch on the snow, and the incident is closed."

It was not just the penguins that were at risk, and after forty-eight hours without sleep Scott came up on deck late the next morning to find six or seven killer whales skirting the fast ice ahead of the ship. As he watched them disappear and reappear to the *Terra Nova's* stern he called up the expedition photographer, and Ponting had just grabbed his camera and run to the ice edge where two of their dogs were tethered when the whole floe exploded under him, as whale after whale smashed into it from below. With the floe fragments rocking fiercely under the assault, Ponting scrambled back to the safety of the fast ice, abandoning the terrified dogs to whine and strain at their chains. By some miracle of physics the ice had split round and between them, and to Scott and the whales' mutual astonishment they remained feet out of reach, watched by successive pairs of "small glistening eyes" as head after head bobbed out of the water to see where they and Ponting had got to. "After this," Scott wrote, "whether they thought the game insignificant, or whether they missed Ponting is uncertain, but the terrifying creatures passed on to other hunting grounds, and we were able to rescue the dogs, and what was even more important, our petrol—5 or 6 tons of which was waiting on a piece of ice which was not split away from the main mass."

Even without the killers to accelerate the process, the ice around the ship was clearly ready to break up, and on the Sunday after they had landed, they suffered disaster with their last motorised sledge. "We realised that the ice was getting very rotten," Priestley wrote in his diary, but when a message came back from an anxious Scott to hurry with the unloading, no one had the courage or the sense to ignore it. The Ship Party had got the sledge down onto the ice when without warning Williamson went through to his thighs, the "car suddenly dipped, the ice gave way beneath her after end and she fell with all her weight vertically on the rope. The rope began cutting through the thin ice, and we were never able to hold her steady for a moment. Man after man was forced to leave the rope through his hands, and when only five of us were left she took charge at a gallop and is now resting on the bottom at a depth of 120 fathoms." It might have been worse, as Priestley, who had gone back to the ship for a lifeline and Day's goggles, abruptly disappeared through the ice. Within a moment he was swept under by a strong current, only to burst up again through the rotten ice "like a cork out of a champagne bottle." "Day, here are your goggles," was Priestley's only reaction.

"A day of *disaster*," Scott laconically wrote, blaming his own hastiness for the loss, but it is hard to imagine he would have taken it so well if he

had kept his old faith in the motor sledges. On the flat surface of the floe and in temperatures only a little below zero they had pulled well enough, but they had already shown enough temperament to suggest that they were never going to be reliable enough for the demands of Barrier conditions and surfaces.

The ponies had also begun to show their distinctive characters and capabilities. "There were the steady workers," Cherry recalled, "like Punch and Nobby; there were one or two definitely weak ponies like Blossom, Blucher and Jehu; and there were one or two strong but rather impossible beasts. One of these was soon known as Weary Willie. His outward appearance belied him, for he looked like a pony. A brief acquaintance soon convinced me that he was without a doubt a cross between a pig and a mule. He was obviously a strong beast and, since he always went as slowly as possible and stopped as often as possible it was most difficult to form any opinion as to what load he was really able to draw."

If it was difficult to get any estimate of Weary Willie's character, Christopher and Hackenschmidt—so called "from his vicious habit of using both fore and hind legs in attacking those who came near him"—left no one in doubt of their malice. "There were runaways innumerable, and all kinds of falls," and "a breathless minute," Cherry wrote, "when Hackenschmidt, with a sledge attached to him, went galloping over the hills and boulders. Below him, all unconscious of his impending fate, was Ponting, adjusting a large camera with his usual accuracy. Both survived."

And if the dogs, suffering badly in the heat and exhausted by even light loads, did "not inspire confidence," Scott could not have been more pleased with the men's work. Priestley was rather more sceptical of their performance, but "Nothing like it has been done before," Scott wrote on 10 January, after just six days' work, "nothing so expeditious and complete . . . Our camp is becoming so perfect in its appointments that I am almost suspicious of some drawback hidden by the weather."

It was the hut in particular that pleased Scott, though for anyone whose terms of reference were framed by the old *Discovery* structure, the word "hut" hardly seemed adequate. "What shall we call it?" he asked in a curious little rush of domesticity. "We have made unto ourselves a truly seductive home, within the walls of which peace, quiet, and comfort reign supreme. Such a noble dwelling transcends the word 'hut' and we pause to give it a more fitting title only from lack of the appropriate suggestion . . . Our residence is really a house of considerable size, in every respect the finest that has ever been erected in the Polar regions; 50 ft. long by 25 ft.

wide and 9ft. to the eaves." The men had practised erecting the hut on the waste ground beside the quay at Lyttelton, and it had gone up on its beach twelve feet above the waterline at Cape Evans without a hitch. The walls had insulated layers of double boarding both inside and outside the frames, and the roof was made of successive layers of match boarding, "ruberoid," seaweed, more match board, and a final three-ply "ruberoid" on the outside.

With as much of the black volcanic sand as they could want to heap up against the walls, compressed forage bales piled up on the south and east sides, the ponies' stalls on the north, and a linoleum floor over four under-layers, the lessons of *Discovery* had been well learned. Within the hut Scott ordered a bulkhead of cases to divide the officers' quarters from the men's, "to the satisfaction of both messes," and allotted the space between his own bulkhead and the men's quarters—"The Tenements"—to Bowers, Oates, Atkinson, Meares and Cherry-Garrard. "These five are all special friends," Scott wrote, "and have already made their dormitory very habit-able. Simpson and Wright are near the instruments in their corner. Next come Day and Nelson in a space that includes the latter's 'Lab.' near the big window; next to this is a space for three—Debenham, Taylor, and Gran; they also have already made their space part dormitory and part workshop."

Unlike Shackleton at Cape Royds, who had a cubicle to himself, Scott shared his corner space with Evans and Wilson. And for the moment, at least, there was nothing too jarring in an arrangement that put Owner and second-in-command together. The frictions were latent—"it will make things uncomfortable . . . if they start slinging plates at each other," Oates wrote—but Kathleen, Hilda Evans and New Zealand belonged to a differ-ent world, and to the past. "I knew when I first met Capt. Scott that I had met a man," Bowers wrote, as if waking from a bad dream. "If seeing little of him for 6 months & then only under the wing of his ambitious & ener-getic wife made me forget for a moment, I know now that my first impres-sions were right. He is undoubtedly a leader & a good one at that & I am only glad that things have turned out so happily to enable us all to realise it."

With the exception of "young Gran"—"a lazy posing fellow" and the unfortunate lightning rod for all Scott's Norwegian hostilities—the sense of satisfaction was general. It was impossible to think what they would have done without Oates. Rennick was "a good fellow" whom they were going to miss. Clissold, the cook, was "splendid." Ponting "a very nice fellow."

"Each man in his way," Scott wrote, "is a treasure." "If you picture us after communications are cut off," he wrote in buoyant mood from their new home to Teddy Evans's wife, "it must be a very bright picture, almost a scene of constant revelry, with your husband in the foreground . . . I am sure we are going to be a very happy family and most certainly we shall be healthy and well cared for."

And the odd thing was, it was almost true. If Camelot and McMurdo had not exactly joined hands, Sir Clements would still have been proud.

Twenty-six: Depot-Laying

Never in the history of Polar exploration can the scientists of an expedition have drawn their inspiration from . . . a leader whose insight into pure science made him so well able to appreciate the results of their researches.

CHARLES WRIGHT *and* RAYMOND PRIESTLEY

For all the genuine satisfaction that Scott took in the hut, it was not domestic comfort he was interested in but time. The sledging season on the Barrier only realistically stretched until the end of March, and with ice conditions in the bay to the south of Cape Evans threatening to cut off their access, it was touch and go if there would be a first season of any kind.

The first priority was to depot the route across the Barrier in preparation for the following season's polar bid, but that was simply one part of a comprehensive plan that demanded every week still available to them. In Scott's initial scheme he had planned for a group of the scientists to remain at Base Camp while two mixed parties of navy and scientists were taken off by ship, an "Eastern Party" under the command of Victor Campbell to explore the coastline of King Edward VII Land, and a Western Geological Party under Griffith Taylor, to work in the mountains first penetrated by Armitage eight years earlier.

On the face of it, there could be no plan better designed to balance science and exploration, but hidden behind the ambition and sweep is that curious paradox that lies at the heart of Scott's last expedition. It is a paradox that is not very easy to address for anyone who admires Scott, yet if one can for a moment separate the immense achievements of his scientists and look instead at what he did himself, one is left with an expedition leader who in intellectual, geographical and imaginative terms cannot begin to compare with the man who commanded *Discovery*.

That is a harsh thing to say about anyone who did as much for polar science as Scott did, and still harsher when one remembers the debt to him that every scientist on the expedition proudly acknowledged. The men that Scott took down on this last expedition were of a different calibre from any of the RS stalking horses from 1900, and to a man they looked on him as essentially one of their own, a latent scientist with a wonderful ear and mind for science, against whose standards every theory and hypothesis had to be rigorously argued and defended. "Over and over again," the meteorologist George Simpson—no friend to amateurism—recalled after Scott's death, "as point after point was cleared up I have longed to be able to show the results to Captain Scott, for there is hardly a problem of Antarctic meteorology which we have not discussed together. His interest in every scientific problem was intense and I do not think I have ever met a man who had the true scientific spirit so unalloyed . . . He was constantly looking forward to the successful completion of the journey to the Pole, the exact value of which was perfectly clear to him, in order that he might spend his remaining time in the Antarctic in opening up new country and making new discoveries."

"It will not perhaps be out of place," Griffith Taylor—again no flatterer, and always happy to argue with Scott or anyone else—concluded his introduction to the Physiography volume of the expedition results, "[to state] how much I owe to Captain Scott for the ever present interest which he showed in my special subject. Indeed the extraordinary acumen he showed in handling many of the broader problems we all discussed together is one of my pleasanter memories of the six months at Headquarters."

There was nothing woolly or uninformed about Scott's encouragement—he could be quite sharp about the relevance of Taylor's particular interests—but when all this is conceded, there was a daring, range and inventiveness about everything he did on the first expedition that is no longer there on this second. It is perhaps as much a reflection on the quality of the men under his command as of anything else, but there was *nothing* done on the *Discovery* expedition that did not bear the stamp of Scott's personality, nowhere that he did not personally go, no gadget or device he did not think up, no problem of temperature, tides, currents, wind, ice or sledging to which he did not turn his mind.

The conditions of ignorance that surrounded *Discovery* were perhaps made for a gifted amateur, but if Scott was in a sense no more than a victim of his own success, there is no disguising the shift of focus. With men of the stamp of Simpson or Taylor at work, it would be absurd to expect the same restless activity from him, yet if one had asked the Scott of 1904 which of the three 1911 expeditions he would lead—the eastern, the western, or the southern slog in the footsteps of another man who had left no geographical problem to solve?—it is inconceivable that he would have plumped for the last.

If there had to be an attempt on the Pole, of course, it was inevitable that Scott would lead it, but it is astonishing to find a man of his originality content with the ninety-odd miles of meaningless plateau that Shackleton had left to him. When he had first mooted his plans to Skelton four years before, the route had been an unknown quantity, but with the Beardmore "cracked" and the way to the Pole opened up, there was nothing on a Southern Journey more intellectually or imaginatively interesting to look forward to than the brute satisfactions of sledging and the scraps of another man's "failure."

With the agent, Kinsey, talking up Shackleton in New Zealand, and Priestley and Day singing his praises on the journey down, Scott can scarcely have been unaware of this, yet it seems to have made no difference.* Back in London Markham had warned him against the folly of empty "Pole bagging," but as the preparations for the depoting journeys accelerated, the Pole and the autumn parties were *all* that had come to matter. "After Service," Scott wrote on 15 January, after discovering that Oates had assigned two of the better ponies to the Eastern Party, "I told Campbell that I should have to cancel his two ponies and give him two others. He took it like the gentleman he is, thoroughly appreciating the reason."

---

*The one criticism that Day or Priestley brought against Shackleton was a habit of "digging out for No 1." On Scott's part, it is worth noting that he never allowed personal feelings to cloud his judgement of Shackleton's achievements or his generosity in acknowledging them. On the voyage south, Bowers wrote that it was impossible to get Scott or Wilson to do anything "except . . . crack up his success." "The 'Discovery' factions have never been given vent to by him [Scott]," he went on. "He has stood by his friends & never said—in private—a word against anyone. I think he has done his part right through in a public & delicate position & ought to have the friendship & support of everybody."

The best ponies, the best men, the dogs, they were all earmarked for the Barrier, but before they could even complete their preparations there was a scare that for a few desperate hours threatened to end the expedition before it had even started. During the early hours of the twenty-first an anxious Scott had gone out of the hut, and the sight of the *Terra Nova* hard up against a lee shore in a freshening wind and breaking ice was enough to conjure up nightmare memories of *Discovery*'s last hours off Hut Point. "Visions of the ship failing to return to New Zealand and of sixty people waiting here arose in my mind with sickening pertinacity," he later wrote, after all Pennell's manoeuvres had only ended in the *Terra Nova* grounding. ". . . The first ray of hope came when by careful watching one could see that the ship was turning very slowly, then one saw the men running from side to side and knew that an attempt was being made to roll her off. The rolling produced a more rapid turning movement at first and then she seemed to hang again. But only for a short time; the engines had been going astern all the time and presently a slight movement became apparent. But we only knew she was getting clear when we heard cheers on board and more cheers from the whaler."

"At such times of real disaster," Cherry recalled, Scott was "a very philosophical man," but with the ice gone in the north bay and breaking up in the south, there was little time for philosophy. There was still a land road for the ponies that would take them to firm sea-ice, but with even that threatening to disappear at any moment, Scott pushed his men through the last preparations for their autumn campaign "in a state of hurry bordering on panic."

For all the old "panic," however, and a workload that meant he had already gone ten days without a wash or shave, Scott was again in his element. "It would rejoice your heart to see your husband in the weather beaten condition he is in at present," Wilson reassured Kathleen. "He is in the most excellent trim for hard work. I am sure he feels, as I do, that it was only yesterday we were here and that the seven years which have passed over have left no trace, except in your husband a very much more confident grasp of conditions & possibilities, in which he simply excels . . . There is nothing I wouldn't do for him. He is just splendid."

"Captain Scott is simply extraordinarily nice to me," Bowers wrote home on the eve of their departure, though after seventy-two hours without sleep, a less modest man might have expected nothing less. "My most vivid recollection of the day we started," Cherry wrote, "is the sight of Bowers, out of breath, very hot, and in great pain from a bad knock which he had given his knee against a rock, being led forward by his big pony Uncle

Bill, over whom temporarily he had but little control. He had been left behind in the camp, giving last instructions . . . and had practically lost himself in trying to follow us over what was then unknown ground. He was wearing all the clothing which was not included in his personal gear, for he did not think it fair to give the pony extra weight. He had bruised his leg in an ugly way, and for many days he came to me to bandage it. He was afraid that if he let the doctors see it they would forbid him to go forward."

While the ponies were being led across land as far as Glacier Tongue on the morning of 24 January, Scott and the dog teams were ferried round to their rendezvous by *Terra Nova*. As the dogs and sledges were disembarked onto the ice, Scott had Pennell draw up the men aft, and with Ponting photographing to his heart's content, thanked them for their "splendid work." "They have behaved like bricks," he wrote gratefully of the last occasion he would see any of the Ship or Eastern Parties, "and a finer lot of fellows never sailed in a ship. It was good to get their hearty send-off . . . I do most heartily trust that all will be successful in their ventures, for indeed their selflessness and their generous high spirits deserve reward. God bless them!"

Scott knew that for a man like Rennick, it was particularly hard to leave an expedition for which he had originally been earmarked, but from his own point of view it was Pennell he would most miss. The admiration was mutual. "Captain Scott was very good to me," his navigator later wrote to Kathleen—a letter that wonderfully illustrates the kind of leader Scott was with men he admired and trusted.

> From the first meeting with Captain Scott in London till saying good bye when he started on the Depot journey in January 1911, he never in any way showed me anything but the greatest kindness and forbearance, & I cannot say how truly grateful I have always been to him.
>
> It seems almost a mockery to say that his example helps one now & will help in the future in getting over difficulties & despising one's own troubles & petty worries; but I do feel that to have been allowed to serve such a man & to have been trusted by him in work that was his life's work is far & away the greatest reward the expedition could have given me.

After their chaotic exodus from Cape Evans, the eleven-man depot party was now one again, but even with their ponies, dogs and sledges safely united, Scott knew they were not out of trouble. At this time of the year it might be another two or three days of progress south before they could be sure of the ice under their feet, but after the weariness of their first day's sledging everything was too exhilarating to the new men in the party for them to worry about what they were sleeping on. "Those first days of sledging were wonderful!" Cherry wrote. "What memories they must have brought back for Scott and Wilson when to us, who had never seen them before, these much-discussed landmarks were almost like old friends."

The state of his old *Discovery* hut, in fact, packed with hard ice from when *Nimrod's* men had forced an entry through a window, filled Scott with a bitter sense that not even his past was safe from Shackleton,* but to Cherry every landmark came straight off the unsullied pages of *The Voyage*. "The peak of Terror . . . Erebus . . . Castle Rock . . . Danger slope . . . tins of the old *Discovery* days . . ." he enthused. "And around the Bay . . . the Heights of which we had read, Observation Hill, and Crater Hill separated from it by The Gap—through which the wind was streaming; of course it was, for this must be the famous Hut Point wind."

The unstable condition of the ice around Cape Armitage entailed a wide detour, but by the afternoon of the twenty-eighth they were bringing their first stores up onto the Barrier. "I expect we were all a little excited," Cherry wrote again of his first experience of a phenomenon he knew so well at second hand, "for to walk upon the barrier for the first time was indeed an adventure . . . what kind of surface was it, and how about those beastly crevasses of which we had read so much? Scott was ahead, and so far as we could see there was nothing but the same level of ice all round—when suddenly he was above us, walking up the sloping and quite invisible drift."[†]

Oates was already taking a "gloomy view" of the ponies, but with Meares in charge of one team and Wilson the second, the dogs were doing Scott proud, and later in the afternoon of the same day the first loads were

---

*Scott's reaction seems to go beyond a reasonable irritation at the carelessness of Shackleton's party. "It is hard to conceive the absolutely selfish frame of mind that can perpetrate a deed like this," he had scrawled in an edited-out passage of his diary after a preliminary reconnaissance to Hut Point with Meares. "The names of some of the Nimrod sailors were actually written on the outer planking of the hut." In a second expurgated passage he returned to the attack: "Boxes full of excrement were found near the provisions and filth of a sordid condition was thick under the veranda & some in the corners of the hut itself . . . it is extraordinary to think that people could have lived in such a horrid condition."

[†]Like the problems of judging distances with any accuracy, this is another phenomenon of polar travel that is hard to get used to. The evenness of the light can make it impossible to detect irregularities or obstructions even when they are virtually under your feet.

dumped about half a mile in from the Barrier edge. Scott was all but certain that their stores were safe enough at this depot, but he was determined that their first real camp was going to "deserve its distinctive title of Safety," and by the morning of the thirtieth all their stores were up on the Barrier and they were ready to begin the haul across to the chosen position.

It was not long, however, before Scott found out what deep snow could do to the ponies, and the inevitable tensions between him and Oates began to surface. "Scott and Evans boss the show pretty well," Oates had written to his mother just before they set off, but "their ignorance about marching with animals is colossal, on several points Scott is going on lines contrary to what I have suggested, however if I can only persuade him to take a pony himself he will learn a lot this autumn—That is all the growl I have got. Scott having spent too much time of his life in an office, he would fifty times sooner stay in the hut seeing how a pair of Fox's spiral puttees suited him than come out and look at a ponies legs or a dogs feet— however I suppose I think to [sic] much of this having come strate [sic] from a regiment where horses were the first and only real consideration."

The first days on the Barrier had not narrowed the gap, and neither Scott's innovations nor his plan to go on for another twelve days rather than push south and kill the weakest ponies impressed Oates. "Tuesday, January 31. Camp 3," Scott noted. "We have everything ready to start—but this afternoon we tried our one pair of snow-shoes on 'Weary Willy.' The effect was magical. He strolled around as though walking on hard ground in places where he floundered woefully without them. Oates hasn't any faith in these shoes at all."

The state of the sea-ice behind them, cutting the party off from their equipment at Cape Evans, made the dispute an academic one, and with no shoes and no retreat, there was nothing to do but plod on and hope for a firmer surface. For the last few days Atkinson had been adding to their anxieties with an infected foot, and when lancing did no good, Scott was forced to leave him behind with the experienced Crean to look after him: "very hard on the latter," he noted curtly, in a passage later doctored by his editor. "Atkinson suffering much pain and mental distress at his condition—for the latter I fear I cannot have much sympathy, as he ought to have reported his trouble, long before and kept silent fearing to be left out of the party—He might have wrecked it—small consideration . . . concealing ailments in this way. Crean will manage to rescue some more of the forage from the Barrier edge—I am very sorry for him."

After another day's progress, they shifted from day to night marching in search of a firmer surface, but the patches of soft snow still caught out the wretched ponies. It was an agony for Scott to watch them floundering, to see them plunge deeper and deeper, "panting and heaving under the strain," until they had fought themselves to an exhausted standstill or collapsed prostrate and trembling in the snow. And the worst of it was, an exasperated Scott railed, that if they had just remembered the other shoes they would have been spared the misery. "Then came the *triumph of the snow-shoe* again," he wrote in an unambiguous side-swipe at Oates, after another pony had been transformed by their application. "If we had more of these shoes we could certainly put them on seven out of the eight of our ponies—and after a little I think on the eighth, Oates's pony, as certainly the ponies so shod would draw their loads over the soft snow patches without any difficulty."

Behind these immediate miseries loomed a larger worry, with the contrasting performance of the dog teams further underlining the bizarreness of their whole transportation "policy." It almost beggars belief that Scott had been mulling over the options since at least 1907, because after just a month in the south all there was to show for it—apart from a motor on the sea-bed and eight struggling ponies—was a hopeless shortage of the one animal for which the Barrier held few fears. Gran had already shown what an accomplished skier, utilising all the recent technical advances in equipment, could achieve, and after a week with Meares, even Wilson could see what a different business dog-driving could be. "Dog-driving like this, in the orthodox manner," he wrote long after the depoting journey, "is a very different thing to the beastly dog-driving we perpetrated in the Discovery days. I got to love all my team and they all got to know me well, and my old leader even now (I am writing this six months after I have had anything to do with any of them) never fails to come and speak to me, and he knows me and my voice ever so far off."

The first real blizzard on the Barrier that kept them at Camp 6—"Corner Camp"—for three days had further rubbed in the difference between dog and pony. "Wednesday, February 8.—No 7 Camp . . . Lat.78°13," Scott noted. "The ponies were much shaken by the blizzard. One supposes they did not sleep—all look lifeless and two or three are visibly thinner than before. But the worst case by far is Forde's little pony . . . The poor thing is a miserable scarecrow and never ought to have been brought . . . they cannot stand more blizzards in their present state . . . The dogs are in fine form—the blizzard had only been a pleasant rest for *them*."

The blizzard had also brought home to Scott that they were not going to get as far south as he had hoped with the depot-laying, and the priority now shifted to getting back as many of the ponies alive as was possible. By 13 February and Camp 11 Scott had decided to send back three of the weakest, but even with the five strongest remaining ponies, and the dogs still working well, the 80th parallel that they had been aiming at was looking increasingly problematic.

If there was little else to cheer him up, there was always the sight of Bowers, who remained indifferent to anything the Barrier might throw his way. "Bowers is wonderful," Scott wrote. "Throughout the night he has worn no head-gear but a common green felt hat kept on with a chin stay and affording no cover whatever for ears. His face and ears remain bright red . . . I have never seen anyone so unaffected by the cold. To-night he remained outside a full hour after the rest of us had got into the tent. He was simply pottering about the camp doing small jobs to the sledges &." Bowers had proved his value in other ways too, helping to broker a peace between Oates and the "dirty and lazy" Gran, but the tensions between "the Soldier" and Scott showed no signs of easing. On the march out of Camp 13 they hit very bad surface conditions, and with Gran and Weary Willy dropping behind, Scott consulted Oates as to the distance they might manage, "and he cheerfully proposed fifteen miles [half again over their usual rate] for the day! This piqued me somewhat and I marched till the sledge meter showed 6½ miles."

Scott's pique and Oates's sardonic challenge almost immediately cost them one of the ponies, because by the time the vanguard had completed its forced march, Weary Willy was almost a mile behind. "What happened never became clear," Cherry wrote, but with "Poor Weary" stuck in a snow drift, one of the dog teams had set upon him, "to all purposes a pack of ravening wolves," until Gran and Meares armed with just their ski and dog sticks flung themselves into the fray and got the pony to his feet. "One way and another," Scott noted in a curiously squint-eyed comment on a casualty list that ran from multiple wounds for Willy to one broken ski-stick and a broken dog-stick, "the dogs must have had a rocky time, yet they seem to bear charmed lives when their blood is up, as apparently not one of them has been injured." "The incident is deplorable and the blame widespread," Scott concluded, blaming himself as much as anyone else, but it had its uses in so far as a spell man-hauling Weary's load was enough to remind him of what the poor animal had endured. They had still not reached the 80th parallel he had been hoping for, but two more night marches were enough to convince him that the ponies could take no more.

They had reached Camp 15, the most famous of all the Antarctic's invisible landmarks, "One Ton Depot." It was situated in 79°28½'s. Two thousand one hundred and eighty-one pounds of stores were deposited, including seven weeks' full provision bags for one unit, eight weeks of tea, six weeks of butter, seven weeks' full rations of biscuits, eight and a half gallons of oil, five sacks of oats, four bales of fodder, 250 pounds of dog biscuits, sledges, ski-sticks, cocoa and matches. "With packing cases we have landed considerably over a ton of stuff," Scott noted. "It is a pity we couldn't get to 80°, but as it is we shall have a good leg up for next year and can at least feed the ponies full up to this point." Scott was careful, too, to make sure that the depot could not be missed. A black flag was raised above it on a flagstaff, the sledges stood on end, and biscuit boxes, full and empty, piled up to act as reflectors. "The depot cairn is more than 6ft above the surface," he recorded with satisfaction, "very solid and large; then there are the pony protection walls; altogether it would show up for many miles."

The decision to turn back north here again found Oates and Scott at loggerheads over the ponies. "Oates proposed to Scott that the animal (Weary Willie) should be killed," Gran recalled many years later, "and that we should push on with the other ponies, but Scott refused this suggestion. He had, as he himself put it, felt quite sick on account of the animal's sufferings. Even though Oates was of course a highly disciplined officer, he felt obliged on this occasion to press his views on his chief. 'Sir I'm afraid you'll come to regret not taking my advice.' 'Regret it or not,' replied Scott. 'I have taken my decision as a Christian gentleman.'"

It sounds too good to be true, too completely and perfectly neat—Scott was only eleven statute miles from One Ton Depot when he died—but if Gran is taking liberties with literal history, his exchange does contain an essential *poetic* truth that everyone on that expedition would have recognised. From the very start there had been a fundamental divide between the realist and the sentimentalist, and at its root lay Scott's old inability to square a theoretical acceptance of the animals' role on the expedition with a deep-seated hatred of the cruelty this entailed. On paper and in his planning Scott was always ready to think of the dogs and ponies as a "wasting asset," but between the conception and the act always fell the same shadow of that Southern Journey with Wilson and Shackleton. The irony of it was that Scott's kindness was probably in the end the crueller option, but to argue the issue in this way is to miss it altogether, because Scott's attitude and decisions came from a part of his nature and experience that was beyond the reach of reason or demonstration.

There is again a muted echo here of the psychology of military life, because for all the difference of scale and morality, one might as well ask a general brought up on the horrors of the First World War to be prodigal with his men's lives in the Second as expect Scott to erase the memory of his Southern Journey. In both cases a deeply felt sense of responsibility and compassion can in the end become the enemy of decision-making, and the very human qualities that made a Scott or a General Percival at the fall of Singapore the *men* they were, become precisely those that disabled them from taking the hard decisions that were required of them in command.

There is a well-documented linkage, too, between a certain kind of lachrymose sentimentality and the ability to oversee disaster in military life that resonates uncomfortably through the story of Scott's last expedition. On both this first depoting journey and the subsequent polar journey the animals and men under his command suffered almost unimaginable levels of hardship, and yet no one could have been more tender than Scott, no one suffer more himself for the misery he was inflicting on others, no one, as Cherry-Garrard famously remarked of him, have cried so easily. "I've always found that to describe Scott's character is quite difficult," Frank Debenham later said, struggling to resolve the apparent contradictions of Scott's character that were not in fact contradictions at all. "I've usually said, well he was very much the Naval officer, he certainly was—on duty—but you gradually found there were certain very sentimental things about him—his care for dogs, his horror of killing dogs, and so on . . ."

It was not that, as in Shelley's wonderfully bitter jibe, "he wept well"—there was *nothing* cynical about Scott—but that does not make Oates's exasperation any the less understandable. It is unlikely that in terms of the expedition the decision to return with all the ponies made any real difference at all, but the fact remains that it was a decision Scott took for reasons that had nothing to do with the demands or the logic of their coming polar journey. It was almost as if he could not bear to watch the animals' misery any longer. As they turned back for home, Scott again divided his party into two, leaving Oates, Bowers and Gran to nurse back the ponies while he and Cherry joined Wilson's and Meares's dog teams. The ostensible

Outlands: the "sleepy hollow"
of Scott's childhood.

John Scott: "The inherited vice
from my side of the family is
indolence . . . My father was idle
and it brought much trouble."

Hannah Scott: "If ever children
had cause to worship their mother,
we feel we have."

Scott at thirteen.

Scott's discipline
sheet from the
naval training
ship *Britannia*.

Name	Mr. Scott			Date of Entry September 81	Page 231

Date. 1882	Offence.	Punishment.	By whom Punished.
March 11th	Skylarking at Morning Study	1 days 3	Lieut Login
June 16	Inattention in the ranks	1 " 3	" — "
Sept 18th	September 82		
Sept 18th	Late for Muster	1 days 4	Lieut Login
Oct 5th	Not being into his place in the ranks when Sounded	1 " 3	
" 6th	Talking in his Hammock after hours	1 " 3	1st Lieut
" 11th	Being into Hindostan Contrary to regulation	1 " 4	Lieut Login
" 13th	Going on the Middle deck in his Night Shirt	1 " 4	" "
" 15	Creating a disturbance on Sleeping deck	1 " 4	1st Lieut
" 16	Making a noise in his Hammock after hours	1 " 3	Lieut Login
Nov 5th	Talking in his Hammock after hours	1 " 3	
" 9th	Improperly dressed at Muster	1 " 2	1st Lieut
" 22	Delaying to come out of the bath	1 " 3	
1883	January 1883		

| No. 21 | Name | Scott R. F. | Entry 15 July 81 | 225 |

Progress at end of	Relative Standing.	Study.	Seamanship.	French.	Conduct.	REMARKS.
1st Term.	10	V. Sat	Sat	Sat	V. Good	
2nd "	6	Sat	Sat	Fair	V. Good	
3rd "	8	V. Sat	V. Sat	Aus at	V. Good	
4th "	7	Sat	V. Sat	Fair	V. Good	

		No. of Days.		
Date.	Offence.	Cockpit Mess.	Defaulters' Mess.	Remarks.
19 Oct 81	Entering an Orchard whilst on Half holiday			
1882 1 Dec.	Damaging Library Books			
1883 17 Mch.	Inattention in the Lecture Room while at Study			
17 apl.	Going out of bounds while away in Sailing Cutter			
19 apl.	Did as Cadet Captain allow some of the Cadets to humbug Mr. Poynter Chief Capt. in the Sanctuary, and did also take part in annoying him			
7 May	Very inattentive in Study			

Sir Clements Markham, KCB, FRS:
"the father" of the *Discovery* expedition
"and its most constant friend."

The first balloon ascent: "If nobody is
killed it will only be because God has pity
on the foolish."

Discovery's officers, 17 July 1901.

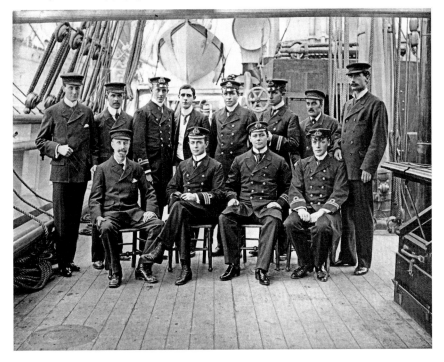

Football on the ice: a "good deal of
promiscuous kicking and foul play."

Discovery in the ice.

Return from the Southern Journey:
Shackleton, Scott and Wilson.

Escape from the ice: *Discovery*,
Morning and *Terra Nova*.

Pauline Chase: "as pretty as they're made."

Captain Scott, ambition fulfilled:
among "the ranks of the advancers."

Marriage, 2 September
1908: "the only thing
that alleviated the
distress of that function
was to see the faces of
Charles, Billy &
Michael wreathed in
many smiles."

Kathleen at work on a statuette,
Veronica (1912), in her Buckingham
Palace Road studio with Peter.

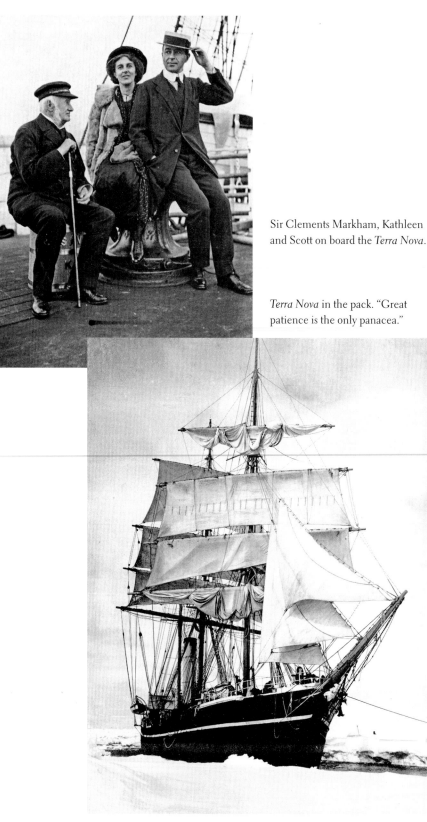

Sir Clements Markham, Kathleen and Scott on board the *Terra Nova*.

Terra Nova in the pack. "Great patience is the only panacea."

Grotto in an iceberg: "a veritable
Aladdin's Cave of beauty."

Cape Evans: hut with Erebus—"an enormous
mountain but looks like a rotten little hill behind."

Castle Berg: "the most wonderful iceberg
ever reported in the polar regions."

Scott's birthday dinner, 6 June 1911.

Oates and the ponies: "the greatest lot
of crocks I have ever seen."

Meares and Oates at the Blubber Stove.

Teddy Evans, Scott's
second-in-command.

Lashly with the motorised sledge.

Crean and PO Evans.

Scott at his desk. "He is in the most excellent trim for hard work . . .
There is nothing I wouldn't do for him. He is just splendid."

Wilson at work. "He stands very high in the scale of human beings—
how high I scarcely knew till the experience of the last few months."

Without priority: Oates, Bowers, Scott, Wilson and Evans at the Pole.

The last tent, Gran's sketch.

Scott's final resting place.

reason was that he wanted news of Campbell's Eastern Party as soon as possible, but there is no mistaking the new bounce in his tone as he and the dog teams sped past the trundling ponies.

The ponies seemed to be doing better than he could have hoped — Scott could now envisage "little difficulty" for them in covering ten or twelve miles a day — but all the animals were showing the grim signs of undereating. The party had realised for some time that their fodder was clearly inadequate under Barrier conditions, but with a very characteristic shift, Scott's sympathies now lay with the dogs under his immediate eye. They were, he noted the next day, "desperately hungry," and, like the ponies, reduced to eating their own excrement. "With the ponies it does not seem so horrid," he wrote in a bid to convince himself, "as there must be a good deal of grain, & etc, which is not fully digested. It is the worst side of dog driving. All the rest is diverting. The way in which they keep up a steady jog trot for hour after hour is wonderful. Their legs seem steel springs, fatigue unknown — for at the end of a tiring hour any unusual incident will arouse them to full vigour."

With a hard surface to travel over on the twentieth, and the dogs still defying their diet, seventeen miles was done by lunchtime, and the next day they were only twelve and a half miles from Safety Camp. By this time, however, the light and the surface had both deteriorated enough to make sledging dangerous, and Wilson had no sooner shouted back a warning to Scott than the middle dogs of Scott's team suddenly disappeared, two by two, into a crevasse they had not seen. "Osman the leader exerted all his strength and kept a foothold," Scott wrote; "it was wonderful to see him. The sledge stopped and we leapt aside. The situation was clear in another moment. We had actually been travelling along the bridge of a crevasse, the sledge had stopped on it, whilst the dogs hung in their harness in the abyss, suspended between the sledge and the leading dog."

Why dogs, sledge and men had not all gone down Scott never knew, but another ounce of weight would have ended the expedition there and then. Anchoring the sledge as best they could, Scott and Meares peered into "the depths of the crack," where they could see the dogs still harnessed in pairs, "in all sorts of fantastical positions" as they swung snarling and snapping into each other's range. Even further down, indistinctly visible in the blue light of the crevasse, were two more which had slipped through their harness onto a snow bridge below.

It looked at first as though there was no chance of saving any of them, and with the leading line biting deep into the crevasse edge, they could not even get enough slack on the main trace to stop Osman beginning to choke. Passing the tent poles across the four-and-a-half-foot crevasse, Scott and Meares finally managed to get sufficient leverage to cut the trace, but they were only able to haul up one dog from beneath before the Alpine rope that they had tied to the leading rope had cut too deep into the ice to budge. With rapidly freezing fingers they manoeuvred the sledge across the crevasse to form a working platform, and retying their rope to the stronger main trace, began to haul up the remaining dogs until all except the last pair on the snow bridge below were released.

With an Alpine rope of ninety feet, and a drop of sixty-five feet down to the dogs, Scott made a bowline, and had himself slowly lowered to the bridge. He had no sooner managed to get hold of the two dogs and watch them safely hauled up, than from somewhere above he heard the distant howls of dogs, and discovered that his "rope-tenders" had been forced to abandon him to separate the rescued dogs from Wilson's team, that had seized the chance to turn on them. When the dogs were eventually separated, and the men back in place, Scott was "with some effort" hauled to the surface.

"All's well that ends well," he noted economically in his diary, and it was again, typically, the dogs and not himself that exercised him. "The dogs are wonderful," he wrote, "but have had a terrible shaking—three of them are passing blood and have more or less serious injuries. Many were held up by a thin thong around the stomach, writhing madly to get free . . . The crevasse for the time being was an inferno, and the time must have been all too terrible for the wretched creatures. It was twenty minutes past three when we had completed the rescue work, and the accident must have happened before one-thirty. Some of the animals must have been dangling for over an hour."

There was no disguising the effect on the dogs, but the injuries sustained in the crevasse were not their only problem. Even Wilson's team were now "as thin as rakes." They "are ravenous and very tired," Scott wrote anxiously the day after their near-disaster. "I feel this should not be, and that it is evident that they are underfed. The rations must be increased next year and we *must* have some properly thought-out diet. The biscuit alone is not good enough. Meares is excellent to a point but a little pig-headed & quite ignorant of the conditions here. One thing is certain, the dogs will never continue to drag heavy loads with men sitting on the sledges; we must all learn to run with the teams and the Russian custom must be dropped. Meares, I think, rather imagined himself racing to the Pole and back on a dog sledge. This journey has opened his eyes a good deal." "It is evident," Scott decided, "that I have placed too much reliance on his experience." He would only have needed to look at his own tables to see how even an ailing dog team could outstrip the ponies. The figures are not of course fair, in so far as the return journey was unladen, but even when this is taken into account, the difference was startling—four, four, one, three, ten, ten, eleven, twelve, eleven, ten, nine, seven, seven and eight miles a day for the outward journey to One Ton Depot, as opposed to twenty-two, twenty-six, seventeen, twelve, sixteen and ten for the homeward run to Safety Camp.

Reunited with what was left of Evans's party there, Scott had this dispiriting truth rubbed in again. He was glad to find the men bursting with health, but of the three ponies they had brought back early, only James Pigg had survived the effects of the blizzard. "The loss is severe," Scott consoled himself as best he could, "but they were the two oldest ponies of our team and the two which Oates thought the least use."

There had been no sign of Crean or Atkinson at Safety Camp, not even a note, and after four hours' sleep, Scott, Meares, Wilson and Cherry-Garrard marched on to Hut Point to see what had happened. Scott was mystified to find their old hut cleared and a message from Atkinson to say that there was a mail bag inside, but when neither mail nor men were to be found, he correctly guessed that they must have unwittingly crossed somewhere on the Barrier, and set off back towards Safety Camp to find them.

The ice around Cape Armitage was weaker than ever, with great expanses of water holes off it, and Scott was relieved to see Crean and Atkinson's tent next to their own. From the tone of his diary it is clear that he had been planning a rocket for them for leaving no message behind for him, but when he was handed the mail bag with its letter from Campbell, anything else seemed an irrelevance.

Amundsen was in the Bay of Whales. "One thing only fixes itself in my mind," Scott wrote, repeating the old New Zealand mantra. "The proper, as well as the wiser, course for us is to proceed exactly as though this had not happened. To go forward and do our best for the honour of the country without fear or panic. There is no doubt that Amundsen's plan is a very serious menace to ours. He has a shorter distance to the Pole by 60 miles— I never would have thought he could have got so many dogs safely to the ice. His plan for running them seems excellent. But above and beyond all he can start his journey early in the season—an impossible condition with the ponies."

"Of one thing I am certain," Gran had written in his diary out at One Ton Depot, "we shall need luck if we are to reach the Pole next year." Now, with the news of Amundsen, they were going to need a lot more than luck if they were to reach the Pole first.

Twenty-seven: Disaster

> For an hour or so we were furiously angry and were possessed with an insane sense that we must go straight to the Bay of Whales and have it out with Amundsen and his men in some undefined fashion or other there and then. Such a mood could not and did not bear a moment's reflection; but it was natural enough. We had just paid a first instalment of the heart-breaking labour of making a path to the Pole; and we felt, however unreasonably, that we had earned the first right of way. Our sense of cooperation and solidarity had been wrought up to an extraordinary pitch; and we had so completely forgotten the spirit of competition that its sudden intrusion jarred frightfully. I do not defend our burst of rage—for such it was—I simply record it as an integral human part of my narrative.
>
> APSLEY CHERRY-GARRARD, *The Worst Journey in the World*

If there was any man in the party other than Scott who fully saw how bad the news was, it was Tryggve Gran. For some curious reason Wilson was sceptical of Amundsen's chances from the start, but after a month's experience of British depot-laying and animal management, the *Terra Nova's* one Norwegian was in no doubt. "I felt as if the glacier had opened under me and a thousand thoughts rushed into my head," Gran wrote. "Was I to compete with my own compatriots, with my own flag? No it was not pleasant to contemplate. I believe from what I have seen that Amundsen's chances are better than ours. First, he is one degree further south than we are and, secondly, his speed is far superior to ours, since our horses are not first class. *If we reach the Pole Amundsen will reach the Pole and weeks earlier.* Our prospects are thus not exactly promising. The only thing that can save Scott is if an accident happens to Amundsen. I hear Scott took calmly the news about Amundsen, but sees clearly the danger."

There was little enough in the reports the Eastern Party brought back to Cape Evans, either, to suggest they were up against anything other than a formidable rival. After dropping off first Scott and then Taylor's Geological Party, Pennell had taken the *Terra Nova* along the Barrier edge as far as

170°W, surveying the ice-face as she went. He had intended to drop Campbell and his five men somewhere on the coast of King Edward's Land, but, driven back by heavy pack and unable to find a suitable landing place, he had headed instead for Barrier Inlet, which in *Discovery* days had been known as Balloon Bight.*

Pennell's sights and angles confirmed what Priestley, at least, already knew: that Scott's Balloon Bight and Shackleton's Bay of Whales were one and the same place. In the three years that had elapsed since he had been there in *Nimrod*, the bight had evidently broken back still further, and the western side altered, but "Otherwise," Priestley wrote, "it was the same, the same deceptive caves and shadows . . . the same pressure- ridged cliffs, the same undulations behind, the same expanse of sea-ice and even the same crowd of whales."

It was here, in the bay that Shackleton had rejected as too dangerous, that Priestley was woken at one in the morning by Lillie with "the astounding news that there was a ship . . . at anchor to the sea-ice." "In two minutes we recognised the 'Fram,'" Scott's brother-in-law, Bruce, reported back to Kathleen. "Curses loud & deep were heard everywhere, and we ran close by her & made fast to the floe ahead without them knowing."

They had been seen from the Barrier, though, and Campbell, the one expert skier among them, raced on ahead to find out the news. "They reached the pack about 6 January," Priestley was soon recording, "and were through it by the 12th, so they did not have as bad a time as we did. They inform us that Amundsen does not intend to make his descent on the Pole until next year. This is encouraging as it means a fair race, though the news we are bringing to them will keep the Western (Main) Party on tenterhooks of excitement all the winter."

In line with the code that Shackleton had reluctantly breached, Pennell and Campbell immediately abandoned their plans to land, and in one stroke of tactful good breeding turned the Eastern Party into the Northern Party. It was a particular blow to Campbell, who had seen the "KEVII Land show" as "*the* thing of the whole expedition," and yet if the sacrifice

---

*Scott's Instructions to Campbell are a model of clarity and flexibility. "Whilst I hope you may be able to land in King Edward's Land," he had written on 23 January, "I fully realise the possibility of the conditions being unfavourable and the difficulty of the task which has been set you . . . Should you succeed in landing, the object you will hold in view is to discover the nature and extent of King Edward's Land. The possibilities of your situation are so various that it must be left to you entirely to determine how this object may best be achieved . . . Should you be unable to land in the region of King Edward's Land you will be at liberty to go to the region of Robertson Bay after communicating with Cape Evans."

seems a piece of punctilio now, it casts an interesting light on Shackleton's behaviour that not a man on board thought so then.

"Our plans have of course been decided for us," Priestley wrote in his journal that night, but even his thoughts were more for Scott's party than for his own "show." Amundsen had been out of camp when they arrived, but the next morning he was back and the rest of the day was spent in a round of diplomatic courtesies and a salutary glimpse for Scott's officers of the formidable organisation behind their rival's bid for the Pole. "Well! we have left the Norwegians and our thoughts are full, too full, of them at present," Priestley wrote. "The impression they have left me with is that of a set of men of distinctive personality, and evidently inured to hardship, good goers and pleasant and good-humoured. All these qualities combine to make them very dangerous rivals, but even did one not want to, one cannot help liking them individually in spite of the rivalry."

The only danger to Amundsen seemed to lie in the site of his base camp, and the risk of calving ice that had put Shackleton off in *Nimrod*. After his bold coup he possibly deserved all the luck that he got at "Framheim," but it is worth noting that his choice of the site was based on error rather than bravado, and on the mistaken belief that the Barrier ice at this point was grounded on land that broke through its surface to the southeast in the shape of Roosevelt Island. It says all that needs saying for this theory that the Bay of Whales is no longer *there*, but if Amundsen's luck could only hold through the winter, there was no question of the advantage he had won himself. "Individually they all seemed charming men," Bruce told Kathleen. "Even the perfidious Ammundsen [sic]. They have 120 dogs, and are going for the Pole! No science, no nothing, just the Pole! . . . if their dogs are a success, they are more than likely to be there first."

If it was typical of Scott that he should have taken the news as well as anybody, it marked the start of a disastrous few days. He had decided to employ the time waiting for the rest of the ponies to arrive in taking further supplies out onto the Barrier, and on the twenty-fourth he set off with two sledges and Keohane's pony towards Corner Camp to meet Bowers and his party. After their ordeal in the crevasse, the dogs were in no state for work, but Scott was determined that the men were going to be in "hard condition," and was glad of the chance some man-hauling gave to bring them up to scratch. He was not over-impressed with the performance of Teddy Evans's sledge party on the first day, and by the next was back to his old exacting sledging self. "Except for our tent," he complained in the same language he had used on *Discovery*'s voyage south, "shall have to tell people that we are out on business, not picnicking."

By this time they had already seen the pony party in the distance, hurrying in the opposite direction, and after depoting another six weeks' provisions at Corner Camp, Scott, Cherry and Crean turned back to catch them up. There was an anxious delay the next day when an unexpected blizzard kept them to their tent, but by the morning of the twenty-eighth they were at Safety Camp and united again with the rest of the Depoting Party. "Found everyone very cold and depressed," Scott noted. "Wilson and Meares had had continuous bad weather since we left, Bowers and Oates since their arrival. The blizzard had raged for two days. The animals looked in a sorry condition, but all were alive."

The ponies might have been alive, but that was about all, and when their coats came off for the march back Scott saw how emaciated they were. With a hard, cold wind blowing from the east, he knew that it was vital to get them off the Barrier before another blizzard, but even without a load to haul another march was more than Weary Willie could manage. "We made desperate efforts [to] save the poor creature," Scott noted after he had collapsed, "got him once more on his legs and gave him a hot mash . . . 500 yards away from the camp the poor creature fell again and I felt it was the last effort. We camped, built a snow wall round him, and did all we possibly could to get him on his feet. Every effort was fruitless, though the poor creature made pitiable struggles. Towards midnight we propped him up as comfortably as we could and went to bed."

In his determination to get the other ponies off the Barrier as soon as possible, Scott had already sent them on with Bowers, Crean and Cherry, and when he woke the next morning to find "Weary" dead, his haste seemed justified. "Well, we have done our best and bought our experience at a heavy cost," he wrote in his last entry for February. "Now every effort must be bent on saving the remaining animals, and it will be good luck if we get four back to Cape Evans, or even three. Jimmy Pigg may have fared badly; Bowers's big pony is in a bad way after that frightful blizzard. I cannot remember such a bad storm in February or March."

The next day Scott, Oates and Gran struck camp early, anxious to catch up with Bowers and the other ponies. Scott had been worrying for at least a week about the condition of the sea-ice off Cape Armitage, but none of his worst forebodings had prepared him for the view that greeted them as they approached Fodder Depot, and saw what seemed to be a mirage of broken floes and open leads criss-crossing the surface he had ordered Bowers and his party across. "My thoughts flew to the ponies and dogs," Scott wrote, "and fearful anxieties assailed my mind. We turned to follow the sea edge and suddenly discovered a working crack. We dashed over this and slackened pace again after a quarter of a mile. Then again cracks appeared ahead and we increased pace as much as possible, not slackening again till we were in line between the Safety Camp and Castle Rock."

His anxieties were well enough founded, but if he could have seen where Bowers and his party were at that moment, they would have been a lot worse. "My orders [had been] to push on to Hut Point over the ice without delay," Bowers later wrote, "and to follow the dogs; previously I had been told to camp on the sea-ice in case of the beasts being unable to go on. We had four pretty heavy sledges, as we were taking six weeks' man food and oil to the hut, as well as a lot of gear from the depot, and pony food etc. Unfortunately the dogs misunderstood their orders and, instead of piloting us, dashed off on their own. We saw them like specks in the distance in the direction of the old seal crack. Having crossed this they wheeled to the right in the direction of Cape Armitage and disappeared into a black indefinite mist, which seemed to pervade everything in that direction."

Bowers had managed to follow the dog tracks in the soft snow as far as the "seal crack"—an old pressure ridge running many miles out in a southwesterly direction from Pram Point—and crossed it onto newer ice on the other side. Crean had been over this surface earlier and thought that it would hold, and Bowers decided that if they gave Cape Armitage a wide enough berth to the west they would be able to make it safely round to Hut Point. "However," he continued, "about a mile farther on I began to have misgivings; the cracks became too frequent to be pleasant, and although the ice was frozen from five to ten feet thick, one does not like to see water squelching between them, as we did later. It spells motion, and motion on sea-ice spells breakage."

A moving crack was eventually enough to halt even Bowers, and after a "beastly retreat back across the seal crack," they got as far from it as the exhausted animals could manage before setting up camp. With only a defective Primus to cook on, it took an hour and a half to heat their water, but after a cup of pemmican and cocoa made in the dark with curry and sugar by mistake—Crean drank his without noticing—they turned in at two.

Two and a half hours later, Bowers was disturbed by a noise, and thinking his pony had got at the oats, stumbled out of the tent. "I cannot describe either the scene or my feelings," he wrote. "I must leave those to

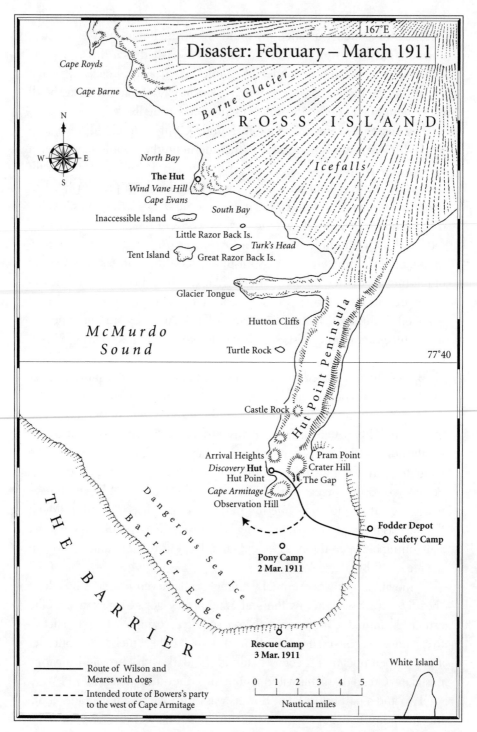

Disaster: February – March 1911

167°E

Cape Royds

Cape Barne

Barne Glacier

R O S S   I S L A N D

Icefalls

N
W — E
S

North Bay

The Hut
Wind Vane Hill
Cape Evans

South Bay

Inaccessible Island

Little Razor Back Is.

Turk's Head

Tent Island   Great Razor Back Is.

Glacier Tongue

Hutton Cliffs

McMurdo
Sound

Turtle Rock

77°40

Castle Rock

Arrival Heights   Pram Point
Discovery **Hut**   Crater Hill
Hut Point   The Gap
Cape Armitage
Observation Hill

D a n g e r o u s   S e a   I c e

B a r r i e r   E d g e

T H E   B A R R I E R

Fodder Depot
Safety Camp

Pony Camp
2 Mar. 1911

Rescue Camp
3 Mar. 1911

White Island

———— Route of Wilson and
              Meares with dogs

– – – – – Intended route of Bowers's party
              to the west of Cape Armitage

0   1   2   3   4   5

Nautical miles

your imagination. We were in the middle of a floating pack of broken-up ice. The tops of the hills were visible, but all below was thin mist and as far as the eye could see there was nothing solid; it was all broken up and heaving up and down with the swell. Long black tongues of water were everywhere. The floe on which we were had split right under our picketing line, and cut poor Gus's wall in half. Gus himself had gone, and a dark streak of water alone showed the place where the ice had opened under him."

The floe they were on was no more than fifteen yards across, and with an easterly wind working on it, was drifting westwards out to open sea. Bowers managed to salvage two of their sledges from an adjoining floe before they floated off, and getting the tent packed and the horses harnessed as quickly as they could, they struck south across the moving ice, leaping the gaps or bridging the open leads with their twelve-foot sledges. "We found the ponies would jump the intervals well," he wrote. "At least Punch would and the other two would follow him. My idea was never to separate, but to get everything onto one floe at a time, and then wait until it touched or nearly touched another in the right direction, and then jump the ponies over and drag the four sledges across ourselves."

With agonising slowness and a constant westward drift, they inched their way south towards the Barrier edge. Sometimes they would have to wait ten minutes for the right floe to touch, only to see it bounce off and drift away again before they could make their way across. "Meanwhile a further unpleasantness occurred in the arrival of a host of the terrible 'killer' whales," Bowers wrote. "These were reaping a harvest of seal in the broken-up ice, and cruised among the floes with their immense black fins sticking up, and blowing with a terrific roar."

It never occurred to any of them that their real difficulties still lay ahead, and after more than six hours they were close enough to fast ice to begin to hope. They had sighted some way off a large, tilted floe that seemed to slope upwards to the Barrier edge, and getting the ponies and sledges onto its lower lip, made a last rush up to what Bowers thought would mean safety. They "were little prepared," Bowers wrote. "All along the Barrier face a broad lane of water from thirty to forty feet wide extended. It was filled with smashed-up brash ice, which was heaving up and down to the swell like the contents of a cauldron. Killers were cruising there with feverish activity, and the Barrier edge was a sheer cliff of ice on the other side fifteen to twenty feet high. It was a case of so near and so far."

There was clearly no hope of getting the animals up that cliff, but if one of the men could make his way windward along the line of the ice edge, a touching berg might give him a moment's chance to scramble onto the Barrier and fetch help. There could be no question of Bowers leaving the animals in such straits, and with Cherry too short-sighted to see much farther than the next floe, Crean was soon edging his way eastward along the open lead in search of a way up to safety.

"It was not a pleasant day that Cherry and I spent all alone there," Bowers later wrote, with only "a zephyr from the south" needed to send them "irretrievably out to sea," but the sight of a distant speck crawling on the Barrier surface was enough to confirm the Hand of the Lord in their day's work. But if one of them was "out of the woods," that still left the other two of them and the ponies, and they only had to look out into the bay to see how real their danger was.

Where they had been only hours earlier was now open water. Nor was the threat only out in the sound. Beside them, the Barrier edge was calving even as they watched, with huge chunks of ice capsizing into the sea, crashing down onto other floes and shattering across the turmoil of heaving brash that filled the lead. The floe they were on had already split as well, and the killers were beginning to take too close an interest "to be pleasant." In a pool between their berg and the next no bigger than the size of a room, Cherry could count six. "They had a habit of bobbing up and down perpendicularly," Bowers wrote, "so as to see over the edge of a floe, in looking for seals. The huge black and yellow heads with sickening pig eyes only a few yards from us at times, and always around us, are among the most disconcerting recollections I have of that day. The immense fins were bad enough, but when they started a perpendicular dodge they were positively beastly."

"I suppose there is no doubt we are in the devil of a hole," Cherry scribbled in his diary as they waited, but to Bowers the whole nightmare seemed no more than one long demonstration of the sustaining power of the Lord. To a more sceptical mind it might have seemed that the day had in fact not gone well, but Bowers's trust in God and Cherry's in him were both rewarded when, fourteen hours after their ordeal had begun, Crean reappeared at the Barrier edge opposite with Scott and Oates.

There was now a berg jammed in the lead between Barrier and floe, but there was still no way of getting their animals across. " 'What about the ponies and the sledges?' " Bowers shouted across to Scott. " 'I don't give a damn about the ponies and sledges. It's you I want, and I am going to see you safe here up on the Barrier before I do anything else.' " Dumping the kit from two of the sledges, Bowers and Cherry had soon made a bridge with their frames, and were safely across to the other side. Bowers had been expecting a "blowing up," but "Captain Scott was so pleased, that I realized the feeling he must have had all day. He had been blaming himself for our deaths, and here we were very much alive. He said: 'My dear chaps, you can't think how glad I am to see you safe—Cherry likewise.' "

Bowers had not nursed the ponies and sledges this far to abandon them now, and in the teeth of Scott's better judgement, wheedled permission to rescue what he could. While he and Scott haggled over each article that Bowers wanted to save, Oates began to cut a slope in the Barrier edge, carving out an ice-ramp for the ponies to cross over from their floe to the safety of fast ice. It was going to take hours, and it was risky work, but Scott and Bowers were agreed it was worth trying when a sudden movement of the floe took the decision out of their hands. As Bowers scrambled to safety, the gap between floe and Barrier began to widen "almost imperceptibly, 2 feet, 6 feet, 10 feet, 20 feet, and, sick as we were about the ponies, we were glad to be on the safe side of that."

There seemed nothing more they could do for the ponies, and with the Barrier edge still dangerously calving, they pitched their tents half a mile in. While they waited for supper to cook, Scott and Bowers returned to the ice cliff, only to find that the crack had widened to seventy feet, the killers "were chasing up and down it like racehorses," and the three ponies were on a floe drifting westwards parallel with the Barrier. "If ever one could feel miserable I did then," Bowers recalled in a revealing passage, but "My feelings were nothing to what poor Captain Scott had had to endure that day. I at once broached the hopeful side of the subject, remarking that, with the two Campbell had left [when the Eastern journey was aborted], we had ten ponies at Winter quarters. He said however, that he had no confidence whatever in the motors after the way their rollers had become messed up unloading the ship. He had had his confidence in the dogs much shaken on the return journey, and now he had lost the most solid asset—the best of his pony transport. He said: 'Of course we shall have a run for our money next season, but as far as the Pole is concerned I have but very little hope.' "

Even now, Bowers was reluctant to abandon his ponies, and time and again after supper he went back alone to the Barrier edge. If he could have killed the creatures to spare them any worse suffering he would gladly have done so, but "hope springs eternal," and when some hours later he returned with glasses, he saw in the distance three dots on a mass of ice that had butted up against a Barrier spur stretching out into the bay.

After his own solo ordeal, Crean's eyes were too bad for him to be of any help, but with Cherry and Oates in pursuit, Bowers had soon leaped his way across the floes to reach the ponies. The cracks between the bergs now were nothing like as wide as they had managed the day before, but, frozen stiff from a stationary night on the floe, Punch jibbed at the first that Bowers put him to and went in, floundering helplessly among the brash and killers of the open lead. For all their efforts, there was nothing Bowers, Oates or Cherry could do to get him out, and sooner than watch him be torn apart, Oates finished him off with a pick. Scott was again more alarmed for the men than the ponies, but with his blood up and Uncle Bill and Nobby still to be saved, Bowers ignored Scott's protests and began to jump them from floe to floe towards a spot where they could scramble them up onto the Barrier and safety.

Once they had been got to the Barrier edge, Scott soon succeeded in rushing Nobby up, but with only a crumbling soup of brash ice between the rest of them and the killers, Uncle Bill was doomed. At the last leap between two floes his hind legs had slipped into the freezing water, and disabled by the shock and exhaustion, he could struggle no more. Even with a rope round him, and Scott, Oates, Bowers and Cherry pulling for all their worth, they could not get him through the slush of ice that had become their only road out of danger. The brash was now so thin, too, that any moment a killer could have burst through and hurled them all "like chaff" into the water. Yet still Bowers could not bear to abandon him, determined that if he could do nothing else for the poor creature, he could at least spare him the horror of the killers. "Sick with disappointment," and impervious to orders or the sudden list of the Barrier edge itself, he held on to Uncle Bill's head. "I said: 'I can't leave him to be eaten alive by those whales.' There was a pick lying up on the floe. Titus said: 'I shall be sick if I have to kill another horse like I did the last.' I had no intention that anyone should kill my own horse but myself, and getting the pick I struck where Titus told me. I made sure of the job before we ran up and jumped the opening in the Barrier, carrying a blood-stained pick-axe instead of leading the pony I had almost considered safe."

It was the end of a nightmare that had seemed to stretch on without end. But even now there was no rest. Anything near the Barrier edge was unsafe, and it was midnight and a two-mile march before Scott and his exhausted men could finally turn in. "So here we are," he wrote in his diary on the morning of 4 March, after "a terrible pull" to cover the short distance to the camp where forty-eight interminable hours earlier he had

After his own solo ordeal, Crean's eyes were too bad for him to be of any help, but with Cherry and Oates in pursuit, Bowers had soon leaped his way across the floes to reach the ponies. The cracks between the bergs now were nothing like as wide as they had managed the day before, but, frozen stiff from a stationary night on the floe, Punch jibbed at the first that Bowers put him to and went in, floundering helplessly among the brash and killers of the open lead. For all their efforts, there was nothing Bowers, Oates or Cherry could do to get him out, and sooner than watch him be torn apart, Oates finished him off with a pick. Scott was again more alarmed for the men than the ponies, but with his blood up and Uncle Bill and Nobby still to be saved, Bowers ignored Scott's protests and began to jump them from floe to floe towards a spot where they could scramble them up onto the Barrier and safety.

Once they had been got to the Barrier edge, Scott soon succeeded in rushing Nobby up, but with only a crumbling soup of brash ice between the rest of them and the killers, Uncle Bill was doomed. At the last leap between two floes his hind legs had slipped into the freezing water, and disabled by the shock and exhaustion, he could struggle no more. Even with a rope round him, and Scott, Oates, Bowers and Cherry pulling for all their worth, they could not get him through the slush of ice that had become their only road out of danger. The brash was now so thin, too, that any moment a killer could have burst through and hurled them all "like chaff" into the water. Yet still Bowers could not bear to abandon him, determined that if he could do nothing else for the poor creature, he could at least spare him the horror of the killers. "Sick with disappointment," and impervious to orders or the sudden list of the Barrier edge itself, he held on to Uncle Bill's head. "I said: 'I can't leave him to be eaten alive by those whales.' There was a pick lying up on the floe. Titus said: 'I shall be sick if I have to kill another horse like I did the last.' I had no intention that anyone should kill my own horse but myself, and getting the pick I struck where Titus told me. I made sure of the job before we ran up and jumped the opening in the Barrier, carrying a blood-stained pick-axe instead of leading the pony I had almost considered safe."

It was the end of a nightmare that had seemed to stretch on without end. But even now there was no rest. Anything near the Barrier edge was unsafe, and it was midnight and a two-mile march before Scott and his exhausted men could finally turn in. "So here we are," he wrote in his diary on the morning of 4 March, after "a terrible pull" to cover the short distance to the camp where forty-eight interminable hours earlier he had with their frames, and were safely across to the other side. Bowers had been expecting a "blowing up," but "Captain Scott was so pleased, that I realized the feeling he must have had all day. He had been blaming himself for our deaths, and here we were very much alive. He said: 'My dear chaps, you can't think how glad I am to see you safe—Cherry likewise.' "

Bowers had not nursed the ponies and sledges this far to abandon them now, and in the teeth of Scott's better judgement, wheedled permission to rescue what he could. While he and Scott haggled over each article that Bowers wanted to save, Oates began to cut a slope in the Barrier edge, carving out an ice-ramp for the ponies to cross over from their floe to the safety of fast ice. It was going to take hours, and it was risky work, but Scott and Bowers were agreed it was worth trying when a sudden movement of the floe took the decision out of their hands. As Bowers scrambled to safety, the gap between floe and Barrier began to widen "almost imperceptibly, 2 feet, 6 feet, 10 feet, 20 feet, and, sick as we were about the ponies, we were glad to be on the safe side of that."

There seemed nothing more they could do for the ponies, and with the Barrier edge still dangerously calving, they pitched their tents half a mile in. While they waited for supper to cook, Scott and Bowers returned to the ice cliff, only to find that the crack had widened to seventy feet, the killers "were chasing up and down it like racehorses," and the three ponies were on a floe drifting westwards parallel with the Barrier. "If ever one could feel miserable I did then," Bowers recalled in a revealing passage, but "My feelings were nothing to what poor Captain Scott had had to endure that day. I at once broached the hopeful side of the subject, remarking that, with the two Campbell had left [when the Eastern journey was aborted], we had ten ponies at Winter quarters. He said however, that he had no confidence whatever in the motors after the way their rollers had become messed up unloading the ship. He had had his confidence in the dogs much shaken on the return journey, and now he had lost the most solid asset—the best of his pony transport. He said: 'Of course we shall have a run for our money next season, but as far as the Pole is concerned I have but very little hope.' "

Even now, Bowers was reluctant to abandon his ponies, and time and again after supper he went back alone to the Barrier edge. If he could have killed the creatures to spare them any worse suffering he would gladly have done so, but "hope springs eternal," and when some hours later he returned with glasses, he saw in the distance three dots on a mass of ice that had butted up against a Barrier spur stretching out into the bay.

first seen the open leads, "ready to start our sad journey to Hut Point. Everything out of joint with the loss of the ponies, but mercifully with all the party alive and well."

The equipment they had left at the camp was gone, and ski and pony tracks pointed towards land. Following them across the Barrier and onto rock, they camped at the highest ridge of Pram Point. There Teddy Evans and his party joined them, and the next day, with the wind blowing hard on the hill, and even harder down at Hut Point, Scott made the final leg of the old familiar journey down to his *Discovery* site. "Found the hut in comparative order and slept there," he recorded in the tired, flat prose of a man who had very little more to give.

It was 5 March, and the end of the depoting journey. "These incidents were too terrible," Scott wrote of its last, disastrous stages, "and the only one comfort is the miraculous avoidance of loss of life." They had, though, bought survival and experience at an even higher price than Scott had imagined possible just days earlier. They still had the eleven men they had started with, and they had all seen the south at its most dangerous. Crean had again shown his worth; Bowers had stamped the imprint of his personality as firmly on sledging as he had on every other aspect of expedition life; Cherry had confirmed the impression he had made on the voyage down; Gran had shown what could be done with skis when given the chance; and they had laid their depots to just short of the 80th parallel.

Against that—and with Amundsen now in the field—they had only two of the original eight horses they had taken with them. Crucially, the condition of the ponies also meant that there could be no early start to the next season. Scott's confidence in the dogs, never high, had been further eroded. His trust in the two experts he had with him, Oates and Meares, was also dented. And just as important, so was theirs in him. "We lost 6 ponies," an embittered Oates wrote to his mother, "including mine which was a long way the best pony we had. I was very upset the more so as I think that he could have been saved if Scott had not been fussing to the extent he was . . . the loss of the ponies was Scott's fault entirely."

Twenty-eight: **Winter**

There must be some of my companions who look back upon Hut Point with a peculiar fondness, such as men get for places where they have experienced great joys and great trials. And Hut Point has an atmosphere of its own. I do not know what it is. Partly aesthetic, for the sea and the great mountains, and the glorious colour effects which prevail in spring and autumn, would fascinate the least imaginative; partly mysterious, with the Great Barrier knocking at your door, and the smoke of Erebus by day and the curtain of Aurora by night; partly the associations of the place — the old hut, the old landmarks . . . the stakes in the snow . . . Vince's cross.

APSLEY CHERRY-GARRARD, *The Worst Journey in the World*

There might once have been times when Scott saw the world with the same freshness as Cherry did, but the March of 1911 was not one of them. From Hut Point there was always a circuitous route onto the Barrier to the south, but the ice falls and crevasses that lay along the slopes of Erebus to the north effectively meant that until the sea-ice froze solid, he and his party were prisoners in a world whose associations and memories had been soured for him by the intrusions of Shackleton's *Nimrod* party.

With old boxes of biscuits to supplement their dwindling rations, plentiful seal for food, fuel and light, a few old copies of *Girl's Own* to read, and the veranda for the two surviving ponies, they were in no danger, but these comforts only seemed to make Scott's frustration worse. On 14 March the arrival of the Western Party swelled their numbers and noise levels, but not even the sparkle of "Griff" Taylor's company or the chance to "fog out the ice problems" with Wright was enough to keep Scott from his daily vigil at the point waiting for the young ice to freeze.

There was enough truth in Oates's criticism to have added an unwelcome edge to his vigil, too, but it was inaction and not introspection that was the enemy. "In spite of all the little activities I am impatient of our wait here," he wrote on 17 March, "but I shall be impatient also in the main hut. It is ill to sit and contemplate the ruin which has assailed our transport. The scheme of advance must be very different from that which I first contemplated. The Pole is a very long way off, alas! Bit by bit I am losing all faith in the dogs—I'm afraid they will never go the pace we look for."

There was one last, unsatisfactory depoting trip that only went to show that the Barrier was not a place to be in March, and by the middle of April Scott had had enough. There was no route for the ponies or the dogs back to Cape Evans until the fifteen miles of sea-ice had frozen hard, but with the right nerve and good men he reckoned that a route could be found over the lower spurs of Erebus to the north of them and down onto the fast ice somewhere to the south of their base camp.

Even without the ponies it was going to be risky—Taylor had gone through the ice only days earlier—but on 13 April Scott and a party of eight began the long, hard haul up their old *Discovery* ski slope above Hut Point. "All gave us a pull up," he wrote in his diary, uneasily conscious that he was not as young as he had been; "it had become a point of honour to take the slope without a 'breather.' I find such an effort trying in the early morning, but had to go through with it."

Their groundbreaking route took them to the east of Castle Rock, and then to the west of two conical landmarks familiar from *Discovery* days, and on as far as a feature visible from Cape Evans known as Hutton Cliffs. From time to time a glimpse of the bays below would give Scott some idea of the condition of the sea-ice in the sound, but it was another five hours' marching before he was able to pick out through the queer April half-light a possible route down from their ridge to the sea cliffs and the safety of fast ice.

The descent was a dangerous business, but it was the kind of challenge that Scott excelled at, and in twenty minutes from the foot of the snow slope he had all his men and their sledges safely onto the floe. "It was a good piece of work getting everything down safely," Teddy Evans wrote with a nice ambiguity, "and I admired Scott's decision to go over; a more nervous man would have fought shy because once down to the sea ice there was little chance of our getting back and we had to fight our way forward to Cape Evans somehow."

It was a brilliant piece of work, in fact, bold, imaginative, decisive— "quite pleased," Scott noted smugly—but a brutal slog in a strengthening wind could only take them that night as far as Little Razor Back Island. Throughout the last hours of the march conditions had been deteriorating all the time, and with the sea-ice around them cracking ominously and the wind now a full-scale blizzard, Scott seized the chance of the first brief lull to find a safer site for their camp on the weather side. "It took two very cold hours," he wrote, "but we gained great shelter, the cliffs rising almost sheer from the tent. Only now and again a whirling wind current eddied down on the tents, but the noise of the wind sweeping over the rocky ridge above our heads was deafening; we could scarcely hear ourselves speak. Settled down for our second night with little comfort and slept better, knowing we could not be swept out to sea, but provisions were left for only one more meal."

The recollection of Bowers's exploits was too vivid to leave anyone unaware of the risks, but a slight improvement in visibility the next morning was all they needed, and three hours' hard pulling brought them safely to land. "I remember on our hazardous march back to Cape Evans from Hut Point," Taylor wrote in 1962, reflecting ruefully on the dangers of a journey that half a century had left as fresh in his mind as ever, "when I certainly thought Scott ought to have waited till the sea ice was thicker . . . This is indeed the sole flaw in Scott's leadership, except his dislike of dogs, as far as my experience goes."

Flaw or not, Scott had carried it off, though after their weeks on the Barrier and with their faces black from the blubber-smoke of the old *Discovery* hut, they looked more like scarecrows than men as they walked in off the sea-ice and into the camp. "I shall never forget the breakfast that Clissold prepared for us," Teddy Evans recalled, sounding very like the Scott of *Discovery* days, ". . . hot rolls, heaps of butter, milk, sugar, jam, a fine plate of tomato soup, and fried seal cooked superbly. The meal over we shaved, bathed, and put on clean clothes, smoked cigarettes, and took a day's holiday."

It was relief enough for Scott just to find that nothing had happened to their base camp while he was away. At ten that night a Verey light was sent up to tell the rump of the Depoting Party still at Hut Point that they had arrived safely,* and while Evans and the others relaxed over Melba and music-hall tunes, Scott realised for the first time just how anxious he had been. "In a normal season no thought of its having been in danger would have occurred to me," he wrote, half-aware that his fears had more to do

---

*An entry from Cherry's diary gives some idea of the anxieties over Scott's party among those left behind at Hut Point. "We all went wild with excitement," he wrote when they saw the distant Verey light, "knowing that all was well. Meares ran in and soaked some awning with paraffin, and we lifted it as an answering flare and threw it into the air again and again, until it was burning in little bits all over the snow. The relief was great."

with superstition than anything more rational, "but since the loss of the ponies and the breaking of the Glacier tongue I could not rid myself of the fear that some abnormal swell had swept the beach; gloomy thoughts of the havoc that might have been wrought . . . would arise in spite of the sound reasons which had originally led me to choose the site."

For all his relief at finding nothing more to disturb him than the death of the vicious Hackenshmidt—Anton reckoned that the pony had died out of sheer "cussedness" and a determination that he was not going to do any work for the expedition—there is something of the same feeling about Scott's return to Cape Evans as there was about his joining *Terra Nova* in South Africa. "It was not many hours or minutes before I was haled around to observe in detail the transformation which had taken place during my absence," he wrote in his diary, sounding more like some visiting dignitary or minor royal than the "Owner" of his own "show,"

and in which a very proper pride was taken by those who wrought it.

Simpson's Corner was the first visited. Here the eye travelled over numerous shelves laden with a profusion of self-recording instruments, electric batteries and switch-boards, whilst the ear caught the ticking of many clocks, the gentle whirr of a motor and occasionally the trembling note of an electric bell . . .

The dark room stands next to the parasitologist's side of the bench which flanks Sunny Jim's corner . . . and my attention was next claimed by the occupant of the dark room.

Long before I could gaze my fill at the contents of the dark room I was led to the biologist's cubicle . . . No attempt had been made to furnish this cubicle before our departure on the autumn journey, but now on my return I found it an example of the best utilisation of space . . .

Day appeared to have been unceasingly busy during my absence . . .

The "cook's corner," the stove, the oven, the acetylene lighting, the new stalls in the stables, the exercise ground, a lean-to for the dogs, Scott was shown it all, and "Finally, in this way," as he put it, "was brought to realise what an extensive and intricate but eminently satisfactory organisation I had made myself responsible for."

Scott was by such a long way the most dominant personality on the expedition, though, that it was only a matter of time before he stamped his own distinctive character on their winter regime. His one fear as he watched the last glow of light disappear behind the Barne Glacier on 23 April was that they would be "*too* comfortable" in their quarters, but with only five months to prepare for the Pole and a full programme of scientific observations — meteorological, magnetic, pendulum, atmospheric electricity, auroras, radioactivity — in place, that was never going to be likely. "One day passes very much like the next," Gran wrote in his winter journal.

> After breakfast Evans goes to his cartography, Scott to his diary, Day to his "make and mend," Meares to his harness-making, Oates (at 12) to his horses, Ponting to his photographic plates, Deb to his rock specimens, Taylor and I to our geographical studies or our diaries. At noon Atkinson with Taylor or Ponting go up to the Ramp. Then comes lunch with cocoa, coffee, cheese, marmalade and honey.
>
> The afternoon is like the morning, except that after five o'clock the pianola starts up . . . Then comes supper. Taylor waits impatiently for the pudding. Finally it comes and the meal ends with the lighting-up of cigars and pipes. Atkinson or I put the gramophone on. Then we play dominoes or chess until ten . . . About ten we begin to turn in; we read in bed, some till nearly midnight . . . Out go the lights at 11 and on goes the watchkeeper's lamp. At midnight and at 4 a.m. readings of the barometer and thermometer are taken. Naturally the watcher is on the look-out every hour for signs of the aurora.

This description is in so many ways reminiscent of the old *Discovery* routines that it is easy to forget the gulf in quality that separated the scientific work carried out by the two expeditions. In many superficial or merely physical ways, of course, the problems and miseries were the same, but if it was just as cold taking observations or doing night duty at Cape Evans as it was at Hut Point, that was about the limit of their similarities.

It had not been Royds's fault, for instance, that he was no scientist, or that he had not been properly trained in the use of his instruments, but nothing could better illustrate this gap than the quality of the meteorological work carried out under George Simpson. "I doubt if an expedition ever sailed with a more complete outfit of meteorological and magnetic instruments," Simpson himself later wrote, and nobody could have been better qualified to exploit the advantage than the future Director of the Meteorological Office. "Irritating as a companion" he might sometimes have been, with his "contemptuous pursing of the lips," but, "admirable as a worker, admirable as a scientist, admirable as a lecturer," Simpson brought to the job precisely that rigour and guarantee of standards that Scott had been looking for when he invited him. The absence of a second trained meteorologist inevitably limited the scope of his work, but the continuous stream of data for 1911–12 taken under Simpson's direction at Cape Evans can compare favourably with modern automated records.

It was not just the painstaking rigour of his record-keeping that distinguished Simpson's work, or the scrupulous cross-calibration of instruments, but the insights he brought to a wide range of meteorological phenomena. At the time of the *Terra Nova* expedition the differences in temperatures between an Arctic and an Antarctic summer were still a mystery to scientists, and it was Simpson who first saw that the answer lay in the intensively reflective quality of the Antarctic snow surface that—in contrast to the northern oceans—radiated solar energy back into space rather than absorbing it. There was corroboration of this when Simpson, with the serio-comic assistance of "Birdie" Bowers, sent up to a height of as much as five miles some of the first hydrogen-filled balloons to be released over the Antarctic. The device they used to release the recording instruments was an ingenious slow-burning fuse, and if this could mean a wild chase over the floes for Bowers to retrieve their equipment, the results in still weather showed the steep inversion of temperatures commensurate with Simpson's theory.

These findings reflected the experience of sledgers on the Barrier, too, explaining the warmer temperatures that followed high winds, as the cold surface air mixed with the warmer air above. For Scott and his men the practical relevance of Simpson's work had largely been confined to summer conditions on the Barrier, but the ferocious temperatures already recorded on the last depoting journey in March ominously attested to a similar relevance to the phenomenon of the "coreless" Antarctic winter. "At the end of summer," Simpson wrote in explanation, contrasting the effect of the warmer Arctic summer on winter conditions with the plunging cold of an Antarctic climate whose base summer temperature is so much lower, "the ice in the north is thinner than at the end of winter, there is some open water, and the surrounding land surfaces are still free from snow, and therefore have a relatively high temperature. All these effects supply heat, and keep the temperature high, thus when the sun sets for the last time in October, the temperature in the north is 24.9 higher than when it rose in February."*

It was not simply the huge chasm between the work of Royds and Simpson that highlights the different cultures of *Discovery* and *Terra Nova*; there was the same gap between the geology of the two expeditions. Given the conditions under which he laboured, Ferrar performed heroics on his Western Mountains journey of 1903, but there was a strict limit to what a young and inexperienced geologist plagued by snow blindness and operating with a broken-down sledge and two seamen to assist him could do in less than a month's exploration. On the *Terra Nova*, by contrast, Scott had in Raymond Priestley (with Campbell's Northern Party), Griffith Taylor and Frank Debenham a mixture of experience, youth, abrasive talent, theoretical vision and systematic "plod" that opened up a different range of possibilities. It needs to be remembered that before their arrival the nearest thing to a technical analysis of a dry valley was Lashly's remark that it would be good for potatoes, but in the two long sledging journeys of 1911 and 1912 Taylor's geological parties revolutionised the understanding of Victoria Land with a systematic exploration of an area that stretched from Granite Harbour on the 77th parallel to the Koettlitz ice delta and its hinterland in 78°20'.

Scott might not always have been at ease with the theoretical thrust of Taylor's physiography—"he strikes doubts . . . I confess a difficulty to grasp his full meaning to the expedition," he noted—but argument and debate were lifeblood to him. In an early character sketch of Taylor, Bowers labelled him "a typical Australian," but it is interesting that while the young Debenham could find his "unkempt, crude, blunt . . . tactless . . . sloppy" fellow-countryman "with not too much idea of cleanliness" something of a national embarrassment, the fastidious forty-three-year-old naval captain clearly had no problem with him.

The work of a man like Taylor, in fact, and the verve, commitment and raw intelligence he brought to it, constituted the *raison d'être* of their presence in the south for Scott, and if his own energies were inevitably harnessed to their polar bid, the "Universitas Antarctica" that their winter quarters became was probably as close to his expedition ideal as could be

---

*The most interesting and original study of the meteorological work of the *Terra Nova* expedition and the effects of climate on Scott's polar journey can be found in Susan Solomon's *The Coldest March*.

realised. "One sees Wilson busy with pencil and colour box," he wrote, in a kind of composite sweep of the hut interior, ". . . filling the gaps in his zoological work of *Discovery* times; withal ready and willing to give advice to others at all times . . . Simpson, master of his craft, untiringly attentive to the workings of his numerous self-recording instruments . . . doing the work of two observers at least . . . Wright, good-hearted, strong, keen, striving to saturate his mind with the ice problems of this wonderful region . . . Adjacent to the physicists' corner . . . Atkinson is quietly pursuing the subject of parasites. Already he is in a new world . . . Constantly he comes to ask if I would like to see some new form, and I am taken to see some protozoon or ascidian isolated on the slide plate of his microscope."

Alongside all this ceaseless activity there were all those other hallmarks of a Scott winter, too, with exercise whenever the weather allowed it, football out on the floe, a slightly feeble revival of the old *South Polar Times* under Cherry's editorship, and lectures three times a week. There were plenty in the hut who thought that number at least two too many, but it is perhaps a measure of Scott's dominance that he could sustain such a remorseless programme of self-improvement in the teeth of a twenty-three to one majority *against*.* "Taylor, I dreamt of your lecture last night," he was overheard saying one morning. "How could I live so long in the world and not know something of so fascinating a subject!"

The mess deck could live only too easily without Taylor's physiography or Wright on "Ice Problems—heaven help me!," and it was only Ponting's slide shows or Meares's reminiscences that could command a full house. "He had no pictures and very makeshift maps," Scott wrote of Meares's account of his Tibetan adventures that had ended in the murder of the expedition leader, "and yet he held us entranced for nearly two hours by the sheer interest of his adventures. The spirit of the wanderer is in Meares's blood: he has no happiness but in the wild places on the earth. I have never met so extreme a type. Even now he is looking forward to getting away by himself to Hut Point, tired already of our scant measure of civilization."

"Yesterday evening Ponting gave us a lecture on his Indian travels"—he had already done Japan—Scott wrote again. "He is very frank in ack-

---

*This represented something less than half the complete complement of the expedition. The last of the Depoting Party returned to Cape Evans from Hut Point on 13 May, but the Ship Party under Pennell had sailed back to New Zealand for the winter after dropping off Campbell and the five men of his now "Northern Party" at Robertson Bay.

nowledging his debt to guide-books for information, nevertheless he tells his story well and his slides are wonderful . . . Jeypore, Udaipore, Darjeeling . . . the wonderful Taj Mahal—horses, elephants, alligators, wild boars, and flamingos—warriors, fakirs, and nautch girls—an impression here and an impression there. It is worth remembering how attractive this style can be . . . A lecture need not be a connected story; perhaps it is better it should not be."

There is nothing to be said about Ponting that Ponting's photographs do not say better, except perhaps that Scott was invariably more generous about him than were many others in the expedition. In some ways Ponting was the *Terra Nova*'s answer to *Discovery*'s Koettlitz, but if he shared the same reluctance to help with anyone else's work and the same capacity for involving everyone in his own, there is no one except Scott and Cherry who has so firmly stamped his vision on our idea of expedition life.* In technical terms his photographs of the Antarctic are as far from the work of his *Discovery* predecessors as Simpson's results are from Royds's, but it is the *vision* his technique serves that distinguishes Ponting's photographs. From the day he first saw McMurdo Sound the landscape seduced him as completely as it did Scott, but it was constantly the dramatic contrasts of expedition life that caught his imagination—the ship in the ice, the carefully posed figure at the foot of Castle Berg ("to pont" became an expedition verb), the isolated sledger against a background of the western mountains—and that feed most directly into the common romantic image of the "Heroic Age."

As well as his wonderful portraits—there is something of Wright of Derby about his picture of Meares and Oates over their blubber stove— Ponting could turn an engaging pen-portrait. "Captain Scott and Bowers applied themselves to the work with extraordinary enthusiasm," he recalled of Scott's photographic apprenticeship, in terms that conjure up a vision of the same Scott who had poor Royds's clock manically striking the hour.

---

*If anyone doubts this, it is worth putting Ponting's austerely beautiful, monochrome image of the *Terra Nova* seen from an ice cave side by side with Scott's description of the same view. "Ponting has been ravished yesterday by a view of the ship seen from a big cave in an iceberg," he wrote. "This afternoon I went to the iceberg with him and agreed that I had rarely seen anything more beautiful than the cave. It was really a sort of crevasse in a tilted berg parallel to the original surface; the strata on either side had bent outwards; through the back the sky could be seen through a screen of beautiful icicles—it looked a royal purple, whether by contrast with the blue of the cavern or whether from optical illusion I do not know. Through the larger entrance could be seen, also partly through icicles, the ship, the Western Mountains, and a lilac sky."

Indeed, Scott's zeal outran his capability; he craved to be initiated into the uses of colour-filters and telephoto lenses before he had mastered an exposure-meter. I had to express my disapproval of such haste, and firmly decline to discuss these things until he could repeatedly show me half-a-dozen correctly exposed negatives from as many plates. When he had achieved this result under my guidance, he would sally forth alone with his camera.

He would come back as pleased as a boy, telling me quite excitedly he had got some splendid things, and together we would begin to develop his plates—six in a dish. When five minutes or more had elapsed and no sign of a latent image appeared on any of them, I knew something was wrong, and a conversation would follow, something in this wise:

"Are you quite sure you did *everything* correctly?"

"My dear fellow" (a great expression this of Scott's), "I'm absolutely *certain* I did. I'm sure I made no mistake."

"Did you put in the plateholder?" "Yes."

"Did you draw the slide?" "Yes"

"Did you set the shutter?" "Yes"

"Did you release the shutter?" "Yes"

"Did you take the cap off the lens?" "Yes"

Then he would rub his head, in that way he had, and admit:

"No! Good heavens! I forgot. I could have sworn I had forgotten nothing."

He would then fill up his holders again, and be off once more. He fell repeatedly into every pitfall in his haste—with unfamiliar apparatus. One day he would forget to set the shutter, another time he would forget to release it, and each time he would vow not to make the same error again—and then go out and make some other. But I liked him all the more for his human impatience and his mistakes.

If Scott's men were taking the measure of him, he was similarly taking stock of them. The one man in the expedition who could induce in him the kind of icy contempt that he reserved for indolence and brag was the young Gran, but after their autumn season on the Barrier and at Hut Point it was his second-in-command who was the real worry. "Evans himself is a queer study," he wrote in an excised passage of his diary on 5 May; "his boyish enthusiasm carries all along till one sees clearly the childish limitations of its foundations and appreciates that it is not a rock to be built on—He is altogether a good fellow and wholly well meaning but terribly slow to learn and hence fails altogether to grasp the value of any work but his own—very desirous to help everyone he is mentally incapable of doing it. There are problems ahead here for I cannot consider him fitted for a superior position—though he is physically strong & fit for a subordinate one. It was curious to note how his value (in this respect) suddenly diminished as he stepped ashore—The ship's deck was his trained position—on the land he seems incapable of expanding beyond the limits of an astonishingly narrow experience."

"So the 'gods' dwindle and the humble supplant them," Scott mused, and if the most startling reversals in reputation were those of Evans and Bowers, Evans was not the only one whose stock had fallen in the ice. "Nelson is also a disappointment," Scott wrote to Kinsey, his New Zealand agent, conscious that the worldly sophistication that had carried his biologist through South Africa with such éclat seemed somehow less impressive within the confines of an Antarctic hut. "A clever little fellow, but idle. I think the biologist's honours will all be with Lillie."

He could be as irritated by Simpson's "cocksureness," too, as he could by "master Gran's thick crust of vanity," but these were trifles when set alongside the huge respect and affection he felt for his scientific and non-scientific staff. After the humiliations over Discovery's science he knew precisely what he owed to Simpson, and if none of the others was the ultimate "treasure" that Bowers was, none of them—Wright, Cherry, Ponting, Oates, Aitch—seemed "far behind." "I am very much impressed with the extraordinary and general cordiality of the relations which exist among our people," Scott wrote gratefully in the middle of May. "I do not suppose that a statement of the real truth, namely that there is no friction at all will be credited . . . there is no need to draw a veil, there is nothing to cover . . . It is a triumph to have collected such men."

This was not just a self-deluding fantasy of Scott's, because in the letters and diaries of Gran, Taylor, Wilson, Ponting, Bowers and Cherry it is the same story time after time. There were endless arguments and brawls between the colonials and the Tory "Right" in the expedition, and Keohane in his cups would wander around in search of anyone who might argue the toss with him over Irish politics, but there was, as Scott wrote, "no sign of sharpness or anger, no jarring note, in all these wordy contests; all end with a laugh."

"Everything here is just as happy as can be," Cherry wrote home to Reggie Smith, and while much of this was down to Wilson's influence, even an occasionally critical Debenham could recognise the value of Scott's distinctive blend of discipline and informality. "I like Scott very much," Cherry again wrote home, and Bowers, as ever, was still more robustly enthusiastic—"Captain Scott is a topper," he declared. "I cannot say too much for him as a leader & as an extraordinarily clever & far seeing man."

There was confirmation of this, too, with Scott's birthday. "June 6 . . . my birthday," he recorded with a kind of avuncular content unusual in a man who hated "show,"

> a fact I might easily have forgotten, but my kind people did not. At lunch an immense birthday cake made its appearance and we were photographed around it. Clissold had decorated its sugared top with various devices in chocolate and crystallised fruit, flags and photographs of myself.
>
> After my walk I discovered that great preparations were in progress for a special dinner, and . . . we sat down to a sumptuous spread with our sledge banners hung about us. Clissold's especially excellent seal soup, roast mutton and red currant jelly, fruit salad, asparagus and chocolate—such was our menu . . .
>
> After this . . . everyone was very festive and amiably appreciative. As I write there is a group in the dark-room discussing political progress . . . another at one corner of the dinner table airing its views on the origin of matter and the probability of its ultimate discovery, and yet another debating military problems . . . It's delightful to hear the ring of triumph in some voice when the author imagines that he has delivered himself of a well-rounded period or a clinching statement . . . They are boys, all of them, but such excellent good natured ones.

It was the same at the great mid-winter dinner, and as in *Discovery* days, it was particularly the gratitude of the scientists that touched Scott. "Needless to say, all were exceedingly modest and brief," he wrote of the after-dinner speeches, "all had exceedingly kind things to say of me—in fact I was obliged to request the omission of compliments at an early stage. Nevertheless it was gratifying to have a really genuine recognition of my attitude towards the scientific workers of the Expedition, and I felt very warmly towards all those kind, good fellows for expressing it."

It was not all light, of course—Teddy Evans, Atkinson, Taylor, Gran, Debenham, Meares, even Bowers, would all catch the rough edge of Scott's tongue—but the single real exception to this general amity was the brooding figure of "the Soldier." "Scott has put two or three peoples back up lately," Oates wrote to his mother at the end of the winter, "and Meares, who looks after the dogs and is a pal of mine had a regular row with him, myself I dislike Scott intensely and would chuck the thing if it were not that we are a British expedition and must beat the Norwegians— Scott has always been very civil to me and I have the reputation of getting on well with him but [these next words are crossed out] the fact of the matter is he is not straight, it is himself first and when he has got all he can out of you it is shift for yourself . . . I must knock off for a minute, as I am getting hungry and must get something to eat I may then feel a little more kindly to Scott."

Oates was not the first man to level this accusation against Scott— Armitage did, Teddy Evans would, Skelton more legitimately might have done—but it is hard to think that anyone ever understood Scott as little as Oates did. He was the first to admit that what he wrote of him was often scrawled in the heat of the moment, but at the heart of his problem was a fundamental inability to see through the accidents of temper or habit to that bedrock of solid decency and truthfulness that Cherry so wonderfully defined.

If this feels like a failure of intelligence in Oates—his predictions of Scott's reactions were always hopelessly wrong—it was also a failure of nerve, because what he could never forgive Scott for was the burden of responsibility he had thrust on him. "I could not but hint that in my opinion the problem of reaching the Pole can best be solved by relying on the ponies and man haulage," Scott had written on 8 May, after he had first sketched out his plans for the polar journey to his men. "With this sentiment the whole company appeared to be in sympathy. Everyone seems to distrust the dogs when it comes to glacier and summit. I have asked everyone to give thoughts to the problem, to freely discuss it, and bring suggestions to my notice. It's going to be a tough job; that is better realised the more one dives in."

It was one thing for the rest of the hut to be "in sympathy" with Scott's proposals, but it was Oates who was going to have to nurse "the greatest lot of crocks" he had "ever seen" to the foot of the Beardmore Glacier, and it was little wonder that he did not thrive on the thought. His anxieties would have been acute enough if the ponies had been just part of the overall plan, as Scott had originally envisaged, but the more marginal the role of the motors and dogs became in his thinking, the more squarely the whole success or failure of the Pole attempt sat on Oates's shoulders.

It cannot have eased tensions that through the dead heart of winter the one man in the expedition who could always mediate between Scott and his men was not there to do that job. The historic winter journey of Wilson, Bowers and Cherry to the Emperor penguin colony at Cape Crozier belongs, as Scott himself said, to their story and not his, but as a reflection on his leadership and on the logistics of the whole expedition few things could be more revealing.

The horrors or the heroism of the journey are not what is of interest here—Cherry's account has made any other redundant—but the basic question of why Scott should ever have allowed it to take place. He must have known at this stage that Wilson and probably Bowers would be in the Polar Party with him, and yet here he was in the last week of June, prepared to see them march off into the darkness in temperatures that no one had ever experienced for a nightmare landscape of crevasses and blizzards from which only Bowers and The Lord could possibly hope to bring them back.

In Scott's defence, there were important scientific issues involved, and the fact that the science on which they were based was faulty cannot retrospectively change that. There was a belief at the time that the penguin was the world's most primitive bird, and if one couples that notion with the theory that the evolutionary history of a species is rehearsed in its embryonic development, then the irresistible lure of an egg in its first stages for a good Darwinist like Scott is obvious.

Even when that is conceded, though, a feeling remains that it was not his head but his heart that lay behind his decision. It is hard to imagine that Scott could have refused Wilson anything that he wanted so badly, but even while he tried to dissuade him, there nestled alongside the rationalist in him a romantic, alongside the pragmatist busy measuring out their journeys in ounces and grams a visionary who was always the first to see that the value and appeal of what they were doing was not to science but "to our imagination—That men should wander forth in the depths of a polar night to face the most dismal cold and the fiercest gales in darkness is something new; that they should have persisted in this effort in spite of every adversity for five full weeks is heroic. It makes a tale for our generation which I hope may not be lost in the telling."

There was a certain scientific respectability to be salvaged from the journey, too, when the three unrecognisable men finally staggered back into camp. "The Crozier Party returned last night," Scott noted in his diary on 2 August, "after enduring for five weeks the hardest conditions on record. They looked more weather-worn than anyone I have yet seen. Their faces are scarred and wrinkled, their eyes dull, their hands whitened and creased with the constant exposure to damp and cold."

Atkinson could find no sign of scurvy, and by the next day Wilson seemed his "keen, wiry self" and Bowers "quite his self." Cherry had clearly suffered more than the other two from the conditions, but he had lost less weight than them — a mere pound to Wilson's three and a half and Bowers's two and a half. "For our future sledge work several points have been most satisfactorily settled," Scott went on, rallying to a more analytical view of the journey once his anxieties were allayed. "The party went on very simple food ration in different and extreme proportions; they took pemmican, butter, biscuit and tea only. After a short experience they found that Wilson, who had arranged for the greatest quantity of fat, had too much of it, and C.-G., who had gone for biscuits, had more than he could eat. A middle course was struck . . . In this way we have arrived at a simple and suitable ration for the inland plateau."

And with the return of the sun only three weeks away, Scott's thoughts were increasingly on the detailed planning for the spring. "I have been working very hard at sledging figures with Bowers' able assistance," he wrote. "The scheme develops itself in the light of these figures, and I feel that our organisation will not be found wanting, yet there is an immense amount of detail, and every arrangement has to be more than usually elastic to admit of extreme possibilities of the full success or complete failure of the motors. I think our plan will carry us through without the motors (though in that case nothing else must fail), and will take full advantage of such help as the motors may give."

Try as he might to envisage the worst, planning was always a narcotic to Scott, inducing in him a kind of euphoria that was proof against even his own natural gloom. The more he looked at the figures and the men, the more it seemed that success was within their grasp. "I fear to be too sanguine," he cautioned himself, "yet taking everything into consideration I feel our chances ought to be good." The animals were all in "splendid form," the ponies putting on muscle "day by day," the dogs "wonderfully fit and strong," and as for the Southern Party, "Of hopeful signs for the future, none are more remarkable than the health and spirit of our people. It

would be impossible to imagine a more vigorous community, and there does not seem to be a single weak spot in the twelve good men and true who are chosen for the Southern advance. All are now experienced sledge travellers, knit together with a bond of friendship that has never been equalled under such circumstances. Thanks to these people, and more especially to Bowers and Petty Officer Evans, there is not a single detail of our equipment which is not arranged with the utmost care." "It is grand to have daylight rushing at one," he exclaimed, and even Oates's "cripples" seemed to have caught the mood. "The ponies were so pleased," Scott wrote on 14 August, "that they seize the slightest opportunity to part company with their leaders and gallop off with tail and heels flung high. The dogs are equally festive and are getting more exercise than could be given in the dark."

He had already told off each pony to its different minder—Victor to Bowers, Nobby to Wilson, Michael to Cherry, Jehu to Atkinson, Chinaman to Wright, Snatcher to PO Evans, Bones to Crean, Jimmy Pigg to Keohane, Christopher to Oates, and Snippets, the one pony bizarrely prepared to eat seal-blubber, to himself and Oates—and on 13 September was ready to unveil his plans. They were in essence the scheme he had outlined at the beginning of the winter, with an intricate combination of motor, dog and man-hauling parties laying down a chain of depots stretching out to the Beardmore. The whole polar journey—1,530 miles there and back—would take 144 days, and beyond the Beardmore it would be straight man-hauling. As far as their own plans were concerned, he again stressed, Amundsen did not exist. "Everyone was enthusiastic," he noted, with the general feeling being "that our arrangements are calculated to make the best of our resources . . . The scheme seems to have earned full confidence: it remains to play the game out."

"I saw Scott's plan for the journey," Gran wrote more hesitantly a week later, after he had returned from a short journey with Teddy Evans to re-mark Corner Camp. "My goodness, it is an involved proposition. The thought behind it is no doubt marvellous, if only he can carry it out."

Preparations were now accelerating. A second Geological Party under Taylor—and including, to the Norwegian's bitter disappointment, Gran—was destined for the Western Mountains again, but it was inevitably the Pole that dominated expedition life. A short "acclimatiser" of his own among the mountains gave Scott another chance to test their general condition, and with the Southern Journey beckoning, it was a relief to find that

he was still up to the task, and PO Evans everything he remembered. "The objects of our little journey were satisfactorily accomplished," Scott wrote, after they had mapped out the movement in the markers on the Ferrar Glacier that Taylor had put down the previous autumn and charted the Geological Party's best route to Granite Island for the coming season, "but the greatest source of pleasure to me is to realise that I have such men as Bowers and P.O. Evans for the Southern journey. I do not think that harder men or better sledge travellers ever took the trail."

The balance for Scott between buoyancy and gloom was always a fine one, and within days of his return to Cape Evans a series of accidents had seen the optimism of his western "jaunt" gutter away. On 3 October Atkinson reported his fear that Jehu was not even going to make the start of the journey, and in quick succession a fright over Taylor's safety, the mysterious death of a dog, a negligent case of frostbite and a ludicrous injury to Clissold, while "ponting" on a berg for their photographer, sent him into a predictable downward spiral. "Troubles rarely come singly," he noted on the eighth—"Hamlet" to the fore again—"It is trying, but I am past despondency. Things must take their course . . . it is hard to have two sick men after all the care which has been taken."

It was at moments like this that Scott's tongue could do most damage, but Taylor for one, who felt the full force of Scott's anxiety when he went missing out on the ice on one of the expedition's bicycles, never bore him a grudge for it. "I had a few keen arguments with Scott—the only ones I knew about," he recalled many years later. "He scolded me very deservedly when I was lost some six miles south of the hut . . . Yet in spite of this he gave me command of the *second* Western Party."

Not everyone was so forgiving. The naval men might take their punishment as if they were used to nothing else, but the fall-out from a football injury was harder for the young Debenham to bear. "I am afraid I am very disappointed in him, tho' my faith dies very hard," he wrote of Scott to his mother. "There's no doubt he can be very nice and the interest he takes in our scientific work is immense, he is also a fine sledger himself and as an organiser is splendid. But there I am afraid one must stop. His temper is very uncertain and leads him to absurd lengths even in simple arguments . . . What he decides is often enough the right thing I expect, but he loses all control of his tongue and makes us all feel wild . . ."

It might have been "difficult to judge one's leader," as Debenham admitted, but it was harder still to be one. A late start for the Pole inevitably meant a second year in the ice, and a second year meant money that the

expedition did not have.* Sometime in October Scott was compelled to ask any officer who could afford it to forgo future payment, but even a generous response left him staring at a sickly financial prospect. "I am afraid Speyer and others will be anxious about funds," he wrote to Kathleen, and to Sir Edgar Speyer himself, the expedition treasurer, after listing all their actual and possible assets—ship, cinematographic rights, authorship, lectures, commemorative stamps, press releases, donations, a signed indemnity relieving the expedition of his own and his officers' salaries—he came to the nub of the matter:

> I realise none of this can be called good security from a business point of view, but as such things as Antarctic expeditions go, it would seem fairly good security for a guarantee.
>
> This brings me to the point of asking you whether in the event of an overdraft you can get it guaranteed till I return.
>
> As regards myself, of course I stand or fall by the expedition. I am set to carry it through to a finish, scientific publications included, with all the resources I could command. My wife is entirely with me.

Scott knew, too, precisely what that last sentence meant. "All this in one sense," he confessed to Kathleen, enclosing with his letter a copy of his proposal to Speyer, "seems to be asking you to sacrifice your own interest and the boy's to the expedition—but I know that you would wish it that way, so we can act straight to ourselves and the world. But you must understand the whole case, for after due consideration I have myself signed the indemnity document referred to in Speyer's letter; that means that my salary from the expedition will cease to be paid, over and beyond the term which it would have been paid had I returned in the 'Terra Nova' in 1912."

This was not the ideal backdrop to the polar bid, and in the anxiety of the final days, and the constant pressures from all sides—reports from the mechanics, news from Meares who was out depoting, messages on the newly laid telephone to Hut Point, another sick dog, fractious ponies—it was no surprise that tempers frayed. "This is annoying . . . These capers

---

*Scott had made this clear to his party when he first briefed them on the polar bid. If he was reckoning on a journey of 144 days starting at the beginning of November, he could not hope to be back until late March, by which time the *Terra Nova* would already have had to leave McMurdo Sound if she was to avoid *Discovery*'s fate.

promise trouble . . . I am annoyed with this." "The day terminates very unpleasantly," Scott recorded grimly after the Taylor incident, and the troubles were not over. "Things not going very well," he wrote again on the seventeenth, when the axle casing on the best of their two motors split within thirty yards of starting on their first journey out onto the floe. "I am secretly convinced that we shall not get much help from the motors, yet nothing has ever happened to them that was unavoidable. A little more care and foresight would make them splendid allies. The trouble is that if they fail, no one will ever believe this."

By 22 October the repairs had been completed, and with the loads out on the floe, the motors under trial, Scott was hopeful that they could get off the next day. "Wretched" weather intervened, however, and it was the twenty-fourth, and another abortive start with the motors, before the long, staggered exodus could finally begin. As Scott returned to the hut at lunchtime, and sat down to his journal, with the motors a mile out in South Bay and going steadily, he allowed himself a moment of visionary hope. "I find myself immensely eager that these tractors should succeed," he wrote, "even though they may not be a great help to our southern advance. A small measure of success will be enough to show their possibilities, their ability to revolutionise polar transport. Seeing the machines at work to-day, and remembering that every defect so far shown is purely mechanical, it is impossible not to be convinced of their value."

"On the whole things look hopeful," Scott wrote, and with the ponies "getting above themselves" on their pre-Barrier feed, and little for the men to do but pose for Ponting's cinematograph, there was nothing but some last letters to hold the rest of the party back. Scott wrote to PO Evans's wife, Oates's mother, and to Kinsey in New Zealand, enclosing his diary, to be sent on to Kathleen after Kinsey had read it. In a letter full of praise for all his men, only Teddy Evans was excepted. He "is a thoroughly well-meaning little man," Scott wrote, "but proves on close acquaintance to be rather a duffer in anything but his own particular work. All this strictly 'entre nous,' but he is not at all fitted to be 'Second-in-Command,' as I was foolish enough to name him."

He had written to his mother from New Zealand, reassuring her that there would be no slacking over Divine Service, and he now wrote briefly again. "As far as I am concerned I could not possibly be in better health. I am a thousand times fitter than I was in London—you see my dear we know all about things down here now—exactly how to feed and clothe ourselves and how to set to work. It is a simple life and therefore very healthy. I

could not wish for better companions than I have got . . . I can't say how it is all going to work out but I have taken a lot of pains over the plans so I hope for the best . . . Well my own dear Mother you must take care of yourself and remember that there is no one to whom I shall be prouder to tell of my successes or more willing to confess my failures."

It was to Kathleen, though, that he opened himself up, in a long letter that was part business and part personal. "I am quite on my feet now," he told her in a revealing passage. "I feel both mentally and physically fit for the work, and I realise that others know it and have full confidence in me. But it is a certain fact that it was not so in London or indeed until we reached this spot. The root of the problem was that I had lost confidence in myself. I don't know if it was noticed by others consciously, but it was acted on unconsciously, as a dozen incidents in my memory remind me. Had I been what I am now, many things would have been avoided. I can trace these things to myself very clearly and can only hope that others do not."

It was not just in himself that he had confidence. "Words must always fail me when I talk of Bill Wilson," he continued in a long tribute to his men. "I believe he really is the finest character I ever met—the closer one gets to him the more there is to admire. Every quality is so solid and dependable; cannot you imagine how that counts down here? Whatever the matter, one knows that Bill will be sound, shrewdly practical, intensely loyal and quite unselfish . . . I think he is the most popular member of the party, and that is saying much."

Bowers, Wright, Oates—"a delightfully humorous cheery old pessimist"—they all come in for the same generous praise. "Edgar Evans has proved a useful member of our party," he reassured Kathleen, with memories of his performance in New Zealand still fresh. "Crean is perfectly happy, ready to do anything and go anywhere, the harder the work the better . . . Lashly is his old self in every respect, hard working to the limits, quiet, abstemious, and determined. You see altogether I have a good set of people with me, and it will go hard if we don't achieve something." "Everything in these seventeen pages seems to have been of myself and my work," he apologised, his last thoughts, as ever, with his family,

and so far not a word of my thoughts of you and the boy and our home, but I know that I cannot tell you too much of things as they are with me, and I know you will not think yourself forgotten when I ask so much of you.

Your postman [Teddy Evans] has very faithfully delivered

your little notes, and I treasure them not only because they are yours, but because they express the inspiriting thoughts which I would have you hold. At such a time as this it thrills me most to think of your courage. It is my greatest comfort to know that you possess it, and therefore by nature can never sit down and bewail misfortune. I can imagine you nothing but sturdily independent and determined to make the most of the life you possess . . .

Do you know that I sometimes feel guilty about mother. In these last strenuous years I seem to have had so little time to spare to her. She is getting old and I am sure you will be good to her . . .

It seems a woeful long time since I saw your face and there is the likelihood of a woefuller time ahead, and then what. I want to come back having done something, but work here is horribly uncertain and now of course the chance of another man getting ahead.

Scott was not the only one writing letters. "It is perfectly wretched starting off with a bunch of cripples and Scott won't believe how bad they are," Oates wrote to his mother, telling her that he thinks he might be in the final party, "that is if Scott and I don't fall out it will be pretty tough having months of him, he fusses dreadfully . . ." "I have half a mind to see Scott," he wrote again, "and tell him I must go home in the ship but it would a pity [sic] to spoil my chance of being in the final polar party especially as the regiment and perhaps the whole army would be pleased if I was at the Pole . . . recall that when a man is having a bad time he says hard things about other people which he would regret afterwards."

"Dear Mrs. Scott," Bowers—ever the counter to Oates—wrote,

. . . We have had to put up with an almost unparalleled succession of initial reverses, and if any man had to endure the trials of Job again, I am sure Captain Scott did when the Depot Journey terminated with such a chapter of accidents following hard upon the news of Amundsen's little game to the eastward. However, good often comes out of the worst and perhaps the necessary reorganisation of the original plans has been the best thing for our object. Certainly to trust the final dash to such an uncertain element as dogs would be a risky thing, whereas man-haulage, though slow, is sure, and I for one am delighted at the decision. After all, it will be a fine thing to do that plateau with man-haulage in these days of the supposed decadence of the British race. Anyhow, whether we succeed or not, we all have confidence in our leader and I am sure that he will pull it through if any man will.

"I shall consider no sacrifice too great for the main object," Bowers wrote home to his own family, "& whether I am one of the early returning parties or not I am Captain Scott's man & shall stick by him though God knows what the result will be but we will do all that man can do & leave the rest to His keeping in which we all are & shall remain."

Back in England, as these last preparations were under way, Kathleen wrote in her diary: "I had rather a horrid day today. I woke up having had a bad dream about you and then Peter came very close to me and said emphatically, 'Daddy won't come back,' as though in answer to my silly thoughts."

Scott had less than five months to live.

Twenty-nine: **The Barrier**

Jehu to be murdered tomorrow night.

CHARLES WRIGHT, *diary, 23 November 1911*

On the morning of 1 November, when Scott and his party finally set out from Cape Evans for the last time, Amundsen had just left behind his depot in 81°s. The previous autumn the Norwegians had laid their depots to a farthest south of 82°, and on 19 October a streamlined team of five, with fifty-two dogs and four lightweight sledges, had set off on their polar journey.

There had already been one abortive attempt in early September, when Amundsen had defied sense and the instincts of his men in a bid to forestall Scott. In temperatures that plunged to −69°F they got no farther than their first depot, however, and as dogs froze to death and frostbite crippled the party, a disgruntled retreat turned into a panic that saw Amundsen abandon his men in the wild rush to get on the first sledge back to Framheim alive.

It was the most inglorious and uncharacteristic episode of his whole exploring life—and one that is seamlessly glossed over in his account of the polar race—but with the toughness that typified his leadership, Amundsen managed to turn even this crisis to his account. The most vocal critic of his behaviour on their return to Framheim was Nansen's old companion Hjalmar Johansen, and in a ruthlessly orchestrated counter-putsch that left Amundsen more firmly in command than ever, he first isolated and then banished from the polar team the one man in the party with the pedigree and the skills to challenge his own authority.

The spring start was possibly the last error he made, and by the time Scott was ready to start, it and Johansen's mutiny were nothing more than a distant and improbable memory. For very good reasons Amundsen had always backed his own and his men's experience against any group of Englishmen, but as his Norwegian party moved swiftly southward across the Barrier, the one uncertainty that still threatened his dream of polar priority was the performance of the motors Scott had with him.

It had only been the fear of Scott—or more particularly of what those motors might achieve—that had driven Amundsen to an early start in the first place, but if he could have seen what was happening three hundred miles to the west of him, he would have known his worries were over. "On the 31st October," Taylor wrote,

> the pony party started. Two weak ponies led by Atkinson and Keohane were sent off first at 4:30, and I accompanied them for about a mile . . .
>
> Next morning the Southern Party finished their mail, posting it in the packing case on Atkinson's bunk, and then at 11 a.m. the last party were ready for the Pole. They had packed the sledges overnight, and they took 20lbs personal baggage. The Owner asked me what book he should take. He wanted something fairly filling. I recommended Tyndall's *Glaciers*—if he wouldn't find it "coolish." He didn't fancy this! So then I said, "Why not take Browning, as I'm doing?" And I believe that he did so.
>
> Wright's pony was first harnessed in the sledge. Chinaman is Jehu's rival for last place, and as some compensation is easy to harness. Seaman Evans led Snatcher, who used to rush ahead . . . Cherry had Michael, a steady goer, and Wilson led Nobby—the pony rescued from the killer whales in March. Scott led out Snippets to the sledges, and harnessed him to the foremost, with little Anton's help—only it turned out to be Bowers's sledge! However he transferred in a few minutes and marched off rapidly to the south.
>
> Christopher, as usual, behaved like a demon. First they had

to trice his front leg up tight under his shoulder, then it took five minutes to throw him. The sledge was brought up and he was harnessed in while his head was held down on the floe. Finally he rose up, still on three legs, and started off galloping as well as he was able. After several violent kicks his foreleg was released, and after more watch-spring flicks with his hind legs he set off fairly steadily. Titus can't stop him when once he has started, and will have to do the fifteen miles in one lap probably! . . .

Bowers was last to leave. His pony, Victor, nervous but not vicious, was soon in the traces. I ran to the end of the Cape and watched the little cavalcade—already strung out into remote units—rapidly fade into the lonely white waste to southward.

The contrast between this comedy and Amundsen's lean operations is stark enough, but it reveals only the tip of Scott's logistical problems. The injury to Clissold had enforced one late change of plans, but even with Hooper slotting easily into his place, Scott was still left with three distinct teams travelling at different speeds and dependent on different resources—the motor party in the van with Evans, Day, Lashly and Hooper; his own pony party following somewhere in their wake; and, finally, the dog teams under Meares.

Griffith Taylor's last sight of the pony party, already stretched out across the floe, was a pointer to the difficulties ahead on a journey in which clear communications would make the difference between life and death. It would have been hard enough to keep these various elements in unison with trained handlers and decent horses, but with the "bunch of cripples" that Scott had to work with, it was tougher still. "A mile south of [Razor Back] island"—some 760 miles short of the Pole, that is, if Scott was looking on the dark side of things—"Bowers and Victor passed me, leaving me where I best wished to be—at the tail of the line. About this place I saw one of the animals ahead had stopped and was obstinately refusing to go forward again. I had a great fear it was Chinaman, the unknown quantity, but to my relief I found it was my old friend 'Nobby' in obstinate mood."

As a puzzled observer of Shackleton's and Scott's dedication to ponies, Amundsen would not have been unduly surprised at this, but like Scott himself he would still have been on tenterhooks over the motors. It would be another six weeks before his fears on that front were finally allayed, but for Scott disillusionment was immediate and brutal. "It appears they had a

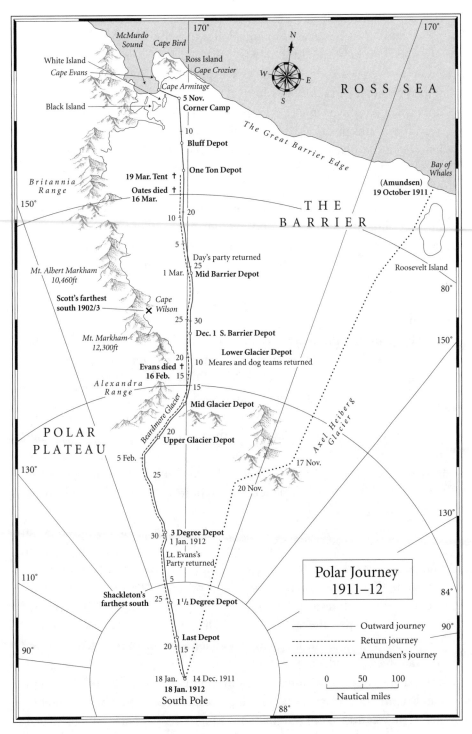

Polar Journey
1911–12

Outward journey
Return journey
Amundsen's journey

0   50   100
Nautical miles

bad grind this morning," he noted, after coming across a cache of dumped petrol and lubricant, and some four miles into the Barrier a "pathetically inscribed" tin confirmed the worst. " 'Big end Day's motor No 2 cylinder broken' . . . half a mile beyond, as I expected, we found the motor, its tracking sledge and all. Notes from E. Evans and Day told the tale. The only spare had been used for Lashly's machine . . . They had decided to abandon it and push on with the other alone . . . So the dream of great help from the machines is at an end! The track of the remaining motor goes steadily forward, but now, of course, I shall expect to see it every hour of the march."

The next day at Corner Camp, Scott's party could see three black dots in the distance to the south, and another march told the rest. A further note from Teddy Evans explained that Lashly's engine had suffered the same failure as the first. For Scott it was the end of a five-year dream. In the great tradition of English polar exploration, the motor party that only twenty-four hours earlier had been talking of the 80th parallel, had now become a man-hauling team.

The failure of the motors also meant that the better ponies would be carrying loads of over seven hundred pounds, but marching at night in search of better surfaces they made light of them, pleasing even the "cheery old pessimist" himself. As they reached Camp 4 a blizzard threatened to blow up, however, and although the animals seemed to stand up to the cold better than Scott had feared, the thick, driving snow was another matter. "We men are snug and comfortable," he wrote, "but it is very evil to lie here and know that the weather is steadily sapping the strength of the beasts on which so much depends. It requires much philosophy to be cheerful on such occasions."

By 9 November they were at Camp 6, travelling in the main over good surfaces and averaging ten miles a night, but even with a staggered start to compensate for their different speeds, confusion was never far away. "He was some time at his lunch camp," Scott wrote of Atkinson, in charge of the first pony party away each night, "so that starting to join the rearguard we came in together the last 2 miles . . . Obviously it is not an advantage to be together . . . An amusing incident happened when Wright left his pony to examine his sledgemeter. Chinaman evidently didn't like being left behind and set off at a canter to rejoin the main body. Wright's long legs barely carried him fast enough to stop this fatal stampede, but the ridiculous sight was due to the fact that Jehu caught the infection and set off at a sprawling canter in Chinaman's wake . . . Christopher is troublesome as ever at the start; I fear that signs of tameness will only indicate absence of strength. The dogs followed us so easily over the 10 miles that Meares thought of going on again, but finally decided that the present easy work is best."

Within forty-eight hours, too, surface conditions had added to their difficulties. Snow had fallen during the day, and lay soft and flocculent on top of hard sastrugi. "In pits between these in places the snow lay in sandy heaps," Scott wrote, as he ruefully surveyed the results of his transport decisions. "A worse set of conditions for the ponies could scarcely be imagined . . . In spite of the surface, the dogs ran up from the camp before last, over 20 miles, in the night. They are working splendidly so far."

As Scott trudged slowly southward, his only company on the march his pony, his thoughts would inevitably drift to Kathleen and home. "Just a little note from the Barrier to say that I love you," he scrawled. "There are long hours in which to think of you and the boy." His diary was, in fact, part addressed to her, and hers, a long, unselfconscious monologue, to him. Side by side, they give a vivid picture of the strange, successful, unknowable, loyal but semi-detached thing their marriage was as it moved blindly towards its end. "There was a return of that sad girl who stopped to lunch and cried unceasingly for several hours," she was writing in their London home, as he was coming to terms with the failure of the motors. "You were right when you recommended me not to mix myself up in it . . . But of course you weren't here, and didn't recommend anything; but you would have done if you had been here, being wise."

"I went to Nansen's lecture on Norsemen in America," she told him the following day. "It was stiff and his delivery dull, and his accent made it very difficult to attend; but I enjoyed it very much, everyone is so very kind to me. Afterwards Major Darwin made me talk to Nansen, but I was shy."

"I went to the bronze foundry about Sir Mathew Nathan's head," she wrote as he watched Chinaman's antics, "and then I took my infant on to Hugh Walpole to tea, and there Henry James hugged him and kissed him; but he said loudly, 'Do things,' which is a nursery saying, and implies that he must be speedily removed."

17 November, Scott's diary:

Camp 13 . . . 13¼ (geo.) miles.

On the whole, and considering the weights, the ponies did very well, but the surface was comparatively good . . . It is early days to wonder whether the little beasts will last; one can only hope

*they will, but the weakness of breeding and age is showing itself
already.*

17 November, Kathleen's diary:

*I meant to go to Paris to-day, but went to meet Nansen at lunch
instead and I'm glad I did. Sir Lewis Beaumont had told me he
had failed to induce him to discuss Amundsen, but he seemed
ready enough to do it to-day. He said he had no notion of
Amundsen's intentions till he got his letter from Madeira in
which he said "I wish I had told Scott." Nansen said when he saw
him off he asked him why on earth he'd got so many dogs.
Amundsen had been rather evasive, but said they might be useful
for coming back. He said it was very nice of Amundsen not to tell
him about it and ask him for secrecy, as it would have made
Nansen's position untenable. He hopes you will meet and go on
together. He said the most popular thing Amundsen could do
would be to let you get there first and then go on himself. I think
that's silly.*

18 November, Scott's diary:

*The ponies are not pulling well . . . The crocks are going on very
wonderfully. Oates gives Chinaman at least three days, and
Wright says he may go for a week. This is slightly inspiriting, but
how much better would it have been to have had ten really reliable beasts! It's touch and go whether we scrape up to the Glacier; meanwhile we get along somehow.*

18 November, Kathleen's diary:

What nonsense, that "virtue is its own reward"!

*What reward have I for refraining from getting my pilot's cer-
tificate? There is nothing I want so ardently as to learn to fly . . .
Everybody is shocked at my flying even as a passenger. "My
duties to you two!" I see their point, but I want to fly, and what
reward have I? Worse—I believe you'd like it if I did fly. Damn!*

*I planted bulbs in my garden so that it may be gay when you
come back and, do you know, I am growing house-proud. Isn't
that comic? I shall settle down into the most conventional of
middle-aged matrons with immaculate house-linen and polished
silver and stair-rods.*

19 November, Scott's diary:

> *Camp 15. We have struck a really bad surface, sledges pulling well over it, but ponies sinking very deep. The result is about to finish Jehu. He was terribly done on getting in to-night. He may go another march, but not more, I think.*

19 November, Kathleen's:

> *I worked all morning. Then a "Daily Mirror" man came to see me and upset me greatly. He said if I would allow a photograph of the infant writing a letter asking for money for you to appear in the "Mirror" he was convinced he could get four thousand pounds . . . My dear, I do humbly beg your pardon if I have done wrong, but I said no. Not only can I not bear my weeny being bandied about in the half-penny press, but also I doubt greatly that any sum approaching four thousand pounds would be got. Dearest, I do hope you approve. I couldn't bear it though.*

27 November, Scott's:

> *Camp 23 . . . Quite the most trying march we have had . . . the surface . . . unspeakably heavy for pulling . . . It is several days since we had a glimpse of land, which makes conditions especially gloomy. A tired animal makes a tired man, I find, and none of us are very bright now after the day's march.*

27 November, Kathleen's:

> *I went to Nansen's lecture at the Bechstein Hall and Shackleton was there. I was asked before whether I minded meeting him, and I said no. I hope I was right.*

28 November, Scott's diary:

> *Camp 24. The most dismal start imaginable. Thick as a hedge, snow falling and drifting with keen southerly wind . . . Second march almost as horrid as the first . . . Chinaman, "The Thunderbolt," has been shot to-night. Plucky little chap, he has stuck it out well and leaves the stage but a few days before his fellows . . . we are less than 90 miles from the Glacier.*

28 November, Kathleen's:

> *Knowing Nansen was leaving I wrote him a little note to ask him*

to lunch. He came at 1:30 and stayed till 5:30. He is the most charming individual imaginable. We talked about the most unexpected things — all about his ambitions and fears for them, and about how he originally studied anatomy, chiefly of the brain, and only crossed Greenland at first by accident, to get away because he was overworked and unhappy.

"I had an amazing letter from Nansen," she wrote again the following day.

What with Professor David saying "Life was the better for having known you" and Nansen saying, "It is nice to know there is a woman so like what one has dreamt of but never met," I am inclined to think explorers are a rather comprehending race. I worked hard and well all day. It does my work good to have the admiration of a person like Nansen. You won't, maybe, believe that, any more than you believe that dancing is good for it, but I have proved it too often to doubt it.

Oblivious as Scott would always be to it, this was the beginning of something more than a flirtation — though never an affair "a outrance," Kathleen insisted — that has inevitably provoked questions over their marriage. Kathleen had first met Nansen in Norway at the time of the motor trials, but it was in London, and later again in Berlin in January 1912, that their friendship changed to something much more romantically, and *hyperbolically*, charged. Her letters to him have not survived, but his to her hover somewhere between the language of medieval courtly love and a gloomily Scandinavian romanticism. It is possible that Kathleen lied about their relationship, and yet given not just her love of truth but her almost absolute conviction that whatever she did was right, it seems much more likely that if there had ever been an affair she would have been the first to acknowledge it.

She might send him Wells's *New Machiavelli* to read, and his vanity might stretch to seeing themselves emancipated from the moral restraints of the herd, but if previous "form" offers any sort of guide, the kind of celibate devotion that she had always demanded of her male friends was still precisely what she wanted. It is plain from his letters and a telegram from him asking her to book a hotel room in Berlin for them that he wanted more, but the adolescent maunderings of his correspondence suggest she

food calculated from the Glacier depot has been begun . . . Resignation to misfortune is the only attitude, but not an easy one to adopt. It seems undeserved where plans were well laid and so nearly crowned with a first success . . . It is very evil to lie here in a wet sleeping-bag and think of the pity of it."

It was the morning of the ninth before they were able to get away, and the heavy snow of the last four days had made the surface a nightmare for the ponies. The exhausted creatures would only move at all for the lash, but by eight that evening they were at Camp 31—Shambles Camp—and the other side of the coastal chasm across which Shackleton had found a snow-filled ramp to the Beardmore. "It was a grim business," Cherry recorded of the ponies' last march. "My impressions of that day are of groping our way, for Bowers and I were pulling a light sledge ahead to make the track, through a vague white wall. First a confused crowd of men behind us gathered round the leading pony sledge, pushing it forward, the poor beasts barely able to struggle out of the holes it made as it plunged forward . . . There was not one man there who would willingly have caused pain to a living thing. But what else was to be done . . . Hour after hour we plugged on: and we dared not stop for lunch, we knew we would never start again. After crossing many waves huge pressure ridges suddenly showed themselves all round, and we got on to a steep rise with the coastal chasm on our right appearing as a great dip full of enormous pressure."

Teddy Evans was surlier about it, as much, however, on his own account as that of the ponies. "I think it would be fairer to shoot them now," he had written in his diary before they set off from Camp 30, "for what is a possible twelve miles help? . . . Why, our party have never been out of harness for nearly 400 miles, so why should not the other eight men buckle to and do some dragging instead of saving work in halfpenny numbers?"

Scott had always been determined to postpone man-hauling for the main party for as long as possible, and the ponies had seen out their task. As soon as they were got to Camp 31 the "slaughter of the innocents" began. "Poor beasts!" Scott wrote, tougher about these deaths than he had ever been in similar circumstances in the past. "They have done wonderfully well considering the terrible circumstances under which they worked, but yet it is hard to have to kill them so early."

If the ponies had done "wonderfully well," so too had Oates. "Crocks" or not, he had got them to the foot of the Beardmore. If his suffering was only just starting, his responsibilities were over. "Oates came up to Scott as he stood in the shadow of Mount Hope," Cherry recalled.

"Well! I congratulate you, Titus," said Wilson.
"And *I* thank you, Titus," said Scott.
And that was the end of the Barrier Stage.

Thirty: **Without Priority**

> I have never seen a sledge sink so. I have never pulled so hard, or so nearly
> crushed my insides into my backbone.
>
> H. BOWERS, *journal, 14 December 1911*

It might have seemed to Teddy Evans in retrospect that "no part of the Southern Journey was enjoyed more thoroughly than the . . . ascent of the Beardmore Glacier," but it is not clear that it felt so enjoyable at the time. After the monotony of the Barrier there was a variety and interest to their surroundings that made an immense difference, but for Scott at least it seemed business as usual, as the luck that he had been railing against since the start of the journey still went against them. They were already behind schedule and eating into rations, and at the glacier foot where Shackleton had found blue ice, Scott found instead deep, soft snow. For the first couple of miles of man-hauling his sledge moved easily enough, but as the incline steepened and the men sank up to their knees, the pulling became even by Scott's standards "extraordinarily fatiguing."

It was the kind of challenge that Scott had always relished, but if his team of Oates, Wilson and PO Evans could hold their own with him, there was worse news from Atkinson of Teddy Evans's sledge. It is clear from Wright's journal that the problem lay with Teddy Evans again, but Atkinson reported that Wright himself was "getting played out," and even Lashly was "not so fit as he was owing to the heavy pulling since the blizzard."

"I have not felt satisfied about this party," Scott wrote, his tone hard and unsympathetic as it could sometimes be in such circumstances, "The finish of the march today showed that there was something wrong. They fell a long way behind, had to take off ski, and took nearly half an hour to come up a few hundred yards. True, the surface was awful and growing worse every moment. It is a very serious business if the men are going to crock up. As for myself, I never felt fitter . . . P.O. Evans, of course, is a tower of strength, but Oates and Wilson are doing splendidly also."

This was not so much vainglory on Scott's part but relief, because at the back of his mind he had been as anxious about his own performance as he was about anyone else's. "Just a tiny note to be taken back by the dogs," he wrote to Kathleen. "Things are not so rosy as they might be, but we keep our spirits up and say the luck must turn. This is only to tell you that I find I can keep up with the rest as well as of old."

With the departure of Meares and the dogs, they were at last into a world of pure man-hauling. "The great thing is to keep the sledge moving," Scott noted again the next day, "jubilant" at the performance of his own team, "But Evans's party didn't get up till 10 [three hours after Scott's]. They started quite well, but got into difficulties, did the wrong thing by straining again and again, and so, tiring themselves, went from bad to worse. Their ski shoes, too, are out of trim. Just as I thought we were in for making a great score, this difficulty overcomes us—it is dreadfully trying. The snow around us tonight is terribly soft, one sinks to the knees at every step; it would be impossible to drag sledges on foot and very difficult for dogs. Ski are the thing and here are my tiresome fellow-countrymen too prejudiced to have prepared themselves for the event . . . A plentiful crop of snow blindness due to incaution."

It might legitimately be wondered what Gran had been doing with the expedition if Scott was not going to compel his men to learn to ski, but it was too late for that now. "Scott came back to discover why we were behind the other teams," Wright noted at the end of the same march. "I was in front with Evans and had found one could do better by pulling at an angle of about 15° to the side and thus get a grip on the surface without my ski sliding back. Scott then said to Birdie, 'See, that's the way to do it,' to which Birdie unthinkingly replied, 'Yes, but look at the loss of pull due to the angle.' I felt like reminding Birdie that the cosine at 15° would not lose more than 1 per cent effort of the straight pull . . . However I kept my peace, for conditions were then at their worst and any argument . . . should be avoided."

Wright's forbearance was wise. It was not a good time for arguments. Behind them lay the Barrier and weeks of hard slog, and ahead of them a nine-thousand-foot and 120-mile climb up the immense, arterial Beardmore Glacier that Shackleton and his men had discovered three years earlier. "From the top of the ridge," Shackleton had written of his first, dramatic sight of the Beardmore, "there burst upon our view an open road to the south, for there stretched before us a great glacier running almost south and north between two huge mountain ranges. As far as we could see, except towards the mouth, the glacier appeared to be smooth, yet this was not a certainty, for the distance was so great . . . we could see the glacier stretching away south inland till at last it seemed to merge in high inland ice."

To the men in Scott's party who knew the Ferrar Glacier, there was something unattractive about the Beardmore, but as so often in the Antarctic, it was the very vastness of its scale that militated against any real sense of grandeur. On either side of the main flow were tributary glaciers and tumultuous ice-falls that "anywhere else would have aroused admiration," but like the mountains that flanked it, these were dwarfed into insignificance by an icy pathway to the summit that in places measured forty miles across.

For the twelve who were now left to haul loads of two hundred pounds each it was a brutal enough challenge, at any rate, and for Teddy Evans and Lashly still worse. There was already a disgruntled sense in Evans's mind that they had more than done their share, and with Scott desperate to catch up on the lost time, the simmering competitiveness natural—and essential—to such men threatened to break out into a less healthy rivalry between the three teams. "Lost one hour on Owner's sledge today," Wright noted on the twelfth. "Looks bad but Teddy and Lashly had pulled all the way from Corner Camp. Teddy a quitter." "Scott set a hot pace," he wrote again. "May I never again be the only long-legged one in such a team. All did their best but I am damn sure I had to provide the extra speed." "Our sledge is slow and can't keep up with the owner's," he complained the following day. "Teddy, the damn hypocrite, as soon as he sees the Owner's sledge stopped and they watch us come up puts his head down and digs in for all he is worth."

Wright had been no more impressed with Teddy Evans on the depoting journey the previous March, and if it seems bitterly harsh to judge a man who had already been man-hauling for seven weeks, he was not the only one who wanted to push Evans down a crevasse. There can be no doubt of Evans's courage when it came to a crisis, but if his performance in the *Terra Nova* or subsequent war record are any guide, his was a temperament that was better suited to the drama and dangers of battle or the high seas than the grim, unglamorous slog of hauling.

There was another side to Evans's conduct on this march, too, that Cherry—the repository of everything that was best in the expedition—would never forgive him for. "Now I am not going to enter into Evans's character in detail," Cherry would write the following year to Reggie Smith, bitter at the thought of Evans usurping the credit for the journey that belonged to other men, "but I wish to put it down in black & white for being one who knows that Evans is no man to whom to entrust the account of this expedition . . . That he has spoken when sledging continually disloyally of Scott, not only to officers but also before the men is the main reason why . . . That he did not pull probably interested those who manhauled with him mainly—I was thankful that I was never on the same sledge as him. Bowers was the most loyal friend & companion that any friend or superior officer could have—he spoke to me once of Evans's behaviour as 'sedition.'"

Cherry was probably more sensitive about the reputation of the expedition—and of Bowers and Wilson in particular—than anyone, but a letter from Teddy Evans bears out his alarm. "I have come to the conclusion," he wrote vindictively during his subsequent convalescence in New Zealand, "that *private* Antarctic expeditions are public frauds for the glorification and selfish ends of the leader alone . . . Scott treated me rather worse than Peary did Bartlett."

With Scott's old stomach acidity doing nothing for his temper either, half the party suffering from snow blindness, and sweat, cramps and sunburnt hands and lips adding to the misery, it had been a grim introduction to the Beardmore. A five-hour march on the morning of the twelfth produced no more than half a mile's progress, and the thirteenth was even worse, "perhaps a half-mile in the forenoon," Bowers recorded, followed by "a shock" in the afternoon.

> We bust off full of hope . . . but pride goeth. We stuck ten yards from the camp, and nine hours later found us little more than half a mile on. I have never seen a sledge sink so. I have never pulled so hard, or so nearly crushed my insides into my backbone by the everlasting jerking with all my strength on the can-

vas band round my unfortunate tummy. We were all in the same however [sic].

I saw Teddy ahead and Scott astern, but we were the worst off as the leading team had topped the rise and I was too blind to pick out a better trail. We fairly played ourselves out that time, and finally had to give it up and relay. Halving the load we went forward about a mile with it, and, leaving that lot, went back for the remainder. So done were my team that we could do little more than pull the half loads . . . Tomorrow Scott decided that if we could not move our full loads we should start relaying systematically.

The next day, however, brought the first hint of relief, with the hard blue ice first two feet and then less than a foot below the surface. The advent of the better surface brought with it the dangers of crevasses, but these were too well bridged to end a rivalry that had now become an integral part of their march. "Did a splendid bust off on ski, leaving Scott in the lurch," Bowers crowed, "and eventually overhauling the party which had left some time before us. All the morning we kept up a steady, even swing which was quite a pleasure." "Evans' is now decidedly the slowest unit . . . Bowers' . . . not much faster," Scott crowed in his turn. "We keep up and overhaul either without difficulty."

As Bowers had said, however, "pride goeth," and another snowfall made the next day tough for all three teams, with the soft crust constantly giving way under their weight. "We must push on all we can, for we are now 6 days behind Shackleton," Scott wrote in response, mercifully unconscious that Amundsen was smoking a victory cigar at the Pole even as they stumbled on. There were times when only their skis saved them from the crevasses, and if that was galling enough in the light of British prejudice, even worse was the dawning reality that they had so far met with nothing that dogs could not have managed.

On the seventeenth an area of bad pressure might have done something to relieve this niggling thought, but a good afternoon run along the centre of the glacier took them up past the "Cloudmaker" before they camped that night at a height of about 3,600 feet. "If we can keep up the pace, we gain on Shackleton," Scott noted. "For once one can say 'Sufficient for the day is the good thereof.' Our luck may be on the turn—I think we deserve it."

Another good day's march buoyed him further, and by the following nightfall they had narrowed the gap with their "ghostly pace-maker" to only five days. "Things are looking up," he wrote in his diary on 19 December, "2 miles or more an hour, with the very satisfactory result of 17 (stat.) miles to the good for the day. It has not been a strain, except perhaps for me with my wounds [leg injuries from falling down a crack] received early in the day . . . Evans and Bowers are busy taking angles; as they have been all day, we shall have material for an excellent chart. Days like this put heart in one."

It was the opposite story for four of them the next day, when at 84°59'6" and 6,500 feet, Scott told off the returning party for the following night. "Atkinson, Wright, Cherry-Garrard, and Keohane. All are disappointed— poor Wright rather bitterly, I fear. I dreaded this necessity of choosing— nothing could be more heart-rending." Scott was not imagining Wright's feelings. "Aitch, Cherry, Keohane and I turn back tomorrow night," he wrote in his diary, "Scott a fool. Teddy goes on. I have to make course back. Too wild to write more tonight. Teddy slack trace ⅞th of today."

"Cherry was, I know, very disappointed, and so was I," Wright later and more reasonably recalled. "The reason for my disappointment was that I was quite certain that both Cherry and I were in better shape than at least one who was chosen to go on. I must have shown my disappointment since the Owner, most kindly, softened the blow by pointing out that I would have the responsibility as navigator of the party, of seeing that we did not get lost on the way back. It did soften the blow to a great extent. I was not entirely happy but soon recovered and indeed, probably took this responsibility too seriously."

Scott could not have been kinder to Cherry in his disappointment either, but he had almost no room for manoeuvre. For all their tireless efforts, Cherry and Keohane had already been identified as the weakest in Bowers's party, and with Wilson, PO Evans, Bowers, Lashly, Crean and Teddy Evans, his second-in-command and navigator, all choosing themselves for one reason or another, the final choice lay between Cherry and Oates. "Scott was very put about," Cherry wrote in his diary. "Said he had been thinking a lot about it but had come to the conclusion that the seamen with their special knowledge, would be needed: to rebuild the sledge, I suppose. Wilson told me it was a toss-up whether Titus or I should go on . . . I said all I could think of—he [Scott] seemed so cut up about it, saying 'I think somehow, it is specially hard on you.' I said I hoped I had not disappointed him, and he caught hold of me and said 'No—No—No,' so if that is the case all is well. He told me that at the bottom of the glacier he was hardly expecting to go on himself: I don't know what the trouble is, but his foot is troubling him, and also, I think, indigestion."

In spite of their disappointment, the return party remained with the main body for another day, criss-crossing the ice in search of a route through the hideous "mass of crevasses" that marked the junction of glacier and plateau. "Teddy Evans and Atkinson were down to the length of their harness this morning," Scott wrote to Kathleen, as he resigned himself to a fogbound wait in the middle of the disturbed ice, "and we have all been half-way down. As first man I get first chance, and it's decidedly exciting not knowing which step will give way. Still all this is interesting enough."

It was largely down to Scott's ice-craft, learned on his Western Journey with Evans and Lashly, that they did not have it harder. "We did not go quite so close to land as Shackleton did," Bowers wrote, "and therefore, as had been the case with us all the way up the glacier, found less difficulties than he had met with. Scott is quite wonderful in his selection of route, as we have escaped excessive dangers and difficulties."

It was not so much Scott's skill, though, as his remorseless *drive* that seized Bowers's imagination. At 3 p.m. the fog cleared enough for Scott to decide to "make a dash for it," and with "Mount Darwin, a nunatak" now visible, an appreciative Bowers went on, "This we made for, and some two miles on exchanged blue ice for the new snow which was much harder pulling. Scott was fairly wound up, and he went on and on. Every rise topped seemed to fire him with a desire to top the next, and every rise had another beyond and above it. We camped at 8 p.m., all pretty weary, having come up nearly 1500', and done over eleven miles in S.W. direction." "So here we are," Scott concluded another volume of his diary, "practically on the summit and up to date in the provision line. We ought to get through."

At 85°7's, where they established their Upper Glacier Depot, they still had 293 miles to go to the Pole. The loss of the returning party meant heavier loads for the two teams that were continuing south, but by five o'clock the next afternoon, after a last series of upward slopes, the hard, crevassed surface they had been marching over abruptly "changed to regular sastrugi and [their] horizons levelled in every direction." It was a moment Scott had been anticipating with a mixture of hope and anxiety, but now that it had come, and he found that at forty-three he could still "go with the best of them," his only feeling was elation. "I hung on to the S.W. till 6 p.m.," he noted, "and then camped with a delightful feeling of security that we had at length reached the summit proper. I am feeling very cheerful about everything to-night. We marched 15 miles (geo.) (over 17 stat) to-day, mounting nearly eight hundred feet and all in about 8½ hours . . . To me for the first time our goal seems really in sight. We can pull our loads and pull them much faster and farther than I expected in my most optimistic moments. I only pray for a fair share of good weather."

Another area of troubled ice two days later—Christmas Day—failed to dampen Scott's spirits any more than a heavy fall into a crevasse did Lashly's. "It appears that Lashly went down very suddenly," Scott noted with a connoisseur's relish, "nearly dragging the crew with him . . . Lashly says the crevasse was 50' deep and 8 feet across, in form U, showing that the word 'unfathomable' can rarely be applied. Lashly is 44 today and as hard as nails. His fall has not even disturbed his equanimity."

That night, birthday, Christmas and survival were all concelebrated in style with a four-course meal that began with pemmican "full whack," "with slices of horse meat flavoured with onion and curry powder and thickened with biscuit; then an arrowroot, cocoa and biscuit hoosh sweetened; then a plum-pudding; then cocoa with raisins, and finally a dessert of caramels and ginger. After the feast it was difficult to move. Wilson and I couldn't finish our share of plum-pudding. We have all slept splendidly and feel thoroughly warm—such is the effect of full feeding."

It would be nice to know whether Wilson or Scott recalled another plum pudding stowed away by Shackleton nine years earlier, and if they did not offer him a silent word of thanks now, they ought to have done. For the first time on the journey their more westerly course from the top of the Beardmore was taking them away from his footsteps, but Shackleton's route and his timetable had got them onto the plateau in better shape than Scott could have ever hoped for.

"It seems astonishing to be disappointed with a march of 15 (sts.) miles," he was writing two days later, but not everyone was so buoyant. As early as Christmas Day Teddy Evans had detected a lack of spring in the communal step, and by the twenty-seventh his new team of Lashly, Crean and Bowers was struggling hard to keep up with Scott. It was plain to everyone that the problem could only lie with either their method or their sledge, and the simple expedient of exchanging with Scott the next day solved the dilemma, if it did little for morale. "In the afternoon we exchanged sledges," Scott wrote, "and at first went off well, but getting into soft snow, we found a terrible drag . . . So the sledge is the cause of the trouble, and talking it out, I found that all is due to want of care. The runners are excellent, but the structure has been distorted by bad strapping, bad loading, &c. The party are not done, and I have told them plainly that they must wrestle with the trouble and get it right for themselves. There is no possible reason why they should not get along as easily as we do."

One very "possible" reason was that Evans and Lashly had been man-hauling now for over six hundred miles, but when Scott was "fired" there were no excuses. As Cherry memorably wrote, there is nothing that better shows the sheer "shove of the man" than Scott's diaries for these first weeks on the plateau, the ruthless determination, in the battle with time and physical weakness, to get "every inch out of the miles, every ounce out of his companions. Also he was in a hurry, he always was. That blizzard which had delayed him . . . and the resulting surfaces which had delayed him in the lower reaches of the glacier! One can feel the averages running through his brain, so many miles today: so many more tomorrow. When shall we come to an end of this pressure? Can we go straight or must we go more west? And then the great undulating waves with troughs eight miles wide, and the buried mountains, causing whirlpools in the ice—how immense, and how annoying. The monotonous march . . . Always slog on, slog on. Always a fraction of a mile more." It was this "drive" that kept his men going through exhaustion, and made them so badly want to go on even when their bodies had no more to give. For five of the men there was still a chance of making the final party, and yet as they all buckled down to one last push, it would have been hard to say whether it was the raw ambition of a Teddy Evans or the collective desire to prove themselves to Scott that was the greatest motivation.

By 30 December they had "caught up" with Shackleton, and the next day the second party jettisoned their skis and a hundred pounds of weight, in preparation for their return journey. Teddy Evans and Lashly had long suspected that their weeks of man-hauling had put them out of the picture for the Pole, but for a few hours that night all the ambitions and resentments that had built up on the ascent of the Beardmore dissolved into the magical interlude of their last New Year's Eve together.

For the first time they had added an inner lining to the tent, and celebrating the New Year with an extra cup of tea, the five officers sat in their bags, writing and talking until two in the morning. For the first time, too, in Scott's company Oates relaxed and talked—and "talked on and on," Evans recalled, "and his big brown eyes sparkled as he recalled little boyish escapades at Eton . . . Oates talked for some hours. At length Captain

Scott reached out and affectionately seized him in the way that was itself characteristic of our leader, and said, 'You funny old thing, you have quite come out of your shell, Soldier. Do you know, we have all sat here talking for nearly four hours?' "

That night, as Teddy Evans put it, "we warmed to each other in a way that we had never thought of, quite oblivious to cold, hardship, scant rations, or the great monotony of sledge hauling." For Evans, in particular, the evening must have had an extra poignancy, because three days later, on 3 January, at a height of more than ten thousand feet and 150 miles from the Pole, Scott broke the news to him that he was going back with Crean and Lashly.

It was especially hard for Scott to disappoint his two old "Discoverys," but how a tale that Crean later told to Gran has been distorted into a vignette of moral cowardice is a mystery. In the version given in Gran's diary and later "improved" with time, Scott went into the second tent after he had spoken to Evans, heard the pipe-smoking Crean cough and, seizing the chance to escape an unpleasant confrontation, said, "You've got a nasty cough, Crean, you must be careful with a cold like that!" "Crean's 'cough' was an excuse for Scott," Gran wrote, "but Crean understood his Captain and saw though him," replying, "'You think I can't take a hint sir!'" There seems no reason to doubt that this conversation, or something very like it, took place, but Gran had been with the *Terra Nova* long enough to know that naval captains did not need "excuses" for anything they did, and that if Scott's remark was in "code," it was the coded kindness between two men and friends who had known and worked with each other for more than ten years.

For Evans, however much he must have expected the news, it was still a bitter blow. In his *South with Scott* he made a decent fist of his disappointment, but anticipation and reality are quite different things, and as second-in-command he had seen himself at the Pole with Scott from the day he had abandoned his own expedition plans. "I never thought for a moment that he would be in the final party," Bowers wrote, "but he had buoyed himself up with the idea of going till the last moment . . . Poor Teddy—I am sure it was for his wife's sake he wanted to go. He gave me a little silk flag she had given him to fly at the pole."

It is certainly true that Scott did not want Teddy Evans along with him, and did not trust him, but all these personal considerations apart, past performance and future events both underline that he was also *right* to send him back. The one, overriding aim that Scott had when he announced his

surface of the plateau, the focus for all those anxieties that the ponies had inspired on the Barrier. On 7 January they had tried to do without skis, but a brief taste of what Bowers was doing was enough to put a stop to that, and after a mile and a half they went back to recover them.

On the ninth the single word "RECORD" marked Shackleton's far-thest south, but a new and untrodden world—or what they imagined a new world—brought no change. "The surface seems to be growing softer," Scott wrote the next day, and, on the eleventh "heavy pulling from the beginning . . . I never had such pulling . . . and the rest of the forenoon was agonising . . . We have covered 6 miles, but at fearful costs." They were now only seventy-four miles from the Pole, but whether they could manage a rate of eleven miles a day for another seven was the question. "It takes it out of us like anything," he confessed. "None of us ever had such hard work before . . . Our chance still holds good if we can put the work in, but it's a terribly trying time."

Day after day, it was the same struggle, the same misery, the same com-plaint. On the twelfth a chill wind hardened the surface enough for the runners to slide more easily, and such was the relief it brought Scott it felt like the first breeze did to Coleridge's mariner—"I had got to fear that we were weakening badly in our pulling," he wrote, but "those few minutes showed me that we only want a good surface to get along as merrily as old. With the surface as it is, one gets horribly sick of the monotony and can easily imagine oneself getting played out . . . It is an effort to keep up the double figures, but if we can do so for another four marches we ought to get through. It is going to be a close thing." There was another ominous indication of things to come. "At camping tonight," he noticed that same evening, "everyone was chilled and we guessed a cold snap, but to our sur-prise the actual temperature was higher than last night, when we could dawdle in the sun. It is most unaccountable why we should suddenly feel the cold in this manner." "Again we noticed the cold," he noted at lunch two days later; "all our feet were cold . . . Oates seems to be feeling the cold and fatigue more than most of us, but we are all very fit . . . Oh! For a few fine days."

On the fifteenth they made their last depot, and at 89°26'57", were only two good marches from the Pole. They had nine days' provisions with them for the last phase "so it ought to be a certain thing now," Scott wrote, "and the only appalling possibility the sight of the Norwegian flag fore-stalling ours . . . Only 27 miles from the Pole. We *ought* to do it."

The next morning they went well, covering seven and a half miles, and started the afternoon "in high spirits . . . feeling that to-morrow would see us at our destination." The first part of the afternoon march had gone just as promisingly, when "about the second hour Bowers's sharp eyes detected what he thought was a cairn; he was uneasy about it, but argued that it must be sastrugus. Half an hour later he detected a black speck ahead. Soon we knew this could not be a natural snow feature. We marched on, found that it was a black flag tied to a sledge bearer; near by the remains of a camp; sledge tracks and ski tracks going and coming and the clear trace of dogs' paws—many paws. This told the whole story. The Norwegians have forestalled us and are first at the Pole. It is a terrible disappointment, and I am very sorry for my loyal companions."

It was hard to guess the age of the tracks, but the flag of black bunting had begun to fray quite badly at the edges, and Wilson reckoned that they must be two or three weeks old, or even more. That night Scott's men camped beside this symbol of defeat, mulling over the evidence, trying to work out just how many men had been in the Norwegian party and from what direction they had come. "We have picked up the Norskies' tracks pointing straight here," Oates wrote. "Scott is taking his defeat much better than I expected." "I am awfully sorry for Capt. Scott," Bowers also wrote, "who has taken the blow very well indeed." Or he was, at least, putting a brave face on it for his companions, though neither Scott nor any of them slept much "after the shock of our discovery." The next morning they were away by 7:30, and followed Amundsen's tracks south-south-west for three hours before striking out on a beeline of their own for the Pole.

It was the coldest march Wilson could ever remember, with a force 4 to 6 wind in their faces and temperatures of −22° penetrating their double layers of woollen and fur mitts. The burnt and blistered face of Birdie Bowers had long looked more like a "ham" than anything else, but it was the badly frostbitten Oates and Evans who were Scott's chief worries. Evans's hands were now so bad that at 12:30 they had to stop early. "It was," Wilson soberly recorded, "a very bitter day . . . The weather was not clear—the air was full of crystals, and driving towards us as we came South, and making the horizon grey and thick and hazy."

They were at 89°53'37", and after another six and a half miles' march due south, camped at the Pole. "The Pole. Yes," Scott wrote, "but under very different circumstances from those expected." It was 17 January, 6:30 p.m. That night they had double hoosh, some last bits of chocolate, and some cigarettes provided by Wilson. In spite of the cold Bowers was outside, taking sights. At five the next morning sights were taken again, and after summing up their observations, they calculated they were three and a half miles from the Pole itself, a mile beyond it and three miles to the right. In more or less the same direction Bowers spotted something, and after a two-mile march they came to the Norwegian tent. Inside was a record of the five men who had defeated them: Roald Amundsen, Olav Olavson Bjaaland, Hilmer Hanssen, Sverre H. Hassel and Oscar Wisting, and the date: 16 December 1911. "The tent is fine," Scott wrote. "A small compact affair supported by a single bamboo. A note from Amundsen, which I keep, asks me to forward a letter to King Haakon!"

Amundsen had left a few things: three half-bags of reindeer skins with an odd assortment of mitts and sleeping socks, a Norwegian artificial horizon, "a sextant and hypsometer of English make." While Wilson sketched and Bowers photographed, Scott wrote "a note to say I had visited the tent with companions," and prepared to leave Amundsen's "Polheim." Sights at lunch gave them half to three-quarters of a mile from the Pole, and there "we built a cairn, put up our poor slighted Union Jack, and photographed ourselves—mighty cold work all of it."

Less than half a mile from their cairn to the south, they saw an old sledge underrunner sticking out of the snow, marking, they supposed, the exact spot as far as Norwegian calculations could fix it. "There is no doubt that our predecessors have made thoroughly sure of their mark and fully carried out their programme," Scott wrote. "I think the Pole is about 9500 feet in height; this is remarkable, considering that in Lat 88° we were about 10,000. We carried the Union Jack about ¾ of a mile north with us and left it on a piece of stick as near as we could fix it."

They took the Norwegian underrunner as a yard for their floorcloth sail, and turned northwards. "What a place to strive so hard to reach," wrote Bowers, sustained to the end of the earth by the consciousness of national superiority. "It is sad that we have been forestalled by the Norwegians but I am glad that we have done it by good British manhauling."

Scott did not even have that consolation. "Great God," he burst out, "this is an awful place and terrible enough for us to have laboured to it without the reward of priority . . . Now for the run home and a desperate struggle. I wonder if we can do it."

Thirty-one: **Ars Moriendi**

In the Eastern story, the heavy slab that was to fall on the bed of state in the flush of conquest was slowly wrought out of the quarry, the tunnel for the rope to hold it in its place was slowly carried through the leagues of rock, the slab was slowly raised and fitted in the roof, the rope was rove to it and slowly taken through the miles of hollow to the great iron ring . . . So, in my case; all the work, near and afar, that tended to the end, had been accomplished; and in an instant the blow was struck, and the roof of the stronghold dropped upon me.

CHARLES DICKENS, *Great Expectations*

If Scott did not feel something of Pip's presentiment of coming evil as they turned for home, he should have done. Between the Polar Party and Cape Evans lay a march across plateau and Barrier of eight hundred miles, and success or failure—survival or death—depended on a hundred decisions that had already been made, on a network of communications already in place, on a series of judgements, assumptions, expectations, orders, calculations, risks, omissions and projections now irretrievably beyond recall. For more than a year of planning, measuring and depoting, he had either been assuring their safe return, or meticulously plotting their deaths, and he could not have been sure which it was. In his last letter from Cape Evans he claimed that he had become more relaxed about things that were beyond his orbit, and yet in this case there was nothing for which he was not responsible, nothing he had not ordered, not a morsel of food that he had not calculated, nor a depot site he had not chosen and marked himself.

"Sole author I, sole cause"—Scott knew his Milton well enough to recognise his "text" for the march—and for a man of his temperament and sense of responsibility there can have been few heavier loads. In his *Worst*

Journey in the World Cherry wrote perceptively of just how easy it was for the "footsoldier," but even with the emotional support of Wilson to call on, Scott could never sink into the amnesiac luxury of thoughtless and irresponsible suffering to take his mind off his cares. Only Bowers, perhaps, was in any position to share the burden of responsibility, but for all his virtues, the faculty of self-doubt was not amongst them. "With such splendid companions," he had written home the day that Evans's party turned back, "& everything so carefully arranged in the food line (by myself) we ought to journey through this lifeless land without mishaps."

It was a lonely burden that Scott carried, and doubly so as man-hauling, with its endless equations of weight and time, left no room for the generous margins of error that Amundsen could afford. There is no doubt that a love of "theory" left Scott especially open to the lure of a good plan, but from the day his transport had "failed," he had precious little choice other than to put in place the complex and vulnerable chain of life-supports that he was now dependent upon.

The real dangers were going to be on the Barrier at the extreme end of the season, when blizzards could throw out all calculations, but at least the immediate task must have seemed consolingly within their scope. He knew that when they set off north they had seven days' food with them, and with a further four cached at their final depot on 15 January and a week's worth laid on the tenth, there was a clear margin of safety for the first stage of a journey that had taken sixteen days on their way south. At "Three Degree Depot," as this first target was called, Scott had left another week's provisions, enough to carry them through to the Upper Glacier Depot laid where Cherry, Atkinson, Wright and Keohane had turned back on 22 December. The next caches beyond this were the Mid and Lower Glacier Depots, and then just three more—Upper, Mid and Mount Hooper—until One Ton Camp some six hundred miles from the Pole.

The other critical issue that was also now beyond revision was their food. "Henceforth our full ration," Cherry had recorded in his diary at the foot of the Beardmore, "will be 16 oz. biscuit, 12 oz. pemmican, 2 oz. butter, 0.57 oz. cocoa, 3.0 oz. sugar and 0.86 oz. tea. This is the Summit ration, total 34.43 oz., with a little onion powder and salt. I am all for this: Seaman Evans and others are much regretting the loss of chocolate, raisins and cereals."

These Summit Rations gave Scott and his men 4,500 calories a day, or probably 2,500 or more a day less than they burned man-hauling on the summit. Scott had used Cherry, Wilson and Bowers as guinea-pigs on their

Crozier journey, but the demands at plateau altitude are more acute than they are at sea level, and the body's capacity to absorb calories—seven thousand a day—simply will not match the expenditure of man-hauling under such conditions. "When I manhauled across the Antarctic continent with Mike [Stroud] in 1993," Sir Ranulph Fiennes wrote, "his meticulous measurements showed that over a sixty-eight-day period (of our ninety-three-day journey), we burned up a daily average of well over 7,000 [calories] and lost forty-four pounds of bodyweight. During our glacial ascent from sea-level to 10,000 feet, we burned more than 11,000 calories every day. This was 5,500 calories more than we were eating."

Fiennes and Stroud were hauling far heavier loads than Scott and his men, but they were pulling more efficient sledges as well, and if the calorific deficiencies were roughly similar, the implications are clear. As late as 8 January Bowers was still congratulating himself on the quality of their rations, but three weeks before that—even before they were halfway up the Beardmore on the way south—he had recorded that he was getting noticeably thinner, and the same was true of the others.

The one area of life over which Scott did retain some control was morale, and for all the disappointments of the Pole, only Evans seemed to be losing heart. It is impossible not to speculate on the psychological effects of their "failure," but if journals throughout the next weeks, or the meticulous meteorological records Bowers kept, are any guide, these were not men on the verge of collapse. For Scott in particular there was the commercial incentive of getting the news back first, but more important than that, none of them was—to borrow Wright's term—a "quitter." In his diary entry for the seventeenth Wilson was insistent that they had achieved precisely what they set out to do when they started, and with the wind now behind them, and their cairns easy to spot, they could at least—if nothing else—look forward to warmer and more pleasant marching.

There was always going to be an element of anxiety until they reached Three Degree Depot, however, and with the surface as gruelling as ever, Scott knew they were "going to have a pretty hard time this next hundred miles. If it was difficult to drag downhill over this belt, it will probably be a good deal more difficult to drag up." In spite of a following wind and a full sail, they were also feeling the cold more than they had done, and by the twenty-second Scott was recording "the most tiring march we have had." The one piece of luck they were still enjoying was that they could follow their old tracks with ease, but on the next day, as they were being carried along by the wind at a rattling pace to their 10 January depot, there came the first real intimation of what lay ahead. "Wilson suddenly discovered that Evans's nose was frostbitten . . . white and hard," Scott wrote. "There is no doubt that Evans is a good deal run down—his fingers are badly blistered and his nose is rather seriously congested with frequent frost bites. He is very much annoyed with himself, which is not a good sign. I think Wilson, Bowers and I are as fit as possible under the circumstances. Oates gets cold feet. One way and another, I shall be glad to get off the summit! . . . The weather seems to be breaking up. Pray God we have something of a track to the Three Degrees Depot."

"Things beginning to look a little serious," he wrote the next day, as first a slanting sun and then a blizzard added to their worries. "This is the second full gale since we left the Pole. I don't like the look of it. Is the weather breaking up? Then God help us, with the tremendous summit journey and scant food. Wilson and Bowers are my standby. I don't like the easy way in which Oates and Evans get frostbitten."

There was relief the next day when they found their depot, and could go on with nine and a half days' provisions to last them the eighty-nine miles to Three Degree Depot. But Scott's anxiety over Evans and Oates was becoming a continuous refrain. "Oates suffers from very cold feet," he recorded again. "Evans' fingers and nose are in a bad state, and to-night Wilson is suffering tortures from his eyes. Bowers and I are the only members of the party without troubles at present."

Their cairns were still serving their purpose, which was just as well, as their outward tracks were often obliterated, but for the first time they were beginning to feel hunger. "If we can get to the next depot in a few marches (it is now less than 60 miles and we have a full week's food)," Scott wrote on the twenty-seventh, "we ought to be able to open out a little, but we can't look forward to a real feed till we get to the pony food depot. A long way to go, and, by Jove, this is tremendous labour."

They were all getting thinner, too, especially Evans, and as on the Southern Journey, talking a "good deal" of food. "I sometimes spend much thought on the march," Bowers wrote in his diary, "with plans for making a pig of myself on the first opportunity. As that will be after a further march of 700 miles they are a bit premature."

Given the conditions and the state they were in, they were putting together a sequence of astonishing performances, with successive marches of sixteen, nineteen and a half and nineteen miles taking them by the thirtieth within reach of Three Degree Depot. But if that was "the bright side," as Scott wrote that night, "the reverse of the medal is serious. Wilson has strained a tendon in his leg; it has given pain all day. Of course, he is full of pluck over it, but I don't like the idea of such an accident here. To add to the trouble Evans has dislodged two finger-nails to-night; his hands are really bad, and to my surprise he shows signs of losing heart over it. He hasn't been cheerful since the accident."

Picking up their depot and Bowers's skis the next day, they trudged on towards their next target, Wilson walking alongside the sledge to save his leg. A cairn on 1 February reassured them that they were only seven days from the Upper Glacier Depot, and with eight days' full rations and Wilson's leg improving, one more anxiety was at least briefly allayed.

Wilson's medical notes, however, make increasingly grim reading. "Evans . . . has a lot of pus in it tonight . . . Evans has got 4 or 5 of his finger-tips badly blistered by the cold. Titus also his nose and cheeks . . . Titus' big toe is turning black . . . Evans finger-nails all coming off, very raw and sore . . . Titus' toes are blackening, and his nose and cheeks are dead yellow . . . Evans' fingers suppurating . . ." Wilson himself was getting almost no sleep from the pain of his eyes, and an injury to Scott's shoulder when he "came an awful 'purler' " added to the casualty list. On 5 February difficulties with their tracks again slowed them down, and with the temperature twenty degrees below what it had been on the way up, the descent was becoming a dangerous scramble to get off the plateau while any of them were still unhurt.

Evans's deterioration, after a fall the previous morning, was gathering pace, and that night Scott noted that he was becoming "dull and incapable." The only consolations seemed, as ever, Bowers and food, but even those were soon in jeopardy. On finally reaching the Upper Glacier Depot on the seventh, they found a whole day's ration missing. "First panic," Scott noted. "Certainty that biscuit-box was short . . . Bowers is dreadfully disturbed about it."

There was relief, however, in the shape of a note from Teddy Evans saying that they had passed safely through, and the next day Scott was sufficiently himself to send Bowers on skis towards Mount Darwin to obtain some rock samples. It is astonishing, in fact, how keenly both Scott's and Wilson's scientific faculties were still working, and after a "cold and cheerless lunch" they spotted a moraine that was "so obviously interesting," Scott wrote, "I decided to camp and spend the rest of the day geologising. It has been extremely interesting. We found ourselves under perpendicular cliffs of Beacon sandstone, weathering rapidly and carrying veritable coal seams. From the last Wilson, with his sharp eyes, has picked several plant impressions, the last a piece of coal with beautifully traced leaves in layers, also some excellently preserved impressions of thick stems, showing cellular structure . . . To-night Bill has got a specimen of limestone with archeocyathus . . . Altogether we have had a most interesting afternoon, and the relief of being out of the wind and in a warmer temperature is inexpressible."

Shackleton had already brought back geological samples from the Beardmore, but interesting as they were as the "first undoubted record of an arborescent plant from the Beacon Sandstone series," they were too imperfectly preserved to provide any accurate information. "The specimens collected by [Wilson] and Lt. Bowers," on the other hand, Debenham later wrote of their Beardmore haul, "are perhaps the most important of all the geological results. The plant fossils collected by this party are the best preserved of any yet found in this quadrant of the Antarctic, and are of the character best suited to settle a long-standing controversy between geologists as to the nature of the former union between Antarctica and Australasia."

After the miseries of the plateau, being among rock again was like stepping ashore after weeks at sea, but the Beardmore had by no means finished with them yet. In his own experience Cherry had found it a harder glacier to come down than to go up, and for the first time now on the descent to the Mid Glacier Depot, Scott's instinct for ice navigation let him down. "For three hours we plunged on on ski," he wrote of "the worst day we have had, first thinking we were too much to the right, then too much to the left . . . There were times when it seemed almost impossible to find a way out of the awful turmoil in which we found ourselves. At length, arguing that there must be a way out on our left, we plunged in that direction. It got worse, harder, more icy and crevassed. We could not manage our ski and pulled on foot, falling into crevasses every minute."

It was twelve hours before Scott could even begin to "*think*" they had recovered their track, but lost time meant short rations, and that night their three remaining pemmican meals were converted into four. After a short night's rest a sight of their 18 December Camp buoyed spirits, but another error took them too far to the left, and "finally at 9 p.m. we landed in the worst place of all. After discussion we decided to camp, and here we are, after a very short supper and one meal only remaining in the food bag; the depot doubtful in locality. We *must* get there to-morrow. Meanwhile we are cheerful with an effort."

By the next morning snow had compounded their problems, reducing .

effective visibility to zero and keeping them cocooned in their bags. "The fog still hung over all," Scott wrote, after a momentary glimpse of the Cloudmaker gave them their chance, "and we went on for an hour, checking our bearings . . . Evans raised our hopes with a shout of depot ahead, but it proved to be a shadow on the ice. Then suddenly Wilson saw the actual depot flag. It was an immense relief, and we were soon in possession of our 3½ days' food. The relief to all is inexpressible."

It is so rare that the sheer nightmare of glacial work among a labyrinth of crevasses makes itself felt in Scott's diary that it is easy to forget it, but this had shaken even him. "Yesterday was the worst experience of the trip and gave a horrid feeling of insecurity," he wrote. "Now we are right, but we must march . . . We mustn't get into a hole like this again. Greatly relieved to find that both parties got through safely."

The relief from one worry only gave Scott time to face another, and Evans was now a desperate concern. It had been clear for days that he had been "going steadily downhill," and his actions now were slow and "stupid." "There is no getting away from the fact that we are not pulling strong," Scott recognised. "Probably none of us . . . but the worst case is Evans, who is giving us serious anxiety. This morning he suddenly disclosed a huge blister on his foot. It delayed us on the march . . . Sometimes I fear he is going from bad to worse." "Evans has nearly broken down in brain, we think," he wrote the next day, "He is absolutely changed from his normal self-reliant self." "It is an extraordinary thing about Evans," Oates brutally wrote in his diary, "he has lost his guts and behaves like an old woman or worse . . . Evans is quite worn out with the work and how he is going to do the 400 odd miles we still have to do I don't know . . . God knows how we are going to get him home. We could not possibly carry him on the sledge."

With the benefit of a good sleep, Evans looked a little better on the seventeenth, but half an hour in his traces was enough for him to work off his ski-shoes and he had to leave the sledge. On an awful surface progress was desperate for the four still pulling, but even so he lost ground. After about an hour the others waited for him, and Scott cautioned him to try to keep up. He "answered cheerfully as I thought," Scott wrote. "We had to push on, and the remainder of us were forced to pull very hard, sweating heavily. Abreast the Monument Rock we stopped, and seeing Evans a long way astern, I camped for lunch. There was no alarm at first . . . After lunch, and Evans still not appearing, we looked out, to see him still farther off. By this time we were alarmed, and all four started back on ski. I was the first to reach the poor man and shocked at his appearance; he was on his knees with clothing disarranged, hands uncovered and frostbitten, and a wild look in his eyes. Asked what was the matter, he replied with a slow speech that he didn't know, but he thought he must have fainted. We got him to his feet but after two or three steps he sank down again. He showed every sign of complete collapse."

By the time they had got him back to the tent he was unconscious, and by 12:30 a.m. he had died. "On discussing the symptoms we think he began to get weaker just before we reached the Pole," Scott wrote that "very terrible day," as much at a loss as everyone since to explain how the strongest man in their party could have collapsed so totally, "and that his downward path was accelerated first by the shock of his frostbitten fingers, and later by his loss of all confidence in himself. Wilson thinks it certain he must have injured his brain by a fall."

Weight loss, dehydration, possible head injury, vitamin deficiency, hypothermia, mental collapse, the effects of scurvy in its earliest, undetectable stages?—whatever the reason or the combination of reasons that lie behind Evans's death, the two myths that can be thrown out are the notion of the "isolation" of a lower-deck man in a tent full of officers, and the egregious error of Scott in taking Evans in the first place. From the way that a number of historians have written about him he might have been the loneliest man on the planet since Adam, but he was not just an old *friend* of Scott's, but someone who had always got on well with the officers in the expedition, utterly at ease with them, confident of his own abilities, incomparably the finest sledge-master, secure in his position, full of stories and always happy to lend out his copy of Dumas—Dum-ass he called him—when required. It is possible that Lashly or Crean might have done better, and Wilson thought so, but there is no certainty that they would have withstood the rigours of an extended period on the plateau any better than Evans did. There was almost certainly an element of sentiment in Scott's choice of him for the final party, but affection and admiration were rooted in years of experience and a sense of obligation that was as well deserved in the week immediately prior to the Pole as it had been on the plateau in *Discovery* days.

"It is a terrible thing to lose a companion in this way," Scott wrote, but there is no mistaking the relief that the need for any decision was taken out of their hands: "calm reflection shows that there could not have been a better ending to the terrible anxieties of the past week. Discussion of the situation at lunch yesterday shows us what a desperate pass we were in with a sick man on our hands at such a distance from home."

Within half an hour of Evans's death they had struck camp, and coming down over the pressure ridges, found their Lower Barrier Depot without difficulty. After the "horrible night" they gave themselves five hours of sleep, and a short march took them across the divide to Shambles Camp where the last ponies had been shot. "Here," Scott wrote, "with plenty of horsemeat we had a fine supper, to be followed by others such, and so continue a more plentiful era if we can keep up good marches."

It was not even as though they had to keep up anything like their pace on the plateau, because with supplies available at the intermediary depots, they had four weeks' full rations to cover the 240 miles to One Ton Depot. They had averaged on the summit a distance of fifteen miles a day, and after 112 days out, a little under an eleven-mile average would get them back to Cape Evans in the 144 days Scott's plan had originally envisaged for the whole return journey.

There were still the questions of the surface and the lateness of the season, and a short march with a fresh sledge they had picked up at Shambles Camp more than bore out Scott's fears. "We have struggled out 4.6 miles," he wrote on 19 February; "it has been like pulling over desert sand, not the least glide in the world. If this goes on we shall have a bad time . . . In all other respects things are improving . . . To-night we had a sort of stew fry of pemmican and horseflesh, and voted it the best hoosh we had ever had on a sledge journey. The absence of poor Evans is a help to the commissariat, but if he had been here in fit state we might have got along faster."

Another morning's march across the same terrible surface brought them to Desolation Camp, where they had been held up by the blizzard, but the total for the day was no more than seven miles. Scott still had hopes that the Barrier surface would improve as they cleared the land, but a repeat of the same conditions and the same funereal progress the following day brought on "the gloomiest thoughts." They were entering a critical phase, with their marker cairns spread wide across the featureless Barrier surface, and while Amundsen had marked his more-frequently-spaced depots latitudinally, Scott had not. On the afternoon of the twenty-second a stiff wind erased their outward tracks, and as they steered out to the east in search of them, they were rewarded with a grim glimpse of their future. "There is little doubt that we are in a rotten critical time," Scott wrote. "Result, we have passed another pony camp without seeing it . . . It's a gloomy position, more specially as one sees the same difficulty recurring even when we have corrected the error."

Bowers's sharp eyes again came to the rescue the next day, and a march

northerly wind came ahead." "Worse and worse . . . poor Oates' left foot can never last out," he noted the following day, "and time over footgear something awful." It was becoming obvious, in fact, that not only was Oates spent, but he was now a burden on the others.

> March 10.—Things steadily downhill. Oates' feet worse. He has rare pluck and must know that he can never get through. He asked Wilson if he had a chance this morning, and of course Bill had to say he didn't know. In point of fact he has none. Apart from him, if he went under now, I doubt whether we could get through . . . With great care we might have a dog's chance, but no more . . . At the same time of course poor Titus is the greatest handicap. He keeps us waiting in the morning . . . again at lunch. Poor chap! It is too pathetic to watch him; one cannot but try to cheer him up.
>
> Sunday, March 11.—Titus Oates is very near the end one feels. What we or he will do, God only knows. We discussed the matter after breakfast; he is a brave fine fellow and understands the situation, but he practically asked for advice. Nothing could be said but to urge him to march as long as he could.

With the Mount Hooper depot the previous day bringing small comfort— "shortage on our allowance all round"—Scott "practically ordered Wilson to hand over the means of ending" their troubles to them. They had to threaten him with ransacking his medical case to get their way, but it is hard to believe that for Scott any more than for Wilson or Bowers suicide could have been a genuine option.

"I should like to keep to the track to the end . . . Must fight it out to the last biscuit," Scott wrote, but for the helpless burden that Oates had become that was no longer an option. "It must be near the end," Scott allowed himself to hope on the twelfth, "but a pretty merciful end . . . Poor Oates got it again in the foot. I shudder to think what it will be like tomorrow."

There is no "tomorrow" in the diary, and the next entry is for the fifteenth or sixteenth—"Lost track of dates, but think the last correct. Tragedy all along the line. At lunch the day before yesterday, poor Titus Oates said he couldn't go on; he proposed we should leave him in his sleeping-bag. That we could not do, and we induced him to come on."

That night Oates was done, and they knew it was the end. "Should this be found," Scott wrote in his diary, shifting for the first time from private mode to an invisible and posthumous public, "I want these facts recorded. Oates's last thoughts were of his Mother, but immediately before he took pride in thinking that his regiment would be pleased with the bold way in which he met his death. We can testify to his bravery. He has borne intense suffering for weeks without complaint, and to the very last was able and willing to discuss outside subjects. He did not—would not—give up hope till the very end. He was a brave soul. This was the end. He slept through the night before last, hoping not to wake; but he woke in the morning— yesterday. It was blowing a blizzard. He said, 'I am just going outside and may be some time.' He went out into the blizzard and we have not seen him since."

It was of growing importance to Scott, as he faced the fact that none of them was going to live, that what they had done and what they had been should be fully understood. "I take this opportunity of saying that we stuck to our sick companions to the last," he went on. "In case of Edgar Evans, when absolutely out of food and he lay insensible, the safety of the remainder seemed to demand his abandonment, but Providence mercifully removed him at this critical moment. He died a natural death and we did not leave him till two hours after his death.* We knew that poor Oates was walking to his death, but though we tried to dissuade him, we knew it was the act of a brave man and an English gentleman. We all hope to meet the end with a similar spirit, and assuredly the end is not far."

The cold was so intense now that Scott could write no more than the odd line at lunch, and only then occasionally. Wilson and Bowers were "unendingly cheerful," and they all still talked of "fetching through," though "none of us believes it in his heart." They still marched, but "dreadfully slowly." Wilson could barely get his skis on, and every encampment had become a torture and a danger. They were now just two pony marches from One Ton Depot. "We leave here our theodolite," Scott wrote, "a camera, and Oates's sleeping bags. Diaries, &c, and geological specimens carried at Wilson's special request, will be found with us or on our sledge."

They were now all but worn out. By the eighteenth, Scott's right foot had gone—"two days ago I was the proud possessor of best feet. These are the steps of my downfall. Like an ass I mixed a small spoonful of curry pow-

---

*There is a small apparent discrepancy here between this statement and Scott's earlier account of Evans's death. There seems no reason, however, to read anything sinister into this.

der with my pemmican—it gave me violent indigestion. I lay awake and in pain all night; I woke and felt done on the march; foot went and I didn't know it. A very small measure of neglect and have a foot which is not pleasant to contemplate."

By the nineteenth Scott knew that the most he could now hope for was amputation, but with three days still to go to reach One Ton Depot, and only two days' food and a day's fuel to do it on, it can have been no more than the remotest fear. One last, dreadful march that afternoon narrowed the fifteen and a half miles to eleven, but that was it. There would be no more hauling.

The next day a blizzard kept them to their tent, and the same the next day dashed the "forlorn hope" that Bowers and Wilson might make it on to the depot for fuel. "Wilson and Bowers unable to start," a helpless Scott recorded; "to-morrow last chance—no fuel and only one or two of food [sic] left—must be near the end. Have decided it shall be natural— we shall march for the depot with or without our effects and die in our tracks."

The entry is dated 22 March and 23 March, the last Scott wrote except for one brief paragraph on the twenty-ninth: "Since the 21st we have had a continuous gale from w.s.w, and s.w," he wrote. ". . . Every day we have been ready to start for our depot 11 *miles* away, but outside the door of the tent it remains a scene of whirling drift. I do not think we can hope for any better things now. We shall stick it to the end, but we are getting weaker, of course, and the end cannot be far."

As late as the twenty-fourth, Bowers still believed himself strong, but feet apart, he and Wilson were as near their end as Scott was, Wilson possibly nearer. Their decline would have mirrored or anticipated his, and without food, without fuel, without hope of the dogs, without hope, as Scott put it, "from man," all that was left was a courageous acquiescence in the will of God. "We have had a long struggle against intense cold on very short fuel, and it has done us up," Wilson wrote to Reggie Smith on the twenty-first or twenty-second.

> We shall make a forlorn-hope effort to reach the next depot to-morrow, but it means a 22 miles, and we are none of us fit to face it.
>
> I want to say how much I have valued your friendship and your example . . . God be thanked for such as you. We shall meet in the hereafter.

I have no fear of death — only sorrow for my wife and for my dear people — otherwise all is well.

To Ory he wrote:

> To my Beloved Wife.
> . . . Don't be unhappy — all is for the best. We are playing a good part in a great scheme arranged by God himself, and all is well . . .
> I would have liked to write to Mother and Dad and all at home, but it has been impossible. We will all meet after death, and death has no terrors . . .
> I leave you in absolute faith and happy belief that if God wishes you to wait long without me it will be for some good purpose. All is for the best to those that love God, and oh, my Ory, we have both loved Him with all our lives. All is well . . .
> We have struggled to the end and we have nothing to regret. Our whole record is clean, And Scott's diary gives the account . . . The Barrier has beaten us — though we got to the Pole . . .
> I feel so happy now in having got time to write to you . . . Dad's little compass and Mother's little comb and looking-glass are in my pocket. Your little testament and prayer book will be in my hand or in my breast pocket when the end comes.

It was, small, black-bound, heavily used. In faint pencil at the front, and in the underlinings and the marginalia beside his favourite prayers and psalms, can be read the same faith, the same certainty, the same sense of wonder at God's creation which had filled his life. "*It is finished*," he transcribed in a minuscule hand. "This teaches us that everything is ready . . . that we haven't to save ourselves that we haven't to make our atonement — that is done. All is ready for us."

"They that go down to the sea in ships, that do business in great waters," he had underlined,

> These are the works of the LORD, and his wonders in the deep.
> For he commandeth, and raiseth the stormy wind, which lifteth up the waves thereof.
> They mount up to the heaven, they go down again to depths: their soul is melted because of trouble:

They reel to and fro, and stagger like a drunken man, and are at their wit's end.

Then they cry unto the LORD in their trouble, and he bringeth them out of their distresses.

He maketh the storm a calm, so that the waves thereof are still.

Then are they glad because they are quiet; so he bringeth them unto their desired haven.

It is an almost unbearably moving document. And it was not Wilson alone who gratefully embraced the time of those last days in the tent to reaffirm his faith and hope. "My own dearest Mother," Bowers wrote, bullish to the end,

> . . . We have had a terrible journey back. Seaman Evans died on the glacier & Oates left us the other day. We have had terribly low temperatures on the Barrier & that & our sick companions have delayed us till too late in the season which has made us very short of fuel & we are now out of food as well. Each depot has been a harder struggle to reach but I am still strong & hope to reach this one with Dr. Wilson & get the food & fuel necessary for our lives. God alone knows what will be the outcome of the 23 miles march but my trust is still in Him & the abounding grace of my Lord & Saviour whom you brought me up to trust & in who has been the stay of my life. In His keeping I leave you & am only glad that I am permitted to struggle on to the end. When man's extremity is reached God's help may put things right—although the end will be painless enough for myself I would so like to come through for your dear sake. It is splendid to pass however with such companions . . . Oh how I do feel for you when you hear all. You will know that for me the end was peaceful as it is only sleep in the cold. Your ever loving son to the end of this life & the next where God shall wipe away all tears from our eyes.
>
> My gear that is not on the ship is at Mrs. Hatfields, Marine Hotel, Sumner, New Zealand.

Scott, too, was preparing himself. In a way that trivialises nothing, faith made death "easy" for Wilson and Bowers, but for a man who did not share their belief, who had nothing firmer than a vague sense of a merciful "Providence" to summon up, there was nothing to hang on to except a sense of self and a loyalty to those convictions that had shaped his life.

It is very difficult in a different culture and age to feel the loneliness of the late-Victorian agnostics as they faced death, bereft of all the consolations of faith and hope that surrounded the nineteenth-century "Christian" end. In the diaries and letters of the time, however, one can glimpse the darkness of extinction that faced Scott, the finality of loss, the agony of separation, unrelieved by any certainty of reunion. Scott did not expect an afterlife. He did not expect to see his mother again. He did not think he would be joined with Kathleen in everlasting bliss. He did not believe he would see his son Peter or—whatever he might say to reassure his mother—find Arch waiting for him. All he had was himself.

"Now is the time to be brave"—the traditional phrase of the French executioner as he entered the condemned cell, and a favourite of Mason's—and it was now Scott's time. And if in small things he was often found wanting, in big things very seldom. The worse the crisis, as Cherry noted, the better was Scott, and it was not likely that the ultimate crisis would find him exposed. He knew death was coming. He had looked steadily at it for weeks. He had watched Evans die. He had let Oates stumble out to his death, and all he had asked of life then was the strength to see it out with the same courage that Oates had shown.

If courage, however, was one of the great hallmarks of Scott's life, so too was *justice*, and he was not going to die unheard. There was no guarantee that their bodies or anything he wrote would ever be found, but in an extraordinary act of willpower and self-control, Scott usurped the traditions of his mother's evangelical faith to transform his tent into the deathroom beloved of Victorian tracts. Racked by cold and hunger and pain, weakening by the day, he wrote with his pencil stub to Sir Edgar Speyer, apologising for the financial muddle he had left the expedition in; he wrote to Sir Francis Bridgeman, telling him that he had *not* been too old for the Pole; he wrote to Egerton, thanking him for all his kindness; he wrote a message to the public; and he wrote to Barrie, with whom there had been some coldness in his last weeks in England. "We are pegging out in a very comfortless spot," he told him.

> Hoping this letter might be found and sent to you I write a word of farewell—It hurt me grievously when you partially withdrew your friendship or seemed so to do—I want to tell you that I

never gave you cause . . . We are showing that Englishmen can still die with a bold spirit fighting it out to the end . . .

We are in a desperate state feet frozen etc, and a long way from food but—it would do your heart good to be in our tent—to hear our songs and the cheery conversation as to what we will do when we get to Hut Point . . . as a dying man my dear friend be good to my wife & child. Give the boy a chance in life if the state won't do it—He ought to have good stuff in him—and give my memory back the friendship which you once found—I never met a man whom I admired & love more than you, yet I never could show you how much your friendship meant to me as you had so much to give and I nothing.

He had already written to Kathleen while the issue was still in doubt, telling her to remarry and be "your happy self again."

I wasn't a very good husband, but I hope I shall be a good memory. Certainly the end is nothing for you to be ashamed of, and I like to think that the boy will have a good start in his parentage of which he may be proud.

It isn't easy to write because of the cold—40 below zero and nothing but the shelter of our tents. You must know that quite the worst aspect of this situation is the thought that I shall not see you again. The inevitable must be faced, you urged me to be a leader of the party, and I know you felt it would be dangerous. I have taken my place throughout, haven't I?

"I think the last chance has gone," he wrote again, determined to live up to his tenets. "We have decided not to kill ourselves but to fight to the last for that depot, but in fighting there is a painless end, so don't worry." It was still his wife, his son, his mother, his family, his duties, his failings, that engrossed him. "You see I am anxious for you and the boy's future," he went on. "Make the boy interested in natural history if you can. It is better than games . . . Try and make him believe in a God, it is comforting—"

"But take comfort that I die in peace with the world," he wrote to his "Own Darling Mother," as ever ready to ease her anxieties, at whatever cost to his own intellectual doubts, "and I myself am not afraid—not perhaps believing in all that you hold so splendidly, but still believing there is a God—a merciful God. I wish I could remember that I had been a better son to you, but I think you will know that you were always very much in my heart and that I strove to put you into more comfortable circumstances . . . For myself I am not unhappy, but for Kathleen, you and the rest of my family my heart is very sore."

Sometimes the thought of that was too much. There was a piece of the Union flag he had flown at the Pole in his kitbag, he told Kathleen, and Amundsen's black flag—"Send a small piece of the Union Jack to the King, a small piece to Queen Alexandra, and keep the rest, a poor trophy for you—What lots and lots I could tell you of this journey. How much better has it been than lounging in too great comfort at home. What tales you would have for the boy, but oh what a price . . . Oh but you'll put a bold strong face to the world, only don't be too proud to accept help for the boy's sake. He ought to have a fine career and do something in the world. I haven't time to write to Sir Clements, tell him I thought much of him, and never regretted his putting me in command of the 'Discovery.'" Freed from the shackles of life, he could be at last the person he had always wanted and so often failed to be, the accidents of personality shed to reveal the nature of the man. The peevishness, the irritation, the ambition, even the reserve were gone.

"Had we lived," he concluded his Message to the Public, the language, the rhythms and frustration of the dying Hamlet living again in his final words,

> I should have had a tale to tell of the hardihood, endurance and courage of my companions which would have stirred the heart of every Englishman. These rough notes and our dead bodies must tell the tale, but surely, surely, a great rich country like ours will see that those who are dependent on us are properly provided for.

The rest is silence. With Wilson on one side, and Bowers on the other, he wrote no more until his last, spare entry:

> I do not think we can hope for any better thing now. We shall stick it out to the end, but we are getting weaker, of course, and the end cannot be far.
>
>> It seems a pity, but I do not think I can write more.
>> R. Scott.
>> For God's sake look after our people.

EPILOGUE

I almost envied Captain Scott as he lay on the field of honour. He had achieved something great for his country, for his family and indeed morally for the whole of mankind.

TRYGGVE GRAN

It was a quite simple creed . . . it amounted to no more than this: that to die decently was worth a good many years of life.

A.E.W. MASON, *The Four Feathers* (1902)

One would be a poor creature indeed if one could not face one's world with such words to inspire one.

KATHLEEN SCOTT, *27 February 1913*

Wright was the first to see it. He was at the head of the advance party, navigating. Some way behind them, with the dogs, were Atkinson and Cherry. "I had been plugging away along my chosen course when I saw a small object projecting above the surface on the starboard bow," Wright recalled, "but carried on the chosen course until we were nearly abreast of this object . . . I decided [it] had better be investigated more closely, but did not expect it was of great interest . . . It was the 6 inches or so tip of a tent and was a great shock . . . I tried to signal my party to stop and come up to me, but my alphabetical signals could not be read by the navy and I considered it would be a sort of sacrilege to make a noise. I felt much as if I were in a cathedral and found myself with my hat on."

It seemed a desecration to camp by the tent, and Wright went out to meet the rest of the advance party, halting them a hundred yards away until Atkinson and Cherry could arrive. The tent had been covered with snow and looked just like a cairn, with the drift piled up against it to the windward. Beside it the tops of two pairs of skis and the bamboo flag mast of a buried sledge poked out of the snow. " 'It is the tent,' " Wright said, as Atkinson and Cherry came up to the waiting men. "I do not know how he knew," Cherry recalled. "Just a waste of snow: to our right the remains of one of last year's cairns, a mere mound and then three feet of bamboo sticking quite alone out of the snow; and then another mound of snow, perhaps a trifle more pointed. We walked up to it. I do not think we quite realized—not for very long—but someone reached up to a projection of snow, and brushed it away. The green flap of the ventilator of the tent appeared, and we knew that the door was below."

Two of the men crawled in through the funnel of the outer tent, but with the drift piled up around, it was too dark inside to see anything. "There was nothing to do but dig the tent out," Cherry wrote. "Soon we could see the outlines. There were three men here." Scott lay in the middle, half out of his sleeping bag, his frozen arm flung out across Wilson. Wilson lay to his left, his arms folded quietly across his chest, Bowers to his right. "The cold had turned their skin yellow and glassy," Gran wrote, and their faces were badly frostbitten. "Scott seemed to have fought hard at the moment of death, but the others gave the impression of having passed away in their sleep."

The tent had been pitched as well as Scott's always were, and was as neat as ever, with the canvas spread "taut and ship-shape," and the inside lining free of snow. There were some loose pannikins from the cooker, some personal belongings, letters and, beside Scott, a lamp fashioned out of a tin with a wick from a finneskoe. "It had been used to burn the little methylated spirit which remained," an awed Cherry wrote. "I think that Scott had used it to help him to write up to the end. I feel sure that he had died last.—and once I had thought that he would not go so far as some of the others. We never realised how strong that man was, mentally and physically, until now."

Under the head of Scott's sleeping bag lay the green wallet in which he carried his diaries, and on the floorcloth beside it were his last letters. On the front of the diary was written an instruction for the finder to read the diaries and then to take them home. "Hour after hour it seemed to me," Cherry wrote, "Atkinson sat in our tent and read . . . Atkinson said he was only going to read sufficient to know what happened—and after that they were brought home unopened and unread. When he had the outline we all gathered together and he read to us the Message to the Public, and the account of Oates's death, which Scott had expressly wished to be known."

The sledge and the rock samples were uncovered, the three men's possessions sorted through, the diaries, letters—including Amundsen's for

King Haakon—records, chronometers, flag and Wilson's prayer book collected up, and the bamboo pole of the tent collapsed. Snow was piled high over it to make a great cairn—"a mark which must last for many years"—and at "the midnight of some day," with the sun dipping low above the Pole, and the Barrier almost in shadow beneath a "blazing sky," "Atkinson read the lesson from the Burial Service from Corinthians. Perhaps it has never been read in a more magnificent cathedral and under more impressive circumstances—for it is a grave which kings must envy. Then some prayers from the Burial Service: and there with the floor-cloth under them and the tent above we buried them in their sleeping bags—and surely their work has not been in vain."

All that was left was to make a cross over the cairn from two skis, and to flank it with the two sledges, dug upright into the snow like a pair of sentinels. Atkinson wrote a note and all eleven men signed it.

> 12 November 1912.
> Lat. 79. 50'S.
> *This Cross and Cairn are erected over the bodies of Capt. Scott C.V.O., R.N.; Dr. E.A. Wilson, MB. B.A. Cantab.; Lt. H.R. Bowers, Royal Indian Marines. A slight token to perpetuate their gallant and successful attempt to reach the Pole. This they did on the 17th January 1912 after the Norwegian expedition had already done so. Inclement weather and lack of fuel was the cause of their deaths.*
>
> *Also to commemorate their two gallant comrades, Capt. L.E.G. Oates of the Inniskilling Dragoons, who walked to his death in a blizzard to save his comrades, about eighteen miles south of this position; also of Seaman Edgar Evans, who died at the foot of the Beardmore Glacier.*
>
> *The Lord gave and the Lord taketh away. Blessed be the name of the Lord.*
>
> *Relief Expedition.*

They never found Oates's body, only his bag, socks and finneskoe—one of which was slit open so that he could get his frostbitten foot into it—and on the morning of the fifteenth built another cairn near the spot where he had walked to his death and erected a cross above it. "Lashed to the cross is a record, as follows," Cherry wrote:

Hereabouts died a very gallant gentleman,
Captain L.E.G. Oates of the Inniskilling Dragoons.
In March 1912, returning from the Pole,
he walked willingly to his death in a blizzard
to try and save his comrades, beset by hardship.
The note is left by the Relief Expedition 1912.

For the search party, as they marched back past the great cairn they had raised over Scott's grave, it was the end of a harrowing eight-month wait. Since 30 March—the day after Scott's last diary entry—Atkinson had been "morally certain" that the Polar Party must all have perished, but time and again over the next weeks a mirage or the distant speck of a seal by a tide-crack would raise hopes that Scott and his men were coming in. "Last night we had turned in about two hours when five or six knocks were hit on the little window over our heads," Cherry recorded in his diary. "Atkinson shouted 'Hullo!' and cried, 'Cherry, they're in.' Keohane said, 'Who's cook?' Someone lit a candle and left it in the far corner of the hut to give them light, and we all rushed out. But there was no one there. It was the nearest approach to ghost work that I have ever heard."

It was not just the Polar Party they were on the lookout for, because the Northern Party under Campbell—the old "Eastern Party" that had stumbled upon Amundsen's Barrier camp—were still stranded somewhere along the coast on which they had been landed by Pennell. The *Terra Nova* had put them ashore at the site of Borchgrevink's old hut at Robertson Bay in February 1911, returning at the start of the following January to transport them and six weeks' worth of sledging rations farther south to Evans Coves with a promise to collect them again in the middle of February.

The Northern Party's previous winter at Robertson Bay had passed uneventfully enough, but when the *Terra Nova* had failed to show by the middle of March, Campbell began to prepare for a second winter under very different conditions. They had already been eking out their sledging rations since the last week of February, and with their tents shredded by gales and a need to preserve supplies for a spring march to Cape Evans, settled into a tiny ice cave they had quarried themselves, with nothing to survive on but a blubber stove and a cache of eleven seals, 120 penguins, some biscuits, enough cocoa for a very thin mug of it five times a week, sufficient tea once a week, and—by way of luxuries—"a very small amount of chocolate and sugar . . . to give us a stick of chocolate every Saturday and every

and not in the other, but instead of the "whirling drift" of Scott's description, what Atkinson recorded were the mild temperatures and light breezes
that are the classic *aftermath* of all Barrier blizzards. They are also the
meteorological conditions—warmer temperatures, following wind, better
surface—that Scott and his men had been praying for since they got onto
the Barrier, so *why* was it that Bowers and Wilson did not attempt to reach
One Ton Depot? In a letter to his wife, Wilson spoke of Scott's "frozen
feet," and of a last attempt by him and Bowers to get to the depot and back,
and yet with everything seemingly in their favour, it was not only a bid that
was never made, but never even attempted.

   Confusion? Exhaustion? Delirium? Scurvy? Self-sacrifice?—
meteorology might be able highlight the problem, but it cannot answer it,
and as with so much in this story, it comes down in the end to a gut sense of
the kind of men they were. It is highly unlikely in any conditions that Bowers and Wilson could have made it to the depot, but what is absolutely certain is that against a south or south-westerly wind they would never have
made it *back*. To leave the tent was in effect to abandon Scott, and neither
of them could have done that. Wilson had once told Markham there was
not a crevasse in Antarctica he would not have been proud to go down
with Scott, and Bowers had not declared himself "Scott's man" to desert
him at the end.

   It would have required no decision, either, no self-conscious moment
of sacrifice, no dramatic weighing of odds—only a creeping, but irre-
versible, postponement until it was too late. It would, above all, have
required no moral compulsion from Scott, and of all the charges levelled
at him this is the most grotesque. There is such a profound sense of
decency in all that he wrote from the last tent that only the most derelict
sense of human nature could imagine that anyone as self-consciously
aware of his own limitations as he was could have spurned the chance to
live up to his ideals that death gave him.

   It is no coincidence, either, that it was only through his journals and
letters that Scott achieved the posthumous dominance over people's minds
that he never did alive. It is easy enough to argue that the Scott of "myth"
bore only a passing resemblance to the living man, but the more central
truth is that it was only in his written legacy that the values to which he
aspired stood shorn of those accidents of character and temper that always
came between him and his ideals.

   After the long years of slide, too—the pettiness of his battle with Shackleton, the shoddiness of his treatment of Skelton, the growing distance

from his family—it was in death a legacy that he at last reclaimed for himself. For most of his life there had been a widening gap between the idealist on the page and the flawed man, but it is the Scott of the page, and not of everyday life, that is the *real* Scott, and in the tent they at last became one.

Death was not an "escape" for Scott in the way that has sometimes been suggested—an escape from failure or public accountability—but it was an opportunity to anchor his character to his most fundamental values, and he seized it. It is clear from his journal that he could be as irritable and impatient on the march as ever, but in those last days the man who had the courage to write as he did in the pain and loneliness of that tent, and the man who had the imaginative power to imprint its image on human consciousness, are the same.

It is above all this profound ability to make real the experience of human nature at the limits of its endurance that is Scott's greatest gift to posterity. His achievements as a leader of two of the greatest of all Antarctic expeditions are unarguable, but in the very nature of science or geographical exploration, if Scott had not done it, someone else would. The same is not true of the legacy of his last days. His testimony has the same appeal as great literature, and has it for the same reason. His letters, diary and last message extend our sense of what it is to be human. No one else could have written them; no one else, at the point of defeat and dissolution, could have so vividly articulated a sense of human possibilities that transcend both. It is as if, too, his followers who raised the cairn over his grave in some way at last sensed that. Cherry famously said that no one could know Scott who had not sledged with him, but as he stared at Scott's body in the gloom of the tent, and listened to the journal of his last days, even Cherry seemed to be seeing him for the first time. "We never realized," he wrote, "how strong that man was, mentally and physically, until now."

And, he might have added, morally. " 'You know,' " Shackleton told Kathleen, " 'I know your husband very well—perhaps better than any man. I have *never* seen him hesitate, he is the most daring man I ever met—extraordinarily brave'—I said—'Yes he's brave morally as well as physically,' & he said 'Yes I agree.' "

Those who knew Scott best had always known that. For his mother, it was the memory of his "goodness" and not his fame that she cherished through the last decade of her life. For Kathleen—successful in her own right as a sculptor by now, and as ready to live and eventually to remarry again as Scott had wanted—he remained the "conscience" she had tied herself to when she first agreed to marry her difficult, moody naval officer. For old Sir Clements, only three years from the end of his long, turbulent life and "plunged in grief," he was simply "the greatest polar explorer that ever lived . . . Chivalrous, noble-minded, forbearing and warm hearted beyond anyone I ever met."

It was not just those who had never known him in the field who saw this. The presence of Wilson and Bowers in his last tent proves that. Crean, "Taff" Evans, Lashly—the best of the polar explorers—they had all, as Evans confessed, been willing to go to "Hell" for him. And if it was perhaps Scott's fault that so many never fully understood him while he was alive, it was a recognition that did finally come. As the rump of his last expedition trudged back past the great cairn they had erected over his grave, it had already in their minds metamorphosed into a "cathedral." They did not know what was coming or how the public would respond, but they were ready for it. Their complicity in the burgeoning myth that surrounded his name was not the silence of a "cover-up" but a tacit acknowledgement of the central truth of Scott's life. Men like Gran and Atkinson who had felt the edge of his tongue needed no reminder that it was not the whole truth, but it was the truth that mattered. Scott might not have been, as he put it, "a great explorer" in the sense that Amundsen was. He might not have been a charismatic leader in the way that Shackleton was. He might not even have been, as he confessed to Kathleen, "a very good husband." But he had been something more.

Except in a theological sense, there is no such thing as a "good death," only a good life lived out bravely to the end, and Scott had done that. As the *Terra Nova* prepared to leave McMurdo Sound for the last time, a party under Atkinson that included Cherry, Crean and Lashly hauled a heavy wooden cross of Australian jarrah up the steep climb of Observation Hill, and set it up high over the Barrier on which Scott's body lies. On it were carved the names of the five dead men and an inscription from Tennyson's "Ulysses":

TO STRIVE, TO SEEK, TO FIND,
AND NOT TO YIELD.

"When I think of Scott," Barrie told the post-war generation of St. Andrews University students in an address on "Courage" that queerly yokes Peter Pan and Laurence Binyon, "I remember the strange Alpine story of the youth who fell down a glacier and was lost, and of how a scientific companion, one of several who accompanied him, all young, computed that the body would again appear at a certain date and place many years afterwards. When that time came round some of the survivors returned to the glacier to see if the prediction would be fulfilled; all old men now; and the body reappeared as young as the day he left them. So Scott and his comrades emerge out of the white immensities, always young."

It is a lie—the same "old lie" that Wilfred Owen damned in his "Dulce et Decorum Est"—but it disguises a truth. Scott is still there, until the ice of the Barrier calves into the sea. He is not, though, eternally young. He is lying with Bowers and Wilson. They are in their bags, quietly acquiescent in their fates; and between them, his face yellowed and badly frostbitten, his arm flung out across Wilson, his emaciated body half in and half out of his sleeping bag as if he had "fought hard at the moment of death," Scott lies, struggling to the last.

Acknowledgements

I am very grateful to Lady Scott and to Lord Kennet for allowing me access to family papers in the Scott Polar Research Institute and the Cambridge University Library; to the Scott Polar Research Institute for permission to quote from material in its archives, and from Apsley Cherry-Garrard's *The Worst Journey in the World*; to the Royal Geographical Society for permission to quote from Sir Clements Markham's papers and documents relating to Scott's *Discovery* and *Terra Nova* expeditions; to the Canterbury Museum, Christchurch, for permission to quote from documents in its collection; and to John Murray for permission to quote from George Seaver's *Edward Wilson of the Antarctic* and *"Birdie" Bowers of the Antarctic*.

I hope the bibliography and notes will underscore just how much this book owes to other writers, but five years' work on Scott has brought many more personal debts. I am again very grateful to the staffs of the Admiralty Library; the Bodleian Library; the British Library; Cambridge University Library; the Library and Museum of Freemasonry; the Public Record Office, the Plymouth and West Devon Record Office; the Royal Naval College, Dartmouth; and the Canterbury Museum for their unvarying kindness, and in particular to Sarah Strong at the Royal Geographical Society and to Bob Headland, Lucy Martin, Caroline Gunn, Heather Lane and all the other staff at the Scott Polar Research Institute for their expert help and patience over many weeks of research in the Institute archives.

Readers of this biography will recognise the influence of the late David

Yelverton's pioneering history of Scott's *Discovery* expedition, but I am even more grateful for the memory of his generosity in putting his own notes and unpublished material at my disposal. I would also like to thank the Master and Fellows of Jesus College for their hospitality over a summer spent in Cambridge; Mr. and Mrs. David Mason for their kindness in allowing me to see the house that Scott and Edward Wilson stayed in near Glen Prosen before their final expedition; Dr. Barrie McKelvey for his patience in answering questions on Antarctic geology; Diana and Michael Preston for many hours of conversation about Scott; and Lisa Chaney for mulling over Scott's friendship with J.M. Barrie with me. Thanks are also due to many other people who helped with suggestions or advice at one stage or another: to the late Commodore Sir John Clerk, for plugging some serious gaps in my naval knowledge; to Louisa Young, Evan Davies, Freddy Markham, Sara Wheeler, Sir Robert Clerk, Eric and Joyce Will-cocks, and to Mark Blackett-Ord for eradicating some of the worst of my social solecisms. To Min Stacpoole and Elisabeth Green, for all their care in reading and rereading this in manuscript; to Celia Darling for saving me from my own incompetence with computers and—in a more chastened vein—to Christopher Swann and Rupert Ashmore for their immense toler-ance in sparing me the consequences of a far more general incompetence out on the sea ice off Baffin Island.

I would especially like to thank Derek Johns, whose role in this book goes far beyond that of a literary agent. I am also very grateful to everyone who has worked on it at HarperCollins, and in particular to Arabella Pike for her enthusiasm and support from the very start; Kate Hyde, who has made the final stages of this book so much easier than they might other-wise have been; and Robert Lacey, for a scrupulous and sensitive job of editing. I would also like to thank Carol Janeway for editorial suggestions that have helped make this a fuller and more balanced biography. Finally, this book is for Honor, without whose help and support throughout it could never have been written.

Notes

Abbreviations

Antarctic Obsession: Clements Markham, *Antarctic Obsession*, ed.
   C. Holland, Huntingdon 1986

Armitage: Albert B. Armitage, *Cadet to Commodore*, London 1925

BAE: British Antarctic Expedition

Bernacchi: Louis Bernacchi, *Saga of the Discovery*, Royston 2001

BNAE: British National Antarctic Expedition

Cherry-Garrard: Apsley Cherry-Garrard, *The Worst Journey in the World*,
   London 1994 edition

Christchurch: Canterbury Museum, Christchurch, New Zealand

Evans: Admiral Lord Mountevans, *South with Scott*, London 1947

Gran: *Tryggve Gran's Antarctic Diary 1910–1913*, ed. Geoffrey Hattersley-
   Smith, London 1984

Gwynn: Stephen Gwynn, *Captain Scott*, Harmondsworth 1929

Huntford: Roland Huntford, *The Last Place on Earth*, London 2000

Huxley: Elspeth Huxley, *Scott of the Antarctic*, London 1977

Kennet Papers: Cambridge University Library, Kennet Papers

Lady Kennet: Lady Kennet, *Self Portrait of an Artist*, London 1949

Limb and Cordingley: Sue Limb and Patrick Cordingley, *Captain Oates*,
   London 1982

Pound: Reginald Pound, *Scott of the Antarctic*, London 1966

PRO: Public Record Office

RGS: Royal Geographical Society

Royds: *The Diary of Lt Charles W.R. Royds RN, Expedition to the Antarctic
   1901–4*, ed. T.R. Royds, Braidwood, NSW 2001

Seaver: George Seaver, *Scott of the Antarctic*, London 1940

Shackleton: E.H. Shackleton, *The Heart of the Antarctic*, London 1909

Silas: *Silas, The Antarctic Diaries and Memoir of Charles S. Wright*, ed.
   C. Bull and Pat F. Wright, Ohio 1993

SLE: *Scott's Last Expedition*, arranged by L. Huxley, London 1913

SPRI: Scott Polar Research Institute
TVOTD: R.F. Scott, *The Voyage of the Discovery*, Thomas Nelson edition, London 1905
Wilson: George Seaver, *Edward Wilson of the Antarctic*, London 1933
Yelverton: David Yelverton, *Antarctica Unveiled*, Boulder, Colorado 2000
Young: Louisa Young, *A Great Task of Happiness*, London, 1996

One: **St. Paul's, 14 February 1913**
The principal sources for this chapter are documents among the Scott family papers, newspaper reports from the time and the letters of Scott's contemporaries. The most valuable study of the impact of Scott's death is Max Jones's paper " 'Our King Upon His Knees': The Public Commemoration of Captain Scott's Last Antarctic Expedition."

3 *I am more proud* . . . SPRI 1/181, 21.02.1913N-N
4 *There is a dreadful report* . . . RGS CB5, Markham, 11.02.1913
8 *Flintshire and Denbighshire* . . . quoted J.M. Brown and W.R. Louis, *Oxford History of the British Empire*, Vol V, Oxford 1999, p. 50
8 *smothered in its own fat* . . . Robert K. Massie, *Dreadnought*, New York 1991, p. 272
9 *The great house* . . . H.G.Wells, *Tono Bungay*, London 1933, p. 9
9 *Children, you are* . . . Arthur Machen, quoted Max Jones, *Heroic Reputations and Exemplary Lives*, ed. Geoffrey Cubitt and Allen Warren, Manchester 2000, p. 110
9 *Oh! England* . . . SPRI 1453/31, Box J, 1913
10 *Amundsen says he won the Cup* . . . SPRI 1453/31, Box J, 1913
10 *I found an essentially* . . . Trevor Griffiths, *Observer*, 17.03.85
13 *To me, and perhaps* . . . A. Cherry-Garrard, postscript to *The Worst Journey in the World*, privately printed 1951

Two: **Childhood and Dartmouth**
The sources for Scott's childhood are largely contained in family anecdotes repeated to his earliest biographers, J.M. Barrie, George Seaver and Stephen Gwynn. The only substantial addition to these traditions is a series of notes (now in the archives of Canterbury Museum, Christchurch, New Zealand) put together by A.G.E. Jones and left unpublished for fear that even in the iconoclastic 1960s a hostile portrait of the Scott family would not be acceptable. The details of his time in *Britannia* can be found in his service and discipline records in the archives at Dartmouth.

14 *There was a time* . . . Gilbert Cannan, *The Road to Come*, London 1913, p. 1
15 *The Scotts were* . . . Gwynn, p. 10
16 *Mr. Scott girded* . . . Seaver, p. 11
16 *The inherited vice* . . . quoted Gwynn, p. 163
17 *Whatever we have cause* . . . Ibid., pp. 23–4
17 *As children we were* . . . quoted Ibid., p. 13
17 *enters history* . . . SLE, Vol I, Biographical Introduction by J.M. Barrie, p. x
18 *His first knife* . . . Ibid., pp. xi–xii
18 *Our tastes for sailing* . . . quoted Seaver, p. 16
20 *That training* . . . S.W. Roskill, *Earl Beatty*, London 1981, pp. 21–2
20 *brave, helpful, truth-telling* . . . Thomas Hughes, *Tom Brown's Schooldays*, London, ill. edn 1874, p. 73

20 *I call the whole system* . . . quoted Robert K. Massie, *Dreadnought*, New York 1991, p. 392

Three: **Scott's Navy**
The primary sources for Scott's naval career can be found in the Admiralty records at the Public Record Office. The most penetrating study of the late Victorian navy is provided in Andrew Gordon's brilliant *The Rules of the Game*, which alongside Mark Girouard's *The Return to Camelot* and Norman Dixon's *On the Psychology of Military Incompetence* gives the most vivid insight into the cultural and professional background of the service Scott joined.

24 *The Naval Salute* . . . *Manual of Seamanship*, London 1908 (revised and reprinted 1915), Vol 1, pp. 4–5
24 *I have* never *realized* . . . Edward Wilson, *Diary of the Discovery Expedition to the Antarctic Regions in 1901–1904*, ed. Ann Savours, New York 1967, pp. 171–3
25 *An Englishman enters* . . . quoted Andrew Gordon, *The Rules of the Game*, London 1996, p. 156
26 *A gentleman may be forgiven* . . . Richard Hough, *Admirals in Collision*, London 1959, p. 28
28 *cowardice or disaffection* . . . quoted Tom Pocock, *Battle for Empire*, London 1998, p. 35
29 *A good deal has been* . . . Hough, *Admirals in Collision*, p. 157
30 *9.am Read articles* . . . PRO ADM 53 12193–5
31 *Mr. Kirkby* . . . Idem
31 *Sublt the Honble* . . . Idem
31 *British barque Guyana* . . . Idem
31 *All yesterday* . . . Lady Wester Wemyss, *The Life and Letters of Lord Wester Wemyss*, London 1935, p. 123
32 *As to horsemanship* . . . quoted Seaver, p. 16
33 *To Campbeltown* . . . PRO ADM 53/15803
34 *My dearest old Gov* . . . SPRI 1160/7/3

35 *Alas! the skipper* . . . SPRI 1160/7/3, 24.01.1889
35 *Captain Hulton* . . . RGS RFS/9b, 05.07.1891
35 *After many* . . . quoted Huxley, p. 28
36 *It is only given* . . . Idem
37 *In the late winter* . . . SLE, pp. xvi–xvii
37 *But what happened* . . . Huntford, p. 114
38 *invalided home* . . . PRO ADM 1 6981
38 *Discharged* . . . *to SS Serena* . . . PRO ADM 53/14315
40 *ever fresh memories* . . . RGS RFS/9c, 03.08.1899
40 *Warrender & Scott called* . . . SPRI 1148/1
40 *How lovely it must be* . . . RGS RFS/9b, 05.07.1891
41 *as regards physical* . . . RGS RFS/9a, 02.12.1890
41 *bound to confess* . . . Idem
41 *hit on a capital method* . . . Idem
42 *At Honolulu* . . . Idem
42 *I was very despondent* . . . Idem
43 *great stay-at-home* Idem

Four: **Crisis**
The primary sources for this chapter are the logs of the ships in which Scott served, which can be found in Admiralty records at the PRO, and family letters.

44 *Lives there the man* . . . SPRI 352/7
44 *He felt that things* . . . quoted Seaver, p. 18
44 *looked forward to* . . . RGS RFS/9b, 05.07.1891
45 *trifle insipid* . . . Idem
45 *When Con* . . . quoted Seaver, p. 17
45 *The night has* . . . SPRI 352/7
46 *Do you remember* . . . Kennet Papers, D/5, KS Diary 1913
46 *Well-built, and alert* . . . *Daily Graphic*, 11.02.1913
46 *Lieutenant Scott is a young* . . . SPRI 352/7
47 *The work of the Torpedo School* . . . Andrew Gordon, *The Rules of the Game*, London 1996, p. 327
48 *severe injury to propeller* . . . PRO ADM 53 16285

48 *due care and attention* . . . PRO ADM 196/42

48 *cautioned to be more* . . . Idem

48 *considered good* . . . quoted Gwynn, p. 19

48 *are firstly that I* . . . Ibid., pp. 18–19

49 *The ship is still very* . . . SPRI 1160/5–9

50 *somewhat disastrous* . . . SPRI 1160/7/3

50 *On the 23rd October* . . . quoted Huxley, p. 32

51 *He never seems to have* . . . SLE, p. xv

52 *I hate to think* . . . SPRI 1160/5–9, 22.11.1896

53 *Dear Mother* . . . Idem

53 *My Own Dearest Mother* . . . quoted Gwynn, p. 22

53 *mixed entertainment* . . . Somerset & Wilts Journal, 22.12.1896, 09.01.1897

53 *I am longing to see* . . . Pound, p. 25

54 *My dearest girl* . . . SPRI 1542/5/10

54 *Isn't Arch just splendid* . . . quoted Gwynn, pp. 22–3

54 *My dearest Girl* . . . quoted Pound, pp. 25–6

54 *My Own Dearest Mother* . . . quoted Gwynn, pp. 23–4

55 *It seems to me* . . . SPRI 1542/5/10, Autumn 1898

56 *whether the game* . . . RGS RFS/9c, 03.08.1899

56 *the ranks of the advancers* . . . quoted Gwynn, p. 27

56 *if this can be worked . . . forget me* SPRI 1160/5–9

56 *I want you to tell father* . . . Idem

56 *I fear it will disappoint him* . . . Idem

57 *but at any rate* . . . quoted Gwynn, p. 27

57 *Everything went well* . . . Ibid. pp. 28–9

58 *Egerton joined today* . . . SPRI 1160/5–9, 28.06.1899

58 *green . . . pretty much* SPRI 1542/5/4

58 *The new Captain* . . . SPRI 1542/5/5, 15.10.99

58 *The naval officer* . . . SPRI MS 1160/3

58 *In 1899* . . . Seaver, p. 31

59 *We leave here* . . . quoted Gwynn, p. 29

59 *What he wanted* . . . quoted Seaver, p. 31

59 *bring me to greater* . . . quoted Gwynn, p. 29

Five: **Enter Markham**

The story of Scott's appointment to the command of the *Discovery* expedition can best be traced in the vast archives of Sir Clements Markham held by the Royal Geographical Society and in Admiralty records. An entertaining and heavily biased version of events is contained in Markham's later account published as *Antarctic Obsession*.

60 *It is almost a reproach* . . . quoted The Forum, Feb 1898

61 *a fat old doctor* . . . Admiral Markham, *Life of Sir Clements Markham KCB FRS*, London 1917, p. 18

61 *volatile, emotional, strong willed* . . . Ibid., p. 82

63 *To what purpose* . . . quoted Fergus Fleming, *Barrow's Boys*, London 1988, p. 1

63 *knight sans peur* . . . quoted Mark Girouard, *The Return to Camelot*, New Haven 1981, p. 8

63 *No one on board* . . . quoted Fergus Fleming, *Ninety Degrees North*, London 2002, p. 163

64 *the hardest day's work* . . . Ibid., p. 167

64 *it rests for German* . . . Ibid., p. 95

64 *Hardly one of them* . . . Ibid., p. 177

65 *In laying down their* . . . quoted Fleming, *Barrow's Boys*, p. 424

65 *In recent times* . . . Clements Markham, Address to the Seventh International Congress, 1899

65 *at once the cleanest* . . . Cherry-Garrard, p. vii

66 *Although it is not* . . . RGS AA/3/2/4

67 *The greatest part* . . . quoted Richard Hough, *Captain James Cook*, London 1994, p. 306

68 *burst forth to the south* . . . TVOTD, p. 34

68 *After all the experiences* . . . Idem

69 *in many respects* . . . Bernacchi, p. 34

69 *All honour* . . . quoted Yelverton, p. xxxii

72 *Referring to the communications* . . . PRO ADM 116/591

73 *On grounds of polity* . . . quoted Yelverton, p. 12

74 *the rag, tag and bobtail* . . . RGS CB2 Markham, undated

74 *We initiate the whole* . . . RGS CB2 Markham, 24.07.1899

74 *Murray talking rubbish* . . . RGS CB2 Markham, 29.09.1899

74 *Murray very troublesome* . . . RGS CRM/1/7, 04.11.1899

74 *I think Murray is trying to wreck* . . . RGS CB2 Markham, undated, 1900

74 *He is an ill conditioned* . . . RGS CRM/1/7, 03.11.1899

74 *Murray's conduct looks* . . . RGS CRM/1/7, 27.10.1899

74 *Greely pompous and* . . . RGS CB2 Markham, undated, 1899

74 *Professors know nothing* . . . SPRI BNAE, Vol 5, piece 29, 24.07.1899

74 *The important questions* . . . RGS CB2 Markham, 31.07.1899

75 *really severe work* . . . RGS AA/3/2/1–7

75 *He should be a* . . . *is to be found* Idem

76 *the best man* . . . Idem

76 *(Sun) to church* . . . RGS CRM/1/6, 11.06.1899

76 *On June 5th* . . . *Antarctic Obsession*, p. 13

76 *In the forenoon* . . . *God bless them!* RGS CRM/1/6, 01.03.1887–10.05.1887

77 *My bright young friend* . . . RGS CRM/1/7, 20.07.1887–24.07.1887

77 *great ability* . . . RGS AA/3/2/1

77 *entire satisfaction* . . . RGS AA/3/3/32

78 *You have nothing* . . . SPRI BNAE, Vol 5, B to S, 04.07.1899

78 *I am at a loss* . . . RGS AA/3/3/33

78 *You certainly could not* . . . RGS AA/2/3/34

78 *predilection* . . . TVOTD, Vol I, p. 42

78 *I told Captain Egerton* . . . SPRI BNAE, Vol 5, piece 25, 23.06.1899

79 *to do nothing* . . . SPRI BNAE, Vol 5, piece 26

79 *I see no possible* . . . SPRI BNAE, Vol 5, piece 27

79 *You have your hands* . . . SPRI BNAE, Vol 5, piece 28

79 *I am glad you saw* . . . SPRI BNAE, Vol 5, piece 29

79 *The hydrographers* . . . RGS CB2, Markham, 31.07.1899

80 *I have written to* . . . PRO ADM 1/7463B

80 *I read my letter* . . . RGS CRM/1/14, 18.04.1900

81 *thorough grounding* . . . *mining survey* RGS AA/3/3/38

81 *That officer's* . . . RGS AA/3/3/40

82 *There were six* . . . *Antarctic Obsession*, Appendix A

82 *always courteous* . . . Idem

82 *We take the opportunity* . . . RGS AA/3/3/42

82 *My Lord and Sir* . . . RGS AA/3/3/43

Six: **Preparations**

In addition to the Markham papers in the RGS, there is an interesting collection of letters in the Scott Polar Research Institute relating to the "Gregory Question" that underlines just what was lost when the *Discovery* expedition sacrificed its one scientist of proven distinction.

83 *Oh Lord!* . . . SPRI 367/23/9, 26.02.1901

84 *I am delighted* . . . SPRI BNAE, Vol 5, piece 46

84 *I must have complete* . . . *Antarctic Obsession*, p. 14

85 *nervously pulling his moustache* . . . Ibid., Appendix

85 *I was influenced* . . . RGS AA/4/1/21

85 *medical man of endurance* . . . *its best men* RGS AA/4/1/3

86 *It is quite clear* . . . SPRI BNAE, Vol 5, piece 46

87 *So many things* . . . *put things in order* SPRI 352/2BJ

89 *The German expedition* . . . TVOTD, p. 44

89 *The horror of slackness* . . . SLE, p. xiv

90 *I may as well say* . . . SPRI 1329, 21.01.1901

90 *Before perusing your* . . . RGS RFS/4a, undated 1901

90 *A preposterous draft* . . . RGS CRM/1/14, 22.01.1901

90 *quite inadmissible* . . . *Antarctic Obsession*, pp. 134–5

91 *Dear Gregory* . . . RGS AA/4/1/10

91 *misconception* RGS AA/4/1/12

91 *that he should be* . . . RGS AA/4/1/11

91 *How far* . . . Armitage, p. 134

92 *It was a rotten* . . . Ibid., p. 139

92 *If a murderer* . . . Ibid., p. 138

92 *My Dear Armitage* . . . Ibid., p. 140

92 *I called and found* . . . Idem

92 *Scott came in the* . . . RGS CRM/1/14, 07.05.1901

92 *Gregory question* . . . *incompetence Antarctic Obsession*, Appendix C

93 *It will be understood* . . . *Antarctic Obsession*, p. 147

93 *I admire immensely* . . . RGS AA/4/2

93 *I went to see Scott* . . . Armitage, p. 120

94 *To Savile Row* . . . *Scott there* RGS CRM/1/14, 17.11.1900

95 *I am of course* . . . RGS AA/6/2/15

95 *a charming young fellow* . . . *Antarctic Obsession*, p. 15

95 *Colin Archer* . . . quoted Ann Savours, *The Voyages of the Discovery*, Rochester 2001, p. 11

96 *Achilles' heel* . . . *less than three feet* TVOTD, pp. 58–9

96 *1¼ days* . . . SPRI 367/23/9

97 *After waiting a short* . . . RGS CRM1/14, 21.03.1901

98 *1 senior carpenter's mate* . . . PRO ADM 1/7463B

98 *Went over Discovery* . . . RGS CRM/1/14, 30.05.1901

98 *fine weather with* . . . Ibid., 04.06.1901

99 *I think* . . . quoted Seaver, *Wilson*, p. 75

100 *you had scarcely* . . . SPRI 774/1/1, 04.08.1901

100 *The relatives were frequently* . . . *Antarctic Obsession*, p. 32

100 *The bishop came* . . . Ibid., p. 34

100 *The Bishop's address* . . . RGS CRM/1/14, 15.07.1901

101 *The venerable white* . . . Armitage, pp. 150–1

102 *At 1 sharp* . . . SPRI 352/1/1, 31.07.1901

102 *all the steamers* . . . SPRI 689/12, 31.07.1901

102 *As His Majesty* . . . (MVO) RGS CRM/1/15, 05.08.01

103 *Very young* . . . SPRI 595/1, 06.08.1901

103 *We have had* . . . SPRI 989/1, 05.08.1901

103 *in spite of being* . . . SPRI 342/1/1, 06.08.1901

103 *My Dear little Phoebe* . . . SPRI 1542/6/1, 05.08.1901

103 *It was entirely due* . . . SPRI 1542/6/4, 28.08.1901

103 *People here like* . . . SPRI 1542/7/1, 12.08.1901

103 *I am not going to* . . . SPRI 1542/7/1, 09.08.1901

103 *It was so lovely* . . . SPRI 1542/7/2, 15.08.1901

104 *sad to see* . . . SPRI 352/1/1, 06.08.1901

104 *a sad time indeed* . . . Idem

104 *How willingly* . . . TVOTD, p. 90

104 *but gradually* . . . Idem

Seven: South

The main primary sources for this chapter are Scott's diaries and official reports, and the letters and diaries of the members of the expedition. Where no reference is given, the quotations come from Scott's *The Voyage of the Discovery*, Volume I, Chapter 3, a later account of the expedition largely based on his journals.

105 *This is an awful ship* . . . Royds, 22.08.1901

105 *The same routine* . . . SPRI 774/1/1, 09.08.1901

105 *INSTRUCTIONS TO THE COMMANDER* . . . quoted Yelverton, pp. 353–6

106 *terribly small* . . . quoted Ibid., p. 74

106 *The ship is a magnificent* . . . SPRI 1452/6/2, 16.08.1901

106 *It is quite impossible* . . . SPRI 1542/7/3, 28.08.1901

107 *the skipper at last* . . . Royds, 23.08.1901

107 *ship building firm* . . . SPRI 342/1/1, 06.08.1901

107 *Those responsible for* . . . SPRI 774/1/1, 23.08.1901

107 *in the cutter* . . . RGS AA/12/1/2

108 *I cannot sufficiently* . . . SPRI 366/11, BNAE, Vol 1, p. 33

108 *It's a blessed* . . . quoted Seaver, *Wilson*, p. 79

108 *He is a most capable* . . . Ibid., p. 84

108 *pleasanter company* . . . *Antarctic Obsession*, p. 111

108 *Captain Scott has* . . . SPRI, 1542/7/1–12, 30.08.1901

109 *I expected to be* . . . 1st Lieut. Royds, 16.08.1901, 18.07.1902

109 *Charles Rawson Royds* . . . SPRI 1456/66, 1955

109 *emblazon* . . . RUSH Jan Morris, *Fisher's Face*, London 1995, p. 136

109 *"Knock off everything"* . . . Royds, 16.08.1901

110 *A better pace* . . . SPRI 352/1/1, 23.09.1901

110 *These delays are* . . . Ibid., 21.09.1901

110 *usual amount of church* . . . SPRI 774/1/1, 25.08.1901

111 *with the doctor* . . . SPRI 575/2, 31.08.1901

112 *The party was rather* . . . SPRI 352/1/1, 31.08.1901

112 *Some of the naval* . . . SPRI 1227/1, 05.11.1901

113 *old Shackles very* . . . Wilson, 08.09.1901

113 *Moderate wind* . . . SPRI 575/2, 29.09.1901

113 *weird, blighted island* . . . quoted Seaver, *Wilson*, p. 80

113 *There is not a single* . . . quoted Idem

114 *had crossed the line* . . . SPRI 352/1/1, 12.09.1901

114 *These twists of fortune* . . . SPRI 352/1/1, 24.09.1901

114 *Best of the sport* . . . SPRI 774/1/1, 25.09.1901

114 *Morning service as usual* . . . Wilson, 10.11.1901

114 *It is always woe* . . . SPRI 1542/6/5, 29.09.1901

115 *Coaling is filthy* . . . Royds, 04.10.1901

115 *inundated with sightseers* . . . SPRI 342/1/1, 03.10.1901

115 *I had great trouble* . . . Idem

115 *From tonight my* . . . Royds, 04.10.1901

116 *the coins were not* . . . Francis Spufford, *I May Be Some Time*, London 1996, p. 250

116 *Now that I know* . . . quoted Seaver, *Wilson*, pp. 68–9

116 *Took up my quarters* . . . SPRI 352/1/1, 05.10.1901

117 *As usual didn't know* . . . SPRI 352/1/1, 09.10.1901

117 *Heard an amusing* . . . Royds, 11.10.1901

117 *As we got under* . . . SPRI 352/1/1, 14.10.1901

117 *working very well* . . . SPRI 352/1/1, 23.10.1901

117 *worse all this gets* . . . Wilson, 22.10.1901

118 *The waves we are* . . . Wilson, 27.10.1901

118 *an enormous wave* . . . Wilson, 28.10.1901

118 *checks were in* . . . SPRI 774/1/1

118 *indeed* . . . *living* Wilson, 22.10.1901

118 *Fast ice seen* . . . RGS AA/12/1/13

118 *A most marvellous* . . . SPRI 342/1/1, 16.11.1901

118 *The sky was grey* . . . Wilson, 15.11.1901

119 *At 4 a.m.* . . . . RGS AA/12/1/13

119 *We saw great flocks* . . . SPRI 1415, 22.11.1901

119 *no prejudice more* . . . RGS AA/12/1/13

119 *which it will so often* . . . Idem

119 *Had penguin for* . . . SPRI 352/1/1, 24.11.1901

120 *has been of excellent* . . . RGS AA/12/1/13

120 *He is indeed* . . . SPRI 352/1/1, 22.11.1901

120 *There is one thing* . . . quoted Seaver, *Wilson*, p. 85

120 *I like Captain Scott* . . . RGS AA/12/1/7

120 *One of the best* . . . quoted Seaver, *Wilson*, p. 84

Eight: **Into the Ice**

Primary sources for this chapter are again expedition diaries and letters, Scott's official Letters of Proceedings to the Presidents of the RS and RGS. Where no reference is given, the quotations come from Scott's *The Voyage of the Discovery*, Volume I, Chapters 3, 4, 5 and 6.

121 *New Year's morning* . . . SPRI 1415, 01.01.1902

121 *Mayor Rhodes* . . . SPRI 352/1/1, 01.12.1901
121 *It is awful* . . . Royds, 03.12.1901
121 *We have dismissed* . . . SPRI 342/1/1, 02.12.1901
122 *men very fat-headed* . . . SPRI 352/1/1, 03.12.1901
122 *big AB* . . . *strapping AB* Idem
122 *How we get along* . . . SPRI 1542/6/2, 18.12.1901
122 *We had a visit* . . . SPRI 1415, Dec 1901
123 *I for one* . . . SPRI 774/1/1, Dec 1901
123 *in a manner* . . . SPRI 352/1/1, 03.12.1901
123 *an excellent chap* . . . SPRI 1542/6/2, 18.12.1901
123 *For my own part* . . . SPRI 352/1/1, 03.12.1901
123 *thud of a fall* . . . Idem
123 *He appears to have* . . . Idem
124 *Very dull day* . . . SPRI 774/1/1, 22.12.1901
124 *We gave full naval* . . . SPRI 1542/10/15, 29.07.1907
124 *The cheers of the* . . . SPRI 774/1/1, 24.12.1901
124 *much depressed* . . . *all concerned* SPRI 352/1/1, 03.12.1901
125 *line of retreat* . . . quoted Pound, p. 52
125 *continued to distinguish* . . . SPRI 1160/5/9, 18.12.1901
125 *My dear girl* . . . SPRI 1542/6/6, 17.12.1901
125 *At home they are* . . . SPRI 575/2, 25.12.1901
125 *Rather erotic* . . . SPRI 575/2, 26.12.1901
125 *Paolo and Francesca* . . . SPRI 575/2, 27.12.1901
125 *Had to make an example* . . . SPRI 353/1/1, 30.12.1901
125 *I myself call mine* . . . SPRI 774/1/1, 27.12.1901
126 *which is the custom* . . . SPRI 575/2, 31.12.1901
126 *Midnight* . . . SPRI 342/1/1, 31.12.1901
126 *What indeed may* . . . SPRI 352/1/1, 31.12.1901
127 *My seal started* . . . SPRI 342/1/1, 05.01.1902
127 *he hates the sight* . . . Wilson, 07.01.1902

127 *are now eating seal flesh* . . . SPRI 352/1/1, 07.01.1902
127 *Our pleasure in* . . . SPRI 352/1/1, 08.01.1902
128 *rather ridiculous* . . . SPRI 342/1/1, 09.01.1902
129 *The Captain is strangely* . . . Wilson, 05.01.1902
129 *The only objection* . . . SPRI 989/11
130 *Hodgson was awfully* . . . SPRI 342/1/2, 13.01.1902
130 *Hodgson is glorified* SPRI 352/1/1, 13.01.1902
130 *"Moss! Moss!!"* . . . SPRI 575/2, 20.01.1902
132 *moral certainty* SPRI 352/1/1, 30.01.1902
132 *Two little points* . . . SPRI 575/2, 30.01.1902
132 *New Land* . . . SPRI 774/1/1, 30.01.1902
133 *Its local name* . . . SPRI 1415, 30.01.1902
133 *It is intensely* . . . SPRI 352/1/1, 30.01.1902
133 *There was a panic* . . . Royds, 01.02.1902
133 *A strange thing* . . . Wilson, 01.02.1902
133 *The courses were logged* . . . SPRI 352/1/2, 01.02.1902
134 *The Captain said* . . . SPRI 575/2, 04.02.1902
135 *If nobody is killed* . . . Wilson, 04.02.1902
135 *The good spirits* . . . SPRI 575/2, 04.02.1902

Nine: **Harsh Lessons**
Where no reference is given, the quotations come from Scott's *The Voyage of the Discovery*, Volume I, Chapters 6, 7 and 10.

137 *All experience must* . . . RGS AA/3/3/40
137 *The whole place* . . . SPRI 575/2, 08.02.1902
138 *There was* . . . Bernacchi, p. 45
139 *Routine while the light* . . . SPRI 774/1/1, 09.02.1902
140 *The cook Mr. Brett* . . . SPRI 1415, 10.02.1902
140 *Had trouble* . . . SPRI 352/1/2, 10.02.1902
140 *There was one* . . . Bernacchi, pp. 48–9

141 *Eyes were turning* . . . SPRI 352/1/2,
13.02.1902

144 *At 11:30 the wind* . . . Wilson,
19.02.1902

145 *As far as the eye* . . . quoted Seaver,
Wilson, pp. 92–3

146 *very tired, but* . . . Royds, 22.02.1902

146 *the effects of sunset* . . . SPRI 352/1/2,
15.02.1902

147 *like a bear* . . . SPRI 595/1, 03.03.1902

149 *All five of us* . . . SPRI 753, 15.03.1902

150 *He must have been* . . . SPRI 352/1/2,
13.02.1902

151 *There can be no* . . . SPRI 352/1/2,
11.03.1902

151 *He was tall* . . . Christchurch, L.
Quartermain (LQ) MS 303/folder10/482,
26.02.1961

151 *Now that one can* . . . SPRI 352/1/2,
12.03.1902

152 *Honeycombed with crevasses* . . . Royds,
07.03.1902

152 *Yesterday the skipper* . . . SPRI 342/1/4,
12.10.1902

153 *All Fools Day* . . . SPRI 1415, 01.04.1902

153 *I have never realized* . . . Wilson,
18.08.1902

154 *was rather an enigma* . . . SPRI 1456/66,
10.10.1956

Ten: **Antarctic Night**

Where no reference is given, the quotations
come from Scott's *The Voyage of the
Discovery,* Volume I, Chapters 8, 9 and 10.

158 *I have often* . . . Christchurch, LQ MS
303/2/folder 37/74a, 16.03.1960

158 *I turned in* . . . SPRI 575/2, 14.07.1902

159 *The windmill is* . . . SPRI 352/1/2,
01.03.1902

160 *The traditions of* . . . Bernacchi, p. 46

160 *simply an exhibition* . . . SPRI 342/1/4,
17.06.1902

161 *This is Victoria Day* . . . SPRI 572/2,
24.05.1902

161 *I have been reading* . . . Royds,
24.06.1902

162 *a really awfully pretty* . . . Royds,
25.06.1902

162 *Taking one thing* . . . SPRI 352/1/2,
23.05.1902

162 *still as the grave* . . . SPRI 1415,
20.06.1902

162 *The idea that we* . . . SPRI 575/2,
22.06.1902

162 *Say what you like* . . . Royds,
14.06.1902

163 *If one couldn't work* . . . Wilson,
13.08.1902

163 *Scott came into* . . . Royds,
08.08.1902

163 *The Captain spoke up* . . . Royds,
18.07.1902

163 *like all human beings* . . .
Christchurch, LQ MS 303/Part H/folder
37/74a, 14.03.1960

164 *My first job* . . . SPRI 761/7, 1965

165 *I had a long yarn* . . . SPRI 342/1/4,
06.07.1902

165 *The Capt called me* . . . Wilson,
12.06.1902

166 *I was called into* . . . SPRI 575/2,
13.06.1902

166 *This is to be a big* . . . SPRI 1415,
22.08.1902

167 *Old Jamaica* . . . SPRI 774/1/1,
23.08.1902

Eleven: **Man Proposeth . . . God Disposeth**

Where no reference is given, the quotations
come from Scott's *The Voyage of the
Discovery,* Volume I, Chapter 12.

168 *Nothing could be* . . . SPRI 352/1/3,
30.09.1902

169 *& determined to start* . . . SPRI 595/1,
02.09.1902

169 *Against our sledging* . . . SPRI 352/1/3,
19.09.1902

170 *party much done up* . . . Idem

171 *Shackleton and Barne* . . . SPRI 342/1/4,
17.09.1902

171 *gallant, uncompromising* . . . Andrew
Gordon, *The Rules of the Game,* London
1996, p. 380

174 *L'homme propose* . . . Wilson,
15.10.1902

Twelve: **The Southern Journey**

As before, in Chapters 12 and 13 where no reference is given, the quotations come from Scott's *The Voyage of the Discovery*, Volume II, Chapters 13 and 14; but the crucial and controversial sources for this Southern Journey are the sledging diaries of the three men concerned, which reveal occasional discrepancies with Scott's later published account. D. Harvie's *Limeys* provides an interesting account of the cultural and historical background to scurvy.

175 *A dread disease* . . . Luis de Camoëns, *The Lusiad, or The Discovery of India*, translated by William Mickle, Oxford 1776, Bk V, p. 224

177 *the great Cambridge* . . . SPRI 595/1, 26.09.1902

177 *Our conclusion was* . . . SPRI 366/12, 01.10.1902

177 *Prior to September* . . . RGS AA/12/4/13

178 *I felt that we . . . interloper* Armitage, pp. 130–2

179 *Ice navigation* . . . Albert B. Armitage, *Two Years in the Antarctic*, Bungay 1984, pp. 45–6

179 *What a wonderful* . . . Armitage, pp. 121–2

179 *Armitage made rather* . . . SPRI 342/1/4, 10.06.1902

179 *The Pilot has been* . . . SPRI 342/1/2, 03.02.1902; 342/1/3, 31.03.1902

180 *I had the cook* . . . SPRI 366/12, 01.10.1902

180 *Render the daily lives* . . . Idem

180 *Service conducted by* . . . SPRI 595/1, 28.09.1902

180 *During Armitage's regime* . . . SPRI 595/1, 04.10.1902

180 *Shackleton has fairly* . . . SPRI 595/1, 05.10.1902

180 *We have got a new* . . . SPRI 774/1/1, 06.10.1902

181 *where we shall see* . . . quoted Seaver, Wilson, p. 107

181 *anyhow* . . . Wilson, 25.10.1902

181 *His party have only* . . . SPRI 342/1/4, 16.09.1902

182 *a good record* . . . SPRI 342/1/4, 02.11.1902

182 *No dogs need . . . shan't be long* Wilson, 30.10.1902

182 *Dogs in splendid* . . . SPRI 1464/4, 02.11.1902

182 *Very comfortable* . . . SPRI 1464/4, 03.11.1902

183 *a persistent and* . . . Wilson, 06.11.1902

183 *I feel more equal* . . . quoted Seaver, Wilson, p. 102

183 *The dogs, I find* . . . Armitage, *Two Years in the Antarctic*, p. 153

183 *Barne leaves us* . . . Ibid., p. 156

184 *so utterly unlike* . . . SPRI 1464/4, 12.11.1902

187 *dash for the South* . . . SPRI 1464/4, 19.12.1902

187 *a conspicuous . . . bearings* SPRI 1464/4, 15.12.1902

188 *Wilson spent 3 hours* . . . SPRI 1464/4, 18.12.1902

188 *Wilson's eye giving* . . . SPRI 1464/4, 26.12.1902

188 *We are really . . . the time being* SPRI 1464/4, 23.12.1902

188 *The talk constantly* . . . Wilson, 05.12.1902

189 *very rarely . . . he examined me* quoted Seaver, Wilson, pp. 110–11

189 *Wilson is the most* . . . Ibid., p. 111

190 *We are looking to* . . . SPRI 1464/4, 24.12.1902

191 *A red letter day* . . . SPRI 1464/4, 25.12.1902

191 *Christmas wash & brush up . . . supper* Idem

191 *I have never . . . delightful* quoted Seaver, Wilson, p. 112

192 *Shackleton is butcher* . . . SPRI 1464/4, 26.12.1902

192 *burnt black &* . . . SPRI 1464/4, 27.12.1902

193 *Marched again the whole* . . . quoted Seaver, Wilson, p. 112

194 *To be idle &* . . . SPRI 1464/4, 29.12.1902

Thirteen: **Survival**

195 *A fool always* . . . Wilson,
11.12.190

195 *pushed mankind's knowledge* . . .
Yelverton, p. 198

196 *Taken altogether* . . . SPRI 1464/4/,
05.01.1903

196 *the spirit of the* . . . A. Cherry-Garrard,
postscript to *The Worst Journey in the
World*, privately printed 1951

197 *What pulled Scott* . . . Cherry-Garrard,
p. 206

197 *Behold, how good* . . . SPRI 352/ 1/4

198 *I am more thankful* . . . quoted Seaver,
Wilson, p. 103

198 *How far was his* . . . Ibid., p. xiv

200 *"Our little systems* . . . SPRI 575/2,
10.06.1902

200 *I do not seem* . . . SPRI 1456/78

200 *practically identical* . . . E.M. Forster,
A Passage to India, London 1924, p. 83

200 *HOMEWARD* . . . SPRI 1464/4,
31.12.1902

201 *It is ludicrous* . . . SPRI 1464/4,
02.01.1903

201 *Le Bon temps* . . . Wilson, 04.01.1903

201 *To add to our* . . . SPRI 1464/4,
08.01.1903

203 *Truly there appears* . . . SPRI 1464/4,
14.01.1903

203 *During a halt* . . . SPRI 575/2,
14.01.1903

204 *Both I and* . . . SPRI 1464/4, 16.01.1903

204 *easy to see he is* . . . SPRI 1464/4,
17.01.1903

205 *Shackleton gave in* . . . SPRI 1464/4,
18.01.1903

205 *Shackleton is improving* . . . SPRI
1464/4, 21.01.1903

205 *The Captain and I* . . . Wilson,
23.01.1903

206 *I am feeling worse* . . . SPRI 575/2,
28.01.1903

207 *no dogs with them* . . . SPRI 342/1/6,
03.02.1903

207 *Amidst cheer upon* . . . SPRI 774/1/1,
03.02.1903

207 *A lovely day* . . . Royds, 03.02.1903

207 *champagne unlimited* . . . SPRI 774/1/1,
03.02.1903

207 *I say Shackles* . . . G.S. Doorly, *The
Voyage of the Morning*, London 1916,
p. 110

Fourteen: **A Second Winter**

The arrival of *Morning* opened a fresh
window on *Discovery* life, but the principal
sources are still the expedition diaries and
letters home. Where no reference is given,
the quotations come from Scott's *The
Voyage of the Discovery*, Volume II,
Chapters 15 and 16.

208 *Shackleton & nine* . . . SPRI 595/1,
31.03.1903

209 *Early in 1903* . . . quoted Yelverton,
p. 357

209 *You will then be* . . . quoted Ibid.,
p. 246

210 *On the way up* . . . SPRI 1476,
17.08.1944

211 *What would Capt. Scott* . . . SPRI
774/1/1, 03.11.1902

211 *endless privileges* . . . SPRI 342/1/4,
15.11.1902

211 *Sing song in Ward* . . . SPRI 774/1/1,
22.11.1902

212 *I was quite ready* . . . SPRI 342/1/4,
24.01.1903

212 *like fighting cocks* . . . SPRI 595/1,
26.01.1903

212 *beside himself* . . . Royds, 25.01. 1903

212 *men have been* . . . SPRI 595/1,
26.01.1903

212 *very great discontent* . . . SPRI 342/1/6,
26.01.1903

213 *A good boy* . . . SPRI 352/1/3, 07.03.1903

213 *A thorough hypochondriac* . . . *dirty
little rascal* Idem

214 *a hell of a woman* SPRI 1476D

214 *My dear, please* . . . SPRI 1 542/8/1,
29.02.1903

214 *After church went* . . . Royds,
05.07.1903

215 *Referring to your* . . . SPRI 366/14/24–25

215 *It is certainly wiser* . . . Wilson,
23.02.1903

215 *During the winter* . . . quoted Huxley,
p. 134

216 *He was in great* . . . Idem

216 *This gentleman has* . . . RGS
AA/12/4/2

217 *All the "crocks"* . . . SPRI 1452/8/1,
29.02.1903

217 *no more than the* . . . SPRI 1456/78

217 *cargo shifter* . . . SPRI 1456/66

217 *a grand ship-mate* . . . SPRI 1456/64,
16.10.1955

217 *the last person on earth* . . . SPRI
1456/66

218 *Royds has improved* . . . SPRI 1452/8/1,
29.02.1903

218 *entre nous . . . acquisition* Idem

218 *just first class* . . . Royds, 02.03.1903

218 *bad characters* . . . SPRI 342/1/6,
02.03.1903

219 *We are all very* . . . Christchurch,
Rhodes MS 50, Item 3

219 *A wave of depression* . . . SPRI 595/1,
02.03.1903

220 *beautifully clean* . . . SPRI 342/1/6,
08.03.1903

220 *Shackleton & nine others* . . . SPRI
595/1, 31.01.1903

220 *promiscuous kicking* . . . Royds,
03.04.1903

220 *glorious black eye* SPRI 595/1,
22.04.1903

220 *The Captain's night* . . . Royds,
17.03.1903

221 *polar winter could scarcely* . . . SPRI
352/1/3, 24.06.1903

221 *Captain . . . quite as much* SPRI 595/1,
27.06.1903

221 *The carpenter asked me* . . . Wilson,
26.03.1903

221 *Altogether the work* . . . Ibid.,
25.05.1903

222 *full of stuff* . . . Ibid., 11.06.1903

222 *Time passes fairly* . . . SPRI 342/1/6,
09.08.1903

222 *I had another dose* . . . SPRI 595/1,
29.02.1903

222 *Apparently he has asked* . . . Royds,
30.05.1903

223 *should have any grievance* . . . SPRI
342/1/6, 28.07.1903

223 *the thing that has* . . . SPRI 774/1/1,
01.07.1903

223 *Turtle soup* . . . SPRI 352/1/3, 25.08.1903

223 *Things rather more* . . . SPRI 774/1/1,
23.08.1903

223 *feel absolute confidence* . . . SPRI
352/1/3, 22.09.1903

223 *this year's trip* . . . SPRI 352/1/3,
22.07.1903

Fifteen: **Last Season**
In addition to the usual sources, Armitage's
journal, which has recently surfaced,
throws interesting light on the growing
estrangement between Scott and his
second-in-command. Where no reference
is given, the quotations come from Scott's
The Voyage of the Discovery, Volume II,
Chapters 17 and 18.

226 *Nothing is more delightful* . . . SPRI
352/1/3, 22.09.1903

227 *a pawnbrokers shop* . . . SPRI 595/1,
30.09.1903

229 *we shall never know* . . . SPRI 342/2/6,
01.11.1903

230 *The skipper gets very* . . . SPRI 342/2/6,
04.11.1903

233 *which he readily* . . . SPRI 342/2/6,
17.11.1903

234 *I said I hoped* . . . SPRI 342/2/6,
22.11.1903

234 *I suppose you would* . . . SPRI 761/16/4,
09.04.1964

234 *a fine clean living* . . . Christchurch,
LQ MS 303, folder 35/56

235 *Chest empty* . . . SPRI 1415,
04.06.1902

Sixteen: **A Long Wait**
Where no reference is given, the quotations
come from Scott's *The Voyage of the
Discovery*, Volume II, Chapter 19.

242 *I am afraid that* . . . SPRI 1542/7,
08.07.1903

243 *the first physically* . . . Yelverton, p. 281

244 *absolutely futile* . . . Royds, 19.12.1903

244 *was the most fearful* . . . SPRI 342/1/7,
13.02.1904

245 *To me it seems* . . . Royds, 21–28.12.1903
245 *Glorious day* . . . SPRI 595/1, 31.12.1903
245 *cut 174 yards* . . . SPRI 774/1/1, 27.12.1903
245 *The Captain asked me* . . . Wilson, 01.01.1904
246 *"Why there's another"* . . . SPRI 352/1/4, 05.01.1904
248 *That wretched obstacle* . . . *cur Balfour* RGS CB6, Markham, 01.08.1903; CB3, Markham, various, undated
248 *I have scarcely* . . . SPRI 352/1/4, 07.01.1904
249 *The King & Con* . . . *before the public* SPRI 1542/7/7, 01.06.1903
249 *I really think* . . . SPRI 1542/7/10, 13.08.1903
249 *seems very down* . . . SPRI 595/1, 08.01.1904
250 *Oh what joy* . . . *man does* SPRI 774/1/1, 01.01.1904; 10.01.1904
250 *Now for the incident* . . . Christchurch, LQ F303, piece 480, 24.11.1960
251 *Whitfield has been* . . . SPRI 352/1/4, 24.01.1904
251 *Whitfield returned* . . . SPRI 352/1/4, 25.01.1904
251 *Yesterday morning* . . . SPRI 352/1/4, 02.02.1904
251 *such as one would* . . . SPRI 352/1/4, 23.01.1904
251 *Things look very bad* . . . Christchurch, Rhodes MS 50, Item 2, 30.01.1904
252 *One scarcely dares* . . . SPRI 352/1/4, 31.01.1904
252 *Everything depends on* . . . *most depressing* SPRI 352/1/4, 03.02.1904
253 *Last night I thought* . . . SPRI 352/1/4, 11.02.1904
253 *I was standing by* . . . Christchurch, LQ MS 303/folder 10/480
253 *What a day* . . . SPRI 352/1/4, 12.02.1904
255 *gave a lurch & leap* . . . SPRI 774/1/1, 16.02.1904

Seventeen: **Escape from the Ice**
The row surrounding *Discovery*'s return can best be followed in the papers of Sir Clements Markham, and in Scott's letters

to his family. Where no reference is given, the quotations come from the final chapter of Scott's *The Voyage of the Discovery*.

259 *continually on the* . . . Royds, 21.02.1904
259 *never was there* . . . SPRI 352/1/4, 17.02.1904
259 *with a spontaneous* . . . Idem
259 *Officers & men* . . . SPRI 352/1/4, 18.02.1904
260 *but Terra Nova ought* . . . SPRI 1227/2, 09.03.1904
261 *Altogether things looked* . . . SPRI 352/1/4, 22.02.1904
261 *We have done* . . . SPRI 352/1/4, 05.03.1904
264 *that I will never* . . . Royds, 05.03.1904
264 *The worst sufferers* . . . SPRI 352/1/4, 29.02.1904
264 *green and russet* . . . *paradise* quoted Seaver, *Wilson*, p. 140
265 *calling on their* . . . SPRI 352/1/4, 28.03.1904
265 *nearly all people* . . . *inhabitants* SPRI 1542/8/4, 12.05.1904
265 *I never seem* . . . SPRI 1542/8/5, 02.06.1902
265 *Most of our people* . . . *keep him clear* SPRI 1542/8/4, 12.05.1904
265–6 *high time we were* . . . *very nice* SPRI 1542/8/5, 02.06.1904
266 *I fear there is* . . . SPRI 15542/8/2, 28.03.1904
266 *Commander Scott emphatically* . . . quoted Huxley, p. 168
266 *I have always been* . . . Ibid., p. 167
267 *and if they keep* . . . SPRI 1227/2, 09.03.1904
267 *a marked man* . . . *anxiety* SPRI 1542/7/12, 04.06.1904
267 *Scott said what was* . . . RGS CB3, Markham, undated
267 *simply magnificent* . . . *quite unsurpassed* RGS CB3, Markham, 02.04.1904
268 *woken up considerably* . . . quoted Huxley, p. 168
268 *It is a great* . . . SPRI 1542/8/5, 02.06.1904

268 *Anyone that had* . . . SPRI 774/1/1,
  04.08.1904
268 *A few yarns lately* . . . SPRI 342/1/7,
  13.06.1904
269 *I realise that* . . . SPRI 1542/8/7,
  18.07.1904
269 *One of the most* . . . SPRI 1342/4,
  22.12.1905
269 *And the deed* . . . SPRI 352/1/4,
  10.09.1904
270 *a luncheon in* . . . *echoing cheer* RGS
  CB3, Markham, 28.08.1904
270 *People do not understand* . . . RGS
  CB3, Markham, 30.08.1904
270 *From all accounts* . . . SPRI 1542/8/7,
  18.07.1904
270 *Scott's complaint* . . . RGS CB3,
  Markham, 15.07.1904
271 *I am much annoyed* . . . RGS CB6,
  Markham, 16.07.1904
271 *very charming letter* . . . RGS CB6,
  Markham, 16–17.07.1904
271 *I despair* . . . RGS CB6, Markham,
  17.07.1904
271 *About the present to* . . . SPRI 342/1/7,
  30.08.1904
271 *There was one slight* . . . Idem
272 *Without a doubt* . . . quoted Huxley,
  pp. 168–9

Eighteen: **The Reluctant Lion**
The major primary source for this period
of Scott's life is the correspondence with
his mother. There is also an interesting
insight into the wider world that opened
out for him in a collection of letters by
J.M. Barrie held in the Scott Polar
Research Institute.

273 *5 mortal hours* RGS CB3, Markham,
  11.09.1904
274–5 *entitle him to* . . . *National Antarctic
  Expedition 1901–4, Physical
  Observations*, London 1908, p. 40
275 *With regard to Captain* . . . *National
  Antarctic Expedition 1901–4*, London
  1907, Introduction
275 *contained his soul* . . . SPRI 1542/8/7,
  18.07.1904

275 *Will you tell Captain* . . . quoted
  Yelverton, p. 327
275 *Commander Scott and his* . . . quoted
  Huxley, p. 174
275–6 *Dear Lord Walter Kerr* . . . quoted
  Gwynn, pp. 65–6
277 *My Dear Captain Scott* . . . SPRI
  1453/171/1, 03.09.1904
277 *very jolly evening* RGS CRM/1/15,
  15.09.1904
277 *I feel that it is* . . . quoted Gwynn,
  pp. 66–7
278 *The Royal Society gives* . . .
  Christchurch, Bernacchi MS 276/2,
  04.11.1904
278 *I must tell you of* . . . SPRI 1542/8/8,
  01.09.1904
279 *Balfour's brazen impudence* . . . RGS
  CB3, Markham, 13.10.1904
279 *Well built and alert* . . . *Daily Graphic*,
  11.02.1913
279 *The Lecture came off* . . . SPRI
  1542/8/9, 12.11.1904
280 *Shackleton as you will* . . . SPRI
  1542/8/10, 17.11.1904
280 *because some stupid man* . . . Idem
280 *a miserable depressing town* . . . *social
  ambitions* SPRI 15432/8/10, 17.11.1904
280 *good form and doubtless* . . .
  Idem
281 *nice people* . . . *apology of a dinner*
  SPRI 1542/8/11, 20.11.1904
281 *I cannot conclude* . . . quoted Gwynn,
  p. 67
282 *My Dear Keltie* . . . RGS RFS/4a,
  24.01.1905
282 *I wrote to Scott* . . . RGS CB3,
  Markham, 23.08.04
282 *Of all things* . . . quoted Huxley,
  p. 177
283 *The question is* . . . SPRI 1542/8/6,
  30.06.1904
283 *Will you go ahead* . . . SRPI 1542/8/8,
  01.10.1904
283 *I don't like going* . . . SPRI 1542/8/12,
  06.04.1905
284 *I have been trying* . . . SPRI 1542/8/13,
  24.04.1905
284 *I am glad* . . . SPRI 1542/8/14,
  03.05.1905

284 *It is eight years* . . . quoted Seaver,
   Wilson, p. 178
286 *I had no idea* . . . quoted Pound, p. 122
287 *I worked very hard* . . . SPRI 1342/4
   RFS, 12.12.1905
287 *It is beautifully* . . . SPRI 1453/171/2
287 *The facts were* . . . M. and J. Fisher,
   Shackleton, London 1957, p. 60
287 *My Dear Sir Joseph* . . . quoted Pound,
   p. 120
288 *On the night when* . . . SLE,
   Introduction, p. ix
288 *If Barrie liked* . . . Cynthia Asquith,
   Portrait of Barrie, London 1954,
   pp. 101–2
288 *iron self-control* . . . SLE, Introduction,
   p. xviii

Nineteen: **The Pull of the South**
The primary source for the row between
Shackleton and Scott is the exchange of
letters between Scott, Shackleton and
Keltie, and the most interesting recent
discussion of it can be found in Beau
Riffenburgh's *Nimrod* (2004).

289 *Gold medals* . . . SPRI 1574/2/5,
   18.07.1904
290 *I return to* . . . RGS RFS/9g,
   05.07.1906
291 *all goes smoothly* . . . SPRI 1542/9/1,
   21.10.1906
291 *I am dreadfully sick* . . . SPRI 1547/2/9,
   21.03.1907
292 *Then to some old* . . . SPRI 1453/3/283,
   08.01.1909
293 *Before his arrival* . . . quoted Robert K.
   Massie, *Dreadnought*, New York 1991,
   p. 439
294 *that his whole soul* . . . Lady Wester
   Wemyss, *The Life and Letters of
   Lord Wester Wemyss*, London 1935,
   pp. 142–3
295 *I had none of those* . . . A.E.W.
   Mason, *The Turnstile*, London 1912,
   pp. 95–8
296 *She saw something* . . . Ibid.,
   p. 301
296 *"I had no suspicion* . . . Ibid., p. 339

297 *As regards my* . . . RGS RFS/4a,
   28.01.1907
298 *looking out the position* . . . *at night*
   SPRI 1452/10/2, 20.02.1907
298 *everyone condemned* . . . Ibid.
298 *except as an amusing* . . . SPRI
   1542/10/6, 25.03.1907
298 *I had quite a long* . . . SPRI 1542/10/2,
   20.02.1907
298 *I went to the C-in-C's* . . . SPRI
   1542/10/8, 06.04.1907
299 *He told me he had* . . . RGS RFS/4a,
   18.02.1907
299 *The situation is awkward* . . . SPRI
   1456/23, 18.02.1907
300 *I ought perhaps to* . . . SPRI 1456/23,
   undated
301 *I would rather* . . . SPRI 1456/23,
   05.03.1907
301 *as Britishers* . . . SPRI 1456/23,
   07.03.1907
301 *He has evidently been* . . . RGS RFS/4a,
   01.03.1907
301 *As to his chance* . . . RGS RFS/4a,
   undated
302 *I took the letter* . . . SPRI 1456/23,
   27.02.1907
302 *You do not say* . . . RGS RFS/4a,
   undated
302 *Your letter makes* . . . RGS RFS/4a,
   01.03.1907
302 *I am sorry to have* . . . SPRI 1456/23,
   07.03.1907
303 *I confess your silence* . . . RGS RFS/4a,
   11.03.1907
303 *The question now is* . . . SPRI 1456/23,
   26.03.1907
303 *I do not agree* . . . SPRI 1456/23,
   11.03.1907
304 *If you in consultation* . . . RGS RFS/4a,
   26.03.1907
304 *on either side* . . . Idem
304 *I am leaving the McMurdo* . . . RGS
   RFS/4a, 17.05.1907
304 *My Dear Shackleton* . . . SPRI 1456/23,
   17.05.1905
305 *On the whole it is* . . . RGS RFS/4a,
   undated
306 *But indeed you mistake* . . . RGS
   RFS/4a, 27.05.1907

Twenty: **Of Lions and Lionesses**

The main primary sources for Scott's
courtship are the collections of letters held
in the Scott Polar Reasearch Institute and
Cambridge University Library; the most
interesting published materials are
Kathleen's own autobiography, *Self Portrait
of an Artist*; Louisa Young's biography of
her, *A Great Task of Happiness*; and Diana
Farr's *Gilbert Cannan: A Georgian Prodigy*.

307 *but lions they were* . . . Lady Kennet,
     p. 76
308 *Dear Miss O'Reilly* . . . RGS RFS/9g,
     05.07.1906
309 *as pretty as they're made* . . . Denis
     Mackail, *The Story of J.M.B.*, London
     1941, p. 364
309 *I DO love you so* . . . *he wont forget it*
     Pauline Chase, *Peter Pan's Post Bag*,
     London 1909
310 *So Scott did* . . . *Mackail*, The Story of
     J.M.B., p. 381
312 *only a slender knowledge* . . .
     Bernacchi, p. 187
312 *the last of a huge* . . . Lady Kennet,
     p. 17
312 *an old Presbyterian lawyer* . . . Idem
313 *She was of medium* . . . Elizabeth Jane
     Howard, *Slipstream*, London 2003, p. 128
314 *shapeless, sacklike garments* . . . James
     Lees-Milne, *Ancestral Voices*, London
     1975, p. 31
314 *She was strangely seductive* . . . quoted
     Young, p. 32
314 *It's the only thing* . . . Lady Kennet,
     pp. 25–6
315 *Then life confirmed* . . . Ibid., p. 83
316 *Dearest Professor* . . . SPRI 1543/3/10,
     02.11.1907
316 *I've tried the telephone* . . . SPRI
     1543/3/12, undated
316 *Somebody said Friday morning* . . .
     SPRI 1543/3/13, undated
316 *There's such strength* . . . SPRI
     1453/3/14, 07.11.1907
316 *Uncontrollable footsteps* . . . SPRI
     1543/3/15, 08.01.1907
317 *To 'know only* . . . SPRI 1543/3/16,
     09.11.1907

317 *"Kathleen"* . . . *if you mind* Lady
     Kennet, p. 84
318 *with his head* . . . Ibid., p. 85
318 *My Dear Con* . . . SPRI 1574/1/2,
     09.01.1908
318 *My Dear Ettie* . . . SPRI 1547/2/11,
     11.01.1908
319 *It's really nice* . . . SPRI 1547/2/10,
     22.06.1907
319 *My own dear Con* . . . SPRI 1453/3/35,
     31.12.1907
320 *Dearest Con* . . . SPRI 1453/3/37,
     04.01.1908
320 *I've just had your* . . . SPRI 1453/3/38,
     05.01.1908
321 *Estimates for 2* . . . SPRI 1453/3/43,
     10.01.1908
321 *I'm looking at poverty* . . . SPRI
     1453/3/57, undated
321 *Your letter made me* . . . SPRI 1453/3/57,
     undated
322 *I dare not think* . . . SPRI 1453/3/24,
     20.11.1907
322 *Dear dear sweet heart* . . . SPRI
     1453/3/25, Nov 1907
322 *I seem to have* . . . SPRI 1453/3/28,
     25.11.1907
322 *I'm sad tonight* . . . SPRI 1453/3/87,
     11.05.1908
323 *I am afraid of what* . . . SPRI
     1453/3/157, 27.07.1908
324 *corn-haired* . . . Lady Kennet,
     p. 79
324 *a rather vacant* . . . quoted John
     Paterson, *Edwardians*, Chicago 1996,
     p. 251
324 *My dear K* . . . quoted Young,
     pp. 91–2
325 *Dear you really must* . . . SPRI
     1453/3/89, undated
325 *freedom, light, purity* . . . quoted
     Young, pp. 94–5
326 *Dear You* . . . Idem
326 *You shall not do* . . . Idem
326 *Why no word* . . . SPRI 1453/3/84,
     07.05.1908
326 *that is if things* . . . SPRI 1453/3/86,
     08.05.1908
326 *The weather here* . . . SPRI 1542/11/1,
     12.05.1908

327 *"Oh this," thought I* . . . Lady Kennet, p. 85

327 *I can't breathe here* . . . SPRI 1453/3/94, undated

327 *You must stop* . . . SPRI 1453/3/97, 25.05.1908

327 *How dare you* . . . SPRI 1453/3/102, 26.05.1908

327 *Do you realize* . . . SPRI 1453/3/107, 03.06.1908

327 *Oh I love you* . . . SPRI 1453/3/111, 04.06.1908

328 *dull and limited* . . . SPRI 1453/3/106, undated

328 *god . . . conscience . . . motive power* Kennet Papers, D/5, 21.02.1913

328 *I'm really falling* . . . SPRI 1453/3/28, undated

328 *I'm loving you so much* . . . SPRI 1453/3/141, undated

328 *Here I am* . . . SPRI 1453/3/159, undated

328 *To be honest* . . . SPRI 1453/3/207, 30.10.1905

328 *a dear little girl* . . . SPRI 1453/3/129, 27.06.1908

328 *And now dear* . . . SPRI 1542/11/15, undated, June 1908

329 *I'd been hoping* . . . SPRI 1542/11/16, 23.06.1908

330 *My Dear Old Girl* . . . SPRI 1547/2/12, 18.06.1908

330 *Ettie was more than* . . . SPRI 1453/3/118, 21.06.1908

330 *sweetest letter from* . . . SPRI 1453/3/115, undated

330 *My Dear Mrs. Scott* . . . quoted Young, p. 86

331 *Of course Kathleen* . . . SPRI 1452/11/17, 23.06.1908

331 *So glad . . . forbearing to all* SPRI 1453/3/118–121, 23–24.06.1908

332 *I'm extremely frightened* . . . SPRI 1453/3/142, 12.07.1908

332 *Precious man* . . . SPRI 1453/3/145, undated

332 *I'm trying to write* . . . SPRI 1453/3/129, 27.06.1908

332 *Con dear I've just* . . . SPRI 1453/3/140, undated

332 *I've written to Barrie* . . . SPRI 1453/3/142, 12.07.1908

333 *I hate the fact* . . . SPRI 1453/3/147, 17.06.1906

333 *There is one important* . . . SPRI 1453/3/160, 28.07.1908

333 *Kathleen's dear heart* . . . Christchurch, Thomson Collection, MS 54, 13.07.1908

334 *very quiet wedding* . . . SPRI 1453/3/l47, 17.06.1906

334 *Give me a word* . . . SPRI 1547/2/16, 19.08.1908

334 *a dress of white* . . . quoted Young, p. 100

335 *I just hated your* . . . SPRI 342/28/49, 31.10.1908

Twenty-one: **Marking Time**
The main primary sources for this chapter are Scott and Kathleen's letters to each other, and the ships' logs for Scott's time in *Bulwark* and *Essex* held at the Public Record Office.

336 *You shall go to the S. Pole* . . . SPRI 14543/3/138, 11.07.1908

336 *Can you really mean* . . . SPRI 1453/188/4, 31.03.1907

337 *the key to everything* . . . SPRI 342/28/20, 25.05.1907

337 *dived into the motor . . . exercise tact* SPRI 342/28/20, 25.05.1907

337 *pushed out of that* . . . SPRI 1456/23, 23.05.1907

338 *As regards the future* . . . RGS RFS/4a, 27.05.1907

338 *Is the Public Press* . . . Idem

338 *I should explain* . . . RGS RFS/4a, 01.06.1907

339 *Rupert England* . . . RGS RFS/4a, 04.06.1907

339 *a small* . . . Shackleton, Vol I, p. 16

340 *I hope we shall* . . . SPRI 1542/10/11, 25.08.1907

340 *worked him up* . . . SPRI 342/28/24, 11.07.1907

340 *June is a bad* . . . SPRI 1542/10/12–14, 08.06.1907–12.07.1907

341 *to be near getting* . . . SPRI 1542/10/17,
      18.08.1907

341 *It has been a great* . . . SPRI 1453/22,
      25.08.1907

341 *a very special* . . . SPRI 1542/10/17,
      18.08.1907

341 *I don't want you* . . . SPRI 1542/1/10/18,
      29.07.1907

342 *Yesterday I walked* . . . SPRI 1453/3/73,
      05.04.1908

342 *I come next* . . . SPRI 1452/11/1,
      undated

342 *We play at war* . . . SPRI 1452/11/22,
      12.05.1908

342 *I'm writing in the* . . . SPRI 1453/3/72,
      02.04.1908

342 *Tomorrow we start* . . . SPRI 1453/3/73,
      05.04.1908

342 *just faintly* . . . SPRI 1453/3/100,
      25.05.1908

343 *It has been* . . . SPRI 1453/22,
      undated

343 *The name of Mr. P.F. Hickman* . . .
      PRO ADM 52/1830 8, 14.11.1908

343 *breakfast, lunch and dinner* . . . SPRI
      1453/3/107, 09.10.1908

343 *I ought to explain* . . . SPRI 1453/3/227,
      10.10.1908

343 *Here's a curious thing* . . . SPRI
      1453/3/110, 04.06.1908

344 *To what stroke of* . . . SPRI 1157/2,
      15.03.1904

344 *You felicitate me* . . . SPRI 1157/3,
      28.10.1918

345 *Con dear* . . . SPRI 1453/3/150–231,
      undated 1908

345 *Oh girl dear* . . . SPRI 1453/3/251,
      25.11.1908

345 *bad pain* . . . SPRI 1453/3/214,
      03.11.1908

345 *Oh I could cry* . . . SPRI 1453/3/259,
      11.12.1908

345 *Oh really dearest* . . . SPRI 1453/3/279,
      Dec 1908

345 *Still I'm dreading* . . . SPRI 1453/3/282,
      02.01.1909

345 *My own wife* . . . SPRI 1453/3/284,
      04.01.1909

345 *proper parental dignity* . . . SPRI
      1453/3/291, 07.01.1909

346 *Oh my Darling* . . . SPRI 1453/3/318,
      13.03.1909

346 *Oh girl dear* . . . SPRI 1453/3/294,
      17.01.1909

346 *Dear sweetheart* . . . SPRI 1453/3/294,
      17.01.1909

346 *What on earth* . . . SPRI 1453/3/246,
      19.11.1908

346 *Write, write, write* . . . SPRI 1453/3/278,
      31.12.1908

346 *a strange thing happened* . . . Lady
      Kennet, p. 89

347 *I've been dining* . . . SPRI 1453/3/291,
      07.01.1909

347 *I seem to be* . . . SPRI 1453/3/294,
      17.01.1909

347 *with a heavy heart* . . . Shackleton,
      Vol I, p. 82

Twenty-two: **Making Ready**
The primary sources are Scott's family
letters and correspondence with the RGS,
and the most interesting published sources
are the subsequent accounts of expedition
members. For the development of the
motorised sledge and the controversy over
Skelton's position, Skelton's own papers
held in the Scott Polar Research Institute
provide the best insight.

348 *I think all present* . . . RGS RFS/4a,
      undated

348 *This was a great* . . . Shackleton, Vol 1,
      pp. 76–7

349 *I have been through* . . . quoted Roland
      Huntford, *Shackleton*, London 1996,
      p. 206

349 *The letter was an* . . . RGS RFS/4a,
      28.03.1908

350 *As for "cogent* . . . RGS RFS/4a,
      02.04.1908

350 *I'll send also* . . . SPRI 1453/3/66,
      undated

350 *I wish to God* . . . quoted Huntford,
      Shackleton, p. 307

350 *It is awkward* . . . Christchurch,
      Bernacchi Collection, MS 276/8,
      25.03.1908

351 *insufferably hot* . . . *glory of it* SPRI
      1453/3/60–1, 8–13.03.1908

351 *Exhaust cam . . . assisted* SPRI 342/10/2, 7–17.03.1908

352 *dreadfully slipshod* SPRI 342/28/51, 04.11.1908

352 *The hyper-sensitiveness . . .* quoted Huntford, p. 230

353 *I have the highest . . .* quoted Yelverton, p. 412

353 *How much longer . . .* quoted Huntford, p. 230

353 *Mark Kerr has been . . .* SPRI 1453/3/261, 01.12.1908

354 *I think all things . . .* SPRI 1453/3/256, 30.11.1908

354 *I think we'd . . .* quoted Huxley, p. 215

354 *"You open it . . .* A.E.W. Mason, *The Turnstile*, London 1912, pp. 202–3

355 *The private feeling . . .* SPRI 1456/23, 23.03.1909

355 *Shackleton's exploit . . .* SPRI 342/28/54, undated

355 *Thanks for sending . . .* RGS CB4, Markham, 28.03.1909

355 *most generous . . .* RGS CB4, Markham, 13.04.1909

356 *gloomily discussing . . .* quoted Huxley, p. 216

356 *very proud . . . Observer*, 20.06.1909

356 *The campaign is opened . . .* RGS RFS/4a, 12.09.1909

356 *The main object . . . The Times*, 13.09.1909

357 *I have thought . . .* quoted Pound, p. 169

357 *At this juncture . . .* Ibid., p. 171

357 *Scott is a man . . .* quoted Seaver, *Wilson*, p. 182

357 *bitten up by . . .* RGS CB4, Markham, 13.04.1909

358 *The offices of . . .* T. Griffith Taylor, *With Scott: The Silver Lining*, London 1916, p. 4

358 *Stop Murray's letter . . .* RGS RFS/4a, 14.09.1909

359 *Ask all the Mayors . . . even that* quoted Gwynn, pp. 118–19

359 *Poor little ship . . .* Evans, p. 27

359–60 *It is anticipated . . .* quoted Pound, p. 177

360 *I have heard . . .* SPRI 1453/85, 04.03.1907

361 *profits — big profits* quoted Pound, p. 179

361 *I should be delighted . . .* SPRI 342/28/65, 21.03.1910

362 *I am forced . . .* SPRI 342/28/67, 20.04.10; 342/28/66, 03.04.1910

362 *I'm sorry . . .* SPRI 342/28/66, 03.04.1910

362 *I was lying abed . . .* quoted Gwynn, pp. 120–1

362 *I know Scott intimately . . .* quoted Sara Wheeler, *Cherry*, London 2001, p. 60

363 *I was drawn strongly . . .* Herbert Ponting, *The Great White South*, London 1921, p. 2

363 *Scott is just what . . .* Taylor, *With Scott: The Silver Lining*, p. 4

363 *nothing of the braggart . . .* quoted Pound, p. 176

364 *a multitude of necessities . . . damp free* Evans, pp. 27–9

364 *manhood of our nation . . .* Ibid., p. 32

Twenty-three: **South Again**

The fullest description of the journey south can be found in Teddy Evans's *South with Scott*, along with the letters home of the crew members. The main primary source for Scott's time in South Africa is Kathleen's diary. The vividest portraits of Bowers and Oates exist in their own letters. In the case of Oates, Sue Limb and Patrick Cordingley's biography also offers one of the fairest accounts of expedition life.

365 *One does pall . . .* Silas, 10.07.1910

365 *At Weymouth . . .* SPRI 1/1/3/86, 09.06.1910

366 *Mayor (Lord) . . .* Idem

366 *I enclose P.O. . . . .* SPRI 1453/135, 15.12.1911

366 *Please convey my . . .* quoted Pound, p. 185

367 *I've just had . . .* SPRI 1453/3/289, 05.01.1909

367 *must be comfortable . . .* SPRI 1547/2/20, July 1910

367 *I don't forget* . . . SPRI 1547/2/21, 30.10.1911

367 *heart-searchings* . . . Lady Kennet, p. 89

367 *There is only one* . . . quoted Gwynn, pp. 126–7

368 *See you at the South Pole* . . . quoted Roland Huntford, *Shackleton*, London 1996, p. 329

368 *We were simply* . . . SPRI 1453/188/5, 12.11.1908

368 *We both disregarded* . . . SPRI 1453/3/223, 18.11.1908

368 *I gather he thinks* . . . quoted Young, p. 113

369 *a prig* . . . James Lees-Milne, *Ancestral Voices*, London 1975, pp. 31–2

369 *Met their excellencies* . . . Kennet Papers, D/2, 13–18.08.1910

369 *in great luxury* . . . Ibid., 11–20.08.1910

369 *Everybody was charmingly* . . . Ibid., 22.08.1910

370 *I wish with all* . . . quoted Seaver, Wilson, pp. 202–3

370 *Bowers, whom you will* . . . Idem

370 *He really was* . . . George Seaver, *"Birdie" Bowers of the Antarctic*, London 1938, Introduction by Apsley Cherry-Garrard, p. xiii

371 *Godless heedlessly happy* . . . SPRI 1/1/2/38, 02.06.1907

371 *If ever I could* . . . SPRI 1/1/2/44, 01.09.1907

372 *No body will give* . . . SPRI 1/1/2/38, 02.06.1907

372 *Daughter of the Harlot* . . . SPRI 1/1/2/261, 23.04.1909

373 *Dr. Simpson is known* . . . Kennet Papers, D/2, 22.08.1910

374 *I have now* . . . SPRI 1016/328, 27.01.1910

374 *We had pictured* . . . E.G.R. Evans, *Strand Magazine*, Dec 1913, pp. 114–15

375 *make out who* . . . quoted Limb and Cordingley, p. 115

375 *I was very glad* . . . Kennet Papers, D/2, 22.08.1910

375 *I have never seen* . . . quoted Gwynn, p. 124

375 *Mrs. Scott is another* . . . SPRI 1/1/3/95, 11.09.1910

376 *They are a capital* . . . SPRI 1016/335, 14.07.1910

376 *"The Owner"* . . . Silas, 02.10.1910

376 *It was an enormous* . . . Evans, p. 43

377 *A programme was* . . . Idem

377 *I doubt if a class* . . . quoted Seaver, Wilson, pp. 202–3

377 *I don't think that* . . . SPRI 559/40/3, 14.10.1910

377 *So as I insisted* . . . Kennet Papers, D/2, 12.10.1910

378 *Madeira* . . . Cherry-Garrard, p. 40

Twenty-four: **Challenges**

The most detailed primary source for Scott's time in Australia and New Zealand is again Kathleen's diary, supplemented by the opening entries of Scott's own. For the fraught relations between the expedition wives, Bowers's letters home are incomparably the most vivid.

379 *Acquiring knowledge* . . . Norman Dixon, *On the Psychology of Military Incompetence*, reprinted London 1983, p. 30

379 *I decided long ago* . . . SPRI 1453/127/2, 28.10.1911

382 *I have had a long letter* . . . RGS CB4, Markham, 15.10.1910

382 *What rascals these* . . . RGS CB4, Markham, undated

383 *And when you pass* . . . quoted Huntford, p. 283

383 *turn turtle* . . . RGS CB4, Markham, 15.10.1910

383 *I think the "Fram"* . . . RGS CB4, Markham, 04.11.1910

383 *Amundsen seems to be* . . . RGS RFS/4a, 19.11.1910

383 *Lunch with minister* . . . *which was pleasant* Kennet Papers, D/2, 14–16.10.1910

384 *sad and fiery* . . . Kennet Papers, D/2, 17.10.1910

384 *frail & old* . . . Kennet Papers, D/2, 19.10.1910

384 *He is wonderful* . . . BM MS FACS 777 (1), 21.10.1910

384 *Dined with Lord Mayor* . . . BM MS
FACS 777 (1), 19.10.1910
384 *Isn't it fine* . . . quoted Pound, p. 203
384 *His pictures were* . . . Kennet Papers,
D/2, 20.10.1910
385 *wretchedly uncomfortable* . . . BM MS
FACS 777 (1), 24.10.1910
385 *the only pleasant recollection* . . .
Kennet Papers, D/2, 26.10.1910
385 *pathetic little meteorological* . . . *things
went badly* Kennet Papers, D/2,
28.09–04.11.1910
385 *He didn't like it* . . . Kennet Papers,
D/2, 08.11.1910
385 *he must go* . . . BM MS FACS 777 (1),
31.10.1910
385 *Mr. Feather is leaving* . . . SPRI
324/23/1, 24.11.1910
386 *Sahib* SPRI 1/1/25/102, 21.10.1910
386 *The killings of the ponies* . . .
Shackleton, Vol 1, pp. 290–1
387 *exploring and mapping* . . . C.H.
Meares, *Badminton Magazine*, 1909,
p. 438
387 *I have been kept* . . . SPRI 1246,
18.03.1910
388 *I have arrived here* . . . SPRI 1246,
22.08.1910
388 *To Quail Island* . . . BM MS FACS
777 (1), 31.10.1910
388 *first class* SPRI 1016/337, 23.11.1910
388 *I don't know how* . . . SPRI 1016/336,
17.11.1910
389 *If he gets* . . . SPRI 1016/337, 23.11.1910
389 *Scott will have nothing* . . . SPRI
1/1/25/102, 21.10.1910
389 *Captain Scott has left* . . . SPRI
1/1/3/100, 24.11.1910
389 *Mrs. Wilson has not* . . . SPRI
1/1/25/104, 28.11.1910
390 *went a happy climb* . . . Kennet Papers,
D/2, 26.11.1910
390 *had a reserved carriage* . . . Kennet
Papers, D/2, 28.11.1910
390 *Found all well* . . . BM MS FACS
777 (1), 28.11.1910
390 *Mrs. Scott and Mrs. Evans* . . . SPRI
1016/337, 23.11.1910
390 *Only one cloud* . . . SPRI 1/1/3/103,
07.12.1910

392 *bored at both* . . . *attractive about [him]*
Kennet Papers, D/2, 29.11.1910
392 *I didn't say goodbye* . . . *departing ship*
Idem

Twenty-five: **Return to the Ice**
The primary sources for all the *Terra Nova*
chapters are the letters and diaries of the
expedition members and in particular those
of Scott himself. Scott's journals were
published in a lightly edited form the year
after his death as *Scott's Last Expedition*,
but where there is any significant
discrepancy between the original journal
entry and the published version, or where
there is an omission, the original diaries
have been used. Unreferenced quotations
in this chapter come from *Scott's Last
Expedition*, Chapters 1, 2, 3 and 4.

394 *There is no deck* . . . Cherry-Garrard,
p. 46
395 *I can't remember* . . . quoted Limb and
Cordingley, p. 126
396 *like a young Niagara* . . . SPRI 279/1,
01.12.1910
396 *I never wish to see* . . . Idem
396 *It was a sight* . . . Evans, p. 52
397 *If Dante had* . . . SPRI 296/6/1, Dec
1910
397 *to find out how* . . . Evans, p. 53
397 *unspeakably dirty water* Idem
397 *Captain Scott was simply* . . . SPRI
1/1/25/106, 10.12.1910
398 *We are not out* . . . BM MS FACS 777
(1), 02.12.1910
398 *Its impossible to* . . . BM MS FACS
777 (1), 09.12.1910
399 *Three weeks in the pack* . . . SPRI
1488/2, 27.02.1911
400 *The invitation is peculiar* . . . SPRI
279/1, 23.12.1910
400 *Capt. Scott who has to* . . . SPRI 1/1/3/
104, 25.12.1910
401 *No good!!* . . . BM MS FACS 777 (1),
03.01.1911
401 *We could see the* . . . Cherry-Garrard,
p. 82
402 *the most restful* . . . Ibid., p. 80

403 *a panorama of such* . . . Herbert
Ponting, *The Great White South*,
London 1921, p. 59

404 *We realised that* . . . SPRI 298/6/1,
08.01.1911

404 *like a cork out of* . . . Idem

404 *"Day, here are* . . . Cherry-Garrard,
p. 94

405 *There were the steady* . . . Ibid.,
p. 90

405 *There were runaways* . . . Ibid., p. 91

406 *it will make things* . . . SPRI 1317/1–2,
22.01.1911

406 *I knew when I first* . . . SPRI 1/1/3/105,
01.01.1911

406 *a lazy posing fellow* BM MS FACS 777
(1) 06.01.1911

407 *If you picture us* . . . quoted Evans,
p. 84

Twenty-six: **Depot-Laying**

Where no specific reference to Scott's diary
is given, quotations come from *Scott's Last
Expedition*, Chapters 5 and 6.

408 *Never in the history* . . . C. Wright and
R. Priestley, *British Antarctic Expedition
1910–13, Glaciology*, London 1922,
Preface

409 *Over and over* . . . G. Simpson, *British
Antarctic Expedition 1910–13,
Meteorology*, Calcutta 1919, Vol 1,
Preface

409 *It will not perhaps* . . . Griffith Taylor,
*British Antarctic Expedition 1910–13, The
Physiography of the McMurdo Sound
Granite Harbour Region*, London 1922,
Preface

410 *except . . . of everybody* SPRI 1/1/3/105,
01.01.1911

411 *At such times* . . . Cherry-Garrard, p. 94

411 *in a state of hurry* . . . Ibid.,
pp. 108–9

411 *It would rejoice* . . . SPRI 1488/2,
17.01.1911

411 *Captain Scott is simply* . . . SPRI
1/1/3/108, 23.01.1911

411 *My most vivid* . . . Cherry-Garrard,
pp. 108–9

412 *Captain Scott was very* . . . SPRI 1488/2,
02.03.1913

413 *Those first days* . . . Cherry-Garrard,
p. 110

413 *The peak of Terror* . . . Idem

413 *It is hard to conceive* . . . BM MS FACS
777 (1), 15.01.1911

413 *Boxes full of excrement* . . . BM MS
FACS 777 (5), 02.02.1911

413 *I expect we were* . . . Cherry-Garrard,
p. 111

414 *Scott and Evans* . . . SPRI
1317/01–02.02.1911

414 *very hard on* . . . BM MS FACS 777 (5),
02.02.1911

415 *Dog-driving like this* . . . Seaver,
Wilson, pp. 219–20

416 *What happened never* . . . Cherry-
Garrard, p. 118

417 *Oates proposed* . . . Gran, 16.02.1911

418 *I've always found* . . . Christchurch, LQ
MS 1/folder 45, 26.01.1962

421 *It is evident* . . . BM MS FACS 777 (5),
22.02.1911

422 *Of one thing* . . . Gran, 17.02.1911

Twenty-seven: **Disaster**

The unreferenced quotations from his
journals come from Chapter 6 of *Scott's
Last Expedition*. The description of the
pony disaster is largely based on Scott's
diary, and above all on quotations from the
letters and diaries of Bowers and Cherry
incorporated into Cherry's matchless
account in Chapter 5 of *The Worst Journey
in the World*. The source of this narrative is
indicated in the text.

423 *I felt as if* . . . Gran, 26.02.1911

424 *In two minutes* . . . SPRI 1488/2,
27.02.1911

424 *KEVII Land show* . . . SPRI 1488/2,
27.02.1911

425 *Individually they all* . . . SPRI 1488/2,
27.02.1911

430 *I suppose there is* . . . quoted Sara
Wheeler, *Cherry*, London 2001, p. 98

433 *We lost 6 ponies* . . . SPRI 1317/1/3,
22.10.1911

493 *The specimens collected* . . . A.C. Seward in *British Antarctic Expedition 1910–1913, Natural History Report, Geology*, London 1964, Vol 1, p. 7

494 *It is an extraordinary* . . . quoted Limb and Cordingley, p. 198

498 *This morning he wished* . . . quoted Cherry-Garrard, p. 414

498 *nice home-baked cake* . . . Ibid., p. 418

498 *once more* . . . *a bright spot* . . . Ibid., p. 419

503 *We have had a long* . . . quoted Seaver, Wilson, p. 293

504 *To my Beloved Wife* . . . Ibid., p. 294

504 It is finished . . . SPRI 984

505 *My own dearest Mother* . . . SPRI 1/1/5/115, undated

506 *We are pegging out* . . . BM Add Ms 46272

507 *your happy self again* . . . quoted Gwynn, p. 163

507 *But take comfort* . . . Ibid., p. 164

508 *Send a small piece* . . . Ibid., pp. 163–4

Epilogue

Atkinson, Wright, Lashly and Gran all left accounts of the discovery of Scott's body, but as ever it is Cherry's that is the most resonant. The most original work done in recent times on Scott's last expedition is Susan Solomon's *The Coldest March*, and the meteorological details in this chapter are based on her findings.

509 *One would be* . . . Kennet Papers, D/5, 27.02.1913

509 *I had been plugging* . . . Silas, *Memoir*

509 *"It is the tent"* . . . Cherry-Garrard, p. 497

510 *There was nothing* . . . Idem

510 *The cold had turned* . . . Gran, 12.11.1912

510 *taut and ship-shape* . . . *Relief Expedition 1912* Cherry-Garrard, pp. 496–502

512 *morally certain* SLE, Vol II, p. 241

512 *Atkinson shouted* . . . Cherry-Garrard, p. 440

512 *a very small amount* . . . SLE, Vol II, pp. 99–100

513 *The question of what* . . . Cherry-Garrard, p. 457

513 *The first object* . . . Idem

515 *the daily minimum* . . . Susan Solomon, *The Coldest March*, New Haven 2002, p. 294

518 *We never realized* . . . Cherry-Garrard, p. 498

518 *"You know* . . . Kennet Papers, D/3/A, 14.06.1911

519 *the greatest polar explorer* . . . RGS CB5 Markham, 11.02.1913

519 *cathedral* Cherry-Garrard, p. 496

519 *When I think of Scott* . . . J.M. Barrie, Address to St. Andrews University, 03.05.1922

520 *fought hard* . . . Tryggve Gran, *The Norwegian with Scott*, London 1984, p. 216

Select Bibliography

Unpublished Sources

By far the most important collection of manuscripts relating to Scott is held in the Scott Polar Research Insitute (SPRI) at Cambridge. There is also an invaluable Antarctic archive at the Royal Geographical Society (RGS) which is of particular interest for the *Discovery* expedition, and a wealth of material relating to both *Discovery* and *Terra Nova* in the Canterbury Museum archive, Christchurch, New Zealand. The records of Scott's naval career and the log books of the ships in which he served can be found among Admiralty papers in the Public Record Office (PRO), Kew, and in the Royal Naval College, Dartmouth. Scott's last diaries are in the British Library; Kathleen Scott's diaries are among the Kennet papers in Cambridge University Library (CUL).

Published Sources

Anon, *HMS Vernon: A History*, London 1930

Armitage, A.B., *Cadet to Commodore*, London 1925

Armitage, A.B., *Two Years in the Antarctic*, Bungay 1984

Asquith, C., *Portrait of Barrie*, London 1954

Bernacchi, L., *Saga of the Discovery*, Royston 2001

Brown, J.M. and Louis, W.R., *Oxford History of the British Empire*, Vol V, Oxford 1999

Bull, C. and Wright, P.F. (eds), *Silas, The Antarctic Diaries and Memoir of Charles S. Wright*, Ohio State University Press 1993

Cannan, G., *The Road to Come*, London 1913

Chase, P., *Peter Pan's Post Bag*, London 1909

Cherry-Garrard, A., *The Worst Journey in the World*, London 1922

Cook, Dr. F.A., *Through the First Antarctic Night*, London 1900

Cubitt, G. and Warren, A. (eds), *Heroic Reputations and Exemplary Lives*, Manchester 2000

Debenham, F., *In the Antarctic*, London 1952

Dixon, N., *On the Psychology of Military Incompetence*, London 1976

Doorly, G.S., *The Voyage of the Morning*, London 1916

Fiennes, R., *Captain Scott*, London 2003

Fisher, M. and J., *Shackleton*, London 1957

Fleming, F., *Barrow's Boys*, London 1988

Fleming, F., *Ninety Degrees North*, London 2002

Girouard, M., *The Return to Camelot*, New Haven 1981

Gordon, A., *The Rules of the Game*, London 1996

Gran, T., *The Norwegian with Scott*, London 1984

Griffith Taylor, T., *With Scott: The Silver Lining*, London 1916

Griffith Taylor, T., *British Antarctic Expedition 1910–13, The Physiography of the McMurdo Sound Granite Harbour Region*, London 1922

Gwynn, S., *Captain Scott*, Harmondsworth 1929

Harvie, D., *Limeys*, Stroud 2002

Hattersley-Smith, G. (ed.), *Tryggve Gran's Antarctic Diary 1910–1913*, London 1984

Holt, K., *The Race*, London 1976

Hough, R., *Admirals in Collision*, London 1959

Hough, R., *Captain James Cook*, London 1994

Howard, E.J., *Slipstream*, London 2003

Hughes, E.A., *The Royal Naval College, Dartmouth*, London undated

Huntford, R., *Shackleton*, London 1996

Huntford, R., *Nansen*, London 1997

Huntford, R., *The Last Place on Earth*, London 2000

Huxley, E., *Scott of the Antarctic*, London 1977

Jalland, P., *Death in the Victorian Family*, Oxford 1996

Jones, A.G.E., *Polar Portraits*, Whitby 1992

Kennet, Lady, *Self Portrait of an Artist*, London 1949

Lees-Milne, J., *Ancestral Voices*, London 1975

Lewis, M., *The Navy in Transition*, London 1965

Limb, S. and Cordingley, P., *Captain Oates*, London 1982

Mackail, D., *The Story of J.M.B.*, London 1941

Manual of Seamanship, London 1908 (revised and reprinted 1915)

Markham, Admiral Sir A., *Life of Sir Clements Markham KCB FRS*, London 1917

Markham, C., *Antarctic Obsession*, ed. C. Holland, Huntingdon 1986

Mason, A.E.W., *The Four Feathers*, London 1902

Mason, A.E.W., *The Turnstile*, London 1912

Mill, H.R., *Autobiography*, London 1951

Mill, H.R., *Siege of the South Pole*, London 1905

Morris, J., *Fisher's Face*, London 1995

Mountevans, Admiral Lord, *South with Scott*, London 1947

Nansen, F., *Farthest North*, London 1898

National Antarctic Expedition 1901–4, Introduction, London 1907

National Antarctic Expedition 1901–4, Physical Observations, London 1908

"Navilus," *A Few Days in the Life of a Royal Naval Cadet on board HMS Britannia*, London 1894

Pack, Capt. S.W.C, *Britannia at Dartmouth*, London 1966

Paterson, J., *Edwardians*, Chicago 1996

Pocock, T., *Battle for Empire*, London 1998

Ponting, H., *The Great White South*, London 1921

Pound, R., *Scott of the Antarctic*, London 1966

Preston, D., *A First Rate Tragedy*, London 1997

Roskill, S.W., *Earl Beatty*, London 1981

Royds, T.R. (ed.), *The Diary of Lt Charles W.R. Royds RN, Expedition to the Antarctic 1901–4*, Braidwood, NSW 2001

Savours, A., *The Voyages of the Discovery*, Rochester 2001

Seaver, G., *Edward Wilson of the Antarctic*, London 1933

Seaver, G., *Scott of the Antarctic*, London 1940

Seaver, G., *The Faith of Edward Wilson*, London 1945

Seaver, G., *"Birdie" Bowers of the Antarctic*, London 1947

Seward, A.C. (ed.), *British Antarctic Expedition 1910–1913, Natural History Report, Geology*, London 1964

Shackleton, E.H., *The Heart of the Antarctic*, London 1909

Simpson, G., *British Antarctic Expedition 1910–13, Meteorology*, Calcutta 1919

Smith, Michael, *Tom Crean*, London 2000

Solomon, S., *The Coldest March*, New Haven 2002

Spufford, F., *I May Be Some Time*, London 1996

Tuchman, B., *The Proud Tower*, London 1966

Wells, H.G., *The New Machiavelli*, London 1911

Wemyss, Lady Wester, *The Life and Letters of Lord Wester Wemyss*, London 1935

Wheeler, S., *Cherry*, London 2001

Wilson, E., *Diary of the Discovery Expedition to the Antarctic Regions in 1901–1904*, ed. Ann Savours, New York 1967

Wolffe, J., *Great Deaths*, Oxford 2000

Wright, C. and Priestley, R., *British Antarctic Expedition 1910–13, Glaciology*, London 1922

Yelverton, D., *Antarctica Unveiled*, Boulder, Colorado 2000

Young, L., *A Great Task of Happiness*, London 1996

Index

(RFS — Robert Falcon Scott)

A Note on the Type

The text of this book was set in Electra, a typeface designed by W. A. Dwiggins (1880–1956). This face cannot be classified as either modern or old style. It is not based on any historical model, nor does it echo any particular period or style. It avoids the extreme contrasts between thick and thin elements that mark most modern faces, and it attempts to give a feeling of fluidity, power and speed.

Composed by North Market Street Graphics,
Lancaster, Pennsylvania
Printed and bound by Berryville Graphics,
Berryville, Virginia
Designed by Anthea Lingeman